W9-AMY-101

AFRICAN PERSPECTIVES ON SOUTH AFRICA

BLACK AND WHITE PERSPECTIVES ON SOUTH AFRIC

Series editor: Hendrik W. van der Merwe

This series is sponsored by the Centre for Intergroup Studies, Cape Town, and the Hoover Institution, Stanford University, Stanford, California

Vol. 1: African Perspectives on South Africa

Hendrik W. van der Merwe is the director of the Centre for Intergroup Studies. He is the principal editor or author of several books including *Student Perspectives on South Africa, The Future of the University in Southern Africa, Looking at the Afrikaner Today,* and *White South African Elites.*

Nancy C.J. Charton, senior lecturer in Political Studies at Rhodes University, is co-author of *White South African Elites* and the author of various articles and mono-graphs on politics, employment and related fields.

D.A. Kotzé is professor of African Politics at the University of South Africa and th editor and author of several books and articles including *Local Government in Southern Africa* and *African Politics in South Africa.*

Åke Magnusson was assistant lecturer in Political Science at the University of Gothenburg, Sweden, and is now Secretary of the Government Commission on South Africa. He is author of *Swedish Investments in South Africa* and *South Afric in the World,* as well as other publications on Southern Africa.

BLACK AND WHITE PERSPECTIVES ON SOUTH AFRICA

African Perspectives on South Africa

A COLLECTION OF SPEECHES, ARTICLES & DOCUMENTS

Edited by Hendrik W. van der Merwe
Nancy C.J. Charton, D.A. Kotzé & Åke Magnusson

In association with the Centre for Intergroup Studies, Cape Town

HOOVER INSTITUTION PRESS STANFORD CALIFORNIA
DAVID PHILIP PUBLISHER CLAREMONT CAPE TOWN
REX COLLINGS 69 MARYLEBONE HIGH ST LONDON

The Hoover Institution on War, Revolution and Peace, founded at Stanford University in 1919 by the late President Herbert Hoover, is an interdisciplinary research center for advanced study on domestic and international affairs in the twentieth century. The views expressed in its publications are entirely those of the authors and do not necessarily reflect the views of the staff, officers, or Board of Overseers of the Hoover Institution.

Hoover Institution Publication 167

First published in 1978 by:
David Philip, Publisher (Pty) Ltd, 217 Werdmuller Centr
Newry Street, Claremont, Cape Province, South Africa
Hoover Institution Press, Stanford University, Stanford
California 94305
Rex Collings Ltd, 69 Marylebone High Street, London W.1

ISBN 0 949968 84 6 (David Philip, Cape Town)

Printed in South Africa by Citadel Press, Polaris Road, Lansdowne, Cape Province

Contents

Acknowledgements xi
Preface / H.W.E. Ntsanwisi xiii
Map of Black Homelands xvii
General Introduction / T.V.R. Beard 1

THE HISTORICAL AND TRADITIONAL BACKGROUND

Some Aspects of African Literature / Lennox L. Sebe 29
African or Black Nationalism / M.T. Moerane 34
Afrikaner Ascendancy and the Challenges of the Seventies / M. Gatsha Buthelezi 42

THE COMMON AREA

POLITICAL ASPIRATIONS: THE FEDERAL IDEA

White and Black Nationalism, Ethnicity and the Future of the Homelands / M. Gatsha Buthelezi 51
The Political Future of the Homelands / Lucas M. Mangope 62

DIGNITY AND CONSCIOUSNESS

A Black Man Looks at White Politics / K.M.N. Guzana 69
Black Solidarity and Self-Help / M. Gatsha Buthelezi 77
Our Common Heritage / M. Gatsha Buthelezi 82
Petty Apartheid / H.W.E. Ntsanwisi 84
Are You Coming Along, Brother? / M.T. Moerane 88
Black People's Convention: Extract from Constitution 91
Black People's Convention: Rejection of Foreign Investment 93
The Disease of 'Mental Whiteness' / Sibusiso M. Bengu 94
SASO: Black Students' Manifesto 97
SASO: Statement of Objectives 98
SASO: Policy Manifesto 99
SASO: Understanding SASO 101
SASO: Alice Declaration: Boycott of Black Universities 106
The League of the African Youth: Objectives 107

The League of the African Youth: Principles 108
Towards Black Fulfilment / M. Gatsha Buthelezi 110
Black Renaissance Convention: Declaration and Resolutions, 1974 118
Why the Students Acted / Temba Nolutshungu 121

ECONOMIC DEVELOPMENT

Traditional Attitudes towards Agriculture and a Practica Agricultural Policy / Lennox L. Sebe 123
KwaZulu Development / M. Gatsha Buthelezi 130
Economic Development of the Tswana Homelands / S.J.J. Lesolang 138
Decentralisation and Border Industries / S.J.J. Lesolang 144
Capital Investment in the Homelands / S.M. Motsuenyane 148
National African Chamber of Commerce: Regionalisation and Bantu Investment Corporation Policy 150
Comments on the Bantu Investment Corporation / P.G. Gumec 158
Ethnic Commerce / S.M Motsuenyane 161
The Buy Home Week / S.M. Motsuenyane 163
The Beginnings of a Black Bank / S.M. Motsuenyane 165
Black Entrepreneurship / S.M. Motsuenyane 171
Trained Black Labour / Wilby L. Baqwa 177
The Management of Black Labour: Welfare Facilities / Wilby L. Baqwa 180
My Plea to I.L.O. / Lucy Mvubelo 188
Black Workers and Unions / Lucy Mvubelo 191
Black Allied Workers' Union: Policy Statement 200
KwaZulu Executive Council: Black Trade Union Rights 202
The Development of Effective Labour Relations / B.I. Dladla 204
Black Trade Unions and TUCSA / B.I. Dladla 210

EDUCATION

Education for Development / W.M. Kgware 214
Consultative Education Committee of the KwaZulu Government: Education Manifesto of KwaZulu 228
Medium of Instruction in African Education / A.L. Mawasha 234
Transvaal United African Teachers' Association: Language and Communication: Freedom to Choose the Medium of Instruction for Children 243

History in Black Schools / E.P. Lekhela 245
Education for Democracy / Cedric N. Phatudi 253
Higher Education for Blacks / T.S.N. Gqubule 255
Words of Identification / M. Gatsha Buthelezi 260
What Do We Say? / Curnick M.C. Ndamse 266
Education as an Instrument for Liberation / Ernest Baartman 273
SASO: The University - What Does it Mean to You? 279
SASO: Historical Background 281
Transvaal United African Teachers' Association: Statement of Objectives 285
Transkei Teachers' Association: Statement of Objectives 286
Black Academic Staff Association: University Autonomy 287

RELIGION

The Black Man and the Church / Ernest Baartman 293
The Church Confronts South Africa / Alphaeus H. Zulu 300
The African's Spiritual Concepts / E. Sikakane 306
SASO: Resolution on Black Theology 309
Black Theology in South Africa / Peter John Butelezi 311
Church Brings Change / Sol Selepe 315
Black Ministers of the Dutch Reformed Church: Statement on Apartheid 318
Pastoral Problems of the Migratory Labour System / T.S.N. Gqubule 320
God-given Dignity and the Quest for Liberation / Desmond Tutu 324
Black Caucus of the S.A. Council of Churches: The Soweto Disturbances 328

COMMUNITY DEVELOPMENT

Black Community Programmes: Aims and Objectives 330
Black Community Programmes: Excerpts from Annual Report, 1973 334
SASO: Community Projects, 1972 341
ASSECA: Objectives and Programmes 347
Women's Association of the African Independent Churches: Report Covering 1969-71 349
Edendale Lay Ecumenical Centre: Location and Nature 352

THE HOMELANDS

The Regional Political Dynamic / D.A. Kotzé 355
Profile of the Homelands / Nancy C.J. Charton 364
The Significance of the Tribal System for the Development of the Homelands / E.S. Moloto 372

THE INDEPENDENT TRANSKEI

Manifesto of Paramount Chief K.D. Matanzima, Transkei General Election, 1963 385
Transkei National Independence Party: Programme of Principles 388
Transkei National Independence Party: Declaration of Loyalty by Members 391
Transkei National Independence Party: Manifesto, Transkei General Election, 1968 392
The Need for Land / K.D. Matanzima 398
Separate Development / K.D. Matanzima 403
Manifesto of Paramount Chief K.D. Matanzima, Transkei General Election, 1973 407
Transkei National Independence Party: Manifesto of Candidates, Transkei General Election, 1973 409
Transkei Democratic Party: Statement of Objectives in the Constitution 410
Transkei Democratic Party: Statement, General Election, 1968 411
On Being a South African / K.M.N. Guzana 413

THE NON-INDEPENDENT HOMELANDS: CISKEI

Change for Development / Lennox L. Sebe 421
Manifesto of Lennox L. Sebe, Ciskei General Election, 1973 425
Ciskei National Independence Party: Principles 430
Ciskei National Independence Party: Objectives in Draft Constitution 431
Policy Statement of Chief Justice T. Mabandla, Ciskei General Election, 1973 432
Ciskei National Party: Policy 437
The Problems of Homeland Transition / Justice T. Mabandla 440
Bantu Affairs Administration Boards / A. Dunjwa 445

THE NON-INDEPENDENT HOMELANDS: KWAZULU

My Role within Separate Development Politics / M. Gatsha Buthelezi 456
Explaining Our Case to Africa / M. Gatsha Buthelezi 461
KwaZulu Executive Council: Comments on Land Consolidation 464
In Defence of the 'No Opposition' Policy / M. Gatsha Buthelezi 468
KwaZulu Executive Council: The Role of the Zulu King 470
No Confidence in KwaZulu Executive Council / Charles Hlengwa 473
Issues in KwaZulu / M. Gatsha Buthelezi 479
The National Cultural Liberation Movement (Inkatha) / Sibusiso Bengu 490
Inkatha (The National Cultural Liberation Movement): Resolutions, 1975 494

THE NON-INDEPENDENT HOMELANDS: BOPHUTHATSWANA

BophuthaTswana Today / Lucas M. Mangope 499
African Liberation / Lucas M. Mangope 505
BophuthaTswana National Party: Manifesto, BophuthaTswana General Election, 1972 507
Seoposengwe Party: Manifesto, BophuthaTswana General Election, 1972 513
Tswana National Party: Manifesto, BophuthaTswana General Election, 1972 515

THE NON-INDEPENDENT HOMELANDS: LEBOWA

Challenges in Homeland Development / Cedric N. Phatudi 516
Policy Statement / Cedric N. Phatudi 519
Manifesto of C.N. Phatudi, N.S. Mashiane, S.S. Mothapo, and C.L. Mothiba, Lebowa General Election, 1973 523
Manifesto of Collins Ramusi and Hebron Leshabane, Lebowa General Election, 1973 524
Lebowa People's Party: Manifesto 526
Statement by the Hon. Chief M.M. Matlala, Lebowa General Election, 1973 530

THE NON-INDEPENDENT HOMELANDS: GAZANKULU

The Hour of Decision / H.W.E. Ntsanwisi 532

THE NON-INDEPENDENT HOMELANDS: QWAQWA

Dikwankwetla Party: Extracts from the Manifesto 536

THE NON-INDEPENDENT HOMELANDS: VENDA

Venda Consciousness / Patrick R. Mphephu 538
On Terrorism / Patrick R. Mphephu 540
Mphephu Faction: Policy Declaration, Venda General Election, 1973 541
Mphephu Faction: Manifesto of Candidates Supporting Chief Mphephu, Venda General Election, 1973 547
Venda Independence People's Party: Manifesto, Venda General Election, 1973 549
Mphephu Faction: Whither the Venda Party?, Venda General Election, 1973 553
Venda Politics Today / J.P. Mutsila 555

THE NON-INDEPENDENT HOMELANDS: SWAZI TERRITORY

Political Development amongst the Republican Swazis / D. Lukhele 557

CONCLUSION

How to Promote Peace in South Africa / Manas Buthelezi 565
Report Back / M. Gatsha Buthelezi 569

Biographies of Contributors 587
References and Sources 598
Index of Contributors 603
Index of Organisations and Documents 604
General Index 606

Acknowledgements

This is the first volume in a series on the African, coloured, Asian, Afrikaans and English population groups. This volume was compiled in 1975. Typesetting of the manuscript was delayed due to circumstances beyond our control. When this was finally completed the bannings of 19 October 1977 affected 4 organisations from which 14 documents are included in our manuscript and legal procedures caused further delays.

The original idea to produce this book was suggested to me by Åke Magnusson. Nancy Charton assumed responsibility for selection and editing and D.A. Kotzé collected most of the documents and also assisted in the selection and editing.

I am grateful for the Preface and Introductions prepared by H.W.E. Ntsanwisi, D.A. Kotzé, Nancy Charton, and Terence Beard.

Helen Albertyn, the Administrative Assistant of the Centre for Intergroup Studies that sponsored the project, assisted with general editing and together with Barbara Chapman, the Secretary, was responsible for typing the manuscript. Over a period of three years the project benefited from the assistance of three assistants: Angela Solomon, a graduate of Fort Hare intimately familiar with African perspectives; Sue Sturman, a social science graduate from the University of Cape Town; and Alex Petersen, an anthropology graduate from the University of Cape Town.

The documents and speeches are intended to give some indication of the opportunities provided for public expression of opinions by Africans in South Africa in the decade until the middle 1970s. Regulations of a general and universal nature have been omitted from the constitutions of organisations and parties. Only typographical errors have been corrected. In editing a book of this sort it seemed necessary, for ease of reading, to delete certain asides or references which may be clear to a live audience, but not to a reader. Brevity, or attempts to avoid repetition, have dictated other deletions. Where substantial modifications have been made we have specifically stated that excerpts are being presented.

As in any society stratified largely according to ethnic or racial groups, the terms used to denote various groups can be a contentious and bitter issue. Choice of terminology can often reflect nuances of political stance. In various papers in this book the terms used are those of the individual authors. In editorial notes we have used 'African' in preference to the official 'Bantu' and the more traditional and offensive 'Native'. We have also used 'black' in preference to 'non-white'.

In presenting these African views which have been elicited from a wide range of people and organisations in public life in South Africa, it is important to stress that they are not representative of all Africans. Many important and articulate African leaders have been silenced by imprisonment or 'banning' or have left the country, and leading organisations have been banned.

This volume is thus restricted to contemporary public figures some of whom are extremely critical of the system within which they operate. As Gatsha Buthelezi puts it: 'This is not a policy of options and to pretend that the question of accepting or not accepting the system ever arises at all, is grossly misleading'.

The full set of documents from which this selection was made is kept by the Centre for Intergroup Studies.

We are grateful to the Hoover Institution Press for a subsidy towards publication costs.

Hendrik W. van der Merwe
Director
Centre for Intergroup Studies
c/o University of Cape Town
Rondebosch
Republic of South Africa
7700

April 1978

Preface

H.W.E.NTSANWISI
Chief Minister of Gazankulu

This book comprises documents of black political, cultural and educational organisations as well as recent speeches and articles by black leaders in South Africa and manifestos of contemporary black political parties and various black organisations. Rural and urban problems facing black communities are thoroughly discussed.

It presents new forms of African nationalism in answer to Afrikaner nationalism. Most of the contributors, especially the homeland leaders and black intelligentsia, express the view that the most frequent delusion to which Afrikaner nationalism has fallen prey is the belief that the majority of the black population welcome the opportunity of running their own affairs in their own fragmented homelands and that they accept the philosophical soundness of apartheid and the concept of the 'andersoortigheid' of the other man. The concept of 'otherness' is indeed the cornerstone of the present policy of apartheid, more euphemistically called multinational or parallel development. Cornerstone it may be but the evidence one gains from the book is that this view is not held or accepted by the black masses or by the black intelligentsia of South Africa. The book projects the view that the sooner the ruling class ceases deluding itself in thinking that they have gradually won African backing for the philosophy of 'andersoortigheid' the sooner will black and white in South Africa come to real grips with the issues that divide them. The view expressed forcibly by most of the writers is that whereas blacks are all proud of their cultural, linguistic and ethnic differences the belief that the salvation of black and white in South Africa lies in the perpetuation of these differences defies logic and the lessons of history. One cannot think of a single human experience in history where two divergent groups have successfully maintained political or social isolation after coming into contact with each other by conquest or otherwise. South Africa is not likely to be the exception with a white minority facing a black majority. Some of the homeland leaders still support the homelands as an interim measure because they see in them at least the first crumbs falling from the rich man's table. There are many Africans, particularly in the towns, who will have nothing to do with the homeland concept because of its emphasis on the differences between the races rather than the similarities, and particularly because it provides the white man with some kind of spurious moral backing for denying the black man in the towns the rights of ordinary human beings whether in the political or in the recreational sphere. It is evident from this book that even those who were prepared to give the homeland concept a try are fast running out of patience because they do not see in the approach of its protagonists a realistic appreciation of the time factor, of the urgency to spend more and of genuinely making the enormous financial sacrifices which might make these homelands work. I believe that it is primarily because of the complete inadequacy and non-viability of the homelands that the black urban dweller rejects them.

It is often said that apartheid has been introduced precisely because of the necessity to recognise aspirations of black men as human beings, leaving them to fulfil their aspirations in areas in which they do not have to face the competition of the white man. But where are these homelands? In small distant areas, far away from the labour markets, in areas so miserably poor and uninviting that therein no professional or middle-class black can hope to find professional, spiritual or material fulfilment. What the contributors try to bring home is the realisation that these homelands are far too fragmented and agriculturally non-viable for black men in the towns willingly to return to them.

Another important theme which runs right through this stimulating book is that discrimination based on colour is no longer acceptable to all sections of the black population. Black South Africans realise that the rest of Africa and its leaders are committed politically and emotionally to what they refer to as the liberation of the black peoples of South Africa and Rhodesia from bondage. This is one unifying factor on which all African political movements are agreed. Freedom and all that it implies has captured the imagination of every black man and especially the youth. This struggle for recognition is as deep in the African soul as it is, and was, in the

Afrikaner nation throughout its history. This recognition involves the right to choose one's political affiliation irrespective of colour and language affinity, the right to sell one's labour to the highest bidder in the labour market, and the right to live and move where one wants.

All homeland leaders have in their speeches expressed the desire to work amicably with their white compatriots in seeking a just formula for their mutual co-existence and interdependence in South Africa, by their pragmatism and willingness to advocate peaceful change. My one fear is that the whites of this country, especially the 'verkrampte' element will not give the black pragmatists an opportunity to prove their genuine desire to work together with the whites. The pragmatists have appealed to the white man to bring about peaceful change by sharing with them the good things with which this country is richly endowed. From the speeches of the homeland leaders the message which rings out loud and clear is that in South Africa the white man is not expendable but he must make it possible for the black man to live in peace and harmony with him by respecting his human dignity and sharing with him. From the pages of this book it also emerges very clearly that modern African youth is tired of dialogue which up to now has brought meaningless change. They are tired of being pushed around. They are tired of keeping the bridges open. They have been driven to the conviction that their only salvation lies in their own people, not in the whites at all. And indeed for all I know the intransigence of all ruling classes may prove them right. It is now up to those who have political power to prove them wrong by giving them a place in the sun. Continuation of enforced separation and ignorance of the other man will result in untold misery for this country - not only for the white man but for the black as well.

The views expressed in this collection deserve the serious attention and thought of all South Africans irrespective of colour, creed, race or age. I commend the work, however, to the whites, particularly to the Afrikaners who wield political power, for it will enable them to understand what the African leaders and their people are thinking as well as the dilemma which faces them.

I have found reading this book immensely exciting - and at times touching. The editors Hendrik W. van der Merwe, Nancy C.J. Charton, D.A. Kotzé and Åke Magnusson have done South Africa a great service by collecting and editing the articles and speeches. Special mention must also be given to Terence Beard for a very scholarly, stimulating and analytical general introduction.

Black Homelands: Consolidation Proposals, March 1975 (Map by courtesy of Africa Institute of South Africa, Pretoria)

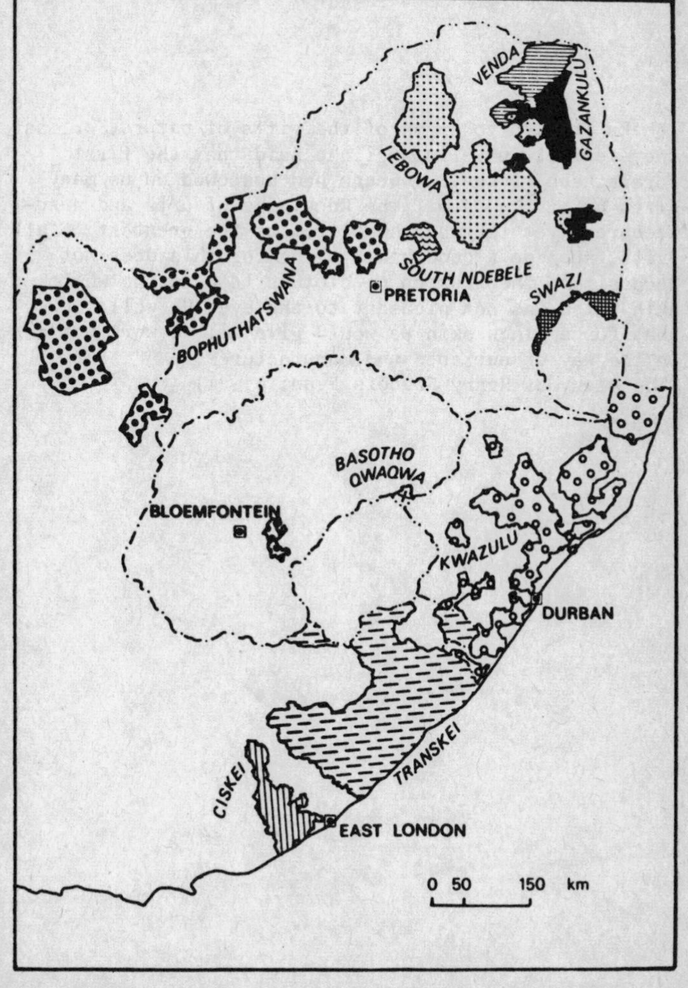

'Shaka went on to speak of the gifts of nature, or, as they term it, uMvelinqangi. He said that the first forefathers of the Europeans had bestowed on us many gifts by giving us all the knowledge of arts and manufactures, yet they had kept from us the greatest of all gifts, such as a good black skin, for this does not necessitate the wearing of clothes to hide the white skin which was not pleasant to the eye. He well knew that for a black skin we would give all we were worth in the way of our arts and manufactures.'
(The Diary of Henry Francis Fynn: p. 81)

General Introduction

T.V.R.BEARD
Professor of Political Studies, Rhodes University, Grahamstown

One of the most striking developments in South Africa over the past few years has been the gradual acknowledgment among the white ruling elites of the necessity for political, social and economic change. The belief that the status quo might be maintained has been steadily eroded away, so that by the General Election of 1974 all the white political parties except the Herstigte Nasionale Party had adopted policies of change with either manifest or latent and perhaps unintended radical implications for the long term. In this atmosphere, created in no small measure by South Africa's increasing isolation in the world, Mr Vorster's detente policy was welcomed by the parliamentary opposition, itself undergoing changes in party alignments under the pressures for change, and whose reactions have been characterised by continual stressing of the need for dialogue and change within South Africa itself.

African politicians such as Chief Gatsha Buthelezi of KwaZulu have continually emphasised this need, and perhaps for the first time in South Africa's history, it can be said that the elites of all racial and ethnic groups are at one at least about the need for change and, to a degree, about the direction which such change should take: that of a sharing of power with blacks. The form and extent of such 'sharing' are subjects of such deep controversy, however, that there is no question of a consensus existing or developing. The concept of 'sharing power' is itself far from clear and little can be said beyond the significant fact that there are clear signs that South Africans of all colours are more and more coming to believe that the status quo cannot be maintained and that change in some form or another is both inevitable and necessary.

The coup in Portugal and the consequent independence of Moçambique under Frelimo with its avowed Marxist ideology and goals, followed by the civil war in Angola, in which South Africa intervened, culminating in the coming to power of yet another Marxist regime in Southern Africa; the acceptance by Mr Smith of the Kissinger proposals for Zimbabwe/Rhodesia, followed by the Geneva conference; all these have been developments of the greatest importance for South Africa. For the first time there has been 'great power' involvement in Southern Africa, an involvement which is likely to continue, and there are indications that the pressures against 'white' rule in South Africa will steadily mount. Not even the possibility of mandatory sanctions against South Africa can be discounted, although at present they seem unlikely.

The changes in Southern Africa and the pressures against South Africa itself have had a dramatic effect upon the perceptions of South African blacks. For the first time for well over a decade, blacks have begun to question the immutability of 'white' domination and to anticipate processes of change in which their roles will not be those of mere subordinates dictated to by a 'white' government. The civil unrest which broke out in June 1976 was symptomatic of this new hope, for, although it began in Soweto, ostensibly over the place of instruction in Afrikaans in school curricula, it rapidly spread to other parts of South Africa and continued long after the government had given way over the school-language issue. It was marked, too, by the participation of coloureds in the demonstrations, a development of signal significance considering the traditional political apathy which had characterised the bulk of the coloured population over the years. It is not too much to say that 'Soweto' marks a watershed in South African recent political history, for, despite the fact that the unrest has posed no really serious threat to the regime, insofar as it has been contained by the police without need to call in the army, it is nevertheless likely that civil unrest will either continue or recur. The new mood which is evident in the black population, buttressed as it is by developments in other parts of Southern Africa, is not likely easily to be broken by governmental countermeasures as happened in the mid-1960s, for the external pressures are steadily mounting, 'white' domination is becoming increasingly beleaguered, so that set-backs to black aspirations are likely to be regarded as no more than temporary.

Against this background the need for a new dispensation in South Africa is becoming self-evident and the judgment of Aristotle that 'a state with a body of disfranchised citizens who are numerous and poor must necessarily be a state which is full of enemies' was never more pertinent for the white-dominated oligarchy in South Africa. It might be said that it is precisely this problem to which the white political parties have addressed their attention, offering two main alternatives to the white electorate.

The first of these alternatives is separate development, the policy of the National Party government, which seeks to solve the problem by the creation of new states for the African disfranchised, so holding out the hope of continued white autonomy within 'white' South Africa; and the second consists of variations upon the federal theme, so opting for a multi-racial state with a 'sharing' of power among the various races and ethnic groups. Critics of the first alternative point to the fact that the creation of separate and autonomous states for Africans will not alter the fact that for the foreseeable future there will be more blacks in 'white' South Africa than whites, and that to denominate them resident aliens suggests sleight of hand, and offers no real solution to the problem stated by Aristotle. Critics of the second alternative lay stress upon white 'identity' and claim that a federal solution can result only in black majority rule and consequently in the loss of white power, 'identity', and standards of living.

That the disfranchised in South Africa are not only poor and numerous (roughly three-quarters of the population) but are also black (to employ that term in its modern and more inclusive sense) is a factor of fundamental importance, for the most significant cleavages in the society are not only consistent but cluster around the variable of colour. That the poor and the powerless are also black is a consequence of white domination and exclusiveness, which has led to colour coming to assume more importance than class in the dynamics of change within the system at least at the level of politics and ideology. The placement of blacks in the system then, relates directly to their colour, and is explained by blacks themselves in these terms. The polarisation between black and white which appears to be steadily developing in South Africa is a process whereby blacks are becoming, to adapt a Marxian term, 'a group for themselves', and Black Consciousness and Black Power are particular manifestations of this process. Thus, although class and colour cleavages are consistent to a high degree, colour is generally seen to be more important if only because class position is taken to be dependent upon colour owing to the ascriptive nature of the latter.

It is against this background of racial polarisation that the development of the 'homelands' and the speeches and writings of the 'homeland' leaders should be seen. To what extent does the creation of homelands diffuse and inhibit black solidarity? To what extent will the economic gap between black and white be narrowed in the short term; and to what extent will the 'daily-life' experiences of blacks, probably the single most important factor in the determining of black attitudes towards whites, be changed for the better? The internalisation of these attitudes and their articulation at the political level has been evident throughout the history of African nationalism in South Africa, and is a theme frequently referred to by black leaders in every sphere (see for instance Ciskei National Party Policy; Ntsanwisi: Petty Apartheid; Mangope: The Political Future of the Homelands; Buthelezi: Report Back; as well as numerous other references in this book). And it is safe to assume that these attitudes will continue to be articulated and will play no small part in the determination of black goals in South Africa.

The views which are expressed in this book, while important to South Africans of all colours, are of perhaps greatest importance to whites as the custodians of power, for they will enable them to gauge to some extent what African leaders and their followers are thinking. At the same time it should not be forgotten that these leaders are all in varying degrees prisoners of a system not of their own choosing (Ntsanwisi: The Hour of Decision), and furthermore that the pressures of the system result in a toning down or muting rather than an amplification of the most heartfelt feelings of both writers and speakers.

The ideas, sentiments, feelings and goals expressed

by African leaders in the South Africa of the early and mid-1970s are for the most part, like the articulation of attitudes referred to above, variations upon themes which emerged during the formative years of African political movements, although indeed some themes such as the land question go back even further. All these themes are played upon within a context changing and yet unchanged, a society more open and yet more closed, more free and yet less free. They are being played out within the context of what is now commonly called 'separate development', a term which has replaced the now rather time-worn and discredited 'apartheid'.

One of the first questions which must occur to anyone interested in contemporary developments in South Africa is whether or not separate development carries with it any significant changes from the old policy of apartheid, or whether it is simply the old policy in a new guise. And the answer to this is by no means a straightforward one. In the first place there is no doubt that the announcement by Dr Verwoerd, in January 1959, of the policy of self-governing 'homelands' signified a departure from what had been declared government policy during the previous eleven years of National Party government rule. This new policy, after further elaboration and clarification, had as its defined goal the sovereign independence of the 'homelands', and was given the name of Separate Development. The declaration of policy was followed up by a draft constitution for the Transkei and subsequently a Transkei Constitution Act was passed by the South African parliament. This in turn was followed by a general constitutional enabling Act (the Constitution of the Bantu Homelands Act, 1971) in terms of which other 'homelands' have been given constitutions. The Transkei has now been operating as a separate but subordinate legislative entity since 1963, and received formal independence in October 1976. It is therefore possible to point to what appears to be a fundamental change in policy dating from the 1959 speech of Dr Verwoerd, for prior to this 'apartheid' had meant no more than a system of devolution under white 'baasskap'.

This change in policy was in part a response to overseas pressures on South Africa, for as Dr Verwoerd himself put it '... we tell the people of South Africa that we cannot govern without taking into account the tendencies in the world and in Africa. We must have regard to them. Our policy must take them into account. And we can only take them into account and safeguard the white man's control over our country if we move in the direction of separation - separation in the political sphere at any rate' (Kruger, 1960: 437). On the other hand it is a policy which its proponents seek to justify on moral grounds. Dr C. P. Mulder, for instance, describes separate development as being 'in accordance with both the wording and the spirit of the United Nations Charter, when it speaks of the self-determination "of peoples", in that it respects the identity and dignity of the diverse peoples of the Republic and seeks to lead them each and all to a state in which they may competently manage their own affairs' (Rhoodie, 1972: 49).

The implementation of the policy of separate development has resulted in its generating a momentum of its own. This is due to three main interlinked factors: the continuing isolation of South Africa and the pressures from without, the demands emanating from the newly created 'homelands' themselves, and the necessary implications of the policy itself. The first factor has led to an accelerating drive for economic 'autarchy' and so to increasing emphasis being placed upon economic growth. As Prime Minister Vorster has stressed, South Africa has to maintain a high economic growth rate because in an uncertain world with many enemies it is of great importance for South Africa to be economically strong. A higher rate of growth would also raise the living standards of all South Africans, including the poorest and least-developed of the country's population groups, and furthermore it would be needed to curb an urgent economic problem - economic unemployment among the African population (Rand Daily Mail, 6 November 1973). This partly explains the shift towards increasing economic development within the 'homelands' in addition to the previously enunciated policy of 'border industries'. The present economic recession in South Africa therefore constitutes a serious threat to the success of this policy of growth.

The demands for economic development from 'homeland' governments and leaders are likewise steadily increasing and, what is more, these demands are not restricted to development within the confines of the 'homelands' but increasingly include demands from blacks in white urban complexes (Sebe: Change for Development; Mabandla: Election Statement).

Thirdly, the policy of separate development itself has important implications, for given the need for economic growth and given that the policy aims at a decrease in the relative proportion of blacks dependent upon the migratory labour system, development within, as well as outside the 'homelands', is the only rational policy. In any case the policy would hardly be meaningful without economic as well as political development.

As a result of this momentum which is being generated it is possible to discern a new emphasis in the patterns of government policy. Especially since 1968, with the passing of the Promotion of Economic Development of the Homelands Act, and subsequent administrative decisions, the pace of 'homeland' development has quickened.

And yet, apart from some of the leaders who have emerged within the 'homelands' system, the tradition among the African elites has been to reject separate development, and apart from the Transkei and recent developments in BophuthaTswana, there is as yet little evidence to show that this tradition is being displaced; in fact the civil unrest has revealed and increased its strength. The government, for its part, regards the existing system in South Africa as a conflict model, perceiving opposition to the policy of separate development as a manifestation of this, and the policy itself as a means of creating a consensus system in Southern Africa. White control is seen as being obviously incompatible with black political rights except on the basis of a geographical division into separate power blocs. Government strategy therefore involves the containment and stifling of 'left-wing' pressures, which include political and para-political organisations emerging in 'illegitimate' contexts (e.g. the banning of trades union leaders, and leaders of SASO and the Black People's Convention), while building up the 'homeland' structures with their 'legitimised' governments and leaders.

In the international context, government strategy would appear to be to play for time, while hoping that the independence of the Transkei will prove the vindication of its whole policy. As yet it has met with scant success for not only the United Nations and the Organisation of African Unity have withheld recognition of the Transkei, but the European Economic Community have also refused to afford it recognition. Despite an ambitious propaganda campaign, the South African government has thus clearly failed, at least for the immediate future, to persuade even those countries with which it has the closest ties to give to the Transkei the recognition without which the policy of separate development cannot be vindicated.

Separate development is not seen by all its proponents as a final goal. For some it is a kind of halfway house to a future commonwealth of Southern Africa or to a confederation of Southern African states. What is clear, is that the policy does mark a departure from the old policy of apartheid.

In 1948, the Malan government had been returned largely on the basis of its commitment to the policy of apartheid, which meant among other things 'baasskap' or white domination. While apartheid was built upon the foundations of the traditional racial policies of segregation, it came to embody a new ideologically based set of structures providing segregation policy with a new rationale. Over the years a vast volume of legislation was passed, firstly in the name of segregation and then of apartheid, and this legislation remains on the statute book virtually unaltered. Furthermore the murmurings of discontent and later the civil disobedience which ensued from 1948 through to 1964 and after, resulted in further legislation designed to bolster up, secure, and maintain, white domination. Apartheid legislation thus came to comprise two kinds, legislation reinforcing and extending racial segregation, and legislation ensuring the efficacy of that racial legislation in the face of opposition (which included civil disobedience) to it. This latter kind is generally termed 'security' legislation.

The implementation of apartheid thus necessitated an ever-increasing growth of government and bureaucratic power and with it an ever-narrowing area of personal liberty not only for blacks but for whites as well. The price of apartheid has been a substantial loss of the democratic rights of whites, let alone its effects upon blacks.

The constitutional struggle of the 1950s saw the

translation of the constitutional doctrine of parliamentary sovereignty that parliament could make or unmake any law whatever, into a political doctrine giving carte blanche to the government. At the same time, it began to be clear that sayings such as those of St Paul, that governments are ordained by God, were interpreted to mean that the acts of government were so ordained. In this atmosphere of political absolutism, South Africa has moved steadily away from western democratic norms towards the norms of authoritarian and even totalitarian states. Disagreement with government policies, due in part to a tendency to identify the government with the state, has increasingly come to be equated with a lack of patriotism and with subversion.

The change of policy from apartheid to separate development has seen no significant changes either in apartheid or in security legislation, the latter having been steadily added to since 1959 under Dr Verwoerd himself, and subsequently under Mr Vorster. On the other hand security legislation, it can now be held, is necessary to ensure stability during the transition to a 'multi-state' system. But the important point remains that apartheid legislation remains intact in the statute books and thus far separate development has not involved the repeal of a single major apartheid Act. There thus coexist two sets of structures, one designed to ensure the social, political and economic subordination of blacks, and the other, purporting to be, in Dr Mulder's words, 'in accordance with both the wording and spirit of the United Nations Charter...'

It is against this background that present developments are occurring (see Mabandla: Problems of Homeland Transition). On the other hand the legislation passed in pursuit of 'baasskap' remains intact and new legislation passed in the name of state security accumulates at every session of parliament, while on the other hand several 'homelands' are now progressing towards self-government and possible eventual independence. The two sets of legislation are not seen as contradictory by their proponents, and one of the main questions to be answered over the next few years is the extent to which they are mutually compatible, and to what extent the old policies will have to give way to ensure the viability of the new, if indeed the new policies can be made viable.

In this context pertinent questions arise. For example, how valid is the analogy, frequently appealed to by government supporters, between migrant labour in Europe and migrant labour in South Africa? Again to what extent is racial discrimination in 'white' South Africa compatible with the sovereign independence of the 'homelands'? These are crucial questions, for the African population of 'white' South Africa will always exceed the white population, and even granting that the status of Africans resident in 'white' South Africa will be that of foreign visitors, will South Africa be able to continue to discriminate against Africans by refusing to accord them the same rights and privileges as are accorded to white resident aliens and visitors from abroad? It would seem safe to assert that racial equality is not envisaged by the National Party government, and 'baasskap' cannot be eliminated as long as people are classified and accorded rights and privileges purely on the basis of race or colour.

South African policies thus appear to be paradoxical or even self-contradictory, and once this is realised the full force of the opinions expressed in this book becomes apparent. On the one hand separate development gives to Africans a degree of power and a relative security from harassment which they have never before enjoyed, at least since white hegemony was finally established, but on the other hand the position of Africans in 'white' areas has never been more uncertain and the position of leaders who have emerged in politica and para-political organisations which do not enjoy government sponsorship has never been more insecure. It means that leaders established by government-instituted legislatures, councils and boards are in a new position of power, but that leaders and activists who emerge outside the ambit of these 'legitimised' institutions have never been more vulnerable.

Two sets of legislation with incompatible goals lie uneasily side by side, a fact which has important repercussions for the contemporary scene. It helps explain for instance how a leader such as Sonny Leon can emerge through the elective processes of the Coloured Persons Representative Council and become firstly official leader of the opposition and, later, Chairman of the Executive Committee (a post from which he was later dismissed). His position of prominence is a direct result of the government policy of separate development. At the same time it explains why, while he was still leader of the opposition, Leon was refused a passport, an action which points inter alia to the policy of white domination. Similarly Chief Gatsha Buthelezi owes his position of power in KwaZulu to the policy of separate development, while on the other hand there would seem to be reasonably reliable evidence to the effect that his opposition to that policy and to the structures of apartheid has led to clandestine attempts by government agents to undermine his position and to create an opposition party (Sunday Tribune, 26 May 1974 and 18 April 1971). The coexistence of apartheid and separate development is seen also in the incidents which have occurred from time to time and which have been reported in the daily press, where African leaders 'legitimised' by government-created institutions have been subjected to humiliating and embarrassing experiences at the hands of whites, sometimes government officials, in hotels, restaurants, and at the Jan Smuts Airport. The reason for this kind of occurrence is perhaps to be found in the fact that these leaders are treated as exceptions to general rules relating to the use by blacks of 'white' hotels and restaurants, and the managers of these establishments have difficulty in interpreting the administrative rulings which make exceptions of black leaders. The position has changed slightly with the opening of certain 'international' hotels to people of all races so that the frequency of these incidents may be reduced, but the class of hotels which are now 'open' ensure that it is only the black elite which is being catered for.

The continued presence of the structures and practices of apartheid undermines the newly established status of African 'homeland' leaders and complicates the whole question of their roles and their status. White domination remains a basic fact of life and with it the subordinate status of all persons who are not classified as white (Guzana: On Being a South African; Ntsanwisi: Petty Apartheid; Mangope: The Political Future of the Homelands). While Africans now do have the new 'homeland' structures in terms of the concept of 'Separate Freedoms', these freedoms are nominal rather than real for the approximately 56 per cent of Africans who reside and work outside the 'homelands', most of whom will continue to do so at least for the rest of their working lives. In their daily lives the master-servant relationship remains virtually unchanged; despite the repeal of the Master and Servants legislation which applied in the four provinces, and the passing of legislation legalising strikes by Africans under certain circumstances, it remains true that blacks suffer serious disadvantages in terms of the law which make it difficult to form meaningful trade unions or conduct meaningful bargaining with employers in government-sponsored work committees. The daily life experiences of Africans have undergone no significant changes in these respects.

A significant proportion of Africans who reside and work outside the 'homelands' were born in 'white' areas, some having no relatives in or connections with the 'homelands' whatever. The fact that these classes of persons are accorded 'homeland' citizenship and are enrolled as 'homeland' voters confirms their positions as 'strangers' in the rest of South Africa where they are employed. As foreigners without votes they cannot influence the South African political process. It means furthermore that the most sophisticated of the African population, the urbanised Africans, play the smallest part in the African political processes which are controlled and run largely by the rural populations. The manpower thus lost must be very considerable, for unlike the development of any other underdeveloped area, the bulk of the educated elites play little or no part in the processes of political development. On the other hand this elite participates in and contributes to the economic development of the developed sectors of the economy, the 'white' sector. The problem of 'the urban African' as it is usually referred to, is then not simply a problem of how this class of African is to be given meaningful political rights, it includes the question of how they are to contribute to the development of areas of which they are nominally citizens, but with which they have no physical contact.

These are the factors which help to explain the continuity in the themes played upon by African leaders from the beginning of the century through to the present day, such changes as there are being, for the most part, changes in emphasis rather than changes in theme. The single important exception is the new theme of 'homeland status'. It is not surprising therefore that the 'homeland' leaders should be concerned about the deprivations from which blacks suffer, or indeed that they have gone so far as to press the South African government for the release of political prisoners and the return of the political exiles who are perceived as symbols in the struggle for black emancipation.

And yet separate development is something new. It does envisage the sovereign independence of the 'homelands' and with it the creation of a new set of 'nation' states - the dividing up of the territories of present day South Africa, or its Balkanisation, depending upon one's point of view. One of the most important questions which arises out of the implementation of this policy is: to what extent will it involve the dismantling of the structures and practices of apartheid? For on the answer to this question hang the answers to several other questions, such as the extent to which the sovereign independence of the 'homelands' can be meaningful; and whether the new policy will do any more than partially to replace colonial-type subordination with neo-colonial subordination; and, as already mentioned, whether Africans in 'white' South Africa will remain subject to apartheid and all that it implies once the 'homelands' attain independence. It seems not unlikely that only after the complete abandonment of apartheid in every form can separate development have a chance of success. And yet while there remains a large African population in the 'white' areas, such a dismantling process would undermine the policy of separate development itself. And so the paradox reemerges. Apartheid is the major impediment to the success of separate development, and yet without it separate development would appear to stand little chance of success. One possible way out of this impasse lies in a more radical redistribution of land to the extent that 'homelands' can become viable enough to support the overwhelming majority of Africans, and for this to be feasible the 'homelands' would have to include areas which are both industrialised and rich in natural resources, a price which whites appear unprepared to pay. But I shall return to the question of land.

The contradictions which characterise present-day policies can be traced in the speeches of 'homeland' leaders. Leaders who, like Chief Kaiser Matanzima, accept the policy of separate development, have made it clear that they do not like discrimination against their peoples in 'white' South Africa. White domination is rejected by the overwhelming majority of Africans if not by all. (See for example Mabandla on Ciskei politics; Guzana: On Being a South African; Ntsanwisi: Petty Apartheid; Mangope: The Future of the Homelands; Buthelezi: Report Back.)

White domination and the racial discrimination on which it is based are indirectly the driving forces behind Black Consciousness. As the reference to Shaka makes clear, black was beautiful before the advent of the white man, but subordination in all its guises, military, technical, social, economic and political, fundamentally affected the self-image of Africans, and Black Consciousness manifests a new striving for self-identity and self-pride, a striving for the creation of a new modern man inferior in no way to people of other races and colours. Black Consciousness essentially is linked to modernity. And yet it is necessary to be aware of the difficulties of accurately identifying the driving forces behind Black Consciousness and of defining the concept itself, for we are dealing with a subject about which comparatively little is known and about which there is scant research. It is of some value therefore to stress what Black Consciousness is not, before attempting a few tentative comments on its nature. Zulus, Xhosas, Tembus, Sothos and members of the various other tribal groups in South Africa are not only usually well aware of their tribal histories but take pride in their tribal identities, even in cases of people who see themselves primarily as Africans and who feel that tribalism is an anachronism in the modern world. But Black Consciousness has little or nothing to do with tribal identity, although it is not necessarily incompatible with it. Neither has Black Consciousness to do with personal identity as such, although the personality problems of individual Africans may be directly related to their 'being-black-in-the-world'. Black Consciousness is what it prima facie purports to be; it is an awareness and an acceptance of being black and an assertion of equality of black people as human beings among other human beings who have subordinated them in manifold ways. It therefore transcends tribal and personal identity, and relates to African desires to be recognised as Africans and as men. This is evidenced not only in the non-tribal nature of most African political movements of the past, but by a continuance of this tradition. Black Consciousness continues to make itself felt politically in such organisations as the South African Students' Organisation, the Black People's Convention and the League of the African Youth. Mangope even sees it as being compatible with the 'homeland' structures (Mangope: The Political Future of the Homelands). The League of the African Youth defines an African as 'anybody who cannot trace his genealogical origin outside the continent of Africa', while the Black People's Convention sees Black Consciousness as embracing liberation from psychological and physical oppression, education of black by black for black, equality, communalism, black theology, and non-cooperation in white-created structures. Guzana, on the other hand, sees it as 'counter-arrogance born of frustration and despair, manifesting itself in rejection and exclusivity, in emphasis on black identity to measure up to and counterbalance the arrogance of the white South African' (Guzana: On Being a South African).

Today most African organisations, apart from 'homeland' political parties (but not all of them) and with the significant exception of Inkatha, are non-ethnic in their membership. This applies particularly to professional and cultural organisations, African Churches, the National African Chamber of Commerce, the South African Students' Organisation, the National Council of African Women, teachers' associations and many sports associations and, perhaps most importantly, the black trade union movement.

Black Consciousness is also manifest in the demand for an education which is oriented towards blacks, of blacks, and by blacks. In religion it is apparent in the demands for self-help and self-evaluation, and in the new black theology. At community level Black Consciousness is seen in the demand for community development and the growth of cultural associations. Black Consciousness is evident at all levels of the black communities, and it retains, for the most part, its non-tribal nature, a feature which finds support from many 'homeland' leaders (see Mabandla: The Problems of Homeland Transition; Principles of the C.N.I.P.;

Buthelezi: Words of Identification and Report Back).

While separate development envisages ethnic or tribal separation, the structures and practices of apartheid tend to make Africans ever more aware of their common identity as underprivileged blacks. Black Consciousness unites all Africans whether or not they accept the ideology of Black Power, in terms of which blacks reject the aid and cooperation of whites, in the belief that only through purely black organisations can they achieve their goals. Their dominant position enables whites to practise policies of divide and rule, and yet this very dominance serves to draw blacks together and militates against the success of such policies of division. The dismantling of white domination may release tribal forces and bring about deep tribal cleavages, especially between smaller tribal groups and larger ones, but its presence acts as a catalyst enabling the pressures towards wider unity to outweigh tribal considerations. And this unity continues to gather strength under the psychological umbrella of Black Consciousness. The civil unrest which began in Soweto has amply demonstrated the strength of Black Consciousness among urban blacks and has revealed the growing attraction of the Black Power movement.

The policy adopted in all the 'homelands' to have English as the language of higher education carries with it not only the desire to be knowledgeable in a world language, but points also to two other implications which may be partly intentional. These are firstly that the 'homelands' will have a language common to all of them and, secondly, the identification of Afrikaans with white domination. It is not uncommon for blacks to refer to Afrikaans as 'the language of the oppressor', and so to link it with the rationale of Black Consciousness and Black Power. This again was demonstrated at Soweto in June 1976.

It would be a gross distortion, not to say over-simplification, not to acknowledge that there exist tensions between tribal and/or regional pressures on the one hand and the pressures for a wider unity on the other. One indication of this is the decision by the Transkei to opt for independence in spite of Matanzima's being a signatory to the Umtata Declaration in which a 'summit meeting' of 'homeland' leaders publicly stated that they would not unilaterally opt for independence within the existing confines of land distribution and political power. On the other hand, that particular expression of Black Consciousness which has come to be known as Black Power, whose chief overt proponents are students, has tended to be identified with the repudiation of the 'homelands' policy in its entirety, for it is seen as a policy of divide-and-rule which is intended to forestall the growth of black political power. Black power movements have rejected even the idea that the 'homelands' should be tactically employed as power bases for the achievement of black goals (see chapter by Pityana in Van der Merwe and Welsh (eds), 1972: 178). And in turn Black Power has been condemned by the 'homeland' leaders. Chief Buthelezi, perhaps the chief supporter of the Umtata Declaration, has made no secret of his rejection of separate development and his decision to employ it only because there is no alternative and because it does provide a platform and a power base for the articulation and the pursuit of African goals and interests, but even he is rejected by some of the Black Power leaders and has condemned them in return. Events in Soweto led to a widening of the gulf which separates Chief Buthelezi and his Black Power critics.

Chief Kaiser Matanzima, who accepts the policy of separate development, has frequently referred to a Transkeian (regional) identity, the growth of which poses even greater problems for the proponents of African and black unity. The South African government, on its part, would seem to be relying upon the growth of local, tribal and regional power blocs with strong vested interests of their own which would militate against future unity or federation and, hopefully, prevent its eventual attainment. This would explain the refusal by the government to entertain the possibility of a federal plan for the 'homelands' prior to their independence.

The failure of attempts at closer union to the north, as in East Africa, seems to point to the unlikelihood of states coalescing once they achieve independence, and the attempts in the Arab world would seem to carry the same lesson. On the other hand, the drive towards greater Arab unity, despite its failure to date, has by no means lost its momentum and the analogy with the South African situation is striking. The movement for Arab unity has gained its main impetus from the

Arab-Israeli confrontation. The very presence of the state of Israel has done more to foster Arab unity than any other single factor, and possibly outweighs all the other factors combined. In South Africa the very presence of a dominant white minority has a similar force. So long as whites remain paramount in South Africa, pressures for black unity are likely to grow, however strong 'homeland' governments might become, for white domination of the developed areas of South Africa means in effect white domination over Southern Africa through control of the economic system.

Having said all this, however, we should not assume that African unity in some form or other is inevitable - what is being argued is that the drive for some such unity is likely to continue and to be reinforced by developments in Rhodesia/Zimbabwe and in South West Africa/Namibia. And the continuation of this drive is likely to lead to a greater polarisation between black and white, with confrontation and conflict becoming more probable. The possibility of parties dedicated to Black Power being formed and gaining support in the 'homelands', or of existing parties adopting Black Power policies cannot be ruled out. To put it colloquially, these are early days yet, and a priori assumptions can be dangerous. It is as dangerous to assume that separate development will provide a simple solution to South Africa's race problems as it is to assume that revolution or violent change is inevitable.

Political power must perforce operate within a geographical framework, and central to white domination over blacks in South Africa both historically and in the present is the control of land. Land starvation has been an issue for Africans for at least a hundred years. The frontier wars, the Great Trek, and the Zulu wars resulted in Africans being dispossessed of much of their land, and this is true of all four provinces of South Africa and of present-day Lesotho as well. This dispossession was made legal both by conquest and by legislation passed by the former colonies and republics, and consolidated by the Land Act of 1913, the purpose of which, ironically, was to ensure inter alia that no further land could be alienated from Africans in the areas reserved for them, the price for such security being the prohibition of the purchasing of land in 'white' areas by Africans, except in urban townships set aside for African occupation. The

Land Act of 1913 accepted as de facto and legal the white occupation of land which had been traditionally occupied by Africans in the past, placing such areas beyond African acquisition by confirming their classification as 'white' areas. Some land which was traditionally African was declared Crown Land, as was, for example, a part of the traditional Tongaland south of the Moçambique border in northern Natal, a region which has been occupied by the amaTonga since early Portuguese exploration. Parts of this land have since been opened to white occupation.

The Land Act had immediate repercussions among Africans, as is recounted by Sol Plaatje in his Native Life in South Africa, which was written to publicise the plight of Africans as a result of the new legislation, and a deputation was sent to the United Kingdom to try to persuade the British government to disallow the Act, but to no avail. The Land Act was considered pernicious by Africans even at a time when the populations of the reserve areas were small by modern standards, and when there was no thought of separate development in the modern sense. Africans complained that they had been allocated only a small portion of the land of their birth and that they were being condemned to starvation.

The Native Trust and Land Act of 1936 was to an extent an acknowledgment that the 1913 Act had been unfair to Africans, for the Minister of Native Affairs, in introducing the Bill, not only pointed out that the 1913 Act had been designed as an interim measure but that the existing 'native reserves' were inadequate. However, the 1936 Act, while adding substantially to the reserves by demarcating 'Released Areas', within which, as the Minister put it, 'the restrictions upon the purchase of land for native settlement will be removed', still meant that the Released Areas together with the areas reserved in 1913 comprised no more than thirteen per cent of the land area of South Africa.

The consolidation of the 'homelands' in terms of the policy of separate development will involve a radical redrawing of boundaries, but the total area to be allocated is still to be based upon the 1936 allocations. Land areas which were considered to be totally inadequate under the old segregation policy, when the reserves were no more than regions set aside for exclusive African occupation, are now to form the territorial bases of independent states. When the growth in population since 1936 is taken into account it becomes obvious that land areas which were inadequate then are now quite unrealistically so. (Principles of the C.N.I.P.; Mabandla: The Problems of Homeland Transition; Buthelezi: Afrikaner Ascendancy and the Challenge of the Seventies; KwaZulu Development; Mangope: The Political Future of the Homelands.) The single partial exception is the Transkei - for there the land problem is relatively less acute, although like the other 'homelands' it is heavily over-populated.

What makes the problem less acute is that most of the historical Transkei is part of the 'homeland', and Chief Matanzima, having already successfully negotiated for the inclusion of Port St John's, Herschel, and Glen Grey, has made claim to other areas such as Matatiele. On the other hand, the acceptance of the independence proposals by the Transkei government in 1976, particularly as expressed in the Status of the Transkei Act, however, would seem to imply a tacit acceptance of the existing land allocation.

There is not a single 'homeland' leader who has not taken up the land question as an issue, and Chief Buthelezi of KwaZulu, which is to be 'consolidated' into ten 'islands' each surrounded by 'white' territory, has questioned the bona fides of government policy, claiming with every justification that KwaZulu could not possibly opt for independence under such conditions. Only a small part of historical Zululand is included in KwaZulu and it is probably true to say that large parts of Natal now designated 'white' were African-occupied land prior to white settlement. Richards Bay, in particular, has become a bone of contention.

The same principles apply to most other parts of the country. For example, the frontier wars of the Eastern Cape are widely known among Africans as the Wars of Dispossession, the 'white' parts of the Ciskei being the areas referred to. Lesotho, too, claims parts of the Orange Free State which were lost to the baSotho in the wars of the 1860s. The assumptions by the South African government and its supporters that the 'homeland' policy will settle the land question once and for all is no more than wishful thinking, and land is likely to be one of the most important issues in the immediate future and one which can be settled only by a radical re-allocation or by the adoption of a policy other than separate development.

The prospect of 'homeland' independence gives a new urgency to the land question for no 'homeland', with the possible exception of Transkei, is going to be satisfied with a territory which holds no prospect of viability even in the limited sense of enabling it to employ a majority of its labour force within its own boundaries. White conquest was the deciding factor in the division and ownership of land, and white domination the deciding factor in the consolidation of the 'homelands' - in both cases the decisions have so far been unilateral.

One of the main characteristics of the African National Congress and the Non-European Unity Movement (All Africa Convention) was their commitment to socialist goals, however vaguely these goals happened to be defined. The A.N.C. did not have a social blueprint for the future, perhaps for two main reasons, firstly that there was no ideological consensus within the organisation and, secondly because, as had been the case in African territories to the north, future goals tended to be subordinated to the more immediate and overriding goal of liberation. The closest that the A.N.C. came to defining its goals lay in its acceptance of the Freedom Charter, a compromise document intended to accommodate communists, socialists and liberals in the movement, which at once ruled out any attempt at precision or detail.

'Homeland' leaders have not so far propounded socialist principles per se but they have appealed to the concept of 'sharing' and to the idea of co-operatives (see Buthelezi: Issues in KwaZulu; Afrikaner Ascendancy and the Challenge of the Seventies; Ntsanwisi: The Hour of Decision; Sebe: Traditional Attitudes Towards Agriculture). The position of the 'homelands' as parts of the Republic of South Africa places them in a particularly difficult position regarding the choice of alternative paths to development, and alternative means to be employed in developing.

Their options are, doubtless, considerably reduced by these geographical, as well as the economic, political and social facts of life. The South African economy is a single economy, albeit dualistic in having an advanced industrial sector co-existing with an underdeveloped sector. But while the 'homelands' lie in the underdeveloped sector, the vast majority of their labour force, which is largely unskilled, is employed in the developed sector. The 'homelands' are thus dependent upon this developed and industrialised sector, which lies outside their borders, for the subsistence of their populations. Their options are therefore curtailed in several ways: by the fact that only a small proportion of their labour force is available for internal development; by the fact that labour employed in the 'white' developed sector is being socialised in the values of the 'white' capitalist economic system; and by such facts as the high cost of diverting industry from the developed to the undeveloped areas. They are also affected by the fact that 'border industries', the main foci of diverted industries, lie on the 'white' side of their borders, so affecting their own internal development. 'Border industries' which lie close to 'white' urban areas such as Durban, Pinetown and Pretoria tend to result in the labour force spending their income in the 'white' towns and cities and so not benefiting the revenues or the trade of the 'homelands'.

There is also the dilemma as to whether or not the 'homelands' ought to continue to regard themselves as regions within the South African economic system, or to aim at the creation of economic systems of their own. The latter choice would seem to involve extremely high costs, probably beyond the means of any of the 'homelands' even with substantial overseas aid. Would it, for example, be possible for 'homelands' to pursue socialist goals, given that they are regions within the South African economic system, and given that the majority of their labour forces are employed within a capitalist system? The same problem arises with regard to the level of living standards aimed at. In short, the shape and pace of development in the 'homelands' depend upon the policies and the cooperation of the Republic of South Africa. Is South Africa, whose policies have always been designed to ensure that Africans do not compete economically with whites, likely to change this policy and encourage competitive development in the 'homelands'? The vetoing by the South African government of the agreement between Lesotho and the Honda company of Japan to assemble motor-cycles in Lesotho was hardly an encouraging sign, but since then it has been announced that a motor assembly plant is to be set up in Transkei, and

Swaziland has been permitted to set up a factory for the assembly of television sets, 20 000 of which may be exported to South Africa per annum. Government policy with respect to the growth of industry in the 'homelands' remains unclear, but this in itself serves to underline the power of that government vis-à-vis the underdeveloped states of southern Africa, especially those underdeveloped states which are wholly dependent upon South Africa for access to the sea. The fact that Transkei is not recognised by the rest of the world will serve to reinforce its dependence upon South Africa.

If the 'homeland' governments are to be restricted in their choice of industries, the whole question of their ability to trade with each other arises. Is there any assurance that they will not be producing the same kinds of goods for the South African market, so finding themselves in a position where they are unable to trade with each other? Such a position would be archetypical of neo-colonialism, the most notable example of which was to be found in Eastern Europe during the postwar Stalinist era (Mamadou Dia, 1962). It is difficult at this point in time to prognosticate about the economic future, but what seems indisputable is the overwhelming dependence of the 'homelands' upon 'white' South Africa.

Of course, it might be argued that this dependence works both ways, the 'white' economy being dependent upon the 'homelands' for the major part of its labour force. Already this is producing a new set of interactions between the 'homelands' and 'white' South Africa. The strikes by African labourers in Natal have been of great concern to the government of KwaZulu, and the unilateral decisions of the South African government no longer go unchallenged. The low wage rates in Natal have been attacked by both the former KwaZulu Councillor for Community Affairs, Mr Barney Dladla, and by Chief Buthelezi. Both also came out strongly in favour of African trade unions, and the 'homeland' leaders are unanimous about the need for living wages for blacks. The South African government remains opposed to the official recognition of African trade unions, but there is no doubt that the de facto power of unofficial unions is greater than their de jure powers. At the same time it remains true that the balance of economic power lies heavily in favour of 'white' South Africa.

There are very broadly two main schools of thought on the question of the influence of economic development upon the future of the South African economic and political systems. These schools of thought diagnose the long-term effects of the increasing mobility of African labour in semi-skilled and even in skilled work in very different ways. The first school of thought contends that this mobility will lead to stability in the economic system, and so in the political system, via the increasing embourgeoisement of African workers, with the gradual formation of an African middle class. This class, they argue, will come to have an increasing interest in the preservation of stability - and they envisage a slow evolutionary process whereby Africans gradually assume more and more economic power, so enabling their accommodation within the political system. And some writers go so far as to assert that this will enable the sharing of power and the growth of a liberal-democratic state. Apart from the fact that the disputants have paid little or no attention to the growth of the 'homelands' and their supposed part in economic development, it can be argued that the very creation of a class of semi-skilled African workers, far from bringing about the predicted economic and political stability, could have precisely the opposite effect. As Crane Brinton has argued, revolutionary activities are often at their greatest at times of rising expectations when new affluent classes are in the process of being formed. In short, it is not possible to make predictions in contexts where so little is known of the more important variables.

The second school of thought contends that present trends are of only minimal benefit to the African labour force, and that the whites who control the system ensure that such developments as are permitted to take place are consistent with continued white domination, and that political and economic power in South Africa reinforce each other. Two different kinds of conclusions are drawn from this. Firstly, that there is no a priori reason why white domination should not continue indefinitely. This invites a comparison with the Soviet system in which a party elite has managed to retain control of the system for sixty years, during which period the U.S.S.R. has progressed from an undeveloped country to a highly industrialised state, in which the managerial, technical and professional classes are successfully contained and enjoy minimal power. Excluding (per impossibile) the intrusion of external pressures, is there any reason why white political power in South Africa cannot be maintained indefinitely? The second possibility which flows from this kind of argument is the increasing polarisation of black and white, of black interests and white interests, until open conflict ensues. Again, contradictory conclusions can be drawn from the same set of premises, which simply goes to show how wide open the theoretical possibilities appear to be.

One of the most important defects of both lines of argument has been the tendency to concentrate on the economic variables to the neglect of the political and sociological variables. The events in the townships since June 1976 reveal the extent to which these socio-political factors play a role, revealing a clash between the ideological interests of the youth and the economic interests of workers. The youth aim at transcending class boundaries and at achieving solidarity of all blacks. At the same time the new African elite has shown a concern for communication with the masses at the grass roots level and likewise has revealed a desire for solidarity. The establishment of Inkatha by Chief Buthelezi is an example of a striving for solidarity in KwaZulu. While it is true that political participation is now circumscribed by the separatist model, the demands for dialogue increase, and the Prime Minister's conferences with 'homeland' leaders have undoubtedly set a precedent for the future. Furthermore, black leaders are very conscious of the world beyond, and this, together with the government's own awareness, serves to enhance if not to enlarge the powers wielded by 'homeland' governments. All these are factors which must be taken into account. Again, what are the effects of colour discrimination in the total system? To what extent is the colour variable related to economic factors? To what extent do the daily-life experiences of blacks determine the attitudes and policies of leaders?

The example of Great Britain in the nineteenth century is possibly of great importance in obtaining insights into the South African situation. Deep class cleavages in Britain, with a small and very affluent class on the one hand and a large and poor working-class on the other, were to a large extent accommodated, with a large middle class emerging and the working-class eventually achieving relatively high standards of real wealth in the twentieth century. The process was evolutionary, but the recent industrial history of Britain reveals that the class cleavages still remain. The South African situation resembles the British nineteenth century one in many respects, but here the large and poor working-classes have one other characteristic in common: that of colour. And it is simply not possible at this stage to say exactly what effect this additional variable will have in the process of change. But the rise of the new Black Consciousness suggests that it will be an important role, for, as Fynn's conversation with Shaka indicates, we have come full circle, with blacks rediscovering their identity and self-assurance. Given a racial polarisation, economic and political developments brought about by whites could have little more than ripple effects determining the strategy and tactics of blacks, rather than bringing about the defusing and diffusion of racial antagonisms within the overall system.

When all is said and done, separate development is a policy adopted, as Dr Verwoerd himself said, 'to safeguard the white man's control' of South Africa, so that the benefits which accrue to blacks are in a sense by-products of a policy designed to protect whites. That whites will have to give up more than they had initially bargained for there can be no doubt, for even the moral rhetoric which has been developed to justify the policy implies this, let alone black demands which have been both created and unleashed in the setting up of the 'homelands'. On the other hand the strength of this moral ingredient is counteracted by what is prescribed by white interests. The conflict between what interests prescribe and what morality dictates is, in the circumstances of South Africa, not only deep but pervasive. And, to adopt a point made by T.S. Eliot in another context, the compulsion to live in such a way that moral behaviour is only possible in a limited number of situations is a very powerful force against moral behaviour. For, as he says, 'behaviour is as potent to affect belief, as belief to affect behaviour'. The re-interpretation of scripture to justify racial segregation is an example of this.

Much depends then upon how whites perceive their own interests, and the pace of change will be affected by the extent to which the conflict between morality and interests is lessened. Change is more and more perceived by whites as a necessary condition for the preservation of their interests, provided that it is controlled and stable change. At the same time, as the necessity for change is seen as increasingly urgent, the time factor assumes more and more importance. For time is essential for controlled and stable change, and when it is in short supply mistakes are more likely to be made and cool judgements become more difficult to make. And this is where the influences from the outside world have their biggest impact. While on the one hand outside pressures have a direct effect upon white interests and are largely responsible for the fact that changes are occurring, on the other hand as these pressures mount, the likelihood of their being counterproductive and reinforcing the 'laager' complex becomes greater.

One thing is certain, and that is that black demands will grow apace, and as these demands are met a climate of rising expectations will be created, expectations which will be further stimulated by the events in former Portuguese Africa, Rhodesia/Zimbabwe, Namibia/South West Africa, and the growing realisation of the latent power which lies in the hands of blacks. Nevertheless, the future may still be fundamentally affected by the extent to which whites are prepared to negotiate meaningfully in allowing for the real needs of blacks to be met and, in particular, for a transformation of the daily-life experience of blacks, which is possibly the most important single factor in the formation of black attitudes towards the political system and towards whites. The new confidence of blacks, together with the black consciousness of which it is one manifestation, and the continuing militancy of black youth, all suggest that unless fundamental changes are brought about soon, the stage for massive conflict will be set.

THE HISTORICAL AND TRADITIONAL BACKGROUND

Some Aspects of African Literature

LENNOX L. SEBE

(Address delivered at the celebration of the 150th year of the publication of the Xhosa language in 1973. Reprinted from South African Outlook, June 1973)

In African thinking, the universe consists of a network of living forces. The universe is a field of forces. Man and woman, dog and stone, even yesterday and east, beauty and laughter - all these are forces related to each other and in continuous interaction. The universe is a unity, in which each part depends on the others, and no part is changeless. If you take possession of part of a thing, you thereby participate in its life force. If you tear a leaf from a tree, not only does the tree quiver, but the whole universe is affected since nothing stands alone. For Europeans, according to Janheinz Jahn, force is an attribute: a being *has* force. In African thinking, force *is* being, being is force, a physical-spiritual energy and potency. The totality of all these living forces is Ntu, Being, which however, is never conceived of as separable from its manifestations. In Ntu, the cosmic universal force, all single forces are tied together. The individual forces fall into four groups, within each of which is a hierarchical ordering: Muntu, Kintu, Hantu and Kuntu.

The Kuntu group contains the forces of relationship, of acting on and of manipulating, of way and manner of acting. They answer questions about the *how* of a culture - that is, about its style. Kuntu-forces are function-forces.

With the foregoing remarks still fresh in our minds let us now touch on yet another important aspect in African literature, namely, African oral literature.

Meinhof once remarked on the surprise people (by people here we mean the non-Africans) felt on every new publication of proverbs, fairy-tales, songs, short stories or novels from Africa, that 'the African, whom we hardly credit with any deep feelings, is infinitely rich in fairy-tales' and that 'these are so like our own fairy-tales'. On the other hand, when Leo Froebenius's twelve-volume anthology, Atlantis, appeared in the 'twenties, European reviewers pointed out basic differences and called African oral literature a complete surprise, revealing 'a world undreamed of'.

Up to now the average European still feels a slight unease on hearing that the 'black man' has a literature at all. In the Introduction to the first great anthology of African oral literature in 1896, August Seidel wrote the following words:

'A wild African! A black beast! Fancy him actually thinking and feeling, his imagination proving vocative! More than that even, fancy him having a sense and appreciation of poetic form, of rhythm and rhyme! It sounds quite incredible, yet it is true. Missionaries should have the credit of first outlining a correct picture of Negroes' natural talents. Philologists, with a more accurate knowledge of native languages, were able to amend this outline. And everyone was amazed to find that the Negro thinks and feels as we ourselves think and feel.'

Seidel's picture of the 'amending' philologists needs some amendment itself. He and Meinhof saw Africa's oral literature as a new and rich field of activity for literary historians - as indeed it could and should have been. For if philologists had explained the common humanity and common feelings as a background against which to point out the style - that factor determined by specific civilisations - they would certainly have reduced the amazement at this literature and gained it wider appreciation. In 1911 Meinhof suggested what needed doing:

'The poetry flows on in irregular lines, of course without rhyme. So far as I can see, the rhythms are different from prose rhythms. At any rate I could register a special poetic rhythm with the Venda. But little research has been done on this, and it presents great difficulty, for the European. I have, it is true, found out the rules of stress for some of the African languages, and have shown that two different kinds of stress occur side by side in the same language. This in itself is something new for the European ear. Moreover, the pitch plays a very important part. So it will be some time before we establish the rules of poetic sound. So we cannot hope to make much progress until all the material has been more thoroughly examined.'

Meinhof's remarks could have provided a programme for research, but they were not acted on.

Scholars continued to collect African poetry, but did not investigate it as poetry, looking for its stylistic rules. They let it be used as hand material for ethnology, anthropology, linguistics, theology, psychology, etc. It has remained a treasure house of manners and customs, a storehouse of vocabulary, a reservoir of archetypes, an inexhaustible source for the historian, a training ground for the phonetician, a quarry for the anthropologist, a paradise for re-mained unexplored territory.

The question arises, of course: how far are the oral texts collected for linguistic, ethnological and missionary purposes to be considered as literature? What exactly is literature? And how is oral literature to be distinguished from mere speech? If we do extend the term 'literature' to oral matter, is any text literature, that gets handed down and preserved? Art is never formless, never without structure. Thus music is structured sound, and visual art has to be constructed out of raw material. In the same way literature is 'made' from language, regardless of any particular period of time, regardless of whether the author happens to be identifiable or not, regardless also, one must admit, of race. The form and the medium depend on convention. This convention will, in turn, differ from society to society. Unless there is an aesthetic element and a principle of form, there can be neither art nor literature. Every text must, at some time or another, have received the formal approval of a group. This applies not only to the form of a literary work, but even more to the method by which it is produced or performed.

In the introduction to Yoruba Poetry Beier wrote that 'most translations of African literature are in fact collections of myths, legends and fables.' Thus the false impression is sometimes created that African literature consists of nothing but tales about the tortoise and the spider. A mere glance at a catalogue of Xhosa works of literary art shows that this is not the case.

Although it is always dangerous to take a work of art and to abstract from it particular qualities, let us now attempt to classify our literature according to whether it is 'Apprentice' or 'Protest' literature.

Anyone who writes begins as an apprentice. His school supplies him with the tools, literacy and the models for him to follow. Many writers remain imitators all their lives, while others sooner or later achieve a individual style. Since the African civilisation had no written alphabet of their own until they came into contact with Islamic and Western civilisations, the African 'apprentice', learning to write, is also an apprentice to foreign cultural influences.

The term 'apprentice literature' may therefore serve as a convenient way to distinguish literary works produced according to the instructor's pattern and the standards of the script-bearing civilisation. But of course the script is shed again afterwards, and the apprentice may even adopt the foreign language as his own means of written expression. So where does the individuality begin which will allow an author to stop being an apprentice?

However convenient, the term 'apprentice literature' has its dangers. There are many people who would like to dispose of all modern African literature by giving it that name or at least putting it in that category. For them the oral tradition from Africa is genuine, all 'letters' are derivation, a surrender to the spirit of Europe.

By content and attitude the Southern Africa literature could almost be considered 'apprentice literature'. But it is not that in the narrower sense, because it is written in African languages and based stylistically on African oral traditions of story-telling. On the other hand 'protest literature' written in European language is European in style and uses European arguments to oppose tutelage by Europeans. Stylistically, apprentice and protest literature belong together.

By content, however, 'apprentice literature', and all early literary works in African languages sponsored by European missionaries and officials (up to about 1950), belong together in one group, which might all go under the main heading of 'mission literature'.

No hard-and-fast line, of course can be drawn dividing 'apprentice' and 'protest' literature. Between them there is a wide field of 'hedging' or 'neutral' works, for, to avoid having to approve their tutelage, many writers glorified the traditional life of the tribe and the tribal chiefs and heroes: this can be interpreted as a form of indirect protest. Look for example, at the quotation chosen by A. C. Jordan in his famous novel Ingqumbo Yeminyanya (The Wrath of the Ancestors): 'For God's sake, let us sit upon the ground and tell sad stories of the death of Kings.' I wish to suggest that Jordan's choice of that particular quotation from Shakespeare is very significant, in the light of what has been said above.

Some books may basically be 'conformist', i.e. 'apprentice literature', but protest against the ways of the Europeans and the missions being brought in too fast. The Africans who accepted the Western innovations with enthusiasm were just the ones who would feel bitterest at the discrimination against themselves as individuals. So acceptance was constantly turning into resentment, the cry of protest is heard between the poems of conformity.

Let us now specially consider Xhosa literature. The spiritual centre of the Xhosa authors was Lovedale, a Church of Scotland mission station. Even before this was established about 1824, Joseph Williams from the London Missionary Society, who died in 1818, had been active as a missionary near there. He converted to Christianity Prince Ntsikana, who survived him by only a few months, and who composed hymns for the little community, although unable to read or write.

The first important author in Xhosa literature is Samuel Edward Krune Mqhayi (1875-1945), whose novel Ityala Lamawele appeared in 1913 or 1914, though it had been written earlier, about which Mqhayi himself writes: 'I had never thought much of it, and the manuscript had been lying about at home for a long time. So I was all the more surprised that it gained general approval among the blacks and also the whites who knew Xhosa...'

In conclusion, may I congratulate all those authors who have constantly contributed to Xhosa literature, and the Lovedale Press which has made it possible for them to boast of their treasured heritage that has been preserved in their literature. Moreover, as the Rev. J. J. R. Jolobe once said, '... the future is pregnant with promise in many spheres and also in connection with literature. It beckons with a flaming hand challenging writers and publishers to make the vision a reality.'

African or Black Nationalism

M.T. MOERANE

(Address delivered at the 23rd Summer School of the University of Cape Town, 16 February 1973)

I have had the great privilege of travelling fairly widely through the continent of Africa, and in my cursory observations I have realised that the African people of this sub-continent are part of a large family stretching today through East, Central and West Africa. East African people like Jomo Kenyatta's Kikuyu are of our Bantu-speaking stock. So are the Baluba and Lulua tribes of the Kasai in Zaire.

I found that people of the Cameroons in West Africa also have a language whose origins came from the same stock as our Sotho Nguni. And when in Eastern Nigeria among the Ibo, I heard them call a child 'ngwa', when our Sotho say 'ngwana', I began to suspect that they, too, may be of common stock with us. Africans here are people who, parting from their brothers further north, have traversed and braved the rigours of the unknown, of jungle and the wilds as pioneering stock, till they settled this sub-continent, over centuries. It is not by accident that recently, when ruins of an ancient city were discovered in Rustenburg, they were found to have the same features as the Zimbabwe Ruins of Rhodesia. Over the centuries our people settled and spread over this sub-continent so much so that the first Western explorers found, for instance in the Transvaal, large cities with their own civilisations and evidence of mining and industrial history, proof of long and peaceful settlement.

In 1652, there came a new factor, a provision station on the coast, right here. This new group - Europeans - were over the centuries to spread, clashing with the inhabitants, first the Bushmen and Hottentots and next the people of Bantu language stock. There followed a hundred years of war which left the white man the undisputed conqueror and ruler of this land. Spearheading this war on the black man were the

Afrikaner trekkers who sought a country and a home and gained it in legitimate war, sharing it as the spoils of war. Most of the time they conquered through our black people's divisions. Thus when that great dynast, King Shaka, had built his tribe into a fighting and conquering machine, his split with his leading general Mzilikazi sent the latter on a ravaging expedition that wreaked havoc on the unprepared tribes of the Transvaal. Travel with me from Johannesburg through the Magaliesberg (Mohale's mountain) and through the Marico (Madikwe) valleys past Chief Mangope's enclave to Zeerust and you are traversing land that belonged to the Hurutshe and Tswana people. This land was terrorised by Mzilikazi until the Hurutshe chiefs sent for the Trekkers, then camped in Thaba Nchu, to come and help them. And indeed fighting side by side these black and white allies drove Mzilikazi into Rhodesia. Now that land is white area and I have seen myself some of the descendants of the Hutshe being evicted from their land in Leeuwfontein farm in Zeerust now designated as a 'black spot'. And when the tribe refused to move, the authorities withdrew all facilities such as schools and other services and you saw the area going wild in resistance. So also, when Sekhukhuni's people had fought the Trekkers to a stand-still there came the Swazis, who indeed helped the Voortrekkers conquer the Pedis and seize their land. What of the Free State, where for protection, as the story goes, the whole land of the blacks was ceded, so that today the black man has absolutely no land there except at congested Thaba Nchu, and a whole people was turned into serfs while the whites divided the country into farms for themselves.

Through these troubled times one ray of hope was hovering in the clouds - the influence of the British Empire which was struggling not only to rule and control South Africa but was inculcating the spirit of justice and protection and equal treatment to all British subjects, black and white. Indeed when our people finally laid down their arms it was with the firm assurance that they were becoming subjects of a new and just regime. They heard Cecil Rhodes declare the dictum of 'equal rights for all civilised people'. They thrilled at the opportunities of the white man's education and civilisation and did their best to deserve the citizenship of the new regime. And at the Cape they won the franchise and exercised it with wisdom and efficiency. The black man at this time - the late 19th Century - had indeed conceded defeat and staked his orderly future development and destiny on the benign and just policies of His Majesty's Government. He learnt from example the democratic way: how to demand and assert rights through organised pressure. He established congresses in every province, established newspapers which spoke out for the people, their needs and rights. Thus in the 1880s we see the emergence of newpapers like Imvo Zabantsundu of John Tengo Jabavu, father of D. D. T. Jabavu, and the uniting of the tribes to form Imbumba (Unity) to consolidate their social and political rights.

While thrilling at the liberal policies of the Cape, the black man was worried about what was happening in the other provinces where discrimination, political and economic, was rampant. The more these things happened in the Republics which were rebelling successfully against the British empire, the more he asserted the principles of British just rule and feared for the future if rule should indeed fall into local white hands. But this indeed was what happened. Thus in 1906 the South African Native Congress sent a resolution to the Home Government: 'The Native Congress feels called upon to record its deep regret at the apparent decline of British views in the treatment of the Native question from those high standards which were once the pride and the crown and the glory of British statesmanship'. They referred to the regrettable conditions in which native affairs were placed in those times in the several South African colonies, and especially in Natal and the Transvaal:

'Congress feels that responsible government has been prematurely granted to the colonies, considering the very low moral tone of the average colonist in regard to native treatment and their feeling and demeanour towards native races. It is also regrettable to observe that the moral influence of the church appears to have declined in its power to counteract these degrading tendencies or to raise the standard of thought and feeling towards the aborigines.'

The same year, the Orange River Colony Native Congress was appealing for 'Native representation' in that colony when self government came. They regretted that this condition was not included in the Vereeniging

Peace terms. Union was approaching; the black man was not invited to the 1909 National Convention; so he called his own convention to make representations to the National Convention specifically on representation in the proposed Union Parliament: full and equal rights for all, without distinction of colour, class, or creed, equality before the law; and condemned the principle foreign hitherto to the law of His Majesty's colony of the Cape, that of the colour line running through the various sections of the Act, e.g. exclusion from Parliament of blacks and non-extension of the franchise to the blacks of the northern provinces. But Union was established without any amendment suggested by the Africans. The colour policy of the north had won the day.

The black people replied to the challenge of exclusion by intensified political national organisation, bringing into being the African National Congress representing the chiefs, leaders and people of all the tribes, Provinces and the Protectorates in January 1912. Discriminatory legislation followed fast, starting with the Colour Bar Act of 1911 and the Land Act of 1913. The Africans saw the Land Act as a deliberate freezing of the opportunity for the black to own land on an equitable basis. The Act, influenced by the segregation policy of General Hertzog, who in the debate had declared that if parliament did not act the white man would be pushed out of South Africa, or a large part of it, was bitterly opposed by the Africans.

Mr Sol Plaatje, Congress General Secretary, was bitter about the abandoned pledges of the British. He asked what had suddenly happened to the Briton's word - his bond - that the solemn obligations of the Imperialists should cease to count. And if it were decided that the Victorian Englishman and the Twentieth Century Englishman were creatures of different clay, the latter's honour binding only when both parties to the undertaking were white, then this action desecrated the memories of their forebears. He continued:

'If there is to be a return to the contented South Africa of other days, both the Native Land Act and the Report of the Lands Commission - its climax - should be torn up. They talked of having 'doubled' the native areas. They found us in occupation of 143 million morgen and propose to squeeze us into 18 million. It never occurred to us when we fought hard for British influence that British dominion would culminate in consigning us to our present intolerable position ...'

So strongly did our fathers feel on the land question in 1913. May I add that Mr J. W. Sauer, the then Minister of Native Affairs, piloting this Bill before parliament, had gone to great pains to reject segregation and asserted that total separation was 'too crude'. What they should have was not prohibition but restriction, and the whole principle underlying the Bill was not absolute prohibition but restriction. You know how the congress sent a deputation to England to protest against the Land Act and the discrimination enshrined in the Act of Union but were put off by the British pre-occupation with the first world war.

There were to follow more discriminatory Acts such as the 1925 Native Taxation law and the 1927 Native Administration Act which, the congress declared, served to restrict free speech and also limit the protection of the African on the basis of common law, as did the Pass laws. Protest against these was to become the stock-in-trade of African nationalism for decades. This movement did serve to unite the African people and to throw up national leaders whose significance went beyond just politics. In this era, too, under leaders like Dr Abdurahman of the Coloured community, and Professor Jabavu, the struggle for rights was from 1927 co-ordinated among Africans and Coloureds and also Indians. Workers' trade union efforts were pioneered by the Industrial and Commercial Workers' Union (I.C.U.) under the leadership of Mr Clements Kadalie and Mr A. W. G. Champion. More activity of this kind was undertaken by white liberal groups such as the churches and joint councils and latterly the Institute of Race Relations.

A climactic point in the evolution of the discriminatory policy of the establishment in South Africa was reached in 1936 when the Hertzog segregation bills became law. A furious battle under the auspices of the All African Convention had been mounted by the Africans and Coloureds to resist these bills becoming law, but in vain. The Cape franchise went, after years of cherished existence. A promise of 7 million morgen more of land was made to add to the land set aside for African occupation in 1913. A few token members of parliament and senators (white) were elected by the

Africans and a dummy Representative Council was appointed for Africans to give advice to the Government, and the Group Areas Act was passed. The black people's movements protested and appealed in vain against the injustices of this legislation.

Meantime a new factor was emerging in the national movement. The younger, educated university men like Anton Lembede, possibly influenced by the disciplines of social science and anthropology, were revolting against the attitude of the blacks to seek admission to the white society as if to be of a different culture meant to be inferior to the whites. Thus in 1948, after the Nationalists had come into power, the African was no longer seriously interested in which white political party was in power. He was disillusioned with the efficacy of white leadership and believed that his salvation lay not in his white friends or British liberalism but in his own hands. This trend was to split the national movement later with the emergence of the Pan-African Congress which asserted that South Africa was part of Africa - the black man's land - and he must rule it with all those who accepted that they were Africans, whatever their colour. The momentum of the struggle for black emancipation and political rights mounted to such a degree that it precipitated the events at Sharpeville. There followed the most drastic measures of detentions and bannings and house arrest this country has ever known, which silenced the black people for a decade.

The will to gain freedom has once more reasserted itself in this decade. Its basic characteristic is a faith in the black man's ability to work out his own salvation and chart his own destiny and the destiny of this country. He realises that, dazzled by the excellence of things white, especially the material gadgets, he has over the centuries idolised the white man and his ways and in the process despised himself and the ways of his fathers. In retrospect he discovers that this god he has worshipped, the white man, has feet of clay. That in fact he is not a god at all but an ordinary frail human being subject to the human weaknesses of fear, self-interest and greed. In certain respects he is a victim of a materialism which makes him a captive who, while wallowing in plenty, is not able to fulfil his desire of creating a happy equitable land.

And so the black man takes up the challenge to build

in South Africa an egalitarian society with justice for all, as the Black People's Convention has dedicated itself to do. His first task is to develop faith and pride in himself as a human second to none, indeed to believe that black is beautiful and truly created in the image of God, and that the spirit of the Lord is within him. That he must muster his solidarity is a categorical imperative because, according to the age-old tenets of his fathers, every black man is his brother whom he may not exploit for his own gain but with whom he must hold hands for the welfare of the family in all its extensions. With his solidarity he is going to assert his democratic rights in a way that cannot but be effective, for no power can resist the united will of a people to be free.

The black man is under no illusions about the wrongness of a system which can unashamedly propagate human suffering and exploitation, and he seeks to bring back a world that has lost its way, into the ways of righteousness and peace where the value of an individual is sacred, whatever the colour of his skin. In his traditional heritage he finds his inspiration for now he knows that even before he met the white man he was not a savage and in fact his civilisation had evolved a social stability which is the envy of cultures with more sophisticated material assets. He seeks his own institutions and the right to administer them and chart his road to the future. Here is a cry for the recognition of the dignity of a man whatever his colour and we must accept that the basic sin of South Africa is the refusal by the white man to accept the black man as a human being with a soul and his own dignity.

How else can you account for the fact that it is the policy of this country to pay a white man doing the same job as a black man twice or ten times as much? How else explain the philosophy of a government which boasts that it will protect at all costs the interests of those workers who are white against those who are black? How explain a system which seeks to save civilisation by denying education and jobs to black people, when in a civilised society work, education and opportunity would be accepted as the rights of all? Answer these questions and you will understand the motivation of the black man. Faced with the mockery of the Bantustan policy with its arbitrary division of land which gave 87 per cent to the minority whites, faced with the rejection of the black man over the centuries, faced with laws that divide families and impose suffering for white ideologies and an electorate that is too much part of the status quo to challenge and change it, it is inevitable that the disenfranchised blacks decided to go apart, find their identity and work out their salvation.

Men of goodwill have begun to be touched by these things, like those whites who will rather go to jail than be party to an action that violates God's injunction that 'whom God has joined together let no man put asunder'. If these men of goodwill can act quickly and realistically there may yet be an alternative to eventual racial confrontation - I do not necessarily mean violent confrontation. Then the alignments finally will be between those who believe in right against those who believe in the paramountcy of their sectional group interests. Otherwise, if men sacrifice their consciences and close their minds to truth and the call of justice, then the blacks, who are the have-nots, will indeed struggle and organise till they are strong enough to assert right and bring justice to this land.

We all can have a part in this task, for in the final analysis the challenge, to my mind, is to accept every man as a human being, as Mr Vorster has recently seen, and to be part of the force in this country which lives for the recognition of this fact in practice; for if we do that, we are the true patriots and will create a South Africa which may yet be the example of how men should live. Then we shall indeed be able to solve our own practical problems of providing work and welfare for everyone. What is more, the threats of outside attacks, that consume so much of the income of this country, will disappear, for if we unite no outsider can attack us. We shall once again regain the respect of the nations of the world and be able to render services that can illuminate the whole continent, which, with our human and material resources, should really be our destiny. Nothing short of this is the motivation of black nationalism today.

Afrikaner Ascendancy and the Challenges of the Seventies

M. GATSHA BUTHELEZI

(Address delivered to members of the Aktuele Aangeleentheidskring, University of Stellenbosch, September 1971)

I consider it a great break-through in terms of human relationships in our own country for me to stand here before you, to communicate with you as my fellow compatriots. It is also historic for me to be here, a descendant on my mother's side of King Mpande, who was a brother of King Shaka, the founder of the Zulu nation, and King Dingane. It is historic for me to speak at this great university to the descendants of the great Voortrekker volk. Your people, like my people, were forged in the African wilderness.
In the United States, I was invited by black students from Africa one evening. In the course of the conversation I stated that the black-white problems of South Africa differ to a great extent from the black-white problems of the rest of Africa. In the rest of Africa, black people had a confrontation with white foreign settlers, whereas in South Africa the white people were indigenous. My fellow blacks waxed indignant and accused me of not knowing the meaning of the word indigenous, to which I responded by saying that the majority of the South African whites had become as indigenous to South Africa as white Americans and black Americans were to America.

I consider it a good omen which should augur well for the future well-being of our Fatherland for me to be a guest speaker at Stellenbosch University. This university has been truthfully described as the pace-setter for Afrikanerdom. I feel it is a great moment to stand here, as I do, at this source of Afrikaner nationalism and Afrikaans culture. This university has given South Africa six of her seven premiers. It has given South Africa several members of the cabinets right from the time of Union to our present day. It is also my very first opportunity to communicate with students of any white university on their campus.

I have come here when the Afrikaner people have reached their ascendancy in South Africa. This the Afrikaners have reached after more than a century of strife and struggle. Today it can be truthfully said that they are masters not only of their own destiny but also of the destinies of other peoples of South Africa, both white and black. To me the Afrikaner in South Africa is faced with a challenge which is greater even than that faced by the Voortrekkers during the last century. The Afrikaners are in perfect control of the political situation in South Africa and have been in such control for almost a quarter of a century. The denouement of our political problems and the form such unravelling takes, will depend almost entirely on what the Afrikaner majority does with the power it wields, and on how much real self-determination it apportions to those race groups, such as mine, which have been subjects of white South Africa for almost a century.

The Afrikaners, just like my people, were victims of colonisation for a very long time. But whereas the Afrikaners have finally shaken off the shackles of colonisation, my people still feel shackled in so far as blacks have had no real voice in the running of affairs for scores of years. Quite obviously the Afrikaners are not solely responsible for this denial of a voice in our affairs. The Afrikaner inherited the situation when they reached their ascendancy and took over the running of the affairs of South Africa. Going back into history is a useful exercise in the understanding of the way events have evolved. I am a student of history and always look at events against the wider background of history. Some people seem to think that the purpose of history is to justify their conduct within the contemporary scene and to justify the apportioning of blame and credit to various groups in our common fatherland. However, the motivations of empire-builders baffle us and seem beyond our comprehension. For example Cecil Rhodes said in 1895: 'In order to save 40 000 000 inhabitants of the United Kingdon from a bloody Civil War, we Colonial Statesmen must acquire new land to settle surplus population, to provide new markets for the goods produced by them in the factories and mines. The empire, as I have always said, is a bread and butter question. If you want to avoid civil war (in the U.K.) you must become imperialists'.

It is beyond the purpose of my address, and would in any case be a little presumptuous for me to narrate the vagaries of imperialism with which you are so familiar. The imperialists wielded power and as someone has said: 'Power corrupts and absolute power corrupts absolutely'. It is a good habit to view these things lest we find ourselves perpetrating the same things against other people. In this case the Afrikaner people stand in relations to us as some kind of metropolitan power that is controlling our destinies and that intends to hand over to blacks the reins of self-determination 'as soon as they are ready to take them'. The challenges of this responsibility are immense and I am the last person to say that this is an easy job. My great hope is that the memories of oppression and colonisation are still fresh enough in their minds to give them that delicate balance they need between doing what is right or wrong in this situation.

We Zulus were, as you know, provoked into an unnecessary war in 1879 by British settlers in Natal in order to 'break the Zulu power once and for all', in the words of Sir Bartle Frere. We finally ended up as a British Colony. We were unlucky because all the people who were British subjects have recently become masters in their own houses, when the process of decolonisation started unfolding. The British settlers in Natal cornered my grandfather King Dinizulu when he returned from banishment on St Helena by insisting that he should agree to the annexation of Zululand to Natal in the year 1897. Our tragedy became complete when Union was formed in 1910 by whites without bothering to enquire whether we wanted to be part of this or not. This union of former enemies inspired Dr Pixley Ka. I. Seme, a Zulu who married King Dinizulu's eldest daughter, and other blacks to found the now banned African National Congress. It was because the whites, who as Afrikaners and British had had such strife, had united on the basis of their colour that blacks also emulated their example and founded a body which would ensure black solidarity, where ethnic grouping would be of secondary importance. The voice of blacks continued to be ignored, just as the voice of the Afrikaners had been ignored. Even in 1931, when by the Statute of Westminster South Africa became autonomous, the feelings of black people were never regarded as of any consequence.

There were many attempts by the Zulus and other blacks to offer resistance throughout the years, which all came to nought. The Afrikaners have many 'blood-stained beacons', to use an expression of a graduate of this university, General J. C. Smuts, throughout their history. Slagter's Nek, the Anglo-Boer War, the fate of Jopie Fourie during the First World War, the 1922 Strike and others are regarded as such in the history of your great people. For this reason blacks have a hope that the Afrikaners whose history is so recent are bound to understand that blacks also have their 'blood-stained beacons', and that their heroes, would, like Jopie Fourie, be regarded by blacks as having had a mission similar to that of Afrikaner leaders who attempted to work for their real self-determination and self-realisation, and in the process incurred the wrath of those in power.

The segregationist policies which have been pursued by various white governments of South Africa have always been formulated and imposed on us without any consultation with blacks. This has led to a general feeling amongst blacks that on the whole blacks have been regarded at most by white South Africa as not much more than pets. This stems from an attitude of presuming to know what is good for them. The present policies which are supported by the majority of white people have also been formulated for us and not with us. As in the past we have co-operated as subjects of white South Africa regardless of how we felt about many aspects of such policies. We have seen between the fifties and sixties how those who attempted to oppose these policies were rounded up. Let me say by way of digression that although I do not deny some Communist infiltration in one of these banned organisations, this fact is always exaggerated.

The blacks hope that the Afrikaners who are governing South Africa at present will appreciate that many black leaders like Robert Sobukwe and Albert Luthuli rose for the same reasons as General Hertzog and President Steyn. I recall the names of the latter two in particular because of the role they played in saving the Afrikaners from committing suicide in 1915. For the same reasons some of us disagree with the view that prescribes violence as the solution for our problems. When black states were given self-determination by their former colonisers, this inevitably had its impact on our own situation in South Africa. Self-determination has become a fact of life on the continent of Africa, and this has made our eagerness to acquire it not just a remote possibility but an urgent requirement particularly after we imbibed from our governors the flattery that we blacks of the South are more advanced than many blacks who are self-governing and free today. When we are, therefore, promised self-government, it must be clear that we do not expect a sham self-government but the real thing. If the majority of whites have now decided to set up blacks in separate states, we have no means to resist it, even had we wanted to.

But the great test is the extent to which this is meant. We expect a sympathetic application of the policy from the Afrikaners, who have a recent history of being oppressed. We know that they know the poverty that faces us, they know what ignorance and illiteracy mean for a people. Our kind of 'decolonisation' is unique in the history of the world because it is being offered us by white South Africa. Even the accusation that we want too much too soon cannot legitimately be levelled at us. We assume that this is done in acknowledgment of the fact that every people on earth have 'the right to bread and liberty'. So that when this eventually happens it will depend on how quickly white South Africa wants us to get the same right. Although it is true that it will also depend on how we co-operate and measure up to our new responsibilities, it does not depend just on us. One of the facts which the Afrikaners who are wielding power have to face is that we have also contributed towards the production of the wealth of South Africa. We will, therefore, not be eager to receive independence if it will be in the spirit of 'since you want independence take it and starve'.

In the seventies and beyond one of the great challenges that face the Afrikaners under present policies is the extent to which they are prepared to give us the opportunity to share in the wealth of South Africa. I regard paying my people on the basis of rate for the job and dispensing with disparities in earnings as a way of giving us a share of the wealth which we have helped to produce. I regard giving my people a free and compulsory education as a way of ensuring that they have equal opportunity to do so. I also regard the equipping of my people with technical skills in the same light. And last but not least, if the people are going to believe that the promised self-government is a serious proposition, their areas must be consolidated by adding more land to existing homelands. People cannot govern themselves in a vacuum. The talk that we will not get more land than was promised us by General Hertzog's Government in 1936, makes talk of independence for our homelands sound a hollow dream, as the quota of land promised at that time was promised long before present policies of setting up separate states were ever contemplated.

To me these are the greatest challenges which the descendants of the Voortrekkers face in the seventies and beyond. Our future survival in South Africa depends on the extent to which they meet our expectations. We have hope that they will rise to the occasion, and equipped as Afrikaners are with the knowledge gained from their own history of deprivation and oppression by other people, many of my people are optimistic that they will measure up to these challenges. If the experiment should fail for any reason, the Afrikaner majority will still be faced with finding an alternative, as their ascendancy has placed the whole mantle of white leadership on their shoulders. The success or otherwise of all these attempts will depend also on the extent to which blacks in urban areas - the most articulate group of our people - are given security of tenure in the urban areas or, alternatively, the extent to which they are made part and parcel of the black machinery set up for them in the homelands by their government. As long as their future is insecure and uncertain our whole future is insecure and uncertain. One of the greatest challenges that faces my people will be to develop an eagerness and a determination to learn from your people. My people will have to learn to work for themselves as faithfully and as diligently as they have done in the development of South Africa in order to promote their own development meaningfully.

I feel certain that if the above things take place, my people will be in a position to face one of the greatest challenges that face the whole human race. In the next twelve years the population of developed nations will increase by 150 million and that of underdeveloped nations will increase by 850 million. The population of Africa was 330 million in 1968 and is estimated to reach 860 million in the year 2000. According to the same publication: 70 people per minute or 35 million per year die of starvation in the world. This stresses the urgency for our full development more than any other single factor. Black areas are underdeveloped and we are an underdeveloped people. The optimum production of our areas is a matter of life and death not only for us, but for South Africa. The problem of population explosion is something that frightens you and me because our minds are trained sufficiently to comprehend it. So long as my people, a largely illiterate people, do not get the maximum opportunity to have their minds trained, then one can only say that one is alarmed by what the problem of population explosion means to the future of our peoples of South Africa.

Perhaps the most significant import your ancestors brought to Africa is your Western Christian tradition. As the wagons of the Voortrekkers moved north to the unknown, the family Bible was the most treasured possession of practically every family. The polarisation between extreme wealth and extreme poverty in South Africa does not help my people, fairly newcomers to your Christian faith, to understand what your Christian tradition means. Through our history extreme wealth tends to be associated in their minds with whites, and extreme poverty with blacks. The more educated our people become, the more disillusioned they get about the feasibility of applying your Christian tradition in practical terms to their lives in South Africa. Problems such as the migratory labour system make them laugh at anyone who tells tham that the family is the unit of the Western Christian society. These are the lines along which they have been trying to model their own society for three centuries.

The late Dr H. F. Verwoerd once described separate development as 'good neighbourliness'. I have often thought to myself that the choice of these words could not have been accidental. I find it significant that Christ used those very words to sum up in simple terms the meaning of Christianity. One of His best parables, that of the Good Samaritan, dealt with the meaning of good neighbourliness in a Christian society. This parable seems to have been well tailored by our Lord for South Africa. Perhaps all our efforts will be judged by generations to come by the extent to which Dr Verwoerd's words on 'good neighbourliness' will have been meaningful in terms of your great Western Christian tradition. This, I wish to submit, is probably the greatest challenge that faces all of us in the seventies and beyond.

THE COMMON AREA

POLITICAL ASPIRATIONS: THE FEDERAL IDEA

White and Black Nationalism, Ethnicity and the Future of the Homelands

M. GATSHA BUTHELEZI

(Excerpt from the Alfred and Winifred Hoernlé Memorial Lecture, delivered under the auspices of the South African Institute of Race Relations at the University of Cape Town in January, 1974 and published with kind permission of the speaker and the South African Institute of Race Relations)

Let us agree that the homelands policy means the emergence of states in which African interests are paramount. Let us also get clear the point that independence or autonomy of these new states should not be conditional on the breaking up of the integrated economy which is the life blood of all the peoples of South Africa. The change should revolve on allowing each and every group to maintain its identity through new constitutional and political arrangements. After all, some people have even spoken of a Common Market for Southern Africa. Some South African economists envisage the formation of a Common Market comprising all ten countries of 'Southern' Africa (south of the Zaire-Zambezi divide).

Among the reasons given for such a step is the fact that South Africa has invested large sums in neighbouring territories. South Africa's own mines and industries provide work and wages, and therefore foreign exchange, for more than a million foreign African immigrants who send back between 30 per cent and 60 per cent of their earnings to their own 'homelands'. South Africa sells large quantities of machinery, food, clothing and manufactured goods to all these territories and is in a position to supply technical aid at any time. Economists, however, point out that a successful common market relies on the fact that the economies of all its members are roughly about the same level. But the fact that at the present moment different stages of economic development of the ten countries militate against any closer association in the immediate future, should not entail abandoning the idea.(1)

If we all accept that the economy of South Africa belongs to all, let us also accept that the emergence of independent homelands is not contradictory to the idea of all the states, white or black, being associated on certain matters of general concern.

A Federation?

As I have stated before, I believe, together with the Chief Minister of the Transkei, Paramount Chief K.D. Matanzima, that this can be reduced to concrete constitutional terms through the federal formula or a federal commonwealth, such as we see in Canada, Australia or the United States.

When South Africa was made a unitary state, there was a strong move in favour of federation. The strong delegation of the Transvaal was, however, solidly behind the idea of a unitary state, led by General J.C. Smuts. The main reason why the unitary state lobby won the day was that all accepted the main argument that there was a nee for a common policy on the native questions or 'problems' in the four provinces. In view of the present homelands policies pursued here there is no longer any need to adhere to this argument. The very fact that the Nationalis government states that it is, through its homelands poli cies, giving Africans self-determination, is in itself a bold admission of the fact that the aspirations of Africans and of other blacks are not yet fulfilled or satisfied.

That point having been conceded, there is justification for a harder look than was taken in 1910 at the present constitutional position in South Africa. The whole concept of separate development presents an ideal opportunity for the presentation of a federal structure in which black and white fulfilment can be justly reached. One can sense a certain fear within Afrikanerdom that the creation of a federal state would not remove competition for power at the centre between the African majority and the white minority. However, it is complete separation that is fraught with more hazards we cannot predict than our togetherness in separate autonomous states linked together through a federal formula. These states would cooperate on certain vital matters of common concern. This would eliminate possibilities of the so-called 'sacrifices' and 'disasters' about which we have heard so much in the past decade or so. Black people are opposed to any idea of robbing the whites of their birth-right and interests in the benefits of the South Africa they have contributed so much to build. At the same time this takes into account the understandable fears of the white people in relation to their economic position and standard of living. This will satisfy most aspirations of blacks for the foreseeable future. This is the time when we should define problems in greater detail by leaving the ideological plane and getting to practical facts and figures.

We should start debating over which matters each state should exercise full authority and which they would wish to share. It should be debated now for which purposes the states should fall under the federal government. It seems obvious that a federal formula of the kind that raises the whole issue of power at the centre should be avoided. This seems to be the actual point of conflict between white and black in our land. It should be possible to establish a common machinery for certain matters without raising the hardy annual of demand for control of a central parliament. This issue which bedevils any mutual understanding and mutual confidence could at least be postponed for several generations. During that time mutual confidence could grow to a point where agreement could be reached at the centre as well. The emphasis here is on constituent independent states that should be established in terms of the government's policy of separate development. If the homelands and other states are established justly in a manner which accommodates the aspirations of the African people and their economic interests, South Africa could have solved her problems through the homelands policy.

The financial implications of establishing such states will cost millions of rands. The cost should, however, not exceed the astronomical figures that are at present set aside for defence. The need for spending so much would be eliminated once present inter-racial tensions in South Africa were eased by every group's security being guaranteed under this federal structure.

Three types of states could be envisaged in a federal republic or commonwealth:

1 / States in which the interests of an African

ethnic group are paramount;

2 / States in which the interests of white people are paramount;

3 / Special or federal areas which are multi-ethnic in character in which no particular group interests are designated.

It should not be impossible to agree on actual boundaries through negotiations, provided due regard is taken of the point already mentioned, namely, that the boundaries, as agreed upon, will include within a particular state farms or property owned by non-citizens of that state. For instance, if a state is established within boundaries of the Great Fish River in the west, the Katberg and Drakensberg mountains, the Umzimkulu River and the East Coast, such a state would be one in which the Xhosa national group's interests are paramount. This would be so without depriving white farmers or coloured workers of the right to own farms or work and live there, or the right, if they so desired and had the requisite qualifications, to be citizens of this state. It is nonsensical to imply that the establishment of a state in which a certain group's interests are paramount, means that all others must leave the area It is this very failure to draw a clear distinction between state boundaries and the protection of vested interests, particularly of white voters, which causes the government to hesitate in the consolidation of states. Moreover, the talk of the concept of independence as meaning the total break-up of the Republic of South Africa bedevils the issue. It is a confusion of issues that is not necessary and that should be clarified now.

Matters such as various aspects of the economy and finance should be left to a federal authority in order to preserve the essential dynamism of the South African economy. At the same time we should dispense with old-fashioned constraints and restrictions such as those contained in the pass laws and influx control regulations. The harnessing of the labour force by means of compulsion and restraints of all kinds is chiefly associated with these methods of control. In the distant past there could have been justification for the passes as a crude and effective means of ensuring that labour flowed in certain directions. Now that South Africa has reached such a high level of economic development this is unnecessary. I also think that no African state worth its salt would allow the humiliation of its citizens under the pass laws as they are operated at present. This is the time to design a system of labour and employment exchanges such as those that operate in European countries, for instance, for their so-called 'guest workers'. These function without any of the constraints and compulsion found in South Africa under our pass laws and influx control regulations. The emphasis should shift from a prohibition of 'entry' into towns to a prohibition of entry into states. We should now work out effective state boundary regulations, so that the whole question becomes one of controlling movement from one state to another. An internal passport would ensure free travel outside a state provided the necessary formalities had been completed. A person travelling to another state would have a local passport or combined identity travelling document. This travel document would be endorsed for travel to that state either for a visit or to work. If it is the latter there should be in the passport a work permit issued in the home state in conjunction with the immigration department of the state to which the person is proceeding.

I and my executive council presented these suggestions to the Prime Minister of South Africa, Mr B.J. Vorster, in a comprehensive memorandum in March last year. He appeared willing to listen to us and he conceded that a discussion of these suggestions was necessary between us and the Minister of Bantu Administration and Development. These discussions have not yet materialised. We hope we shall have the opportunity to pursue the matter with the Minister even before independence.

It should be clear, therefore, that the policy of establishing states in which this or that group's interests are paramount does not necessarily mean the break-up of the economic integration achieved in the economy of South Africa. All it means in effect is that provision is made for a common federal citizenship in addition to any state citizenship each person will enjoy. A common citizenship of South Africa as a whole is something which I believe all South Africans, whatever their colour or ethnic identity, will want to preserve.

The distribution or devolution of power from a unitary centre to a number of autonomous states would greatly reduce or even eliminate altogether for a long time the obsession of all groups with central power or control thereof, which at the moment threatens the country with unrest and revolution.

Political power within each state must be based on popular will. Each state will naturally have the right to determine or draw up a constitution that suits itself as is already happening within the various homeland governments. Attempts would have to be made to ensure that in our participatory democracy in the black states the educated African elite is included. These are people who would help the smooth running of the government machinery in these new states.

Each state would determine the question of franchise rights for itself. In most homelands anyone who has reached the age of 18, male or female, has a vote.

I have not come here to draw maps. I believe that the drawing of maps should be a matter of negotiation between representatives of blacks and representatives of whites. I am therefore giving the following examples of what I have been talking about without drawing actual maps in seriousness. I have no mandate to draw such maps either from the KwaZulu government or from any other homeland government, nor, for that matter, from the Republican government which reserves for itself the right to determine these at present.

1 / By way of illustration, there will be states in which a particular group's interests are paramount. Such states would be the white state or states, say, covering the Southern Transvaal, the Free State and the Western Cape. Likewise, within this group fall states such as KwaXhosa or KwaZulu covering the 'traditional' lands of these large African groups.

2 / The other type of state would be that designated a federal state or a special area. This could be confined to a particular city or to an area. I am thinking here of something like the city-state of New York, or West Berlin in Germany. These are areas which it may not be expedient to designate for one particular group. For instance, it might be desirable to designate Cape Town as a federal area. This in practice would mean that the area or city is under one federal control. This will be clearer when the organisation of government at state or

federal level is considered.

It might be helpful in fixing the boundaries of states to be guided in certain areas by what was the historical area of a particular people. Let me illustrate my point hypothetically by saying that for the Xhosa people, for example, it might cover an area encompassed by the Great Fish River; the Katberg range; the Drakensberg mountains; the coastline from the Umzimkulu River to the Great Fish.

In the same hypothetical sense it might be suggested that KwaZulu should, historically speaking, include the whole of the territory of present-day Natal. But at the very least then it can be suggested that such a territory should cover the areas over which King Cetshwayo ruled before the Zulu War of 1879.

In the same sense a third state of African paramountcy would be Sekhukhuniland (present-day Lebowa) as it was in the day of King Sekhukhuni.

A fourth would be the area previously known as British Bechuanaland which was always the land of the Batswana (present-day BophuthaTswana).

There would be other areas of African paramountcy, but I will not go into all of them since I do not want anyone to misunderstand my illustration as an attempt on my part to produce any blueprint.

In these circumstances the central part of the white-controlled states might include the area known as the Natal Colony; the Southern Transvaal; the Orange Free State; the Cape; excluding the Tswana and Xhosa states. Since this would include virtually all the major cities of the Republic except East London, a major concession of this nature could only be possible within the framework of a federal structure. The rights of all the people permanently resident in such states, including urban and rural Africans, coloured people and Asians, would have to be guaranteed to ensure that they would enjoy full citizenship status. In such states, the ethnic origin of their African citizens would be irrelevant. Africans, like whites, would not be divided into ethnic groups for residential and other purposes, as is the position now.

All states, whether a specific group has paramountcy or not, will have the same legislative and executive powers and functions. There will, obviously, be no first and second-class states. Far-reaching change of this nature entails the abolition of the present provincial system as it exists under the present unitary form of government. Parliament in its present form would also cease to exist. Its place would be taken by a federal parliament composed of representatives of all the constituent states. It would be empowered to carry out those functions which by agreement have been vested in it.

The establishment of central and state parliaments would mean a shift of political attention from the single all-powerful parliament which we have in South Africa at present. The advantage of the federal concept is that the federal principle ensures that the states and their legislatures will not be subordinate to a central parliament. The powers of a federal parliament and those of the states will be co-ordinated except in regard to those few matters which it is agreed should be left to the central federal parliament.

At present in the homelands, the powers of the legislature are specified. These powers are not exclusively held by the homelands' legislature, as the central parliament can still legislate on the same subjects and in that event the will of the central legislature prevails. This makes the legislative powers of homelands' legislatures almost shadow powers.

The powers under a federal formula consist of:

1 / those matters over which each state has exclusive control;

2 / those matters over which the federal or central parliament has exclusive control;

3 / those matters in which there is concurrent control in which case it must be specified which body has over-riding authority in the event of conflict. It would have to be agreed as to where residual power resides.

It might be wise to discuss whether the central or federal power should, generally speaking, control external immigration; boundaries and coastlines; currency and coinage; federal citizenship; defence and security except such specified local or state security as does not affect national interests; posts and telegraphs; external borrowing and loans and general banking control; have the right to declare a state of emergency either in each state or nationally. Then all other matters other than these might be vested in the states. Any matters which are unspecified or unforeseen which require legislation might fall under residual powers given to the central federal legislature.

State governments, as at present in the homelands, should continue to be led by a chief minister and a cabinet responsible to him. The representation of the central government in each state could be through a governor who would be the head of the state and whose duties would be to perform the constitutional functions at state level which are performed by the head of state at national or federal level.

From experience we know that the belief that the white people need security forces to preserve their property and vested interests is not correct. There can be no lasting security through oppressing other people. The maintenance of such forces to keep under control unarmed people has the effect of oppressing them and creating hatred and resentment. After all, it is almost a century since whites and blacks were involved in any pitched battle. This is apart from the skirmishes during the Bambata Rebellion in KwaZulu in 1906.

This matter would therefore need delicate and careful handling as it is a sensitive issue. Each state or homeland needs its own state police force. Federal police should only interfere during a state of emergency. The presence of security forces in the homelands keeps homelands' citizens under great fear. As long as the security forces are so active in homeland areas, it is false to say we can look forward to unrestricted politics without fear of victimisation. The exclusive control of military and security matters by whites is cause for great resentment by Africans and is cause for great mistrust, since it is plain that whites do not trust us either. A KwaZulu government without any para-military force to patrol our own boundaries and to look after our own property is like a hornless bull. If this situation is perpetuated, it would mean that we were still hostages of whites and independent only in name. It is essential that the control of these important spheres of activity is shared.

Foreign policy should be determined through participation by all citizens of a country, regardless of race. African officials at the O.A.U. spoke for the African countries when they told me last month that they are not interested in dialogue with white South Africa unless there is meaningful dialogue in South

Africa between black and white. Africans in other states seem more attractive than Africans here. Is it because another man's grass always looks greener than one's own? Or because Africans here, on account of the subordinate position they are placed in, lack the mystique and charisma of Africans from independent states? Is is just a human trait that the girl from far away looks more exotic and attractive than the girl next door who, because of familiarity, looks plain and unattractive? Is it not true that invariably the girl next door tends to be more stable and more reliable? It is only if Africans in South Africa participate in the formulation of South Africa's foreign policy that they can be in a position to assist in carrying it out and defending it anywhere in the world. It might be advantageous for individual states to have their own trade representatives, but to have unified political representation by the federal state on behalf of all the states.

Conclusion

Under the circumstances I have attempted to set out here, it should be possible for the homelands policy to be used as the basis of a formula for the South Africa of the future. My great concern is that we have so little time. It is urgently necessary for us to move in the directions I have indicated if the homelands policy is to be accorded any credibility within this country or abroad. Otherwise this policy will appear as no more than a form of neo-colonialism without the finesse of the former colonists. If the policy is static and no progress is made, what Professor Adam states, will be seen to be accurate:

'Afrikaner domestic neo-colonialism, at least the Verwoerd and Vorster version, is much more enlightened than the traditional colonial methods of an Ian Smith in Rhodesia or of Portugal in Moçambique and Angola, both of whom manage without formal racial separation. Under the pressure of world opinion and the growing urbanised African proletariat, as well as a small non-white professional elite with a fifty-year-long struggle for emancipation behind them, Verwoerd realised that he had to create a political outlet for African Nationalism. The Bantustan policy is supposed to fulfil this function. It deflects political aspirations to areas where they are no danger to white rule. It meets the world-wide demand for African political rights in a fading colonial period by granting them the vote in remote areas, but not in their living and working places where they are merely given the status of rightless "guest workers".' (2)

In this connection it is just as well to look at another comment by another political scientist worth reading:

'In the light of the external as well as the internal pressures that formed the setting within which the South African government embarked on the Transkeian experiment, would independence for the territory do anything to assuage foreign criticism and African resentment? By itself, and with its extremely limited resources, such a development would seem almost meaningless except, perhaps, to its small group of leaders and local inhabitants. The almost total dependence on the South African economy for even the livelihood of those in the territory, the lack of attractiveness of rural life to Africans brought up in urban areas, and the relatively small numbers affected in relation to the total African population of South Africa would all seem to make independence for the Transkei relatively unimportant in the total context. Even if the South African government should decide to pour massive funds into the Transkei and other African areas for which it plans comparable developments, it can hardly be expected that either the Africans themselves or the outside world would feel that what was virtually a unilateral settlement by whites for a small, impoverished area could compare with the progressive extension of political, social, and economic rights for Africans within the present boundaries of South Africa.' (3)

This comment applies to all the homelands, and this will be a final verdict on the future of all of them unless there is a radical change of attitude by the powerful in this land.

It is no attempt at pontification about the crisis in our land. It represents our attempts as black people to bend over backwards in our attempts to meet our white countrymen who wield power over us. We are still willing to participate in meaningful dialogue even on the basis of formulae such as separate development, which were conceived by whites solely from all-white perspectives. What more can we do?

The Political Future of the Homelands

LUCAS M. MANGOPE

(Excerpts from address delivered to the South African Institute of Race Relations Conference, Cape Town, January 1974, and published with kind permission of the speaker and the South African Institute of Race Relations)

We embrace in one single citizenry, or expanded 'polis', a multiplicity of cultures and groups, with problems of so many facets and such complex and intertwining implications as have never before in history been thrown together in one pot. In this situation the creative politician has to find and steer a safe course. But such a course has never been mapped out for him before. And no chart is available which indicates the rocks and dangerous currents ahead of him, and there are plenty. Nobody who has not lived and identified himself with our unique situation can even remotely form an adequate and reliable notion about its overwhelming complexity.

I must mention something about which we must be as clear in our minds as we must be honest in our hearts: to talk about the political future of the homelands, is to talk about the political future of South Africa, or, even more correctly, of Southern Africa. Whatever is fulfilled or not fulfilled, whatever is achieved or not achieved, in the political future of the homelands, is of much more than academic interest to white South Africa and all our neighbouring countries. Whether one likes it or not, it will relentlessly and permanently decide all basic trends in the political, economic and social future of our subcontinent, for better or for worse.

I cannot think of a more disastrous self-delusion than the idea still ghosting around in the minds of some white South Africans, namely: create the homelands, give them independence, yes, even fully-fledged sovereign independence, and then – push them out of your thoughts, forget about them. How completely different are the hard facts. Our present survival is rooted in our interdependence and, even much more so, will our future survival depend on our expanding interdependence. Be it independent homelands or not, be it whatever formula one cares to put forward, the fact is that blacks and whites in South Africa are crowded together in one little boat. And this frail boat is being tossed by wild and unpredictable waves on the ocean of history. Do we realise that we have only each other to rely upon in the life and death struggle to reach the safety of a distant port? Do we realise that we will either reach that port together, or, failing this, will perish together? As for the little boats of our neighbouring countries, if they think that they are not attached to our boat, and can ride out the storms of history alone, and reach the harbour alone, then that is clearly a case of wishful thinking. This fact, of being and remaining in one and the same little boat, needs urgent clarification in terms of the homelands policy, and in terms of the pattern along which its immediate evolution will take place.

I want to sound a word of grave warning to those who still consider the homelands concept as a mere theory or hypothesis, who still make the 'to be, or not to be' of the homelands the subject of an academic exercise. They are the ones that fiddle while Rome burns. I want to state most emphatically that the homelands are a reality, and a reality with which we have to learn to live. Whether it was a wise thing or not to create them has become irrelevant. That is an issue which has been consigned to the pages of history books. Of overriding relevance is the question whether we are happy with the various facets of this new reality. Today the burning issue about the homelands is the question: where do we go from here, and how do we get there, and without rocking or perhaps even overturning our boat? That is by far the most urgent challenge any politician in this country is faced with, be he black or white. After all, the homelands and their problems are, and will remain, an integral part of South Africa.

It is safe to say that no political party in this country, whether among blacks or whites, which proclaims its intention to abolish the homelands, has the remotest chance at the polls. With all the grievances, inconsistencies, obstructions, insecurities and frustrations which bedevil the homelands issue today, let one vital fact be spelt out clearly, once and for all: the black man sees in the homeland concept a positive acknowledgment and vindication of his particular stamp of black identity. This principle is immensely more important and dynamic today than at the inception of the policy some 25 years ago. At that time, the terms 'Black identity' and 'Black consciousness' were never heard of.

It is, therefore, equally safe to say that, as from now, the success of any political party in this country will depend first and foremost on its homelands policy: it will depend on the honesty, justice, imagination and speed with which it gives meaning and fulfilment to the homeland ideal. It will depend on the wisdom with which it reconciles and eliminates the tensions and confrontations which will unavoidably build up in the process. Such tensions and misgivings in most cases are based on conflicting 'group interests'. These arise each time when adjustments and sacrifices are necessary to permit, or speed up, the establishment of meaningful homeland complexes.

Here again, it must be pointed out with grave emphasis that such conflict situations will continue to arise, until all South Africans, and here I must specifically refer to the whites as being the most privileged group, have learnt the lesson which will make or break our future, which will determine the fate of the boat in which we are all fellow-passengers and fellow-crew. It is to subordinate our immediate and short-term personal and sectional interests to the long-term and ultimate interest of ensuring a safe passage for our little boat.

This principle, undoubtedly the most basic for our future, boils down to the question of existential security, the deepest and most potent human need, both individually and collectively. In view of our interdependence, what is needed surely is a positive willingness to accept such adaptations, hard as they may be, that will establish and entrench the existential security of all groups. This, I am convinced, is an absolute sine qua non for a peaceful future, and no imaginable power-structure can ever be a substitute for any length of time.

Building on the principles that I have outlined, I will venture to elaborate on some more concrete details in line with the political evolution as I visualise it. In view of my belief in black-white interdependence, more specifically in the economic field, as the only key to any form of peaceful co-existence, it would obviously be inconsistent if I put them in the form of rigid, militant demands. All the same, what I have to say comes from my heart and is put forward as a basis for constructive dialogue. After all, interdependence only works out if the two parties involved sit down with an honest willingness to thrash out the mutually most acceptable formula.

As the ultimate ideal I can never depart, in South Africa as elsewhere, from the principle of 'one man one vote'. But it would be utterly futile, at this stage, to disregard the historical realities and their practical implications. The fear on the part of our four million whites of the power falling overnight into the hands of sixteen million blacks is a natural and not unreasonable reaction of any privileged and highly developed minority.

At the same time, it is not unreasonable either to postulate that, in the long run, developments may bring about a situation where this fear loses all substance. With educational, training and economic opportunities increasing with gathering momentum, a process which is unavoidable, the present colour-bound stratification will in due course be superseded and disappear. A society will then emerge in which responsibility for the security and welfare of the country as a whole will be evenly distributed, and where all will have an equal stake in peace and progress, and will equally be losers if these are not maintained. It is inconceivable that under such circumstances the present fears would continue to be operative in the minds of people of goodwill.

On the basis of our uncompromising belief that full respect is due to our human dignity, as in the case of all human beings, we confidently expect that our independence will bring about a restitution of privileges, inseparably associated with universal human dignity. Among these privileges I must single out a few:

1 / In the country of our forefathers, and of our birth, the sharing of power is our inalienable right.

2 / That in our country, the country of our birth, there must be a more fair and just sharing of the land, is a principle from which we can never deviate. We

reject outright the present attempts to make the 1936 Land Act the basis of 'settling' this issue. This law was introduced to increase the then 'Native Reserves', or, if one prefers to put it that way, to solve the then 'Native Problem'. In no way did the law claim or intend to provide additional area for future independent sovereign states. In terms of the present policy, therefore, this law has no relevance whatsoever in respect of homeland consolidation negotiations. Any continued reference to this Act in the context of homeland consolidation has the taste of a dishonest subterfuge, and will do untold harm. Provision should further be made that some of the most fertile areas, such as Hartswater and Brits, instead of being monopolised, be shared.

3 / Having contributed and still contributing substantially, through 'cheap labour', to the impressive economic development of white South Africa, we would like an assurance in clear terms of what we will get in return, so as to enable us to make our economically depressed territories more prosperous.

4 / As we will continue to be actively contributing and participating in the economic unit of South Africa as a whole, we in the homelands would have to enter into an agreement ensuring our fair share of the many indirect taxes we are paying.

5 / A labour agreement, mutually beneficial, would have to be entered into.

'We live in the spirit of the times.' Nothing can prevent this spirit from spreading into the remotest corners of today's world. The rest of Africa is free. This cannot but echo every day in the souls of black men here in the South. Freedom, after all, is the birthright of every human being. We are no exception, and there is no reason why we should be. Yet we are honest in acknowledging the presence of providential ties with the white man, which do not obtain further north. That is why we have accepted the independent homeland concept which gives positive expression to our interdependence. We have always lived with whites in South Africa, and actually we have lived together remarkably peacefully. In spite of tensions, differences and quarrels, the basic goodwill which exists is not only remarkable, but almost miraculous. We do not want this heritage of goodwill undermined by unilateral action, designed to exclude whites from our homelands. In fact, we would heartily welcome whites as citizens in our midst. And not only for the sake of their know-how and their capital, but as people. There are many whites who make one feel good to have them around. People of all races who have civilised hearts can and will live happily together, and their different identities and cultures will enrich the quality of human existence. Even if we are discriminated against, we would not find it in our hearts to retaliate by discriminating against anyone.

There is much speculation about the concept of a federation, but the time in history has arrived when we must consider it more seriously. If we cannot have 'one man one vote' in South Africa, then there seems to remain no logical alternative to federation. As independent states, we, the homelands, would sooner or later have to federate with white South Africa, plus those states of Southern Africa which would agree to federation. The federal structure would obviously start off on a rather loose and limited scale and on a narrow range of fields. In accordance with mutual needs and desires it could very well develop into a closer-knit federation, thereby increasing its influence, power and status in the international field.

In brief outline, I would welcome the establishment and gradual strengthening of the following federal ties:

1 / First and foremost, an economic federation, as the most effective safeguard for peace and good-neighbourliness. The European Economic Community is a fine example of its peace-promoting effect. In some respects it could serve as a model, though basically the terms would have to be thrashed out locally to fit our own situation.

2 / A security federation would serve as a formidable bulwark against aggression, terrorism and infiltration.

3 / An educational and cultural federation could achieve much in promoting not only higher training standards, but also the best spirit of good-neighbourliness. Especially at university level, young people would be allowed to study across the border and broaden their outlook and maintain a creative dialogue.

We would of course wish to be treated, then as now, strictly as equals, both as states and as individuals. The whole degrading structure of so-called 'petty apartheid', which is at present doing more damage to South Africa's international image than any other single factor, could then be instantly demolished, without giving anybody any reason to feel threatened. There is of course no reason to wait so long. A federal council, representative of the various independent, sovereign states which have acquired membership, would regulate matters of common concern and interest. Representation in the federal council would have to take the populations of each member state into consideration, but other factors could be agreed upon to determine the formula.

In those services controlled and conducted by the federal council, there would obviously have to be an equality of opportunity. Candidates from all member states would be eligible for posts in the federal services, for instance administrators, defence officers, diplomats, etc., on the understanding of course that appointments are made strictly on merit.

One point which is clearly illustrated by the examples I have just given is that we here in South Africa have already made considerable strides into a new era. It is an era where we can speak out honestly and openly on delicate issues that were still taboo only a few years back and, what is more, where there is a rapidly increasing willingness for responsible, constructive dialogue across the colour line. We still have our own version of holy cows roaming our streets, but already people are less shocked and alarmed as they disappear one by one.

The present times are tough, but the promise on our horizon makes it worthwhile to hold out hopefully.

A Black Man Looks at White Politics

K.M.N. GUZANA

(Address to the Cape Congress of the Progressive Party, 9 June 1973)

The subject of my address is somewhat enigmatic as it requires me to place myself on some detached planet and look at white South African politics as an unaffected person. My first reaction was therefore to ask myself the question: can I be disengaged to such a degree that I can look at this subject without personal involvement to the extent of being unprejudiced in my assessment of white politics, which is also black politics? Are the two aspects of South African politics not so enmeshed together and intertwined as to be inseparable from each other? Living in South Africa as I do, can I not see politics as South African politics so that in touching the trigger of legislation the discharged bullet grazes white South Africa and hits black South Africa? When South Africa's legislation is directed at South Africa's multi-racial population it is race legislation, either reserving certain rights and privileges for one section of the population and/or taking away these from another section. However, I have accepted the challenge implicit in the subject and shall try in a limping fashion to pinpoint what a black man sees when he looks at white politics.

Were I to attempt a legal approach to the subject, I would be operating from a conceited and paternalistic assumption that you do not know the law of the land. Even apart from this aspect, to examine the various laws that grace and disgrace the statute books and to restate what the black man sees in them would be too onerous a task and too tedious an effort to contain in this short address. In the circumstances, allow me to suggest that the black man sees white politics as:

a) attitudes and prejudices enshrined in enactments that physically restrain him;

b) negativing the black man's longing to eat well,

to clothe himself and his family adequately, and to have a clean and hygienic home;

c) robbing him of the simple comforts of living happily with his wife and children;

d) a detraction from his yearning for a full and complete self-realisation as a human being in a Christian country, in which he ought to live without fear or anxiety for his future and liberty;

e) a way of life which drums into his head that he is a lesser human being than others, in a half-way evolutionary stage of development from animal to man, not developed enough to be an equal of the white man, but not so underdeveloped as to be grouped with sheep and cows;

f) assigning to him an undefined existence in which the black man is a 'come and go' human cipher, sufficiently intelligent to be used but not cultured enough to be accepted.

When white missionaries brought Christianity to South Africa and taught the black man that all persons are equal before God and that in life man should be equal in the eyes of other human beings, this ethical basis of human relationship gradually substituted for a rough and tumble existence based primarily on self-preservation in its crudest form. As a trusting individual, the black man accepted this ideal which meant for him physical security, unhindered advancement and protected enterprise. These expectations were nurtured by a benevolent paternalism as the black man tentatively experimented with this new-found concept. He left his rural home to seek work in the urban areas, to join his friend or relative, to enjoy the varied and fascinating experience of equality in the complex and exciting environment of a concentrated and hectic society.

But gradually and inexorably, white politics began to restrain his free movement, to undermine his novel sense of equality. Shop assistants told him to wait his turn when white customers entered the shop; he dare not sit down on that bench at the railway station; he must crowd with other blacks into one railway coach when the next coach has one white occupant; restaurants and cafes sell him sausage-rolls and soft drinks to consume on his feet on the pavement; he must eschew certain entrances and exits; and avoid the front gate.

Equality took on a new shape and meaning: it was

neither between man and man nor between white and black, but between white and white and between black and black. Irritating and frustrating experiences of inequality piled one upon the other for the black man: equality took on a monstrous look; it became colour-conscious, intolerant and aggressive. Laws and by-laws, rules and regulations, all carrying criminal sanctions for any ill-conceived exercise of equality completed the picture and the black man now asks: white South Africa, what do you mean by equality?

Once upon a time, soon after Union, the black man looked forward to representation in parliament and lesser governing bodies which made laws that affect South Africa citizens. He firmly believed that the white man would progressively give him active participation in legislation even if initially such participation were not on an equal footing. Black political organisations made the requests and recommendations through the correct channels, respectfully importuned white South Africans to extend to the black man the right to share in the making of the laws of the land. When these representations became aggressive in tone, cresting in demonstrations and possible physical revolution, the organisations went the way of all things done by the black man which are irritating and provocative.

The white man in South Africa is represented by a white man in legislative bodies; the black man who does not know what is good for him must be represented by a white man and at that, by a numerically insignificant number. Even this might give the black man fancy ideas about equal representation, one man one vote, and so like another nuisance it went. A black man to sit with a white man in parliament! What? Over our white dead bodies, yes, but not otherwise. The black man again asks the question: white South Africa, what do you mean by equality? Your electoral laws permit none other than whites to vote for members of the House of Assembly, and candidates can be none other than white persons who will legislate for South Africa's multi-racial population. Black man, do you see double when you look at white politics?

In a traditional set-up, the black man with his one, two or three wives had a very strong and healthy respect for the stability of his home and family. The black man treasured his family unit which, without him thinking it out, was the basis of a coherent tribe. When white missionaries persuaded him into a monogamous marriage, he was prepared to try it out, liked it in most cases, and settled for it until death us do part. After all, persons, black and white, who embraced western Christian civilisation, accepted this form of marriage as in keeping with Christian ethics and exclusive matrimonial loyalty.

But when the black man went to the mines and towns to work, white politics legislated against his wife accompanying him to his place of employment, restricted her visits to him, neglected, in order to have a plausible excuse for keeping the couple apart, to provide accommodation for him in the urban area as a family man. If he is single, he must choose his life partner from among the urban beauties and not from his hometown or village. If, as a Xhosa, he lets his loving eye rove into Lesotho for a wife, he cannot bring his bride back to the Transkei to live with him.

Turn the coin over, and the white man moves with his family from Johannesburg to take up employment in Cape Town, in Durban or Umtata, the capital of the Transkei homeland. A Capetonian male heart-throb can marry a platteland lass, streamline her via slimming courses and hairdressing salons into his elegant residence in Rondebosch. The black man looks at white politics and asks: do the invariable consequences of marriage differ from race to race in South Africa? Is white South Africa legislating me into default on my marriage vows? Is the white man's law forcing me into infidelity, into extra-marital associations and dehumanising practices? Is the black man's family unit so light-weight and inconsequential that husband and wife and children must be separated by the inhuman dictates of white politics? Is the sanctity of the black man's marriage vows somewhat second grade and fouled by the complexion of the parties to the marriage? Can the marriage last when a black man spends the greater portion of his vigorous life away from his wife and children? Again the black man asks the question: what double marriage standards, white South Africa?

Then again white man's politics becomes so self-concerned and so subjectively self-conscious that certain legislative enactments would be highly ludicrous if they were not so pathetically egotistical. Certain laws prohibit a marriage between a white person and a member of another racial group and will even punish parties to a passing affair. White South Africans flee from their politics into Lesotho and Swaziland to be themselves because their politics is intolerable. In this sensitive situation chivalry has been dealt a grievous blow and white womanhood has had to be reinforced in its sense of what is morally right or wrong by the horror of a public criminal trial and has to behave well as befits a member of the white race. The suspicion of men who invented the chastity belt has indeed ingenious manifestations in South Africa. The black man would like to know why white South Africa thinks in this degrading fashion about its womanhood; and why the womenfolk take this lying down. Is social ostracism not a sufficient deterrent? The black man is unable to explain these crude manifestations of subjective white race consciousness with all its intolerance and impertinence.

All western-orientated societies recognise that rights and liberties are enjoyed fully only when curtailed in the interests of members of the societies. The black man realises this and accepts law enforcement and sanctions as part and parcel of a well-ordered society. Punishment for murder, theft and for many other offences is morally acceptable. But when a black man goes to prison because he is in an urban area without a permit; or because he is not in employment; because he has lost his employment and cannot find another employer soon enough; when the law takes away his right to live permanently in an urban area because he is unable to prove that he has lived in the area since birth; because he has strayed into a white-by-night town, and for breaching multifarious and incomprehensible rules and regulations without any moral guilt attaching to these infringements, then the black man sees white politics as the politics of inequality.

The continuing procession of the black man into prison and out of prison, and again into prison and out of prison for a breach of apartheid strictures has a demoralising effect on the black man. Those in prison ask why they are in prison; those outside prison expect to go inside sooner or later: those in prison are filled with an overwhelming sense of grievance: those outside prison are living in a hell of unabated apprehension. The black man's life is one of evasion and avoidance; of slinking away and of furtive glances. The shadow of uncertainty is darker than the blackest night. The black man asks the questions: where is justice? wher is fair play in white politics?

In a growing impatience with the persistent annoyance from the black man's ubiquitous presence in every corner of South Africa, in the home and at the office; at work and at play: from his becoming uncomfortably indispensable everywhere, white politics dreams up the phantasy of separate freedom, separate political rights, separate towns, separate privileges, separate everything, all of which when summed up give us the homelands solution. The black man will have all these and more in the bantustans which will ultimately become independent. The white government even baits the homeland leader with independence as a matador baits the bull with a red flag - woe unto the bull if it allows itself to be taunted beyond reason! Cut up South Africa into so many irregular and unequal geographical pieces, each straining for recognition. The land tug-of-war is on: the crowds are urging each bantustan leader to pull harder and harder; the game has taken on a bloody menace: black consciousness which might soon crystallise into Black Power lends muscle to the black man; the white man's face is growing pale; the black man's face is getting blacker and more ominous looking.

Tragically, the basis of the bantustan concept is white rejection of the black man, and because separate development is basically race division and is conceived in a white-superior and black-inferior mental and emotional political penthouse, it is discriminatory. The black man who professes to accept the policy is a depressed fatalist who has accepted defeat and slinks back into the strategy of withdrawal. One wants to shout stop! How does white South Africa, in a country which is a compact geographical unit with a South African population of many races, essay into a programme of dividing up liberty and basic human freedoms, patriotism and South Africanism into ethnic compartments? The black mar wants to know how this can be done without injustice; hc the fundamental and intangible pillars of a Christian democratic country can be splintered into halves, quarte and eighths without permanent hurt, injury and inequalit

For the black man in South Africa, patriotism is a

binding, indivisible thread which knits together peoples of all races, colours and creeds, the rich and the poor, the privileged and the less privileged, and even political antagonists in a united loyalty to the country of their birth. He will stand shoulder to shoulder with white, coloured and Indian, with Jew and Gentile, ready and proud to make the supreme sacrifice for his home and country. He is not fooled by unctuous cries for the liberation of the black man by violence and bloody revolution, and in as much as today he has died nobly along South Africa's borders, he is equally as ready to resist the seductive forces of violence inside South Africa.

Not all the security laws in South Africa's statute books would have made South Africa safe and prosperous without the loyal response of the black man. The black man now asks white South Africa for tangible vindication for his loyalty and patriotism. He asks for a living wage, a good home, an opportunity to rise higher and higher, equality before the law and acceptance - a stake protected by the law of the land unfettered by prejudice. Why is white politics overlooking this frontier which it can build for its twenty million odd population in every street and corner, in the urban and rural areas, and at every fireside family circle. A black man can go on in this way, asking questions that are never answered, doubting the bona fides of the white man behind white politics without getting anywhere. Somewhere, sometime, there must be a change of heart and attitudes for both blacks and whites in South Africa. Let us develop a collective emotion round the future of South Africa to fire the imagination and inspire healthy planning; a unanimous concern for the welfare of all South Africans. The black man has tangible reason to believe that the change is taking place in white South Africa, though somewhat painfully and slowly. When a white minister of religion challenges his white congregation to bring the servants along to church, something good is happening somewhere. When a Progressive Party invites a black man in Natal and another today to address its Party Congresses, it is in earnest about its policy which is etched vividly in all hearts impassioned for justice and fair play. When the parliamentary doyen of this party together with the party leader carried the message of hope and the assurance of racial understanding through seven African states and evoked everywhere a warm appreciation of the party's stand for peaceful and meaningful change, the black man's heart was warmed with new hope for the dignity of man in South Africa.

When even in Nationalist parliamentary circles there is thought on the happiness of the urban African, the training of the black man for skilled and semi-skilled jobs, the right of the black man to strike for the improvement of his lot, the African sees the rigidity which characterised race thinking and race legislation acquiring some limited but none-the-less progressive flexibility. The black man is taking hopeful note of these happenings. White politics is responsible for our rejection by many countries of the world; white politics will bring us out of the cold into the fold of countries which have a compassion for the rights of man. The black man stands knocking at the door of white politics, urging change. He even asks the question: why is white South Africa shy of a change of government? You know what? You will not be alone at the celebrations.

Black Solidarity and Self-Help

M. GATSHA BUTHELEZI

(Address to Muslim Assembly, Cape, at the official opening of the Athlone Trade Fair, 17 February 1973)

I thank the Muslim Assembly of the Cape, for I am here today partly because I could not, despite the heavy demands on my time, fail them, when a call was made on their behalf for me to be here. I honour and respect all God's children regardless of colour, creed or religion. To be in this world and to have the privilege of serving them in however small a way, is the greatest privilege one can have, within one's short span of life.

The other aspect of this invitation is that this was a call by the black communities of the Cape Flats to me as a black brother. I believe that black consciousness which ends only in rhetoric is an intellectual pastime which we as blacks cannot afford. I, as a black man, therefore consider it a great privilege to be here and to identify myself with efforts of other blacks to uplift themselves. I believe that coming here to participate in a black event of this magnitude, boils down to black consciousness and identification. Those of us who believe in this kind of identification need to allay the fears of many people who see nothing positive in black identification. It is a unity to uplift and not a unity to oppress. It is a unity not against any creature of God's creation, but a unity of God's creatures in order to emphasise the greatness of the whole of the Lord's creation. In other words, by our efforts and by our identification we are here to praise God or Allah. We are here to say through an identification and through this kind of event, 'He cares for all His creatures'. If we claim, as we do, that we are made in the Creator's image, then we must in our limited way show, as we are gathered here to do, that we also care.

I was informed that the Athlone Fair was arranged

as a source of revenue for a charitable welfare organisation in Athlone which caters for the needs of the community irrespective of creed or colour. The Oxford dictionary defines charity as 'Christian love of fellowmen; kindness, affection'. This, I will admit as a Christian, is a lopsided definition of charity, no doubt showing that the dictionary was compiled by Christians. However, in fairness to them, they also add that it means beneficence, liberality to the poor, almsgiving, alms, bequest, foundation or institution for the benefit of others especially the poor or helpless.

From this definition you will agree with me that, if we take into account that the bulk of black people in this country earn uneconomic wages, there is a lot to commend in the action of the poor caring about the poor. I know that I am on dangerous ground when I commend charitable actions. A view is expressed, which I think we cannot argue against, that owing to the manner in which South African society is ordered, the affluent seem bent on not sharing their wealth with blacks, except in the form of charitable actions. I know that it might be argued that this is not a charitable view of the situation. I,however, think that things like disparities in the pay scales of professional people on the basis of race and things like job reservation are irrefutable evidence that this view, unpalatable as it may be to some, is quite valid. I am personally openminded enough to accept that there are people who do charitable acts for altruistic reasons.

A view is held, particularly by the young, that charitable actions in South Africa are an indulgence to salve guilty consciences. While I am again charitable enough to say that not everyone does so to salve a conscience, I am fair-minded enough to accept that the orientation of our society has categorised the bulk of blacks as a population of recipients of charity not because they could not by their own efforts live a better life, but because certain ceilings to their advancement are placed deliberately for no other reason than that they happen to be black.

It is a fact of course that humans in general do want to appear altruistic either for religious or for humanitarian reasons. I have found in my travels, even in countries where the welfare state is almost an accomplished fact, that certain people do want to involve themselves in charitable work regardless of the godlessness of the post-Christian era in which they are now living.

South Africa is no exception, and I think it would be quite wrong for me not to pay tribute to societies, religions and others whose members have involved themselves in welfare work amongst our black people. Good old South Africa as a state is an 'also ran' in this respect. I am not trying to denigrate my country here. I say this for reasons explained above about the manner in which our society is racially ordered. Furthermore, even where efforts have been made in connection with social welfare work amongst blacks the race issue has dogged the steps of those who have tried to do so over the years, from the cradle to the grave. Let us look at the following figures and then what I am trying to say will be clearer:

	Pensions per month (R)			
Race	Old age	Blind	Disability	War veterans
Whites	39,48	36,14	36,93	47,28
Coloured people	15,77	15,76	16,30	19,85
Africans	5,38	5,21	5,35	-

(Sources: Hansard, House of Assembly, 1972: 10 col.758; 44 col.302; 6 col.511)

From these figures you can see that our country is conscious of its duty to the aged and the disabled, but its concern for these is again completely nullified by our obsession with race, which makes us grade peoples' needs not according to need, but according to race.

The Muslim Assembly responsible for this trade fair deserves our praise and emulation. It is not sufficient to squeal about our plight anymore. In spite of the odds we are facing as blacks let us not wait only for other friends to help us, but let us gird ourselves to face up to our problems without too much flinching. I find the words of Frederick Douglas, a famous black leader who escaped from slavery in the last century, most pertinent in this respect. In his writing under the heading 'What Are The Coloured People Doing For Themselves?' he states the following amongst other things: 'If there be one evil spirit among us, for the casting out of which we pray more earnestly than another, it is that lazy, mean and cowardly spirit, that robs us of all manly self-reliance, and teaches us to depend upon others for the accomplishment of that which we should achieve with our own hands'.

Our white friends can and are rapidly removing barriers to our improvement, which they themselves have set up; but the main work must be commenced, carried on and concluded by ourselves. While in no circumstances should we undervalue or fail to appreciate the self-sacrificing efforts of our friends, it should never be lost sight of that our destiny for good or for evil, for time and for eternity, is, by an all-wise God, committed to us; and that all the help or hindrances with which we may meet on earth can never release us from this high and heaven-imposed responsibility.

It is evident that we can be improved and elevated only just so fast and far as we shall improve and elevate ourselves. We must rise or fall, succeed or fail, by our own merits. If we are careless and unconcerned about our own rights and interests it is not within the power of all the earth combined to raise us from our present degraded condition - 'Hereditary bondsmen know ye not who would be free, themselves must strike the blow?' 'We say the present is a time when every coloured man should ask himself the question, what am I doing to elevate and improve my condition and that of my brethren at large?'(1)

I think the efforts of the Muslim Assembly in having arranged this kind of fair from the year 1968 have everything to commend them to all of us as blacks. Again let me stress that I think it is important for me to have been given the privilege of coming here to identify myself with other black people in their efforts at helping themselves. The Cape is not new to this at all, as that great black leader Dr A. Abdurahman blazed this trail for all of us. His key-note addresses regularly attaked any form of racial discrimination.(2) As early as 1902 Dr Abdurahman initiated the African Peoples Organisation. He realised as early as that that coloured people were of Africa and was not ashamed to form an organisation which he named as he did. It was predominantly composed of coloured members. Dr Abdurahman was unable to acquiesce in unrestrained white power and refused to accept Chamberlain's advice to 'trust to the good feelings of the white colonists' in the Transvaal. The African Peoples Organisation which Dr Abdurahman led argued consistently for rights and privileges regardless of class, colour and creed.

When an African delegation went to London in 1909 to protest against the South Africa Act, Dr Abdurahman's African Peoples Organisation contributed £100 towards the expenses of the African delegates, and after that date Abdurahman remained an important commentator. In this way he helped to clarify African political thought and personally sought contact with African leaders, although his coloured fellowers were not always so enthusiastic about such co-operation.(3) I hope that my invitation by the Muslim Community will strengthen the ties established by Dr Abdurahman between our various peoples. Any doubts at this juncture would be suicidal in terms of our common cause and commitment to one goal of full recognition and full human rights. It is for this reason that it is such a privilege for me to be here this afternoon, to declare this sixth annual Athlone Trade Fair officially open. INKOSI ISIKELELI AFRIKA.(4)

Our Common Heritage

M. GATSHA BUTHELEZI

(Excerpts from statement on visit of Executive Councillors and the Chief Executive Councillor of KwaZulu to Cape Town at the invitation of the Hon. the Minister of Bantu Administration, 25 February to 2 March 1973)

Despite the fact that there is so little to be happy about, if you happen to be born with a black skin in South Africa, we are a rich country, not so much because of our gold which so few enjoy, but because of the variegated backgrounds of people who make up our population. The greatest privilege we do not appreciate in South Africa is our common human heritage, and the fact that we are all created in the image of God despite our different backgrounds. The agony of South Africa is that we despise the image of God in men of colour.

Meeting and talking as freely as I did with my fellow-countrymen of different racial, political and religious backgrounds has enriched me, and although we are an affluent country, we are one of the poorest in things of eternal value, on account of the fact that we close the doors of our hearts to so much that can enrich our souls from our fellow-countrymen of different racial backgrounds. Nothing has emphasised this point more than the profound observation by the Honourable the Prime Minister at the end of the Durban strikes that we are human beings with souls. This may go down as the most significant statement ever made by a white prime minister in South Africa.

But to me, while I applaud it, it is depressing at the same time that the realisation within the power structure is only dawning now, in the twentieth century and in the seventies, that it is so. When one looks at this, against the days of slavery here in the Cape and against the liberation of the Afrikaners themselves, it appears quite a far cry. The challenge of the Prime Minister's observation is that it can either be transformed into action now or South Africa will inevitably face disaster.

The man-made valleys between man and man in South Africa gape before our eyes, without appearing to narrow in any meaningful way. Should we fail to take the hint from the Prime Minister's words, we will all sink and lose our souls in these dark valleys of everlasting death. Do we have the right to destroy such a beautiful country and all the Lord's creation in it? There is only one dignity which all human beings receive automatically from God, and it is almost blasphemous to speak of apportioning dignity or giving status to human beings who are God's creation. Even immigrants can be given full human rights and human dignity after a certain period and on complying with certain requirements. How grossly insulted do we feel that we should not be eligible in our own land for what immigrants can get, merely because we are a few shades darker than the people who control power in our land?

Any solution worked out by Whites on their own will never give us satisfaction. We are the only people who know what we want and we do not need other people to interpret this for us, because we know it better than they can every know it. Even the policies in which we are participating can never be more than a very inadequate stop-gap exercise, so long as we blacks do not fully determine our own destinies as free people do all the world over. What American blacks deplored we deplore too, that while we are co-operating, one side should do all the 'operating' and we merely the 'co-ing'.

Petty Apartheid

H.W.E. NTSANWISI

(Address prepared, but not presented, for the Sociological Symposium, University of Pretoria, 18 August 1973)

Much has been written and heard about apartheid, the policy followed in the Republic of South Africa in which people are grouped for purposes of government and politics into different categories. This policy in the main provides for complete territorial separation of the races in South Africa, with special emphasis on separate political, economic and cultural development of the various ethnic and linguistic groups within the Republic of South Africa. As far as the whites are concerned ethnic, cultural and linguistic differences are not taken into consideration as they are placed in one white homeland.

According to census statistics South Africa has a population of 21 million people of whom 3-3/4 million are whites - the white homeland presently constitutes 87 per cent of the land while 13 per cent has been allocated to the blacks. This aspect of apartheid which is sometimes referred to as macro-apartheid therefore also discriminates against the blacks and is advantageous to the whites.

Meso-apartheid, which is physical separation resulting in homogeneous residential ghettos within multiracial urban areas, is also advantageous to the whites since they live in the best residential areas in the cities. Micro-apartheid is referred to as separation in private and public facilities. This is also advantageous to the whites since they are provided with the best of facilities and enjoy preference in the use of all facilities. In certain instances such as lifts, the whites use facilities meant for the blacks whenever that suits them. All these forms of apartheid have to my mind one thing in common, i.e. discrimination based on colour. For this reason the expression micro-apartheid or petty apartheid cannot be easily defined as it is nothing else but a manifestation of the whole concept of apartheid. It is therefore difficult to isolate petty apartheid from the broad spectrum of apartheid. In this paper, however, we shall discuss petty apartheid as micro-apartheid.

Petty apartheid has been described as discrimination in public and private facilities. This type of discrimination or apartheid is observed in railway stations, trains, buses, public buildings, banks, beaches, etc, where there are separate facilities for whites and blacks. Notices 'Whites Only' and 'Non-Whites' are seen all over the country in parks and lifts in buildings. This discrimination is based on colour; it is a form of apartheid based on racism. It is seen in the Separate Amenities Act and other restrictive legislation which debar any person who is not white from enjoying many facilities and rights in the land of his birth. This petty apartheid is irritating and hurtful to the soul of the black man who is discriminated against and it is an affront to human dignity.

Petty apartheid with its grossly unequal facilities constantly reminds the black of his second class place in the social life of South Africa and it is no doubt a source of emotional pride, economic and other practical advantages to the whites. The gains that the white obtains from petty apartheid are no doubt substantial but one doubts as to whether this contributes anything towards the maintenance of white supremacy other than his ego - especially the ego of those whites who have nothing to pride themselves on except the pigment of their skin. The observance of petty apartheid is definitely not a cornerstone of the socio-political order. The Portuguese in Mozambique and Angola still maintain their rule without resort to petty segregation and thus claim that they are free of racial prejudice.

Petty apartheid generates hatred, bitterness, spiritual and social tensions which bedevil human relations in South Africa. A black man who visits distant countries overseas where there are no notices for 'Whites Only' is forcibly reminded of his second class status as soon as he lands on South African soil because now and then he must stop and watch as to whether he is not treading on forbidden ground. There are white people now who feel that petty apartheid serves no useful purpose, but unhappily they are not many. Many black people, especially the educated and the young, have ceased to respect the white man as a result of petty apartheid, because disrespect begets disrespect. Any man of self respect feels deeply hurt when he is discriminated against on the grounds of his colour.

Indeed the question of dignity goes deeper than anything else in the analysis of race relations in this country - every time you refer to me as 'boy', 'Jim' or 'John', every time you push me from the pavement; every time you tell me to try my shoes on in a dark and hidden storeroom; every time you stop me and ask me for my pass; every time you question my right to work in a certain area; every time you stop me from worshipping where I happen to be; every time you debar me from seeing a rare work of art; every time you pay me less for the same work and equal qualifications, you build in my soul a sense of resentment and helplessness I cannot forget.

All that we black people want is to be treated like men, to believe in our hearts that we are men - men who can stand on our own feet and control our own destinies. We are not interested in the patronising attitude of the white man; we don't seek any favours; we want to be afforded the opportunity to pay our passage through life. What we want is not favours or privileges but rights. For the sake of posterity; and the future survival of this country, discrimination based on colour must go; the matter is urgent and the time is short.

We may indeed be 'andersoortig' (different) in that our cultures and backgrounds differ. But this is surely no justification for hurting my dignity by forcing me to enter by another entrance or pay at another counter. Many people of goodwill are today looking for a solution to this violence on the dignity of man. This will require sincerity, courage and heroic decisions on the part of political leadership, university professors and other educators, businessmen, employers and employees, teachers and students, trade unionists and parents and teachers and, particularly, the white electorate. Those who hesitate to act because of the colossal nature and apparent magnitude of the problem must realise that we are daily moving towards a deep precipice from which we shall not be able to extricate ourselves.

I have pointed out all these things because I firmly believe that there can be no real progress in the crucial race relations in this country unless the hurt to human dignity, by measures inherent in petty apartheid, is pointed out in forthright terms for all to see and understand and take some concrete action to counteract this explosive race problem before our borrowed time is up.

Are You Coming Along, Brother?

M.T. MOERANE

(Address delivered at National Organisations Conference, Johannesburg, 18 December 1971)

A new spirit is moving through our community in these days. It is this spirit which in April 1971 saw representatives of seven African organisations meeting in conference in Bloemfontein. The essence of this spirit was evinced in the manifestation of a re-evaluation of who the black man is, and the need for the black man, proud of his identity, to assume his manhood and evolve his own destiny. This meeting decided to call a wider conference subsequently with the simple theme of how African organisations could pool their resources to move their community forward and to promote our self reliance and awareness of ourselves as a black people.

Thus on Saturday 14 August 1971, twenty-six African organisations met in conference at the Edendale Lay Ecumenical Centre in Pietermaritzburg. The six papers read at that conference and the discussion which ensued made it clear that the Africans as a people had been objects and victims of a vicious system over the years. This system, in essence, consisted of entrenching white privilege and exploitation of the blacks. This cult of exploitation became a way of life and the very core of the attitudes and institutions of the white regimes of this country. The black man, into the bargain, had become progressively dispossessed, rejected and dehumanised. Not only was he dispossessed of his land and denied the opportunity to participate in the economy and industry of this land, beyond menial levels of labour, he was robbed of his own faith, his manhood and his self respect. He had almost completely grown to believe that and act as if indeed he was less than a human. This betrayal had been mediated, sometimes through the most pious of institutions such as those of religion and education. And his oppression was buttressed by the fiercest of discriminatory legislation and ruthless police action. Yes, the black man had now put the white man on a pedestal, regarded him as boss and master and the standard and referee for his values and conduct.

Yet in his own folkways and his own culture and values lay tenets both dynamic and nationally edifying. Values that had evolved for the African cultures which were the envy of Western peoples, e.g. in the stability of our societies and the noble attributes of respect for the dignity of the human personality and social consciousness and social responsibility. The new spirit enjoined the African today to be himself and to do his thing. It was clear we had to rediscover ourselves, while at the same time we grew to recognise oppression, mental enslavement and exploitation in its varied, often so sophisticated, guises. We had, if we were going to evolve our destiny, to recognise how the process of our degradation functioned.

We had to accept our own values and evolve our own philosophies and posit our own goals. We had to de-brainwash our own people and kindle a new pride and will for self determination in their hearts, mind and sinews. We had to get our people involved in this adventure of our lives.

But these things could not be done in vacuo. It was a convenient strategy to take advantage of the existing organisations. But we must recognise that some of them are products or adjuncts of the system we are rejecting. We thus need to take stock of our organisations while recognising the important criterion that the African, as an individual or in association, must make nation building his task.

We are here to lay the foundations of the confederal movement which will maximise our efforts and build our self reliant strategy in our struggle to attain independent freedom. We are here to effect our solidarity as brothers and comrades in arms. We shall have a good and critical look at the way we have lived and acted, thought and believed in the past. We shall re-evaluate the effectiveness of our organisations for nation building and freedom and when we have found the right ones we shall use them to the maximum advantage. But these things cannot be done in vacuo.

In the past the white man was our frame of reference, and our activity was barren. Today our frame of reference is the needs of our people. And if indeed we address ourselves to these needs, our activity cannot but be relevant and creative. This, to me, constitutes the challenge of this conference. By all means let us have the ideological analysts and theoreticians of our cause, doing their thing and illuminating our goals. But also let us go down where our people are in their struggles: to the sloughs of ignorance and poverty, where our people need education, enlightenment, jobs and living wages; to our ghettoes, where our womenfolk are condemned to live in fear for their security without rights of basic human freedom and self determination; among our workers, where wages are below minimal living standards and influx laws make slaves of men, at the beck and call of arbitrary bosses. There is where we belong. I see this force of men and women which we are forging today emerging as a real force, giving new hope to our masses who live a twilight, depressed existence, giving our young people the opportunity of an adventure of exertion and dare that sweeps us on to victory. I see this force rising in the nation and gathering momentum, till the black man has forged his way to regain his own.

Yes, from the broken, dispirited, impoverished remnants that we were yesterday, shall rise this mighty force in the nation that will sweep to victory. And the people will regret, who decreed that the races shall be separate in this country. For tomorrow they shall come running to us, for if we stop mouthing inane solgans and get on with the real job for, through and with our people, the future in this land is ours.

Are you coming along, brother?

(At this, the third successive conference, it was decided to establish the Black People's Convention. Moerane and others then withdrew, being more in favour of a non-political service organisation - Editor)

Black People's Convention: Extract from Constitution

Preamble

We, the black people of South Africa, declare that having examined, analysed, assessed and defined our needs, aspirations, ideals and goals in this country; and noting that there is a dearth of a political movement to articulate and aggregate these needs, aspirations, ideals and goals, and having further unconditionally declared our faith in the effectiveness, relevance and capability of black political movements as the only media through which our liberation and emancipation could be effected and realised, and believing that:

1 / black people in South Africa have unique needs, aspirations, ideals, difficulties and problems pertaining to them;

2 / it is an inalienable birthright of any community to organise itself into a political movement for effective translation of its needs, ideals and goals into reality;

3 / it is necessary and essential for blacks in South Africa to unite and consolidate themselves into a political movement if their needs, aspirations, ideals and goals are to be realised and actualised;

4 / there is a crying need in South Africa for blacks to re-assert their pride, human dignity and solidarity through a political movement; and whereas we are aware and conscious of our responsibility and obligation towards the liberation and emancipation of blacks, we are, nevertheless prepared and determined to accept this responsibility,

we, therefore, resolve to found a political convention; we, further, resolve to adopt this draft constitution as the constitution of this political movement, which would:

1 / articulate and aggregate the needs of black people in South Africa;

2 / represent the black people nationally and internationally.

Principles and aims of the Convention

1 / To unite and solidify the black people of South Africa with a view to liberating and emancipating them from both psychological and physical oppression;

2 / to spread, popularise and implement the philosophy of Black Consciousness and Black Solidarity

3 / to formulate and implement an educational policy of blacks, by blacks and for blacks;

4 / to create and maintain an egalitarian society where justice is meted equally to all;

5 / to formulate, apply and implement the principles and philosophy of Black Communalism - the philosophy of sharing equally;

6 / to create and maintain an equitable economic system based on the principles and philosophy of Black Communalism;

7 / to reorientate the theological system with a view to making religion relevant to the needs, aspirations, ideals and goals of the black people.

Object of the Convention

The object of the convention is to unite the South African blacks into a black political organisation which would seek to realise their liberation and emancipation from both psychological and physical oppression. The convention shall operate outside the white government-created systems, structures, and/or institutions - and shall not seek election into these.

Membership

1 / Membership shall be open to blacks only.

2 / Every member shall subscribe to the principles, aims, policies, goals and philosophy of the convention.

3 / No person who subscribes to the policies, principles and/or goals of any white government in South Africa shall become a member of the convention.

Interpretation clauses

1 / Unless inconsistent with the context, 'black' shall be interpreted as meaning Africans, Indians and coloureds.

Black People's Convention: Rejection of Foreign Investment

(Contents of a letter sent by B.P.C. to 31 foreign firms in South Africa)

At the Black People's Convention national congress at Hammanskraal in December, the following resolution was unanimously passed:

That this congress noting:

the role played by foreign investors in maintaining and supporting the economic system of South Africa,

that this system is designed for maximum exploitation of black people,

that the riches and resources of this country belong to blacks as their birthright,

that foreign investors claim their presence in this country contributes towards the development of the black community,

that this claim is disputed by reality of the black experience in this country,

therefore resolves:

to reject the involvement of foreign investors in this exploitative economic system,

to call upon foreign investors to disengage themselves from this white-controlled exploitative system,

to give the national executive a mandate to make known our stand on foreign investors both in this country and overseas through all available channels.

Your positive response to the above resolution will go a long way towards stamping out naked racism and exploitation of blacks.

The Disease of 'Mental Whiteness'

SIBUSISO M. BENGU

(Excerpted from The Zulu Voice, an English-language supplement to the Zulu newspaper, Ilanga, 13 September 1975)

My remarks to you, young sons and daughters of Africa, are based on one of the oldest yet contemporary enemies of mankind, as revealed in human behaviour - and that is, ethnocentrism. Of all the evil -isms such as imperialism, colonialism and racism, ethnocentrism is the most difficult enemy to fight. Since I have a natural hatred for long and big words, may I hasten to define ethnocentrism.

Ethnocentrism is a belief in the superiority of one's own cultural group or society and a corresponding dislike or misunderstanding of other such groups. This compound word comes from two basic words - 'ethnic', meaning social group or nation, and 'centric', a word formed from centre.

An ethnocentric person places his or her own group at the centre of the world and views or judges the other groups according to his or her group's standards. One's own group is placed at the centre of the world as an in-group and the out-group are seen as conforming or failing to conform to the norms and standards set by the in-group.

Ethnocentrism is, therefore, the projection of one's own group values on to others. Jean Piaget, a French psychologist, attributed ethnocentrism to the group's failure to differentiate between the ego and the world.

In an ethnocentric way the white races believe that their so-called talent and ability to form stable governments belong to them alone. Other races must necessarily 'remain in a state of barbarism or semi-barbarism, unless the white nations undertake the work of state organisation for them'.

Whilst it is true that every cultural group is to some degree ethnocentric, the period of imperialism and colonialism allowed for the drumming in of the belief that white institutions were superior. White ethnocentrism was reinforced by white political and economic domination of the people they had conquered.

The system of education introduced in Africa by the colonial masters discouraged African culture and African values. Since it was established by our ethnocentric colonial masters and since not much change has taken place in the basic orientation, it is still a trip out of Africa, the destination of which is the 'glittering' world of Europe. And yet education as we understand it should be a process by which people acquire or are given knowledge of themselves, of their environment, and of the tangible and intangible forces that tend to control their lives.

It wasn't until very recently that some Africans began to realise just how much they have been victims of white ethnocentrism. The obvious enemies that African nationalists have tried to fight were the visible effects of colonialism, most of which are either political or economic. It does seem that it will never be possible for Africans to eliminate new forms of white cultural domination in Africa until they understand the futility of their lifelong efforts to please the coloniser.

After years of denigration and self-abasement Africans now suffer from a very queer disease, and that is, negative ethnocentrism. The concept of negative ethnocentrism involves the act of a person or group having its own values and going full out to adopt values and habits of other groups. Whilst it is necessary for us to tell the Westerners to develop a less self-centred view of the world which inevitably places them in a position of superiority, we must struggle to come out of our own negative ethnocentrism.

Under the spell of European heroes, Africans make themselves carbon copies of various aspects of European culture, either as a carry-over from colonialism or as a component of development. This admiration for European culture causes complexes for both the European and the Africans. It contributes to European reassurance, European pride and racial arrogance. For the African it produces mental and spiritual whiteness. Large segments of African society look down upon things African and become apologetic about their African heritage.

This malady of negative ethnocentrism plagues the

Africans without them being aware of their thinking and actions which betray their Africanness. In an attempt to fully internalise Western cultural values some Africans become more English than the English.

Ethnocentrism is an enemy because it generates the following evils:
A biased perception of the out-group by the in-group.
Discrimination - members of the out-group are treated in a separate way.
Anti-locution - members of the in-group speak ill of the out-group.
Segregation - a more intense and institutionalised form of discrimination like apartheid is officially adopted.
Finally, ethnocentrism leads to the persecution or extermination of the out-group. This extermination may be physical as in the case of genocide, but it may just be ethnocide which leaves the group alive but takes its culture away from it, as with the West Indians.

The launching of the National Cultural Liberation Movement known as Inkatha is an attempt to have us liberate ourselves from white ethnocentrism on the one hand, and on the other, our own negative ethnocentrism. It is easy to understand why blacks in Southern Africa seek to liberate themselves through their culture.

Not only do Africans wish to liberate themselves from poverty, ignorance, hunger, disease, neo-colonialism and cultural domination by their white masters, but they are also desirous of liberating themselves from what I choose to call 'mental whiteness', that is, a sense of rejection of things African.

SASO: Black Students' Manifesto

We, the black students of South Africa, believing that the black man can no longer allow definitions that have been imposed upon him by an arrogant white world concerning his being and his destiny and that the black student has a moral obligation to articulate the needs and aspirations of the black community hereby declare that:

A. We black students are:

1 / an integral part of the black oppressed community before we are students coming out of and studying under the oppressive restrictions of a racist education;

2 / committed to a more disciplined involvement in the intellectual and physical world and to the consistent search of the black truth;

3 / committed to work towards the building of our people and to the winning of the struggle for liberation and guided by the central purpose of service to the black community on every technical and social level.

B. We, therefore, reject the whole sphere of racist education and commit ourselves to:

1 / the intellectual and physical development of our community and to the realisation of liberation for black peoples of South Africa;

2 / the definition that education in South Africa is unashamedly political and we, therefore, believe that black education is tied to the liberation of the black people of the world.

C. We hereby commit ourselves to:

1 / the assertion, manifestation and development of a sense of awareness politically, socially and economically among the black community;

2 / the belief that black students should maintain a spirit of fraternity amongst themselves, free from the prejudice of white fallacies by virtue of their common oppression;

3 / attempting to break away from the traditional

order of subordination to whites in education and to refuse to be educated for them;

4 / encourage and promote black literature relevant to our struggle;

5 / ensure that our education will further the preservation and promotion of what is measured in our culture and our historical experience.

SASO: Statement of Objectives

Preamble

We, the black students of institutions of higher learning in South Africa believing:

1 / that black students in South Africa have unique problems and aspirations pertaining to them;

2 / that it is necessary for black students to consolidate their ranks if their aspirations are to be realised;

3 / that there is a crying need in South Africa for black students to re-assert their pride and group identity,

Therefore

Adopt this constitution in the belief that unity and positive reawakening will result among the black students of South Africa.

Objects

1 / To promote contact and practical co-operation among black students in South Africa.

2 / To represent black students nationally and internationally.

3 / To establish contact among South African students.

SASO: Policy Manifesto

1 / SASO is a black student organisation working for the liberation of the black man first from psychological oppression by themselves through inferiority complex and, secondly, from the physical one accruing out of living in a white racist society.

2 / We define black people as those who are by law or tradition, politically, economically and socially discriminated against as a group in the South African society and identifying themselves as a unit in the struggle towards the realisation of their aspirations.

3 / SASO believes that
(a) South Africa is a country in which both black and white live and shall continue to live together;
(b) that the white man must be made aware that one is either part of the solution or part of the problem;
(c) that, in this context, because of the privileges accorded to them by legislation and because of their continual maintenance of an oppressive regime, whites have defined themselves as part of the problem;
(d) that, therefore, we believe that in all matters relating to the struggle towards realising our aspirations, whites must be excluded;
(e) that this attitude must not be interpreted by blacks to imply 'anti-whitism' but merely a more positive way of attaining a normal situation in South Africa;
(f) that in pursuit of this direction, therefore, personal contact with whites, though it should not be legislated against, must be discouraged, especially where it tends to militate against the beliefs we hold dear.

4 /
(a) SASO upholds the concept of black consciousness and the drive towards black awareness as the most logical and significant means of ridding ourselves of the shackles that bind us to perpetual servitude.
(b) SASO defines black consciousness as follows:
(i) Black consciousness is an attitude of mind, a way of life.
(ii) The basic tenet of black consciousness is that the black man must reject all value systems that seek

to make him a foreigner in the country of his birth and reduce his basic human dignity.
(iii) The black man must build up his own value systems, see himself as self-defined and not defined by others.
(iv) The concept of black consciousness implies the awareness by the black people of power they wield as a group, both economically and politically and hence group cohesion and solidarity are important facets of black consciousness.
(v) Black consciousness will always be enhanced by the totality of involvement of the oppressed people, hence the message of black consciousness has to be spread to reach all sections of the black community.
(c) SASO accepts the premise that before the black people should join the open society, they should first close their ranks, to form themselves into a solid group to oppose the definite racism that is meted out by the white society, to work out their direction clearly and bargain from a position of strength. SASO believes that a truly open society can only be achieved by blacks.

5 / SASO believes that the concept of integration cannot be realised in an atmosphere of suspicion and mistrust. Integration does not mean an assimilation of blacks into an already established set of norms drawn up and motivated by white society. Integration implies free participation by individuals in a given society and proportionate contribution to the joint culture of the society by all constituent groups. Following this definition, therefore, SASO believes that integration does not need to be enforced or worked for. Integration follows automatically when the doors to prejudice are closed through the attainment of a just and free society.

6 / SASO believes that all groups allegedly working for 'integration' in South Africa ... and here we note in particular the Progressive Party and other liberal institutions ... are not working for the kind of integration that would be acceptable to the black man. Their attempts are directed merely at relaxing certain oppressive legislations and to allow blacks into a white-type society.

7 / SASO, while upholding these beliefs, nevertheless wishes to state that black consciousness should not be associated with any particular political party or slogan.

SASO: Understanding SASO

(Introductory paper to a 'Formation School' arranged by the South African Students' Organisation at Edendale, 1971)

What are we talking about?

Here we are primarily concerned with SASO and its work. We talk glibly of 'Black Consciousness' and yet we show that we hardly understand what we are talking about. In this regard it is essential for us to realise a few basic facts about 'Black Consciousness'.

'Black Consciousness' is essentially a slogan directing us away from the traditional political big talk to a new approach. This is an inward-looking movement calculated to make us look at ourselves and see ourselves, not in terms of what we have been taught through the absolute values of white society, but with new eyes. It is a call upon us to see the innate value in us, in our institutions, in our traditional outlook to life and in our own worth as people. The call of 'Black Consciousness' is by no means a slogan driving people to think in a certain way politically. Rather it is a social slogan directed at each member of the black community calling upon him to discard the false mantle that he has been forced to wear for so many years and to think in terms of himself as he should. In this regard therefore Black Consciousness is a way of life that must permeate through the society and be adopted by all. The logic behind it is that if you see yourself as a person in your own right there are certain basic questions that you must ask about the conditions under which you live. To get to this stage there are three basic steps that have to be followed.

(i) We have to understand thoroughly what we are talking about and to impart it in the right context. This becomes especially necessary in a country like ours where such an approach lends itself easily to misinterpretation. For this reason we have made provision for a historical study of the theory of 'black power' in this formation school.

(ii) We have to create channels for the adoption of the same approach by the black community at large. Here, again, one has to be realistic. An approach of this nature, to be successful, has to be adopted by as large a fraction of the population as possible in order to be effective. Whilst the student community may be instrumental in carrying the idea across to the people and remaining the force behind it, the approach will remain ineffective unless it gains grass roots support. This is why it is necessary to create easily acceptable slogans and follow these up with in-depth explanations. Secondary institutions built up from members of the community and operating amongst the community have to be encouraged and these must be run by people who themselves understand what is involved in these institutions and in the approach we are adopting. One can expand and give many examples of such institutions but we expect this to come out of discussions at this formation school. Let it suffice to say that such institutions must cover all fields of activity of the black community - educational, social, economic, religious, etc.

(iii) People have to be taught to see the advantages of group action. Here one wonders whether a second look should not be taken at the government-instituted bodies like Urban Bantu Councils and bantustans. It is a universal fact that you cannot politicise people and hope to limit their natural and legitimate aspirations. If the people demand something and get it because they have an Urban Bantu Council or 'territorial authority' to talk for them, then they shall begin to realise the power they wield as a group. Political modernisation of the black people may well find good expression in these institutions which at present are repugnant to us. In contrasting the approach adopted in the United States by the black people and our own approach here, it will be interesting to know what this formation school thinks of the various 'territorial authorities' in our various 'own areas'.

There are some dangers that we have to guard against as we make progress in the direction we are pursuing. The first and foremost is that we must not make the mistake of wishing to get into the white man's boots. Traditional indigenous values tell us of a society where poverty was foreign and extreme richness unknown except for the rulers of our society. Sharing was at the heart of our culture. A system that tends to exploit many and favour a few is as foreign to us as hair which is not kinky or a skin which is not dark. Where poverty reigned, it affected the whole community simply because of weather conditions beyond our control. Hence even in our aspirations basic truth will find expression. We must guard against the danger of creating a black middle class whose blackness will only be literally skin-deep. The paper on African socialism will provide us with enough grounds for discussion along these lines.

Secondly we must not be limited in our outlook. There is a mile of difference between preaching Black Consciousness and preaching hatred of white. Telling people to hate whites is an outward and reactionary type of preaching which, though understandable, is undesirable and self-destructive. It makes one think in negative terms and preoccupies one with peripheral issues. In a society like ours it is a 'positive feed-forward' approach that leads one into a vicious circle and ultimately to self-destruction through ill-advised and impetuous action. In fact it is usually an extreme form of inferiority complex where the sufferer has lost hope of 'making it' because of conditions imposed upon him. His actual aspirations are to be like the white man and the hatred arises out of frustration.

On the other hand Black Consciousness is an inward-looking process. It takes cognisance of one's dignity and leads to positive action. It makes you seek to assert yourself and to rise to majestic heights as determined by you. No doubt you resent all forces that seek to thwart your progress but you meet them with strength, resilience and determination because in your heart of hearts you are convinced you will get where you want to get to. In the end you are a much more worthy victor because you do not seek to revenge but to implement the truth for which you have stood all along during your struggle. You were no less angry than the man who hated whites but your anger was channelled to positive action. Because you had a vision detached from the situation you worked hard regardless of immediate setbacks. White hatred leads to precipitate and short-run methods whereas we are involved in an essentially long-term struggle where cool-headedness must take precedence over everything else.

The third point is that we must not make the mistake of trying to categorise whites. Essentially all whites are the same and must be viewed with suspicion. This may apparently sound contradictory to what I have been saying but it is not in actual fact. A study of the history of South Africa shows that at almost all times whites have been involved in black struggles and in almost all instances led to the death or confusion of what they were involved in. This may not have been calculated sometimes but it arises out of genuine differences in approach and commitments. That blacks are deciding to go it alone is not an accident but a result of years of history behind black-white co-operation. Black-white co-operation in this country leads to limitations being imposed on the programme adopted. We must by all means encourage 'sympathetic whites' to stand firm in their fight but this must be away from us. In many ways this is dealt with adequately in an article that appears in the August SASO Newsletter, 'Black Souls in White Skins'. The fact that 'sympathetic whites' have in the past made themselves the traditional pace-setters in the black man's struggle has led to the black man's taking a back seat in a struggle essentially his own. Hence excluding whites tends to activate black people and in the ultimate analysis gives proper direction to whatever is being done. This is a fact that overseas observers visiting the country find hard to accept but it remains very true. Racial prejudice in this country has gone beyond all proportions and has subconsciously affected the minds of some of the most well-known liberals.

Where are we today?

SASO stands today at a very important stage of its life. The establishment of the organisation has had a very great impact in three major directions.

Firstly we have created a mood on the black campuses which has set the stage for a complete revision of thinking. Our 'blacks only' attitude has infused a sense of pride and self-reliance on almost all black campuses. Where originally one met with stiff opposition to all exclusive talk, it is now generally accepted that blacks must go it alone. This attitude is welcome to us but has to be guided very carefully and steadily least it falls prey to some of the dangers we have already mentioned.

It is hoped that we shall translate all the intellectual talk about 'black is beautiful' into some kind of meaningful practical language.

Secondly we have given impetus to meaningful thinking outside the campus. Suddenly black people are beginning to appreciate the value of their own efforts, unpolluted by half-hearted support from the white world. Though this kind of thinking is still limited to the black 'intelligentsia' at present, there are all the signs that it will spread to the rest of the community.

Thirdly we have dealt an almost fatal blow at all black-white movements. One does not know whether to take pride in this or not, but definitely it is obvious that we have wasted a lot of valuable time in the so-called non-racial organisations trying to cheat ourselves into believing we were making progress while in fact by the very nature of these bodies we liquidated ourselves into inactivity. The more radical whites have in fact rejoiced at the emergence of SASO and some of them have even come up with useful support in terms of valuable contacts etc., but radical whites are very rare creatures in this country.

Our strength has been difficult to assess because of the battle we were waging for members. With the latest affiliations by Fort Hare and Ngoye we now stand in a position to get down to practical stuff.

Whither are we going?

At all costs we must make sure we are marching to the same tune as the rest of the community. At no stage must we view ourselves as a group endowed with special characteristics. While we may be playing the tune, it is the rhythmic beating of the community's boots that spurs us to march on and at no stage should that rhythm be disturbed. As the group grows larger and more boots join the rhythmic march, let us not allow the beating of the boots to drown the pure tones of our tune for the tune is necessary and essential to the rhythm.

SASO: Alice Declaration: Boycott of Black Universities

(Issued by a SASO meeting at Alice, May 1972, in support of African students expelled for boycotting classes at several universities)

This Formation School, noting:

1 / the series of expulsions from various black universities/institutions;

2 / the oppressive atmosphere in the black institutions of higher learning as demonstrated by the expulsion of the Turfloop student body;

3 / that the 'wait and see' attitude, if adopted by other black institutions, will be a betrayal to the black man's struggle in this country;

4 / that the black community is anxiously and eagerly waiting to learn and hear of the stand taken by black students on other campuses who invariably are subjected to the same atrocities and injustices suffered by the Turfloop students; and believing;

(a) that this cannot be viewed as an isolated incident;

(b) that black students have long suffered under oppression;

(c) that this can be escalated into a major confrontation with the authorities,

therefore resolves

that all black students force the institutions/universities to close down by boycotting lectures;

that the date when a simultaneous boycott of all classes be effected be on 1 June when it is expected that all Turfloop students will be returning to university.

The League of the African Youth: Objectives

Preamble

We, the African youth, noting the decline of the constructive element in the education of an African child in many respects; believing that it is the duty of the African youth to focus his education on his community, to join hands with others in combating illiteracy and to exert himself in community development; and convinced that a purposeful education is essential to the African youth in promoting the interests and aspirations of his community; do hereby resolve to form a League of the African Youth.

Objects

(a) To spell out the most essential elements in an African education and to prepare and guide the youth to this goal.

(b) To create a spirit of fraternity among the African youth and to establish an extensive co-operation between the youth and the rest of the community.

(c) To combat illiteracy and undertake projects on community development.

The League of the African Youth: Principles

Being

- An organisation for the African youth defines an African as anybody who cannot trace his genealogical origin outside the continent of Africa and anybody who is committed and involved in the struggle and maintenance of the dignity of the African community;

Being

- Not a racialist organisation and prepared to accommodate anybody's contribution towards the liberation of the African nation from psychological oppression, it therefore rejects any form of ethnological dissection of the African nation.

Convinced

- That education, whether it be formal or informal, is the only sure medium of transmitting from one generation to the next the accumulated wisdom and knowledge of the society, and to prepare the young people for their future membership of the society and their active participation in its maintenance or development;
- That in particular education can and must be the principal instrument of the internal cohesion and stability required for any community, and at the same time a dynamic force for the development of a balanced and self-reliant community able to afford its members the standard of living essential to them.

Considers

- That education cannot fully perform its function unless it is relevant to and consistent with the values, attitudes and objectives of a community at a given time;
- That it must emphasise the spirit of self-reliance and co-operative endeavour; and it must also stress the concept of responsibility to give service which goes with any special ability; and in particular induce the attitude of human equality and thus counteract the temptation to intellectual arrogance; for this leads to the better-educated despising those whose abilities are non-academic or who have no special abilities but are just human beings;

- That a campaign to inform and educate public opinion is essential in order that everyone shall understand the primary purpose of education - being in particular, to prepare young people to live in and to serve the society, and to transmit the knowledge, skills, values and attitude of the society.

Believes

- That the development of a community and the social advancement of the individual are not opposing, but rather mutually interacting concepts and that the mobilising of the abilities and resources of all the people who are willing to work hard for their improvement can only lead to real and lasting results if it is carried out through educational methods which serve to inculcate a sense of commitment to the total community.

Affirms

- That all knowledge which is worthwhile is not necessarily acquired from books or people who have been through formal education;
- That therefore the young people should be discouraged from despising the knowledge and wisdom of other old people or regarding them as being ignorant and of no account.

Appeals

- To all who believe in social stability and advancement, either as individuals or organised groups, to take part each within his own sphere of activity or influence in a vast educational campaign for the progress of the community towards the acknowledgement, the respect and promotion of values essential to human existence.

And adopts

- As a whole the Constitution annexed to this Declaration.

Towards Black Fulfilment

M. GATSHA BUTHELEZI

(Excerpts from an address to the students of the University of Zululand on 30 August 1974)

It has been common until recently to say that the native must be kept in his place. That is why the United Party government under General Hertzog attempted to set up political structures which did not go far enough in affording blacks fulfilment. I refer here to the Native Representative Council and parliamentary representation of blacks by whites in the Senate and in the House of Assembly. It does not surprise us that these structures did not go far enough because in the words of General Smuts:

'There are certain things about which all South Africans are agreed, all parties and all sections except those quite mad. The first is that it is a fixed policy to maintain white supremacy in South Africa.'

Little wonder that after ten years, in 1946, African leaders decided to arrest the machinery of the Native Representative Council by passing a resolution which made it defunct. The present regime, as you know, had viewed the Native Representative Council as a forum for agitation and in which there was incitement of 'good natives', against the government, and they undertook to abolish it completely when they came into power. This they ultimately did.

The younger people in South Africa and particularly at the University of Fort Hare were also against these structures which were now described as 'dummy bodies'. Africans throughout the continent of Africa were at this time clamouring for fulfilment in their countries and for freedom or uhuru.

When Africans realised that whites had no intention of including them at their table, they founded the African National Congress in 1912. At the risk of incurring for myself the wrath of some of you, this to me was the beginning of the first phase of Black Consciousness in South Africa.

The first Pan-Africanist movement in South Africa was founded by Robert Mangaliso Sobukwe. This was the second phase of Black Consciousness as one of the things the founders objected to was the influence of white Marxists in the affairs of the African National Congress. The resentment was against the ideological colonisation of the black man.

Both these national movements, the African National Congress and the Pan-African Congress, were banned after the 1960 Sharpeville episode. You are all familiar with the incarceration of the leaders of these movements and the banning orders imposed on them.

The Nationalist government as a result of pressures at the United Nations and by black states at every international conference table, started talking of 'separate freedoms' and of separate self-determination. Clearly this was an old Roman Empire technique of 'divide et impera'. This brings us to the consideration of the question whether the black man can ever reach fulfilment through apartheid structures such as the KwaZulu Legislative Assembly. The Nationalist Party ploy is to set up, once again, the Zulu nation, the Xhosa nation, the Tswana nation, etc.

Whilst I also abhor apartheid or separate development, I would like to say that it is a fallacy and the height of arrogance to say that those of us who are serving our people within separate development perimeters with no other options open to us, are doing so out of a betrayal of the African cause. I say so because one of the symbols of the present phase of Black Consciousness was the emergence of the South African Students' Organisation, and the break-away of SASO from the National Union of South African Students. Before I go any further, shall we all stand up and have a prayerful meditation for the banned leaders of SASO such as Steve Biko, Nyameko Pityana and others and for the souls of Abram Tiro and Nicodimus Mthuli Shezi.

The emergence of the present phase of Black Consciousness coincided with a phase of Black Consciousness in the United States. It is not solely a product of American Black Consciousness, but it would be a lie to say that it had nothing to do with it. There is nothing to be ashamed of in this linkage between the movement in the States and the movement in South Africa, at the same time, as there have always been links between these two similar political situations.

The Nationalists have been in power for 26 years, yet we hear it is envisaged that only in 1976 our brothers in the Transkei will achieve fulfilment separately from the rest of the black people. This is not out of benevolence at all, but a product of pressure both from within the ranks of the Nationalist Party and from without. When we met as black leaders at Umtata in November 1973, it was to continue the ideal of one African nation in which most of us fully believe. When the federal idea was mooted, it was because we did not want anyone to separate us into fragments for his own ends. When we requested an interview with the Prime Minister, Mr Vorster, in March 1974 and discussed with him 'black problems', not ethnic ones, it was because we fully believe in Black Consciousness and in black unity without which we can never find real fulfilment. If there was sincerity on the part of the government in making all the so-called black areas compact countries not in terms of the 1936 Land and Trust Act but on the basis of a new map, then there might even be a hope that blacks might reach fulfilment even through the structures of a philosophy we all abhor.

I am at present not convinced of any sincerity, if for instance Richards Bay is going to remain white, and if KwaZulu is going to remain as 29 separate pieces. Then I should be forgiven if I see this policy as showing the makings of a political fraud. Through a federation we could have remained together as one country and as citizens of the whole of South Africa which is our country. That may be the reason why the Prime Minister has rejected my proposals on federation. In doing so, the Prime Minister also did me the favour of stating that he respected my honesty as I did not regard the federation I proposed as a solution to last forever. How could I? And in any case my proposals were motivated by our being together as we move through this dark abyss of an uncertain political future. It is nonsense to say that I have ever, in my federal formula, given up any part of South Africa. Americans in Texas are as much citizens of the United States as Americans in New York State. They have one passport and one economy.

As far as I am concerned, we cannot afford to quarrel amongst ourselves at this point in history. My own history is a guide here because when I was a university student, we disagreed with our Professor Matthews's stand in not resigning from the Native Representative Council. Our technique was to get into Congress affairs and effect changes from within. We never used denigration methods.

The future leaders of this land will come from amongst you. But it does seem to me that the first condition of real leadership is humility. No one who lacks it can ever hope to be a true leader. I do not think that humility is something in-born but the least any true leader can do is to aspire to attain it.

The danger I see as we move in this dark tunnel, is lack of identification with the masses. One must never despise them and one can only influence them as one of them. The problem and danger we can get into is to think that our university education makes us little saints whose sole work must be pontification for the hoi polloi. It is a wrong assumption to conclude that God never endowed anyone who has not been through university doors with any wisdom. Book-learning without wisdom cannot take us very far in our battle.

Intellectuals have a great role to play as leaders of the community, but there is a great danger we have to guard against. The danger is intellectual arrogance. A sociologist-theologian I know and for whom I have the greatest respect and admiration, warns in these words:

'Intellectuals also play an important part in almost all revolutions, particularly in the pre-revolutionary phase, through their critique of the socio-political system, their leadership and their contribution to setting up a new regime. Sociologically, it is they who are best placed to challenge a political regime, since they are not usually directly involved in political action and yet they are sensitive to innovation. This is also true of students today. It must be added, however, that the "scholarly" role of the intellectual often allows him to play a "clean" part, leaving others to "dirty" their hands.'

Yes, some of us know that we have dirtied our hands by participating in separate development politics. Our people or the majority of them live within the confines of what are termed 'black areas'. If we seek them we find them there struggling in poverty, struggling in ignorance and struggling with diseases of want. The choice is between 'clean hands' and 'dirtying' our hands as we have done, in the interests of our people.

This does not mean that one must not have respect for those who would rather have no part in it. People must be respected for their stands, however much one disagrees with what motivates them. On the other hand one more or less expects people, particularly intellectuals, not to dismiss one's bona fides merely in order to maintain a 'holier than thou' attitude, or merely to maintain intellectual snobbery, regardless of how such a stance affects the day-to-day lives of one's people.

As I travel abroad I am often intrigued by criticism from Marxist quarters directed at those of us who are active in the Black Consciousness campaign or in the struggle for the black man to reach fulfilment. I am certain that some of the members of SASO would be surprised that one finds oneself tarred with the same brush as SASO. I remember reading an article in which both Mr Nengwenkulu and myself were severely dealt with.

They further warn against the advancement of privileged strata while leaving the masses behind; and they warn against the possibility of submerging the African nation with its own languages, culture and traditions into an amorphous movement whose identity is based mainly on skin colour. These are views of critics of those of us who are in the Black Consciousness movement. One does not necessarily agree with every word they say, but one cannot ignore every word they say.

It is most unfortunate that we should quarrel amongst ourselves. It serves the interests only of those who wish us to remain an ineffectual, amorphous mass. That the interests of the powers-that-be are served by divisions and petty quarrels amongst ourselves, is proved by the involvement of Pretoria in the artificial manufacture of pseudo-opposition parties even within separate development politics. There is so much at stake and with unity we can go far. Heribert Adam, in his book Modernizing Racial Domination, puts this problem of divisions serving Pretoria's interests well, when he says:

'Less important political decisions and bureaucratic functions are delegated to various non-white local and regional self-governing bodies, whose members work under white supervision. Apart from the propaganda effect, these institutions prove useful to the central authority in at least three respects: first, upwardly mobile and politically ambitious individuals are absorbed into this administration; second, immediate discontent of non-whites is directed towards members of their own groups, since they represent the overall system; and third, the real authorities are freed from burdensome and tedious spade work and confine themselves to advisory functions without losing control'.

The apparent appearance that we represent the system is more illusory than real. We do not hate the system any less than you hate it. We are not part of the system, any more than you are products of the system, because of having been educated under Bantu Education and having had both Bantu junior and secondary education before enrolling at Bantu universities. At least most of you have done so. I could not boast that I am a better product merely because I have a University Junior Certificate, a Joint Matriculation Board Certificate and a degree from the University of South Africa. In what way are you responsible for having received a 'separate development' education, any more than I can escape black politics within the perimeters of separate development? The mud-slinging sessions between us and our youth can only serve the interests of those who wish to see us remain unliberated.

I respect and love the leadership of your organisation. But owing to the persecution campaign against SASO, it is obvious that some of your best talent is no longer available.

One is only too aware of the derogatory manner in which some lecturers at some of the black universities speak of KwaZulu, of me in particular, and of other black leaders. Students forget that we are spoken of in terms of derogation for daring to challenge the status quo and the whole apartheid bluff. And what comes out at Hammanskraal? Students from African homes do not end up in criticising us, which is good enough, but go on to swear at us as 'Bantustan Boys', and 'Cultural Clowns'. Is it necessary to molest some of the KwaZulu employees who come to this university by calling them 'Gatsha's Stooges'? In what way does it enhance Black Consciousness and our image as blacks to forgo our code of etiquette on the pretext that we are abiding by SASO's ideals? Black Consciousness can only exist within the context of our culture.

I do not for a moment think the measure of our youth's political maturity and self-awareness is going to be determined by the extent to which they can outshine each other in a competition as to who can fling the foulest expletives at us. The cause of this conduct is frustration or boredom. While there is a lot that is frustrating in our South African life if one is born black, let us not treat each other as objects on which to vent our own particular frustrations. It does not advance our black cause one iota.

I know that it is difficult if one is young and sensitive not to be upset about the situation in South Africa. I think however that there can be no doubt that we shall attain our liberation in the end. But it will be tragic if we were to reach that point in a state of unpreparedness. Those of us who are educated owe the illiterate masses of our people a big debt. It is not true that there is nothing one can contribute in the struggle for our liberation within the limits of separate development. If we change our attitudes we have more than enough opportunities to make such a contribution. I think the educated blacks need to cultivate a meaningful identification with the masses of our people.

There are various methods by which this can be done, The Afrikaners who wield power in South Africa have fresh memories of the battle for their own liberation. They, more than any other racial group, understand the clamour for freedom, as they have struggled and attained their freedom within this century. The Afrikaners may not like the language I speak here, but deep down in their hearts will have great sympathy for such a clarion call as I sound for black freedom or black fulfilment.

As the black man's struggle for freedom spreads more and more towards the south, we are virtually becoming the last post of white colonialism. With labour unrest so rife in our land, I think students can make a meaningful contribution in that battle if they humble themselves and identify with us. We are wielding some influence amongst millions of people and whether we are right or wrong in your opinions, we are wielding this power. As we move towards the dawn of our liberation we have an obligation to find each other, hold each other by the hand and move as one man step by step. We have labour bureau offices in all tribal offices. I wish to propose co-ordination of efforts whereby some of you can visit these offices, meet those who are about to go to work and explain their rights as workers and some of the difficulties they are likely to encounter. If either as tribal chiefs or leaders we are lost, as some of you think we are, this is the time to get close to us and possibly 'save us from ourselves'.

There are several other things we need to do and can do together as we move forwards. Sitting down and crying will get us nowhere. Tears of self-pity could drown us! Drinking and swearing about it does not help either. I have come to invite you to play the role God has given you, the opportunity to play in the liberation of your people. I have always maintained that teaching even one or two people to read and write, without any remuneration, is a worthwhile contribution towards freedom.

I have come to appeal to you now that frontiers of freedom and liberation are coming so close to us. This is a time to be collected and calm so that whatever we do should not precipitate disaster that will make us miss the sun now about to rise on the eastern horizon. In this great darkness we find in the tunnel, let us remember that this is the final darkness before dawn when a mistake can be so fatal. We need to join hands and feel the palpitations made by each other's hearts as we move in one direction as one man.

Children of Mother Africa, today I appeal to you, as someone whose area will soon border on the two independent black countries of Swaziland and Moçambique, to realise that we are passing from the era of theoretical politics to practical politics. Let us at this great moment of truth have more light rather than too much heat.

Black Renaissance Convention: Declaration and Resolutions, 1974

DECLARATION

Section A

We, the black people of South Africa, meeting at the Black Renaissance Convention in December 1974, declare that:

(i) We condemn and so reject separate development policy and all its institutions.

(ii) We reject all forms of racism and discrimination.

Section B

We dedicate ourselves towards striving for:

(i) A totally united and democratic South Africa, free from all forms of oppression and exploitation.

(ii) A society in which all people participate fully in the government of the country through the medium of one man one vote.

(iii) A society in which there is an equitable distribution of wealth.

(iv) An anti-racist society.

Section C

We call upon our people and all their organisations to organise their efforts towards securing the release of all political prisoners, detainees and banned people.

RESOLUTIONS

This Convention:

1 / Declares that legalised racism in South Africa is a threat to world peace and therefore calls upon all the countries of the world to withdraw all cultural, educational, economic, manpower and military support to the existing racist institutions.

2 / Expresses its shock and dismay at the expropriation of the Federal Theological Seminary in Alice and calls upon the black community to fight for the continued survival of this institution.

3 / Acknowledges that it is not the first to convene a meeting of black people and states firmly that it wishes to continue with the efforts that have taken place in the past.

This Convention noting that:

(i) the great majority of black people are workers;

(ii) besides being discriminated against, the workers also suffer the most blatant forms of exploitation;

(iii) the wage that workers receive is far below the bread-line and they are therefore frustrated in the attempt to use their bargaining power.

Therefore resolves that:

(a) the government immediately recognise African trade unions;

(b) there is need for workers to organise themselves into trade unions free from government interference.

One of the most dramatic highlights of the Convention was the vehement condemnation of the policy of separate development, its exponents and institutions. By an overwhelming vote, the delegates prevented a prominent homeland leader from addressing the Conference. This was nothing personal, but merely a symbolic gesture to show how totally they abhorred apartheid.

Black Renaissance Convention revealed some non-antagonistic contradictions, which is a healthy sign of a living community. The Black Renaissance Convention achieved the following results:

1 / The Black Renaissance Convention was a nationwide conference which consisted of many disparate ideologies and organisations and managed to get a consensus from the 300-odd delegates. Not a mean feat.

2 / The highlight of the Convention was the passing of the Declaration and Resolutions.

3 / Although black organisations may differ about strategy and method, the Convention demonstrated beyond doubt that black people are unanimous with regard to ultimate objectives. Blacks demand their freedom now! They want their land; they want political and economic powers; and they want to be masters of their own destiny. Admittedly, there will always be a debate about the type of the hoped-for new society. Some will settle for reformism whilst others will stop at nothing short of a complete and radical change of the system.

4 / Finally, the Convention provided a long-needed public platform whereon black people could ventilate their grievances in an atmosphere of freedom. Even disagreements which do not lead to overnight solidarity are useful. They clarify positions and focus attention on fundamental issues....

Dedicated to all our black heroes, living and the dead.

Why the Students Acted

TEMBA NOLUTSHUNGU

(Reprinted from Race Relations News, December 1976)

To say that the present crisis in the African townships has been generated by a desire to break away from imposed educational institutions - namely Bantu Education, Coloured Education and Indian Education - is to catch at the shadow of the problem and lose the substance.

This situation had to come about sooner or later. The students were the catalyst and they have perpetuated the mood that characterises this period of unrest. The students share the same fundamental political aspirations as their parents. The only difference between the youth and their parents is that the parents are basically political negotiators while the students are political activists. That is why the parents have not demonstrated their solidarity with the students even though they share the same grievances.

The parental generation still adheres to the doctrine of passive resistance. They go to church on Sunday and pray for change. They read the newspapers, complain about the spiralling cost of foodstuffs, cry over ridiculous wages, and protest verbally at pass law arrests and general police harassment. They have their own description of what a parent is and the students have their own description of themselves. To the parents a student is somebody who goes to school, does his homework, endorses Bantu Education and bothers about nothing but his career.

The students, however, see themselves as people to whom education is a means to an end, the end being the ultimate realisation of the political aspirations of their people. The students regard going to school as a means of preparing themselves to serve their people. It means being vested with responsibilities towards their people. They look at the past graduates of Bantu Education and find many of them snugly settled in enviable positions. They don't want that to happen to them. They regard it as immoral.

The students of today want future generations to say that they did their best, that they sacrificed everything for the betterment of their people. This is how they want to be remembered.

Their parents have always expressed resentment at the shebeens and alcoholism generally but they have never done anything about it. The students mobilised and issued an ultimatum to the shebeen runners. Now the possibility of a clinically sober community exists through the initiative of the youth, who in most cases had the blessing of their parents.

The students reject allegations that they are skollies. They believe they are in the process of formulating a new morality. The youths have been subjected to parents who have always assumed that they know best. Yet the parents who are supposed to know more about the situation and do not take any meaningful action to change the status quo are becoming alienated from the youth.

Students nowadays are also generally much better informed than their parents. They read the New Statesman, Newsweek, The Observer and The Guardian and they are analysts. This has been demonstrated by their crusade to bring the various groups in South Africa together.

To understand the African youth is to appreciate that they are people imbued with the idea of creating history. For the first time they have brought together the 'coloured', 'Indian' and 'African' groups into one social entity.

We have seen how they physically demonstrated the need to break through the legal and geographic barriers that alienate the different racial groups from each other.

ECONOMIC DEVELOPMENT

Traditional Attitudes towards Agriculture and a Practical Agricultural Policy

LENNOX L. SEBE

(Excerpts from an address to a Colloquium held at the University of the North, 30 October 1973)

Many centuries ago the black people of Southern Africa migrated down the continent from Central Africa. How long it took them to do so is not known exactly. However, according to their old customs and their mode of life, it would appear that they were constantly on the move. No attempt was made to erect permanent homes or other structures. Their dwellings were constructed of saplings and grass and were of a purely temporary nature. From an agricultural point of view they were pastoralists in continual search of new or better grazing areas for their livestock. Their sojourn in an area was determined by the availability of grazing or the arrival of a more powerful and hostile tribe. The traditional role of the man was thus to tend his cattle, hunt and fight.

A shifting agronomy was also practised, in that small areas of land were burned and cultivated. No attempt was made to improve the fertility of the soil. When, because of depletion, the land could no longer yield sufficiently it was simply abandoned and a new area cultivated. Agronomy was the province of the woman and was limited to small-scale cultivation using primitive methods.(1) So life continued over the centuries while the tribes moved slowly down Africa.

This way of life came to an end when they met the Europeans trekking northwards up Africa. As a result of this contact a new pattern of life began to emerge. The tribes then adopted a more settled way of life which led to greater social stability. Nevertheless, many of the old customs and traditions which had been built up over the centuries were retained, in many cases to this day. Some of these customs are, however, incompatible with modern-day requirements. In the case of agriculture they are sometimes deterimental to progress and will need to change. Some examples to illustrate this are the following:

(a) The desire to acquire as many cattle as possible - regardless of the limited carrying capacity of the land. The reason for this is that cattle not only provide meat and milk but also the wealth of a man is reckoned in cattle, as it is with cattle that he must acquire wives for himself and for his sons.

(b) The importance attached to the colour of cattle and shape of their horns. This invariably affects attempts to introduce improved breeding stock based on quality.

(c) Ploughing and sowing of crops would not be done whenever the individual chose but was indicated by various signs, such as the advent of certain migratory birds or position of certain stars in the heavens. In many cases nobody was allowed to plant or reap before the King.(2)

These practices, likewise, affect the principles of good husbandry as perceived by the agricultural scientist. With this in mind, we may now ask ourselves such questions as: how efficiently is agricultural policy operating in the homelands today? Do the people know the policy? Is their attitude towards it positive? Are the departments of agriculture in the various homelands satisfied with the progress they are making with regard to agricultural development? Is the rate of progress being made at least sufficient to ensure that the gap between population increase and food production will close and not widen?(3) A quick glimpse at production figures for the homelands is enough to remove any doubt whatever that sufficient progress is <u>not</u> being made.(4) What are the reasons for this unsatisfactory situation, and what can be done to improve it?

In this paper I will attempt to illustrate what I refer to as the 'clash of interests' between the traditional customs of rural African communities and certain elements of government policy as far as agriculture is concerned. I will not attempt to solve any of these problems. I will, however, mention an idea which has been brought to my notice for an approach which I feel has merit, and may accelerate agricultural development and thereby increase the efficiency of the present policy.

Agricultural extension, as you may know, refers to the process of conveying new knowledge (ideas, recommendations, skills) from the source of discovery to farmers and farming communities in such a way that it is accepted and applied by them as a permanent change to their customary behaviour. To be efficient, this process should be accomplished as quickly as possible. In this way the professional agriculturist hopes to increase food production per area of land cheaply and safely, and so, among other things, contribute towards the closing of the gap which has arisen between population growth and food production in the world. This is one of the agricultural extensionist's main objectives. To do so he must not only have a thorough knowledge of agriculture, but also of human behaviour. He must know how to communicate with people and how to motivate and persuade them to accept and eventually adopt his recommendations. He must, in other words, be a good salesman, because he must sell ideas and recommendations.

Extension work as we understand it, is actually an American idea.(5) It started during the 19th century. In 1914 a national extension service was established in the U.S.A. It was largely the result of the working together of two forces: agriculture (and the need for new products) and education (and the idea that education should be available to any person in any field). Agricultural societies and farmers' institutions became established as channels of communication between agriculturists and farmers. Lectures, demonstrations and finally publications, became the order of the day. What was the result of this effort? Records show that crop production increased by 65 per cent from 1921 to 1961.(6) Output per breeding animal was 88 per cent greater. One farm worker produced food for himself and twenty-five other people. Exports to other countries increased. In 1960, out of a total of 332 million acres under cultivation, 57 million (17 per cent) were used to produce for other countries (i.e. 1 in every 6 acres). Farming has become big business in America today.

For the sake of interest and comparison, some characteristics of this development may be mentioned.

Situation A: The state of American agriculture some 200 years ago:

At first most of the population was rural. Most farmers lacked capital. Farms were relatively small. A large percentage of the population owned land. Markets were either far away or non-existent. There were no proper farmer organisations including agricultural and extension departments (therefore no contact between farmer and researcher). Illiteracy was high. Farming from a social point of view was considered unimportant. The attitude of people, especially young people, towards farming as a career was generally not positive. Most youngsters, attracted by the bright lights, yearned for a life in the developing towns and cities. Farming was not done very scientifically. Production was relatively low. Not much (if any) attention was paid to agricultural research. People had to learn by trial-and-error. 'Farm remedies' were the order of the day.

Situation B: The state of agriculture in the U.S.A. today:

Most people live in cities. Credit is readily available. The number of farms has decreased but their size has increased. Markets, even for export, are readily available. The farmers are well organised (furthermore, farmer and professional sectors work as a team). They have government departments to assist them. Since farming is a business it is managed by well-educated and efficient men. Attitude towards the importance of farming is positive. Many young people seek careers in this direction. The need for only the best students in this field is increasing each day.

Now, if we are prepared to accept the fact that America is advanced, from an agricultural point of view, then we may regard the situation as it was 200 years ago and as it is today, as the opposite poles of a continuum. The homelands may be placed somewhere along this continuum. In most homelands today we find that most families have land, but not enough money to develop it. Production is mainly at the subsistence level. Local markets are lacking. There is very little co-operation between farmers to the benefit of all. Suspicion and jealousy are rife. Illiteracy is high, particularly among the older generations. The younger generation tends to consider farming 'dirty' work. Few matric and junior certificate students are really interested in agriculture as a career. Most of those who go to the agricultural colleges are those who were not accepted at the teachers' training colleges.(7)

From this it would appear that the general situation in the homelands today is, in certain respects, similar to that which prevailed in America long ago. It indicates the direction and nature of change which is required before the state of agriculture can be placed on a sound economic basis in the homelands. It is interesting to note that knowledge of improved methods of farming is only one of the factors involved. It would seem as though a change of attitude among African people towards the importance of farming in the world today should become a major objective. The fact remains that these changes must occur in the homelands before we can expect to reach that stage of agricultural progress which will provide a surplus production for export. Export, of course, means money flowing into the homelands, and thus higher wages for all (both farmer and professional agriculturist). The rate at which Situation A will change to Situation B in the homelands with regard to agriculture is mainly dependent on the people themselves, and on their willingness to change and co-operate among themselves and with their agriculturists.

THE ATTITUDE OF BLACK PEOPLE TO AGRICULTURE

Cultures change with the passing of time. The rate at which they change depends upon various factors. One is the degree to which they are influenced by, and dependent on, a more technologically developed culture. However, the direction of change depends on the needs of recipient culture. Unfortunately the most pressing needs of the recipients are, as far as the donor culture is concerned, not always so perceived by the recipients themselves. Although culture is desirable and essential for man's orderly living, it may sometimes incorporate customs and taboos which are decidedly incompatible with the requirements for modern economic development. The customary roles of the sexes in agriculture is an example of this. The notion that digging in the land is woman's work is decidedly detrimental to agricultural development. The black man's traditional attitude towards agriculture, and envy of those who want to make good, is often an important barrier to development, as the following examples clearly indicate:

'Men who work away from the location and who receive "big" salaries will not allow their wives to make a garden because it is a sign of poverty and it might be said that their husbands do not support them.'(8)

'Young men between eighteen and thirty years of age

will not make gardens because they fear being ridiculed by girls.'(9)

At the trial of a progressive farmer, one Joseph M., the chief of the area warned him not to sell his vegetables in any way other than via the chief's own market and, furthermore, to dissuade people from visiting his property. 'He had', he said, 'noticed that European officials visiting the area were always making a fuss of Joseph's achievements and he wondered if Joseph was not perhaps desirous of establishing himself as a chief.'(10)

The men of a certain region do not like working in the cane fields, because such work is considered 'dirty'. They say that young women prefer men who do clean work. Because of this attitude, the cane farmers of that region are forced to import labour from another homeland.(11)

From these few examples it is clear that the farmer is a person with a relatively low status in the eyes of the African people. If agriculture in the homelands is ever to take its rightful place, then this attitude will have to change. The question is: what must be done to change it? The way I see it, such change will have to be initiated and motivated by the leaders in the homelands. I do not think it will occur quickly enough to make any meaningful difference to the present situation if left to the initiative of the masses. What I am quite confident of is the fact that such change will occur if the people are made properly aware of the need and importance of such change!

I do not think that sufficient has been done in the past to make people aware of the importance of agriculture in the world today, or even in the development of the homelands. Much effort and vast sums of money are being spent on the dissemination of knowledge to would-be farmers, but of what use is this to the majority of land-occupiers, who do not really feel they need it? According to a study conducted in a certain homeland, less than 19 per cent of all the farmers in a particular area could be classed as 'above average' or 'good'. No less than 44 per cent of one of the samples used in the study referred to were classified as 'bad'. Most of those classified as bad, do not co-operate with, or even attempt to contact, their extension worker.(12) For how much longer can this state of affairs be allowed to persist?

A PRACTICAL POLICY

The most practical policy will be the one which is compatible with the needs and interests of the people and which permits meaningful economic development. Although it will not be easy to find or discover the ideal policy to satisfy these requirements, I do nevertheless feel that better progress may be made by somehow trying to graft new ideas on to old customs rather than by trying to get people to change their old habits, for example, trying to persuade people to plough before winter when, according to custom, it had to be done at a particular time of the year.(13)

I have already mentioned the fact, and given an example to illustrate it, that jealousy is still quite rife among communities in the homelands. Because of this I feel that, firstly, any policy should be deliberately aimed at the group as a whole rather than at the individual within the group. This statement must not, however, be interpreted to mean that individual initiative must be completely neglected. It must be interpreted to mean that the emphasis must be placed on community rather than individual efforts. Secondly, because most farmers do not have sufficient money to develop their properties, credit will have to be made available to them. It is here that I see an excellent opportunity for not only satisfying the needs of the farmer, but also for stimulating a rapid increase in production. This could be done, for instance, if credit on a contract basis were to be made available to a group (community) of farmers on certain conditions such as that they follow the recommendations of the extension worker with regard to the production of their crops.

In summary, I would like to repeat that:

1 / The traditional attitude of the black man towards agriculture is not positive enough for the rate of development which we would like to achieve. This attitude must be changed, and the traditional leaders will have to take the initiative. This is an educational problem.

2 / A practical agricultural policy is one which not only recognises traditional customs but also makes progress possible. In the homeland situation today money is an important limiting factor to agricultural development. The provision of credit to communities of farmers on a disciplinary basis will greatly improve the practicability of the present policy.

KwaZulu Development

M. GATSHA BUTHELEZI

(Excerpts from an address to Johannesburg Chamber of Commerce, 16 June 1972, published in S. Biko, ed, Black Viewpoint, Durban: Sprocas Black Community Programmes 1972)

As a layman I cannot make pretensions that I can offer a diagnosis or even hazard a guess at any cures for our economic ills in KwaZulu.

However, being a representative of the patient, I can at least describe the pains, particularly the very sharp ones around the tummy which are so excruciatingly painful! Even the doctor needs this to arrive at an accurate diagnosis.

As early as 1880 The Natal Witness disputed the suggestion that Africans had any right to consider Natal as their country: 'They are here as immigrants on sufferance, and not as citizens'. This was after the Zulu War, when even Zulu territory north of the Thukela was fragmented deliberately in order 'to break the Zulu power once and for all', in the words of Sir Bartle Frere, and Zulu territory was opened up by the conquerors for white occupation. This was not peculiar to Natal, but happened throughout this southernmost point of Africa.

My people were at first self-sufficient because there was enough to eat and no problems of population explosion. This too was soon brought to an end by the new conquerors who called upon chiefs to supply young men to work on what was then known as Isibhalo. They were in other words forced to sign contracts to come to places like Johannesburg and Kimberley and other industrial areas to build the white industrial empires that we see in full bloom in all the metropolitan areas of South Africa. Taxation was one of the methods used to force Africans to move into urban areas to work.

The tragedy deepened when even in the urban areas my people found themselves regarded as temporary sojourners who were there on sufferance, only to minister to the reasonable wants of whites. According to the 1852-3 Commission Report it was recommended that 'All kaffirs should be ordered to go decently clothed. This measure would at once tend to increase the number of labourers because, as they would be obliged to work to procure the means of buying clothing, it would also add to the general revenue of the Colony through customs duties'.

Coming to the question of the so-called homelands, as early as 1849 Earl Grey agreed that it would be 'difficult or impossible' to assign to Africans reserves of such a size that they could continue to be economically self-sufficient. He added that it was desirable that Africans should 'be placed in circumstances in which they should find regular industry necessary for their subsistence'.(1)

Not all Africans could be accommodated on the reserves, and the remainder continued to occupy crown lands and colonist owned farms. Africans ultimately spilled over into the white farms as squatters. The reserves were made up of the worst farming lands in the Colony. According to G.R. Peppercorne, most of the land in the Impofana reserve is 'as worthless as the sands of Arabia'.(2) Only thirty per cent of KwaZulu is arable land.

According to Brookes and Hurwitz there was no increase in land provision for Africans between 1864 and 1913.(3) The promises made by the Hertzog government under the Native Trust and Land Act of 1936 for an additional quota of land to my people and other ethnic groups was a recognition of this fact. Little wonder that whereas other people improve with the times, my people have sunk lower and lower into poverty over the years because they are caught between two devils.

When the Zulu Territorial Authority was inaugurated in 1970 I made it clear that without consolidation of land, the present government's policy would not make any sense. There has been very little done or said about this aspect of government policy until last year when the Prime Minister promised to consolidate the Zulu homeland only to the extent of the 1936 land quota. I pointed out to him then that consolidating in terms of that quota could hardly be adequate in terms of setting us up as a separate independent State in terms of his government's policy.

What happened last week has been merely confirmation of what the Prime Minister said last year and also a few weeks ago in parliament. I refer here to the so-called draft map for the consolidation of KwaZulu. This is a question which is crucial to the whole exercise of setting up KwaZulu as a country and on it hangs the issue of whether we can ever be economically viable or not. I wish also to submit that the whole question of our economic potential depends on it.

Earlier this year I opened a conference at the University of Natal's Institute for Social Research on 'Towards Comprehensive Development in Zululand'. This conference was interesting in so far as we did not try to find cures for KwaZulu's economic ills, but managed to assess the complexity of KwaZulu's economic ills. We found that there are two issues closely interlinked, the problems relevant to the development of the Zulu homeland territories, on the one hand, and those relevant to the development of the Zulu people on the other. Although the two issues are closely interlinked, the problems facing the development of the Zulu people, the amaZulu, relate not only to the Zulu homeland areas, but more directly to the entire economic, social and political structure of South Africa. The development of the amaZulu (or that of other blacks for that matter) is much more closely interlinked with change and progress in the common economy and common area of South Africa, than is the development of KwaZulu.(4)

To me the most important area which concerns all of us is that of the development of my people. At present we have hardly any employment opportunities for the KwaZulu citizens; no wonder we have only about a third of citizens in KwaZulu at any time. More than sixty per cent of our able-bodied males are away most of the time.

We have at present no industrial growth points except Sithebe, which has few Zulus at present, who are paid very low wages. The specious argument used by the Bantu Investment Corporation is that, although Sithebe has low wage levels and ample supply of labour on the credit side, the relatively low level of training is ranking high on the debit side and it is, therefore, not strange to find that an unskilled worker is being paid a weekly wage of R5 to R7. The Bantu Investment Corporation further state that they would prefer wage levels comparable with those in the metropolitan areas but realise that it is far better at this stage of development in KwaZulu to have say 100 Zulus employed at R7 a week than to be able to create say only 10 employment opportunities at R12 per week. It must also be remembered that the cost of living in metropolitan areas is very much higher than in the vicinity of Sithebe.(5)

The argument on the cost of living being lower in rural areas is a partial truth, because people can only live in accordance with their means of livelihood. And in any case this is also on account of poverty and, since we have no cash crops except sugar cane in some parts of KwaZulu, we have a cash economy and it is a remittance economy, as families depend entirely on cash from their breadwinners, who must earn wages elsewhere. The measuring rod as far as wages are concerned is the poverty datum line. Food is cheaper in town than in the rural areas where people are charged extra for transport costs.

The greatest shock so far in this whole question of whether KwaZulu can ever be economically viable now or in the dim misty future has been the decision by the all-powerful South African government in deciding that Richards Bay should be developed as a white port, and in doing so depriving KwaZulu of the only opportunity of having an outlet to the sea. No one disputes the fact that Richards Bay is providing jobs for Zulus, and that this will increasingly be the case as the Richards Bay complex develops. Job opportunities are welcome, as is the concern of governments throughout the world. But the question that arises after that is whether we can really be independent as easily as it is so often glibly said these days, if at most KwaZulu's development means that it is merely going to continue to be a vast labour farm for white South Africa, as all black homelands are at present?

What is not so encouraging is that even in the metropolitan areas of South Africa very few of our people are paid above the poverty datum line. Many surveys have been carried out including one by an employee of the Johannesburg Municipal Non-European Affairs Department. I feel certain you are all familiar with these. On the average it is now well known that the ratio of black to white wages is 1:14. Other industries give what are called fringe benefits and many of them boast that they look after their employees and provide them with a balanced diet. What Dr Francis Wilson had to say on this point is quite illuminating concerning the recent rise in the wages in the gold industry.(6) It is also true to say that any wise person who uses any beast of burden would look after it, feed it well and shelter it so that it can be in good condition to bear its burdens.

One must also thank and encourage all the other industries that are trying to narrow the wage-gap. But we blacks wonder what underlies white thinking in this respect because when one looks around there are no subsidised shops that sell necessaries of life at sub-economic rates. At the same time the majority of white South Africans have for years rejected the idea of accepting black urban workers as anything but temporary sojourners. These people are supposed to send money to their families in the homelands and to help us develop in the homelands. The question is, in view of the above, how does one do it? So far there seems to be no serious consideration of consolidating these homelands, as a result KwaZulu cannot at present take even displaced Africans from white farms as it is congested. We are developing a new class of rural Africans who cannot even have token arable allotments, and cannot keep any stock, who are settled in what are called closer settlements. Owing to the stringent application of influx control regulations these people cannot freely go to look for jobs in urban areas.

An additional burden is caused by lack of a free and compulsory education for blacks, which is available for the white group. So that some of the meagre earnings that are sent for necessities have also to be used to pay for the children's education, in fees, books, in some cases for the privately paid teachers and also to put up school buildings. At this juncture I wish to congratulate those white people who are assisting in providing funds towards the Rand Bursary Fund ASSECA and other similar projects. These are palliatives that are very necessary and which we highly appreciate.

The homelands are all being given 'self-government'. In other words we are supposed to provide facilities for our people from our taxation and from allocations from the Consolidated Revenue Fund made to us by the republican government. At present it is not yet apparent that these homeland governments can provide separate but equal facilities on the basis of this. In fact the KwaZulu budget of 32 million rand for the current financial year is, despite inflation, hardly a drop in the ocean, in terms of providing facilities for four and a quarter million Zulus. Even for our civil service it will be difficult to get the best men in view of this differentiation in salaries on the basis of race.

There is an apparent reluctance on the part of white South Africa to consolidate the homelands realistically, to make them independent countries in a meaningful way. There is an equal reluctance to accept our people who are in the urban areas as permanent residents in these areas. It might also be pointed out that all of us including myself, may be indulging in self-hypnosis by even trying to believe we can successfully create several ethnically oriented economies in South Africa instead of one.

Several questions at once arise such as, does white South Africa hope to have her cake and eat it? At some point we have got to decide one way or the other. Or does white South Africa hope we can all live in a make-believe world ad infinitum through sheer force of arms? This seems to be the time for decision whether we are going to be set up as viable homelands or not. This is the dilemma of white South Africa, in which South Africa alone has placed herself. It is black South Africa's dilemma too, with the difference that since black South Africa does not wield the power of the bullet and the ballot, it is a dilemma in which black South Africa has been placed by white South Africa. So that in a sense we are not equally culpable as far as the apportioning of blame in this dilemma I am talking about is concerned. But we all have equal reason to 'Cry the Beloved Country', since our destinies are so inextricably intertwined.

How long are urban Africans going to remain temporary sojourners in the metropolitan areas of South Africa? If we blacks are as human as whites, can anyone tell me what are these virile able-bodied men in hostels and compounds supposed to do in order to enjoy feminine company? Of the married temporary sojourners from the homelands who are forbidden to bring their wives with them into metropolitan areas, the question can be asked: can our male white compatriots countenance the idea of living in separation 'a mensa et thoro' from their wives, and only make love to their wives during the Easter week-end and during a few days at Christmas time?

Many of you will, I am sure, want to ask me, why then be involved in the homelands policy? I believe that it is a moral duty to be involved in alleviating human suffering, even if that is the most one can do. For this reason I believe that, despite the many snags I have pointed out, there is still some scope to help my people to develop even within the limitations of the policy. That is why I have great admiration for what American firms like Polaroid, I.B.M., and Pepsi Cola, and banks like Barclays Bank and Standard Bank are doing in giving equal pay for equal work regardless of race. These firms should by now have put our own South African firms to shame, if at all we still have a conscience such as I believe South Africans have. Do South Africans feel happy that foreign firms should take this lead, and that South African firms should drag their feet instead of following in their footsteps?

I believe that, apart from the development of people themselves, there is still a little scope for developing these homelands, whether one believes in separate development or not. The homelands to me are a challenge, whether one regards the Homelands policy as a political fact or a fantasy.

I believe that their development even on the basis of establishing micro-economic activities is something in which all of you can assist us. Community development schemes are a necessity in areas such as KwaZulu where people are as a result of poverty still victims of diseases of want such as malnutrition, kwashiorkor and tuberculosis.

I believe that where there is economic infrastructure, industry and commerce in South Africa should not hesitate to help us to establish industries, not necessarily as cures for our economic ills but even as palliatives. To me while South Africa battles in trying to make up her mind about the future, we should not forget that human lives are at stake here. What is more our whole future, yours and ours, and that of our children depends on this. I believe the manner in which the future will unfold, that is, whether it will be peacefully or violently, depends to a large measure on these factors. We cannot hope that the nerves of our black population will stand this insecurity indefinitely both in the urban and rural areas.

We do not ask to be given doles or what we do not deserve. We would like to be self-reliant and, having contributed so much towards the production of South Africa's wealth, we are at least entitled to a little of it, to set up on our own feet, be it in the urban or rural areas.

The Ovambo strike has given us a foretaste of what may one day overtake us, and I do not believe that we need to wait for the trauma of a confrontation of that kind to ensure our peaceful co-existence on this southernmost point of Africa.

Economic Development of the Tswana Homelands

S.J.J. LESOLANG

DEVELOPMENT CORPORATIONS

Over the last decade the government of the Republic of South Africa passed acts of Parliament establishing development corporations of homelands. The main aims of these corporations are more or less the same; they are to give financial assistance and technical advice and to stimulate the development of homelands in various fields of economic activity. They are also given certain powers to borrow white capital, to call for tenders and to employ agents to develop specific projects. Because there is, comparatively, a small capital used in the homelands from the Bantus themselves, the development corporations may establish businesses for themselves where a need arises in the homelands and own them, until such time as the Bantus can buy over these businesses.

The South African Bantu Trust is the present sole shareholder in these corporations. Their respective boards of directors are all white, appointed for their ability and experience in business or administration or their knowledge of the requirements of the Bantu population. In the case of the Promotion of Economic Developments of Homelands Act, the Minister may, in addition to the white board of directors, establish advisory boards with appointed Bantu members selected in consultation with the Bantu government or the Bantu authority with jurisdiction in the area concerned. It is, therefore, quite clear that the capital for these corporations comes from the same source, the South African Bantu Trust. It has to be noted that the entire planning of the implementation and the administration of homeland developments are all in the hands of whites. Blacks are not given the opportunity to make some contributions, not even in an advisory capacity although our authorities repeatedly make open statements to the effect that the Bantus are allowed to carry out the development themselves with the assistance of whites where such assistance is required; and that government white officials in the homelands must be regarded as instruments and as tools placed there to render assistance to the Bantu.

Mr M.C. Botha, then the Deputy Minister of Bantu Administration and Development, in opening the 1963 Session of the Tswana Territorial Authority said, inter alia, 'The impression that the Trust is an enemy or competitor or an undertaking not associated with you (Bantus) has perhaps been created by the fact that it has in the past sometimes acted independently. Actually the Bantu Authorities themselves should undertake all services which the Trust provides'. This statement supports our just claim to share in the handling of the machinery of the Bantu Trust and activities flowing therefrom.

Let us look into the constitution and functions of these Development Corporations. Firstly, the Bantu Investment Corporation Act of 1959 provides for the establishment of a corporate body. As a result, the Bantu Investment Corporation of South Africa was formed the same year with an initial capital of R1 000 000 for all the republic's Bantu national units. The increased capital has this year reached R18 000 000. I wonder how many of our Tswanas seize the opportunity of applying for loans from this capital to boost their businesses.

The Bantu Homeland Development Act of 1965 provides for the establishment of a development corporation in respect of the homeland of each national unit. So far, only the Xhosa Development Corporation has been established under this Act. These corporations, whilst they are non-profitmaking bodies, have power to call for tenders, to employ agents to develop specific projects, for example a mine. The Xhosa Development Corporation was established and commenced its business operations in 1966 with an initial capital of R1 000 000. The capital has since increased to R7 000 000. The corporation took over all business activity hitherto undertaken by the Bantu Investment Corporation during the first two years of its operation. The take-over by the Xhosa Corporation seems to render the B.I.C. redundant in the Xhosa homeland. Moving the second reading of the Bantu Homelands Corporation Bill in 1965 Parliamentary session, Mr de Wet Nel, then Minister of Bantu Administration and Development, said, 'Whites would not be able to invest money in the homelands or undertake development there but the corporation would have the power to employ white organisations as agents for specific projects such as mining, not on profit-making bases, but for a fixed scale of remuneration'. This white employment should be applied where Tswanas are themselves unable to carry out a project because of lack of technical knowhow.

The Promotion of Economic Development of Homelands Act was passed in 1968 to enable the government to set up agencies specialising in industrial, commercial, financial and mining undertakings. The Bantu Investment Corporation of South Africa in its 1968 Annual Reports states, inter alia, 'It is still the policy of the government that the economic development in the Bantu homelands should in the first instance take place: (a) through Bantu entrepreneurs, or (b) through the development corporations established for this very purpose'.

From this statement one finds that Bantu entrepreneurs, as in all other cases of development, should be given a priority or they themselves are expected to take the initiative in all matters affecting them socially and otherwise. This should be the case even where white capital on agency basis is involved. Dr W. W.M. Eiselen, the Commissioner General of Lebowa, would say, 'The Bantus have a natural right to such expectations'.

The Bantu Mining Development Corporation was the first to be set up in terms of the legislation and it started off with an initial capital of R500 000. This corporation or agent acting on its own will investigate mining potential of the Bantu homelands reserves and undertake specific projects. The white directors of this corporation include mining experts, representatives of the Bantu Investment Corporation, the Department of Mines and the Department of Bantu Administration and Development. The Tswanas for whom this development is meant and the ones who are expected to take over eventually do not feature anywhere except as junior clerks and unskilled labourers.

The Minister of Bantu Administration and Development is reported to have said in Parliament on 18 June 1969 that because the government's policy was to create employment the mining corporation would do everything in its power to develop any possible deposit even if it merely covered costs and showed no profit. It would appear that the question of profits in the homelands is not as important as creating employment for our people. But then we must remember that costs can be inflated and this could be the case here. Then the question arises as to who benefits. Is it the Tswana from his low wages of R10,00 per month, the chiefs who receive rents and royalties, or the white investors, directors, managers and the white trade unions? The answer is that the last-mentioned four groups benefit to such an extent that they can be quite happy even if the mines did not make profits. For instance, we understand that the average pay of a white miner in the homeland is R500 per month. This means that if we have 500 mine workers (to be conservative) in our Tswana homelands each paid at the rate of R500 per month, the wage bill would come to R250 000 per month and R3 000 000 per annum for these miners (excluding directors, managers and other members of the administrative staff). This amount together with tax accruing thereon would be drawn from the Tswana homelands yearly to white areas.

INCOME EARNED FROM THE MINING INDUSTRY

The earnings are paid from these mining industries to the people who raised the capital by way of shareholding and by way of loans:

(a) Profit (payable to white shareholders)

These are drawn from Tswana homelands and carried across the border to the white areas making these areas richer and enabling them to open more firms and industries and further stimulating their entire commerce and industry,

(b) Interest

Because the loan capital comes from the white areas, it follows that the interest earned on this capital must also be carried out of the Tswana homeland to the white cities in the same way as profits.

(c) Salaries and Wages

Directors, managers, engineers, accountants including their clerical staffs, artisans and mine workers are all white and earn high salaries and wages. Tswanas who are paid unskilled wages because of constitutional limitations are not allowed to acquire shares in an all-white set-up. Their advancement for higher posts with better remuneration is challenged in their own territory by white mine workers and trade unions, thus forcing our people to remain hewers of wood and drawers of water. This must be so because their low earnings are consumed, leaving them with no provision for investment.

(d) Rent or Royalties

Rents and royalties are usually determined by mining concerns in consultation with the Department of Bantu Administration and Development. The owner of the land has no bargaining power. Moreover, even where royalties are reasonable, their proportion is lamentably low. A study of final accounts of the balance sheet of the platinum mining of the Rustenburg area may be carried out and compared with these facts. I have also to point out that most of the general expenses are incurred in the white cities too, e.g. printing and stationery, protective clothing, spare parts, i.e. replacement of tools and machine parts, oil etc., so that capital continues to flow back to the white areas.

RECOMMENDATIONS

1 / That the South African Bantu Trust Act be so amended that it provides for the inclusion among its trustees of representatives of the Tswana government. This would mean, among other things, a progressive preparation for eventual takeover.

2 / That a Tswana Development Corporation be established without further delay, and that all other existing or about to exist corporations be regarded as redundant and that they be consolidated into this Tswana Development Corporation.

3 / That a provision in the Tswana Development Corporation be made for the establishment of other development corporations in which Tswana individuals or companies may hold shares.

4 / That the affairs of the Tswana Development Corporation be managed and controlled by a board of directors consisting of Tswana men and that a white directorate acts as advisors to the Tswana board of directors.

5 / That the present mining and other industrial contracts be allowed to continue until such time as their period expires but taxes accruing from profits

and all mine workers earnings be paid directly to the coffers of the Tswana government.

6 / That the Tswana Development Corporation, in carrying out its undertakings to finance Tswana corporations and promote other commercial and industrial organisations, should employ white technicians and pay them according to a fixed scale of remuneration.

WAGES

The present wage paid to the Tswana in commerce and industry is terribly low. It is futile to think of a successful economic development of our homeland whilst the earnings of our working community remain so. This is a problem our government should regard as serious and which requires immediate investigation. I recommend a complete overall rise of the basic wage of our Bantu people throughout the republic.

DEVELOPMENT OF WHITE SPOTS

For some time now there has been a mass removal of black spots. There has been comparatively very little removal of white spots. Whites, in anticipation of their removal one day, have continued to entrench themselves in these spots, thus making it impossible for a change-over. White spots like Taung and Thaba Nchu would be among the convenient areas to be handed over to Tswanas for development before entrenchment of whites can take place. Property development companies, financed by the Tswana Development Corporation, when formed, should be given this task. Tenders with attractive concessions should be invited by the Tswana government. In conclusion I emphasise that Tswana must aim at eventual ranking with other world nations and should therefore fight against playing second fiddle in international economic, social, educational and political affairs. To achieve this goal we must avoid anything artificial and have a change of attitude and be honest with ourselves, and we must have a national outlook in all our dealings and undertakings.

Decentralisation and Border Industries

S.J.J. LESOLANG

(Reprinted from The African Trader, 1972)

The decentralisation and establishment of border industries and their effects on the development of the Bantu homelands is an event that is fast gaining favour all over the country, even from those who initially opposed the concept. With the march of time, it has become abundantly clear that this move has created employment facilities for thousands of our people, who hitherto were subjected to various evils associated with lack of employment.

According to a recent survey of the South African Institute of Race Relations, 'these new concerns and expansions involved private investments of more than 177 million Rand, and provided employment for 40 000 Bantu'. It was estimated that schemes contemplated for 1966 would provide employment for a further 4 200 Bantu.

As a result of the establishment of border industries on the fringes of Bantu areas, the problems of employment have to some degree been minimised. One would feel that this development has also stimulated commerce and industry within the Bantu homelands themselves.

According to Dr J. Adendorff, general manager of the Bantu Investment Corpcration, the corporation had at the beginning of 1966 already invested R5m in direct loans and financial aid to African entrepreneurs and in the building of new townships and factories in the homelands. Since its inception in 1959 the corporation has altogether helped 950 businessmen financially.

He stated further that there were 596 undertakings including brick yards, transport, bus services, bakeries, garages, wholesale and retail shops which were assisted to the extent of R2,5m and a further R230 000 that was given as housing loans.

Whilst the implementation of the government policy of establishing border industries is going on, and is in fact receiving more and more support, it is also becoming clear that the process cannot furnish a complete and permanent answer to the socio-economic problems of the homelands. The reasons for this are not far to seek. First, these new industries are patchy, and are mainly situated at certain growth points selected on the European side of the borders, and thus offering to the Bantu nothing more beyond employment. Secondly, only those living nearest to these growth points are taken on for work; people occupying virtually undeveloped parts of the homelands further inland, are left workless and destitute.

It should be borne in mind that the people of South Africa, both black and white, have for the last three centuries focussed their energies on the development of what we now call the white urban areas, where big cities with their skyscrapers and large industries stand out as the pride of this country. In this joint effort for this great achievement, the whites provided the capital and the know-how, whilst the blacks gave their labour. The result is that South Africa today ranks with the foremost countries in the world economically. According to a recent brochure of the Department of Information, South Africa is equalled in the Western world only by Australia, and surpassed only by Japan, Germany and Italy. What a wonderful achievement this is!

But while this admirable and momentous forward drive was carried out, the Bantu homelands remained stagnant in underdevelopment. Most of us who have long yearned to witness the beginning of a new day of progress in the Bantu areas, have viewed as a remarkable break-through the creation of such bodies as the Bantu Authorities; the Bantu Investment Corporation; and the proposed Bantu Development Corporations for all the national ethnic units, whose primary purpose it will be to bring about a more rapid economic growth to the homelands. One can hope that South Africa as a whole will now begin to focus her attention on the development of the Bantu homelands and build there also a balanced economy, similar to what has taken place in our white areas. It is for this reason that the present government should be given full support in their efforts to develop the Bantu homelands.

Border industries would not solve all the economic problems of the homelands. One feels persuaded to think that these industries would serve a more adequate purpose only if established on both sides of the border line, so that those on the Bantu side could be expanded further into the interior. In this way, not only can more and more Bantu take up employment, but many could receive technical training and apprenticeship in their own industries. The Bantu could then also invest their monies in their own industries by taking up shares in them. Such facilities are not afforded them in industries on the white side of the border line.

A further advantage in establishing industries on the Bantu side of the border line would be to enable such industries to share facilities such as transport, communication, power, water and roads, with those on the European side of the border. In this way the enormous cost of developing the Bantu homelands industrially and commercially would be somewhat reduced.

In terms of Act No. 86 of 1965, provision is made for the establishment of development corporations for all the Bantu national units. The Transkei has already established its own development corporation and it is hoped the government will, without much delay, bring about the establishment of the other corporations visualised in the Act. Such corporations will inter alia exploit all natural resources in the homelands, and establish heavy industries similar to those found in white areas, even if these were to be first supervised by white technicians. If such a move was left too long, it might be difficult for the Bantu to start their own industries, because they would have to compete unfairly with long-established white industries on their borders which are even more generously subsidised.

The enormity and urgency of the development programme in the Bantu areas stands as a great challenge to the sincerity and conscientiousness of the people of South Africa. This programme calls for much more capital than has hitherto been made available. The Tomlinson Report indicated that at least R208m was required for the first 10 years of the development plan recommended by that Commission. Unfortunately, that vital recommendation did not at that time meet the approval of the government. It is, however, our hope that the new Bantu Development Corporations visualised for the Bantu national units will be equipped with sufficient capital, so as to make them effective within a minimum of time.

The question now arises, what part are the Bantu themselves to play in bringing about this revolutionary change in our economy? The African businessman, the professional man, and the ordinary man in the street, should answer this question.

In its White Paper of 1956, the Republican government declared that 'the government accepts the policy, that the Bantu enterprise, unimpeded by European competition, should be enabled to develop its own industries with or without assistance inside Bantu areas'. Up till now very few of us have seized this golden opportunity, which must also be regarded as a challenge. Where any attempt was made it was rather too individualistic in its outlook.

The National African Chamber of Commerce and its affiliated subsidiaries springing up all over the Republic, should take the lead in this development. The voice of NACOC should reach out to the Bantu man in the street; in the homes; and up to the uttermost part of the country. And, the voice should say, 'Wake up and develop your own'! Campaigns should be launched to pool financial resources into national investments.

Our people should be taught to invest monies with organisations established to build up their standard of living, and to support their own industries and commerce. On the other hand, the businessman should be taught to meet the needs of the people at the right prices. Let us all understand that our social and economic problems can never be solved for us by a foreign hand, but by our own hand. Let us expel suspicion, fears and eliminate ignorance among our people. Let NACOC free our Bantu people from the vicious circles of starvation and poverty. Has the time not come when NACOC should appoint a special project committee to see to the implementation of a five-year programme for the economic development of the African areas by the Africans themselves?

Capital Investment in the Homelands

S.M. MOTSUENYANE

(Excerpts from the Presidential Address to the Eighth National Conference of the National African Chamber of Commerce, Durban, 13 May 1972)

Two weeks ago, the First Secretary of the Malawi Embassy told our Chamber members in Pretoria that South Africans of all nationalities were free to invest their money in Malawi. If this could happen in Malawi why not with our own African homelands here? Why should it not be possible for a Venda businessman in Sibasa to invest his money in the Transkei or KwaZulu? Our homeland governments have already allowed white industrialists to invest money in their areas by establishing factories on an agency basis. This policy is quite good and realistic and we are all for it. But where two industrialists, a Zulu and a white man, apply for a factory in BophuthaTswana, preference should in all fairness be given to the Zulu businessman, because the policy of separate development requires Africans to serve Africans, and more than this, the Zulu businessman has much more in common and is closer to the Tswana than the white man.

We must in our acceptance of separate development realise that like any other political concept it has its own shortcomings. We have to be wise to recognise that we as a black people share common interests and similar aspirations and problems. We can best solve these common problems and achieve our objectives by working together in a spirit of oneness. The concept of separateness in so far as Africans are concerned will be of short duration. Its continuance depends only on the convictions of the party in power and not so much on the realities of life which constantly call for adjustments in human existence. The important thing we need, like all other human beings, is freedom of association; freedom to choose our friends.

The idea of separateness is to my mind of much less importance than that of development. The economic development of our territories is the most urgent common factor which ought to bind us together in our struggle to uplift ourselves. If the most developed areas of the world like Western Europe perceive and feel the need for a European Common Market to sustain and expand their economies, how much more fitting and necessary is this concept for our poverty-stricken and underdeveloped territories? Our country must find a way of advancing the development of the Bantu homelands much more rapidly.

In our search for solutions, we must be absolutely realistic in our approach. First things must come first. The interests of the country and the people as a whole, should be placed above our narrow ethnic and sectional considerations. In this spirit of nation-building, our homelands should discard altogether the idea of ethnic affiliation as the principal condition governing investment policies. Investors in South Africa, as in Malawi and other states, come from all over the world and represent a diversity of ethnic groups. By encouraging inter-ethnic investment, our homeland governments will not have departed from the same economic policy that is practised by South Africa itself.

Whilst advocating a new sense of realism in our approach towards solving the economic problems of Bantu homelands, I am also stressing the importance of our direct participation at all levels in all the schemes and projects that are intended to benefit us. We are as a people losing faith in having things done for us like grown-up babies. The feeling that we, like the rest of mankind, should now initiate something we can call ours is gaining momentum by the day. Many of us believe that it is now time that we established our own banks, financial institutions and companies which should help to hasten the pace of our development. Our National Chamber of Commerce is unhappy about the policy of the Bantu Investment Corporation regarding direct participation by Africans in its top-level administrative services. In order to construe the Bantu Investment Corporation as our own institution, it must open shareholding to us, and also make it possible for us to be directly represented on its directorate.

National African Chamber of Commerce: Regionalisation and Bantu Investment Corporation Policy

(Memorandum from the National African Chamber of Commerce to the Minister of Bantu Administration and Development, 29 August 1969)

SECTION A

Preamble

This memorandum is the outcome of an interview held on 13 January 1969 in Pretoria between the Honourable Deputy Minister of Bantu Administration and Education and members of the Executive Committee of the National African Chamber of Commerce...

SECTION B

Some proposals and recommendations concerning the rights and interests of Bantu businessmen in their areas

1 / Restriction against business expansion due to policy

In the urban Bantu residential areas, the existing policy is to allow only one shop to a businessman regardless of his financial or managerial abilities. This policy of one man one business, according to our understanding of the present political set-up, was to be confined to European areas only. But, in fact it has been extended to certain Bantu areas especially in places where the Bantu Investment Corporation has established shopping centres. Whereas the shops bought or leased from the corporation are often too small to accommodate any further expansion, current regulations and procedures debar Bantu businessmen from having more than one shop in the same locality; and this constitutes an impediment against the rise of bigger business concerns in the Bantu homelands.

Another kind of policy restriction that adversely affects business expansion in the Bantu areas, is the political and not business qualification that a particular ethnic group shall be served only by members of that specific ethnic group. The effect of this rather unusual requirement in commerce is to hinder economic developments which may be brought about by what could be called outsiders in any particular ethnic group or community...

Furthermore it must be pointed out that Bantu businessmen, having business establishments in the urban Bantu areas, are not easily permitted to open new business concerns in the homelands, without being compelled to close down their older establishments.

In the light of the above findings, our organisation recommends:

(a) that all regulations and requirements relative to the size and number of businesses a Bantu trader may be allowed to have in the Bantu homelands be waived;

(b) that Bantu firms or traders be allowed to establish themselves where conditions are favourable and not necessarily within their own ethnic groups;

(c) that in all cases where white firms have to be allowed to trade in the Bantu areas, preference should be given to existing Bantu firms disregarding ethnic qualifications for any particular area. This will make it possible for a Tswana firm to trade in the Transkei instead of a white firm doing so;

(d) expansion into the Bantu areas of businesses established in urban Bantu areas should be permitted.

2 / Suggested amendments to the policy: structure and operations of the Bantu Investment Corporation

Whereas our association views with appreciation the existence of an organisation such as the Bantu Investment Corporation, an organisation especially constituted for the promotion of economic development in the Bantu areas, it must, however, be noted that there are at present aspects of the policy structure and functioning of the Bantu Investment Corporation which need to be revised and reshaped to enable the organisation to achieve its purpose without arousing too much antagonism and criticism among the Bantu traders.

The following are our suggestions and recommendations, which, if accepted, might make the Bantu Investment Corporation more acceptable to the Bantu traders.

(a) The structure of the Bantu Investment Corporation

According to the constitution of the organisation, the Bantu Investment Corporation has a directorate of ten persons: four representing the Department of Bantu Administration and Development and six businessmen appointed for their special knowledge of business affairs. At present all the members of the board of directors of the Bantu Investment Corporation are white.

Our organisation is of the opinion that the interests of Bantu businessmen would be better served if some of the directors of the corporation were drawn from the Bantu people as well. Not only would this give the corporation the character of a Bantu organisation, but it would open the way for the eventual take-over of the corporation by the Bantu people themselves. Without the involvement of the Bantu in the top administrative machinery of the corporation on an increasing scale, it is difficult to visualise an eventual smooth take-over of the organisation by the Bantu people.

If the above suggestion cannot be accepted for any other reason, we recommend as an alternative the creation of a national Bantu advisory council on commerce and industries comprised of Bantu businessmen representing all ethnic units in the country. Such an advisory body would work in collaboration with the Department of Bantu Administration and the Bantu Investment Corporation.

(b) Land ownership rights of the B.I.C. in the Bantu homelands

Our association has become aware that in most of the new Bantu townships in the Bantu homelands all or most business sites are allocated to the Bantu Investment Corporation, which in turn leases them to Bantu businessmen after erecting shops thereon.

Our organisation maintains that the acquisition of business sites and properties in the Bantu homelands by the Bantu Investment Corporation, in competition with Bantu people who have the necessary capital to purchase such properties, constitutes an encroachment upon the area of the business rights of the Bantu people...

We recommend accordingly that all business sites in the new Bantu townships be advertised for sale to Bantu businessmen and the B.I.C. should come in only when asked by the individuals concerned to do so and that the corporation's sphere of participation be limited entirely to the financing of business transactions. This will give Bantu businessmen the opportunity of deciding what type of shops to build and how big they must be.

(c) Shareholding in the B.I.C. by Bantu

Although shareholding in the B.I.C. is at present the preserve of the South African Bantu Trust, our association feels that for this organisation eventually to fall into the hands of the Bantu people, it must open shares for sale to the Bantu as an initial step in that direction. The acquisition of such shares in the corporation will entitle the Bantu to increased participation in the administration of the organisation at higher levels. This participation will not only build the confidence of the Bantu in the organisation, but shall in a way create the essential feeling that the B.I.C. truly belongs to them.

(d) Exclusion of other wholesalers where the B.I.C. operates

Our association observes with some concern that with the establishment of wholesale stores by the B.I.C. in certain Bantu areas, the Department of Bantu Administration is often prevailed upon to stop the issuing of entry permits to other wholesalers supplying those particular areas. This is done in most cases without regard for the lower prices, better conditions of service, and the quality of goods that the other wholesalers offer...

In view of the difficulties resulting from the above measures applied in certain Bantu areas, we strongly recommend: (a) that the B.I.C. be respectfully urged to take no action against other wholesalers in certain Bantu areas where it operates until it is able to provide all the lines of merchandise required by the Bantu traders concerned at competitive prices; (b) that the B.I.C. be persuaded to regard competition with other wholesalers as a wholesome feature in commerce in general...

3 / The status of Bantu businessmen

Although the matter of the status of the Bantu businessman has been the subject of discussion at an earlier interview between the Honourable Minister of Bantu Administration and Development and our Chamber organisation, it is still our contention that current legislation does not place the Bantu businessman in the position of respectability that befits his high status and responsibilities in his community.

Where a Bantu businessman has completed five years of uninterrupted service, he should be regarded as a professional man and should therefore be accorded all the rights and privileges of other professional persons such as, for instance, doctors, teachers and social workers.

We recommend that recognised professional businessmen be freed from the restrictions imposed by the influx control regulations and accordingly be allowed to establish their business anywhere in the Bantu areas where their service is required.

Further we recommend that such professional businessmen be exempted from the inconvenient and time-consuming practice of having to submit their reference books for endorsement at the end of every month to the labour registration offices in the urban Bantu areas.

4 / The issuing of fire-arms to responsible Bantu traders

In view of the disturbing and alarming increase in the number of cases of armed robbery in which Bantu traders are the victims, our association feels reluctantly compelled to redirect once more its appeal to the Honourable Minister to expedite the issuing of fire-arms to responsible Bantu businessmen and especially those running big concerns and naturally handling large sums of money daily for purposes of self-protection...

5 / Bantu representatives of local Chambers to serve on licensing boards

Our organisation notes with appreciation that in considering the allocation of trading sites and licences certain authorities in the Bantu homelands, e.g. Hammanskraal, include in the committee considering applications a representative of the local Bantu Chamber of Commerce.

It is strongly recommended that such opportunities and privileges be extended to all Bantu business organisations both in the Bantu homelands and in the urban Bantu residential areas.

6 / Development of industries inside the Bantu home-

lands

Much as we appreciate the opportunities which these industries create for our people, it must also be pointed out that the border industries situated in the white areas under present conditions cannot accord the Bantu unlimited scope for development into highly skilled artisans and technicians. Nor can these industries provide Bantu participation above the servant level.

In order to create conditions under which the Bantu in the homelands will have unlimited chances for training, as skilled technicians, managers, and directors of big business undertakings, more emphasis must be placed on the establishment of industries inside the Bantu homelands where the prevailing job reservation regulations will have no effect. In instances where European firms are given permission to trade in Bantu homelands, Bantu should be allowed to participate by way of buying shares.

SECTION C

The advisability of creating ethnically-divided Bantu Chambers of Commerce based in the homelands

From a purely business organisation's point of view, the National African Chamber of Commerce finds it inappropriate to think strictly in terms of ethnic divisions, as this is more a matter of politics than business.

Due to the accidents of history and geography, however, our present local and provincial Chambers are already to a great extent constituted along ethnic lines. This is true of our Natal and Zululand Chambers, which are predominantly Zulu; our Transkei and Ciskeian Chambers, which are altogether Xhosa; and our Orange Free State Chamber, which is Sotho and Tswana. The only provincial Chamber that has more than three ethnic groups comprising its membership is the Transvaal Chamber.

Our National Chamber of Commerce and its constituent branches take full cognisance of the existing policy of separate development and will as far as possible endeavour to adhere to its terms and requirements. In doing so, however, our organisation is also aware of some intricate situations which may make the fulfilment of the policy a slow process of evolution rather than a quick but disruptive one. Thus, the question of time is an important consideration in dealing with a matter as difficult as the division of our cosmopolitan urban Bantu Chambers into ethnic units.

The National African Chamber of Commerce, like all other Chambers of Commerce the world over, is a creation of the urban society, where up to now its leadership and source of strength have emanated from. The organisation developed as one body representing the interests of all Bantu traders without any regard for their ethnic identity.

Whereas in the Bantu homelands it will be possible for our Chambers to re-organise themselves along the lines suggested by the Honourable Minister, in the long run the situation in the cosmopolitan Bantu urban areas, especially in the Transvaal, is going to be very difficult to handle. The practical problems are as follows:

(a) The Bantu people have not yet produced sufficient leaders, especially so in the field of commerce because they are relatively new to it. Some ethnic groups draw leadership from others.

(b) The unevenness of the numbers of members from each ethnic group will make impossible the establishment of local Chambers along ethnic lines.

(c) Chambers based in the homelands cannot adequately minister to the needs of the urban Bantu traders in places like Soweto, owing to peculiar local circumstances which differ in different areas. It is much better to have local Chambers dealing with local problems.

(d) Our present Chambers in the homelands are still very poorly organised, due to lack of leadership and the comparatively lower number of Bantu traders in those areas at present. In the light of the above facts, the National African Chamber of Commerce conference held at Pietermaritzburg in May 1969 decided as follows:

That the conference fully and wholly accepts the establishment of regional Chambers which in turn will federate into provincial federal Chambers. This is done to facilitate better organisation, the creation of more effective Chambers and to ensure the necessary co-operation and consultation between the National African Chamber of Commerce and the already established Regional and Territorial Bantu Authorities. To this end the conference resolved as follows:

(a) that the National African Chamber of Commerce and its affiliated provincial organisations amend their constitutions to accommodate the new concept of regionalisation and federalism;

(b) that the regional Chambers be granted increased autonomy in as far as the administration of the affairs of their regions are concerned;

(c) that regional Chambers shall be constituted to cover the area of each particular territorial authority; but the cosmopolitan urban Bantu areas shall constitute their own regions for as long as they remain.

In terms of the above resolutions, the National African Chamber of Commerce has displayed its readiness to work within the framework of the present policy of the department. It will take some time to re-organise our Chamber along the lines suggested and it is hoped that whilst the re-organisation goes on, the department will continue to work through our national organisation and its provincial branches.

Comments on the Bantu Investment Corporation

P.G. GUMEDE

(Reprinted from African Business, May 1973, by kind permission of the publishers, Keeble-Prins Co. (Pty) Ltd.)

In 1971 this organisation gave my executive a specific mandate regarding the manner of approach which we had to adopt over the Bantu Investment Corporation issue. This Chamber (the Inyanda regional African Chamber of Commerce which operates in Natal and KwaZulu) at a general meeting acknowledged the fact that the corporation was a government-sponsored institution created by Act of parliament whose purpose was to initiate and sponsor economic development in the homelands. This Chamber, however, pointed out in no uncertain terms that it was not happy with the manner in which the corporation operated. It was pointed out that if the corporation is an institution created to promote economic development in our territory, then it must undertake this development in consultation with our Chamber as well as with our KwaZulu government. The effect of this mandate was correctly interpreted by my executive to mean that as an institution the corporation is both desirable and indispensable and has a meaningful purpose, but the modus operandi and certain spheres of operation undertaken by the corporation were found to be undesirable and my executive was charged with the task of bringing these dissatisfactions before the corporation.

This Chamber expressed dissatisfaction with the following:

(a) that there was a great deal of red tape involved in dealing with applications for financial assistance with the result that it took exceptionally long before the applicant knew the outcome of his application;

(b) that the corporation should not acquire and develop business sites but that these should be sold by the Department of Bantu Administration to prospective businessmen who would be left entirely free to approach the Bantu Investment Corporation for whatever help they needed, e.g. erection of building and/or purchase of stock;

(c) that the corporation should be content with reasonable security advanced by the applicant against his loan and not be compelled to pass a comprehensive bond over all his assets in favour of the corporation;

(d) that the corporation should endeavour to employ experienced men as field officials;

(e) that the notorious clause 14 of the Conditions of Agreement be deleted;

(f) that applicants be advanced cash and not pro forma invoices.

SPHERES OF OPERATION

(a) This Chamber strongly recommended that the Bantu Investment Corporation should altogether withdraw from the business of brewing, distributing and selling Bantu beer and that this be passed on to individuals or Bantu companies;

(b) that the Bantu Investment Corporation should withdraw from the screening committee as Bantu Investment Corporation is an interested party in such committee.

This Chamber then gave a mandate to my executive to take up these matters with the corporation. My executive prepared a memorandum and interviewed the territorial manager and territorial administrator of the corporation jointly with the Chief Bantu Affairs Commissioner for Natal. The said memorandum together with its reply was circulated to the members. I shall briefly outline here with pride what my executive achieved as a result of that interview.

(a) The corporation gave an undertaking to withdraw from acquiring sites, developing them and thereafter leasing them to successful applicants. It was agreed upon that the Department of Bantu Administration would advertise vacant business sites and the Bantu Investment Corporation would only come into the picture when requested by such successful applicant, discuss his plans with the corporation and finalise his loan arrangements with the corporation.

(b) All efforts would be made to deal with applications and announce results within the shortest period possible.

(c) A liaison committee between the KwaZulu government, the Bantu Investment Corporation and our Chamber would be established.

(d) Clause 14 was deleted as recommended.

(e) The question of brewing, distributing and selling Bantu beer would be taken up with the KwaZulu government.

(f) Companies would be formed in order to acquire from the corporation already developed projects like Umgababa holiday resort, the hotel at Umlazi, etc. The proviso was that the corporation would initially be a shareholder in such companies until we had trained personnel to carry on with the management and administration of such projects.

The corporation does admit that it is not employing professional people in all spheres - that, if the type of people we want to see in the corporation circles were in fact employed, they would demand fantastic salaries and part of this would be passed on to the interest paid by the applicants, and if the existing 7½ per cent is already felt to be rather high what would be the reaction if this was to be increased further? The corporation endeavours to train its employees and arranges seminars and other courses for them and we have every reason to hope for a gradual improvement in this sphere. I may mention in passing that Mr Smith, the newly appointed branch manager at Madadeni, holds amongst other qualifications, a certificate of achievement in marketing management which he obtained from the American Management Association.

My executive has noted grievances which were raised at our Mondlo meeting and will strongly recommend to our successors in office to carry on with the dialogue which we have established with the corporation and try to arrive at a compromise. We accept that the corporation is here to benefit us and we should not rest until we have, through dialogue, established a formula which should not only improve our relations with the corporation but which should make even the ordinary man in the street realise that the corporation is for us.

...It is also pleasing to conclude by saying that the leadership of the KwaZulu government shares the same view as my executive in this matter.

Ethnic Commerce

S.M. MOTSUENYANE

(Excerpts from the Presidential Address to the Sixth Annual Conference of the National African Chamber of Commerce, Bloemfontein, 23 May 1970)

The Honourable Deputy Minister has appealed to our organisation to consider urgently and seriously the creation of separate ethnic Chambers because, 'in future the Minister would probably not agree to consult with a body consisting of various ethnic groups.' Ladies and gentlemen, this means our conference must today take the most fateful decision ever to face a business association in this country. If we say yes, it means the very death of the spirit of unity which gave birth to this organisation and the objects for which it stands. On the other hand if we say no, then our organisation might be isolated and thereby rendered ineffective in so far as negotiating for a better deal with the department is concerned. We do not want our organisation buried alive, but we also do not want our organisation to follow the path of least resistance, and in this way sacrifice the principles upon which its very existence depends. Somewhere in the middle of the road we hope to find a solution acceptable both to ourselves and accommodative of some of the workable aspects of the present policy.

This brings us now to another very important proposition of our Pietermaritzburg conference, which must be further looked into and discussed at this conference: namely, the establishment of regional chambers of commerce. The idea of establishing regional chambers was accepted by our previous conference as an attempt to meet the Deputy Minister's proposal in part; as a means of attaining a more effective organisation of our provincial chambers; and also to facilitate co-operation of our organisation with the recently constituted territorial authorities throughout the republic.

Although the idea was accepted, it has not been

possible for the national executive to issue any definite instructions to the branches, as the Minister's reaction to our proposed plan of regionalisation was still pending. Secondly, the national executive maintained that the actual plan of breaking up the provinces into regions would have to come from the provinces themselves. Thirdly, the whole plan of regionalisation necessitates far-reaching changes in our present national constitution, especially on the form of representation that these proposed regions would be given at national level. Fourthly, there has been a big query as to whether the new concept of regionalisation in effect nullifies the necessity of retaining our existing provincial organisations.

The Buy Home Week

S.M. MOTSUENYANE

(Message from the President of the National African Chamber of Commerce, October 1969)

The Buy Home Campaign is an effort by the National African Chamber of Commerce to keep as much of the African money circulating in the hands of the African people themselves as possible. The bulk of the hard-earned money obtained by our people in the republic is presently spent outside the African areas. This in effect deprives the African of the money he so much needs for the promotion of his own development and welfare. There can be no real progress and development among a people whose economic power is spent largely outside that nation itself. And accordingly we can anticipate no major advancement in our areas unless and until we capture and utilise our buying power within our own communities.

By supporting our local traders and buying all or most of our requirements at home, we shall not only be supporting our own dealers as is expected of us, but we shall also be stopping our money from draining out, and thereby strengthening ourselves financially. All our plans and schemes for social and economic advancement can be implemented only if we have the necessary capital and know-how to do so. Our capital consists in the main of the very monies we spend in shops outside our areas and, should the present tendency to buy more outside our own stores continue indefinitely, there is no hope of ever building the basis of a sound economy in our own areas.

The African people in the republic have today attained a colossal buying power of over R1 000 000 000 per annum and this is expected to rise sevenfold to R7 500 000 000 within 30 years. This accounts for the profound and unmatched interest shown by businessmen of other races in the African market in recent years.

The African traders who for a long time have witnessed the monolithic flow of money from the African areas with an air of cold resignation and helplessness, have now decided through the medium of the Buy Home Campaign to join the crucial competition for the African customer. To win this competition the African trader is prepared to bring down prices, to become more courteous to his customers and to do everything in his power to render his business attractive to the customer.

From our customers' side we pray for co-operation. We wish them to understand that charity begins at home. We ask them also to realise that by supporting their own local businessmen, they are actually strengthening themselves because money spent in an African shop is money saved for our nation's benefit. Our already enormous and growing buying power can mean something to us only if we spend it wisely at home.

With the increased support that African businessmen can obtain from their own people, they will be obliged to show an ever-increasing measure of appreciation and thankfulness. The National African Chamber of Commerce encourages all businessmen to play a more and more important role in the social and cultural affairs of their communities. We depend on the support of every section of our nation throughout the republic to help ensure the success of the Buy Home Campaign.

The Beginnings of a Black Bank

S.M. MOTSUENYANE

(Excerpts from the Presidential Address to the Ninth Annual Conference of the National African Federated Chamber of Commerce, at Bloemfontein, May 1973)

Concerning the African Bank Project, I would like to state how grateful I am that at long last some progress is being made. Until May 1972, despite constant appeals for contributions towards the national fund which was started in 1964 for the specific object of serving as the nucleus of an African Bank, the response was rather weak and insignificant. The general attitude was one of slackness and undecidedness, and very few members contributed anything above R100.

The meeting with the directors of Barclays Bank in London, who offered to help train African personnel for the proposed African Bank and furthermore to buy shares in the bank, proved to be the key which opened the minds and fired the black people with the confidence and the determination to make a vigorous beginning. Since the meeting of the joint executives of our regional chambers which met at Hammersdale last July, and took an important decision to make a positive start towards initiating an African Bank, much ground has already been covered. After making preliminary contacts with the Barclays Company in South Africa and meeting responsible government officials in this regard, the National Executive convened a special national conference at Mamelodi in November 1972, at which no fewer than 300 Chamber members and delegates were present. This special conference gave the Executive the necessary mandate to go ahead with definite plans for the establishment of the proposed National African Bank.

The Conference agreed to establish an African Bank in which African private investors, homeland governments and European banks could participate together and acquire shares in the proportion of 49 per cent, 21 per cent and 30 per cent respectively. Although the bank could be registered with a capital of R1 000 000 it was decided that the share capital of the proposed African Bank be R5 000 000. In order to get the project off the ground, the National Executive was empowered to open a trust account into which prospective shareholders could deposit their funds for the purpose of building the necessary capital required. A period of six months was specified as the time during which the required capital should be raised. Furthermore, the Executive was authorised to make the necessary formal application for the registration of the proposed banking institution, after seeking and securing the co-operation of all homeland governments.

I have the greatest pleasure in reporting that our Executive has carried out all the instructions of the special conference held at Mamelodi. We opened the Nafcoc Bank Collection Account No. 22652625202, at the Church Square Branch of Barclays Bank at the end of November 1972. Until February 1973, very little money was deposited in the account. The Executive has had to intensify its efforts at getting more people to become aware of this facility. At the beginning of March, deposits began to come in much more regularly and in greater amounts. Although we have received an average amount of R10 000 per month of deposits during the past two months, this you will agree falls far short of our expectations.

Further, I wish to report that the Executive together with our regional committees in the various homeland areas have met all but one homeland government. The only homeland government we have failed to see so far is that of Qwa-Qwa. The general reaction of these governments to our appeal for involvement and acquisition of shares in the African Bank Project is most assuring. Six of the seven governments have indicated that in principle they accept the offer to participate as shareholders in the African Bank. The one government that has not yet indicated whether or not it will participate in the project is the BophuthaTswana government. There is on the whole an overwhelming desire and willingness on the part of homeland leaders to co-operate as far as possible in helping to enhance the success of the project.

In so far as the application for the registration of the proposed banking institution is concerned, this was done, and permission in principle has been granted. In his reply the Registrar of Banks has made it clear that the proposed African Banking Institution will be registered initially as a General Bank, and will remain so until it has accumulated sufficient reserves to rise to the status of a Commercial Bank. The Registrar also indicated that it was the desire of the government that instead of Barclays alone participating in the partnership, a consortium comprised of all the five major banks in South Africa, namely Barclays Bank Limited, Volkskas Bank, Ned-Bank, The Trust Bank, and Standard Bank, be allowed to acquire the 30 per cent shareholding, earmarked for white financial institutions. Further the Registrar has agreed subject to the approval of the Minister of Finance, that the proposed African Bank could receive foreign funds. The development of the bank, he emphasised, should be on sound lines, and the approval of his office would be necessary before the establishment of any new branch or branches.

We have reached the end of the six months period fixed at the Mamelodi conference for raising the necessary capital for the black Bank. But the truth is we are only starting now with our fund-raising. The pledges that were made at the Mamelodi conference which involved an amount of excess R1 million have not yet been honoured. Many of our local Chambers have not as yet called a single meeting of businessmen to discuss the bank, and to decide how they, as individuals and as Chambers, could throw in their lot with the rest of our people in ensuring the success of the project. As a rule we are naturally slow and doubtful starters, and some of us have become unfortunate victims of complacency, doubt and indecision. This time we cannot afford to remain behind without losing too much that is dear to us. We cannot now assume a lukewarm disposition towards a project that affects our very well-being and destiny.

There is much work left to be done. We need to get every black man involved in the project of the black Bank in order for it to succeed. We must raise more than R50 000 at least, to cover the initial organisational and registration costs, quite apart from the R3 1/3 million which must be subscribed for shares by individuals, companies, organisations and homeland governments. The question is, can we really do it? I say yes! It can be done. I maintain that we have the brains; we have the numbers; and if we want, we have money. We need to have a determination and desire to win. I am quite sure we have many sympathisers who will sooner or later come to our assistance, but we must start the ball rolling and place ourselves in a position to carry the greater share of the responsibility and the burden of self-upliftment. We must become enthusiastic and daring to venture, courageous and dedicated to our cause. Above all we must develop faith in ourselves and in the things of our own creation. If we can all leave here determined to go back and work, there is no doubt in my mind that we can raise the capital required. We need more time to organise and talk to our people, pointing out the obvious advantages which we stand to gain by having our own banking institution The Executive, therefore, recommends that we extend our fund-raising period to the end of August 1973, or later as the case may be. During this period it should be possible to prepare the articles of association of the proposed bank, and to register the banking institution. Thereafter, a prospectus will be issued, offering shares to be bought and detailing all the conditions of shareholding. A more detailed plan of action will be formulated later after meeting the representatives of the banks that will be participating in the Black Bank Project with us.

It is unusual for a black company to have white shareholders in South Africa. In the case of our bank, we have no alternative but to enlist all the help, support and co-operation that the existing white banks can offer. And for quite a number of years we shall have to depend on their know-how and experience whilst still training our own people ultimately to take over the complete management of the bank. It should also be quite clear that white capital in the black bank may in due course be phased out gradually to allow greater participation by the African people themselves. Every new step taken in the development of the proposed African Bank, however, must be dictated by the circumstances prevailing at the time, and the ultimate objective of ensuring the uninterrupted growth of the establishment.

There are quite a number of other important considerations that must still be given attention by the Executive. The first one of these is the choice of a suitable place for locating the headquarters of the bank. Whilst the most suitable place would certainly be in the urban areas where the bank would have abundant chances of enjoying a ready and large-scale patronage, it is to be regretted that there are laws in this country prohibiting black companies from establishing their main operations in the urban areas. In view of the fact that it might be necessary for the first few branches of the black bank to be established in the urban areas, the Executive has had to write to the Minister of Bantu Administration and Development to grant certain policy concessions in so far as the location of the first branches of the bank are concerned. Any places found suitable for branches in homeland towns, however, will certainly be made use of with the permission of the homeland governments concerned.

In some quarters the question of the composition of the bank's board of directors is so highly regarded as to create cause for concern. In the mind of our Executive the board will consist principally of shareholders and the representatives of shareholding organisations. The banking institution proposed will and must of necessity operate in co-operation with homeland governments in whose areas specific development projects may be supported or initiated. But to function normally and freely, as all other banks in this country do, the black bank should not be relegated to the control of any particular homeland government or policy. All homeland governments and political parties should construe the African Bank as a non-political institution like the Church, which ought never to be drawn into the arena of party-political differences. It is to be regarded more as a national project, vital to the economic interests of all the black people in this country.

Many black people are delighted at the prospect of having a bank of their own, established in South Africa. But notwithstanding the enormous advantages, the dignity and image-building benefits which this establishment would bring to our people, there may also result frustrations occasioned by restrictive laws that prohibit the growth of black entrepreneurship and enterprise especially in the urban areas. The black bank will certainly not develop as smoothly and as rapidly as some of us are inclined to believe. In a community such as ours, circumscribed with restrictions on the freehold ownership of property, and having limited investment opportunities, the growth of the black bank must necessarily be a slow, a difficult process. We are certainly looking forward with anticipation that the republican government shall stand ready to make adjustments in its policies where necessary to facilitate the fullest participation of the bank in the economic progress of the black people of this country.

Black Entrepreneurship

S.M. MOTSUENYANE

(Excerpts from address to a symposium on 'The Optimum Involvement of Manpower in Business and Industry' under the auspices of the United States-South Africa Leader Exchange Program, Umhlanga Rocks, August 1973)

Black entrepreneurship in South Africa has been circumscribed by harsh restrictions and legal restraints for more than half-a-century. These were largely prompted by the fear of black competition in business and the desire to uphold white economic domination and to perpetuate black dependency and subservience. Although the country started with a negative trading policy for the black people, characterised mainly by the curtailment and denial of business rights to them, especially in the urban areas, there has been a tendency over the past twenty-five years to widen the scope of trading opportunities for the black people in their so-called homeland areas.

The whole policy of separate development in so far as African trading is concerned merits honest reappraisal. The policy is based on an assumption that is entirely false and illogical: that the blacks are temporary dwellers in the urban areas of South Africa; and furthermore on the belief that opportunities created in the homelands can fully and adequately compensate for the rights denied them in the urban areas. The idea of black temporariness in the so-called white areas of South Africa is quite absurd and ridiculous when viewed against the stark actualities of our South African situation. I am inclined to share the same opinion with Professor Richards in his realistic statement that 'the unscrambling of the mixture in race location built up over many years seems impossible both physically and economically: neither mining, agriculture, secondary industry, nor virtually any other activity can eliminate or even greatly reduce dependence on non-whites'.

Considering the size of the homeland areas at

present and the state of their economic underdevelopment, moral justification of a policy advocating the denial and curtailment of business rights to the black people living in the urban areas, stands as wholly questionable. It must be quite clearly understood that the limiting of business opportunities for black people, especially in the urban areas, has the effect of denying them the legitimate right of ministering to the full needs of their own people. A fair policy in a racially fragmented society such as ours should at least accord each racial group the freedom of economic growth within the area of its habitation irrespective of whether it is there temporarily or permanently. The alleged temporary settlement of the black people in the urban areas does not in any way justify their deprivation of human and citizenship rights in these areas, even if the homelands were granted full independence.

Low wage scales and limited employment and promotional opportunities in white employment have caused an increasing number of Africans to take up business. The majority of these people are the professionally better qualified and experienced people. In the urban areas, the people are more sophisticated and less traditionally orientated. Their needs are more complex and cash is more readily available. The business undertakings in the urban areas are therefore more diversified than in the rural tribal areas. The urban market is larger than the rural market.

The lack of capital for business development has been and still is one of the most crucial handicaps confronting growth of black entrepreneurship. Until 1959 when the Bantu Investment Corporation was established, there were no direct or indirect government channels for financing black business in South Africa. There was also little scope for private South African banks and other financial institutions to give direct assistance, by allowing overdraft facilities, owing to the poor credit facilities to Africans due mainly to their poor credit-worthiness resulting from denial of freehold property ownership rights to them, especially in the urban areas. As has already been mentioned earlier, the Bantu Investment Corporation was created specifically to give assistance only to businessmen and projects in the homelands.

This means that the majority of African traders who

live in the urban areas of South Africa are deprived of facilities which they require most urgently. Furthermore, it should be made quite clear that the Bantu Investment Corporation with its present financial resources cannot adequately meet the full requirements for the complete development and industrialisation of the so-called homeland areas. The Tomlinson Commission on the development of the Bantu areas recommended in 1952 a budget of approximately R208 million to be spent in the first 10 years of the development. When the corporation began in 1959, it started with a capital of only R500 000, but this has had to be increased – up to now their capital is much less than R50 000 000.

There is an air of absolute insecurity in sofar as the acceptance of the enormous financial responsibility for homeland development is concerned. The country is more preoccupied with internal defence and the undertaking of expansionary projects in the white areas than with the building of a bright and promising economic future for all its inhabitants. African businessmen thus have few avenues of raising funds to start a business. Until this year, when the Bantu Investment Corporation started an agricultural financing section, there was practically no direct financial assistance to African farmers for productive purposes. The Tomlinson Report noted that the most important pre-condition of entrepreneurial genesis is for a people 'both to sanction business activity and to attach a relatively high degree of prestige to it'. In South Africa until very recently business was, unfortunately, never accorded the importance it deserves as compared with professions like teaching, ministry, law and politics. Business, for the most part, attracted the less educated and the strugglers, who nonetheless possessed the ambition, the daring and the nerve to pioneer and to venture into the unknown.

Entrepreneurs, distinguished by their willingness to take risks, their capacity for innovation and their unlimited managerial ability, are unfortunately found in small numbers in all developing countries. This is sometimes cited as the main reason responsible for the slow economic growth of such areas. The problem of shortage of entrepreneurial talent is more acutely experienced in the rural tribal areas where custom and tradition and institutional social values greatly influence the economic outlook and activity of the people. Because the entrepreneur represents a dynamic force, without which no country can expect to achieve a reasonable and satisfying measure of progress and development, the primary task and responsibility of policy makers and planners is to ensure that ideal conditions are created for entrepreneurial genesis.

Most of the business undertakings started by Africans are 'one-man concerns'. Owing to lack of managerial skills, little education and business experience and also limited capital, African companies have a high mortality rate. Furthermore, African businessmen tend to mistrust one another and, as a result, react negatively towards the suggestion of forming companies. Economic pressures are, however, causing them to begin to work together. The National African Federated Chamber of Commerce, with now about 4 000 members, is a potent force towards unifying African businessmen on various needful schemes such as, for instance, the Black Bank, which will soon become a reality.

African entrepreneurship can be studied from two different environments: the rural tribe environment and the urban environment. As noted from our discussion of the policies affecting African trading, the general tendency over the past four decades has been to provide more numerous and wider opportunities for African business undertakings in rural tribal areas, now referred to in South Africa as the Bantu areas.

By 1936, the total number of independent African businessmen had risen to 556 from 27 in 1910. Between 1936 and 1952 the overall number of general dealers in the African areas more than doubled and numerically there was a significant change in the racial pattern of trading in favour of African traders. Despite the increase in the number of traders, their share of the African trade amounted to about 10 per cent in 1952. Numbers continued to rise from 3 871 in 1951 to 6 032 in 1958. The rate of growth in the late 1950s and 1960s was considerably slower than in the preceding years.

There are no reliable statistics on the growth of African urban trading. It is believed that in 1910 there were only two African traders in the locations on the Witwatersrand, but by 1936 there were more than 600. A survey conducted by L. Reyburn for the South African Institute of Race Relations in 1959 found that owing to high overhead expenses, the poverty of the customers and the keen competition that goes on in the Soweto shops, the majority of African traders don't make any significant profits at all. It is almost solely the general dealers who earn high profits and then only if they carry the optimum amount of stocks. He found lack of capital and the means of raising it to be the most severe problems confronting African traders. He concluded that these problems arose from the inability of Africans 'to obtain freehold rights over land, and hence their inability to advance immovable security for overdrafts, loans and mortgages'. Soweto businesses were found to be more sophisticated, specialised and diversified than those in the reserves.

THE FUTURE OF AFRICAN ENTREPRENEURSHIP

We have surveyed both the policy affecting African trading, generally, and examined trends in the development of African entrepreneurship, both in the urban areas and in the homelands. Based on the findings, the following conclusions can be deduced:

(a) There is a growing demand for African entrepreneurs in both the urban and homeland areas of the Republic of South Africa.

(b) The policy of regarding the black urban residents as temporary sojourners in these areas, and consequently denying them business rights, is both dishonest and unrealistic. As long as the white industries demand the presence of Africans in the white areas of South Africa, for so long will the black people reside in those areas. Logically the time will never come when Africans will not be required in white areas. As long as they live there, they are entitled to human and citizenship rights.

(c) The assumption that the rights and opportunities denied the Africans in the urban areas can be made good by giving them greater or commensurate opportunities in the homeland areas, is both fallacious and impractical. There can be no fair comparison between opportunities available in the underdeveloped homelands with those to be found in the developed so-called white areas of South Africa. The very disparities in population size and land distribution of the black and white people of this country negate the assumption as a just, honest and reasonable solution.

(d) African businessmen need to be allowed free and equal participation in the common economy of South Africa. If white businessmen can have black customers and not be restricted in their service, why must black men not be free to trade among the whites in South Africa?

(e) African businessmen are restricted much too much in the urban areas, and must be given wider scope for serving the needs of their urban communities, at least. They must be given financial assistance for expansion and allowed to establish companies and partnerships, to set up big supermarkets and light industries in their areas, as this would also enable them to help solve the problem of unemployment.

(f) Africans should be allowed to acquire shareholding in European companies, especially those deriving the larger share of their profits by selling to them. In this way, true economic partnership based on fair play to all can result. Otherwise the African can never ever hope to share fully and equitably in the assets of the common South African economy, of which he is a partner.

(g) The economic development of the Bantu homelands, and the opening of increased business and employment opportunities for Africans there, is in the best interests of South Africa and her people. More funds should be made available for this task. It is urgent that the system of joint partnerships between white and black entrepreneurs should be allowed in border industries in order to give the African future industrialist a chance to benefit from the wider experience of white industrialists.

(h) Unless the people of South Africa can develop a new way of accepting one another as equals, entitled each to a fair share of the resources of our country, there can be no bright future for all of us. Our economic interdependence today suggests that we are bound together as South Africans, in the economy. The voice of the black man and his interests must not be completely disregarded and relegated to second place, for this may as well mean the undoing of our great economic success in Southern Africa.

Trained Black Labour

WILBY L. BAQWA

(Excerpts from an address to a seminar on 'Utilisation of Trained Black Labour', Johannesburg, 23 and 24 October 1973)

If you went to a kraal in a rural area and observed the people's movements from sunrise to sunset, you would see how they behaved within the limits of a specific environment. This would not necessarily expose you to their customs or traditions but primarily to the environmental and behavioural attitudes. Subjected to the same environment, all people regardless of their heritage would, I am sure, react in similar ways. Variations or differentiations seem to occur when one sector has better financial resources.

We tend to label as westernised anyone of a group who employs modernised methods of living. Granted, they may be taken as westernised but primarily because of the scientific advancement of western countries. These observations compel me to disagree with the common view that black people have their own way of thinking. On the contrary, I find that the subservient role they are subjected to channels them into a situation where they have to adopt a strategy that will circumvent, obviate or perhaps even obliterate the permanence of this role.

There is no need to try to find queer reasons for the migrant worker wanting to be housed with his fellow tribesmen in a hostel, because this is a human tendency: don't we find some white suburbs in Johannesburg mainly occupied by immigrants from specific areas? This practice is not custom or tradition but a mere convenience for communication and reminiscence. Do we not find the immigrant inclined to move away from this suburb as soon as he has established his permanence in the country? Does he not eventually become one of the volk, or nation, and partake in local activities even to a greater extent than in his own? Why then do we regard similar actions of the black person as unique and attributable to his tradition?

Somewhere along the line, I think there is need for us to draw a line and demarcate the limits of tradition as against tribal or racial practice. It was common practice and not necessarily belief in olden rural days for a dead person to be buried in the skin of the beast that was slaughtered to feed the crowds that would come to the funeral. In urban areas, this slaughtering still takes place but why would this tradition of burying the deceased in the skin have been discontinued if it was a belief and not merely a practice? Why do our T.B. hospitals even in the remotest rural areas have so many patients if the black people believe so firmly in witchcraft?

I believe that black people have fewer beliefs than are actually attributed to them, and I think the most important of them all is that the white person does not want him to discover his human potential, and that he should always look upon himself as subservient and not capable of leadership. This of course means then that he immediately tries to accommodate this purported axiom in his dealings with his white counterpart. He will pretend that he is not aware of the counterpart's fear of competition and will also behave as if he succumbs to the subservient role until he is convinced that there is a genuine effort towards sincerity to the contrary.

Training the black worker is an inevitable or rather unavoidable exercise caused by lack of white artisans, not necessarily brought about by the genuine need to train workers, and will as such always be suspect on both sides of the line but particularly on the black side. The artisan will see it as a means not only of assistance and necessity but of substitution, whilst the black worker will see it as a means of meeting the emergency and also of increasing his emoluments. Whichever way we view it, the worker does not seem to think of it as a necessity for the country's benefit. The whole issue of the utilisation of black workers is confused in the first instance by the fact that it is handled from two different platforms. Government has its own way which in some instances does not necessarily tally with the methods or aspirations of the businessman but has to be adopted by law. Hence it becomes difficult to find a situation where the industrialist is in a position to implement his methods without having to accommodate the dictates of the law.

In the interim, here is a black worker who is trained and is convinced within himself that he knows the ins and outs of a particular skill. He feels ready and keen to put his knowledge to practice; he is urged towards this also by the fact that his own group will now look up to him; he has acquired an important image; he sees himself as one who will now be able to handle jobs from an authoritative perspective; he is no longer a 'boy' but a boss in his own right. He is assured in the first instance of an increase in his rate which he normally gets without trouble and lands in the job situation. He gets disgruntled in the first encounter when he realises that he is still not allowed to use his knowledge in an independent capacity; he eventually realises that his charge-hand is determined to 'keep him in his place' and of course from then on there is a tussle between the two usually resulting in a black versus white situation and not, as it really should be, artisan versus trainee. I think the ball is on the white side of the court with the black worker waiting anxiously for a return.

The whole structure would change, I believe, if our foremen and charge-hands handled the trained black worker in the same way as they handle a trainee. He needs to be guided onto his new platform, he should be afforded opportunity to implement his knowledge, he should be wedged into the responsibility for which he was trained and of course he should be made to feel wanted. This involves and necessitates a change of heart and outlook particularly on the part of the charge-hand, who will be working with the trained worker. Here, I believe, the foreman should play an important role by impressing on the charge-hand the need to do this. There are of course occasions when the system cracks down even on the foreman level and reaches a distorted proportion at charge-hand level.

The Management of Black Labour: Welfare Facilities

WILBY L. BAQWA

(Presented at a seminar of the South African Institute of Personnel Management, Johannesburg, 11 and 12 June 1973)

My first duty is to thank the South African Institute of Personnel Management for its laudable effort in endeavouring to solve labour problems through these exchanges of ideas. This type of bold and determined effort is bound to result ultimately in a labour policy that will be reasonably acceptable, and suggests the need for a concerted effort to implement those things necessary for good human relations not only in the work situation, but also in our everyday life.

We are now starting to communicate positively rather than in the usual apologetic manner. The evolutionary period into which the South African black man has now entered is subjected, amongst other things, to the same problems that face what are generally known as 'developing nations' or 'modernising societies'. In the words of Professor Freeman Butt, these are:

(a) ethnic and racial integration
(b) religious and cultural pluralism
(c) technical and intellectual specialisation
(d) rural transformation and industrial urbanisation
(e) popular participation in public affairs
(f) national-building and national development

I find it difficult to separate behavioural attitudes from culture, hence my inclination to focus our scope and basis of research on Clyde Klickhohn's definition, which says culture constitutes 'that part of learned behaviour which is shared with others. It is our social legacy, as contrasted with our organic heredity'. Herein, I think, lies the answer to the questions which have brought us here today. How do we get profitable productivity from our black worker - do we have to know his likes and dislikes, do we have to accord him the same procedural treatment that used to prevail in his hereditary past, or do we merely have to accommodate him withi within the framework of industrial programmes? These questions are not rhetorical; on the contrary, their answers open up the gateway to solutions of our industrial, and in many ways also, social and co-existence problems. My contribution is based predominantly on the building construction industry and should be viewed from that angle even though there will be much that is of universal application. Let us now look at the various aspects of welfare facilities.

Feeding Schemes

I gather from Mr Hersov of Anglo-Vaal that the gold mines provide free meals in their compounds. This seems a generous and considerate gesture. I have had meals in some compounds and have found the diet reasonably good. I do not know if this is so in all compounds but I believe that there is an acceptable standardisation. It is possible to prepare meals on mines because the work situation, the compound and the hospital are in the same environment. Hence the atmosphere in a mine situation becomes domestic rather than purely industrial. In industry the black worker tends to view the various aspects of his working life separately. He does not regard items like feeding as being a company responsibility but tends to accept this as his own commitment. He is prepared to adjust his hunger and thirst to the limits of his meagre budget, and no one else is competent enough to advise him on this.

I have found sufficient justification for such views when considering that the budget spoken of here is in the region of some R10 to R12 per week and needs superhuman expertise to handle. In the final analysis, it does not even matter whether the diet in question is sumptuous or not, the main point for this type of worker is that his pay-packet should be untouched. Any deductions should be at his request and not the result of any foreign or official inducement. Feeding-schemes even if heavily subsidised are always looked at sceptically, and very rarely go on for long particularly in urban work situations. In secluded rural areas the worker usually has no choice but to use whatever amenities are available. I am inclined to side with the view that a cafeteria service is the answer to feeding problems. In that way the worker is able to adjust his needs to his pay-packet. My experience in our company has led me to conclude that it is futile arranging for a subsidised feeding-scheme. In fact the few trials we have had along the Reef have all since been discontinued at the demand of the employees.

Accommodation Facilities

This section of welfare service always generates many problems. For the migrant worker, the only official amenities available are compounds or hostels, which come under direct control of local authorities. Some municipal authorities do make available separate sections of these hostels to individual concerns, in which case administration and general security can be improved to the standard codes of the particular organisation. Compounds made available to industry are usually those of discontinued mines. These are understandably neglected and usually outmoded in outlay and structure. The general trend then is to use available amenities and to improve them within permissible limits. Some companies like the organisation I am attached to will, after securing separate blocks for their exclusive use in a particular hostel or compound, have their own cleaners and security personnel. They will also have an administration office on the premises where all employees will have their matters handled. These will range from security to hospitalisation. Quite frequently after the initial handling these matters will then be given over to the welfare department for finalising.

The housing shortage in the locations makes it necessary for an organisation to have close ties with local authorities, whose sympathy in such matters is always vital. The assistance given to workers in their search for houses in the location is, besides putting some official tag on the application, time-saving as well. Normally if a worker had to negotiate on his own he would initially be off work for some two days. Thereafter he would have to frequent the local authority for days on end, whereas a letter or phone call could easily do the trick, perhaps even with better success. People will try to acquire for themselves a good name with an organisation so as to be able to have the necessary qualifications (10 years with one organisation or a total of 15 years with different organisations in the same area), to own or rather rent a municipal house.

Black accommodation usually just means four walls and a roof. On taking occupation of a new municipal house, it is not uncommon to find the tenant spending the first fortnight cementing floors, plastering walls and installing ceilings. These seem to be luxuries that the black person officially does not appear entitled to. I was envying a new white township that is in the planning stage, with excavating machines and cranes digging trenches, laying pipes and going through all the necessary pre-planning stages long before the houses are erected. This type of operation takes place long after black houses are erected. The same applies to hostels. I read with interest the other day that the City Council of Johannesburg was planning to instal a heating-system in the already occupied hostel in Alexandra Township.

I once went to fetch an employee who had been injured on duty to take him to hospital for treatment. I got to his compound room in the early hours of the morning when workers were getting ready to go to work. In this particular compound, the beds were (still are) three concrete tiers one above the other from slightly above the floor right up to near the ceiling, or rather where the ceiling would normally be. The patient was sleeping on the bottom bed and his two colleagues were seated on his bed pumping their primus stoves so as to boil water to wash or to make themselves a cup of tea. The same thing happened right round the room which could easily have housed some 21 people. This was the type of home workers had inherited in the work situation. It is always argued that this type of accommodation was no different or perhaps even better than the homes of the workers. Actually, this subject is one that needs special attention and study, quite urgently too.

Transport Systems

Casting your eyes northwards on your way from Soweto into town via the new Soweto Highway, just before you get to Ophirton, you see the mine dumps. If it is between 6 a.m. and 8 a.m. or between 4 p.m. and 7 p.m., you are bound to start wondering whether there is a location on the mine dumps. You come across all sorts of sights but the common one of the men pulling the women up the mine dumps so as to get to the nearest railway station always strikes me as a joke in planning. The hundreds of light industries in the area employ numerous people from Soweto. There is no direct transport programme, the nearest station being some miles away, necessitating the climbing of mine dumps, crossing of river beds and, worst of all, crossing the notorious Soweto Highway which has already claimed many lives. Just recently a footbridge was built over the highway and this at least reduced one risk. The highway itself is used by buses, taxis, pirate taxis, private cars and company vehicles. Peak hours in the highway bring one face to face with a most confused and unorganised traffic disorder, with cars travelling on the extreme right side of the road in over-taking.

Board any of the Soweto trains and you start wondering what would happen if traffic cops were empowered to ticket trains for overloading. A woman boarding a train at Park Station after work is lucky if she can disembark at her normal station owing to this unbelievable overcrowding. One can only praise the designers of the coaches for they must have allowed for at least four times the permissible stress load. Bus transport is often hardly adequate, and is unavailable on routes that are served by the railways regardless of the need for feeder services from the station to the work place. Individual concerns do not readily make available private transport for their employees except perhaps where overtime is worked and knocking-off times are at awkward hours. There also seems to be very little co-operation by various companies in tackling this transport problem on a regional basis. One feels that if industries in an area got together and tackled the problems jointly, local and central governmental authorities would be more sympathetic.

I was travelling to the Free State the other day following a tipper truck. I was about to overtake it when I noticed that an accident was about to happen. This truck had a load of black workers possibly en route to a site. I saw the back end inclining gradually and the load was tipped onto the road. Fortunately the driver was travelling slowly and the load thus merely slid down with no casualties. This type of makeshift transport seems to be the order of the day for black workers. It seems that anything that can get them to point X is all right; whether on a cold wintry morning or a rainy summer day an open truck will still do the job. I notice with pleasure that local authorities are now demanding canopies over any transport used for the black worker. It does seem evident that not the employer, nor the local authority, nor the government give full attention to the transport needs and requirements of the black worker. Where some consideration is given, it is very rarely adequate and appropriate.

Contract Labour System

It was on the findings of the Stallard Commission in 1924 that the contract labour system, which had in actual fact been in operation since the days of diamond digging, became legalised. There are close to two million migrant workers in South and South West Africa and all indications point towards a tremendous expansion of the system following the government's decision in 1968 to base the country's economy on this system. Already in Johannesburg there are giant hostels in Alexandra Township which will house 40 000 men and 20 000 women. Black labour is recruited from the homelands or from countries outside the Republic under contract for a year and in some instances for two years. On completion of this period the contract is either renewed or the worker goes back home. These workers are accommodated in hostels and compounds, where essential facilities are not always available. In compounds provided by mines, the administration is solely in the hands of the mining house concerned and essentials like kitchens, bathrooms, halls and sports grounds are usually provided. Hostels, on the other hand, fall under Bantu Regional Boards. Until recently they were on the outskirts of towns but it is now common to find them dwarfing location houses. Soweto alone has about seven hostels and the population forms quite a portion of the township.

From this system emerges a unique society, a society that could perhaps be singled out as being responsible in one way or another for the numerous anomalies attributed to the black people. Basically there are two types of workers: the urban and the rural dweller (hostel group). The rural dweller, on being subjected to restricted and sometimes even unnatural conditions in the hostel, usually finds himself envying his westernised counterpart who stays in the location. He breaks ties completely with his rural background, stops writing home, ignores his family commitments and starts making local contacts. Eventually this worker hardly ever sleeps at the hostel, becoming an illegal sub-tenant generally in a shebeen or some such loose house. Others find their way into the backyards in the white suburbs and end up by having new wives. Some of our notorious gangsters and criminals have come from this drop-out society. Some of them manage to wangle out of the contract permits and soon have their urban qualifications through backdoor means. It is this desperate society, bent on making or even bettering the urban grade, that creates numerous complications. Whilst staying in the hostels they will terrorise their mates in an endeavour to display their urban attainments. With the recent innovation of hostels in the locations, they will even challenge the prowess of the neighbouring elements and terrorise them. So they go on and on until they even get to learn how big-time criminals make their money, and emulate them. Their aim is to dominate, in the work situation as well. They become agitators and not necessarily leaders, to the extent that even the urban stalwarts dwindle into silence. In trying to quell a feeding-scheme strike the other day, I was stunned by the reticence of the majority of the workers. After a private session with an innocent hand-picked worker, I got to know that they all feared X and his gang, who had told them not to eat the food any more. By mere coincidence the worker X was transferred to another site and the same type of strike started there in a matter of days. Sometimes we make the drastic error of making this type of worker an induna or gang-boss. The work force then becomes a crowd of frightened workers who are never at ease in their jobs. Contract labour systems, to my mind, are only suited to mine settings and should not be encouraged in other industries. The social menace created by this system both in towns and in the homelands makes one feel that it should either be revised drastically or scrapped completely.

In an endeavour to obviate some of these evils, some companies, like the one I am attached to, arrange with the local authorities for some blocks of a particular hostel to be allotted to them and then these are run under company administration with closer supervision over the individuals. In this way it takes a shorter time to notice any inmate whose movements tend to be irregular, and disciplinary measures can always be speeded up to prevent his influence spreading. In practice these workers are supposed to stay for the duration of the contract but so many of them find themselves back home much earlier because the charge-hand regards them as stupid. 'They cannot even understand English or Afrikaans.' A clerk once asked why we did not say the same of immigrant artisans who could speak neither of the official languages. I notice the official description of a contract labourer is a chap who will learn to use his pick and shovel.

Whether industry really can afford to have such expensive cheap labour is a questionable thing. The contract worker is responsible also in many ways for spreading venereal diseases and illnesses like tuberculosis. This is the logical result of his desire to become human. For fear of being sent home or to hospital after having contracted such diseases, he will try by all means to conceal his plight and will only be discovered at an advanced chronic stage. By then, he will have been in contact with thousands of other people.

Suggested Corrective Measures

(a) Contract labour should have similar amenities as on the mines - their stay in the hostels should be accorded as much human consideration as possible.

(b) The practice of having these hostels in the locations should be discouraged completely.

(c) Different companies should be allotted their own blocks in the hostels to allow for closer scrutiny and individual administration. Perhaps individual companies who have need for such labour should be allowed to build their own hostels which could conform to set codes.

(d) Provision should be made, even on a temporary basis, for families of these workers to visit them for a week or two.

My Plea to I.L.O.

LUCY MVUBELO

(Address prepared for (but not delivered at) meeting on Apartheid, International Labour Organisation, Geneva, 15 June 1973)

Mr President, Ministers of different portfolios, and fellow workers. I wish to thank first and foremost all those who have been instrumental in giving me the privilege of speaking at this workers' parliament, and you, Mr Chairman, and all the Trade Union movement, which has shown great concern over the problems of black workers in South Africa.

My purpose in coming before you is to correct the record and to make the truth known to all as interested working class. I am a trade unionist and a worker who knows how the ordinary African worker suffers under the discriminatory and harmful effects of apartheid in South Africa, because I am a practising union leader in South Africa.

I represent over 18 000 African workers employed in clothing factories in Johannesburg. Fortunately, my union also has members in the predominantly Nationalist area of the Orange Free State and Northern Cape. It is unfortunate that at this stage clothing factories established in the newly formed Bantustans or homelands cannot be organised in terms of the legislation, and the claim of the South Africa government that they are looking after these workers' conditions and wages. I repeat that it is unfortunate, because many of my union members were taken to these areas to train workers. I have to deal daily with the problems of the workers under the apartheid system. I am not fortunate enough to look at them from outside South Africa or from a position of safety and distance; this is why I can speak with sincerity, feeling and authority, because I am there and not somewhere else.

For years I have heard all the arguments, the proposals and suggestions for removing the apartheid system and I must express my doubts as to whether what has up until now been suggested be either desirable or effective for me or my fellow African workers in South Africa. I do not discount the help and assistance which could be furnished by well-meaning people and organisations who desire what I personally want, but any programme and action for the elimination of apartheid, and the improvement of the black workers' conditions of life, must be jointly planned with the actual representation of the resident South African workers. This will be the only effective way to bring change and the elimination of the apartheid system.

Don't isolate us, don't break off contact and don't advocate disengagement and withdrawal of foreign investments, because you will still be talking in another ten years' time and the situation in South Africa will not have changed to any degree. The trade union movement in South Africa for Africans, coloureds, Indians and whites is the only instrument which will bring about change, and this is what must be considered and must be achieved. This was demonstrated by African, coloured and Indian workers in the recent strike actions which took place in Durban, Johannesburg and other major urban areas. These workers proved to the world that they need trade union rights, and also that the economy of the country depended on their labour. In short, there are over 400 000 black workers who are ready to be unionised. What they need is leadership.

Investments from foreign countries have created job opportunities for thousands of African workers who would otherwise have been unemployed. Thanks to the pressure of trade unions in these foreign countries, black workers employed in these foreign companies have recently gained large wage increases, much larger than the wage increase obtained by black workers employed by South African companies.

In the textile and clothing industries, the minimum wage of a male worker has been increased from R8,50 per week to R20,00 per week. Married workers get another R2 per week plus R1,50 for each child up to four children. This brings the minimum wage up to R29 per week. Workers are given educational bursaries for their children for high school and universities.

I appeal to our trade union colleagues not to make the task of the black people of South Africa more difficult by asking for withdrawal of these companies from South Africa, or for boycotting South African goods. By so doing, the black workers will lose their employment and the government will tell them that their jobs have been closed by the insistence of their fellow trade unionists overseas. We are all against apartheid, but do not make the life of African, coloured and Indian workers unbearable by throwing them out of work.

Knowing the conditions and the South African policy, may I make use of an old adage that governments come and go, and so the policies of the government may also change, but the policy of the trade union movement shall always be one. Hence my contention is that the I.L.O. Workers' Committee should hold a dialogue with the non-racist South African Federation of Trade Unions, which will lead to a better understanding and education, not only for South Africa, but for all other countries who suffer at the hands of segregation and apartheid.

Black Workers and Unions

LUCY MVUBELO

(Address delivered at a symposium on 'The Optimum Involvement of Manpower in Business and Industry' under the auspices of the United States-South Africa Leader Exchange Program, Umhlanga Rocks, August 1973)

Recent developments show a steadily widening gap between the rising aspirations of black workers and the offerings of employers. The initiative for industrial change has gone over to the black workers, and it is only with the formation of black worker unions that an impetus is created for the good intentions of some managements to be carried out in practice. It is industrial activity on the part of black workers which is forcing the pace of change.

From the beginning of this year it has become clear that black workers are not tolerating the position into which they have been driven by inferior education, legislation, and the strict implementation of repressive labour regulations. Strikes by black workers have always an element of surprise since such activity does not conform to the image of the docile black worker who is quite unready for the responsibilities of trade unions. In Natal, where a series of strikes paralysed the Durban-Pinetown industrial complex in February 1973, the rising anger of black workers was felt by certain registered trade unions which had evolved some form of direct contact with black workers in various industries. Warnings made by these unions, in particular the Textile Workers' Industrial Union and the Garment Workers' Industrial Union of Natal, had no effect whatever. But although specific warnings were made, neither the trade unionists nor the employers expected the popularity of the strike movement and the dynamism of the workers. There were at least 65 000 workers at 130 factories on strike in the period of a month.

Behind the wage demands of the workers lay a clear perception of the needs of themselves and their families. Workers justified their demands for considerable wage increases by their desire to educate their children, to feed and clothe the family, to pay the rent, and to get to and from work. The workers milling about outside the factories, to a large extent leaderless, but with heightened expectations and the weight of numbers, were testament to the government's refusal to recognise African unionism or to allow recognised trade unions to include African workers. The government, by refusing to adjust labour policy to the reality, which is that the majority of the workers are black, had to abide the chaos of shopfloor demands which ranged tremendously between a desired wage and a negotiable demand and other demands which were difficult to reduce to specific industrial grievances.

It is worth quoting the words of the workers to understand the extremities to which they had been driven. 'We are men and women who want to see if tomorrow can be better than today because today is a struggle which is very heavy and we would like to have hope for the future.' 'Everything costs more these days', said a textile worker. 'It even cost more to sleep! The blankets I weave I cannot buy in the shops.'

The strikes were more widespread and determined than at any time previously by black workers in South African labour history. The table below gives some indication of the rising mood of anger of black workers.

Number of black (African, coloured, and Indian) workers on strike:

1960	5 266
1965	3 540
1970	3 303
1973	85 000 (estimated)

From Natal the strikes spread to the Transvaal and the Eastern Cape, although some of the momentum was lost in the process.

In striking, workers have secured some immediate relief from the poverty wages earned by most black workers. Immediate increases of between R1 and R2 were given by employers in most cases in Natal, while increases in the Transvaal clothing industry on average were R1 or less. The increases which were granted by no means brought the mass of black workers within reach of the poverty datum line, and many workers still earn below R10,51, at which point African workers contribute to the Unemployment Insurance Fund and are entitled to its benefits. Mass action by black workers to raise wages is likely to occur again until industrial workers (who are really a privileged section of the black community) earn at least above the poverty datum line without having to rely on overtime or production bonuses. It is estimated that about 80 per cent of African workers earn below the poverty datum line which was averaged for the principal urban areas.

The workers' struggle for a living wage in the industrial sector is a formidable one, but when we look at other sectors the picture is even bleaker. African workers constitute the highest proportion of workers in the most unrewarding occupations: mine work, domestic service, and farm labour. In these occupations wages are extremely low, and it is no exaggeration to say that farm workers in particular live in conditions of desperate poverty. The table on the next page shows the breakdown of African workers into the major occupational divisions.

The disproportionate number of African workers in the agricultural sector is an indication of the forced occupational immobility of African workers, particularly on white farms, who are immobilised by a special set of limiting regulations. African workers in the 'service' category are mainly in domestic service with exceptionally long hours and low wages.

Yet the people in these lowly occupations are fortunate in one sense in that they are not part of the large pool of black unemployed. Census statistics concerning African people are never very reliable, but the 1970 Census found that 300 000 African people were unemployed. Even with a projected growth rate of 5,5 per cent per annum (which now seems unlikely) the number of black unemployed will rise to 414 000 by 1975. But even these figures are conservative. A leading Stellenbosch academic has spoken of black unemployment in the region of 1,25 million people, and a leading industrial consultant, Dr Lawrence McCrystal has estimated that, given the current rate of economic growth, there would be 728 000 unemployed by 1975, virtually all of them black people (Survey of Race Relations, 1972, p. 253).

Whatever the precise figures may be, there can be no

doubt of tremendous black underemployment and unemployment. Workers who demand higher wages and who are in lowly occupations are readily replaced, and wages are kept to below poverty levels because of the threat of displacement by the labour pools in the reserves.

Major occupational divisions	Total	Percentage of economically active Africans (rounded off)
Professional, technical and related worker	93 300	1,7
Administrative and managerial worker	3 400	0,6
Clerical and related worker	96 280	1,7
Sales worker	110 880	2,0
Service worker	1 011 940	18,1
Farm and forestry worker, fisherman	2 051 600	36,6
Production and transport worker, miner and labourer	1 688 840	30,1
Not classifiable by occupation and unspecified	548 900	9,8

Provisional figures (Statistical News Release, 19 February 1973, p. 11 no. 70)

Given this situation, one would have expected the state to adopt emergency programs to absorb the starving unemployed and to relieve the pressure on those workers with jobs. In other countries labour-intensive public works would be brought into operation to absorb such a large pool of unemployed.

Because of the low wages, inequitable employment structure, labour regulations, enforced migrancy, victimisation, and a high proportion of unemployment, it is not surprising that there are few African trade unions. African trade unions are not recognised by the basic industrial relations legislation in South Africa: the Industrial Conciliation Act. Despite this fact, which acts as a tremendous inhibition to the formation of African trade unions, and a high incidence of bannings of black trade unionists, African trade unions continue, new ones are formed, and membership is rising. The following are the existing African trade unions:

Membership of existing African trade unions	
National Union of Clothing Workers	18 464
Engineering and Allied Workers' Union	500
Transport and Allied Workers' Union	400
Laundry and Dry Cleaning Industries Union	500
African Chemical Workers' Union	300
African Tobacco Workers' Union	360
Metal and Allied Workers' Union	400

The figures on African unionisation are extremely depressing given the vast potential for organisation. With a few notable exceptions, registered trade unions just have not been giving African workers in their industries the assistance in the formation of African trade unions.

Following the destruction of mass movements among African workers, in particular SACTU (South African Congress of Trade Unions) which combined political and industrial demands, the growth of membership of surviving African trade unions and the establishment of new unions have been problematical. The best (and at present the only) example of a large-scale African trade union is the National Union of Clothing Workers (S.A.) (N.U.C.W.), which works closely with the Garment Workers' Union of South Africa in Johannesburg The N.U.C.W. originated after the passage of the Bantu Labour (Settlement of Disputes) Act in 1953, which specifically excluded African women from the definition of an 'employee'. With the close co-operation of the Garment Workers' Union of South Africa, the N.U.C.W., which has 400 elected shop stewards, now enjoys considerable recognition from employers at the industrial and plant level. During a recent series of work steppages in the clothing industry in the Transvaal, the N.U.C.W. organisers negotiated on behalf of the workers for cost of living increases, despite the hostility of the Department of Labour. Despite the relatively fortunate position of the N.U.C.W., the Union is denied any form of direct representation on the Industrial Council of the Transvaal Clothing Industry. When the Union requested observer status during cost-of-living negotiations, the representative of the Department of Labour threatened to walk out, as he claimed personally to represent all African clothing workers.

Instead of the expansion of African unionism, the government is proposing the expansion of various types of works committees with a view to eradicating existing African trade unions. After the strikes in Natal, the government was faced with the problem of the legitimate representation of the interests of African workers. Either the Bantu Labour (Settlement of Disputes) Act of 1953 would have to be amended to allow changes in representation or the Industrial Conciliation Act of 1956 would have to be amended to allow for the recognition of African trade unions. The government decided on the former course, the expansion of works committees and the destruction of African trade unions. The position of African trade unions is threatened by the new Bantu Labour Relations Regulations Amendment Act. As the Minister of Labour said in reply to a question from Helen Suzman: 'If we had wanted to prohibit these trade unions, Minister Schoeman would already have done so in 1953. This has never been done; we have felt that they could simply struggle on like that. I think that the establishment of these works committees will really deprive those favourite Bantu trade unions of the Honourable Member of their life's blood and any necessity for existence' (Hansard 18, 11 June 1973, column 8779). It is obvious that the Department of Labour will concentrate on the development of works committees to exclude the possibility of the formation of African trade unions, and those trade unions already in existence will face a hard future.

There is evidence that works committees are expanding at a steady rate, although they constitute a small fraction of their potential, which has been estimated at around 30 000.

Number of works committees

	'Non-statutory'	Statutory
February 1973	117	18
March 1973	161	31

The 'non-statutory' works committees of the past are not the liaison committees of the present Act. The workers who attempt to work within the 'Bantu labour relations system' face the following problems:

1 / They cannot negotiate with employers when negotiations are taking place on an Industrial Council level. They are limited to seeking improvements only for each plant.

2 / The works committees do not have the opportunity of meeting regularly amongst themselves to formulate a distinct policy.

3 / The top management does not attend meetings: usually it is the labour officer or welfare officer who chairs the meetings, which cannot make any decisions or express any definite point of view.

4 / There is no established procedure for the handling of grievances, as in the case of shop stewards.

5 / There is no opportunity for workers to hear from their representatives what was decided at the meeting; i.e. there are no facilities for a report-back meeting.

6 / The white front-line supervisors feel that the works committee members are trying to undermine their authority and refuse to take up complaints.

7 / There is no opportunity for works committee representatives to get education in negotiation or even basic literacy.

8 / There is always the feeling (which is often justified) that workers will be victimised if they say the wrong thing or speak their minds. Managers do not like to hear criticism from workers, especially if the criticism is justified.

9 / Fundamentally, the workers stand in awe of the authority figures in the plant and do not express legitimate complaints. The atmosphere in the South African plant is highly authoritarian, and communication is generally a one-way process.

Homeland leaders have made their position on the works committee system quite clear. They were not consulted on the changes which have been introduced, and feel that if trade unions are good enough for white, coloured, and Asian workers, then they should certainly be good for African workers.

The introduction of the Physical Planning Act has tremendously affected African workers, particularly African workers on the Rand. One of the provisions of the Act has been to implement a 2,5 : 1 ratio in the Pretoria-Witwatersrand-Vereeniging area, of African workers to white workers at every plant. This has limited tremendously the number of African workers who are taken on in industry in urban areas. The Transvaal garment industry has been hit particularly hard, and skilled African workers are finding it increasingly difficult to get work, even although there is a shortage of skilled labour in the industry.

As a result the clothing industry is expanding in other areas, and dying on the Rand. The growth rate is now 39,6 per cent in the Western Cape, 61,9 per cent in Natal, 68 per cent in the border industrial areas, but only 5,4 per cent in the Transvaal, which has always been the centre of the women's garment industry.

The government has now announced that the lax manner in which the Act had previously been administered will be changed. The Department of Planning has told employers that the law will now be strictly enforced, and African garment workers may be discharged because they are illegally employed.

Possibly even more worrying for black workers is the extension of repressive labour regulations by Bantu Administration Boards which will fall directly under the control of the Department of Bantu Administration and Development. Control over African labour is being removed from the labour offices of the local authorities and centralised on a regional and national basis. Africans are anticipating that people regarded as economically 'superfluous' will be deported to the already overcrowded Bantustans at an increasing rate.

The chairman of the East Rand Bantu Administration Board, Mr Kallie van der Merwe, has already said that one of the greatest aims of the boards is that economically inactive Africans will in time disappear from 'white' South Africa. An estimated 300 000 African people under his board's jurisdiction are likely to be affected and removed to the reserves.

The increased mobility of labour which, it was promised, would accompany the inauguration of the new labour control areas has in practice turned out to be far less than originally anticipated, and if the regulations are to be strictly implemented then a harvest of bitterness will be reaped.

Finally I must mention the position of foreign firms

in South Africa. Wild claims are being made for the enlightened wage and personnel policies of various foreign companies in South Africa, particularly now there is so much criticism of foreign capital in South Africa. There is no doubt that certain foreign companies are doing a good job in revising their labour policies, but it is also true that all this is taking place only with tremendous external pressure. In some cases, however, foreign companies have done nothing at all to improve the wages and working conditions of their African workers. In giving evidence to the Parliamentary Commission of Enquiry into the employment practices of British companies in South Africa, it appears that a leading Natal concern, which has had a fair reputation for good labour relations in South Africa, does not even have a plan to bring the wages of its workers up to the poverty datum line. The issue of foreign firms recognising African trade unions has not been faced yet, and in many cases South African firms show more understanding.

The task which I have had to perform has not been a pleasant one. I had wished it would have been possible to be able to say everything is changing and that African workers were benefiting from industrial development in South Africa and enjoying full industrial rights. This is still far from the case.

What is needed is a clear and forceful demand for the recognition of African trade unions, and the will to work with African workers to make this dream possible in our time.

Black Allied Workers' Union: Policy Statement

The Sales and Allied Workers' Association (S.A.), which is a trade union for black workers engaged in sales and other allied jobs in the Commercial-Distributive Trade, was founded in June 1971.

This Union:

(a) realising the peculiar unique economic position in which members of the black community are;

(b) being aware of racial discrimination, lack of job opportunities, traditional colour prejudice, wage disparity between black and white workers, lack of trained, skilled and technical knowledge among black workers;

(c) realising the urgent need for a change in the labour system in commerce, industry and private sectors;

(d) realising that single, autonomous trade unions are limited and powerless to bring about that desired change in a labour system that is entrenched in the existing industrial laws, tradition and prejudice;

(e) and, further realising the need for black workers' unity and solidarity in the approach to labour problems peculiar to the black worker and the country as a whole,

accepted a mandate given them at the Black Workers' General Meeting, held at the St John's Berchman R.C. Mission Hall, Orlando East, Johannesburg, on 27 August 1972 - to found an 'umbrella trade union' that would cater for and embrace all workers in various job categories (crafts) - the Black Allied Workers' Union.

The Black Allied Workers' Union is a trade union for all those who are by law, tradition, racial prejudice and attitude, discriminated against, and find themselves in a position of economic deprivation, with denial of the right for collective bargaining through the process of trade unionism; and who are being discriminated against in the work field because of race and colour of the skin.

The Black Allied Workers' Union's purposes and aims are:

1 / To organise and unite all black workers into a powerful labour force that would earn the respect of and de facto recognition by both employers and the government.

2 / To consult with existing black trade unions to effect the calling of a 'Black Workers' Conference' where the Black Allied Workers' Council shall be elected;

3 / To improve the workers' knowledge through the process of general and specialised (occupational) education programmes and thus better the worker's skill and know-how by conducting of leadership courses; labour seminars; lectures and specialised commercial courses; circulation of pamphlets and other information materials.

4 / To establish labour training centres, vocational and technical schools (where possible) for black youth.

5 / To enlighten and assist black workers where and how to obtain their rights and benefits as contained in various industrial legislations such as unemployment money, accident money, maternity and death benefits.

6 / To negotiate (on behalf of workers) with employers for better wages and acceptable working conditions.

7 / To protect workers from exploitation and victimisation by employers.

8 / To encourage savings and found a cash loan bank where black people could invest; to organise cooperatives and other commercial schemes in order to improve the black workers' community and economic life.

9 / To make the black worker realise his significance as a human being in a job situation.

10 / To be spokesman for black workers in any matters that affect them in the work field.

KwaZulu Executive Council: Black Trade Union Rights

(Press release by the Executive Council of KwaZulu, 19 September 1974)

A letter was laid before the Executive Council in which the Secretary of the Department of Bantu Administration and Development explains the implications of the amendment to the Bantu Labour Relations Act, making it 'The Bantu Labour Settlement of Disputes Act No. 48 of 1953'.

The purpose of the Secretary's letter is to inform homelands leaders and their urban representatives that they have no legal powers to intercede in labour disputes in white areas. It was stated in the letter that such intercession by homelands leaders and their urban representatives only impedes the task of the Department of Labour and neutralises the machinery that the Department has at its disposal. Where liaison may be necessary between homelands leaders it was stated that such liaison can only take place through the medium of the Department of Bantu Administration and Development. The prescribed procedure is that if we receive requests from other departments, employers' organisations, trade unions, industrial councils, employers or employees, the homelands leaders must bring the request to the notice of their Commissioner-General, whilst urban representatives must advise their governments immediately of any requests addressed to them. The Honourable the Minister of Bantu Administration and Development will discuss with Commissioners-General the task of homelands leaders in connection with strikes in the white areas. In the interim it is desirable that homelands leaders' attention be invited to the provisions of the law in this regard and to request them not to react to requests for intercession unless such requests emanate from this Department.

Whilst we noted the implications of the Act in question as explained to us by the Secretary, we stated that the continued refusal of the Republican Government to give black trade union rights places us as a so-called government in our relations with our people in a most invidious position. We cannot see ourselves turning a deaf ear to any pleas from our people for intercession, as our people have no proper machinery for negotiation, and we cannot be insensitive to any alleged exploitation of our people. Were we to adopt this attitude we might as well fold up as a government. We therefore wish to state that the solution is not the procedure proposed here but the granting of trade union rights to our people.

The Development of Effective Labour Relations

B.I. DLADLA

(Address to the Natal Midlands Personnel Management Institute at the University of Natal, Pietermaritzburg, 28 May 1974)

Let me say at the outset that, although there has been progress in Natal in the area of labour relations, we still have a long way to go. We are at the stage where we are only getting an outline of the major problems which we have to face, where people still talk of unique problems and refuse to acknowledge that we have to rely on established procedures for resolving industrial problems. We still have to guard against over-optimism and the feeling that things will get better without any effort. I am glad to be speaking on the development of effective labour relations because nothing is inevitable and we need a conscious will to improve working conditions.

I would like to distinguish between labour relations and human relations in my talk because this distinction is important to my conclusions. I am sure you as personnel managers are very conscious of the human relations approach in industry: the approach which deals with the worker as a human being with a definite scale of wants and desires which have to be satisfied at work and at home. I am more concerned, however, with labour relations: the approach which acknowledges that a labour force is not simply a collection of individuals but has a collective will. I feel that it is right that workers should express themselves as a collective unity, and in my talk I will be dealing with ways in which this healthy solidarity among workers can be channelled in the most constructive way. And possibly more important for personnel managers, I want to deal with what I feel to be the correct response from management to the upsurge of activity among workers we have all recently experienced.

As personnel managers you will know that in every industry there are firms with outstanding labour relations, and others with a painful history of bitterness and antagonism. It is this problem which is faced by the workers in industry when they establish themselves as a trade union. This is a most important point for an understanding of why trade unions and, in particular, the African trade unions springing up in Natal have rejected works committees as a means of improving labour relations. They have learned from hard experience that while some firms will listen with respect to the opinions of the works committees or liaison committees, in other firms workers who express similar views will find themselves out on the street. It is also a hard fact that the Department of Labour has done very little indeed to protect representatives of workers on works committees or liaison committees. Despite a number of cases of obvious victimisation handled by trade unions in Natal, and referred to the Department of Labour, not one case has been resolved to the worker's satisfaction, either by getting his job back or by receiving satisfactory compensation as due in terms of the Bantu Labour Relations Regulation Act of 1953.

But there are wider objections which can be made to works committees or liaison committees and in my view these can be summed up by saying that the approach involved in representation of workers at each factory is a modified human relations approach. Works committees and liaison committees are unsatisfactory for effective labour relations because they do not crystallise the collective will of the workers and bring it out in the open. Representatives on works committees and liaison committees are tongue-tied in the presence of management and often do not come out with what are legitimate grievances, and so the issues escalate into major industrial unrest. Representation in the factory in the form of works committees and liaison committees is based on trust, which is a moral attribute and not an industrial characteristic. Instead of allowing the inherent opposition between labour and capital to come into the open and be resolved, representatives often rely on trust in a particular manager, while the trust of the workers in their representatives becomes rapidly eroded, unless there is a trade union to monitor the system. It is a sad fact that in a strike it has been my experience that trust between workers and their representatives on works committees and liaison committees becomes completely eroded and there is a loss of face all round. I am the last person to decry trust of one man in another, but in the difficult problems of industry we need more: we need an effective labour relations system.

Thus my first suggestion is that management should come to realise that there is a legitimate difference in viewpoint between capital and labour, that the collective will of labour be allowed to express itself, and that trade unions are the best vehicles for sound labour relations.

In Natal the following trade unions have been established which are open to all workers but have mainly African membership:

The Metal and Allied Workers' Union
The National Union of Textile Workers
The Union of Clothing Workers
The Furniture and Timber Workers' Union
The Chemical Workers' Industrial Union
The Transport and General Workers' Union

These unions, which are based at Bolton Hall in Durban, are trying to represent the legitimate interests of the workers and maintain industrial peace at the same time. Altogether these trade unions represent 12 000 workers, and there are a further 10 000 workers who have joined the General Factory Workers' Benefit Fund and are in the process of organising themselves. These trade unions are growing day by day, and it looks as though Natal will soon have more workers in trade unions representing mainly African workers than all the other provinces put together. It has been said that there is no stopping an idea whose time has arrived, and African workers find no difficulty in understanding the idea of trade unionism. It is these facts which I would like you to keep in mind when I discuss labour relations as a general issue.

The attitude of management is crucial in the formation, development, and attitude of trade unions. This is a fact which trade unionists are not always ready to acknowledge, but it remains a fact nevertheless. Where management is tough and arrogant, one can expect the union in the industry to be uncompromising and militant in response. On the other hand where management is reasonable and friendly, a trade union, which has its hands full already, is loth to be militant for the sake of militancy. So management should assess its position very carefully before refusing to co-operate with a trade union which already has members in that factory. I would suggest that management could soften much of the antagonism which African trade unions have toward works committees and liaison committees if these committees are not used to forestall the formation and growth of membership of trade unions.

Now just what is involved in working with African trade unions? I would suggest that the following practices would build a good relationship between the trade union and management:

1 / guaranteeing no victimisation for union representatives in the factory;

2 / permitting the union officials reasonable and regular access to the workers outside of working hours;

3 / accepting that the union officials have the right to bring up complaints;

4 / permitting the election of shop stewards for the purpose of taking up complaints and collecting subscriptions;

5 / recognising shop stewards as the authentic voice of workers in the factcry and as the proper persons to settle complaints;

6 / co-operating with the trade union in establishing systematic collection of union dues and/or subscriptions to benefit societies administered by the union;

7 / giving wage increases only in consultation with and through negotiation with the union;

8 / at times of dispute calling in the trade union officials and not the police.

These are the steps I feel will build up a good relationship between trade unions and management. These are the practices which are common in all varieties of industrial societies, and South Africa is no exception to the rule.

But I would suggest that these practices are only the start of a good relationship between the trade union and management. The second step, after recognising the African trade union, is to work toward a civil contract between the trade union and management which would crystallise the good practices established in a particular firm. I am quite aware that present state policy does not provide for the legal recognition of African trade unions, but we are here today to discuss realities and new practices to meet new situations.

A civil contract between the trade union and management would involve the following subject matter:

1 / recognition of the trade union as representative of the workers;

2 / the categories of work and the wages for the categories;

3 / the hours to be worked;

4 / a guarantee of job security for workers who meet the requirements of the conditions of service; and

5 / the administration of benefit schemes such as medical benefit and pension schemes.

As a start both parties could study industrial legislation as it presently exists in South Africa and make sure that conditions are being observed and that workers know of the benefits to which they are entitled. Then both parties could look at the standards laid down by the International Labour Organisation in various conventions and recommendations. The I.L.O. has quite specific standards which have been agreed to by countries from all over the world. These international standards concern such items as sick pay, holiday pay, incentive bonus schemes, maternity leave, hours of work, and other issues which relate generally to all industrial and agricultural workers. Then there are conventions and recommendations for specific industries, such as those which relate to plantations and mines. Since South Africa was expelled from the I.L.O., there has been a serious lapse in observance of these standards in industrial agreements, and it is the responsibility of enlightened firms to write these conditions into civil agreements with African trade unions.

I would suggest that firms do not try to compete with the African trade unions with regard to benefits. All these trade unions provide funeral benefits for the workers at a level which the workers can afford and much cheaper than insurance companies can offer. It has come to my notice that some firms are wanting to compete directly with African trade unions at the level of these benefits. Instead of competition, which is bound to lead to future antagonism, I would suggest that both parties should get together and then be able to improve on the benefits offered by each party.

I would suggest either that the civil agreements should provide for jointly administered medical benefit and pension schemes, or that employers should contribute to schemes established by the trade unions. In America, for example, the trade unions administer the benefits for the workers, which have come about through negotiation, and I think that this is the best alternative in South Africa. I would like to sound a warning about pension schemes, if I may. Many of these schemes run by employers for a particular factory are totally deficient in the contributions made by both parties and these benefits often only come into operation at age 65, while many African workers do not live to that age. I understand that even some industrial pension schemes do not have any workers on pension and that the benefits are pitiful. Too few pension schemes really benefit the workers. Most are old-fashioned, badly run, and do not have the best features of modern far-seeing pension schemes which have been developing rapidly overseas, such as built-in clauses which compensate annually for inflation, or which allow easy transferability of pension rights and obligations to another employer. Often the workers earn no interest on their contributions to pension funds. Generally workers face a severe decrease in their income when they retire, and some pension schemes provide such low payments per month that these do not compensate for the loss of pension from the state.

I would suggest that if private or industrial pension schemes interfere with the right of a worker to draw a state pension, then they should be transformed into provident funds, as is the case in many industries. With the lump sums of money which come from the provident funds, workers could then buy themselves or their sons and daughters adequate accommodation. These are only suggestions but they do, I feel, merit attention from the African trade unions and employers. The best alternative in all cases is that these benefits should be provided by the trade unions which understand the exact problems of the workers and can provide for benefits accordingly....

I would also appeal to foreign companies in South Africa to set the example, to work as yeast in building up enlightened employers' associations, and to recognise the existing African trade unions. We have a long way to go, but at least let us avoid all those mistakes which have been made in the history of other industrial societies.

Black Trade Unions and TUCSA

B.I. DLADLA

(Excerpts from policy speech to KwaZulu Legislative Assembly, 1974)

A start in labour organisation was made in 1971, when the General Factory Workers' Benefit Fund was established. Workers had asked trade union officials in Durban to provide a way in which they could legitimately get together and gradually organise trade unions. The idea, backed up by good funeral benefits, soon caught on and at the moment the General Factory Workers' Benefit Fund has 20 000 members on its books, which makes it the largest black workers' organisation in the country. Gradually workers were brought together from the same factories and industries to discuss the formation of trade unions.

It was at this stage that this government started to become involved in discussions with officials of trade unions and the benefit fund, at their own request. I was invited by these officials to talk to workers about the attitude of the KwaZulu government towards trade unions for black workers. I addressed the inaugural meeting of the Metal and Allied Workers' Union in Pietermaritzburg in May 1972, the first blacks' trade union to be formed in Natal for a long time. Following the February-March strikes in 1973 there was a great upsurge in interest in black trade unions by workers. At the same time there was a recognition by trade union officials that tremendous effort was needed in the field of industrial education, as thousands of black workers were ignorant of what rights they were entitled to at work.

The Institute of Industrial Education was formed on 30 May 1973, to meet this real need. Various institutions such as the registered trade unions in Durban, the South African Institute of Race Relations, and academics, gave the Institute their blessings; and this government was represented at the inaugural meeting by the Honourable Mr J.A.W. Nxumalo representing the

Department of Education and Culture, and by myself representing the Department of Community Affairs. The Chief Executive Councillor had already agreed to serve as Chancellor of the Institute.

Again, this government was requested to address the inaugural meeting of the National Union of Textile Workers held in August, 1973. In the same month, the Union of Clothing Workers was formed.

In January 1974 the Furniture and Timber Workers' Union was formed, and chemical workers are at this moment requesting help in organising themselves.

All these important developments have tended to involve the KwaZulu government for very good reasons, and we must remember that our involvement would not have been necessary had the Republican government provided for recognition of black trade unions, or had Natal employers agreed to recognise these trade unions. In fact there has been tremendous hostility from these two sources, a matter which compounds the difficulties of black workers in seeking out peaceful ways of resolving disputes.

I have been requested by black trade unions to intervene to help solve problems when these unions have exhausted all other forms of negotiation. At Alcan factory in Pietermaritzburg, for instance, the Metal and Allied Workers' Unions requested me to intervene to make sure that they got a seat at the negotiating table when wages were being negotiated between the Boilermakers' Union and the management. In other cases I have responded to urgent calls from the National Union of Textile Workers, which faces tremendous opposition from textile employers, and shocking conditions. Hundreds of workers employed in textile mills in Pinetown faced imprisonment in January 1974 and at times like these the KwaZulu government has to consider the fate of its citizens very urgently.

In the past year there have been important developments affecting black workers on the international scene. At the International Labour Organisation the trade unions resolved to bring about international boycotts of South African goods, and following this decision the British Trade Union Congress sent a mission to South Africa to study conditions at first hand. The British T.U.C. wrote approvingly of the work done in Natal by the Central Administration Services and the Trade Union Advisory

Committee as some of the most dynamic labour organisation seen in the country.

The Trade Union Advisory Committee was formed by the black trade unions in Natal getting together to work out their policy and the way in which we could work together to ensure that black trade unions will eventually be recognised by employers, the registered trade unions, and ultimately the State. It was during discussions with the Advisory Committee that it became clear just how little support the black trade unions were getting from the registered trade unions, which are represented by the Trade Union Council of South Africa (TUCSA). As time went on it became quite clear that not only was TUCSA not helping black trade unions, but it was actually out to control these unions. By establishing parallel trade unions for 'Bantu Workers' these trade unions would hope that the hand of white leadership would rest heavily on these new unions.

Step by step TUCSA moved to isolate the developments in Natal. TUCSA withdrew from a seminar organised by the Institute for Industrial Education and worked on other registered trade unions and such unions as the National Union of Clothing Workers led by Mrs Lucy Mvubelo not to support the Institute. TUCSA then made an announcement that it would start its own education programmes to compete with the Institute.

During the February 1973 strikes, TUCSA did not help in any way and when four trade union officials were banned in February 1974, TUCSA did not condemn these bannings. All that TUCSA has done has been to report what the Minister of Justice has had to say. And now we have seen that TUCSA has taken it upon itself to launch the strongest possible attacks on myself. While it would not be worthwhile to go into all the details of this issue, it becomes clear that TUCSA has a guilty conscience in that it is trying to support white trade union control over black unions. At a time when black trade unions are being harassed by the Security Police and the Bureau for State Security, their officials have had not a word of sympathy from TUCSA.

But we must remember that TUCSA is not composed only of white trade unions; in fact, it is coloured and Indian workers who are in the majority. It is the registered trade unions representing coloured and Indian workers who should be providing support for the development of black trade unions. Instead of this we are finding that in Natal the registered trade unions mainly representing Indian workers are turning their backs on the African workers. When officials of these unions are working with African workers the executive committees are telling them to stop. It is these trade unions which are responsible for negotiating for thousands of African workers and, in many cases, I am sorry to say they agree to the most shocking level of wages for labourers by which they understand they are only 'Bantu workers'. If there is to be goodwill and harmony between all black races in South Africa, then those workers who enjoy legal recognition for their trade unions must extend aid to the new black trade unions. Is it too much to ask that they should make offices available, that they should consult black trade unions, and that instead of black trade unions having to rely on financial aid from international trade union movements, these unions make grants and loans from hundreds of thousands of rands they are storing up in the banks? Is it too much to ask that they support officials who are working with African workers?

Ultimately we will have to consider taking up the policy of the Republican government in respect of trade unions, and the KwaZulu government should consider legislation to this effect. Possibly the way to work out a path through the maze of legislation for black workers is to set up a commission of enquiry with authority to report and propose legislation on this subject, always remembering that the KwaZulu government must find ways in which the aspirations of its citizens at work can be represented, whether these citizens work within its boundaries or outside.

EDUCATION

Education for Development

W.M. KGWARE

(Paper presented to the National Colloquium on 'Significant Facets of Development with regard to Man and His Environment in the Northern Homelands' held at the University of the North, 30 October to 1 November 1973)

From 15 to 25 May 1961 there was convened in Addis Ababa in Ethiopia '... a Conference of African States ... with a view to establishing an inventory of educational needs and a programme to meet those needs in the coming years ...'. The conference was jointly organised by the Director-General of UNESCO and the Executive Secretary of the United Nations Economic Commission for Africa.

The purpose was to provide a forum for African states to decide on priorities in the provision of educational facilities, priorities which would promote the socio-economic development of the countries concerned. It was also the intention of the conference to arrive at decisions on short-term and long-term programmes of educational development.

The findings of the conference on the state of educational underdevelopment in black Africa at the end of the colonial era make sombre reading: 80 per cent to 85 per cent of Africans over the age of 15 were illiterate, nearly double the world average; fewer than half of middle Africa's 25 million school-age children would complete primary school; fewer than 3 out of every 100 would enter secondary school, and fewer than 2 out of 1 000 would receive any higher education. (UNESCO Final Report, p. VI)

Clearly, this situation was not consistent with the socio-economic development of the new nations of Africa. Something had to be done to bring about rapid improvement. A twenty-year development plan was set up. In terms of this plan, primary education was to be free to all by 1980, 20 per cent of the pupils were to be enrolled in secondary schools, and about 2 per cent in institutions of higher education. In these twenty years educational expenditure was expected to rise from the 1960 figure of $450 million to $2,2 billion in 1980. African governments were advised to work out their own short-term development plans and were urged to invest as much of their limited funds in education as they could. (UNESCO Final Report, p. VI)

Another UNESCO-sponsored conference of African states was held in Nairobi in July 1968, on education and scientific and technical training in relation to development in Africa. This conference made a careful assessment of the progress that had been made in African education in the period between 1960 and 1965 with a view to the planning of future strategies in development. It was found that primary-school enrolments, which stood at 36 per cent of the relevant age group in 1960, had risen to 44 per cent in 1964, or 3 per cent below the 47 per cent target for that year; secondary-school enrolment, which was 3 per cent of the relevant age group in 1960, had reached just under 5 per cent in 1965, or more than 1 per cent below the 1965 target of 6 per cent. Only in higher education was the Addis Ababa target slightly exceeded: the 0,02 per cent of the relevant age group in 1960 had risen to 0,05 per cent in 1965, or 0,01 per cent above the Addis Ababa target. Nor were Addis Ababa targets reached in the number of trained primary and secondary-school teachers, although substantial improvements had been made. (Jolly, pp. 29-33)

The major finding of the Nairobi conference was that educational development and economic development were inseparable and that there was need to tie educational planning to planned stages of economic development.

The South African experience

I have begun this paper by referring to educational problems in black Africa to the north of us. All too often we in South Africa have approached our study and evaluation of the educational system of black South Africa from the viewpoint of the systems of the other national and racial groups in our country, groups whose historical, socio-economic and cultural backgrounds are often dissimilar to those of the blacks. Whatever merit there may be in that approach, I, for one, have come to the realisation that the problems and challenges encountered in black education in South Africa are seen in clearer light and perspective when viewed against the background of similar experiences in other parts of developing Africa.

In our education, too, we have had to make an assessment of our educational needs in relation to our socio-economic needs. One of the most thorough assessments of this kind was made by the Native Economic Commission as far back as 1932. After a careful study of the type of education provided in mission schools at that time, the commission recommended three objectives which should guide the education of the black man, and it is these criteria that have guided subsequent developments in Bantu education. I quote them in full: (Commission Report, p. 628)

1 / 'Education should aim at freeing the mass of natives from their reactionary conceptions-animism and witchcraft, certain phases of the cattle cult, the "doctoring" of lands as an alternative to proper cultivation, the insistence on a large amount of leisure, and all the mass of primitive fears and taboos, which are the real reasons for their backwardness. The removal of them is the first problem of Native Education.

2 / 'It should not pursue a course which makes the Native dissatisfied with everything in his own background. But it should proceed from the foundations of Native society and build up, giving the Native a pride in his own people and a desire to develop what is good ... in his own institutions.

3 / 'It should aim at making the educated Native a missionary to his own people, an instrument in advancing their material progress, without which they will never as a people achieve cultural progress.'

The Native Education Commission of 1949-1951 made far-reaching recommendations towards the realisation of the above objectives. Its recommendations formed the basis of the Bantu Education Act of 1953. From the point of view of control most Bantu schools are now community schools managed by black school boards and/or school committees; efforts have been made to base the curriculum on the needs of the people; Bantu languages are used as media of teaching throughout the primary school and in some specified subjects in the post-primary schools; and every effort has been made to open the school doors to as many children of school-age as possible.

Setting up educational priorities

One of the major provisions of the Bantu Education Act was the transfer of the central control of the education of blacks from the provincial administrations to the national government; a specially created department, the Department of Bantu Education, took charge of this service.

A task which faced the new department was that of determining priorities in the provision of education at the different levels - primary, secondary and tertiary.

Primary education

The highest priority was given to the development of facilities for primary education. At the time of the take-over of Bantu education by the national government there were some 5 700 schools, just over 21 000 teachers and 869 000 pupils, representing 40 per cent to 45 per cent of the school-age black children. The objective of the Department of Bantu Education was to provide schooling facilities for at least four years for every child who lived within reach of a primary school. As of 1973 nearly 3½ million children attend school, representing over 70 per cent of the potential enrolment. This progress, made in fewer than twenty years, can only be described as phenomenal, especially when account is taken of the current population explosion.

But this rapid development in primary education has been attended by serious problems. Emergency measures such as the double-session system in most sub-standard A and B classes had to be resorted to. According to this arrangement the school day is divided into two sessions, each of about three hours, and a maximum enrolment of 100 pupils per teacher is permitted, 50 pupils attending each session. In that way classrooms, books and other classroom equipment are used by double the number that would normally be provided for. In large urban communities the double-shift system has had to be introduced in both primary and secondary schools. The pupil-teacher ratio is disturbingly high: it has been estimated that 48 000 teachers are doing the work of 60 000. (Van Zyl, 'Bantu Education', pp. 501-2)

In addition to coping with large classes the primary-school teacher has to master the content of new syllabuses, especially in such subjects as the official languages, arithmetic and general science, the content of which is based on the national basic syllabuses. These syllabuses aim to upgrade the quality of work done in primary schools, and for the majority of the teachers who have no more than the Junior Certificate (Std. 8) and two years of professional training, the demands of the work are often very exacting indeed. Aware of this problem, the Department of Bantu Education has provided teachers' guides in most subjects as well as textbooks specially prepared to meet these needs.

Secondary education

The first priority, then, was the promotion of literacy and numeracy as well as a general introduction of the child to his social and natural environment. In 1964 a second priority, secondary education, was given attention, for in Bantu South Africa, as in other parts of black Africa, it was realised that it was at the level of secondary education that manpower is prepared for subsequent training in a great variety of vocations and skills: academic, technical and commercial.

In the past decade the development of secondary education for blacks in South Africa has been accelerated. While the growth pattern in primary education over this period has been at an average of 6 per cent to 7 per cent compound interest per annum, at the junior secondary-school level (the first three years of the secondary school) the growth rate has been around 12 per cent compound interest per year, or double that of the primary level. Some 36 000 candidates are expected to write the Junior Certificate Examination at the end of 1973. At the Senior Certificate level the growth rate has risen to 33 per cent c.i. per annum. In 1960 only 1 out of 20 of the pupils who commenced the five-year secondary school course, reached the fifth year; in 1972 the corresponding figures were 1 in 8. This is a development which needs to be accelerated still further if the black community must provide its share of the trained manpower which the country desperately needs today. (Van Zyl, 'Developments', p. 4)

An aspect of secondary education warrants special emphasis, namely, technical education; for this is the aspect that is currently listed as a top priority by the Department of Bantu Education. From the early days of the Christian mission enterprise in the education of the African until comparatively recently, technical education did not rank as a priority in the educational programme. With the coming of political independence to black Africa in the fifties and sixties of the present century, attitudes towards technical skills began to change for the better. Today technical education is generally regarded as the key to wealth and power. The cry heard all over Africa today is:

'... let us drill our own wells, dam our rivers, manufacture our own materials, pilot our own aircraft; thus shall we increase our national power and play a larger part on the stage of world politics.' (Ward, pp. 114-15)

Black South Africa is also beginning to respond to this call, especially since the granting of partial self-government to its homelands. Ten years ago, in March 1963, the editorial of the Bantu Education Journal had cause to complain that the few then existing technical schools for blacks were far from full; it pleaded with black teachers to encourage their pupils to take up courses offered at these institutions. Today the picture is changing.

Recently a symposium was held at Umhlanga Rocks on the north coast of Natal arranged by the United States-South Africa Leader Exchange Program on the theme 'The Optimum Involvement of Manpower in Business in South Africa'. The Secretary for Bantu Education, Dr H.J. van Zyl, presented a paper on the educational implications of such involvement, and it was my task to lead the discussion on this paper and also to draft the findings of the symposium thereon. An important finding was that there was today an acute shortage of skilled white manpower, a fact which both employers and labour in South African industry have long admitted, job reservation notwithstanding. Government, too, was perturbed by this situation. Last year the government appointed an interdepartmental commission, under the chairmanship of Dr Van Zyl, to study and report on this problem, special attention being given to the on-the-job training of black manpower. The report of this commission is awaited with the greatest interest.

At present the Department of Bantu Education runs six technical secondary schools, four of which are situated in the urban areas of Pretoria, Johannesburg, Durban and Port Elizabeth and two in the homelands. It is planned that each homeland should have at least one such school which will offer courses leading to the Junior Certificate and the Senior Certificate. The Senior Certificate course is designed in such a way as to make it possible for pupils to gain matriculation exemption and thus qualify to enter university. (Van Zyl, 'Developments', p. 13)

A beginning has been made with the establishment of facilities for tertiary technical education. Two centres are now in operation: at Seshego, near Pietersburg in the Transvaal and at Edendale, near Pietermaritzburg. It is to be hoped that many more centres that offer technical training at the post-school level will be established. Thought should also be given to the establishment of schools of engineering and business administration at the black universities. Meantime generous bursaries could be made available to black students who are qualified to enter South African white universities which offer these courses.

Teacher education

Prior to the transfer of the control of the education of the blacks from the provinces in 1955, teacher education was without exception undertaken by the Christian missions. Missionary institutions were, for the most part, multi-purpose establishments which provided primary, secondary, teacher-training and even trade instruction. There were some forty of these centres in the country and together they trained, on the average, 2 000 teachers per year. (Van Zyl, 'Developments', p. 5)

The Department of Bantu Education has not only set itself the task of improving the quantity but also the quality of teachers in black schools. Teacher education has, in recent years, been separated from other types of education and is now concentrated in fewer, larger, and better staffed and equipped schools. About 4 100 primary-school teachers qualified in 1972; the target for 1974 is 5 500, and for 1980, 8 000. (Van Zyl, 'Developments', p. 5) At the take-over in 1955 the majority of primary-school teachers were those who had eight years of primary education followed by three years of professional training; today most teachers have the Junior Certificate and two years of professional preparation as minimum qualifications. With the rise in secondary-school enrolments referred to above, the day may not be far distant when the Senior Certificate will be the entrance qualification to primary-school teacher preparation.

Secondary-school teachers are prepared mainly at the universities. There are usually three levels of training: two undergraduate and one post-graduate. The non-graduate teachers are prepared for service in junior secondary schools, while graduate teachers are prepared for senior secondary schools. But the number of teachers produced by the three black universities has proved to be insufficient to cope with the rapidly rising demand for secondary-school teachers: at present some 35 per cent of secondary-school teachers are not qualified academically or professionally to cope with work at this level. To meet this unhappy situation the Department of Bantu Education has had to establish a number of training schools which offer a two-year course of professional training after senior certificate. The first of this type of teacher appeared in 1970; 388 junior secondary-school teachers qualified at the end of 1972 and the target for 1974 is 600. (Van Zyl, 'Developments', p. 5)

An in-service training centre has been established at Mamelodi, near Pretoria, to serve the whole Republic. It is also used for refresher courses. Similar centres are contemplated in the homelands.

A problem that black South Africa shares with other developing communities in Africa is that of the loss of its more experienced and better qualified teachers to other avenues of employment in the public service and, even more serious, to industry and commerce which offer more attractive employment opportunities.

It is worthy of mention that there are still a number of white teachers and instructors who have continued to do service in black schools, especially at the teacher-training and technical levels. But in South Africa, unlike other parts of black Africa, white teachers are but a small percentage of the total teaching force.

University education

In 1959 parliament passed two Acts of far-reaching

significance in the history of higher education in South Africa. These were the Extension of University Education Act, and the University College of Fort Hare Transfer Act.

The first measure provided for the establishment of four new university institutions for non-whites. These were the University College of the North in the Transvaal, to serve mainly the Sotho, Tsonga and Venda-speaking population groups, the University of Zululand for the Zulu, the University College of the Western Cape for coloureds, and the Indian University College in Durban. The second measure provided for the transfer of the control of the University College of Fort Hare (established in 1916) from the Department of Education, Arts and Science to the Department of Bantu Education. This college was thenceforth to cater mainly for Xhosa students. The University of South Africa, for long the watch-dog of academic standards in the country, took these non-white colleges under its wing. Students at the colleges were prepared for the examinations of the University of South Africa, which also conferred its degrees on successful candidates.

Between 1970 and 1971 all five non-white colleges became autonomous universities. In 1971 student enrolment at the three black universities was 2 368. For medical training black students are enrolled at the University of Natal where the Wentworth Medical School admits non-white students only. In 1971 there were 154 black students in training at Wentworth; an average of 10 to 12 doctors qualify each year. Courses not offered at the black universities may be taken at the 'open' Universities of Cape Town and the Witwatersrand with the permission of the Minister of Bantu Education. (Van Zyl, 'Bantu Education', p. 507) Recently it was reported in the press that the Rand Afrikaans University was of the intention to admit blacks to post-graduate study. In 1971 approximately 2 400 black students had enrolled to study by correspondence at the University of South Africa. (Van Zyl, 'Bantu Education', p. 507)

A university has two basic functions: to disseminate knowledge and to add to the accumulated store of knowledge by research and publication. In underdeveloped communities, such as the black communities of South Africa, the university has a special role to play, namely, to function as a focal point in the development of the human and material resources of the community. Time does not permit me to enumerate the research projects that have been, or are being, undertaken by the black universities of South Africa to meet the requirements stated above. Suffice to state that the faculties of arts have undertaken comprehensive socio-economic studies, especially in the homelands; the faculties of education are continually investigating learning and teaching problems in black schools; law faculties have initiated inquiries into the application of Bantu law and the administration of justice; divinity faculties have undertaken studies of the Bantu separatist church movements and related problems. In short, black universities are striving not only to maintain universally accepted academic standards, but they also render special service to the communities they are designed to serve. But more remains to be done in this direction. A welcome development has been the establishment, in 1973, of the South African Pedagogical Society, membership of which comprises not only the members of the teaching staffs of the faculties of education at the three black universities but also suitably qualified members of institutions of tertiary education which fall under the Department of Bantu Education or the homeland departments of education and culture.

There is also urgent need for inter-disciplinary planning and execution of research projects within a university.

Adult education

The Addis Ababa conference estimated that there were 100 million people in Africa who were unable to read or write. It saw in adult education an essential and vital foundation and complement to formal education, for it could promote an intelligent appreciation of the social and technical changes which faced the new Africa. (UNESCO Final Report, p. 7)

It was therefore resolved that African countries should accord adequate attention to adult education, especially in rural areas. It was further found that mere literacy was not a guarantee of socio-economic development, for experience in other continents had shown that even among illiterate farmers agricultural extension services can effect increases in the yields of crops and animal husbandry.

But where literacy had been achieved, the conference recommended the expansion of library services, the creation of suitable reading and audio-visual materials and the extension of the coverage of educational programmes on radio to reach isolated areas. (UNESCO Final Report, p. 7)

We in black South Africa have yet to give serious attention to the systematic development of programmes of adult education. Sporadic efforts have been made, chiefly by non-governmental agencies, to promote adult education. It is perhaps in this area of education that the black universities can take the lead.

During the last week of September 1973 a seminar on adult education, which was attended by representatives from all but one of the fifteen residential universities in South Africa, was held at the University of Cape Town. The Universities of Rhodesia and Malawi also sent representatives. The purpose of the seminar was to establish the extent to which the universities of Southern Africa participated in adult education programmes. Both Rhodesia and Malawi, like the majority of the white universities of our country, could report that they had established effective institutes or departments of adult education whose main function was to plan, in collaboration with their ministries of education, programmes of adult education for their population groups. I came away from that seminar with a strong conviction that there was urgent need for the establishment of institutes of adult education at our black universities.

Some general problems in black education

I must bring this necessarily cursory survey of the educational needs of a developing black South Africa to a close by referring to two or three problems of a general nature.

Rural education

Africa is, for the most part, a continent inhabited by rural peoples. This was the finding of the Addis Ababa conference, which stressed the need to adapt educational curricula, particularly at the primary and lower secondary levels, to rural and village life. In the years since Addis Ababa, efforts have been made to bring the school to the countryside not only physically but also in terms of a programme more in line with rural needs and interests. The new direction will, it is believed, not only raise the productivity of the agricultural economy, but also diminish the number of school-leavers who flock to the towns and cities in search of employment which in most cases they cannot find. (UNESCO Final Report, pp. 5-6) In several countries of black Africa, such as Malawi and Tanzania, fairly successful experiments have been launched in rural school curricula combined with rural community programmes.

The South African black homelands can, I feel sure, learn something of value from these countries. Two or three years ago representatives of the Department of Bantu Education and of the homeland departments of education and culture visited Malawi to study the rural community development schemes in that country. It remains to be seen what adaptations will be made to our school curricula to make them more relevant to the needs and interests of the people in the rural areas.

The holding power of black schools

One of the oft-repeated cries of black leaders in South Africa is the cry for the institution of a system of compulsory school attendance. Many a candidate for election to the legislative assemblies of the homelands has promised his would-be constituents that he would bring them compulsory education for their children. But compulsory education has, after a decade and more, been achieved nowhere in black Africa: it still remains a consummation devoutly to be wished. Many black nations even doubt that it will have been achieved by the target year 1980.

A more realistic approach seems to be to improve the educational opportunities of the about 70 per cent children who are already at school. One of the serious problems is that of the poor holding power of our schools: there is a disturbingly high drop-out rate among pupils. Thus, of the total school population in the homelands in 1970, no fewer than 95,24 per cent were in primary schools and of these 68,7 per cent were enrolled in the first four classes. Homeland departments of education would do well to investigate the causes of this high pupil wastage which bodes ill for the development of their communities. It has been found that pupils who have received less than four years of schooling easily lapse back to illiteracy, and money expended on their schooling is money wasted.

Financing of black education

Until 1972 the financing of education for blacks was based on the principle that the blacks should, to an increasing degree, provide the money needed to run their educational system. State aid was pegged at R13 million per annum. In 1963 an additional R1½ million was voted by parliament from general revenue to finance the three black universities. But as these sources of income proved inadequate, parliament had to resort increasingly to the Loan Account to balance the Bantu Education Account.

By 1972 the Bantu Education Account had proved to be totally inadequate to meet even the barest essentials required to maintain the educational system, and the need for a new and more realistic system of financing the education of blacks became urgent. In terms of the Bantu Education Account Abolition Act of 1972 the Bantu Education Account was abolished and its assets and liabilities were transferred to the Consolidated Revenue Fund, and the outstanding loan owing to this account was written off.

At the same time the Bantu Trust and Land Act of 1936 was to be amended to provide for part of the money accruing from the general tax of the blacks to be paid to the homeland governments, and part to the S.A. Bantu Trust Fund. Education in the homelands was to be financed from the moneys thus paid to them by the Department of Bantu Administration and Development. (Horrell, pp. 344-7)

It is to be hoped that this new arrangement will place more ample funds at the disposal of black education both in the white areas and in the homelands. Time does not permit even a passing mention of the considerable financial contribution made by parents, local communities and private enterprise to supplement treasury allocations. The doctrine of self-reliance about which we hear so much today has long been accepted and acted upon in black South Africa.

Setting educational objectives

In March 1972 there was held at the University of the Witwatersrand an international conference whose theme was 'Accelerated Development in Southern Africa'. In his address to the education workshop that preceded the conference, Professor Franklin Parker of the Department of Education at West Virginia University in the United States stressed the need for setting clear educational objectives in relation to any programme of community development. I quote him:

'School systems by their very organization and financing have built-in objectives, aims, and goals. But benefit can be derived from stating objectives explicitly, reviewing them regularly, and restating them frequently in the light of changes in the school system and in the society it serves. The hope is that when objectives are under continual and careful review, they may be improved for continual renewal of efficiency, innovation, and service to society.' (Parker, pp. 6-7)

What are these 'built-in objectives, aims, and goals' in so far as the education of the blacks of South Africa is concerned? I trust that at the end of this conversation we shall have found part of the answer to this vital question on which so much depends.

Consultative Education Committee of the KwaZulu Government: Education Manifesto of KwaZulu

(Report by an ad hoc Consultative Education Committee under the auspices of the KwaZulu government, presented on 14 February 1973)

1.1. Whereas hitherto Africans have had no effective control over their education which was European-designed and European-executed, going under the term 'Native Education' and later 'Bantu Education' with no black voice in the decision-making machinery connected therewith, and this education system purported to prepare Africans for inferior status in life;

1.2. Whereas high-level manpower in modern societies includes the following occupational categories:

1.2.1. entrepreneurial, managerial, and administrative personnel in both public and private establishments, including educational institutions;

1.2.2. professional personnel such as scientists, engineers, architects, agronomists, doctors, veterinarians, economists, lawyers, accountants, journalists, artists, etc.;

1.2.3. 'qualified' teachers, defined as those who have had a minimum of twelve years of education themselves;

1.2.4. sub-professional technical personnel such as agricultural assistants, nurses, engineering assistants, technicians, senior clerks, supervisors of skilled workers, the highest level of skilled craftsmen, and skilled clerical workers such as stenographers;

1.2.5. top-ranking political leaders, labour leaders, judges, and officers of police and the armed forces (Harbison & Myers: Education, Manpower And Economic Growth. McGraw-Hill, New York, 1964, p. 16).

1.3. Whereas the dearth of the abovementioned types of people, who, in general, fill the strategic occupations in modern societies, reflects our current educational bankruptcy as illustrated, for instance, by the following 1972 statistics:

1.3.1. KwaZulu population - 4 1/4 million

1.3.2. The school situation:

(a) circuit inspector - 21; assistant inspectors - 42
(b) organisers of special subjects - 4
(c) organisers for culture - 1; school counsellors - 3
(d)

Type of schools	No. of schools	Pupils	Teachers
Primary	1 672	431 876	6 874
Secondary & High	83	23 440	760
Teacher-training	4	1 325	76
Industrial & Technical	6	846	65
School for sons of chiefs	1	94	8
Grand totals	1 766	457 481	7 783

1.3.3. Educational manpower (provisional statistics)

(a)	Professional	1 064
(b)	Administrative	463
(c)	Technicians	52
(d)	Artisans	675
(e)	Operators	239
	Grand totals	2 493

1.4. Whereas it is desirable that the current caricature pyramid constituted by African manpower with an oversize base but no apex be rectified as soon as possible.

2.0 Be it therefore known that an ad hoc Consultative Education Committee under the auspices of the KwaZulu government was charged with the task of drawing up an education manifesto for KwaZulu and this was done in October/November, 1972, as follows:

2.1. AIMS AND OBJECTIVES OF OUR EDUCATION

2.1.1. We need a black-oriented education (in aim, content and organisation) designed to satisfy the genuine needs and aspirations of the African: an educational system adapted to meet the challenges of the scientific-technological age. The outputs of our education must constitute a proper pyramid. Unless there is a clear aim of our education, our efforts will be in vain. Therefore, we adopt the following as the aim of our education: The effective organisation of the African's experience sc that his tendencies and powers may develop in a manner satisfactory to himself and the nation, by the growth of requisite knowledge, desirable attitudes and congenial skills required to face the modern age (cf. Jowitt: The Principles Of Education For African Teachers in Training, Longmans, London, 1932, p. 48).

2.1.2. Our objective is free compulsory education for the first ten years of schooling, that is, from 6 to 16 years of age or Standard 10 whichever comes first. We need to take a bold step forward in order to wipe out the current educational bankruptcy which is our unfortunate lot.

2.1.3. We shall have to adopt a properly organised differentiated education embracing a 12-year school programme divided into four 3-year phases as follows:

Junior primary school	Grade 1 to Std.1
Senior primary school	Stds.2 to 4
Junior secondary school	Stds.5 to 7
Senior secondary school	Stds.8 to 10

Educational differentiation is designed to route pupils to the right course and the right institutions according to their ability, aptitude and interest, viz. academic, agricultural, commercial, technical and domestic science courses. Counselling plays a crucial role in this regard.

2.1.4. The late introduction of a new medium of instruction causes difficulties with our pupils. In the near future mother-tongue instruction will be confined to the junior primary school only, and thereafter a new medium will replace it.

2.2. PRIORITIES

Priorities should reflect the major goals of a society. The country which commits itself to rapid progress and attempts to engage in rational planning to achieve it must make a logical assessment of priorities (Harbison & Myers, 1964 p. 20). The following is our high-priority programme:

2.2.1. Free compulsory education for all children up to the age of 16 with a fully-fledged differentiated programme to enable pupils to follow diversified courses in accordance with individual differences and in response to the manpower needs of KwaZulu. Such a programme involves, inter alia:

(a) Massive school building schemes to augment existing

accommodation;
(b) Provision of additional equipment and facilities;
(c) Large-scale teacher-training programmes;
(d) Establishment of a pedagogical clinic;
(e) Services of non-black specialist senior assistants to serve under black headmasters;
(f) Payment of realistic salaries in order to retain the services of trained teachers and to reverse the present brain drain to commerce and industry and to countries outside our borders.

2.2.2. The improvement and augmentation of existing hostel facilities and the erection of several new hostels to alleviate the hardships suffered by pupils who have to travel long distances between home and school, particularly so in rural villages, and to cater for pupils who have to stay away from their villages which have no post-primary schools.

2.2.3. The establishment of a university of science and technology along the lines of the Kwame Nkrumah University of Science and Technology in Ghana which offers the faculties of agriculture, architecture, art, engineering, science and pharmacy. We could also add the faculties of forestry and veterinary science.

2.2.4. A medical school is urgent. At the moment we are producing virtually no doctors at all.

2.2.5. A big contingent of students including serving personnel should be sent abroad to do university studies as was the case with other pre-independent African states. For instance at the time of independence in 1957, there were 1 716 Ghanaian university students, of whom 846 were studying abroad. In the course of their studying abroad our students will at the same time develop the inevitable mental independence and acquire modernistic cultural experiences to enrich the cultural life of our educational institutions and, ipso facto, that of the nation.

2.2.6. The establishment of a research institute under a trained black director with a professional status (who may be an expatriate on contract) assisted by a team of specialists with lecturers' status who are experts in various fields charged with the task of conducting research continuously regarding the needs of KwaZulu.

ADDENDUM: FURTHER NOTES ON THE MANIFESTO

1.3. Educational bankruptcy

Our educational bankcruptcy is evidenced by the fact that:

(a) There are only 13 black academicians as against 84 Europeans at the University of Zululand, viz. 9 in the Faculty of Arts, 3 in Education and 1 in Science (Botany).

(b) Only 25 science graduates, with mostly biological sciences and psychology as majors, have been produced by the University of Zululand since its inception in 1960. In 1971 the Faculty of Science had a total enrolment of only 51 students in contrast to the 233 science students at the University of Fort Hare.

(c) Three of the teacher-training colleges are staffed predominantly with European personnel.

(d) Industrial and technical education is still almost exclusively in the hands of European instructors.

(e) There are only 1 766 schools with an enrolment cf 457 481 pupils manned by 7 783 teachers in KwaZulu, compared, for instance, with 1 680 schools with an enrolment of 441 507 pupils manned by 7 493 teachers in 1971 in the Transkei, which has a population of only 1,84 million. An even sharper contrast is provided by Ghana with a population of 4 3/4 million at the time of her independence in 1957, when there were 4 988 schools with an enrolment of 602 670 pupils taught by 19 825 teachers.

(f) About 24 per cent of the teachers in the lower primary schools (i.e.. Grade 1 to Std.2) are unqualified, whilst only 17 per cent of the post-primary school teachers are graduates.

1.4 Caricature pyramid

A normal distribution curve is bell-shaped or pyramid-like, in this case the base representing the majority of workers and the apex the minority engaged in sophisticated jobs. A sound educational system must provide for this type of distribution of manpower as opposed to a system which prepares blacks for an inferior status in life. At the moment the apex is out of reach for our people so that the pyramid is rendered an irregular or caricature structure. We are convinced that the launching of an Accelerated Development Plan for Education in

KwaZulu can remedy this abnormality within ten years.

2.1.4. Medium of instruction

Under Bantu Education the medium of instruction in the primary school is mother-tongue (i.e. from Grade 1 to Std.6). At secondary-school level two media are used on a 50:50 basis, viz. English and Afrikaans. This policy has caused untold hardships to black pupils. It has caused perennial difficulties in communication between tutor and student at high school and university. A solution to this problem lies in the early familiarisation with the new medium as was the case prior to the advent of Bantu Education. The use of two media of instruction at the secondary-school level has no pedagogical basis and must be discontinued.

2.2.1. Pedagogical clinic

The chief functions of this clinic will be, inter alia:

(a) To acquaint teachers with the latest developments in their respective subjects.

(b) To upgrade teachers and inspectors.

(c) To train school and hostel administrators.

2.2.2. Large-scale teacher-training programmes

This will involve training three categories of teachers, viz:

(i) junior-school teachers: with an academic qualification of Std.8 (i.e. 10 years of schooling);

(ii) senior-school teachers: with an academic qualification of Matric (i.e. 12 years of schooling);

(iii) secondary-school teachers with a degree.

2.2.3. Medical school

In South Africa there is 1 black doctor for every 44 400 blacks, 1 coloured doctor for every 6 200 coloureds, 1 Indian doctor for every 900 Indians, and 1 European doctor for every 400 Europeans. The numbers of Africans being trained are quite negligible; less than 12 doctors a year for a population of 15 million. This state of affairs is giving cause for concern.

Medium of Instruction in African Education

A.L. MAWASHA

(Excerpts from an address to the National Education Conference of ASSECA (Association for the Educational and Cultural Advancement of the African People of South Africa), Orlando, 31 May 1973)

Basically the debatable question about medium of instruction in African education centres around the question whether the African child should be taught through the medium of the first language, i.e. his mother tongue, or through the medium of a second language, i.e. either of the European languages used in the country. Educational reports at our disposal show that this issue has engaged the attention of educational administrators, teachers and parents throughout the history of African education in this country. No wonder the 1935-36 Interdepartmental Committee on Native Education referred to it as a 'vexed question' (par. 484).

I believe that this issue is going to be topical from now to perhaps 1980 or even longer. The centre of the argument is going to be: who is to decide on the medium of instruction to be used in African education as a whole in this country? It is quite possible that some of the points raised at this conference might be referred to again some day when this issue is discussed at other levels elsewhere. It is for this reason that I have decided to approach the topic from an historical point of view, attempting to place in perspective past and present viewpoints on the issue, hopefully to guide future decisions.

I have divided the topic into three parts: before the Bantu Education Act of 1953; after the Bantu Education Act of 1953; some general conclusions and, finally, a personal viewpoint.

1 / Before the Bantu Education Act of 1953

English, both as a language and as medium of instruction in African education, was predominant before the promulgation of the Bantu Education Act of 1953 in the

Republic of South Africa. There are several reasons why English featured so prominently in African education during this period. Most of the missionary-teachers who were engaged in African education at the time were English-speaking. The aim of the missionary-teacher was not only to evangelise but also to westernise the African convert. This endeavour could hardly be attained without involving and giving prominence to the language of the tutor. The English held an influential position in public life in South Africa at the time, and much business, including education, was conducted through the medium of English. Most Africans were introduced to the Western concept of education and civilisation through the agency of the English language, and as a result many of them naturally came to associate formal classroom instruction and education generally with the English language. The bulk of the reading material available to blacks appeared (and still does) in English, and this obviously tipped the scale in favour of the English language.

Apart from these fairly obvious reasons, there was the belief of the English people themselves that English both as a language and as medium of instruction was necessary in the education of the African. Edgar H. Brookes for example felt that 'English gives the Bantu pupil the breadth and sweep of culture which the Classical languages give to the White pupil'.(1) C.T. Loram on the other hand described it as 'certainly cumbersome' to try to express for example large numbers and, say, lower fractions in an African language.(2) He quoted Zulu as an example of such an African language. Even the renowned Lovedale Institution felt that if a choice was to be made between classical languages and English, then the former 'could be sacrificed if they stand in the way of the pupils' acquiring a thorough understanding of English'.(3) The tendency to give English prominence both as a language and as medium of instruction in African education was not only evident in the utterances of individuals and standpoints of certain institutions, but was equally evident in the policy of certain administrative bodies during the period under review. For example, as early as 1841, in a memorandum setting out conditions upon which allowances were to be granted from the Colonial Treasurer in aid of mission schools and certain other African schools not on the government establishment, it was stipulated: 'The English language shall form a branch of instruction in all schools thus aided and, where practicable, it shall be used as the colloquial language of the school.' (4)

To meet this stipulation, teachers in African mission schools not only preferred English as medium of instruction but also studied it as a language. In fact, as the Welsh Commission put it, they 'devoted a great part of their energies to the instruction of English as a subject'.(5) But for the sake of accuracy it must be mentioned that sometimes administrative bodies did not want to commit themselves on the question of medium of instruction in African education. For example in 1885, when the Language Congress of the Dutch Reformed Church desired information on this issue, it received the following reply from the Superintendent-General of Education in the Cape: 'As regards the language in which the younger children should receive instruction, this Department does not interfere; the matter rests with the managers and the people whose interests they represent'. (6) What I think deserves special note is that many teachers in African education during this period seemed to have preferred English as medium of instruction. This fact is borne out by reports on African education published during this period. A few examples will illustrate this.

In 1931 the Superintendent-General of Education in the Cape observed that, although it was permissible to use the home language of the pupils as medium of instruction in African schools, there was nevertheless still a general tendency among the teachers to introduce the official languages at too early a stage in the education of the child. The choice of the official language usually meant English.(7) Earlier, round about 1929, G.H. Welsh had already observed that teachers in African education 'generally required some coercion' to effect the regulation to use vernacular as medium of instruction in the lower classes of the African schools. Inevitably the language preferred was English.(8)

This tendency of preferring English as medium of instruction in African schools was not only evident in the Cape, but in other provinces as well. In the Transvaal, for example, N.D. Achterberg, an inspector of schools, said in 1920 that in the majority of cases English was preferred as medium of instruction notwithstanding the departmental option that mother-tongue instruction could be used.(9) In 1931 G.H. Franz reported as follows: 'Efforts to introduce mother tongue as medium of instruction aroused violent opposition on the part of the parents.'(10) It would appear, therefore, that the pre-Bantu Education Act era was characterised by the predominance of English as a language and as medium of instruction and that both parents and teachers engaged in African education preferred English as medium of instruction.

2 / After the Bantu Education Act of 1953

Guided largely by the recommendations of the Commission of Native Education 1949-1951, which is also known as the Eiselen Commission, the Bantu Education Act of 1953 provided for an ever-increasing emphasis on the mother tongue as medium of instruction in African schools. The Commission recommended among other things:
(a) that the vernacular of the child should be used as medium of instruction since this was the language the child understood best;
(b) that all education, except in the case of the official languages, should be given through the medium of the vernacular for the first four years and that this medium should gradually be extended to the whole primary school course;
(c) that committees be appointed to compile terminologies which would be necessary in the teaching of school subjects through the medium of the vernacular;
(d) that subjects such as history which did not require an extensive technical terminology should be taught through the medium of the vernacular as soon as possible.(11) 'Strong emphasis must ... be laid on the home language and the principle of home language instruction must be applied ... in order that the pupil may be able to use his own language for his needs in a civilised society.'(12)

Although the Commission of Enquiry into the Teaching of Official Languages and the Use of the Mother Tongue as Medium of Instruction in Transkeian Primary Schools recommended in the final analysis that mother-tongue instruction in the Transkeian schools be retained only up to and including Standard 4, yet it also found it necessary to state: 'Indeed, if the mother tongue is not a suitable medium of instruction, then it must either be developed to become a suitable medium or the people must adopt another mother tongue.'(13)

In a subsequent utterance elsewhere, the chairman of the Commission warned that, while other issues bearing on the problem relating to mother-tongue instruction should not be lost sight of, yet 'care must be taken that they do not colour clear judgement on the soundness, necessity and urgency of mother-tongue instruction in our educational system'.(14)

Let us look at the position in the schools themselves in connection with the issue of mother-tongue instruction. I cite a few reports of the Department of Bantu Education to establish this. 'Mother-tongue instruction was reported as being in full force in the primary schools and that the available terminologies were beginning to bear fruit and were resulting in an improvement in the standard of work and of teaching.'(15) 'The policy of mother-tongue instruction was applied everywhere without much difficulty.'(16) 'A gratifying and encouraging note struck in virtually all reports by inspectors is that teachers have a favourable attitude towards mother tongue as medium of instruction. Progress is evident.'(17) Mother tongue was applied in all primary schools, and the Africans were gradually beginning to clamour for mother-tongue instruction wherever possible. This was said to be partly due to the realisation of the great potential that the Bantu homelands held in store for the Africans.(18)

I think it will be appropriate at this stage to draw some preliminary conclusions. The earlier reports we referred to led us to conclude that many African teachers, and even parents, preferred English as medium of instruction in African schools; but the reports of the Department of Bantu Education led us to conclude that the principle of mother-tongue instruction has not only been successful, but has also been acceptable to many teachers in African education.

3 / Personal viewpoint

Straightaway I want to express the viewpoint that, whilst it is universally agreed among educationists that the first language of the child should as far as possible be the medium through which such a child should receive his entire formal instruction, yet under certain circumstances this principle cannot be applied without substantial modifications. Such modifications usually take cognisance of certain practical problems obtaining at the moment and try to meet them in the best possible manner. African education in South Africa is an example of such an educational system, which cannot wholly rely on the mother tongue of the pupils for instructional purposes. This is quite obvious: African languages in South Africa are fully developed to meet the immediate communicational needs of the Africans, but they are certainly not adequate in themselves to cover all the knowledge that rests enshrined in the Western world and in the older world languages. This knowledge we need as people if we are to cope with such modern demands. A visit to any type of library anywhere in the country will corroborate this fact.

Professor W.M. Kgware, viewing this issue of medium of instruction from a purely didactical and psychological point of view, points out that, although the child would learn better when taught through the medium of his home language since this is obviously the medium of communication the child understands best, yet he does not omit to state that often circumstances render the implementation of the principle of mother-tongue instruction inadvisable, causing for example the African child 'to rely on more than his native language and thanks to the relatively undeveloped state of his language as medium of communication in the scientific and technological age, he must even accept the use of a foreign language as medium of learning'.(19) I tend to feel that while the vernacular must be taught as effectively as possible in African schools, yet as medium of instruction it should be confined to the lower primary school since at this level of his schooling the child is still being introduced to the idea of formal instruction and it will be pointless to use a second language he hardly knows. But from the higher primary upwards a second language as medium of instruction should be introduced and retained throughout his schooling.

But which second language should African education prefer? I think English. My preference is neither arbitrary nor mischievous; it is based on the African's obvious preference. As well as the obvious advantage of this language as a world language, Africans in this country have long accepted English as some sort of lingua franca. At different types of gatherings, from student meetings through African teachers' conferences, to educational, social and cultural gatherings like this one, English seems to be the most preferred of the European languages used in this country. I am fully aware of the fact that knowing a language and being able to use it in day-to-day communication does not necessarily mean that you should use it as medium of instruction in your schools, but it seems quite sensible to me that, since African education has to fall back on a second language as medium of instruction, then the second language most preferred should be the one selected to serve as medium of instruction.

In a paper prepared for the National Language Teaching Conference in July, 1972, K.B. Hartshorn provided facts and figures to give an idea of the African pupils' performance in English at Matric level. He concludes: 'You will note that this indicates a lower level of attainment in Afrikaans than in English.'(20)

Further statistical evidence in support of our suggestion is taken from the Bantu Education Journal of September, 1970, p. 21. In 1970 there were 21 872 Form 1 - 5 pupils who were doing English A as against 2 260 who were doing Afrikaans A - a difference of about 19 612 in favour of English. And let us not forget that, when the Transkei was allowed to make its own choice of medium of instruction in lieu of Xhosa, in 1963, the Legislative Assembly preferred English as from Standard 3 upwards. With reference to this Hartshorn said: 'There is good reason to suppose that in the case of KwaZulu, the Ciskei and possibly BophuthaTswana, all of whom have already expressed themselves in this matter (i.e. of English as medium of instruction) similar decisions will be taken in a year or two.... It is therefore clear that throughout the Bantu schools system there is to be an earlier use of English than of Afrikaans.'(21) On 22 April 1973, Chief Gatsha Buthelezi of KwaZulu is reported as having said: 'But I would like to say that my government will introduce legislation next month which will make English the medium of education from Standard 3 upward in KwaZulu.'(22) And so I repeat: my preference is neither arbitrary nor mischievous; it is based on what the African people themselves seem to prefer.

In addition to my preference for English as medium of instruction in African education from the first year of the higher primary school course, I endorse the contention that: 'Any attempt to make both official languages mother-tongue substitutes must be firmly rejected as a violation of an important educational principle. If there is to be a transfer in medium, then it can only be from the mother tongue to one of the official languages and not both.'(23) Indeed how we arrived at the position of having three media of instruction running parallel in our secondary and high schools is not very easy to understand. The envisaged arrangement of having either English or Afrikaans as medium of instruction is much better, but unfortunately the manner in which this new arrangement is to be implemented seems to have some snags. I quote from the editorial of the Bantu Education Journal of November, 1972, p. 3: 'For the homelands, the governments concerned will decide which of the two media will be used. In the white areas Afrikaans will be used if the majority of the whites in the particular area is Afrikaans-speaking, and English if the whites are mainly English-speaking.'

I have no doubt that this decision was made in good faith and perhaps on the basis of certain considerations which I do not feel competent to go into, but I honestly find it very difficult to understand why homeland leaders should be considered competent to decide on the medium through which their future citizens in the homelands are to be instructed and yet not be allowed the same freedom regarding their subjects in the urban areas.

I wish the envisaged arrangement regarding medium of instruction in African education could be reconsidered with due consideration for the wishes of the African leaders both in the urban areas and in the homelands. This rests on the understanding that such leaders will be representing the interests of the parents whose children are directly concerned. If this wish is not considered wise, then I am afraid homeland leaders in particular are going to find themselves in an unenviable position in which they might find themselves operating on the basis of something bordering very dangerously on a double-standard in the implementation of certain decisions by their parliaments in regard to their citizens. That is to say a decision such as choosing English or Afrikaans as medium of instruction for a particular homeland will only be applicable to those citizens who are resident in the homeland itself but the same decision may not be applicable to urban citizens of the same homeland. I think it is within the powers of homeland leaders to study this arrangement very carefully, desire clarity on certain implications and then declare an official standpoint to guide their people.

But all said and done, an issue such as medium of instruction in African education cannot be decided upon and finalised without prior consultation with African parents through their leaders both in urban areas and in the homelands. I think it will not be enough to let, say, a body controlled largely by the central government (or one or other of its departments) make the final recommendation on this issue, because whatever recommendation such a body may put forward will not necessarily reflect the wishes of the African parents in general and may perhaps even be rejected by them.

I think this is an instance in which the idea of dialogue could be given concrete expression. Let the final decision on the issue be a product of mutual consultation between the parents of the children (acting through their leaders) and the authorities concerned in the implementation of the envisaged arrangement in connection with the medium of instruction in African schools in this country. Such mutual consultation will not only check unnecessary unpleasantness but will also cause all parties concerned to feel committed to whatever decision might be taken.

Let us not rule out the vital role that teachers' associations might play in this matter since they are the ones to put into practice whatever decision is taken on this matter. The success or failure of the final agreement will depend to a large extent on their competence and hard work. And again let us not rule out the possibility of using independent commissions of inquiry to find out what the Africans in general feel about this matter.

Transvaal United African Teachers' Association: Language and Communication: Freedom to Choose the Medium of Instruction for Children

(Editorial in TUATA, Journal of the Transvaal United African Teachers' Association, October 1973)

The question of the choice of the medium of instruction or the medium of learning is a vexed one. The Teachers' Association has always made a very clear stand regarding what medium they prefer. At their 67th Annual Conference at Sibasa, from 1 to 3 September 1973, TUATA again re-affirmed previous resolutions to opt for English as a medium of instruction.

English, teachers contend, is the Africans' lingua franca as used for basic communications across ethnic and tribal barriers. African representatives in all walks of life have, in no uncertain terms, indicated their choice of English as a medium from Standard 3 upwards. Seemingly, the only people out of step, in so far as this thinking is concerned, are those who want to do things for others and not with them.

We as teachers do not doubt their sincerity in their insistence that the mother tongue be used as a medium up to Standard 6 (Standard 4 from 1975). But is it not the right and freedom of a people to enjoy self-determination? This freedom and self-determination has led all peoples in the Western world to enjoy progress as well as to suffer from hasty and ill-timed decisions. But the fact remains that the decisions have been theirs alone.

We lack that opportunity because of imposed tutelage. We yearn for a time when we shall be able to learn from our own mistakes and blunders. We are not aware of any nation that has been annihilated as a result of its mistakes and blunders....

Our mother tongues as presently taught and studied at university are static. There is more emphasis on grammar rather than on practical criticism. They do not equip the young teacher for his task of teaching. They are instead convenient for white researchers to acquire degrees.

We believe, however, that our languages are self-sufficient to express our thoughts, feelings and aspirations. We use them in our gatherings to express certain poignant and related ideas. But we do not accept the imposition of these languages over us by officialdom. We cannot but deplore the apparent, if not intentional, commercialisation of our education by making available textbooks in our various languages when these are already available in English. The expense involved, we contend, could have been used for some other valuable projects.

It is not our intention to down-grade our languages. But we deplore it when they are used to divide and separate us as a people. Let it come from us that we are different.

As for the principle of using English and Afrikaans as media on a 50-50 basis at post-primary school level, we have been betrayed. To us, as expressed by delegates at the aforementioned conference, this principle is educationally unsound and politically motivated. The principle of 50-50 does not apply in white, Indian and coloured education.

While conceding the authority of the department and adherence to state policy, we believe concession by the department on issues about which Africans have very strong reservations would go a long way to foster and improve the currently over-debated race relations.

History in Black Schools

E.P. LEKHELA

(Excerpts from an address to a conference of Tswana teachers at Mafeking on 16 August 1975)

Profound changes in the nature of the education of the black man in South Africa have taken place in recent years. Thus since 1973 the structure of our educational system has altered to keep pace with our expanding educational horizons; the content of the subjects taught in our schools has been reviewed with a view of making it more and more relevant to the circumstances under which we live; methods and techniques employed in the teaching process have been revolutionised; and educational technology has come in to aid and abet the teacher in the classroom and lecture hall.

Let us look at what is prescribed for the black child's instruction in history.

Junior primary school level

At the junior primary school level, i.e. during the first four years of schooling, historical instruction in the form of environmental studies is first given in stories more or less apposite to the environment in which the pupil lives. An anthropological bias is easily discernible. Civil servants and other workers in the area are focussed upon and pupils are led into understanding and appreciating the work done by them.

By way of comparison it might be pointed out that in England, for example, family history is introduced at the Grade 2 level. Basic historical concepts such as time, change, continuity and evidence are gradually introduced. The general strategy is based on the fact that the child is primarily concerned with his own lifetime. It starts with himself and moves back slowly and cautiously to the lifetimes of his parents, grandparents and so on to the more remote ancestors. From this point it is a fairly easy transition to the history of society at large, as Steel and Taylor point out.(1)

There are many advantages for the child's historical education that accrue from the study of family history. Having regard to the time at my disposal I shall mention only three, namely that in the first instance the child is completely involved in the exercise and in the process ropes in father, mother, brothers and sisters who must supply answers to his many questions. In the second instance the child is afforded an opportunity to try his hand at an imaginative reconstruction of the life of his parents and grandparents. Thirdly it can become an interdisciplinary project, as the family history often spills over into many subject areas like art, drama, geography and even sociology as well as creative writing and the use of literature.

It is definitely not too much to suggest that some attempt should be made to introduce family history into the syllabuses in our primary schools even at this stage. In the curriculum of our indigenous education, family history (geneaology) was included. There seems no reason why we should not re-introduce it into our history syllabi even as they do in the schools in England and elsewhere.

Senior primary school level

At the senior primary school level, i.e. the second four-year period in the education of the child, the subject history constitutes a part of the composite study called social studies. In general the aim is 'to extend the intellectual and spiritual horizon of the pupils, and pace must be kept with their development in capacity, comprehension and interest'.(2)

A pleasing feature of the revised syllabi of 1967 is the fact that in all of them provision is made for the teaching of the history of the black man if not in South Africa generally, then certainly in their respective areas of domicile. Consideration has, in the first place, been given to 'the mode of life and existence of the Bantu in South Africa'.(3) But it must be admitted that for the reason that history is more or less integrated into social studies, not enough is provided to include some very important (and essential) themes in the study of the history of South Africa. Black nationalism, and the part played by the black man in the development of South Africa economically, socially, politically and militarily, are only a few of the topics that could with advantage have been included.

As in the junior primary school, family history should be included and in conjunction with local history treated in more detail, if only to afford the pupils further practice in the use of primary sources, and thus ensure their working independently of the usual textbook. It is often erroneously thought that the skilful handling of evidences is a by-product of, rather than a necessary precondition of learning history.

Junior secondary school level

As from 1974, history at the junior secondary school level is treated as a subject of study in its own right, divorced from geography with which it was integrated up to the end of 1973. Accordingly Pamphlet XII of 1974 sets out the contents of history at Form 3 level. It describes the aims of the study of history and delineates the various sections of the syllabus.

The greater portion of the syllabus deals with the development of nationalism and liberalism in Europe up to 1848, whilst of the three themes chosen in South African history one deals with the history of the black man. All told, 66 periods are set aside for the study of general history whilst only 25 are allocated to the study of the history of the black man.

Considering that this syllabus is designed for black pupils as distinct from white pupils, it is not unreasonable to suggest that more time should be devoted to the history of the black man in South Africa. If there is not enough written about the black man's history, then surely the implementation of this suggestion should be an incentive to black teachers and historians to find the material and set it down in book form for use in our secondary schools.

If it was found necessary to suggest that certain topics dealing with movement and periods in the life of the black man per se should be treated at the senior primary school level, then there is absolute necessity that this should be repeated and emphasised at the level of the junior secondary school. Contact between whites and blacks at all levels in the various spheres of activity, inter-tribal and inter-ethnic interactions, as well as affiliation with blacks across the borders of the republic, could well be probed into.

Then, of course, one would suggest that in determining which topics in general history should receive attention, first preference should be given to those that had a direct bearing on the black man in South Africa. The starting point should be the identification of the outstanding features in the life of the black man at this juncture. These should be traced back first to their immediate causes and subsequently regressively back tc the history of the country of their origin to understand why the introducers reacted in this way. History treated in that way will certainly be more meaningful for the black pupil in our schools. As Mrs E.V.N. Motshabi points out in her M.Ed. dissertation entitled 'The use of the text-book in the teaching of history in Bantu high schools, with special reference to the Form II class', (page 2), Fort Hare, December 1973: 'The history as it is found in the Social-studies text-book for Junior Certificate is not part of the experiential background of the pupil'. It fails and will continue to fail to satisfy the wishes of the black man and his children in the junior secondary schools.

Senior secondary school level

The higher and standard grades history syllabuses for the Senior Certificate as published in a departmental pamphlet of 1975, like that for Junior Certificate, consist of two sections, namely, General History 1919-1970 and South African History 1910-1970. Here the greater number of topics, nine, is to be found in the South African history section. Sad to relate, however, is the fact that only one of the nine items deals with the history of the black man in South Africa. For the coloureds and Indians similar treatment has been given. To say the least, this is definitely not enough and is not calculated to elicit good reactions from black pupils in the schools.

Here, too, one would suggest that more of the history of the black man be included in the syllabus and that, where European history is prescribed, only such topics as had a definite influence on the history of the black man be studied. The point of departure should be the main features in the history of the black man. It is also of importance that some place be given to the study at this level of contemporary history of the developing independent states in Africa, Asia and America, if only to understand their problems and aspirations.

The black man as reflected in history textbooks

It is conceded that many of the suggestions made above cannot readily be implemented, that real hard work will have to be done before suitable history textbooks for use in our junior and senior secondary schools are available, and that consensus will have to be obtained as to which sections of European/ general history can be omitted from the syllabuses. But that there is need to revise some of the material in the history or social study textbooks for use in the Junior and Senior Certificate courses cannot be denied. Certainly some of the sentiments expressed and the value statements made are not calculated to engender feelings of admiration and pride for our ancestors.

In a masterly and, indeed, scholarly analysis of three social study textbooks, Mrs Motshabi has revealed how, owing sometimes to ignorance of the black man's life and world view, owing, more often than not, to sheer prejudice, and in a few cases owing to not having a clear grasp of historical methodology and, as a consequence, floundering in the pitfalls of generalisations, the white authors of three social study books failed to live up to Cicero's dictum, namely that 'the historian should tell the whole truth and nothing but the truth'.(4)

Allow me a few minutes to illustrate my point with reference to the Social Studies texts by Dent and Hallowes, Social Studies For J.C.; Strydom, Van der Merwe and Gerber, Social Studies For Forms II and III; and Grove, Le Roux, Geyser and Dugard, Hersiene Sosiale Studie. Generally speaking there is a lot which is historically offensive in all three books. The shortcomings may be categorised in the following ways. I discuss only two in this paper.

Ideological shortcomings

Offensive typologies like 'Bantu barbarian', derogative epithets like 'thieves', 'murderers', 'superstitious ignorant people', 'rapists', etc., occur in all three books. Significantly the highest incidence of the ideological, emotive words occur in the book of Strydom, Van der Merwe and Gerber, a relic from yesteryear. The lowest incidence occurs in the book by Grove, Le Roux and Dugard. There is clear evidence that some white historians and possibly bodies concerned with the nurture of good human relations, like SABRA (the South African Bureau for Racial Affairs), have brought their influence to bear on those who mean to write history textbooks for black pupils.

Lest you get the impression that such offensive epithets have been used in respect of the black man only, let me remind you that Afrikaner historiography is often ethnocentric as against the English; it is characterised by a vituperative tone towards the British. I can only refer you to De Kiewiet's book, The Imperial Factor In South Africa, A Study In Politics And Economics, (Cambridge University Press, London, 1937, pp. 103-4).

The same criticism may be levelled against English historians. In their history books a self-congratulatory attitude features very prominently, and the Afrikaner is described as 'uncouth', 'boorish' and often 'un-christian' in his dealings with both blacks and English whites. Again, this phenomenon is not peculiar to the South African situation. It is found all over the world. The accounts of the same Battle of Waterloo as given by German, French or English historians differ a great deal. Ideological shortcomings deriving from racial or national differences will always be there. What is important to my mind is that efforts should be made to put the record straight as the Afrikaners have done. 'Write our own history books.'

In an address to a conference of history teachers in secondary and high schools held at the Witwatersrand University in May 1974, Robin Hallett focussed attention on shortcomings in three Senior Certificate textbooks, namely those by F.A. van Jaarsveld, New Illustrated History; Boyce, Europe And South Africa; and Fowler and Smit, Senior History. Generally he found them fairly free of ideological bias, and one could expect it, as the four authors have definitely come under the influence of the discipline 'history'. African nationalism, he pointed out, was treated perceptively. It was viewed as 'not unjustified' in Boyce's book, 'a circumstance to be reckoned with' in the books of Van Jaarsveld and Fowler and Smit. However that may be, all three books fail to mention all the reasons why there are 'feelings of frustration' among the blacks in recent times and fight shy of one or another of the basic causes such as the social and economic changes, and the expansion of education and urbanisation of the black man.

Irrelevancies

The history of the black people if it is to be a source of pride and inspiration must portray, inter alia, the wisdom of the past, be bound up with the chief, his tribe, the clan and the milieu in which they operated. It must take cognisance of the philosophy, the life and world view of the black man. It should not undermine the ego and should avoid presenting the black man as a marginal man 'torn from the mooring of (his) cultural and historical world .... scarred and humiliated, stripped of (his) previous identity', as Motshabi puts it.(5)

It is to be regretted that the world and circumstances described in the overwhelming proportion of the history textbooks for the Junior and Senior Certificates epitomise the English and Afrikaans philosophies of life, as often irrelevant and 'diametrically opposed to the world in which the pupil is reared and has his being'.(6)

Let us admit that black pupils need history textbooks with a difference. The attempts made by white historians to habituate them to the European views of life have failed. Those to perpetuate the fallacy that the history of the black man in the Cape Colony began in the eighteenth century, and in the nineteenth century in the northern provinces, are being systematically nullified. In the oral, legendary, mythical and allegorical tales are buried the gems of the history of the black man. No wonder the black historian in his dilemma to find the truth often goes back. 'The Bantu student becomes uncertain and decides to go back into his past...'(7).

Let it not be imagined that this quest into the past of his people is an expression of rebellion and an attempt to start off a revolution against anybody, nor is it a clarion call to the black man to regard his history as indigenous. On the other hand our plea is that it will be seen as Motshabi puts it, as an attempt to imprint African features onto the history of the black man, 'on the basis of those that were embraced by their ancestors... it is a desire to create a system of history which incorporates the relevant aspects of modern civilisation, with a view to evolving something specifically black in order to make their contribution to national and international relations.(8)

Education for Democracy

CEDRIC N. PHATUDI

(Excerpts from an address to the District Conference of TUATA (Transvaal United African Teachers' Association) held at Kgabagare School, Mapela, Potgietersrust, on 8 October 1972)

In South Africa and under the segregation policy, no genuine freedom politically and otherwise was accorded to the black inhabitants. It is common knowledge that such freedom was a right accorded only to the white South Africans. Our society upheld harsh discriminations against the black people in favour of the white citizens. Under this political arrangement, therefore, no black man tasted genuine freedom, although the black people, like all others in the country, read books and literature on freedom and perhaps they sufficiently understood the concept. But in the final analysis their life experiences in this connection were those of people who were excluded from civil liberties as known in a full-blooded Western democratic state.

How then could teachers who were not free teach others about freedom? This is a difficult question but I prefer to leave it to you to find its answer. What I want to suggest however is that that impasse - that predicament - in which the teachers were is no more. Our Bantu society is freer than it ever was before. We are a self-governing state and we want, indeed, to be a sovereign state as soon as possible. Nevertheless in our present state of constitutional development we can exercise a genuine measure of freedom and it is this opportunity that the teaching profession should make use of.

Specifically it must be stated that the teaching fraternity must now prepare pupils for a life of free men. That is, a life that demands the free exercise of the talents endowed upon the children by God Himself. Stated differently, the proposition should be considered this way: the Lebowa citizens have now to enjoy civil liberties - freedom of speech, of communication, of work, of education, of assembly, of human dignity. Along with all these rights are obligations - responsibilities that accrue from participation in shouldering the burdens of society.

The teaching fraternity is called upon to understand this new freedom profoundly and to practice it skilfully and usefully. The relationship between the teacher and pupil in the classroom, between teacher and teacher in the staffroom, between the headmaster and assistant master on the campus, between the teacher and the community, between the teachers' association and the government - all these must be influenced by the teacher's understanding and spirit as also his practice of freedom. If the teacher fails in this connection then he resorts to brute force with undesirable consequences. For example, there is recourse to excessive and not corrective use of corporal punishment, there is friction and more often than not open revolt between teacher and teacher, or headmaster and assistant, or staff members and school committee, or between the local tribal authority and teachers or between teachers' unions and other associations.

In contrast, if the teacher succeeds, he generates mutual understanding and harmony wherever he is and this is a blessing and fulfilment of the highest ideals cherished by a free or democratic community. Under present changes, the teaching fraternity must avoid the use of methods that encourage brainwashing and dictatorship in their dealings with the pupils and other sections of the community. They must encourage respect for human dignity and employ more freely methods that place a premium on democratic practice. Methods like 'discussion methods', 'problem-solving methods', 'discovery methods', 'project methods', are methods that promote the type of mind that is open and can cope with the needs of a democratic society.

I have confidence that teachers in Lebowa will give these crucial matters serious and deep thought and will endeavour with zeal to attune the younger generation in our schools in such a way that they may successfully make use of the new freedoms that our people have gained and are gaining, and will further prepare them through education for the coming of sovereign independence of Lebowa.

Higher Education for Blacks

T.S.N. GQUBULE

(Reprinted from SASO Newsletter, March/April 1972)

Higher education for blacks in South Africa is offered at Fort Hare, Turfloop, Ngoye, Bellville and Durban-Westville. These places came into being, as they are at present, in terms of the Extension of University Education Act 1959 (No. 45 of 1959) to provide education for blacks along ethnic lines. By Acts of Parliament passed in 1969 each of these institutions was given university autonomy with effect from 1970. Thus were born the University of Fort Hare, the University of the North, the University of Zululand, the University of the Western Cape and the University of Durban-Westville, to provide education according to tribal groupings.

Calendars	Professors		Senior lecturers		Lecturers		Junior lecturers	
	b.	w.	b.	w.	b.	w.	b.	w.
Fort Hare 1972	2	28	2	33	9	29	4	1
Turfloop 1971	4	19	2	36	10	23	6	-
Ngoye 1971	1	17	2	40	6	16	-	-
Bellville 1971/72	-	17	-	24	3	26	-	-
Westville 1971	-	19	5	49	23	50	13	10

b. = black w. = white

This process gave further explication of the fact that apartheid means not only the separation of the whites from blacks, but also the separation of blacks from blacks. While the separation of blacks goes on there is a terrific drum-beat for white unity calling the English, Afrikaners, Dutch, Germans, Italians,

Portuguese, etc., into the white laager. Who can believe that these places were established for purely educational and not political purposes?

The racial composition of the teaching staff is interesting as the table shows. It will be seen from this table that there is a vast preponderance of white lecturers and professors over black lecturers and professors. Of the white members of the teaching staff there is an overwhelming Afrikaner majority. With all the goodwill in the world, it cannot be that the best academically qualified men in every field are Afrikaners.

It has also been said that part of the reason for the creation of these tribal institutions is the desire to preserve the culture of the groups concerned. We do not believe that the university exists for this purpose. We do believe that the university exists for the pursuit of knowledge and the unchannelled search for the truth in its universality. If it is still insisted that the preservation of the group's culture is part of the function of the university, then we must also insist that only the blacks themselves can preserve their culture if they feel it needs to be preserved. They must not be told by anybody that they need to preserve their culture. Many years ago Prof. W.M. Macmillan wrote:

'...plans for the "separate development" of the Bantu - too often little more than an excuse for barring them from a share in the privileges of the dominant European - cannot be forced upon them; for without freedom, the Bantu can have no true "culture of their own".' (1)

Culture is a social concept and since there is virtually no social contact between the white staff and the students, when, where, and how can they help to preserve this culture?

Then there is also the fact of discrimination on the salaries of teaching staff. This discrimination was introduced even at Fort Hare where no such discrimination was practised before the Nationalist government took over control of the college. Nationalist apologists use tendentious arguments to defend this policy. Nationalist spokesmen have repeatedly said that they do not regard themselves as superior nor the blacks as inferior. If that be true, what sensible reason can they give for paying differently men with the same academic qualifications, doing the same work, shouldering the same responsibilities?

It is often argued that the reason why there are so few black members of the teaching staff is that there are very few blacks who are qualified. While admitting that there are not as many qualified blacks as there should be I would like to state the following:

1 / There are enough blacks in the country and abroad who can staff every department in every one of the black universities.

2 / Black members of the staff are employed in these places under conditions of service more stringent than and different from those of their white colleagues.

3 / Other blacks would rather go outside the country and work under conditions common to all members of the teaching staff, where they would earn the same salaries, and enjoy the same privileges and facilities and be given the same treatment and human dignity as anybody else. In short, they have gone out to seek pastures new because of their opposition to the apartheid system.

4 / They know that education, the world over, knows no racial barriers, but that it should be made available to all those who are intellectually capable of acquiring it.

5 / If it be true that there are few blacks who are academically qualified, one would have expected that, as a matter of policy, the administrators of the black universities would consistently train black students and prepare them to take their places on the teaching staff.

In the twelve years during which the black universities have been operating very few of their former students have been admitted to the teaching staff. At Fort Hare there are six, at Ngoye there are three. Although I was unable to ascertain the accuracy of the numbers, Turfloop and the Indian university seem to have done better. The situation at Bellville is more serious: apart from the black laboratory assistants, there are only three coloured members of the teaching staff - Mr & Mrs Adam Small in the philosophy department, and Mr M.W. Khan in the Pharmacy department. Mr Adam Small, M.A., who has been on the teaching staff of the university from its inception, is not even Senior Lecturer.

Surely if there was any intention to employ more blacks on the staff of these places, more should have been encouraged, groomed and appointed by now. In fact, it is an open secret that some departments directly or indirectly discourage postgraduate students.

A disturbing feature in all these places is the complete absence of blacks in the decision-making bodies. The university councils, that make decisions on the running of the universities are all white, which means that no blacks have any share in the making of the most vital decisions in the running of these universities.

Ostensibly Fort Hare is meant to serve the Xhosas of the Transkei and the Ciskei, but there is no Transkeian or Ciskeian in the governing council of the university. Yet there is a Transkei Minister of Education and a black official in charge of education in the Ciskei. If there is any meaning in these portfolios, then the cabinet ministers should be able to have a voice in the councils of the universities. How can a man be given the responsible portfolio of education when the man can have no say in the running of the university that trains people who are going to serve these 'homelands'? So the galling truth is that Paramount Chief K.D. Matanzima has no university: Chief Justice Mabandla, Chief Gatsha Buthelezi and other Bantustan heads have no universities, and there is no evidence that in the foreseeable future they will have any. It is to the credit of Paramount Chief K.D. Matanzima that he withdrew from the advisory council of Fort Hare.

In theory the advisory councils which all are black were meant to take over from the university councils which are white. But in 12 years there has been no sign of any intention to hand over the powers of the university councils to the advisory councils. The members of the advisory councils are government appointed: some are in government service and are not, therefore, in a position to say anything against government policy. There is no official meeting between the decision-making university councils and the advisory councils and no official meeting between advisory councils and students. Student opinion has no place in decision-making. Undoubtedly these are white institutions for blacks. Here the omniscient whites play God to us again. They know what is good for us; they make all the decisions for us.

One of the most far-reaching decisions the whites at Fort Hare have ever made, in which no blacks have had a share in formulating and initiating, is Fort Hare's desire to buy the land and buildings of the Federal Theological Seminary in Alice.(2) They claim to be acting 'in the best interests of the Xhosa people'. To this I must reply that they have no mandate whatsoever from the Xhosa people to act in this way. This decision obviously has government support, otherwise Fort Hare would not have the money nor the courage to take such a momentous step. We must see this move in its proper perspective:

1 / It is in line with the government's practice of moving people ruthlessly from one place to another for ideological reasons.

2 / It reveals once more the weakness of the apartheid system, namely its inability to stomach opposition. Unless the Seminary conforms, to a greater or lesser degree, to the apartheid policy, it will not be allowed to exist in security anywhere in the country.

3 / It is part of the church-state conflict which basically is a conflict between the gospel and the apartheid ideology.

4 / It would be far better for Fort Hare - instead of spending large sums of money in buying the land and buildings of the Seminary - to use that money in building on the land which they now have or in expanding to the Transkei where they may obtain the land without paying anything. Certainly the Faculty of Agriculture should be where it is needed most, in the midst of agriculturists.

So an examination of higher education for the blacks makes one point clear and it is that the blacks must not choose for themselves, they must not decide for themselves. Otherwise the whole fabric of apartheid collapses. For under this system the blacks must serve 'their own people in their own areas', in pre-determined ways and numbers, and those who are allowed to do so must be carefully scrutinised lest they bring some foreign body of ideas, and apartheid fears ideas.

If blacks themselves were given the freedom to run their own universities they would strive to give the university its true character - its universality. They would admit into the university community, staff and students from everywhere on academic grounds alone, that is, because of their ability to search for truth and their potential to contribute towards its realisation in life. Thus the university would become a mosaic of culture, colour, class, custom and ideas.

Words of Identification

M. GATSHA BUTHELEZI

(Address to a protest meeting held in Cape Town as a result of the closure of the University of the Western Cape, 8 July 1973; the university was closed after a clash between students and administration after the banning of SASO, the black students' organisation)

When my attention was drawn to today's meeting, the editorial in Die Burger of 21 June 1973 under the title 'Brown Students' rang in my ears. In particular the last paragraph haunts me; its translation reads: 'We believe that the Minister of Coloured Affairs has set everyone an example by the sort of firm but calm and understanding approach which promises a satisfactory ending. Let men of goodwill draw a cordon around this problem and keep out the exploiters and fire-brands.'

Categorisation of people and the throwing around of labels is a well-tried and a convenient way of passing the buck. Red herrings (and in South Africa they are really red!), help us to divert the attention of people from facing up to real issues in order to defer conveniently any situation which has the makings of the moment of truth. Whenever black men take the initiative, with no violent intentions whatsoever, it is an easy way of shelving the problem to interpret their taking the initiative as an attempt at confrontation. This attitude is taken regardless of the fact that blacks are an unarmed people and could therefore not be expected to initiate any violence worthy of that name.

The kind of sabre-rattling we have seen at the University of the Western Cape in the past couple of weeks is a smoke-screen generated deliberately in order to hide the fact that we are living in a society in South Africa structured on real violence, with men of colour at the receiving end. As far as this situation is concerned let me confess at the very outset that having been expelled from Fort Hare University College (as it was then) myself in 1950, I come here as someone whose words will be shrugged off because of this similar political past.

I come here as a duty to blacks in South Africa to identify myself with you against the injustices perpetuated against black society. I come here as someone who is deeply concerned about the future of this country and that of all her people. I come here as someone whose anguish is as intense as yours at seeing the fulfilment of the words, 'Those whom the Gods seek to destroy, they first make mad' drawing near in South Africa every day. Any imbalance that causes anyone or any people to commit suicide is a sad thing to watch, but it is tragic when people who are bent on a suicide course seek to destroy the rest of the people in the process. The people dragged into the quagmire of self-destruction have a right to protest and this I believe is what we are assembled here to do.

If South African society was not structured on racism we would not be in the situation we are in today. Had policies pursued by the all-white regimes since 1652 not been based on racism we would not be experiencing this trouble our young people find themselves bogged in at the University of the Western Cape. This is not peculiar to this university but to all black universities. This trouble began when the first Superintendent-General of Public Education in the Cape in the last century succumbed to pressures for the exclusion of coloured children from public schools for colonists, by ruling that all pupils 'should be decently clothed and of good deportment'. In this way some lee-way was made for white parents to raise objections to the attendance of schools by coloured children who inevitably came from poorer families.

The technique is old: deprive black people of the means of living and then blame them or their children for being poorly clad or for their environment to which they have been confined by laws. The struggle to push coloured children out of schools went on to 1861 when government schools had to all intents and purposes become schools for whites only. The climax came when the Appellate Division of the Supreme Court ruled against the attendance of coloured children at Keimoes Government School. This meant that just like their darker brothers and sisters, the coloured children were relegated to a poorer and an inferior type of school.

We see the entrenchment of these racist theories in the findings of the Wilcocks Commission of Inquiry in

1937. In particular the report stated that the ultimate aim of education for all racial groups was to make better human beings of the children, but that in the case of the coloured group various factors had to be taken into account, for example the home environment which was often unsatisfactory and for which compensation should be made; the fact that the greater majority of coloured children did not proceed beyond the fourth standard; and lack of economic opportunities.

Thus, we see, as a result of this kind of thinking, figures of expenditure per head for children of all racial groups as given by the National Bureau of Educational and Social Research in 1969-1970 (page 37). In all the four provinces the average was R83,98 for whites, R33,10 for coloureds and Asians, and R12,82 for Africans. We see differential scales for teachers' salaries based on race. We see the birth of Bantu education tailored to fit the products of such a system to their station in life. We see the Extension of University Education Act No. 45 in 1959 under which the University of the Western Cape and other black universities, further segregated on the basis of ethnic grouping, were established.

We see that, even when we were supposed to be on our own and with our own universities, this was far from being the case. The principle of separate but equal did not apply as black professors and lecturers had to earn 'kaffir, coolie, and coon' salaries, and their white counterparts had to receive higher salaries which their white skins and not their qualifications earned them. We see the white man's hypocrisy in telling the world that he is establishing black universities when these are new areas of a new type of colonisation. Thus we see that these black universities are under white control with all-white councils assisted by subservient impotent black advisory councils. We see ministers of various groups clothed with powers to determine the establishment of each college, and for a start also with the power to appoint and promote members of staff. We see the 'conscience clause', which is included in the constitutions of all white universities except two, omitted in the case of the new black universities. In the regulations gazetted as Government Notice 239 of 19 February 1960, we find included, in addition to clauses similar t other universities, other unusual clauses such as one restricting membership of students to organisations within and outside the campus except with the approval of the council. We see another restricting meetings within the precincts of the university except with the approval of the rector. Another clause of an unusual nature is one restricting publications or distribution or a display of any notice or placard without the permission of the rector, and one which has caused this rumpus restricting the issuing of statements to the press by or on behalf of students without the rector's permission.

There is no doubt that the whole nature and style of running these universities was influenced by the fact that they were for a voteless and therefore a voiceless people who had no means of giving effect to their objections. It is obvious that it was an educational system tailored by the powerful for the powerless with the intention of ensuring that these universities produced 'good Kaffirs, Hotnots, and Coolies'. We hated this 'benevolent despotism', but in the absence of anything else we had to use what was there, despite the simmering discontent within the black community.

Is it therefore surprising that young sensitive minds of our youth find this so sickening that they have expressed their indignation in such an unorthodox manner? If their reaction appears odd to those of us who are their elders, it is logical to me as a reaction to an odd situation in which the youth find themselves. Is it surprising that these young sensitive minds reject the further ethnic subdivisions of black people even at university? Can we say that they cannot detect that the motive in this compartmentalisation is divide and rule? I say so without any fear of contradiction being a graduate of Fort Hare when it was truly a black university which catered for all black groups. It was an enriching experience, and it consolidated our common identification as the oppressed of this land. No wonder our rulers decided to dismantle this kind of set-up at Fort Hare.

I think we should be grateful for the moderate protestations of students despite all this provocative set-up in their so-called universities. I wish to appeal to the powers-that-be to save these young people and this country by acting reasonably in this particular case. They will be acting in a mature way becoming what they would like to see themselves as, that is, responsible trustees. What students have done simmers in the heart of every black man in South Africa, and the only thing they have done is to express it in a dramatic manner typical of students throughout the world. Immature people react like children by pouring fuel on the fire, whereas mature people such as we hope the government are, should rather pour oil on troubled waters. I say this, with every right to say it, as one of the voiceless millions of South Africa. It might interest our rulers to read with me this expression of our feelings in poetry by a black man:

Those who invented neither gunpowder nor compass
Those who never learned to conquer steam or electricity,
Those who never explored the seas or the skies
But they know the farthest corners of the land of anguish,
Those who never knew any journey save that of an abduction
Those who learned to kneel in docility
Those who were domesticated and Christianised
Those who were injected with bastardy ...

He went on to say, 'Yes, all those are my brothers - "bitter brotherhood" imprisons all of us alike.' I think our black brother expresses here what is innermost in our hearts.

I appeal to the government of South Africa not to force our people to indulge in foolish actions that will destroy South Africa. This is the most challenging time of all, when South Africa should show maturity becoming to her three hundred years. It is appropriate for me to end my appeal with a poem by a black American poet, Pauli Murray:

TO THE OPPRESSORS

Now you are strong
And we are but grapes aching with ripeness
Crush us!
Squeeze from us all the brave life
Contained in these full skins.

But ours is a subtle strength
Potent with centuries of yearning,
Of being kegged and shut away
In dark forgotten places.
We shall endure
To steal your senses
In that lonely twilight
Of your winter's grief.

What Do We Say?

CURNICK M.C. NDAMSE

(Excerpts from an address to the ASSECA Conference (Association for the Educational and Cultural Advancement of the African People of South Africa), Orlando, 31 May 1973)

... Bantu education is not of our creation. It was imposed on us. Analysis of it is absolutely irrelevant to our cause. The weakness of the black man's struggle in the past lay in his over-reaction to what other people say to him, write about him, think for him and plan for him. Valuable time, which could have been used profitably, is spent on pointless analysis and pious resolutions which leave the conqueror hilarious and assured, and ready for the next onslaught.

Time and money were spent on the analysis of the Act of Union which also affected the education of the black child. The further onslaught was ushered in with the Land Act of 1913. Precious time was spent on the analysis of the 1925 Taxation Act, by which enactment blacks were required to pay for the education of their children, and further came with force in 1927. Meetings were called and papers were read on the analysis of the Social and Economic Commission's Report. One reads the painstaking analysis of the report by the enthusiastic delegates to the All-African Convention which met in Bloemfontein in 1935.

The benediction had not yet been pronounced, when the most vicious onslaught fell on the black - in the Native Representation and Land Act of 1936. While the blacks were stunned and thrown into an utter maze of bewilderment, the 1956 Commission on Native Education presented its report, which in no uncertain terms, and most unashamedly, made it clear that the white child was educated as a member of the dominant ruling race, while the black child was educated as a member of a subject race. To my mind, up to this time no fundamental change is discernible. But the point I wish to make is this: If the Commission said so, what do the blacks say? What are they doing about it? Educationists and men and women are agreed that the Eiselen Commission's Report remains the blueprint of what is to be done with African education, as long as power to determine the education of a black remains in the hands of the white man.

But it is our duty to educate our children, for we know, as Joseph Addison once said, 'What sculpture is to a block of marble, education is to a soul.' I am saying this in spite of the well-known statement made by Dr Verwoerd. When he moved the Bantu Education Bill in parliament in 1955, Dr Verwoerd said: 'I just want to remind the hon. members that if the native in South Africa today, in any kind of school in existence, is being taught to expect that he will live his adult life under a policy of equal rights, he is making a big mistake. If they, like we are on this side of the House, are not in favour of the native's development within his own sphere and in the service of his people, then such a person should be reared in that idea right from the start.... Natives must not be given false hopes of green pastures which are meant for the white people.' This is the naked truth. Successive government policies are meant to put us in our right place. They are meant to indoctrinate us into believing that we are inferior. This is their philosophy of our education. What is our philosophy - the aims and objects of our education? What are our national goals in education? In this I suggest we drink from the fountain of wisdom of Thomas Jefferson: 'We hold these truths to be self-evident, that all men are created equal, that they are endowed by their Creator with certain unalienable rights, that among these are life, liberty and the pursuit of happiness.'

This was a mighty vision. We believe we blacks are beings of infinite worth. With this conviction, we believe we are architects of our own destiny. This defies previous commissions' reports. We are bricklayers in the nation-building process involved in laying what we consider to be reliable foundations upon which our children can build a decent and happy future for themselves and the succeeding generations. The preparation of the younger generation for the future ahead is our prime responsibility. We are anxious to induce in them the growth of desirable qualities and character. To equip them fully to deal with problems facing not only South Africa, but also the rest of the world, is a necessity, for we have had our day and a full share of problems and enjoyment where this has been possible. But the future is for the young whom education must mould with the highest degree of perfection. The role of education in this task and in the formation of national character cannot be over-emphasised. The task is considerable....

It should be clear that the establishment of homeland governments has brought about significant changes. Many issues have not only become outmoded, but are irrelevant. Do the various homeland governments agree with the aims and objects of Bantu education? If they agree, then let us analyse the points of agreement. If they do not, then their voice has either been very soft or timid. It should be pointed out that education is one of the matters invariably handed over to the homeland governments. It is my considered opinion, therefore, that whatever venom may be in store, it should certainly not be intended for Pretoria. It should be directed to homeland governments. They cannot have it both ways. There is also a very significant aspect about some of the homeland governments. The portfolio of education seems to be responsible for the rise and fall of cabinet ministers. One wishes more time were spent on planning, instead of fighting.

I wish briefly to touch on the financing of South African education. The details are not called for. It must, however, be emphasised that there can be no justification for the comparatively meagre amount spent on African education. This, to say the least, is a serious reflection on South Africa. People in authority have repeated ad nauseam that never have so few done so much for so many. What five million whites are supposed to have done, and are doing, for the sixteen million blacks in South Africa, is always referred to. Any black man could reverse the quotation and say never have so many (blacks) done so much for so few (whites). Nowhere else in the world do people have as high a standard of living as South Africa's whites - thanks to cheap and abundant black labour. And as for what the whites have done in return, a question may be asked: Is it really for the blacks and not the whites' convenience? Would whites change places to enjoy this alleged bounty?

This is all so terribly irrelevant. To begin with, if

we were to accept that whites have done these worthy things, regardless of motive, where is the point in saying this has not been done anywhere in the world? We are always being told that ours is a unique position, so how can it be compared with any other situation in the world? The claim is therefore as empty as claiming that no other country has Table Mountain. What makes the claim even worse, however, is that our social services in South Africa, reckoned in the light of our mineral and economic wealth, are pathetic. Our pensions are pitiful, our social security virtually nil; and all the care of cripples, the sick, aged and poor that is carried out is done by volunteers of the welfare societies functioning on public donations. In other words, although our public pays more than its taxes for these services, the services themselves are woefully inadequate and depend on private initiative. Education is a shambles, housing is a mess, hospitalisation is a drop in the swelling ocean, and insecurity threatens all sections.

Instead of being proud of the situation, the authorities should be alarmed. The poor blacks pay fees for their children from the primary school to university. For other people primary school education is free. Poor blacks pay for books for their children; other people do not. A feeding-scheme is provided for the children of more affluent sections of the population. Children from the poorest section of the population invariably go to school without a meal, more often than not to traverse inordinate distances. The effect of this on a child can be imagined. Then we ask where is the sublimity to be found? I have often wondered why successive governments, including homeland governments, do not make African education compulsory. I am not naive when I say this is apparently South Africa's way of life. Homeland governments echo the excuses given by successive white governments. Every child has some worth in him. It is the bounden duty of any responsible government to see that every child attends school. Every educated child is an asset. An uneducated child is a liability to the nation and can at best condemned to be a hewer of wood and drawer of water. Compulsory education assures the nation of human investment. I am not aware of anything better. We suggest free compulsory education for all children up to the age of 16, with a fully-fledged differentiated programme to enable pupils to follow diversified courses in accordance with individual differences and in response to the manpower needs of the black people.

It must be emphasised that hitherto Africans have had no effective control over their education. It was European-designed and European-executed, going under the term 'Native Education' and later 'Bantu Education'. There was no black voice in the decision-making machinery connected therewith. This educational system purported to prepare Africans for inferior status in life. We need manpower. High-level manpower in modern societies includes the following occupational categories: entrepreneurial, managerial, administrative personnel in both public and private establishments, as well as in educational institutions. Compulsory education will help tap every source. As far as this is concerned, Bantu education is not reassuring....

Allow me to make some comments on university education. The Extension of University Education Act was passed in 1959 by the republican government. This opened a new chapter in the history of education for Africans in South Africa. Festering sores, whose cure has not yet been found, were opened. The Department of Bantu Education assumed the control and administration of black universities. The black people were hurt. They bowed down as they had done before. Black universities are an accomplished fact. May I say the position in these centres of learning is most unsatisfactory. The Afrikaners have lost a golden opportunity to prove their sincerity of purpose. Afrikaners form more than 90 per cent of the white staff One doubts if many of them have been fortunate enough to meet and know the black man of a certain type. The principal is white. The governing council is all white. The senate is all white. University committees invariably are all white. The black public does not feel itself part of the university community. Communication between the authorities and students is lacking. Students do not consider these universities as their alma mater. Members of advisory councils are despised and are considered of no value. Relations in the lecture-room, with the exception of some honourable men and women, leave much to be desired. What a tragic situation! Black universities are accused of failing to produce men and women of such calibre as those earlier graduates of Fort Hare and the

Universities of the Witwatersrand, Natal and Cape Town. Fort Hare suffered most. In 1916 Fort Hare had a mixed governing council, but in 1973 this is not possible or permitted. This is a tragic situation which causes concern. Inter alia, to remedy this situation these universities should be manned by blacks. If, as a result, the blacks should suffer, let it be suffering of our own making. But on this I venture to say our ill-wishers have a shock awaiting them. Homeland governments must consider it as one of the priorities to send students for the sciences, forestry and engineering overseas, as Ghana did before independence. The urgency of the matter needs no further emphasis.

This paper would be incomplete without views expressed on medical training for Africans. The republican government will have to drink all the waters in the sea to allay the fears that the removal of blacks from the University of the Witwatersrand and the University of Cape Town was a disguised plan to thwart the progress of the black man. Coloured and Indian students may be admitted at these two universities. Africans are only admitted at the Durban Medical School, where they are in the minority. At present, less than two per cent of all the doctors produced in South Africa each year are Africans. While the country's six medical schools produce approximately one hundred white doctors annually per million of the white population, they turn out only 0.5 Africans - or half a doctor - per million of the black population. This shocking discrepancy should alarm the authorities.

Up to now, I have dealt with the situation in the classroom and campus. In my concluding remarks, let me say the informal education outside the classroom is most devastating to the black. Children of other races are depicted as superior. Indignities and signs 'Whites Only' have a telling effect on the psychology of the black child. The point here is that, while schools are to be re-organised, social issues should be overhauled. And yet I know if we work hard, we have nothing to fear but fear itself. Our task now, and the task of all of us, as Kennedy would say, is to live up to our commitment.

I close on a note of hope. I know that it is in the period of calm that the fighter must prepare for the onslaught, when the watchman must be on the alert. We are not lulled by the promises of self-determination, by the momentary calm of the sea or the somewhat clearer skies above. We know the turbulence that lies below, and the storms that are beyond the horizon. But we sail with the tide of human freedom in our favour. We steer our ship with hope and, as Thomas Jefferson said, 'leaving fear astern'.

Education as an Instrument for Liberation

ERNEST BAARTMAN

(Address to a fund-raising banquet for the South African Students' Organisation, Durban, June 1973)

I ask you to spend the next few minutes looking, with me, at the subject 'Education as an instrument of liberation'. For some people listening to an address on that subject may sound a waste of time. Is it not true that it is some of the educated people in this country who provide cheap labour? Is it not true that in many townships it is the uneducated who own what appear to be successful businesses? Is it not also true that it is the educated who form the black middle class and then go on to strive to save and preserve what they have? Is it not the educated who are 'reasonable' because they understand the ways of the white man?

To find an adequate answer to these questions would take a great deal of research and a long dissertation. Perhaps for our purpose we need to attempt to verbalise some traditional purposes of education. In our society, i.e. South Africa, we are educated so that we can fit into slots created by society. We get a good education in order to be useful and productive members of society. We go to school in order to avoid being misfits in the world. Then such a purpose is to make a good living, earn a good salary, build some security for ourselves and our children. Thus in any given society it is often the educated who own the more expensive houses with high walls and big dogs, a Mercedes for the madam and a Volkswagen beetle for the man. All this, I want to suggest, stems from a misunderstanding of education, and the kind of education that the ruler wants the ruled to have.

Paulo Freire, a native of Brazil, is the man who through his work with adult illiterates in north-east Brazil brought into existence the word conscientisation. He makes the point that education cannot be neutral. He says, 'It means that no matter if we are concious or not as educators, our praxis is either for the liberation of men, their humanisation, or for their domestication - their domination. Liberation is the opposite of domestication for our purposes. This then means that we can never employ the same methods for liberation as we use for domestication. Education for domestication means the alienation of man. It is then false to say that the end justifies the means because there is always the pre-existence of the end in the means. The methods that lead to domestication can never achieve lasting freedom. This then means those who teach for liberation must reject in their entirety the present methods used in our education. The teacher must re-examine his role and the role of the student and be seen differently. The present teacher-student relationship must be changed.

The teacher-student relationship

In this relationship the teacher is the narrating subject and the students are the patient listening objects. In this relationship the students come with empty heads to be filled with the knowledge the teacher has. If you can picture an empty pail being filled with milk, this gives a picture of what happens in education for domestication. The task of the student is to memorise the contents of the narration. The fact that these contents are not within the existential experience of the student is neither here nor there. Narration turns them into 'containers', into receptacles to be filled by the teacher. The more completely he fills the empty heads, the better teacher he is. The more meekly the empty heads permit themselves to be filled, the better students they are.

The teacher is the one who is knowledgeable and therefore is the opposite of his ignorant students. He justifies his role through the absolute ignorance of the students, and the students accept him because he has the knowledge. They never see themselves as educating the teacher, and the teacher never sees himself as a student. The teacher deposits knowledge into the mind of the student, thus projecting ignorance upon the student. This, of course, is the favourite tactic of the oppressor. This is the banking concept of education.

In education for liberation we need to see that both the teacher and the student are simultaneously teachers and students. The banking concept of education, Freire maintains, highlights the contradictions in the teacher-student relationship. These also reflect oppressive society.

1 / The teacher tells, the student accepts.

2 / The teacher is the one who knows everthing, the students are absolutely ignorant.

3 / He cogitates and the object of his cogitation is the students.

4 / The teacher lectures, and the students are all ears.

5 / The teacher exercises discipline, and the students are there to accept it.

6 / The enforced choice is the teacher's, and the students do as they are told.

7 / The teacher is the actor, and the students see themselves acting through what the teacher does.

8 / The teacher, without consulting the students, chooses what is to be taught and the students have to try and fit themselves to the programme.

9 / In the learning situation the teacher is the subject of the process, and the students are no more than objects.

10 / The teacher restricts the freedom of the students through confusing the authority of knowledge with his professional authority.

The black teacher needs to ask himself, 'Why am I a teacher, anyway?' If he begins to deal with that question seriously he will need to ask, 'Who am I?' In their book, Teaching As A Subversive Activity, Neil Postman and Charles Weingartner list these honest answers to the first question:

I can control people.

I can tyrannise people.

I have captive audiences.

I have my summers off.

I love seventeenth-century non-dramatic Elizabethan literature.

I don't know.

The pay is good, considering the amount of work I actually do.

Education for liberation must first of all resolve the teacher-student problem. The teacher who seeks to liberate his students helps them learn how to learn. Primarily it is learning how to deal with problems. He engages in a problem-posing education. He builds the students' confidence in tackling problems. Not problems for which there are already cut and dried answers. He shapes the thinking of the students but he is so open that his thinking can be shaped by other students. I want to suggest that what we lack in this country are people who can think. Our schools, colleges and universities churn out people who can only remember. Do you or can you remember how at school your teacher said, 'Now think Mohamood,' and you knew what she meant was, 'Try and remember what I told you'.

This problem-posing concept of education must be the aim of every educator of any oppressed people. This is one way to reject our desire to be like those who are determined to keep us down. Even as I speak I begin to have doubts of our seriousness about being fuller human beings when we are going to put people through a system of education which equips them to fit into a machine; when we give them an opportunity to go through an educational system that changes 'to be' into 'to be like', and 'to be like' is 'to be like the oppressor'. Surely our aim or purpose in education is not to become oppressors ourselves. We cannot seek full humanness in order to dehumanise. In our dehumanisation we could say that we have deteriorated with the dehumaniser but the tragedy is that we are dehumanised because of the inhumanity of man to man.

Problem-posing education must help us deal with change. Any education that only changes our consciousness and has that as its sole purpose is enslaving education. We are living through a change revolution. You may not believe it but it is true, the gospel we are supposed to preach is one of change. I cannot be a minister of religion and Christianity in particular if I fear change. Change has as its aim to make man a fuller being, to enable man to fulfil an aim and purpose in life that makes life meaningful. Change must work towards greater freedom. Therefore education must aim at change as man struggles to find reality and what the truth is.

As has already been pointed out our education helps us to adapt to a world designed and created by others. If the others are the oppressors then the oppressed can never hope to get out of their oppression through that education. They will be better equipped to serve the oppressor. They will understand their role a little better. They will accept their higher status in an oppressed community. Thus the teacher compares his salary with that of a street sweeper but never with that of a teacher in the privileged community.

We must equip our students for change. This you may find interesting. Postman and Weingartner use the image of a clock.

'Imagine a clock face with sixty minutes on it. Let the clock stand for the time men have had access to writing systems. Our clock would thus represent something like three thousand years, and each minute on our clock fifty years. On this scale, there were no significant media changes until about nine minutes ago. At that time, the printing press came into use in Western culture. About three minutes ago, the telegraph, photograph, and locomotive arrived. Two minutes ago: the telephone, rotary press, motion pictures, automobile, aeroplane and radio. One minute ago the talking picture. Television has appeared in the last ten seconds, the computer in the last five, and communications satellites in the last second. The laser beam - perhaps the most potent medium of communication of all - appeared only a fraction of a second ago....'

Problem-posing education leads us to question what is being transmitted to us. Many a teacher is in the transmission business. His task in educating others is passing on what has been handed down to him. It does not matter whether what he passes on is outdated or not. People have observed that 'if you are over twenty-five years of age, the mathematics you were taught at school is "old"; the grammar you were taught is obsolete and in disrepute; the biology, completely out of date; and the history, open to serious question. The best that can be said of you, assuming that you remember most of what you were told and read, is that you are a walking encyclopaedia of outdated information'.

Our education is so conducted that we are trained to accept authority without ever questioning it. To make the grade the student must figure out what is in the mind of the teacher when a question is asked. The authority must be satisfied. This is so true even in life outside school. In school, have you ever seen a student taking notes from what another student says? Even in public meetings what matters is what the guest speaker says. The student in the class, the person from the audience who makes a contribution does not have the authority so what he says is of no consequence. This is just what the oppressor wants. It matters a great deal who is invited to address people, especially people who have been through our system of education. You cannot speak of liberation and invite any speaker from the privileged community. Rather put up with inferior, shallow freedom than with sophisticated oppression.

Education that seeks to liberate people is one that must produce good learners. These are people who can never be satisfied with what they are just told. These are people who enjoy struggling with problems. When they are beaten they never give up but tackle the following one with new zest, vigour and determination. Good learners are the ones who are never quick to give an answer. They pause until they have gathered enough information to work through the problem. They value their freedom and seek to free others.

In this country, truly educated men will be those who will day in and day out struggle with the problems we face as black people. The service that doctors give patients will not be confused with eradicating disease. The services by undertakers will not be confused with preventing unnecessary death. The services lawyers give their clients will not be confused with the struggle for just laws. Education must seek to affirm the being of people, black people in particular. Our degree diplomas and certificates will mean nothing until they spell freedom from ignorance, fear, dehumanisation and oppression. Our education will be effective when we transcend our state of oppression and work for liberation. Education will be liberation when we learn to be for others, when we are led out of ourselves, free to free others, black and white.

SASO: The University – What Does it Mean to You?

(From a pamphlet of SASO, the South African Students' Organisation, 1972)

Not many of us are thinking seriously about a university among our people except to suggest a craving for higher education. To many of us this is a passport, a key to affluent living, and a university degree bestows us with a status and earns us the respect of the community. Beyond just thinking about the university we need to discover its relevance to us black people and place it in context with the entire black community it purports to serve (in our case).

A bird's-eye view of a university and one commonly held is that a university is simply a school of idealists, dreamers who have no desire to be anything else but that. Yet it must be realised that a university is a community of people involved in a common search for the truth. TRUTH, this is the operative word. This entails a search for the self and an awareness of your community. Hence it would be quite easy to define TRUTH in terms of the needs, goals and aspirations of a people.

University education for blacks has had the effect of creating a black elitist middle class that is far removed from the true aspirations of the people. Thus the result is a poor imitation of white values and they have become blurred images of their white master. The universities have produced graduates who would never understand themselves and their people. These universities have been 'the secular refuge of mediocrity ... the safe hospital of all intellectual invalids - and what is worse - the place where all forms of tyranny and insensibility found the chair where they could be taught'. You will, no doubt, agree that they are the faithful mirrors of this decadent society.

Is it worth it?

Black students are today faced with a value system. They seek to understand why a particular human model which they identify as 'part of the problem' should be imposed upon them by a white society which has never exhibited any profound love for them. Universities today are extensions of 'the system'. They do not offer black students an attitude of intimacy with the masses. In order for the social structure to be maintained in existence it is necessary for blacks to acquire the kind of behaviour pattern which is consistent with its survival. Thus the university, as it is, is there to entrench the exploitative system and white culture models. Black students have rejected this.

What then does a university mean to us?

To blacks, university students are part of a wider suffering community. To them, the meaning of a university projects the idea of a community. Love and cooperation with one's fellows is a participation in a human model of fulfilment through creative involvement in the social processes.

The university offers oneness and intimacy with the people. Black students must take over the responsibility of the people's destiny and devote themselves to the task of eradicating all evils, resolving all problems and generally transforming the spirit of the people. This is the leadership role black students are destined to play towards the development of their people.

With the emergence of SASO and its aim 'to heighten the sense of awareness and encourage them to become involved in the political, economic and social development of the black people' has come the idealism of the black revolution, a revolution of ideas, of values and standards. To us this is a challenge and a commitment to put our ideas into practice. This involves making a community conscious of a need to undertake a venture jointly in order to meet those needs and priorities which are essential for its survival. Community development is the direction which black students must take if they are to transform their idealism into stark realism.

This is the era in which we must make the mission of the university real to the world it serves. We face new realities, we are the new peoples with vast possibilities and vast horizons between us. Within our frontiers lives true humanity. We have to bring forth a new humanity with a higher conscience. This is the challeng of the university. Are you with us?

SASO: Historical Background

(From a pamphlet of SASO, 1972)

The emergence of SASO was a manifestation of a mood which had been spreading in the black campuses ever since the collapse of other black students' organisations which preceded SASO.

The complexity of the South African scene makes it impossible to have a pluralistic organisation that satisfies the aspirations of all member groups. Social and political stratifications in the country coupled with preferential treatment of certain groups result in different aspirations prevailing in the different segments of the community. Thus it often becomes almost impossible to show allegiance to both sides of the colour line. Attempting to keep both opposing segments more often than not results in internal strifes within the organisation. This is the mood in which black students have decided on several occasions to go it alone.

Dissatisfaction with the white-dominated NUSAS led to the establishment of several black student organisations. The Durban Students' Union and the Cape Peninsula Students' Union, who later merged to form the Progressive National Students' Organisation, were fanatically opposed to NUSAS initially and adopted the emotional slogan of the Non-European Unity Movement (NEUM) - 'non-co-operation with the collaborators'. The C.P.S.U. refused to co-operate with NUSAS in their protests and other forms of activity. They saw NUSAS as a student wing of the imperialist front whose interest was to control the blacks.

In 1961 and 1962 the African Students' Association (ASA) and the African Students' Union of South Africa (ASUSA) were established. Both ASA and ASUSA were concerned much more with national issues and saw themselves as student wings of the national movements. The differences between ASA and ASUSA were ideological. Attempts to unite the two organisations failed. Perhaps the fact that the blacks never attained a strong solidarity on the campus was attributable to these divided loyalties. Lack of co-ordination prevented progress in any recognisable direction as the various groups were bound to compete with each other. Moreover at the time NUSAS was by no means a spent force on the black campuses and commanded quite a following, which capitalised on the differences of opinion between ASA and ASUSA. The fact that this was coupled with intimidation and victimisation of the individual leaders of these organisations served to hasten the collapse of both ASA and ASUSA.

A period of isolation of the black campuses followed the collapse of ASA and ASUSA. The new university colleges which had been established in 1960 for blacks were born into a tradition of restriction. Their S.R.Cs. were under strict surveillance and served more the function of a prefect body than that of student representatives. Not one of the colleges was allowed any interaction with NUSAS although branches existed underground on some of the campuses. In the meantime NUSAS assumed the role of being a spokesman for these campuses. More often than not this accompanied debates on the 'Separate Universities' Act.

The formation of the University Christian Movement in 1967 gave black students a greater chance of coming together. Because of its more radical stance and also because at that stage it had not developed a 'bad' complexion politically in the eyes of the black campuses' authorities, U.C.M. tended to attract more black students to its conferences and this opened channels of communications amongst the black students.

Amongst the black students, one of the most talked about topics was the position of the black students in the open organisations like NUSAS and U.C.M. Concern was expressed that these were white-dominated and paid very little attention to problems peculiar to the black student community. In fact some people began to doubt the very competence of a pluralistic group to examine without bias problems affecting one group, especially where the unaffected lot is from the oppressor camp. It was felt that a time had come when blacks had to formulate their own thinking, unpolluted by ideas emanating from a group with lots at stake in the status quo.

At the 1968 U.C.M. conference about 40 blacks from

Fort Hare, Ngoye, Bellville, theological seminaries, Turfloop, U.N.B. and teacher-training colleges resolved themselves into a black caucus and debated the possibility of forming a black students' organisation. The U.N.B. group was asked to investigate the chances of holding a conference of black student leaders that same December.

Back at home the U.N.B. representatives openly argued the case for a closer co-operation amongst the black centres and as a result the student body mandated the S.R.C. to convene the conference.

SASO was ultimately formed at the 1968 December Marianhill Conference of black student leaders and inaugurated at the 1969 July SASO Conference at Turfloop. At both conferences the student leaders were faced with a complex problem. On the one hand there were accusations by the right-wing elements on the black campuses to the effect that the move to establish a blacks-only student organisation was a manifestation of conformism. This attitude was more expressed in liberal white circles.

Then, too, there were several warnings from the middle-of-the-roaders that SASO wouldn't survive for long and therefore its establishment did not warrant the breaking of old ties.

In the face of this the SASO leadership adopted a cautious approach to the 'relations' question. While still maintaining their recognition of NUSAS as a National Union, SASO constantly took a very critical stand regarding NUSAS and refused to consider the possibility of affiliation to the organisation. They maintained their distance from NUSAS and gradually explained themselves to their black campuses, with whom they quickly found favour.

In the 1970 SASO Conference the attitudes that had been carefully hidden came to the surface. At once SASO withdrew its recognition of NUSAS as a National Union, believing that 'the emancipation of the black peoples in this country depends on the role the black peoples themselves are prepared to play ... aware that in the principles and make-up of NUSAS, the black students can never find expression for aspirations foremost in their minds'. Since the 1970 Conference, SASO has been much more positive in its outlook and is working towards a much more intimate involvement with the black community.

1971 saw SASO rapidly increasing her membership and gradually consolidating her position within the black community. The statement that 'we are black students and not black students' was thoroughly substantiated as SASO set about consulting with many black community organisations in an effort to weld completely the student efforts with those of the rest of the community in this great surge towards attainment of the black man's aspirations. Black Consciousness was highly stressed by SASO as the philosophy and approach to be adopted.

To date SASO has come to be accepted as one of the most relevant organisations in this search for the black man's real identity and of his liberation. The involvement of students with the community by way of community development projects remains a testimony to the oneness of the two, both in plight and in efforts.

On the broader student scene a new and welcome pride is developing amongst black students: a pride in themselves and their achievements; a pride in their own community and a strong faith in the righteousness of their struggle. It is this pride that has ultimately led NUSAS to concede grudgingly that SASO is the only organisation that can effectively represent black students. It is the same pride that has led the black community to welcome the emergence of SASO and to work willingly together with SASO in the setting up of programmes designed to build a self-reliant and a politically conscious black community.

Transvaal United African Teachers' Association: Statement of Objectives

(From the Constitution)

Aims and Objects

The aims and objects of the Association shall be:

(a) To study the educational needs of the African people in particular, and those of the Republic of South Africa in general, with the specific purpose of striving to effect or bring about the necessary improvements called for from time to time.

(b) To establish, or encourage the establishment of educational committees to study the various educational problems and enlighten from their findings both the African teaching profession and the African parents in order that improvements in the various fields of African life can be striven for.

(c) To look after, promote and protect the interests and rights of the African teachers and to employ in this connection any lawful and constitutional means necessary for the achievement of these aims.

(d) To afford members advice and assistance, legally or otherwise, in matters arising out of their profession.

(e) To encourage and promote African literature, art and music and to hold from time to time shows and competitions relating to the above.

(f) To establish a scholarship fund to assist needy and deserving African scholars.

Transkei Teachers' Association: Statement of Objectives

(From the Constitution)

Aims and Objects

1 / To unite the teachers of the Transkei into a body for the purpose of fostering closer relationship by the exchange of educational experience, views and knowledge among members.

2 / To advance the cause of education generally by the advocacy and support of policies designed to improve the school system, to aid the general educational development of the Transkei people and to serve the best interests of the African child.

3 / To uphold and maintain the just claims of its members by negotiating through recognised channels of communication with the educational authorities to achieve acceptable conditions of appointment, service, promotion, remuneration and superannuation.

4 / To educate the public and the teaching profession to the broader principles of education by disseminating information about opportunities and by organising seminars, lectures, festivals, and similar events.

5 / To co-ordinate the activities of the T.T.A. with those of the African teachers' associations in other provinces and abroad by establishing and maintaining connections with them.

Black Academic Staff Association: University Autonomy

(Extract from the memorandum of the Black Academic Staff Association of the University of the North, presented to the Snyman Commission, 1975. (Reprinted from Turfloop Testimony, Ravan Press, 1976)).

It is submitted that there are significant differences between the autonomy of the University at Turfloop and the autonomy of the white universities, and that in the case of the University of the North the state retains a significantly larger measure of control. A comparison of the relevant statutes of application discloses vital areas where it should be possible for the autonomy of the University of the North to be increased and brought into conformity with that which prevails at the white universities. There can be no good justification for discrimination between black and white universities with regard to the degree of autonomy, and such discrimination merely serves to engender the image that the black universities are institutions of lesser status and do not have the characteristics which are generally considered to be essential to the function of a university. The areas concerned are set out hereunder.

(a) The University of the North Act No. 47 of 1969 provides in section 2 (3) that the University shall serve the North Sotho, South Sotho, Tsonga, Tswana and Venda national units. The effect of this prohibition is not only to exclude non-Africans from admission, but also Africans belonging to certain ethnic units not referred to in this sub-section. This is considered to be an unnecessary inroad into the freedom of the University, and most certainly derogates from its image as a universitas.

(b) Section 3 (2A) of Act 43 of 1969 provides that the University of the North requires Ministerial approval to borrow any money or to receive any money or property by way of donation or bequest, or to acquire certain stores and equipment. It is submitted that this constitutes an unnecessary fetter on the University's autonomy which is not found in the corresponding provisions of the statutes governing the white universities. Thus, for example, section 3 of the University of Pretoria Act No. 13 of 1930 confers corporate status on the University, and gives it power to acquire and alienate immovable property, and perform all acts such as bodies corporate perform, including investing, borrowing and lending money. Similar provisions are contained in the statutes of the other universities.

(c) In the case of the white universities there is invariably provision made for a convocation of graduates which is deemed to constitute a part of the University, as much as the Chancellor, the Council, the Senate and the staff and students. Section 4 of the University of the North Act, however, which deals with the constituent elements of the University, makes no reference to the convocation at all, and a convocation in respect of the University of the North does not in fact exist. This is considered to be a very important omission which should be redressed. It may very well be that when the Act was first promulgated, the legislature considered it premature to make provision for a convocation before the University succeeded in producing any students, but at the present time the University has succeeded in conferring 535 degrees and 501 diplomas over a period of 11 years. This constitutes a formidable body of persons with very real connections with the University. Provision should therefore be made forthwith for the recognition of a convocation and for the powers of a convocation similar to the powers which a convocation enjoys at a white university. The report of the Commission of Inquiry into universities under the chairmanship of Mr Justice van Wyk de Vries, at page 20, recognizes the importance of convocation in the government and structure of a modern university. That convocation is an essential ingredient of a university is clearly recognized, inter alia, by the University of Cape Town, (Section 9 of Act 38 of 1959), the University of Port Elizabeth, (Section 11 of Act 7 of 1960), the University of the Witwatersrand, (Section 12 of Act 15 of 1959), R.A.U., (Section 12 of Act 51 of 1966), and the University of Rhodes, (Section 9 of Act 15 of 1959).

(d) The importance of a convocation at a university

is that it has the power to elect the most important officials in the administration of a university. In the case of the University of the North, the convocation would therefore be able to use its powers to encourage Black administration on the highest levels, if it is so minded. At the Universities of the Witwatersrand and Pretoria, for example, convocation elects the Chancellor. Provision is made at most of the universities for the representation of convocation on the University Council. In all cases convocation has the power to discuss matters affecting the University, and the power to make recommendations to the Council.

(e) In terms of Section 7 (1) of the University of the North Act, the Rector is appointed by the Minister of Bantu Education after he has consulted with the Council. This also gives to the State a power not usually available at the White universities, where the Rector is usually elected or appointed by the University itself.

It is submitted that it is undesirable for the Rector to be elected by the Minister. In the first place, this might lead to a situation where the appointee is not approved by the Council. Secondly, it derogates from the autonomy of the University and might in certain circumstances give a political character to the appointment which could be as objectionable as the election of judges in the United States, which is said to be often associated with political influences.

(f) Undoubtedly the most important body at a university is the Council. Most of the statutes of the other universities are at pains to ensure that the Council is constituted by the widest spectrum of society, reflecting all the groups interested in or connected with the university. The University of the Orange Free State, for instance, provides for four members of convocation, three members of the Senate, a person from the City Council of Bloemfontein, a person selected by the donors, two persons appointed by the N.G. Kerk, a person appointed by the Teachers' Association of the Orange Free State, another person appointed by the Helpmekaar of the Orange Free State, an appointee of the Vrouevereniging, three persons appointed by the Provincial Council of the Free State, and not more than four persons appointed by other bodies not expressly referred to in any of the other sub-sections. In varying degrees the anxiety of the legislature to ensure a wide representation on the Council appears also from the statutes of the other universities.

In the case of the University of the North, it is perhaps even more important to ensure a wide spectrum of representation where several homeland governments are involved, a large contingent of students is drawn from the urban areas, and where it is said that the University must be more orientated towards the development of the community. The statute however fails to provide any such machinery. Section 3 (1) of the University of the North Act merely provides that the Council shall be constituted by the Rector, not less than eight persons appointed by the State President and two members elected by the Senate. It is of course correct that the State President in making his appointments, can take account of the different groups, but this is not the same thing as conferring upon each of these groups the legal right to elect their own representatives. The homelands governments, the urban areas, Councils of the large municipalities such as Johannesburg and Pretoria, the various teachers' association and teacher-training colleges, donors and graduates are all groups which should have a right of representation in the University Council. Such a Council would then more accurately portray the aspirations of the community which the University serves, and be less amendable to the impression that it is controlled by the State, which is given by the power of making appointments conferred upon the State President. This particular reform must be considered in the context of the Africanization of the University.

(g) Section 10 (1)(c) of the University of the North Act provides that the Senate shall include only such professors and senior lecturers of the University as the Council may from time to time designate for that purpose. This necessarily implies that no professor has any automatic right to be a member of the Senate, a restriction which does not appear in the other comparable statutes.

(h) The University of the North Act also has other far-reaching powers which are vested in the Minister of Bantu Education, which do not appear from the statutes governing the white universities. Thus, Section 10 (2) (e), which gives power to the Council to appoint members of the Senate, makes this subject to the Minister's approval, and further vests power in the Minister to determine the number of persons who would constitute the Senate. Section 14 provides that the staff appointments of the Council must be approved by the Minister, and Section 15 similarly provides that the Council's powers to determine the conditions of service of staff members must receive Ministerial approval. In similar vein, Section 18 (2) provides power to the Minister to request the Council to act if he thinks that a particular staff member has committed an offence, and Section 18 (3) empowers him to direct the Council to take any action. Upon such direction the Council 'shall thereupon take such action'. Section 26 similarly empowers the Minister to determine the University fees payable by the students, and Section 30, which deals with examinations and other tests of the University, makes the University's discretion with regard to the use of external examiners and moderators operative only as long as the Minister has not otherwise determined.

All this control in the hands of the Minister is alien to the autonomous powers of a free university, and contrasts sharply with the corresponding provisions of application in the statutes dealing with the powers of the white universities. Section 9 (8) of Act 51 of 1966 (R.A.U.), for example, provides that it is the Council which shall administer the property of the University, and have control of the University and its affairs and activities, subject to the provisions of the Act.

The control over academic matters at the white universities generally vests in the Senate, and is subject only to the powers of the Council as the supreme legislative body of the University.

Similarly, any matters relating to discipline, conferment of degrees, the conduct of examinations, fees, the employment of staff and the determination of conditions of service, are all vested within the ambit of the Council and the Senate at the white universities, without any power of interference by the Minister. The only exceptions concern a right of appeal to the Minister where there has been a dismissal of a staff member, Ministerial consent where new departments or faculties are sought to be established and the restriction on the right of admission of non-white students without Ministerial permission, which was introduced by Section 13 (5) of the Extension of University Education Act No. 45 of 1959.

From all the aforegoing, it appears that there is very substantial room for an increase in the autonomy of the University of the North, based on the statutes and provisions of application to the white universities.

(i) It is not intended to suggest that the University of the North has been selected for special discrimination among all the black universities. Most of the restrictions concerned appear substantially in the case of the statutes dealing with the University of Fort Hare and the University of Zululand, but not in the statutes dealing with the white universities.

(j) Attention is drawn to the fact that the University of Botswana, Lesotho and Swaziland, which is easily accessible to black students in South Africa, enjoys a substantial measure of autonomy, comparable with that enjoyed by the white universities. This appears from the calendar of that university in respect of the year 1973/74, on page V, sections 9 and 10. The fact that that university enjoys such autonomy, and the black universities within South Africa do not, might detract from the attraction of the latter in the eyes of potential students, and generally diminish the status and dignity of the South African black universities among the international community of free universities. It is submitted that there is no ground of public policy or otherwise which requires the perpetuation of such restrictions.

RELIGION

The Black Man and the Church

ERNEST BAARTMAN

There is a lot of literature in many theological institutions on 'The Church'. If you have not read any, you are a lucky man because you can go now and read the Bible and learn what it says about the church. The one thing there seems to be agreement on is that Christ is the head of the church. The way some servants of the Lord carry on makes you think that Christ is their servant. Another idea known in many church circles is that the church has a mission. I am not sure that there is general consensus on what that mission is, let alone on how to set about that mission. Sometimes I get the feeling that within my own sect we are not agreed in how to engage in that mission. It is this mission we need to work out and crystallise for the black man. Until we have done that we stand the risk of finding many blacks confused and unable to handle the situation.

What picture does the black man have of the church? The church is composed mainly of elderly people. There are also some young people. The young people who think and ask questions are not encouraged to remain in the church. The Thomases are not made to feel at home. The black church has room only for the good, obedient, well-mannered young person. The result is that the young rebel is not tolerated. By and large the church receives those for whom society has very little use. Not many beauty queens and entertainers are strong church people. This means the church must take a long look at her method of approach.

For many people, young people are to be seen and not heard. The black man is going through this phase of his development. Incidentally, this is not necessarily a cultural trait peculiar to blacks. It is a sociological question in the development of any people. The question asked when any young person took his membership responsibilities seriously was: 'Has he finished with the world?' Nobody was going to listen to a boy. Your grey hairs were your badge of respectability. The book, i.e. education, is beginning to replace this. Again this is not peculiar to blacks. The result is that the church is run, patronised and stifled by old people. She has become the waiting room for the bus to the beyond.

Another characteristic of the black church is that it is run by autocratic or bullying church wardens and stewards. These are men who have become or are becoming power-drunk. If you knew their position in South African society you would understand their behaviour. You have to remember that throughout the week they are 'nobodies', pushed around by some insignificant white boss engaged in that job reserved for useless, unproductive whites, 'Kaffirkyk'. In fact 'Kaffirkyk' is a welfare job. Sunday is therefore the one day when the warden is somebody. Human nature being what it is, he never stops to think what his behaviour does to those in the pews.

The multi-racial church is characterised by white domination. This is changing gradually. It is so gradual that one wonders if it will ever reach the point where it has changed sufficiently to enable us to speak of a truly non-racial church. Unfortunately this is one of those areas where the church reflects those practices of South African society which are against the Gospel of Jesus Christ. The church is God's. This is fundamental to the nature of the church. It is given to man through Jesus Christ. Man joins Christ in His Church. This means that the church is both holy and sinful. Jesus Christ gives it its holiness. Man brings his sinfulness. It is also true to say that man is out to thwart God's plans and purposes when these go against man's selfishness.

The black man is therefore ever grateful to God for His church. He admires those missionaries who came here with the gospel. These men heard the call and came to Africa. The one great thing that the whites missed and missed badly was that Jesus Christ was already at work in Africa. They were not bringing Jesus on a boat to Africa.

The price of that mistake is still being paid by the church and the church still has to pay. She finds her word being doubted by a giant who is stirring from a sleep, as it were. As this giant Africa stirs, he wakes up to the call of many voices. Christianity calls and many -isms are calling. Which way shall he go? Where is the young black to go?

You have the picture that I tried to draw mainly because, at the moment, the black man is finding it very hard to see what he hears or even to hear what he is supposed to hear.

The church in this land is not the church in the New Testament. In the New Testament the fact that Christ is the head of the church is taken seriously. Hence in Corinth you could get a church with such diversity of people. Yet they could workship together. They were bound by the blood of Jesus. In this country people are more bound together by the blood of their fore-fathers. The cross and its message are secondary to the monuments and the messages around those monuments; the blood of our fore-fathers.

The commandment of Jesus Christ was love. 'You shall love the Lord thy God ... and love your neighbour as yourself.' To use the word love in this country is to beg for loneliness. For lonely is the man who loves in South Africa. When I use the word love I use it in the sense of agape. Yet could we say we feel smothered with love in here?

I believe when blacks look at the church they see very little evidence of love. Let me confess something that was a grave shortcoming for me until recently. When I spoke about the church I had in mind the congregation at worship. This was what one talked about as the church. That was very different from what the black man had in his mind. He talked about the church scattered. This is when and where the black man sees and assesses the credibility of the church. It is when Christians in industry, commerce, politics, etc. meet to live out their Christianity that the church is under scrutiny. Behaviour in life outside the church buildings and courts is very different.

The black man finds this very difficult to understand and justify. He never was a religionless or irreligious man. He had his own religion. The difference between his religion and Christianity was that his was part of his life. No matter where you went your ancestors went with you. You were not in touch with them once a week or only when you visited their kraal.

Perhaps it is as well that I deal with one of the -isms that some people would dearly like to see the black man called. That -ism is communism. I am not a student of communism. But let me say here and now that no black man can ever truly be voluntarily a communist. I do not care what the whites say. The communists deny life hereafter. The black man is born into a world of spirits. The supernatural is a strong element in his life. Years of hard work have not removed that element from the blacks. The point here is not indigenisation but simply to emphasise that communism is the one ideology that cannot easily find acceptance among blacks. Therefore the church has a far better chance of attracting the black man than communism has.

The black man, as I implied earlier, wants the church to be involved in life. The life in this world must be a foretaste of the life hereafter. This seems to contradict what is preached in many black churches. We usually hear that we are to endure suffering in this world and in heaven we shall be set free. Pie in the sky. For many whites this may sound silly and backward. Let me remind them that that is partly what is keeping them in a position of privilege. The black man waits for his reward in the next world. This kind of thinking or theology is driving the young and intelligent blacks up the wall. I remember some years back I was walking along the beach at Muizenberg, and a young black man asked me, 'Do you think there is a place for whites in heaven? Surely if our reward and freedom is in heaven, then they have already had theirs'.

It is into this situation that the church is expected to throw herself. For God's children, the blacks, she ought to be saying something to her members about sharing the good things of this life for we claim to share in the godly things of this life. The church ought to be there in Durban alongside the blacks who are striking for their humanness, who are trying to be and live like the children of God. Instead it is Christians who threaten to sack these people. Many are going to be not so much victims of the strike, but of greed and selfishness. What is going to happen on Sunday? We are going to try and preach sermons that are theologically sound.

The church ought to speak to those in power. The church ought to be helping to bring the people in power back to reality. Surely, I do not need an agitator to tell me that I am hungry. I need no agitator to tell me my children are starving to death. I need no agitator to tell me that a stupid white boy with no experience of the work is earning six times what I get with all my experience. What I am saying is that the church would speak much more loudly to the black man if she were engaged in current events or even current affairs.

Another point that troubles the black man, particularly when he looks at the multi-racial church, is the monopoly of power by the whites. This point has been considered before in many places where people have been concerned about the church in South Africa. I know when a black man raises this point the initial reaction from whites is 'these blacks want nothing but power'. That is partly true. The one thing that is not true is the 'nothing but'. Power yes. But much more than that. There is something greater than that. 'Human being-ness.' 'To love.' 'To live a life of abundant joy in Christ.' In South African society the black man takes orders from whites. Some of those orders may be very stupid, but the black man has to take them. When you read the story of the creation, the Bible makes it quite clear that God gave man dominion over all creation. God did not only give man dominion but he also gave him the ability to rule. There is something within me that seeks to be over something. You cannot keep me down forever. The church should be preaching this but it is the church that has been the culprit.

There is hope that gradually she is beginning to bring more blacks into the decision-making bodies. Let us stop for a moment and look at what the black man sees happening.

In every man there is the desire to preserve himself. In the South African context the black man has developed this into an art, the art of saying what the whites want to hear or see. Hence the road gangs appear happy to the 'Kaffirkyker' and he is happy that his Kaffirs are happy because they are singing whilst swinging those picks. And their happy song is 'Abelungu ugoo-Swine'. (The white man is a swine.) The black man in the church has for a long time been guilty of this. What blacks see happening is that the ones who say what the white bosses want to hear, get appointed. The more honest ones are languishing in the back veld of the country because they are difficult. I pray to God that I am wrong. I pray to God that there are no blacks like that. Do I pray in vain?

The other sore point about blacks on these decision-making bodies is tokenism. It is not often that you get an equitable representation of blacks and whites. You get what many people call window dressing.

The church must take this very seriously. If the church is going to make intelligent decisions then she must take into consideration the viewpoints of all her constituencies. When she makes public pronouncements she must speak for all her members.

It would be the height of irresponsibility on my part not to say anything about one of the pressing questions today, that of the World Council of Churches and their aid to the so-called terrorists. The black man in this country knows what violence is. The white structures have not found a way of dealing with him without being violent in the end. It is not necessary for me to enumerate instances of violence. Ask any black man in your group and he will do so. When this violence is practised on blacks it is law and order. It is for the protection of the public, the security of the country and the average white Christian will say, 'We need law and order'. Yet when a white is not satisfied with his employer he can move from one city to the other. When the black does that, the security of the country is threatened.

When some blacks I spoke to heard what the World Council of Churches had done, it was not so much the money but rather the show of concern, love and care which touched them. Many white people say that when the terrorists get here they will oppress everybody. Do you really think that impresses the black man? His retort would probably be, 'join the club'.

The church needs to do something concrete. She needs to join Christ in His struggle for the poor, the oppressed and the hungry. She needs to write more theology along that line. There was a gap which black theology is filling.

Now a few words on church unity and the black man. When the missionaries came into this country they evangelised the country in different geographical areas, according to their denominations. This was possibly the most economical way of doing the work and probably the most convenient way in terms of languages and dialects. It resulted in a further division of the blacks. For many blacks it is an accident of history that they belong to their particular denomination. I have no deep emotional ties to or differences from any of the imported denominations in this country. I have no forefather who was persecuted because he was an Anglican or a Roman Catholic. For many blacks in the pew there are no great doctrinal reasons why they cannot join in the Lord's Supper.

There may be some moral questions, like, 'How am I going to worship together with somebody who drinks and gets drunk?' I think these are the kind of questions that will be asked. The reason for this feeling is that even now in the black church the minister spends a lot of his time on two moral sins, viz. sex and drunkenness. The other great moral issues are seldom if ever discussed in the black church.

With the white government separating us, black from white and black from black, the church needs to bring the people of God together. On the black side, I believe there is an urgency for church unity that is possibly not as easily detectable in the white church. There are some dangers in denominationalism. There are two great dangers for me. I can see that, sooner or later, one of these bantustans is going to choose one denomination and make it its national church. There are advantages in having a national church but the disadvantages outweigh the advantages. Ethnic grouping is going to be deepened by denominationalism.

If we continue as we are, competing in the field of mission, we only add to the black man's confusion. We shall waste our time on competition without really meeting the needs of the black man.

The denominations have made far too many mistakes which cannot be corrected now. A united church can make a new start. A united church could bring the Word of God more strongly and powerfully to South Africa. It could lead her into the paths of God and bring her back to face and meet the demands of the gospel. She will bring heaven to South Africa where man is man, where love is justice and mercy!

The Church Confronts South Africa

ALPHAEUS H. ZULU

(Excerpts from address to the National Conference of South African Council of Churches, Johannesburg, 21 May 1964)

The South Africa which must be confronted by the church is all the people because 'all have sinned' in the sense of becoming a 'law unto themselves'. This is true of individuals and of all groups. In every generation, whenever men live by their own will and desires, friction and disorder follow, on account of suspicion, hatred, injustice and murders that invariably accompany disobedience or indifference to the revealed will of God. The church in South Africa has the duty to call the people in the country to reconciliation with God and with one another. She must make it clear that such reconciliation is a daily conscious taking up of the cross of Christ in deliberate rejection of each person's self-will and acceptance of God's way which the world always considers foolishness. The church in South Africa has the duty to proclaim the good news that in Christ individuals as well as every group and nation can receive the peace of God.

All persons and groups have their own responsibilities and needs. The obedience which God demands of each varies according to circumstances. For this reason, the church must understand the people where and as they are. She will then be in a position to speak the appropriate word. To illustrate our point we shall refer, first of all, to the European group of South Africans. Outstanding facts about their situation in this country are their possession of absolute political power, their superior technical skills and wealth and the history of their race. All three are great privileges. In the eyes of God, the Father of Jesus Christ, all three are, in addition, grave responsibilities. Each one of these facts can be a source of temptation when it leads to arrogance and injustice. Each can be a means of grace when it is recognised as a gift from God to be used for his purposes.

Europeans have enjoyed a monopoly of political power in South Africa since 1910. By denying human rights to non-Europeans, the Act of Union created a situation which has corrupted all legislation in a progressive manner and has made it increasingly difficult to establish a society based upon known and accepted principles of Jesus Christ. While much legislation has benefited all groups in many ways, there has clearly been a selfish trend which provides and ensures privileges for Europeans. Fortunately God continues to love them and so has not left them alone. They seek every day to redeem the situation by giving greater justice to non-Europeans. The tragedy is that their very best and noblest efforts are sure to fail because the foundation, and Constitution of the Republic, is unjust in regarding a section of God's children as less than human. Here are a few things which show that the 1910 constitution is contary to the Christian understanding of God.

The most important thing about Africans is the denial by Europeans of their personality, their humanity. Surrounded by the overwhelming power of Europeans, many Africans have accepted the myth that the African is less than human, and that he is not as good as other races, least of all the European. A grave inferiority complex is caused which inhibits initiative, and leads to despair. That condition confirms the European's original concept so that he comes eventually to believe that he has found proof and that what some may describe as myth is in reality a fact. Those Africans who do not despair seek compensation in various ways. The best of them find it in religion when it becomes their opium. Many find compensation in anti-social behaviour of all kinds. These again serve to convince many Europeans that the African is not human as themselves.

Some Africans reject the European myth. Several who do so for purely natural reasons frequently want to retaliate by encouraging hatred of white men. Those who reject the myth for Christian reasons will forgive the European for his mistaken views. Sometimes they pray that the eyes of white men may be opened so that they may see the tragic results of their attitudes. But so far they have, by and large, failed to do anything practical to assist God in opening the eyes of white men. This omission is disastrous for Christianity. It gives the impression to those outside the Christian faith, that the African Christian accepts the myth; that he considers himself to be less than human and that he is willing to be treated as such by Europeans. I believe that the greatest challenge and trial of African Christian leaders will be found at this point. They have the duty to proclaim to African communities what it is for them to be Christian when so much human behaviour around them is contary to their understanding of the Christian life.

Of recent years, many and loud voices have been heard declaring that it is not the business of the church to be involved in providing for the material well-being of men and women and that activities of this nature are a corruption which springs from humanistic philosophies, either purely social or communistic. Is the Christian religion concerned with the daily living conditions of Africans, with their families, their children, their homes, their hunger, their happiness and their sorrows? According to Christianity, is it sinful for Africans to desire to share responsibly everything that is good in the whole country for which many of their forebears died in the struggle against white occupation? Is it compatible with Christianity for Africans to accept the freedom of the so-called Bantu homelands when in many of them it can be no more than the freedom of cattle on a ranch or of pigs in a sty? What is the Christian African's attitude to be towards banned or imprisoned African politicians? When the African Christian has deplored and roundly condemned all unlawful attempts to seek redress, do not the utterances of many find an echo in every African's heart? And if so, if he is Christian what does he do? Some good African Christians may have had the shattering experience of having their sons leave the country against the law of the land. When that happens what must they do? What must they say?

This is the situation in which the Christian gospel has to be proclaimed. And if gospel means 'good news' then the church in South Africa has the business to show it is good news just here. In my view there is one way only. The African Christian must see the finger of God in all this. That is to say, he must accept this as the situation in which he must see and express the love of God. Remembering that God loves all the people of South Africa, he must consider the problems that surround him as more than temptations. He must see them as opportunities for the testing, not only of his love for, and loyalty to Christ, but also of his manhood. He must tell himself that if the European does not consider him to be truly a human being, it must be partly his own fault. It may be that he has not behaved humanly enough. It may be that he has betrayed the truth of God and lived only to please others so as to gain transient favours. When he was in a privileged position he may have sought mostly those things which were for his benefit and neglected the needs of others less fortunate than himself. And it may be that he has worshipped Mammon and sacrificed principle and virtue to earn wealth. He may have been cowardly and feared to suffer for truth and righteousness. The African has no right to indulge in self-pity. When Europeans criticise themselves he must avoid joining the chorus. Rather he too must look at himself and assess his own shortcomings. He must work out in his mind the full implications of the truth that God loves all men and gives His Spirit without measure upon all so that they can witness for Him. If he understands this he will know that he too has a part to play in the conversion of the people of the country so that they may see and do the will of God.

Above all, Christian African leaders need to begin by speaking the truth to their European brethren. Many of the laws which Africans consider to be unjust have been made by Europeans in good faith but on false premisses on acccunt of the scanty knowledge they have of the true aspirations of Africans. Those Africans who have access to the ears of Europeans, whether as ministers of religion, elders, chiefs, school teachers or police, have the responsibility to say what they know to be the truth about Africans in respect of their hopes and their desires. Many Africans have been labelled as agitators and communists because good Christian leaders have not spoken the whole truth, or at least have not spoken loudly or clearly enough. I am concerned that there is sufficient goodwill among Europeans for many of them to trust us and to accept us as brethren in Christ when they are sure of our love and concern for them. Then they will remember that because we are all human beings and children of God, real solutions of the racial problem in our land must follow Christ's method who is the way, the truth and the life, for individuals and nations.

How is Christ's message to be proclaimed? Members of different branches of Christ's church in this country must gather to listen to the Word of God together without consideration of race or colour, so that hearing the same message they can carry it out together, each in his own environment and group according to gifts possessed from God. Much of such listening will be in joint study of the Bible and of the faith of the Church, as well in prayer and worship.

All Christians need to bear in mind and to meditate upon the fact that in announcing his own mission to the world, Christ, the Lord of the church, said he had been annointed and sent 'to announce good news to the poor, to proclaim release for prisoners and recovery of sight for the blind; to let the broken victim go free and to proclaim the year of the Lord's favour'. (Luke 4: 18) Which is to say that Christ's ministry on earth prevents us from spiritualising his gospel. All, therefore, who know and love Jesus Christ must co-operate in ministering to the material as well as the spiritual needs of the people.

Regular and frequent examination of conscience in respect of motive for preaching and service in the name of Christ is essential on the part of those who will be faithful witnesses to Him. We are told that there is virtue only in things undertaken for love of God and fellowmen.

Ministers of religion must remember their responsibility upon the basis of the prophet Jeremiah's words when he said, 'a wonderful and horrible thing is come to pass in the land. The prophets prophesy falsely, the priests bear rule by their means; and my people love it so ... they have healed the wound of my people lightly, saying "Peace, peace" where there is no peace'. (Jer. 6: 14) In more recent years Dietrich Bonhoeffer, speaking of the costliness of discipleship, says, 'Cheap grace is the deadly enemy of the church ... Cheap grace means grace as a doctrine, a principle, a system ... Cheap grace is the preaching of forgiveness without requiring repentance, baptism without church discipline, communion without confession, absolution without personal confession. Cheap grace is grace without discipleship, grace without the cross, grace without Jesus Christ, living and incarnate'.(1)

Let the church in South Africa be truly the body of Jesus Christ proclaiming His word or reconciliation not only from the pulpits but in every human relationship. Let the church make clear what is the abundant life which the gospel of Christ brings to people in industry, masters and servants; to the unemployed, to rural communities and to dwellers in the cities and town locations; to legislators and to the disenfranchised; and to all who suffer for their convictions. The church must demonstrate the relevance of the gospel in respect of life in this world as well as in the next, to non-Christians and to lapsed Christians and the unfaithful in all groups. The moment through which we are passing is our hour for our witness to the mercy, love and the power of God. We have been entrusted with a glorious treasure. Pray God let us be found faithful.

The African's Spiritual Concepts

E. SIKAKANE

(Excerpts from an address to the National Organisations Convention, 16 December 1971)

African spiritual concepts are what has been revealed by God to the Africans and what is being revealed. God has been in Africa revealing Himself from time immemorial, long before the white man came to settle in Africa. When the missionaries came to Africa south of Zambesi, they found that the African people knew God already and they adopted in the Bible God's Xhosa name Uthixo, the Sotho or Sechuana Molimo, and the Zulu Unkulunkulu. Early missionaries in southern Africa were at a far greater advantage. The South African names of God mentioned above were not in conflict with Christian theology. This was not so in Europe. For more than a thousand years Western theology had considerable difficulty in westernising Christianity, that is, adapting it to Greek philosophy. Christianity came from Palestine. It is Jewish in culture and therefore alien to westerners. Hebrew culture is not western. For instance, Italians, Spaniards, Germans and Slavs had great difficulty in accepting Christianity. They would not part with their gods and so their pagan saints were given Christian names.

Prof. John Mbiti, professor of Theology and Comparative Religion at Makerere University College, in his book Concepts Of God In Africa says:

'In thinking and talking about God, African people often use anthropomorphic images but they also consider Him to be a Spiritual being, a concept which they try to express in various ways. As far as it is known, there are no images or physical representations of God by African peoples. This is one clear indication that they do not consider Him to be physical, even if they may use physical metaphors.'

African spiritual concepts are closely related to the Gospel of St John who says Christ said: 'The time approaches, indeed it is already here, when those who are real worshippers will worship the Father in spirit and in truth. Such are worshippers whom the Father wants. God is Spirit.' John 4: 23-24.

In Prof. Mbiti's earlier book (African Religions And Philosophy, page 75) he supports the almost universal African concept of God which states that the spiritual world of African people is very densely populated with spiritual beings, spirits and the living-dead. Their insight into spiritual realities is extremely sharp. The spiritual world and the physical world are therefore not distinctly separated. They are very closely related. Between God and men are spirits. These are spirits which were created once upon a time, human beings. Africans believe that the spirits dwell almost everywhere, in the woods, bush, rivers, mountains, cattle kraals, around the kraals. They live among men, they protect them and also punish men. Their activities are similar to those of the living.

Mbiti says that becoming spirits is a social elevation and for this reason African people show much respect and high regard for their living-dead. They are the closest links that men have with the spirit world. Moreover, Prof. Mbiti says that the living-dead are bilingual.They speak the language of men with whom they lived and the language of the spirits and of God.

God was in Africa revealing Himself to Africans before the white man set foot on this continent. The prophet Amos said to the Israelites: 'Are you not like the Ethiopians to me, O people of Israel'? Amos 9: 7. We are equal to all the nations of the world. Africans are not inferior beings. They were created in the image of God.

The new covenant of loving one another despite our differences of opinion and background is our great need in Africa. It will be our source and power for creativeness in our land. The covenant of the New Testament by Jesus Christ harmonises with the African spiritual concept of God. 'A new Commandment I give to you, that you love one another, even as I have loved you, that you also love one another.' John 13: 34.

The covenant that God made with Israel, it must be noted, extends to all believers through Christ. It brought us into equality with all the children of God. I think I am in harmony with the spirit of the Scriptures, especially the New Testament, in my opinion that when Dingane's Day was changed to, and designated as, the Day of the Covenant, (1) the Zulus ought to have been invited for reconciliation. This would have meant forgetting the past and sharing all things in common. Both Zulus and Afrikaners should have appeared before God at Blood River for a new covenant. A covenant of reconciliation is still missing; the church, which is ourselves, must do something. If this reconciliation is not effected many of us will ever see the covenant services at Blood River as a continuation of estrangement, increasing the gap.

The significance of the National Day of Prayer should be an act of building the nation as a whole, encouraging creativeness. We were all created in the image of God. God is a creator and therefore we should be creative. The negative aspect of blaming and criticising other organisations and other leaders will not help Africa. We have to be positive and creative in our organisations throughout the year. We need to meet, not to listen to orators, but to share in the survey of our needs and the identification of our goals. We have a great treasure in the resources and talents of our black nation.

NOTE

(1) A national religious holiday, 16 December, set aside to commemorate the victory of the Voortrekkers at the Battle of Blood River over the Zulus. Before going into the battle the whites promised to set aside each year a day of thanksgiving for victory.

SASO: Resolution on Black Theology

(Resolution No. 57 taken at General Students' Council, 1971)

This G.S.C. believes that:

(1) Black theology is not a theology of absolutes, but grapples with existential situations. Black theology is not a theology of theory but that of action and development. It is not a reaction against anything but is an authentic and positive articulation of the black Christians' reflection on God in the light of their black experience.

(2) Black theology asserts its validity and sees its existence in the context of the words of Christ, who in declaring His mission said: 'He has sent me to bring good news to the poor, to proclaim liberty to captives, and to the blind new sight, to set the down-trodden free, to proclaim the Lord's year of favour.'

(3) Black theology, therefore, understands Christ's liberation not only from circumstances of internal bondage but also a liberation from circumstances of external enslavement. Black theology means taking resolute and decisive steps to free black people not only from estrangement from God but also from slave mentality, inferiority complex, distrust of themselves and continued dependence on others, culminating in self-hate.

And noting that:

(a) Christianity as propagated by the white dominant churches has proved beyond doubt to be a support for the status quo, which to black people means oppression. This is clearly demonstrated by their over-emphasis of inter-racial fraternisation as a solution to the problems of this country, whereas they are fully aware that the basic problem is that of land distribution, economic deprivation and consequently the disinheritance of the black people;

(b) we hereby support those Christians in this country who are making a new departure to take the Christian message to the people of God, and consequently welcome the emergence of black theology.

Instructs:

(i) the secretary-general to convey the following message to all black seminaries and faculties of theology in black universities that they take a serious look at the training of black ministers and theologians whose roles SASO sees as being intrinsically interwoven with the surge towards Black Consciousness and liberation;

(ii) and further instructs the secretary-general to convey our belief that black people are best qualified to teach in these institutions, since they are the only ones who are able to focus theologically from the basis of their experience as blacks in a racist South Africa;

(iii) that black seminaries and faculties of theology take a serious look at the syllabuses with the intention of incorporating black studies as a necessary discipline in the training of black ministers and theologians since it is important that they be enabled at least to focus theologically on their blackness, which entails looking back and reassessing one's history, culture, traditions and beliefs, looking at the present and assessing the theological and secular realities of the black experience and looking to the future and their Christian goals.

Black Theology in South Africa

PETER JOHN BUTELEZI

(Extracts from address prepared for Regional Seminar on Black Theology of the Transkei, St Cuthbert's Mission, Tsolo, 1971)

Of late, one hears much about black theology in our South African press. One wonders what is being dealt with, and how this fits into the scheme of things.

What we are after is a real theology, that is, we want to scrutinise the Divine plan. Many a young African wants to know what theology has to say to him of his situation as a black man in South Africa. He wants to hear what God has to say about it all. He has appealed to African theologians to help him out and to provide him with a valid answer. Often he has felt deceived by the white man, or he has lost faith in him. He feels he can appeal to his fellow African, but what he wants is a valid answer, not an evasion of issues.

As theologians we should be grateful for this movement. Our young men show great confidence in us and in theology. They feel there must be an answer somewhere in theology.

As stated above, the origin of this movement lies in the loss of faith in the white man and in the way in which he has presented Christianity to the black man, which has led to the position of some querying the very Christianity itself.

Now what can we say, theologically? In the first place, we must affirm categorically that Christianity and Western culture (and civilisation) are not the same thing. A confusion of the two has led to error.

The problem is not a new one. In New Testament times we find a similar problem. There, the problem was to show the distinction between belief in God leading to salvation and Judaism. (Gal. 5: 6) Some felt that, in order to become a Christian one had first to become a Jew, whereas others did not. We are deeply indebted to St Paul for his work in clarifying this issue. It was especially through Paul's work and influence that the early church finally accepted the fact that a man did not need to become a Jew first in order to become a Christian and to be saved.

We see this problem dealt with in three books of the New Testament in particular. It is dealt with in the book of Acts, in I Corinthians and in Galatians. The teaching in these books is quite clear. There are two problems involved in this matter; one concerns doctrine and the other concerns mutual relations between believers.

On the question of doctrine, it is clearly affirmed that one need not become a Jew in order to become a Christian or a follower of Christ. This can be inferred from the story of Cornelius and Peter in the book of Acts, chapters 10, 11 and 15. In this story, Peter and his party see the Holy Spirit fall on non-Jews and are surprised. We read: 'The Believers who had come with Peter, men of Jewish birth were astonished that the gift of the Holy Spirit should have been poured out even on Gentiles.... Then Peter spoke: "Is anyone prepared to withhold the water for baptism from these persons who have received the Holy Spirit just as we did ourselves?" Then he ordered them to be baptized in the name of Jesus Christ.' (Acts 10: 45-48) Explaining his action later on to the brethren in Jerusalem he said, '... their doubts were silenced. They gave praise to God and said: "This means that God has granted life-giving repentance to the Gentiles also."' (Acts 11: 18)

Many texts could be produced from these three books proving this point, but those quoted here should be enough. A careful study of the footnotes in the Jerusalem Bible to chapters 10, 11 and 15 of the Book of Acts will be very fruitful in this connection.

We can, with full confidence, tell our impatient young men once and for all, that indeed one need not be Westernised to become a Christian. Christianity and Western culture are not the same thing. The same truth can be stated in a positive manner thus: One can become a fully-fledged Christian whilst remaining an African in the true sense of the word.

Having said this, and having accepted it, the road remains open for ennobling the African culture. Just like every other culture, so too the African culture has much to gain from Christianity and revelation. Christ said that he had come that 'men may have life, and that they may have it more abundantly'. (John 10: 10) This is true of African culture just as it is of every other.

A second point touched upon in the three books mentioned above concerns the mutual relations of believers. Paul teaches that once the doctrinal point is clear, then charity must prevail. In I Corinthians 8 we have a good example. He teaches that of itself, eating meat offered to idols is not wrong. He, however, advocates abstaining from this if it will lead to a brother falling away. Many of the prescriptions of the Apostles in Acts 15 refer also to this point of mutual relations. Certain requirements are placed on the Gentiles who are Christians to make their contacts with converted Jews run smoothly. The general principle in this matter is that we should not scandalise our brother.

A difficulty sometimes arises here. What if there is a conflict of interests? Who is to give in? This is a difficult question to decide. In the New Testament we see that Paul had Timothy, as was required by custom, circumcised. His mother was a Jewess. (Acts 16: 1-3) He refused to have Titus circumcised. (Gal. 2: 3; 5: 1-12)

On the one hand St Paul insists on his principle that faith, not Judaism, is required to be a Christian. On the other he sees nothing wrong with indulging in those things which of themselves are licit. In those, charity might oblige us to abandon a thing which of itself is licit, just as the same charity might oblige us to do a thing which of itself is indifferent but which will make relations with our brother easier. This enabled Paul to be able to say that he had become all things to all men.

Black theology demands that Christianity remains consistent with itself. The African finds himself today in the same situation as the first Christians. Like them he does not belong to the ruling race. Christianity tells him that in spite of this he is something, he is somebody, a son of God. He is an inviolable thing - a person. Black theology demands that Christianity acts this through and through and that it should not imitate State attitudes. There should be no racism in the church; the black man should feel a true son, at home.

Much could be said here about the discrepancy between the black man's position in the church, as opposed to his position in society. Very often in society he is nothing, whereas in the church he is a full citizen. Too great an influence of society on the church can lead to the church being a traitor to its call and to its Lord. People should at least be aware of this, so as to avoid being unfaithful unintentionally.

To sum up, we can say that black theology rightly feels that much of what is good in the African heritage has been wrongly thrown overboard. A true position would say that what is good is to be promoted, and what of itself is indifferent should be kept. Black theology also rightly feels that there should be no racism in the church. Is there no danger, one might ask here, of introducing a new black racialism? This might form a good point for discussion. Black theology approaches the black theologian with its questions. Let him not fail it. It has shown its confidence in him. The questions it poses are honest. Thus understood black theology would be Christian. It would be relevant to the South African situation, where the African is a minor in society, whereas he is a major in the church. The black man poses in black theology the questions that worry him most. He makes theology alive for himself. A danger to be avoided is that of affirming things which would not stand scientific scrutiny. As black theology is a new thing, everything is to be done to keep it in the good path.

Church Brings Change

SOL SELEPE

The racial problem creates a crucial difficulty for Christianity in South Africa. The Christian religion predicates a universal order in which men should live together as sons of a common Father, without distinctions or discriminations based on colour or culture.

Yet despite the church's aim and effort racial hatred or, more accurately, racial discimination has invaded every aspect of our national living and has embedded itself even in the church of God. It has split our religion into the unnatural segments of black and white. It violates our sense of Christian brotherhood and vitiates the power of the gospel that we preach. By warping our judgement and blinding our vision it makes clear thought difficult and honest action dangerous. It raises the severest challenge to the church and it weakens the capacity of the church to fight back. Racial discrimination in South Africa stands today as the Christian's vicious dilemma.

I believe that conquering this racial hatred, or whatever you may decide to call it, is a must from which there is no evasion, no escape, if Christianity is to survive in our country. We must conquer it firstly for the salvation of our own souls. We know now, as we have already pointed out, that we cannot simultaneously love God and hate a brother. This is strong language, but it is clear. The church in our country is forced to face the challenge of 'racism' and must overcome it as quickly as possible. I sincerely believe that the conquest of this evil is the high vocation for which the Christian in South Africa has been set apart.

The question now before us is, how can the problem be met and mastered? What part must the church play?

'Believers should be equipped by the church through teaching and discipline to serve God, in all spheres of society, individually, and where possible, corporately.

Believers must also proclaim the commandments of love in race relations and make it applicable to the affairs of civil government and the structures of society.'

It is the contention that the church as an institution and as a group of individual Christians can do as much as and probably more than any single agency in the nation to meet the problem of racial discrimination on Christian grounds and to root it out of our national order.

Racial prejudice in South Africa is based upon suspicion, fear, misunderstanding and antagonism, most of which are groundless but which persist just the same. The popular mind in South Africa needs direction here. Not only are our minds confined by the frictions that arise during the ordinary contact of diverse human groups, but we are also afflicted by the professional hatemongers, the leaders of racist movements who gain prominence and power by means of the dissemination of distorted ideas; men who deliberately appeal to every capacity for hatred within the human mind. These two forces - ordinary antagonism and abnormally aroused fear - keep the popular mind in a constant state of confusion and excitement giving rise to acts of meanness and oppression we normally would be ashamed of.

The church can bring to light the unreasonableness of these popular beliefs through teaching and discipline. It can show that black people are no worse and no better than any other element of the national population. It can show that the black man has played as vital a part in the nation's economic and cultural development as any other element. It can show that, given the opportunity, blacks do as well as anyone else. It can show that giving a black man a decent job does not injure the social structure, neither does it presage black domination. It merely means a higher standard of living for one citizen and thus a contribution to the total economic advancement. As each citizen advances, the whole society does too. The church can help by showing that blacks do not want to dominate the nation. They want only to be good citizens with all the rights and responsibilities that good citizenship, entails.

I believe that many Christians, even within the Dutch Reformed Church, today recognise this, but the truth has been so widely distorted by professional haters and by a heritage of distorted beliefs that it needs constant reiteration.

Let me point out that the role of the individual Christian is important. Action by the church is significant, but vigorously active individuals are important too. I strongly believe that the individual Christian, in his daily walks and talks, can wield a revolutionary influence upon our pattern of life. If tomorrow millions of white church members should begin to act personally towards black men and women as if they were men and women (which they are of course), not black men and women, the faces of the black people and of our country would light up as if a new sun had appeared in the heavens. If to any one the great changes in race relations do not now seem possible then let him set about practising the humbler virtues of courtesy and righteousness in personal relations. That is part of the miracle-working power we seek. Whoever follows such a course can do so with the satisfaction that if it does not bring immediately the national salvation he seeks, it will have the virtue of helping to save his own soul.

Let us Christians in this country remember that we are at war with vicious unchristian forces. And for us there can be no retreat. If antichrist wins, the church dies. We cannot be a sheltered, retired group, chanting and singing on corners in a country run by the devil.

Our way of life must be the dominant way here in South Africa, or our way will go. Thank you, God, for I know that the way of Christ will win!

Black Ministers of the Dutch Reformed Church: Statement on Apartheid

(Statement by Black Ministers of the Nederduitse Gereformeerde Kerk in Afrika (Dutch Reformed Church in Africa) made in Johannesburg on 16 November 1973)

The ministers' fraternal of the Dutch Reformed Church in Africa met to discuss newspaper reports which have recently appeared in connection with our rejection of apartheid. The meeting decided, inter alia, on the following:

1 / The meeting reaffirmed their earlier decision to reject totally the concept of apartheid, in that it cannot be reconciled with the Word of God.

2 / In affirmation of their community in Christ, it was decided unanimously that anyone, of any capacity, status or standing, is duty bound to submit to the authority (of the State) and to honour and respect it, and obey it in all that does not conflict with the Word of God (Art. 36, The Netherlands Articles of Faith) but if any State body advances anything which conflicts with the Word of God, it is the duty of the Christian to submit himself to God's Word and Will. (Acts 5: 29, 'We ought to obey God rather than men'.)

3 / That all those things which promote injustice and unfairness should be opposed in a Christian manner, since they cause social and class conflict and racial hatred; thus we find a hate existing between one part of the nation and the other. Opposition to this should shun all forms of bloodletting, since Christ's blood has been shed for all time, and the shedding of further blood will not solve problems.

4 / The ministers' fraternal noted with regret a rumour, according to news reports, that a possible split may occur between the Dutch Reformed Church in Africa and the Dutch Reformed Church.

At the previous meeting on 10 October 1973, this gathering decided that it was opposed to apartheid, since it cannot be reconciled with the Word of God.

5 / We do not believe that the statement of 10

October 1973, and this one, can disturb the rela ship between the D.R.C. in Africa and the D.R.C. far as mutual relations and financial help are c cerned. But the fraternal believes that help of a nature which the D.R.C. offers to the D.R.C. in Africa should not have the aim of supporting apartheid, but rather of promoting the Kingdom of God in this world. (Matthew 28: 19)

Pastoral Problems of the Migratory Labour System

T.S.N. GQUBULE

(Reprinted from South African Outlook, 103 January/ February 1973)

I used to be a minister at Tsomo in the Transkei. One of our problems as ministers in the area was the pastoral care of migrant labourers. A young man would come from Johannesburg or Cape Town or some place in Natal. He had his three weeks' annual holiday and within the three weeks he must make arrangements for his marriage. The actual marriage usually took place on a Tuesday during his last week at home. On Tuesday and Wednesday the ceremonies took place at the bride's home and on Thursday and Friday the ceremonies took place at the bridegroom's home. The young couple had the Friday night together and on Saturday the newly-married young man went off to his place of work leaving his young bride with his parents until he had his next holiday a year or nine months later. Imagine the physical and emotional strains on both of them!

For the minister there is little or no possibility of preparing the young people for this momentous event which is to last 'till death....' The young couple cannot be helped by their minister through the difficult period of mutual adjustment to each other because for them there is no such adjustment especially in cases where they did not know each other before the marriage. Because the young man is away at work there is no opportunity given for the marriage to develop to a Christian partnership in which the two become 'one flesh'. There is also no question of the couple being prepared by the minister or some other Christian leader for parenthood. It is a miracle of God's grace that some of these marriages do last 'till death....'

The young wife has to face, without the husband's tender care, the ailments and problems of the period of pregnancy. She faces alone the agony and the joy of the birth of her first baby. At best the minister can do only a partial job in counselling and bringing joy to the young mother.

The picture of the young wife of a migrant labourer lulling her babe to sleep, with an appropriate lullaby, with tears rolling down her cheeks, dropping on the chubby cheeks of the babe who is an image of the father, is well-known to those who know this kind of life. One of the immortal descriptions of this picture is to be found in Wesley Bam's song: Lala Baba.

If, as often happens, conception does not take place during the very limited time the newly-weds had together before the husband left for work, she will have to wait for his next holiday when he will come 'to make the child'. Some are advised by the older women: Hamba mntwana wam uye kulanda isisu. (Go, my child, to fetch the stomach.) This means that the young wife must go to the husband's place of work and stay illegally there until she has 'got the stomach'.

The older women who are wives of migrants, who have seen their husbands coming and going every year, do not have an easier lot because they have become accustomed to this kind of life. They have the problems of:

1 / looking after the household, the lands, the live-stock, etc.;

2 / caring for the children and, in their ignorance, trying to give them something of an upbringing. Religious and moral training of the children has to be given by the woman who normally has no authority in the affairs of the home. These children grow up with no knowledge of a complete family life. Those who have never known the joys of children, mother, father living together as a family cannot be expected to appreciate, desire and organise their own family life when they get married. Thus the migratory labour system destroys family life and family religion and cripples the pastoral work of Christian ministers;

3 / they are constantly exposed to untold moral and spiritual problems which they fear to unburden even to their ministers. I found myself being confessor even to women who belonged to churches other than my own and they came at all sorts of hours.

Ministers who have served in rural areas know how Sunday by Sunday they are faced by a solid congregation of women with a sprinkling of men and children. It becomes imperative to appoint women as leaders and stewards.

Let us now look at the other side - the men in their compounds in the urban areas. Most of these men have no personal experience of town life before coming as migrant labourers. To be dumped in these depressing masculine places is not the best introduction to town or city life. They have no alternative but to learn from those who have been there before the way of life in these new bewildering circumstances, and what they learn are the degrading ways of men who have been dehumanised by the system. Some of the men form more or less established associations with women in the urban area in which they work. Thus another family is raised in addition to the one at home, and from their meagre salaries the men have to support two families.

Very few men in this situation can have any connection with the church. It is difficult to trace the Christians among them to begin with; it is difficult to build at the compounds a viable, witnessing Christian community; it is difficult to make the migrants part of an already existing Christian community around the existing churches. There is also the problem of the baptism of their illegitimate children and the standing in the church of their illegal 'town wives', while the standing in the church of a migrant who is known to be in this predicament raises acute disciplinary problems in the church.

There is no possibility of helping these men to have a Christian home life when at the compounds there can be no family life. When they return home for brief periods there is no possibility of helping them to build a meaningful home life with children who must take time to recognise the migrant as father, when he himself does not know how to be father to them and the children do not know how to react to this visitor who only temporarily becomes a father.

The migratory labour system is unchristian because it exposes young men to the evils of homosexuality, perverting their views of sex at a suggestible age. In their degradation men commit shameful acts with other man and burn with passion for one another. It robs young newly-married couples of the opportunity to grow in love for each other and bring up their children in Christian love. It makes it easier for men to be unfaithful to their wives and encourages prostitution. Being conscience stricken because of their misdeeds men slide away from their faith. The whole idea of a woman going 'to fetch the stomach', or a man going home 'to make the child' reduces sex to the level of beasts. The soul is taken out of marriage. Marriage is drained dry of its essence, its joy, its life and love. Marriage is a divine institution; any system that destroys it works against God.

So these compounds are colonies of guilty men each of whom alone knows the depth of his guilt. But the greater guilt and sin is on those who make financial gain and build up an economy on a system that so destroys the personality and humanity of those for whom Christ did not disdain to die.

God-given Dignity and the Quest for Liberation

DESMOND TUTU

(Paper to the National Conference of the South African Council of Churches, July 1973. Reprinted from Ecunews 4 August 1976)

It is generally unacceptable to most people in the world today that a minority should rule the majority without the consent of the latter. Now this is the position in which we find ourselves in South Africa at the present time. And the majority are demanding what they consider to be their inalienable right to self-determination.

The second horn of the dilemma apparently is that the minority, because they have enjoyed such wonderful privileges are determined to retain their privileged position and refuse to consider movement to an open and more just society, one which would rule the roost with the advent of so-called majority rule. The minority fear mainly because it is alleged that majority rule in other parts of Africa has brought in its train considerable chaos and misrule. What we have is, in fact, more an impasse than a dilemma, though the two courses just described are undesirable seen from a particular point of view. The first course - retention of white minority rule - is wholly unacceptable to the blacks, while majority rule is equally unacceptable to most whites.

One of the major questions we need to ask is whether we all still have sufficient control over things to be able to determine how history will develop. Some of us think that there might just still be time for us to discuss with one another - the ruled and the ruler, the privileged and the disadvantaged, the oppressor and the oppressed - for us to emerge into the sort of society in which every person will count for something because he or she is a human being first and foremost. So majority rule is rejected as unacceptable by whites and minority rule is rejected as unacceptable by blacks.

What one fears is that we may soon be overtaken by

events of which the recent disturbances in black townships are perhaps harbingers, such that especially the white man will not have the possibility of exercising any options. He will be compelled to go along with a violent current - and so many of us want desperately to avoid this kind of thing happening. My worry is that it may be that we have another Pharaoh-Moses situation. You will recall how Moses kept going back to Pharaoh to warn him that God said unless he let the children of Israel go free, then all kinds of disaster would befall Egypt. You will recall that Pharaoh became more and more obdurate - he hardened his heart.

It seemed that the warnings had the effect of rendering Pharaoh quite incapable of hearing and so acting rationally - he was set on a collision course with history and that was that.

Those who wield power and their supporters, mainly the white community in this country at the moment, are set on a collision course with history and are on the slippery slope to disaster unless they heed the many warnings that have been sounded and keep being uttered. Their reaction to events has been to become more intransigent and to adopt ever more draconian powers, dangerously unaware that the law of diminishing returns applies in this area of human relations as well. They will have to become more and more ruthless, unjust and repressive, gaining ever less and less security and peace, law and order.

There was a time in England when it was a capital offence to steal but such a stringent law failed to be a deterrent. Actually it made people more reckless since they said 'one might just as well be hung for a sheep as for a lamb'. We will soon reach such a stage in South Africa when the victims of our ruthless and unjust laws will say 'to hell with everything - I don't mind what I do because it will be part of my contribution to the struggle for liberation. After all, we are detained in solitary confinement for needless periods just because we want to be treated as what we are - human beings - and even when we are not harassed by the police and other authorities, when we are not banned and placed under house arrest or restricted in one form or another, our lives in the townships are not really worth living. To die because I have struck a blow for freedom is to have attained a new dignity that was denied me when I was alive.'

Please will somebody realise that the man who shot the Krugersdorp Municipal officials was issuing a serious warning that this is how most blacks feel. Please, please, wake up to the fact that we have been using euphemisms when we have been talking about black resentment and frustration. We have not wanted to shock whites or ourselves by telling it as it is, because what is filling black hearts more and more is naked hatred. I am frightened but that is just the plain truth - when a black confirmation candidate aged 16 years can say 'I don't want to be confirmed by a white bishop' then we have reached a very serious state of affairs. God help us.

The object of our present exercise here, and the S.A.C.C. must be warmly commended for its courage and perspicacity - the object of the exercise is surely to point to a third possibility which _is_ our best chance and that is for all of us to get _together_ and to try to work out _together_ the best and most just ordering of our society as possible. We must desperately, urgently, get down to the business of discussing and talking _together_, arguing with and persuading one another, giving what is due to one another and respecting one another's point of view. Maybe it is now almost utopian - I hope not. The solution for our country must be one that we all accept freely and not one that is imposed, because we are creatures who have been created freely and made for freedom.

Yes, the oppressed must be set free because our God is the God of the exodus, the liberation God who is encountered in the Bible for the first time as a liberator striding forth with an outstreched arm to liberate the rabble of slaves, to turn them into people for his possession, for the sake of all his creation. This liberation is one that is absolutely crucial for both the oppressor and the oppressed, for freedom is indivisible. One section of the community can't be truly free whilst another is denied a share in that freedom. And we are involved in the black liberation struggle because we are also deeply concerned for white liberation.

The white man will never be really free until the black man is wholly free, because the white man invests enormous resources to try to gain a fragile security and peace, resources that should have been used more creatively elswhere. The white man must suffer too because he is bedevilled by anxiety and fear and God wants to set him free, to set us all free from all that dehumanises us together, to set us free for our service of one another in a more just and more open society in South Africa, where true peace, justice and righteousness will prevail, where we will have real reconciliation because we will all be persons in a society where our God-given dignity is respected, where we will be free to carry out the obligations and responsibilities for being human, in which governments and other authorities will be strictly defined so that they do not blasphemously arrogate to themselves powers that no human being should exercise, where we will be able to protest against unjustified inroads on our liberty (something which is nonexistent in the white community, showing just how far we have fallen short of our calling to be human persons).

The struggle for liberation, a truly biblical struggle, is crucial for the survival of South Africa. It must succeed. Yes, liberation is coming because our God is the God of the Exodus, the liberator God. 'If God is on our side, who is against us?' (Romans 8: 32)

(Recommendations of the Black Caucus at the National Conference of the South African Council of Churches, July 1976)

(i) We request the executive committee to investigate an effective means of fully informing the constituency of the events which transpired in Soweto and other areas during the recent disturbances which have been a direct challenge to the church.

(ii) We express our condolences to all the bereaved families who lost their loved ones in the recent disturbances in the townships.

We urge the State to permit open public meetings again in order that:

(a) parents can be informed of the result of delegations to the authorities;

(b) we urge churches to expose their constituency to the full implications of the disturbances through consultation with blacks.

(iii) We affirm the right of the students to have protested non-violently on the language issue and express our solidarity with the black youth in the struggle for liberation.

(iv) We express our support for the officials of SASO, B.P.C. and S.A.S.M. who have recently been detained or arrested without any charges being laid against them. We do this in the awareness of these organisations being amongst the legitimate mouthpieces of the black people of South Africa.

(v) We call upon all those who have relatives missing as a result of those disturbances to contact their local ministers and similarly we ask the constituent churches to request their ministers to list missing parishioners in order to assist in tracing them. If difficulties are encountered an appeal can be made to the S.A.C.C. for legal advice.

(vi) We call upon the authorities to charge or release all those who are detained.

(vii) We call upon the authorities to heed the demands of the community leaders for the withdrawal of the police reinforcements and patrols as they are a serious provocation to the people. We believe that, unless there is a marked improvement in the relationship between the police and the black people, further violence may occur.

(viii) We deplore the continuous reference to black youth as thugs and tsotsis as hurtful in the extreme to black people as this gives rise to misrepresentation of the facts of the situation and is seen as divisive.

(ix) We deplore the fact that the provision of recreational facilities in the black townships has been financed from the profit on liquor sales. We note that the beer halls and bottle stores have long been identified with the exploitation and oppression of the black man. We therefore demand that the money which is being spent in re-erecting beer halls and bottle stores should instead be used for black education.

Black Community Programmes: Aims and Objectives

The Black Community Programmes were established in 1972 sponsored jointly by the South African Council of Churches and the Christian Institute of Southern Africa. In 1973 it became an autonomous black company with a board of directors and was registered under the Companies Act as a company limited by guarantee.

The principal objects for which the company is established are:

1 / To inculcate, foster, organise, direct, maintain and extend in the black community, the principles of self-help and self-determination and to unite and associate the constituents of the black community in their efforts and desire to be self-reliant and to extend these aspirations throughout the Republic of South Africa.

2 / To co-operate with Christian churches and bodies and black organisations in the extension and development of religious, moral, educational and cultural work among blacks.

3 / To promote and develop goodwill, co-operation and fellowship upon a Christian basis, coupled with the realities of black experience, among all members of the black community throughout the Republic of South Africa and elsewhere.

4 / To promote, foster, organise, maintain and direct the moral, mental and physical education and well-being of all blacks throughout the Republic of South Africa and elsewhere.

5 / To extend, develop, maintain, control and direct the work of the various branch offices (both those already established and those which may hereafter be established) in the Republic of South Africa and elsewhere.

6 / To consider and discuss and act on all questions affecting the interests of the black community and further to encourage communities to identify their want and needs and work in co-operation to satisfy them.

7 / To develop and carry on alone or in co-operation

or conjunction with other similar or relevant organisations, the objects of the company.

The goals of the Black Community Programmes are:

1 / To help the black community become aware of its own identity.

2 / To help the black community to create a sense of its own power.

3 / To enable the black community to organise itself, to analyse its own needs and problems and to mobilise its resources to meet its needs.

4 / To develop black leadership capable of guiding the development of the black community.

Our goal, simply stated, is to help in developing a self-reliant black community.

We recognise that a community cannot be self-reliant unless it is aware and proud of its identity and dignity, that a community cannot be self-reliant unless it has 'power' (which manifests itself in the existence of institutions and organisations which make collective decisions concerning the community's destiny), and that a community cannot be self-reliant unless it uses its resources - material, physical, mental and spiritual - effectively for its own benefit.

We recognise also that a community cannot be self-reliant unless it has adequately trained leadership to guide the development of its members.

What we are and what we are not:

1 / We are a 'voluntary organisation' but we are not a 'relief' or 'welfare' organisation in the general sense that a welfare organisation has come to be understood in South Africa.

2 / We are a 'people-centred' community organisation concerned with the mobilisation and motivation of human resources in our community so that these resources can be used for the development of our community. We are concerned that in our community there are not enough mature people in the right places, that whole segments of our community are inadequately prepared for the tasks to be done; that discrimination in various guises robs countless numbers of our people of opportunities to make their contribution to society. To this can be added as further evidence that the inadequacies of our

institutions, social structures and motivational patterns are the core problems of our black community. But we are not a 'political organisation'.

3 / We are an 'initiating organisation'. We are concerned about the lack of facilities in our communities, yet we do not hold ourselves up as the people to provide these. For we believe that only those facilities which are established by the people themselves as a result of their own decision will have any permanent value. But we accept it both as our duty and privilege to initiate action to start projects and programmes which the black community desire and are willing to support once they are started.

4 / We are a 'promoting organisation'. We encourage those activities which the community itself has already started but lacks the means (human, technical and sometimes financial) to enable it to advance beyond the stage of mere existence to a stage of self-confidence, self-respect and self-reliance.

5 / We are a 'co-ordinating organisation'. We accept and encourage individual and organisational autonomy in our community, but believe that uncoordinated action seldom leads to effective work and is quite often wasteful and leads to unnecessary competition between organisations and individuals to the detriment of useful community work. We encourage and remind our community that the pooling of resources between organisations with similar aims is important and can be achieved by common planning.

6 / We are an 'enabling organisation'. We are interested in enabling people to prepare for the tasks they undertake in their organisations. We believe in efficiency because only efficient organisations have any hope of retaining the confidence of the people amongst whom they work.

Efficiency cannot be achieved if people are unsuitably trained or not trained at all for the difficult job of community organisation.

In our communities all over the country there are memories of many 'departed' community organisations which started with enthusiasm and 'fizzled out' for various causes - most frequently inadequate or unsuitable leadership, but also at times inadequate finance or unsuitable premises.

Our staff is appointed and trained to have expertise

in the area of leadership training so that this expertise can be made available to organisations and individuals requiring help.

7 / We are a 'communicating organisation'. We believe that people cannot make proper decisions unless they have information. For information to go beyond the stage of gossip and rumour, it has to be well researched and properly compiled and in most cases interpreted. There are very few agencies in the black community that devote any amount of time to obtaining information, processing it, interpreting it and disseminating it to the people that need it most. Our task and our duty is to become the kind of agency to which people can come for information regarding the many facets of our life in the community. Our publications and research programmes exist for this purpose.

In carrying out our programmes nationally and regionally we see a major portion of our time being devoted to:

Leadership training: To offer the best facilities for leadership training for black organisations is a central purpose in all our projects and programmes.

Economic self-sufficiency: B.C.P. seeks to promote collective entrepreneurship amongst blacks, both rural and urban - through, amongst other things, home industries.

Welfare work: To encourage or undertake only the kind of welfare which has a strong emphasis on self-help. We provide an advisory service to various welfare organisations seeking advice.

Revenue-producing: Finally, for our own survival and for the purpose of carrying out all our programmes and objectives, we are planning to explore revenue-producing programmes which will eliminate the need for us to live on 'hand-outs'.

Black Community Programmes: Excerpts from Annual Report, 1973

Programmes

Our regional or branch offices are the main centres for the planning and execution of relevant programmes for community development.

The branch offices concentrate primarily on programme development in response to identified interests and needs of the black community in ways consistent with our goals.

It is through the branch offices that the Black Community Programmes have expressed their concern and have developed their programmes in response to the critical circumstances of the urban and rural black community.

The staff, along with competent board members in the regions, have produced a variety of effective programmes that have included work and planning with communities in their area to develop their own programmes in youth work, educational work, welfare work, church work, women's work and cultural work.

Head office programmes

At the beginning of this year we appointed onto our head office staff two additional programme assistants, one with specific responsibility for women's programmes and the other with specific responsibility for research. These two staff persons are national staff stationed at head office and are available to assist branch executives with programmes in regions where such programmes fall within the scope of their speciality.

In other words, while this staff plans, initiates, promotes and communicates, it does so in consultation with regional officers in the different areas. For example, the regions wanting to set up women's programmes in their areas will often make use of the women's programmer to assist in training and conducting of such programmes. Similarly, should regions feel a need for research or surveys in their areas, they are able to request the research assistant to undertake such work for them.

In the same way, women's organisations are free to consult with the women's programme assistant on any organisational problem which they might have.

Publications programme

The Director of Black Community Programmes was editor of all our publications until he was given a governmental restriction prohibiting him from editing such work. We are hoping that this work will continue as the community itself begins to take interest in its further development.

During 1973 we published our first major book known as Black Review 1972 which is a survey of events in South Africa particularly those events which affect the black community. This publication has proved very popular with students, teachers and all other institutions interested in race relations. We have found an enthusiastic market for the book here and overseas and we hope that our next publication, Black Review 1973, will be just as useful as a medium of information on the life and contributions of black people to their own development and to the development of the country as a whole.

During 1973 we also published for the first time a Handbook On Black Organisations. This book lists organisations that are controlled by black people in South Africa. It gives a description of the activities each of the organisations undertakes and a description of the structure of each organisation and its location.

This book has been well received particularly by the organisations themselves, but it has also been used by other agencies here and overseas who are interested in the development of the black community. It has also been used by students interested in the humanities.

This publication is not a yearly publication and will be updated in two years' time when changes and additions will be made to the present data. In the future the intention is to extend this work with Black Viewpoint, which is an occasional publication, and poetry, prose, plays by black writers will be collected from workshops held by us in the fields of drama, poetry and literature, art, music and sculpture, and prepared for publication.

Fact papers, study books and essays will also be published from time to time and made available for use in tutorial services and for distribution in the black community.

The community has become aware of the facilities we offer in this department, and our research staff spend a great deal of time looking through manuscripts from persons wishing to have their work published by us. Such advice as is necessary is given.

The volume of data collected during 1973 has also proved very valuable to other people doing research in related fields. Our library of information has been available to all people seeking information. This has proved a very worthwhile service to our community, and one which is going to be even more important in the future.

Consistent with our goal of promoting and initiating we are now planning to hand over this aspect of our work to a black organisation which will extend and expand this work which is so valuable. A new organisation has been formed by the black community to undertake this work which the Black Community Programmes started, and the board of directors has agreed that the time has come for us to enable the community itself to accept this responsibility for publishing and researching. They have also agreed to give what help they can towards the development of this organisation, consistent with the objects of the Black Community Programmes.

This will free the Director and some of his staff to concentrate on the untouched areas of community work which still need to be initiated in the country.

Youth programmes

The youth programmes undertaken by our staff in all regions have already borne results. The programme as a whole was divided into two phases, phase one being a co-ordination phase in which attempts were made to bring together youth clubs at regional and national level. This programme has resulted in the creation of several regional youth co-ordinating groups that seek to sharpen the focus on youth work and to bring about welcome agreement on goals and sharing of ideas.

These groups met during the course of the year and decided to establish a National Youth Movement. While it cannot be said that all youth groups are within this movement it is clear that the majority of youth clubs in the country are benefiting from this new co-ordinated approach to youth work by the youth themselves.

As in all other programmes, our policy is to initiate and enable communities or groups to do what they want to do. Our role is to help them achieve this while they retain full autonomy to develop in the direction in which they wish to develop. Therefore, the final structure or direction taken by an organisation formed as a result of our encouragement is not subject to control by us, and the programmes that develop may not be the action which we feel we necessarily agree with.

But we emphasise the importance of people learning to work together at the problems they conceive to be important. For only when this happens can such projects as the community undertakes have a meaning and permanence which imposed projects cannot have.

In our youth programmes we have now entered the second phase, which is to develop latent leadership in those individuals selected for leadership positions by their youth groups; to equip these leaders with diversified skills necessary for effective fulfilment of their duties; to help the youth leadership to plan ahead and equip them with skills in creative planning of programmes and to help them understand the broad leadership responsibility and its relation to other 'non-youth' activities in the community and in society.

Church programmes

Following our two church conferences held in 1972, we sponsored another conference in February 1973. This was attended by black theologians and laymen interested in black theology, its meaning, its methods and goals. The three-day conference held in-depth discussions on black theology and its role in the life of the church in South Africa.

Our role in the field of church work has been to help existing church groups within the various denominations in carrying out their programmes. We help where we can with advice on programming and leadership training. The Director was this year invited by several church and related groups to address them and/or help in their training programmes. This year the Anglican Challenge groups in the different provinces in particular made use of us in this way. The Roman Catholic 'Justice and Peace' groups also worked closely with us.

In the Eastern Cape Province, where we have a branch office, we work very closely with the Border Council of Churches in carrying out some essential programmes to help the communities in that area develop a sense of confidence and self-help.

Educational programmes

The Eastern Cape Province branch office through its staff has made approaches to a number of people in East London, Umtata and King William's Town about setting up a home education scheme, the main aim of which is to make available to the black population opportunities for furthering their educational standard and to enable those who use the scheme to meet the rigorous demands of modern communications media.

Our staff is attempting to get the community itself to take up the scheme and set up their own trusts and administer these programmes themselves. As our branch staff in the area say:

'The idea behind this is to make the people see the scheme as a local venture and identify with it rather than see it as a paternalistic approach by an outsider group. The role of the Black Community Programmes regional office shall be to assist the independent trust with the technical details that accompany such a scheme and also to provide the necessary initial funds for the scheme. The regional office will also be instrumental in the setting up of the educational trust and maintain steady involvement in the scheme until such time as the scheme runs itself.'

It is envisaged that the scheme will eventually spread throughout the Eastern Cape. Initial places seen as most suitable for this are Zwelitsha, Mdantsane and New Brighton. These areas are selected on the basis of population concentration.

This scheme by its very nature is very involved and takes a long time to organise and a great deal of sacrifice on the part of the community to maintain. Results are therefore not seen within a short period.

Creche scheme

During the year our staff have also been making studies of how best we can assist in the area of child education and care. We are aware that there are several child welfare societies interested in this field. But we are also aware that some areas that sorely need such facilities do not have them and where this is the case we have again brought local people together to discuss ways and means of meeting the need.

In King William's Town, for instance, we are encouraging a local community to revive a creche, initially for 40 children. We have encouraged a small committee, composed of local residents and the local Red Cross Society and Voluntary Aid Detachment to work at the problem. Our involvement in the process is to offer a standing contribution to enable the committee to meet initial costs and participate fully in the organisational and administrative planning.

Health education scheme

We have completed a study of the way in which we could get involved in community health education and after careful study we came to the conclusion that we need to devote an appreciable amount of time to this important aspect of our community life.

The board of directors subsequently agreed that a health education pilot scheme be run in the Eastern Cape as soon as suitable land can be secured. The aim of this project is to provide the black community with essential health services, both curative and preventive, which are so badly lacking especially in the rural and 'resettlement' areas.

The scheme will entail the establishment of community clinics in needy areas. These will serve as nuclei or central points of operation. Because of the pilot nature of the scheme we will start off with one or two clinics in one area and later expand on a nation-wide basis.

The services to be offered by the community clinic are curative medicine, i.e. treatment of already existing diseases in paediatrics, medical, obstetrics and surgical; and preventive medicine, i.e. providing the community with information on causes of diseases prevalent in the particular locality and how these relate to the socio-economic status of the community. Discussions will be held with the community on measures to prevent diseases and all such matters relevant to a sound health education programme.

Workers project

The black workers project is a project to which we seconded our branch executive in the Transvaal during 1972 and 1973.

The purpose of the programme was to initiate and help workers and groups to organise themselves to become aware of their role and importance in the economy of the country and also to be aware of their social responsibilities as individuals, as men and women in the South African society as a whole. The intention was to form a black workers council by the middle of 1973.

Unfortunately our programme officer working in this project was served with 'restriction orders' by the government early in the year and this prevented him from continuing in this capacity. We had to pull him out of the project so that his skills could be used in other directions.

Women's work

With the appointment this year of a woman programme assistant, we are also beginning to make our skills and resources available to women's groups as well as other groups such as social workers, nurses and housewives.

Plans have now been drawn up to help co-ordinate and enable women's groups in the different regions to improve their programmes and develop new ones. Our responsible staff person will be travelling around the country and making her services available to women's groups that need her skills.

Staff

Some important changes took place in our staff structure during this year. Some of the changes were planned, some were forced upon us by events. When we opened a branch office in the Eastern Cape, Mr Biko was appointed branch executive there, following his 'banning' by the government. He is doing excellent work there in spite of the heavy restrictions placed upon him. He has a staff to assist him in the programme.

SASO: Community Projects, 1972

(Extract from Executive Report to 3rd General Students' Council, July 1972)

Community development

Field projects

Field projects are one measure of actively involving students in the physical development of the black community. This is geared at instilling a sense of self-reliance in the minds of both students and the community at large which is a prerequisite for self-emancipation and liberation. Involvement in the black community is necessary for blacks so as to acquaint themselves with the suffering of their people and to give something of their skill to the people.

New farm project on preventive medicine

This project was initiated by the University of Natal (Black Section) SASO local committee last year. Although initially a research project, the second phase of it had to deal with counselling on preventive medicine and the use of medical students at the local clinic run by the Phoenix Settlement Trust. The logical progression of this project involved identifying the great need for a healthy water supply system, the root cause of the diseases there being the stagnant and unhealthy pools people use for water. The rate of illiteracy in the community also necessitated a literacy scheme.

The co-operation of the community was sought and they committed themselves to contribute nominally to the drawing of water and setting up of waterpipes, which project was thoroughly investigated and the first grant towards it came from World University Services in December. Students were organised in December from all the universities but the authorities of the Phoenix Settlement Trust who own the land refused permission at the last moment. No reasons were given. Hence the regular visits of students to the clinic were discontinued and the project is virtually at a standstill.

Attempts to approach the officials of the Phoenix Settlement Trust were not successful. We shall, however, persist in seeking an interview with them or find alternative means to continue with the project.

Winterveld

Ideas for this project were extracted from the New Farm Project. A pilot scheme, though purely experimental, had a successful run there during the summer vacation. The initial project was to help build a school but there were problems with officialdom about the siting of the school.

There is a privately run clinic and maternity home at Mabopane, which is very deficient in its services to the people mainly because of staff shortage and lack of modern amenities. This means that the clinic has to be very expensive for the rural folk because it has no government grant. Attempts to establish it as a welfare organisation have not been successful.

Unfortunately it was not possible to get a team of clinical year students to go to Winterveld, and only one turned up. She did a very good job reorganising the clinic and offering tuition to the staff to keep them up to date with the latest trends in medicine.

With regard to the Health Education and Preventive Medicine Scheme the students conducted a house-to-house investigation with emphasis on home hygiene. There were prevalent slum conditions.

The main thrust of the Winterveld Project was in the area of literacy. With the co-operation of the Catholic parish the project got under way. With only one trained literacy instructor, this meant that teachers had to be trained first. Material was obtained from the Bureau of Literacy. Because of the demand for literacy there were not enough teachers to meet the need. The inhibiting factors of the scheme were poor planning, lack of funds, insufficient teachers and transport problems. Yet this was the only project which went on during the vacation.

Because students had to return to varsity in February, a group under Ben Ramose and Fr Clement undertook to continue with the project. Breakdown in communications between Mr Ramose and the Permanent Organiser meant that the continuation of the scheme was in jeopardy for a while. Subsequently a SASO branch was formed in Pretoria under Mosibudi Mangena which will undertake the continuation of the scheme. Subsequently a meeting with the Winterveld group and the SASO executive resolved to continue with the scheme and co-operation was promised.

PRESO (Pretoria Branch of SASO - ed.) is currently working on a scheme to establish a women's club and a youth club. These, we hope, will be able to bring the local people together.

Dududu

We have had lots of contact with the area of Dududu on the Natal South Coast mainly through Mr Dlamini and his COSEDO, a voluntary welfare organisation. We planned a work camp for the summer vacation with Mr Dlamini. The project was going to consist of health education and literacy. It was indeed very embarrassing when none of the students who had indicated an interest in the Dududu camp turned up and the whole scheme had to be cancelled.

COSEDO's interest in SASO never waned as a result. An unquenchable thirst for learning having been detected by Mr Dlamini, many people in the area are continuing privately with their studies. With the aid of SASO, tuition was provided for students. In this manner was born the SASO-COSEDO Home Education Scheme. In a circular the objects of this scheme were set out as:

1 / to boost adult education where post-literacy awareness and the wider horizons, builds in them an urge to study further;

2 / to provide tuition from formal school to university level;

3 / to stimulate literacy skills and encourage readership, group discussions and debates.

Greater co-operation with Mr Dlamini and COSEDO is promised. We heartily congratulate him for his untiring efforts in the service of his people. We hope to have representatives of COSEDO in this conference.

Education by employment (Edu-Ploy)

This scheme was conceived in conjunction with the Wilgespruit Fellowship Centre Industrial Mission Project. It is designed to help students experience working conditions and together discuss their findings and be able to forge links with the working community and to understand the conditions under which black people work and contribute to the economy of South Africa. Counselling can then be offered on workers' problems and liaison established with them.

A pilot scheme scheduled for December/January failed because the director of Wilgespruit unilaterally cancelled the programme mainly because no adequate preparations were made.

In order to obviate any similar embarrassment the Permanent Organiser has been in contact with industrialists in the Reef and Natal about the possible placement of black students in such jobs. The response has been rather encouraging.

The report on the experiences of a group of theological students in July last year is available.

Leadership training

A highly successful National Formation School on Black Consciousness and Community Development was held at Edendale Lay Ecumenical Centre on 3–8 December 1971. This seminar was very representative and evaluation of delegates indicated that the participants benefited greatly. This was scheduled to provide the motivation for work camps which were planned in various parts of the country afterwards. It is unfortunate that only one of these could be held.

The seminar took the form of the examination of the concept, black consciousness, its practical implementation, the dynamics of student leadership, action training and community development and planning. The seminar was adequately structured with use of trainers from outside and from the SASO leadership as personnel.

A smaller seminar was held on 17–21 January at the same venue mainly for the benefit of the S.R.C., local SASO or any students who are in actual leadership positions on campus. By its very nature the seminar was a technical one, grappling with day-to-day leadership problems on campus: administration, finances, public relations, budgeting, etc.

On 11–13 May another national seminar was held at Alice – a very crucial one indeed since it was the first coming together of black students on a national level since the events which led to over a thousand students from Turfloop being expelled. Hence the seminar had to assume a new form and constitute itself into centre representatives.

A discussion on the obligation of campus in terms of their self-professed solidarity led to the now famous Alice Declaration, which gave rise to the 1 June countrywide boycotts. A wide-ranging discussion on leadership problems was gone into in depth. This was aimed at helping leadership meet its problems.

A purely local effort was undertaken in April under the auspices of the Turfloop S.R.C. when a Transvaal regional seminar was held at Wilgespruit. This is to be applauded and is in keeping with constitutional provision on regional organisation. Although staffed by the Turfloop S.R.C., two executive staff officers were invited to help run this efficient service.

Student benefit scheme

This scheme, still at its embryonic stage, has been organised by the distribution of SASO identity cards, which very few centres bothered to return. Both the December and January seminars recommended that centres organise with local commerce to get discounts for students on production of the I.D. card. Regrettably, very few centres did this. In Durban, various black businessmen committed themselves to offering substantial discounts for students. Unfortunately this wasn't circulated even in Durban, mainly because no centre returned their cards.

Comment

We regret to report that our fieldwork projects still leave much to be desired. As yet we cannot claim one completely satisfactory project. The only one which was partially effective was the Winterveld one and that, too, was bedevilled with many frustrating problems which confronted the participants.

One of the main contributing factors is inadequate finances. This greatly militates against the implementation of self-reliance in our projects. It is again because of lack of funds that we have no vehicle which will make the work of the Permanent Organiser easier. Without transport it is almost impossible to penetrate deep into the rural areas which are our main concern in terms of the programme.

Another reason is that the Permanent Organiser has been rather unwell for a while. This has rather ill-disposed him to the rugged travelling his portfolio requires. Added to that we still require trained literacy managers in this field, hence both the Permanent Organiser and the Secretary-General are taking a course in this aspect. We hope to make more students available for training as literacy managers in the near future.

The fact need not be lost sight of that students are also responsible because of their lethargy towards projects. This is one area which has not really gained much commitment from black students, especially if it means a sacrifice of vacations.

It is then suggested that in order to make a real success of our community development projects we must concentrate on the present projects: Dududu, New Farm, Winterveld etc.

It is our conviction that through literacy projects we will be able to reap an appreciable harvest in terms of progressive awareness. These are the easiest programmes to organise. Hence a real need for a qualified literacy manager on our staff. The training of both executive staff officers as literacy managers is meant to meet this need.

Another recommendation is that our leadership programmes need to be expanded to benefit the wide community. A seminar is being planned, for instance, for schools in August/September over a weekend.

ASSECA: Objectives and Programmes

(Extracts from Secretary's Report for the period 9 February 1968 to 28 February 1970)

Background to the formation of the Association for the Educational and Cultural Advancement of the African People of South Africa (ASSECA).

The appalling 1967 matriculation results prompted the late Mr P.Q. Vundla, our founder and former chairman, to summon a meeting of a few people at the beginning of 1968, to take a close look at African education. The people invited to that exploratory meeting included leaders of various African organisations.

The findings of that first meeting were that the poor examination results were due to inadequate school accommodation, the insufficiency or lack of school equipment, such as desks, teaching aids, library and laboratory requisites.

Unsuitably qualified teachers, the double-session system, the inadequacy of the funds set aside for African education, the use of mother tongue as the medium of instruction, lack of compulsory education, and failure on the part of some teachers to conduct themselves in a manner befitting their profession, were found to be additional contributory causes of the poor examination results.

The people who attended that first meeting felt that if the African people were to take their rightful place among the peoples of the world, they would have to play a positive role in the education of their children.

A decision was taken that a bigger and more representative meeting be called to consider the advisability of forming a national organisation that would mobilise the African people in helping themselves. The immediate objective of this organisation would be to see to it that every African child attended school and received the best education under the best possible conditions.

Short-term programme

Because of the element of urgency brought about by the shocking 1967 matriculation results, and the turning away from our schools of large numbers of children because of insufficient accommodation, ASSECA had of necessity to divide its work into short and long-term programmes.

ASSECA's short-term programme took the form of assisting matric failures, finding school accommodation, establishing branches, and assisting with school equipment.

Long-term programme

ASSECA's long-term programme takes the form of striving to overcome all the obstacles to the educational and cultural advancement of the African people.

In conclusion, it should be pointed out that different African leaders have at different times advocated the need for the African people to strive for their own advancement. What has been lacking so far has been a channel through which the different organisations and individuals could funnel their efforts. By virtue of its being able to tackle our educational and cultural problems at all levels, ASSECA is signally suited to meet this need.

ASSECA was made a non-political body, and this has been done advisedly, so that every African, be he a government or non-government servant, should feel free to be involved in its work.

It should also be pointed out that the improvements ASSECA is trying to bring about are effected through statutory channels.

Women's Association of the African Independent Churches: Report covering 1969–71

The Women's Association of the African Independent Churches two years ago themselves chose as a theme for their organisation: 'How can I help myself and others' and 'How can I as a minister's wife be of better service to my congregation'. The women decided to set up three projects:

(a) Needlework classes
(b) Courses to combat analphabetism
(c) Nutrition

Three experimental projects were set up in Soweto, Johannesburg, and the intention was that these would be organised and led by the women themselves. In the beginning this gave rise to an enormous number of headaches since the women of the African independent churches were simply not sufficiently trained to tackle something of this nature. We were compelled therefore, to draw upon people from outside who were prepared to help us set up the work.

The classes were organised by the wives of the ministers of the various churches in Soweto. The work is decentralised, i.e. the teachers go to the churches and only upon invitation. This system works quite well, far better than if the women had to go to a central venue for their lessons.

Survey of the classes in Soweto

Needlework classes: There are three needlework classes in Soweto of which one is especially for young girls. We hope to reach the youth so much better in this way. Mrs D. Gule is the needlework teacher. There have been two sales; return R84,00. Approximately 50 women have attended the classes.

Classes to combat analphabetism: These are held at three places in Soweto. There are approximately 25 students and the classes are only now starting to swing. There were difficulties: it was almost impossible to find women who were prepared to become teachers; many expected salaries. But W.A.A.I.C. regards teaching as a service to others on a voluntary basis. This principle is now generally accepted by the women and this is a big step forward. There are now 12 people who work without salaries and who only receive some travelling expenses now and again. The classes are also expanding now. There is a particular demand for evening classes.

Nutrition and cooking classes: At the moment there are six classes in Soweto led by Mrs D. Maakwe. Training is also given in hygiene, budgeting, laundering, ironing, etc. The classes are attended by approximately 48 women. Some of the classes which were set up two years ago do not exist any more because the classes last only eight months or because the house in which a particular class was held is no longer made available. New classes continue to come into being all the time and the demand for classes is increasing. We are now busy setting up well-defined programmes for the classes.

As a result of these classes there now exists in Soweto a group of 5 women who can give the lead and who can train other women: 3 needlework teachers and 2 women who attend to the courses to combat analphabetism.

Survey of the classes in the republic

The three projects in Soweto were experimental projects. The model tried out can now be applied to local situations at other places in the republic. The classes are usually preceded by an information week. An information week is held only at the request of the women in a particular place. The week is organised by the local women themselves. It depends on the choice of the women which type of classes are set up. During such an information week discussions are held on 'How does one organise a class', etc. The teachers are also invited to give an introductory lecture on methods of work and techniques. Information weeks differ in nature from place to place: in the city, needlework and nutrition (e.g. 'How must I deal with money'); in the country, nutrition, especially in the context of horticulture, and combating analphabetism.

In Bloemfontein classes in needlework and to combat analphabetism are now being set up. In Maclear, Transkei, the plans are to organise a needlework and handicraft class. In Cape Town an information week is to be held to prepare for needlework classes and courses to combat analphabetism. Young girls in the Transkei have asked for a special information week on sexual education.

In the past year special emphasis has been laid on the structure of the organisation. Without a sound structure one cannot organise classes. The management of W.A.A.I.C. has therefore repeatedly discussed subjects as: What is a district? What is a branch? How does one hold a meeting? etc. The organisation is expanding apace all across the country.

It is of importance that women are realising more and more that they will have to raise funds themselves if they want to work independently.

Edendale Lay Ecumenical Centre: Location and Nature

The Edendale Lay Ecumenical Centre is situated six miles south of Pietermaritzburg, Natal, in a Makholwa tribal area which includes a full range of African types from the rural to the sophisticated town dwellers. It serves the third largest African community in the Province of Natal, an African community of 50 000 people.

Being the only ecumenical centre in South Africa administered by Africans, its services will eventually extend to the whole South African community.

The Centre is a symbol of African initiative. The site was purchased and the Centre is partly supported by Nzondelelo, an African organisation within the Methodist Church in Natal. The trustees, who are dynamic and educated African representatives of various churches, hold free-hold rights to the property under the chief of the Edendale Makholwa tribe, the Edendale district being one of the few remaining areas close to an urban complex in which African people do enjoy free-hold property rights. The advantage of this situation is that all racial groups can meet on the premises.

Objectives

Set within the social network of a divided and apathetic society, it aims to create the type of informed Christian leadership that is prepared to take community responsibility and leadership seriously.

The project will bring together people from different professional and racial groups to develop their awareness of responsibility for community leadership, and to explore ways in which this leadership can be exercised with mutual concern.

The present situation of a professional elite who have become alienated from their fellows causes anxiety in African communities where belonging to each other is an important component of African personality.

This project would attempt to bridge the gap, and integrate this leadership into the African community and confront professional people of other racial groups with the contribution they could make to the welfare of the whole community.

In addition to providing Christian education for the laymen, it aims to serve the emerging African industrial worker and urban dwellers. The Centre believes that the African is a community man who has to regain his awareness of himself as a human and social being at a time of rapid transition in a closed society.

Programmes and courses

To this end the Edendale Ecumenical Centre has embarked on a series of programmes, grounded in the local community but flexible to serve the needs of all communities.

1 / The community leadership programme is a contribution at a new level, directed towards the professional elite as well as to the needs of the whole community.

2 / The changing role of women in the home and family life calls for an attempt to equip and support them in the social upheaval caused by rapid transition, so that they may be a source of strength to other families.

3 / Youth leadership training: There is great need for the promotion of the social, cultural and the spiritual well-being of African youth by means of a healthy and better appreciation of Christian teachings, group discussion, training in speech and drama, and the understanding of civic affairs.

Community leadership programme

If the African community has to acquire skills to help itself a leadership training programme is essential. The plea is: Help us to help ourselves; give us good support at this initial stage.

Conference facilities

At present the facilities consist of a dining hall, which serves for conference room, and two blocks for sleeping accommodation. Further facilities needed for conference and courses are: three further sleeping units, office and meetingrooms, hall and library, nursery school and creche, domestic block and transport. (Some of these facilities have already been constructed.)

THE HOMELANDS

The Regional Political Dynamic

D.A. KOTZE

The African National Congress and the Pan-Africanist Congress never attained the status of mass movements in terms of membership. Controlled by members of the African elite they remained confined to the largest urban centres and failed to gain significant support in most rural areas. The declaration of the A.N.C. and P.A.C. as unlawful organisations in terms of the Unlawful Organisations Act in 1960 nevertheless left a political vacuum. Underground organisations of Africans and whites had been crushed by the South African Security Police by the middle of the 1960s before they could achieve a significant following. A military wing of the A.N.C. was established, the Umkonto we Sizwe, and the A.N.C. established itself as an organisation in exile. The rivalry between the A.N.C. and P.A.C. continued when the latter also went abroad. Poqo, a cell-like offshoot of the P.A.C., dedicated to violence, was banned together with Umkonto we Sizwe, in 1963. The Dance Association, the S.A.A. Football League and the Football Club were also regarded as the P.A.C. in disguise, and banned in 1963. Other unlawful organisations which sprang up in this period were the National Committee for Liberation and its successor, the African Resistance Movement, the Yu Chi Chan Club, the Unity Movement of South Africa, and the African People's Democratic Union of Southern Africa.

The failure of the A.N.C. during its long existence from 1912 to 1960 to forge effective links with voluntary associations was to some extent responsible for its failure to regroup and appoint alternative leaders and achieve effective continuity after its banning. It was only at the beginning of the 1970s that the South African Students' Organisation (SASO), a leading exponent of Black Consciousness, realised that penetration of voluntary associations was essential to the creation of a mass movement in a parochially oriented society.

The implementation of the South African government's separate development policy necessitated the setting up of alternative platforms for African political expression. The first step in this direction was taken with the establishment of Bantu Authorities, commencing in 1951, which consisted of territorial authorities for each of the eight ethnic African groups in the African homelands, and subsidiary regional and tribal authorities. ('African homelands', 'white areas', and similar terms refer to the territorial division of South Africa into white and African areas in terms of the Natives Land Act, 1913, and the Bantu Trust and Land Act, 1936.) The entire constellation was composed mainly of traditional leaders. At the same time (1951), the defunct Natives Representative Council (established in 1936) was abolished. The next step was to abolish the African franchise for the South African parliament, increase the powers for the territorial authorities, and to promise further constitutional advance in the homelands. This was done in 1959 and the enabling legislative machinery was the Promotion of Bantu Self-Government Act.

The third step was the granting of self-governing status to the Transkei in 1963 through the Transkei Constitution Act. Departments of the Interior, Justice, Education, Roads and Works, Agriculture and Forestry, Finance and the Chief Minister came under Transkei government jurisdiction, with Health being added in 1973. Since 1968 territorial authorities for other homelands have been organised along the same lines as in the Transkei government service except in the Swazi homeland where no territorial authority has yet been established. Preparatory to the granting of self-government, the Bantu Homelands Citizenship Act of 1970 conferred on every African citizenship of one or another homeland. The Bantu Homelands Constitution Act of 1971 enabled the South African government to bestow self-governing status on a homeland by proclamation. This is done in two stages - in the first a legislative assembly is established as a brief preparatory stage for the second where the homeland government may legislate in respect of matters under its jurisdiction. At the beginning of the latter stage general elections are held to fill the vacancies for elected members in the legislative assemblies, a minority in all cases. The majority of members are nominated according to prescribed procedures by electoral colleges consisting mainly of traditional leaders.

The constitutional position of the homelands was taken a step further in 1976 when the Transkei became an independent republic, with a titular president as the head of state, and a cabinet and prime minister responsible to a parliament consisting of an equal number of elected and nominated members. The option of independence remained open for all homelands, but at the end of 1976 only BophuthaTswana had indicated that it would ask for it.

Homeland governments have no jurisdiction over their citizens in white areas. In white urban areas, the Africans are still officially regarded as temporary sojourners and are allowed to form advisory councils to the respective urban local authorities.

The position is therefore that, whereas alternative political platforms have to a certain extent been created in the homelands, the position in the white areas remains unchanged.

All government and opposition leaders in the homelands conditionally accepted separate development as a framework for political action, although several rejected it as an ideology. The approach of the homeland leaders is essentially pragmatic. Several of them have adopted the viewpoint of 'take what you can get, and use it in order to get what you want'. While the separate-but-equal doctrine has been accepted by leaders such as Matanzima (Transkei), Sebe (Ciskei), and Mangope (BophuthaTswana), there is a growing disillusionment among them about the equality aspect. Racial discrimination is rejected by all homeland leaders (and has been abolished in the independent Transkei), and most of them are prepared to allow whites as citizens of their territories. The majority of them also favour a single non-racial South Africa where the numerical strength of the Africans would put them in control of the government. Ethnic grouping and ethnically based homeland governments are accepted as the only possible alternative, under the present circumstances, for political expression and consultation with the South African government. The only homeland government that used to accept separate development almost unquestioningly was that of Basotho Qwaqwa, which has the smallest land area and the fourth largest de jure population - i.e. including those in the white areas. After K.T. Mopeli had succeeded Wessel Mota as chief minister, following the former's Dikwankwetla Party's almost clean sweep in the 1975 Qwaqwa election, the Qwaqwa government became increasingly critical of aspects of separate development. Qwaqwa also used the ethnic factor in an attempt to obtain certain areas inhabited by Basotho within other homelands, such as the Matatiele and Mount Fletcher districts in the Transkei, the Herschel district in the Ciskei (which, ironically, was transferred to the Transkei in 1976), and the Thaba Nchu district in BophuthaTswana. (See speeches by Matanzima 11 April 1972 and 22 March 1973; Mabandla; Phatudi, 18 December 1971; Buthelezi, December 1972; Matanzima's election manifestoes of 1963 and 1973; and the manifestoes and statements and objectives of homeland-based parties.)

There is unanimous rejection by homeland leaders of certain separatist measures of the South African government, such as job reservation, the wage gap, influx control, and restriction on land acquirements by homelands over and above the quota determined by the Bantu Trust and Land Act of 1936. Educational needs, agricultural priorities, industrial development, localisation of the civil service, better housing and transport facilities, and improved health and social welfare services are among the most important needs expressed by homeland leaders. The election manifestoes issued by leading candidates of different parties and in different homelands express the unity of purpose in this connection.

Together with the homeland leaders' desire for African unity in South Africa, these common problems and needs and the obvious advantages of a common approach to them provided the initial stimulus for the first conference of homeland leaders held in Umtata on 8 November 1973. Ethnic grouping by the South African government is regarded as detrimental to African unity, but the political relevance of ethnic differences is generally acknowledged. (See 'Political development amongst the Republican Swazis'.)

Numerically the strongest ethnic group in South Africa, the Zulu has perhaps the most articulate government of all the homelands. Politically, it is an exceptionally interesting region with its strong historical tradition, the political intrigues emanating from the royal family, the non-party approach of the KwaZulu government, and the large numbers of whites and Indians living in and between the scattered territories of KwaZulu. Perhaps because of their numerical strength,

Zulu pressure for an African federation was particularly strong. The seeds of discontent, however, were also present, and in the Transkei and Natal opposing leaflets have been issued, while the host to the first homeland leaders' summit, Kaiser Matanzima, did not invite Chief Minister Mota of Basotho Qwaqwa because of a dispute behind the scenes over the Transkei lands inhabited by Sesotho-speaking tribes. (See speeches by Matanzima on 22 March 1973 and Buthelezi in December 1972, as well as the section on federalism.) The Transkei's independence and BophuthaTswana's move towards independence, the 1976 riots and the international situation (Angola, Rhodesia and South West Africa) since 1975 served to relegate to the back-ground talks on a homeland federation, although conferences of chief ministers continue to be held.

The burning issues of the decades preceding the banning of the A.N.C. and P.A.C. are still present, and are now to a certain extent being articulated by the homeland leaders. Bantu education is being transformed in the homelands by introducing English in the place of the vernacular as medium of instruction from Standard 3 upwards, and by adapting curricula to locally determined standards. Africans are not arrested for pass offences within the homelands, and criticism of the South African government over the pass laws continues unabated from the homelands which also continuously seek relief for their citizens within the white areas. The land reserved in 1936 for African ownership and occupation is still regarded as insufficient, and claims for additional land have been issued by all homeland leaders. The inability of homeland governments to accommodate and employ all their citizens, including those in the white area, led them to call for the official recognition that these people are in the white area permanently and should receive civil and political rights there. Economic self-sufficiency and self-help, preached by the A.N.C. in the 1930s, are pursued energetically by the homeland governments. (The above-mentioned needs are articulated in homeland election manifestoes, and several speeches, among which that of Matanzima on 22 March 1973 is a good example.)

Within the white area SASO and the B.P.C. (Black People's Convention) reject separate development completely, and refuse to co-operate with institutions created in terms thereof, or with individuals working within its framework (see the section on Black Consciousness). Both accept Black Consciousness as their point of departure. Black Consciousness and unity are also accepted, at various levels of articulation, by several other organisations, which include the Transvaal United Teachers' Association (TUATA), the Association for the Social, Educational and Cultural Advancement of the African People of South Africa (ASSECA), the National African Federated Chamber of Commerce (NAFCOC), the League of the African Youth, the Swazi National Council, the KwaZulu Executive Council (or cabinet), the Inter-denominational African Ministers' Association of South Africa (IDAMASA), and the Black Community Programmes. Like SASO and B.P.C. they are striving for African advancement through self-help efforts, the main difference from SASO and B.P.C. being that unlike the latter they are prepared to co-operate with South African and homeland authorities and white organisations.

SASO and B.P.C. came into being as a result of the increasing momentum of the Black Consciousness idea in South Africa. While SASO grew out of the now defunct multi-racial University Christian Movement and as a reaction during 1969-70 against the white domination of the National Union of South African Students, the B.P.C. was the result of prolonged consultations among representatives of a number of African voluntary associations in the fields of welfare, religion, sport and education. Starting in April 1971, several meetings were held by a growing number of representatives and organisations, culminating in a decision in December 1971 to establish a political organisation. (See M.T. Moerane's address to the National Organisations Conference.) The B.P.C. was formally established in July 1972 after further study and recommendations by an ad hoc committee. The B.P.C., SASO and Black Community Programmes were crippled through a series of restriction orders served on employees and officials by the South African government during 1972 and 1973. The organisations as such were not affected.

A covert Africanism is expressed in the objectives of most organisations, including homeland-based parties, especially in their emphasis on education for and by Africans, self-help efforts in social and economic fields, the bias towards African culture and development in the Black Consciousness movement, the willingness even in certain organisations to work within the separatist framework of separate development in the homelands, and the desire for an 'African' or 'Black' theology. There is some similarity between the economic, educational and cultural objectives of homeland-based organisations on the one hand, and Black Consciousness-oriented organisations on the other hand, and they differ mainly in respect of political strategy and attitudes towards white South Africans.

Several factors have contributed towards the formation of political parties in the homelands. The establishment of legislative assemblies and the resultant general elections necessitated a concentration of recruitment efforts by candidates. In Venda, KwaZulu and BophuthaTswana, parties were formed before elections could take place; whereas in the Transkei, Ciskei and Lebowa, political parties were established after the first general elections. However, pacts formed before the first elections in the latter three territories afterwards led to the establishment of parties. The incumbent Venda government leaders refused to establish a party - which they regarded as a foreign institution - but formed an election pact for the August 1973 general election. This pact was afterwards converted into the Venda National Party. The first general election (October 1973) in Gazankulu passed without parties and amid great satisfaction with the incumbent government led by Ntsanwisi.

Conflicting leadership aspirations led to the formation of opposing groups which later crystallised into parties. In BophuthaTswana, Lebowa and the Ciskei, personality conflicts overshadowed policy differences and they also played a role in the Transkei in 1963. In the Transkei, however, a serious policy difference on whether separate development should be accepted or not was also an important divisive factor. Policy differences in the Transkei also led to the formation of the Transkei People's Freedom Party which wanted immediate independence for the Transkei in 1967.

Political parties in homelands are to a great extent dependent on chiefs and headmen for recruitment of local support as a result of prevalent loyalties to tribal leaders and the parochialism in political outlook in tribal areas. The building of strong grass-roots organisations and party loyalty is thus inhibited. Although the parties appear to be better organised in the homelands than in the white urban areas, it is in fact not the case, as the homeland organisation is often nothing more than an adaptation of traditional structures for recruitment purposes.

The problems of underdevelopment also retard the development of parties. Homeland governments have small economic and financial resources at their disposal and the power of re-allocation of material goods and privileges is so limited that it offers restricted ground for difference. The government is invariably at a disadvantage because of its relative impotence. An irresponsible opposition could exploit the situation, but the great measure of consensus on priority needs largely dispels this danger and tends to minimise party differences. The KwaZulu government's fear of irresponsible opposition action in this connection contributed to its propagation of a non-party approach, although it is not totally against opposition parties. Under Buthelezi's leadership, Inkatha ka Zulu (a name symbolising Zulu unity) has been revived and transformed into a 'Zulu cultural liberation movement'. Purporting not to be a political party, it has obvious political objectives and overtones such as the promotion of unity among all Africans in South Africa.

Whatever the merits or demerits of separate development, it is a fact in contemporary South Africa that government and opposition leaders in homelands are employing to the fullest extent possible the available opportunities for political articulation, communication and action. They have therefore a tutelary significance. For almost the first time modern-type political parties are spreading their networks into the rural areas. Never before has the Africans' quest for dignity and equality been highlighted so consistently and intensively and to such an extent by African leaders within and outside homelands. (See for example the section on Dignity and Consciousness.) Perhaps this fact, more than anything else, led homeland leaders to compromise with separate development; the volume of political debate has been swelled by those who preferred to remain outside the system and without formal representation in the institutions created under separate development. (See speeches by Matanzima, 11 April 1972 and 22 March 1973; Sebe,

12 March 1973 and 29 August 1973; Buthelezi, December 1972; and Phatudi 28 May 1971.) Homeland leaders generally do not welcome outside assistance on the grounds that it would not materially benefit the African population. (See speeches by Sebe, 29 August 1973; Mabandla; and Mangope's press release on 8 September 1972.)

They have attended the South African Prime Minister's conferences with homeland leaders in full strength, and used these meetings to submit African aspirations and grievances in homelands and white areas alike. The first of these meetings took place on 6 March 1974. Although a measure of disillusionment was expressed by some homeland leaders after meeting the Prime Minister, better understanding for urban African problems seemed to flow from these conferences, e.g. the concession in 1975 that urban Africans could own their houses in urban townships. (See 'Report Back' by Chief Buthelezi.)

Although rejected in certain African circles, represented especially by SASO and B.P.C., the homeland-based parties are establishing themselves as credible political organisations in the respective territories. This credibility extends to a limited extent outside the homelands, but has been increased by the desire of these parties and other organisations for African unity in South Africa, and their understanding of the problems of Africans outside the homelands.

Profile of the Homelands

NANCY C.J. CHARTON

The contribution of homeland leaders to the political debate in South Africa needs to be seen in the context of the political and economic development of these territories. This is clearly reflected in the accompanying chart: Profile of South African Homelands.

It is obvious from the composition of the eight legislatures created to date that the traditional elites, the chiefs and the headmen, have inherited the political kingdom from the Republican government. They first came to prominence with the creation of Territorial Authorities; when elective components were added later to 'modernise' the legislatures, they retained their positions of dominance. Even in Transkei, elective and traditional components of the legislature have only just attained parity with each other. The period of self-government prepared traditional elites for leadership, which in most instances they have retained, in spite of the introduction of the elective principle; it is they who for the most part were elected Chief Ministers, and who founded such political parties as there are.

In the early stages of the development of the homelands, chiefs and headmen were salaried civil servants of comparatively lowly status. In the later stages they became the salaried executive and judicial officers of the homeland administrations. They have gained much materially and in status from the political transformation. It has been in their interests to co-operate with the Republican government.

They came to power endowed with a degree of traditional legitimacy. They have managed in most instances to consolidate their power effectively. In no homeland is there a really effective opposition party; where anything like a radical opposition has shown signs of emerging, it has been dealt with quickly. But it is the politics of the carrot rather than of the stick which has consolidated their power. As in all colonial and post-colonial societies the political elite have been able to reward nascent middle-class groups. In the concentrated development programmes which have been initiated since 1963 the public service in all territories has been Africanised. For instance in 1975 only 2,5 per cent of the officials in Transkei were white. A glance at column 15 of the 'Profile' shows the relative importance of employment in the public sector, which includes bureaucrats, teachers, doctors, nurses and other professionals, as well as technicians and labourers, all relatively highly paid. The availability of many posts in the public sector, the rapid mobility of personnel, and the very limited nature of the private sector, make it possible for the government to reward political support and to penalise political dissent.

There are of course black entrepreneurs, for part of the development programme has been concerned with Africanising the commercial and industrial sectors. Column 16 reflects the extent to which Africans have availed themselves of the loans and training provided by government bodies. The private sector, of which these entrepreneurs form part, is no less tied to the government than the bureaucrats and teachers, for almost all of them have loans from public development corporations. Here, too, there is a chance for the government to reward support and to penalise dissent. There has also been considerable development in the agricultural sphere with resultant differentiation of farmers.

The whole accelerated programme of development, agricultural, industrial, commercial, and bureaucratic, has thus enabled the political elite to build political and electoral support, a fact clearly reflected in election statistics for Transkei and the Ciskei. Not only are the homelands economically dependent on the Republic of South Africa for capital funds, as illustrated in column 12, but their development programmes sustain and extend the political bases of the leaders. This compounds their dependence.

There is a third very effective tie which binds homelands to the Republic - the fiscal tie. Each is dependent on the Republic for a major share of its revenue, with the single exception of Qwaqwa whose subsidy yields only 18 per cent of its revenue. This may presumably be accounted for by its small resident population, only 48 000. The remaining 1 219 000 live and work permanently in the white areas of the Republic. It is taxation levied on non-residents by the Qwaqwa government which yields the bulk of its revenue; this is another variety of fiscal dependency, one common to all the homelands. In KwaZulu no less than 80 per cent of revenue derives directly from the Republican government.

Fourthly, in all the territories there is considerable pressure of population on land. The generally prevailing forms of subsistence production cannot sustain the rapidly growing population. The results if this type of pressure are clearly shown in columns 7, 10, and 11. There is a low per capita income, particularly in areas where people cannot commute to work in adjacent white areas, as they can in BophuthaTswana, KwaZulu and the Ciskei. Many have left the homelands and are now permanently settled in the 'white' areas of the Republic. There is a high rate of absenteeism among those who remain, varying between 10 per cent in BophuthaTswana and 28 per cent in Gazankulu; these absentees are migrant workers, many of whom could not live or sustian their families without a regular spell of contract labour in the 'white' areas. The chief export from these territories is not commodities, but people. Without the work opportunities which white South Africa can offer, black South African homelands starve. The peasants, no less than the elites, are involved in the complicated network of dependent relationships. In evaluating the degree of dependence and its political significance for the homelands, it must be borne in mind that most colonial and post-colonial states in the Third World have similar problems.

However, the problems of South African homelands are compounded in many cases by the lack of a unitary territorial base. Chief Buthelezi once referred to the 'Dalmatian-like' appearance of KwaZulu on the map! Only Qwaqwa, the Ciskei and Swazi, the smallest territories, will be in one piece when consolidation proposals have been finalised. This fragmentation creates administrative problems for the developing territory, which must rely on systems of communication in South Africa for connecting its own internal networks. Furthermore, all homelands are geographically encapsulated, except Transkei with its long coastline and potential harbour at Port St John's.

In spite of these deficiencies there is considerable potential in this system of devolution for pushing regional economic development, and even for pressing territorial claims, a potential which has been singularly effectively exploited by Transkei and Bophutha-Tswana. Because the homelands have many millions of citizens in white South Africa, they have good cause to exert political pressure on behalf of their non-resident citizens. This they have sometimes done, not always successfully. However, the effectiveness of their actions on behalf of their citizens will in large measure depend on their unity of purpose vis-à-vis South Africa.

Unhappily this unity has proved to be very fragile during the past four years. In 1973 a summit meeting of six homeland leaders was held in Umtata; all present agreed that the idea of federation be propagated to the people, and that the Republican government should consolidate the homelands. Even more important was the agreement not to open separate negotiations with Pretoria unless there was revision of the 1936 Land Act.(1)

When negotiations on this issue failed, the Transkei decided to work towards immediate independence, and was accused in some quarters of betraying the Umtata agreement. Subsequently Chiefs Mangope and Sebe were to negotiate land deals within the terms of the 1936 Act. And in March 1976 Chief Buthelezi rejected homeland independence: 'South Africa is one country. It has one destiny.'(2)

The fragility of unity is not really dependent on the personalities and ideas of the leaders. It is inherent in the socio-economic facts of the situation. These territories are in competition with each other, for whatever favours the dominant Republic is willing to bestow. They all export the same commodity, labour, and all have a singularly urgent interest in maintaining, if not in expanding their share of the market. All need capital, and compete in attracting industry to their areas; white government institutions canalise the flow of capital investment. Several homelands have discovered conflicting territorial claims, mainly at the expense of other homelands, for example the Transkei/Ciskei dispute over Herschel and Glen Grey, the Transkei/KwaZulu dispute over territory in the Umzimkulu area, and the Transkei/Qwaqwa dispute about certain Sotho-speaking areas in the Transkei.

It is perhaps astonishing that homeland leaders and politicians have been so outspoken, having regard to the constraints which hedge them in. They do have some purchase on the Southern African system; what they have they use. It is interesting to compare the situation of Lesotho, which is almost as dependent on South Africa as the homelands. In the early years of her independence she pursued a subdued and subservient role. However, membership of the international community and the knowledge that support would be forthcoming both from the Organisations of African Unity and the United Nations Organisation have enabled her to speak out more boldly. Since the early 1970s Chief Jonathan has seldom lost an opportunity of challenging the Republic in international forums.

This particular international power booster is not available at present even to the Transkei, who joined the ranks of the 'stateless' states in October 1976. Political support from the international community would increase the influence of homeland leaders in the South African system; economic support would reduce their dependency on the system. There are signs that economic support may well be forthcoming in the immediate future. But economic aid in developing countries tends to create more problems than it solves, as we have seen in the relationship between South Africa and her black satellites. Whether the international community approves or disapproves, and receives or fails to receive the homelands, the process of fragmentation in Southern Africa is under way.

GOVERNMENT

Status	Chief Minister	Party System: Ruling party	Party System: Opposition	Legislature: Members appointed	Legislature: Members elected	Budget: Own resources R 000	Budget: Subsidy R.S.A. R 000
Transkei Independent since Nov. 1976	President Chief Botha Sigcau Prime Minister Paramount Chief K.D. Matanzima	Transkei National Independence Party	Democratic Party: two factions: Knowledge Guzana, H.B. Ncokazi	75 50 %	75 50 %	*1975/6* 32 848 34,3 % (Benbo 1975, p.66)	62 877 65,7 %
Ciskei self-governing: 2nd stage since 1973	Chief L.L.W. Sebe	Ciskei National Independence Party	Ciskei National Party: Chief Justice Mabandla	30 60 %	20 40 %	*1975/6* 7 131 20,7 % (Benbo 1975, p.64)	27 352 79,3 %
KwaZulu self-governing: 1st stage since 1972	Chief Executive Councillor G.M. Buthelezi	Inkatha	no official opposition	70 56 %	55 44 % no elections yet held	*1974/5* 13 773 19,7 % (Benbo 1975, p.68)	56 177 80,3 %
BophuthaTswana self-governing: 2nd stage since 1972 (to be independent Nov. 1977)	Chief L. Mangope	BophuthaTswana Democratic Party	Seoposengwe: Chief T. Pilane	48 67 %	24 33 %	*1974/5* 6 370 19,5 % (Benbo 1975, p.58)	26 264 80,5 %
Lebowa self-governing: 2nd stage since 1973	Dr C.N. Phatudi	Lebowa People's Party	nil	60 60 %	40 40 %	16 645 39,4 % (Benbo 1976, p.53)	25 605 60,6 %
Venda self-governing: 2nd stage since 1973	Chief P.R. Mphephu	Venda National Party	Venda Independence Party: B. Mudau	42 70 %	18 30 %	*1973/4* 1 568 24,2 % (S.A.I.R.R. 1975, p.125)	4 910 75,8 %
Qwaqwa self-governing: 2nd stage since 1975	Mr K. Mopeli	Dikwankwetla Party	nil	40 66 %	20 34 %	*1973/4* 2 467 82,4 % (S.A.I.R.R. 1975, p.125)	529 17,6 %
Gazankulu self-governing: 2nd stage since 1973	Prof. Hudson W.E. Ntsanwisi	nil	nil	42 61 %	26 39 %	*1973/4* 2 756 31,3 % (S.A.I.R.R. 1975, p.125)	6 051 68,7 %
Swazi self-governing: 1st stage since 1977	no elected leader	nil	nil	appointed only		no budget yet	
S. Ndebele (originally part of BophuthaTswana, now in process of excision) tribal authority only	no elected leader	nil	nil	nil	nil	no budget yet	

POPULATION AND LAND

Population permanently resident: In Homeland 1973 estimate (Source: Benbo 1976, pp. 30, 34)	Population permanently resident: In White areas 1970 Census	Area 1973 (Source: Benbo 1976, p.23): Hectares	Area 1973: No. blocks	Area 1975: Hectares	Area 1975: No. blocks	Percentage Arable (Source: Benbo 1976, p.108)	Absenteeism (Benbo 1976, p.31) (no. of men absent as % of total de facto male population)	Estimated Per Capita Income 1973/4 (excludes income from migrant workers) (Benbo 1976, p.76)	Public Fixed Investment Gross (Source: Benbo 1976, pp.191-2): R.S.A.	Public Fixed Investment Gross: Black
000	*000*	*000*		*000*		*%*	*%*	*R*	*R 000*	*R 000*
Transkei										
1 929	1 297	3 871	2	4 501	3	18,5	24,9	56,00	12 435	12 288
Ciskei										
602	523	942	15 + 11 smaller pieces	770	1	13,3	14,4	111,00	7 192	3 311
KwaZulu										
2 442	1 879	3 273	48 + 157 smaller pieces	3 239	10	14,0	15,4	107,00	7 432	15 348
BophuthaTswana										
1 023	1 073	3 799	19	4 043	6	6,6	9,6	161,00	8 927	4 663
Lebowa										
1 217	603	2 248	14	2 518	6	15,3	18,9	59,00	4 682	4 398
Venda										
301	106	618	3	668	2	9	25,0	42,00	530	1 984
Qwaqwa										
48	1 219	48	1	62	1	19,8	17,1	73,00	290	986
Gazankulu										
298	261	633	4	741	3	12	27,7	51,00	1 050	2 143
Swazi										
155	361	208	3	391	1	15,5	13,4	43,00	2 498	44[illegible]
S. Ndebele (originally part of BophuthaTswana, now in process of excision)										
no information		20	3	73	2	18,1	no information		no information	

ECONOMIC DEVELOPMENT

Mineral Resources (Source: Benbo 1976, pp.86–7)	Industrial Development 1974 (Benbo 1976, p.114) Investment: Agency system		Black Employment (Source: Benbo 1976)				Commercial enterprises owned by blacks (Source: Benbo 1976, p.118)
	Industrialist *R 000*	Public corporation *R 000*	p.115 Agency system*	p.116 Industrial Development Corporations	p.119 Gov. services	p.105 Potential average annual increase in supply of migrants to R.S.A.	
Transkei mines nil; travertine, nickel, tin, titanium, coal	5 239	6 491	2 287	4 007	34 304	21 500	2 592
Ciskei mines nil; titanium	52	100	85	434	13 131	1 489	432
KwaZulu mines 9; employ 114 blacks; coal	1 475	1 651	983	1 077	28 573	4 377	3 416
BophuthaTswana mines 26; employ 67 767 blacks; platinum chrome	18 112	9 239	5 559	664	13 126	2 255	886
Lebowa mines 16; employ 0 322 blacks; sbestos hrome	2 614	470	1 112	744	21 132	6 349	1 380
/enda nines 4; employ 18 blacks; old, asbestos, agnesite, orundum, tanium, aphite	737	372	598	44	6 344	1 350	335
waqwa	86	37	144	22	1 384	700	14
azankulu nes 4; employ 1 blacks; ld	300	609	301	97	6 887	2 144	379
vazi	78	40	125	22	4 877	840	134
Ndebele iginally part of BophuthaTswana, now in process of excision)			no information				22

'Agency system' refers to the conditional permission to White entrepreneurs to invest in the homelands

ırces: *Black Development in South Africa.* Bureau for Economic Research re Bantu Development (Benbo) 1976
nskei *Economic Review* 1975 Bureau for Economic Research re Bantu Development
kei do. 1975
aZulu do. 1975
ohuthaTswana do. 1975
owa do. 1976
urvey of Race Relations in South Africa 1975*, compiled by M. Horrell and T. Hodgson, South African Institute of Race
ations, 1976

The Significance of the Tribal System for the Development of the Homelands

E.S. MOLOTO

(Address delivered at the Colloquium held at the University of the North from 30 October to 1 November 1973. Translated from the Afrikaans by F.E. Auerbach and reproduced by permission of Dr E.S. Moloto and Professor J.L. Boshoff, Rector of the University of the North)

The Tribe

The basic unit of the traditional as well as the present political structure in non-urban Bantu society is the tribe. This consists of wards which in their turn consist of sibs. The core sib (which will also be the noble sib) is the head of all the wards and sibs jointly. The stronger the attraction of the core sib - a factor which, in its turn, depends on the tribal chief's power of organisation - the bigger a tribe can become, and vice versa. Thus there are large and small tribes.

Often, too, it is the availability or otherwise of the natural sources of life, such as water, grazing land, arable land, etc., which causes either cohesion or disintegration. For these and other reasons there is a constant flight from tribal lands and from tribal authority to white areas (farms, towns, mines, factories) where there is a possibility of earning a living. The result is that the number of Bantu really connected with and living in tribal territory and under tribal authority is considerably smaller, than the urban group, a phenomenon which challenges the tribal system if indeed it does not threaten its very existence.

There are four national groups organised or to be organised into eleven national units. Thus at present there are 642 separate and independent tribes each with its own chief. Nearly seven million of the Bantu population are in the homelands while 8 059 325 live in white territories, i.e. 46,5% in Bantu territory. On an average there are 10 900 people per tribal chief in the Republic of South Africa. This appears to make it possible to justify the continued existence of the tribal system. South Africa comprises 317 965 non-South African Bantu, 18 904 in Bantu territories and 299 061 in the white area. The latter has, of course, a stronger power of attraction where it offers employment and income.

Some national units have a low, others again a high average population per tribal unit: for example, the Swazi have 4 872 compared to the Tsonga with 20 697. This suggests a great measure of disintegration on the one hand, and a considerable cohesion on the other. It would seem that in some, possibly in all cases, a great problem of internal consolidation arises. There are cases where there are as many tribal units as there were sons in the house of the patriarch. The late Prof. J.P. Bruwer testified:

'...truly it is the closer tribal unit among the Bantu which shows a recognisable corporate form as a national unit ... Such a Bantu tribe is an autonomous unit by itself with its own tribal organisation, tribal government and tribal land.' (Bruwer, p. 12)

The important point here is that the corporate tribal unit is the tribe, not a people or a nation; that there was no national authority or territory yet, even less a nation, although a national spirit is at times noticeable.

It may be illuminating to mention one or other theory of origin in order to show what the patriarchal tribal authority is founded on, because at present nation-building and the building up of tribes are clashing instead of being complementary. The duties of a nation builder are manifold and complex and demand a division of privileges and authority on a very wide front, while 'the narrower tribal unit' encourages selfishness. Both must be willing to take with one hand and to give with the other. Both do not always do this. A recent issue of South African Panorama tells us:

'According to legend, a certain captain (chief), one Malandela, settled on the banks of the White Umfolozi River with a little band of followers late in the seventeenth century. After his death, Zulu, his son, became captain ... Today the Zulu nation numbers more than four million, consisting of 286 tribes. Their territory covers approximately three million hectares.'

It is understandable that the most senior descendant of Zulu wants to have overall authority vested in him, as well as the right of ownership of the tribal territory, and not in 286 bodies. On the other hand the 286 tribal chiefs claim the right to do as Malandela did. The history of tribal organisation is throughout one of the making and the breaking of the tribe and/or the chief. Among the Tswanas opposition to Kgama the Christian arose twice, when he wanted to oppose his father and later when his son wished to oppose him (Kgama). Prof. I. Schapera states:

'...among the Ngwaketse, Tshosa fought for the chieftainship against his father Makabe II; among the Tawana, Moremi I similarly fought against his father Tawana; while among the Ngwato, Kgama himself succeeded after a long series of struggles in ousting his father Sekgoma I and becoming Chief even though Sekgoma was still alive.' (Schapera, p. 58)

Whatever the case may be, as soon as a member of a noble family can gather together a following and obtain some land of his own, it has, over the years, become the easiest and most common step according to law to apply to the government of the Union or Republic of South Africa, in accordance with Law No. 38 of 1927, for recognition of his following as a separate and independent tribe and of himself as autonomous tribal chief, and thus he also becomes the patriarch of his followers in his own right. The traditional tribal authority resides in this patriarch or in his descendant, who is the ruler, judge and protector of the law, commander-in-chief of the army, the priest of the people and the chief doctor of the tribe. In an address in 1961 the late Mr Bruce Young, Secretary of Bantu Administration and Development, referred to the existence of (the institution of) a supreme tribal chief as well as the lack of such an institution among the Bantu national units of South Africa when he said:

'The history of the Tswanas is, of course, that in the past the various tribes and clans were split up. The result is that there is no paramount chief here as you have, for example, in Zululand. Anybody who seeks to aspire to a paramountcy here may be looking for trouble ... A Chairman and a Vice-Chairman have been elected. This does not mean that they will exercise powers or functions over the individual tribes.' (Proceedings of Tswana Territorial Authority, 1961.- Speech by Bruce Young).

And yet he had just said: '...self-government must be centred in a constitutional governing body'. He also foreshadowed further change:

'There are people who refer to all the indigenous people of South Africa as Natives or Bantu or Africans, whichever they prefer ... Possibly the stage may be reached, in the future, when the several Bantu national groups will be referred to as ... as Tswanas, Zulus, Xhosas, Vendas, South or North Sothos and so on.'

The Role of the Tribal Chief

From the foregoing it is clear that a tribe must have a tribal government and a tribal territory, and that the head of a tribal government has clearly defined duties and privileges. Thus the tribal system shows a course of development. Schapera said of the Tswana (p. 53): 'A chief is never elected'. On application, the most senior male heir or a specific tribal chieftainship gets recognition as head of the tribe in accordance with the Native Administration Act No. 38 of 1927. He is also invested with a measure of criminal and civil jurisdiction. But it was only in 1957 that the duties of the tribal chief were more closely defined by law. We refer here to Proclamation 110 of 1957: 'Regulations prescribing the duties, powers, privileges and conditions of chiefs and headmen'. As far as my knowledge goes, this was the first time that conditions of service were laid down for these officials as well, and in my view this was an important step forward. In the duty rules it is laid down, inter alia, that an appointed tribal chief shall see to the composition of a tribal authority according to the Bantu Authorities Act No. 68 of 1951 within thirty days of his appointment. In other words he is expected, and even compelled, to act as chief-in-council 'according to the laws and customs of the tribe concerned'. If this is not done, the Minister himself can nominate such a council. The chief and his council must look after the 'material, moral and social welfare of his people and/or the development and improvement of the soil in his territory, and mainly measures providing for, supporting, actively encouraging or himself initiating the active participation of his tribe or community in the administration or management of its own affairs'. He is entitled to the loyalty, respect and obedience of all the Bantu in his territory. He gets a stipendium and 'may not become a member of or participate in the affairs of a political organisation or of an association whose aims, in the opinion of the Minister, undermine or adversely affect the established administration of law and order'. Article 8 reads:

'He must carry out all the lawful orders which he receives from or through the Native Affairs Commissioner or another government official properly authorised thereto in writing by the Secretary, the Chief Native Commissioner or the Native Commissioner.'

Periods of absence from his territory without the approval of the Bantu Commissioner are limited to seven days, and, if it is longer than 30 days, the consent of the Chief Bantu Affairs Commissioner must be obtained. Dereliction of duty, disregard of orders or any form of misconduct is punishable by either reproof, suspension, reduction in salary or summary dismissal. One comes to the conclusion that the appointed tribal chief is a civil servant of a special category. His position is more or less similar to that of a municipal administrator who gets his licence from the State, but who is employed by a particular local authority. Thus the tribal chief must, inter alia, look after the economic welfare of his people, most of whom have no income. According to tradition there are, however, tribal lands which are worked by age groups of men or women. Harvests are gathered and kept by the chief. Members of the tribe are entitled to rations during periods of famine, or they buy the grain at a fairly low price. The resultant income is kept by the chief from year to year. Often he is the wealthiest citizen.

The chief is also on the lookout for spheres of work for members of the tribe. He negotiates with labour bureaux and industrialists on behalf of the members of his tribe. When the Second World War broke out, there was not only an opportunity for members of the tribe to defend their land and people, but (they could) earn an income, and the chiefs in their turn were on the lookout for work opportunities for members of their tribe.

The economic concerns of a tribe are very close to the heart of the chief-in-council. The tribal territory is divided into three districts (wards), for grazing, agricultural lands and residential purposes. Natural sources of water are protected, dams are dug and boreholes sunk. Businessmen are recruited. Tribesmen themselves start business enterprises: general dealers grocers, livestock speculators, transport riders, bus owners, etc. All this is still on a small scale. It is the duty of the chief-in-council to encourage and assist with all this. In spite of the above, or partly because of it, the proportion of the urban to the homeland Bantu population is about 8:7. If it is remembered that most men and women who can bear arms and pay taxes will be in the towns, and grandfathers, grandmothers and grandchildren in the homelands, it can rightly be stated that most homeland Bantu must be dependent for their livelihood on relatives in the towns, a situation that should be rectified by industrialisation in the homelands in order to prevent large-scale famine and sickness there, and to curtail the ever greater emigration. Therefore the central homeland authority must concentrate on the strengthening of tribal authority. We have already said that the traditional tribal chief is also the priest of his tribe. Dr. P.L. Breutz writes of the (Tswana) tribes in the Mafeking district:

'Old beliefs have survived in magical acts for the purpose of protection and cures, in fear of witchcraft, in the influence ascribed to the spirits of the ancestors on the life and progress of the living individual and occasionally in rain ceremonies ... Through the influence of the Christian Missions, ancestor worship, and with it the traditional rain ceremonies, have become an unimportant factor in Native life." (Breutz, p. 56, p. 71)

What is stated here is certainly true of many of our present-day Bantu tribes. It is of importance that the tribal chief willingly transforms his priesthood, that it is he who allows the Christian church within his tribe and, in many cases, invited it. The name Botshabelo for more than one mission station among the Sothos, which means 'place of refuge', is evidence of the flight of members of a tribe, in the distant past, from an unconverted tribal chieftainship to Christianity. But the fact remains that 'old beliefs' have become 'an unimportant factor'. In order to illustrate the degree of acceptance of the Christian faith we take 23 tribes (1953) in the Rustenburg District (including Pilanesberg). Certainly this will differ from district to district in the Northern homelands, and possibly this district is, in this respect, one of the more 'enlightened' territories. Nineteen of the twenty-three chiefs or 83%, profess the Christian faith. There were already two hospitals in the district, as well as a clinic in each of the larger chiefs' kraals. Before the authorities system (1951) there was a strong local council under the 1920 Bantu Affairs Act, which, inter alia, looked after the establishment of clinics and the employment of district nurses. Together with the school the clinic was the pride of the tribal authority. Funds for this service were provided from the so-called local tax of R1 per hut per year payable by married men. Many urban taxpayers did not pay it. Again one has the position where the active men of the tribe suffer in favour of the town. One wonders whom a homeland government is actually expected to tax!

The foregoing means that both religious provision and medical services were fairly complex and there was a strong tendency for these to be entrusted to experts, i.e. in lesser degree to either the tribal chief or to the traditional medicine man. This shows a division of labour in comparison with the traditional way of handling matters where these were vested in the chief. However it may be elsewhere, the chief practises ever less often as chief doctor and priest. He is proud of his church. He respects what is left of belief in the ancestors. In this way he gains recognition both by the Christian church and by the traditional doctors.

Socially the tribal chief always remains a cohesive force. It is always excellent for a tribesman to be able to claim kinship with him. His clan is the most senior and he himself is senior to all irrespective of his age/youth. Leaders of age-group regiments are found from those of his line. He administers the 'laws' for the young and the aged, for the family and for property, and encourages home activities. He remains the representative of the ancestors. He should have knowledge of illness, death, departure for the cities, return from there, and should be greeted with presents. This ensures the approval of the ancestors and promotes blessings and good fortune. If he is ill-treated, there will be no rain.

We have already referred to the Bantu Authorities Act, according to which the tribal chief establishes a tribal council. This tribal authority fits in with a

Regional Authority and the latter with a Legislative Assembly. A tribal authority is concerned with a single tribe and the chief is its chairman, working no longer only according to tradition and custom but also in accordance with written regulations. Tribal chiefs and councillors from two or more tribes sit in the Regional Authority, one of them as chairman, and they are responsible for the common affairs of the tribes concerned, e.g. roads, high schools, exhibitions, the status and stipends of the tribal chiefs, cattle diseases, etc. The Legislative Assembly is the overall body which exercises authority over all the regional and tribal authorities. According to Proclamation 151 of 1972 the Tswana Legislative Assembly, for example, has 48 members appointed by the tribal and regional authorities. Preference is given to chiefs and only if a regional authority has too few chiefs, bodies of lower rank may be considered. There are also 24 elected members. Tribal chiefs not appointed may offer themselves for election. This ensures an overwhelming majority of tribal chiefs. We read the following about KwaZulu:

'In the Constitution Proclamation, provision was made for the reconstitution of the Legislative Assembly on the basis of 55 members elected by citizens of KwaZulu entitled to vote, three chiefs appointed by each regional authority and the paramount chief and his representative.' (South African Panorama, p. 46)

According to The World, 10 August 1973, the following applies to the Venda Legislative Assembly: 'The new Assembly will have 60 members, made up of 42 nominated chiefs and headmen and 18 elected persons'.

The point I wish to make here is that tribal chieftainship entrenched in the authorities system is protected. Chiefs have the duty and privilege to join an authority without going through the noise and fury of an election. That also seems to be the aim of the legislation abolishing the former Native Representatives Council. The Bantu Authorities Act No. 68 of 1951 envisages:

'...to provide for the institution of certain Bantu authorities and to outline their activities, to abolish the Native Representative Council, to amend the Bantu Affairs Act, 1920, and the Native Representation Act, 1936.'

The Native Representative Council consisted of

educated black politicians of western orientation. Most of them were elected by the masses and not on an ethnic basis. At one stage they asked for the abolition of all racial discrimination from the laws of the land, and then there was trouble. On the contrary, the authorities system is based on the ethnic group and assures a majority of tribal chiefs on the councils. On top of that there is Proclamation 110 of 1957, article 18 of which lays down that the chief 'may not be a member of, or take part in the affairs of a political organisation or an association the aims of which, in the opinion of the Minister, undermine or adversely affect the established administration of law and order'. There are two absurdities here. Maintaining a majority of tribal chiefs is an alien institution, because traditionally there is one chief on a council and the majority on the side of his subjects. This can be seen as a recognition of weakness or of possible rejection by the masses. It suggests that the chief has no following and that the elected members are the real leaders of the masses.

The wording of the article quoted above means that the official, the tribal chief, may take part in politics as long as it does not threaten the established administration or law. This implies that he is forbidden to support another political viewpoint than that of the ruling party of the central government of the Republic. If the tribal chiefs clearly understand this article it would not be in the least surprising if they, in their turn, expected those they give favours to - businessmen, social institutions, professional associations, officials, village councils, tribal councils, etc. - also not to take part in politics unless this does not threaten the ruling party. That, then, would not be politics but 'partitics'. The only honest and sound prescription would be that an official should not take part in any politics, and that would include the tribal chief. In the Transvaler of 20 July 1971, Mr Barend Venter expresses it as follows:

'We shall hear of still more Bantu leaders in the next few years. Strong men are coming forward, schooled to speak within the framework of the national policy, who are going to gain positions of power among the Bantu peoples' (my underlining).

Whether the leaders will speak 'within the framework' is a question that causes one serious reflection. Was the tribal chief trained to know that the quoted article 18 is his condition of service? Can one ever expect a politician to adhere to this article? Or is this a case where 'stupid' has caught 'clever'? In the meantime, what will become of the tribal system? It is true that, without the support of his tribal chief 'a Bantu politician (ordinary tribesman) does not usually get very far', as Barend Venter says further, but if the tribal chief is also a politician they will have to compete (kragte meet), something which ought to be avoided for the sake of the tribal system. Politics is becoming more and more demanding and specialised. This applies to administration as well. In my view a tribal chief ought to choose between the two, and all politicians should be elected. But now let us be warned: 'first given, then taken away, is stolen by a thief'.

The fact is that we have moved from one extreme - the Native Representative Council with its six official members (Secretary for Native Affairs and 5 Chief Bantu Commissioners), four nominated members and 12 elected members - to the other extreme, to traditional leadership on an ethnic basis with a majority of nominated tribal chiefs. Just as a tribal chief can hardly remain the ruler and the priest, he can scarcely be tribal ruler, tribal lawgiver, national executive authority, national politician and all that goes with these, in modern society. The tasks are specialised and he will also have to specialise in one direction.

That such a politician must also make appointments, decide on applications for trade licences, etc., must necessarily encourage corruption irrespective of a person's colour, education or religion. Admittedly tribal chiefs are traditional or natural leaders, but not, by any stretch, the most logical leaders in every sphere. In my view this will be the reason why the legislative assemblies will travel the same path which the abolition of the Representative Council was designed to end.

Instead of the tribal chief remaining the judge and deciding whether the politics of his subjects are attuned to the interests of the nation, he himself is a politician and the judge's seat is vacant. The entirely acceptable reasoning on which the position of the King of Lesotho outside politics is based, is valid for anyone who occupies an office of which justice and impartiality are required. The Botswana system, where a tribal chief must resign - any official must resign - when entering politics seems to be justified.

Has economic development kept pace with political development? It is to be doubted. The initiative has been shifted from the tribal authority and the regional authority to the legislative assembly. The latter controls all funds, and has the first right to tax the citizens. In the meantime there are three types of land ownership:

(a) Trust land which belongs to the legislative assembly;

(b) Tribal lands for which the tribe has the title deed;

(c) Reserves which in fact are also government territory.

Most certainly development under (a) will have preference, with the result that people will be lured out of tribal territory. When one hears of twenty towns and a further 23 for KwaZulu, at the same time one sees, in one's mind's eye, just as many tribal kraals empty. All the homelands will be affected in this way. The towns cannot be reserved exclusively for Bantu from the cities. If they are, it would mean that the tribal chief, the authorities system, would put the interests of the urban Bantu first and thus possibly neglect the tribal Bantu. It would be ironical for the tribal system to work in this way. Would a chief promoting such a system keep his chieftainship? Should we not rather change the tribal kraals into towns, with tradesmen and industries, before we build new towns? Should we not rather change the whole way of life in a Bantu village and modernise it and thereafter build new towns? What are we doing at present? To extend the cities to the homelands and thereby to contract the homeland territory, or to develop the homeland territory? For us Mabopane and Seshego are extensions of Pretoria and Pietersburg. When and how will the tribal chief develop the actual tribal territory? We repeat Mabopane gets preference although it is trust territory, not tribal land, and this encourages unfair competition.

The personal attention of the tribal head is urgently needed for (b) and (c), more urgently than it is needed in politics, in order to look after education, the economy, homecraft and the general social welfare, so that the tribal territory can equal the power of attraction of the towns. If not, he will lose his subjects. And how could this fail to affect his position as ruler and as a politician? The question is whether the common tribal lands should not be resuscitated on an economic basis, perhaps under irrigation and for a great variety of crops. What of forestry, not just for firewood? If a town must provide everything, and at a price, then the town is living on the tribal village, the town is exploiting the tribal system, and one day all will be off to the town for good, and then the tribal chief will also have to follow there, possibly without his chieftainship.

I wish to conclude by mentioning the existence of schools for the sons of chiefs in all the homelands, a silver lining in a dark cloud. In my view these sons will have to consider very carefully whether they wish to inherit their fathers' tribes or the whole nation in one. The signs are fairly clear that one cannot inherit both. If the tribal chief loses his hereditary hold on the basic unit of the traditional society, the tribe, just for the sake of the secondary political area, then he will give up the permanent in favour of the temporary.

There is a large number of tribal chiefs per national unit. If they will not join politics by the purifying process of a general election, they will ultimately either have free access to it or stay out entirely. We believe that strong tribes will provide strong regional authorities, strong regional authorities again a virile legislative assembly. It does not look as if the opposite would also be true. If the traditional chieftainship fails, the tribal system and the authorities system will collapse. If the speculation of Mr Bruce Young is correct, and a black nation is being born in South Africa, without the tribal chieftainship first being properly established, then the tribal system will experience even more violent shocks (skommelinge).

Thus it would seem that a real future must be thought out for the tribal system, and that this will not happen unless we go straight to the tribe and provide it with measures of improvement, reinforcement, attraction, modernisation and development; we put our money in what we believe in, and not alongside it; we do not surround it with competing, wealthier, more attractive, cosmopolitan towns which in their nature are extensions of the white cities; and the tribal chieftainship limits itself to the tribe and does not itself become the personification of divisive political quarrelling.

Perhaps the future can see the tribal authority take over most of the administrative duties of the Bantu Affairs Commissioner's office and the chief himself, if he is educated and capable, might develop in the direction of District Magistrate/Administrator. In that case the tribal area of a town would fall under his jurisdiction. His own kraal must be developed just like the town. Then the town would be an addition to the tribal system. That challenge would provide us with stronger characters than the present system which provides much too much protection. If I may speak for the younger generation I firmly believe that they would not be frightened by this challenge.

On the regional level a tribal chief might let himself be relieved of his post with the consent of his tribe in order to allow himself to be incorporated in the civil service and to shine as Regional Magistrate/Administrator because of his education and competence. And nothing would prevent such a career from splitting further, on the one hand towards the higher judicial posts and on the other to the higher administrative posts of the secretariat of state departments. The fact that the central or territorial authority of the authorities system controls and develops the towns and that the tribal kraals are just left as they are can rightly be seen as a recognition that the chief cannot handle a town, that the tribal kraal does not deserve development, and that the traditional system and the Western system do not come together anywhere; but this can also be recognised as the death knell of the traditional authority.

THE INDEPENDENT TRANSKEI

Manifesto of Paramount Chief K.D. Matanzima, Transkei General Election, 1963

As the future Chief Minister of the Transkei I wish the people to know that:

1 / I stand for the policy of separate development which is the cornerstone of the Transkei Constitution Act which has granted self-government to the Transkei.

2 / Chieftainship should be preserved and, in order to do so, chiefs should participate in the body that makes the laws - the Transkei Legislative Assembly.

3 / The Transkei should have its own industries but no European private enterprise should be allowed. Initially the Transkei government acting with the Republican government on the commonwealth relationship should start industries which can later be taken over by Bantu companies or individuals.

4 / All the land in the Transkei should belong to the Bantu including municipal land in the 26 villages of the Transkei. This will be done by the gradual elimination of the whites. In other words, the land that formerly belonged to the British King (Crown land) and later to the South African Native Trust, will be transferred to the Transkeian government and land held on freehold title by whites should be purchased by the Republican government for occupation by Bantu in terms of the 1936 legislation. Municipalities will be zoned on a gradual process until they are wholly occupied by Bantu. Additional land formerly occupied by Bantu will, after consultation with the Republican government, be added to the Transkeian territories. I refer to such land as in the districts of Queenstown, Lady Frere, Indwe, Maclear, Elliot, Ugie, Mount Currie, Harding and Port Shepstone.

5 / The Department of Education in the Transkei should be solely responsible for the nature and standard of education to be given to the Bantu child. The Republican government should stop interfering. The people of the Transkei should decide on the medium of instruction and syllabi.

6 / The Transkei civil service should be entirely black and the salaries paid to the staff should compare

favourably with those paid to the white civil servants in the Republic of South Africa. The principle of equal pay for equal work would be demanded if the Transkei were a multi-racial society, but since the Transkei is to be a black state we can only promise high salaries for our staff and compare these with those of the whites in the Republic. This is my objective.

7 / Agriculture should be put on a high standard. It means that every able-bodied man owning land should use modern methods of farming. The whole country should be completely rehabilitated. Irrigation schemes, such as that under construction at Qamata, should be undertaken. Soil erosion should be stopped. Dams should be constructed. Stock should be of good quality.

8 / Roads and bridges should be so well constructed that quick communication will be facilitated.

9 / The Transkei will require financial stability. Good relations with the Republican government will have to be maintained in order to facilitate the flow of money from that country to the Transkei by way of grants and employment of the people of the Transkei in the border industries and elsewhere.

10 / The expeditious transfer of the departments presently left in the care of the Republican government will be considered. The Department of Public Health and Labour should be the first to be transferred as soon as conditions become favourable.

11 / I propose to make representations to the Republican government for the establishment of a Bantu battalion of the Transkei government in the Republican defence force. The object is to train our young men for military service in the event of war involving South Africa and to prepare for the establishment of a Department of Defence in the Transkei.

12 / I will strive to induce the Republican government to employ Bantu men and women in all the departments that have not been transferred to the Transkei government so as to train them for independence.

13 / In granting licences for trading, Bantu traders will receive first consideration and the radius rule between Bantu and European trading stations will be abolished.

As a graduate of the University of South Africa in Arts, having majored in Roman Law and Politics, with English II, Latin I, Psychology I, Native Law, South

African Criminal Law and Roman Dutch Law as subsidiary subjects and having passed the Attorneys Admission Examination, obtaining the first position amongst Cape candidates, I feel positive that I will be able to discharge my duties as head of the Transkei government with all the competence that is expected from a distinguished statesman. My achievement in piloting discussions between the Transkeian Territorial Authority Executive Committee and the Minister of Bantu Education, resulting in the appointment of an all black Commission of Inquiry into complaints levelled against Bantu education is sufficient evidence of my statesmanship and is a pointer to the achievement of much greater things for my people in future.

As an administrator with 23 years service, I am competent to deal with any situation on a national or international level. My colleagues, the chiefs of the Transkei, will admit that their status socially and economically improved as soon as the Bantu Authorities Act was introduced. In 1954 the United Transkeian Territories General Council resolved unanimously that the Transkei did not want Bantu Authorities. But as soon as I joined the Bunga in 1955 a motion from Emigrant Tembuland challenged the 1954 decision and asked for the abolition of that puppet body, the Bunga, and the substitution therefor of Bantu Authorities - hence Proclamation No. 180 of 1956.

If anybody wants to see what I have done for my people during the last 23 years of service to them, let him visit Emigrant Tembuland for personal observation. The present Act was piloted by me. During the struggle for self-government, Paramount Chief Botha Sigcau and I experienced the most trying and difficult time resulting from revolts engineered by communists. Were it not for our bravery and statesmanship, the position of the chiefs and other colleagues who assisted us would have been in jeopardy. We should be allowed to continue our work until men of similar calibre appear who are prepared to carry on similar work. There is no room for Communists and Liberals in the Transkei.

Actions speak louder than words.

Transkei National Independence Party: Programme of Principles

1 / The party, whilst striving to conserve and foster all beneficial tribal law and custom, will observe democratic government and recognises the Christian faith under the guidance of God.

2 / It is the purpose of the party to promote the welfare of the various tribes living in the Transkei through political action, based on the principle of separate development. It seeks to instil a sense of national pride and unity and an urge to develop in gradual stages towards greater self-determination, culminating in eventual independence.

3 / The party pledges itself to preserve the office of chieftainship and their automatic membership of the Transkei Legislative Assembly. Since chieftainship is the traditional form of authority with the Bantu of the Transkei, it forms the framework of the political structure.

At the same time the party will safeguard the franchise extended to the citizens in terms of our constitution, thus linking the traditional political system with the modern concept of democracy.

4 / Whilst not allowing Europeans to become members of the party or to participate in the Transkeian franchise, the party wishes to stress the spirit of friendship prevailing between the Bantu of the Transkei and the Europeans living in their midst. It guarantees just and considerate treatment to these citizens of the Republic of South Africa living in the Transkei. The gradual withdrawal of Europeans from the Transkei is a matter of paramount concern to the party. It will therefore strive, in close co-operation and collaboration with the government of the Republic of South Africa to achieve such repatriation with as little loss or hardship as possible.

Europeans or Bantu who will endeavour illegally to foil this purpose will be dealt with according to the directives of the law pertaining.

5 / The party stands for the preservation of friendly

relationship between the Transkei and the Republic of South Africa, who has undertaken to assist the Transkeian State to attain greater self-determination in stages towards independence. After full independence for the Transkei has been achieved it is the policy of the party that the Transkei should continue its close and friendly relations with the Republic of South Africa as well as with other Bantu homelands created in terms of the policy of separate development.

The party guarantees just and equal treatment to the various tribes living in the Transkei and will foster a spirit of true Transkeian loyalty and dedication. It will strive incessantly to achieve all its aspirations, bearing in mind the sanctity of its special customs and traditions of each tribe.

6 / The party recognises the constitution of the Transkei as its statutory basis and will only alter the constitution when it becomes necessary for the more efficient functioning of administrative action. It will however never alter the principle of separate development embodied in the constitution. It will contest any attempt to alter the principle of separate development to one of integrated multi-racialism.

7 / The party accepts Nkosi Sikeleli Afrika as the national anthem and will endeavour to create a flag for the Transkei at an early date.

8 / It is the policy of the party to improve agricultural production through the introduction of sound scientific and progressive farming methods. It envisages the creation of an agricultural bank to assist Transkeian farmers with loans to finance their farming operations thus enabling them to enhance production. The creation of as many irrigation schemes as possible is a matter of great urgency, thus harnessing the water of numerous Transkei rivers.

It will assist and encourage farmers in all spheres of animal and field husbandry to acquire the best bloodstock, seed, fertiliser and expert advice.

9 / The party will investigate every possible avenue of industry and will sponsor local industrial development. Since secondary industry usually has its source in the raw material produced by private industry it is the party's policy to encourage the establishment of such primary industries as may prove to be the basis of secondary industry.

10 / It is the policy of the party to have a proper geological survey made of the Transkei, to establish its mineral potential. It envisages the development of such mineral deposits that could be developed economically.

11 / It is the conviction of the party that commercial concerns at present in the hands of Europeans must progressively be taken over by Bantu, with the co-operation of the government of the Republic of South Africa. Wherever possible Bantu business must be sponsored.

12 / The party stands for a progressive educational system under the guidance of educational experts. It is the policy of the party to embark on large scale technical training.

13 / It is the policy of the party to discuss all matters affecting labour conditions of those Transkei citizens working outside the Transkei, with the government of the Republic of South Africa, if and when it becomes necessary. In this way it will endeavour to ensure the best possible labour conditions and terms.

14 / The party subscribes to a policy of national health services, which will be expanded progressively as trained Bantu staff becomes available.

15 / To implement these general principles the party will establish itself as an independent political group on a national basis. It will announce its programme of action from time to time.

16 / This programme of principles can only be altered by a national conference of the party which will normally be held every April or by a special conference summoned for the purpose of altering these principles.

Transkei National Independence Party: Declaration of Loyalty by Members

'I hereby solemnly and sincerely declare that I acknowledge the sovereignty and guidance of Almighty God in the destiny of countries and people;
- That I shall seek in a spirit of brotherhood with my fellow party members the development of the Transkei's national life along Christian-National lines;
- That I shall with undivided loyalty and to the best of my ability uphold and encourage the declared principles of the National Independence Party as the political national front of the African nation;
- That I bind myself of my own free will to an undivided loyalty to my party and testify faithfully to fulfil the obligations attached to my membership of the party as stipulated in the constitution;
- That I submit to the authority and discipline of the party organisation as stipulated in the constitution;
- That I am not a member of any other political party or any other organisation with a political intent.'

Transkei National Independence Party: Manifesto, Transkei General Election, 1968

How does the Transkei National Independence Party envisage the future and what are its policies?

1 / We believe in the policy of separate development, since it has proved that it is the only policy that can successfully be applied in South Africa. Since it is the hereditary right of the people of the Transkei to govern themselves in their own country and according to their own wishes, we honour and observe the Transkei constitution and will act in accordance with the principles laid down in it. Whenever we find that the constitution needs amendment on account of political, administrative or economic developments, we shall not hesitate to approach the Republican government to effect such amendments.

2 / We strive for the entire independence of the Transkei along the lines of steady constitutional development.

In the process of development towards independence we shall approach the Republican government, as we have done in the past, to hand increasingly more administrative responsibilities over to us, until those departments at present still administered by that government have been transferred to the Transkei. When this has been achieved the Transkei will be virtually independent and its recognition as an independent state will be a matter of formality.

We are in fact at present awaiting the reply of the Republican government on representations we have made to it, requesting the transfer of certain departments to the Transkei.

3 / Since we appreciate that independence would yield but scant satisfaction if the viability of the country is not developed, assuring the citizens of the Transkei a higher standard of living and in consequence the state a higher revenue, we pledge ourselves to develop the agriculture of the Transkei, its most valuable natural resource, to the fullest possible extent. The development of our agriculture is of paramount importance for the establishment of secondary industry, since this can

only be profitably established if the general economic condition is such that raw materials will be available at a competitive price level to prospective industrialists. Agriculture, together with the labour of our people, is the greatest asset of the Transkei and will enjoy priority attention from the T.N.I.P. government. The progressive agricultural methods applied by the T.N.I.P. government during the past five years will not only be continued, but will be applied more intensively. The T.N.I.P. will strive to make more land available to Transkei citizens.

4 / The T.N.I.P. government has set a fine example of its responsible attitude towards education during the first five years of its administration and intends increasing the tempo of educational development during the forthcoming period of its government over the Transkei.

The expansion of primary, secondary and higher education will continue as in the past five years. Serious attention will be paid to the development of technical education and the training of technical staff. The Transkei Technical College, the buildings of which are under construction, will be able to teach our sons and daughters those very necessary trades and professions which they did not have the opportunity to acquire in the past. The training of technicians is very important to the development of our country, especially in the industrial field. The T.N.I.P. will negotiate with the Republican government to relax all labour and industrial laws impeding the process of training our own people in the field of trade and commerce in the Transkei.

We pledge ourselves to the advancement of education in all fields, because we recognise the necessity of education as a means of establishing ourselves indisputably as a people who can manage our own affairs in peace with efficiency and dignity.

5 / In close collaboration with the Xhosa Development Corporation we shall develop such industries as can be established in terms of existing economic conditions and strive to improve the economic structure of the country thus enabling it to accommodate more industrial development.

6 / The T.N.I.P. will observe the bonds of friendship existing between itself and the Republican

government. We intend to achieve our aims by means of friendly relationships between the Transkei and the Republican governments. History has proved beyond any doubt that cordial relationships and friendly negotiation have achieved much more than revolutionary extremism or political expediency.

7 / The T.N.I.P. wishes to state that it is opposed to any form of Communism or related forms of political expression. It will oppose with all facilities at its disposal Communist or Communist-inclined infringement on the liberty of the Transkei. It will not tolerate terrorism in any form, but especially terrorism emanating from leftist subversion, such as that experienced in Rhodesia at the present moment.

8 / In the event of Communist-inspired attack on the Republic of South Africa, the T.N.I.P. pledges its support to the Republic.

9 / The T.N.I.P. wishes to live in peace and harmony with all neighbouring peoples and governments. We are not interested in their internal politics or policies, but would co-operate in good-neighbourly activities that are of mutual importance to us. We think especially of such countries and nations as Lesotho, Botswana and Swaziland as well as, of course, all the other Bantu homelands in the Republic of South Africa.

You know our associations and our policies. They are honest and straightforward!

The T.N.I.P. stands for Transkei Nationalism and Transkei Independence!

Because we have a policy to offer you, we offer you a future of happiness and opportunity!

Because of our unquestionable achievements, the T.N.I.P. can in all sincerity expect your support.
Vote T.N.I.P. and be free!

Appendix to Transkei National Independence Party Manifesto, 1968. 'Our achievements as governing party.'

To any unprejudiced person it must be quite clear that great progress has been experienced in the Transkei during the past five years of T.N.I.P. government.

Here are a few of the outstanding achievements:

1 / The Transkei has established its own civil service. There were 2 446 posts in the civil service when the T.N.I.P. took over the government in 1963. Of these posts 455 were held by Europeans. At present there are

more than 3 400 posts of which 365 are held by Europeans. Thus the posts held by Europeans were decreased by 19 per cent, Bantu replacing the Europeans. The number of Transkei citizens employed in the civil service increased by 39 per cent.

2 / Expenditure by the Transkei government has steadily increased and government spending on capital works was responsible for an upsurge in the buying power of our people.

It is interesting to note that the circulation of money has increased substantially. Thus the local branches of two commercial banks operating in Umtata have had a turnover of R152 000 000 during 1967. Such a phenomenal economic growth is the most eloquent sign of progress. The six government departments are efficiently run, with the assistance of white officials seconded to the Transkei government by the Republican government. The white officials are progressively being replaced by Transkei citizens and the time is not far off when all departments will be run by our own people.

3 / Spectacular progress has been experienced in the educational field where 80 000 more children than in 1963 are attending school, making a total of 335 000 school-going children. The education vote has been increased by 50 per cent since 1964 and represents more than 27 per cent of the total budget of the Transkei. The T.N.I.P. government is aware of the fact that the people of the Transkei need education to enable them to improve their own standards of living and to develop their country and their nation to the fullest possible degree. Thus the curriculum of 100 primary schools was extended to standard 6, seven new high schools and nine new secondary schools were established. No less than 1 691 additional teachers and administrative officers were appointed, thus bringing the total number of teachers in the Transkei to over 6 000.

The Transkei Department of Education is well organised and compares very favourably with that of any other country in Africa.

4 / The Department of Roads and Works spends R1 000 000 annually on building and maintenance of roads and the number of machine operators rose from 181 in 1963 to 360, thus doubling the number of Transkei citizens employed in this capacity. More than 1 500 additional labourers were given employment on the

roads.

Unskilled labour employed in the Transkei rose from 32 000 in 1964 to 41 000 in 1967. During the 1965/66 drought, 67 565 men and women were employed on relief works.

5 / Pension beneficiaries increased from 51 755 in 1964 to 62 551 in 1967.

6 / The well-known 'five mile radius restriction' on rural trading stations was abolished. People were assisted by the Bantu Investment Corporation (B.I.C.) and the Xhosa Development Corporation (X.D.C.) to buy shops and trading stations and the number of business concerns owned and run by citizens of the Transkei virtually doubled when they increased from 663 in 1963 to 1 201 in 1968.

7 / Law and order was maintained and subversive activities were entirely stamped out. Action taken against people like Hjul, Vigne and other Europeans and their Bantu henchmen ensured that this territory enjoyed a period of undisturbed peace.

In the Department of Justice there was a steady replacement of European officials by Transkei citizens. Two magistrates have already been replaced by Transkei citizens. There are six assistant magistrates and six public prosecutors who have been promoted during the past five years and the time is drawing near when all districts in the Transkei will have Transkei citizens as magistrates, as well as other judicial functionaries.

8 / A Transkei police force has been created and will progressively be expanded until it can replace the South African police. Already there are seven police stations that are manned entirely by Transkeians.

9 / Great progress has been made in the agricultural field where the T.N.I.P. government has embarked on projects calculated to enhance the development of our agriculture, which we recognise as our main asset and can yet make the Transkei a very prosperous country. We name only a few:

(a) The Lubisi dam at Qamata has been opened and we are proceeding to place settlers on the Qamata irrigation scheme.

(b) We have continued the establishment of phormium tenax plantations in Butterworth and Lusikisiki. We have overcome practically all the technical snags in connection with the decortication of this fibre and the

establishment of a grainbag factory is imminent.
(c) We have established a tea and coffee plantation in Eastern Pondoland, which promises to become a real and lasting source of income for the Transkei since our tea seems to compare very favourably with similar plantations elsewhere in the Republic.
(d) A meat factory was established to process beef and farmers who sell their cattle to the factory are very satisfied with the prices they receive.
(e) There has been a great improvement in the production of wool and if the tempo can be sustained, as it must, the sheep farmers of the Transkei will have a very good quality sheep, yielding more profits in the not too distant future.
(f) The building of yet another irrigation scheme in the Umgazi River has been announced and work on this scheme will commence in the very near future, thus developing one of the most fertile areas in our country.
(g) Afforestation continues at unabated tempo and has become the Transkei government's largest single source of revenue.

10 / Through negotiations with the Republican government, more Transkei citizens who had to look for work because of the unprecedented drought were accommodated in the Republican urban areas, the number of people who went to work in the Republic having increased from 32 000 to 41 000.

There are still numerous matters that have not been mentioned in this appendix to the Election Manifesto of the T.N.I.P. We do, however, appeal to the Transkei voters to take note of the irrefutable progress made under T.N.I.P. government during the past five years when they go to the polls on 23 October. These are hard facts, not pipe-dreams such as the hollow slogans of the Democratic Party as well as the Freedom Party.

Vote for steady and concrete development. Vote T.N.I.P. A vote for the T.N.I.P. is a step nearer to total independence, based on sound and sensible development.

The Need for Land

K.D. MATANZIMA

(Excerpts from an address delivered to congress of the ruling Transkei National Independence Party held at Umtata, 11 April 1972)

Twelve months ago I made significant and relevant statements on relations between the Transkei government established in terms of the separate development policy nine years ago and the Republican government of South Africa. Today it is my duty to give a true and unbiased report of the events which followed. It pleases me to report to this congress that much has been done by the Minister of Bantu Administration and Development to implement the remaining stages in the transfer of the departments which formed the basis of my protestations.

During the year 1971/72 we witnessed the accelerated purchasing by our own people of white businesses and residential properties not only in the rural areas of the Transkei but also its urban areas. This was particularly done by the most vehement opponents of the policy which has enabled Transkeian citizens to acquire freehold rights to property - a situation which has not existed anywhere in the Republic. In other words we saw curious characters who behaved like a man who takes the honey from a beehive and in the process says to his colleagues while he is enjoying the honey alone, 'do not come near, they sting', meaning the bees. The opportunism of these queer characters has been exposed to the voters of the Transkei. Hence they are in the process of quarrelling amongst themselves in a bid for leadership.

During April 1972, the Department of Prisons and five police stations will be transferred from the Republic to the Transkeian Department of Justice. The further transfer of other police stations will be undertaken in the not-too-distant future. During April 1973 the Health Department will be transferred wholly to the Transkeian administration with its own minister who may take control of the social services now under the Minister of the Interior. This will result in an additional portfolio to the present number of cabinet ministers. During 1973 the road transportation control services will also be transferred from the Republican Road Transportation Board in Pretoria to the Transkeian administration.

In the Departments of Posts and Telegraphs and the Railways much is being done to accelerate the training of the young Transkeian citizens to take over control of these departments with the object of transferring them to the Transkeian government. This is being done in spite of the objections of the Republic's major opposition political party which has consistently charged the National Party with placing important services under ignorant and incompetent people - the Africans of the Transkei - people who may at any time, they allege, align themselves with a Communist attack on the Republic. I am sure we can only charge these people as being the most backward, stupid and inhumane racialists amongst their own people. We have witnessed the intensified efforts of the Republican government in a bid to convince the world that the policy of separate development has received the blessings of all black races in South Africa. This has been done through the radio and the English and Afrikaans press.

But the refusal of the Republican government to release that portion of the Transkei which was unilaterally expropriated after the Union of South Africa Act was passed, has now politically put the Transkei people in their relations with white South Africa back to pre-1963 days and the struggle between the two governments may destroy existing good relations. For it is inconceivable to expect a dispossessed people to connive at injustices particularly when they enrich one people to the total exclusion of the other. My government has had discussions with the Prime Minister on this matter and his Cabinet's reaction has been negative despite conclusive documentary evidence produced in support of our submissions.

The land we claim formed part of the Transkeian administration under the British government, but was unilaterally and cynically raped by the Union government. Claims by us to such land are now referred to as claims to white land. This is confusing the issue and is most stupid and irrelevant as it is not based on fact. It is more so when a Transkeian citizen like Mr Guzana calls it a claim on white land and another,

Mr Ndamse, calls it a claim falling outside the Transkei Constitution Act. Who does not know that the land we claim was not included in our territory under the Transkei Constitution Act? We all know that in as much as all the towns in the Transkei remained white spots and are still white spots they are, through our efforts, in the process of being transferred to our government.

My government has conceded that white land-owners in the area claimed have legitimate rights to the land they occupy, but our submission is that these lands, in the process of re-inclusion in the Transkei, should be open to purchase by Transkeian citizens by repealing the provisions of the Land Act of 1913 and the Urban Areas Act of 1923 which preclude Africans from ownership of land in the white areas of the Republic. Our claim is reasonable and affects a small fraction of the land occupied by white South Africans.

When one considers that the population of the Transkei, including those squatting in the Republican towns and farms, is almost equal to the whole population of white South Africa, one is compelled to come to the conclusion that the policy of separate development is basically in the best interests of the white people and that less consideration is given to those of the black people. I say so because land is the determining factor which will reflect the altruism of white South Africans in their pronounced bid to satisfy the aspirations of all racial groups. The policy of separate development would, if the land question were settled equitably, be accepted even by the doubting Thomases. For its alternative, racial integration, would lead to endless quarrels cultivated by racial differences.

I wish to give friendly advice to the Republican government and say that they should reconsider their decision, if harmonious relations amongst the races of South Africa are to be maintained. As the people of the Transkei will be advised not to ask for independence without first getting their land, the land issue between the Republic and the Transkei will remain a very bitter issue which may gradually estrange existing harmonious relations and cause resentment amongst the Transkei citizens. This advice is being given by a moderate leader who puts realism above ideological political concepts.

Coming now to the progress made in the six government departments, I am happy to say that much development is imminent. In education, agricultural development and extension services, land administration, social services, administration of justice in the government department and the chiefs' courts, in road building, school buildings, etc. there is no doubt that development has taken place. Industrial development is forging ahead slowly but surely under the auspices of the Xhosa Development Corporation. Our problem in this respect is the continued migration of our manpower to labour centres under the notorious influx controls.

Every effort is being made to harness the rivers of the Transkei in order to step up industrial development in the towns and to improve agricultural holdings by way of irrigation. I wish to appeal to T.N.I.P. adherents to take our struggle for survival seriously. They cannot do so without developing a true spirit of nationalism. My government has stepped up the payrolls of our civil service but unless these ladies and gentlemen consider service to their country more than their persons, nothing will be achieved in the struggle for emancipation.

The political relations between the Transkei and the Republic of South Africa have reached a stagnant point because of the latter's refusal to face the facts submitted by the former for an equitable agreement on land partition. Never before has the unity of our people been more essential in their struggle for the attainment of human rights enjoyed by all people in the free world. Never before has a demand for principled decisions devoid of all opportunism become so strong as is the case in our resolve to regain all that portion of our land which was taken from us without consultation. This will always remain the only cause of resentment and irreconcilable difference between the blacks of the Transkei and the Republic.

While we acknowledge the government's attempts to bring about a solution of previously strained race relations, it must be conceded by all reasonable men that land is basic to the successful establishment of such cordial relations. In the not-too-distant future, those of us who constitute this moderate government may announce their retirement because of old age. The question is: what attitude will our successors adopt? I appeal to the Republican government to initiate full and open consultation with us on this land question and to try to persuade the most hardened racialists in their ranks of the desirability of an equitable partition of the land occupied by whites in order to accommodate the dispossessed blacks.

Ladies and gentlemen, in conclusion I am bold to say a day will come when we shall say: 'At last we have got our country back'.

Separate Development

K.D. MATANZIMA

(Address delivered at the opening of the congress of the Transkei National Independence Party, Umtata, on 22 March 1973)

Let me allude to the most important ramification in the natural growth of a nation, namely human relations, and say that never before have human relations been so eminently the characteristic feature in the building of a nation. From speeches of important personalities in the political circles of the Republic of South Africa a spirit of cordiality, a desire to solve the racial problems of our country amicably, has appeared. I refer to such outstanding statesmen as the Honourable Prime Minister of South Africa, Mr B.J. Vorster, Mr Theo Gerdener, Dr Connie Mulder, the Minister of Interior, Sir de Villiers Graaff, and Chiefs Mangope, Matlala, Buthelezi and Ntsanwisi, all leaders of their respective communities.

Allow me to say that the Transkei government has acquitted itself as the equal of the Republican government in the discharge of its duties in all the departments under its charge. The transfer of the prison department and health services to our administration is a little step up the ladder towards self-realisation. But what is the reason for the non-transfer to our establishment of all the remaining departments to complete the stage leading to full independence? These are pertinent questions that require answers, not from me but from the Republican government. My government has repeatedly solicited the Republican government to transfer all departments, irrespective of their intricate nature, to our administration. The last of these dialogues raised hopes of preparedness to hand over bus transport, the police, information services and posts and telegraphs after protracted investigations for a take-over were made. I want to make a bold declaration and say the Transkei is now ready for full self-government and will not tolerate any reactionary forces militating against its constitutional development to full independence.

On my return from America, I made a pertinent statement in East London relating to the South African racial situation. I warned white South Africa that their country is becoming more and more isolated and that every country in the world is anti-South Africa because of the latter's discriminatory laws. Many people interpreted my statement as being Democratic Party orientated, as if my party stood for racial discrimination. I want to make it clear that I stand by my declarations during the years of our existence as a governing party. I stand for separate development provided it is carried out to its logical conclusion. If it fails, as it seems to be failing, the alternative is an integrated South Africa with full equality amongst all races. What is meant by the 'carrying out of the policy of separate development to its logical conclusion'?

A self-governing state should have a constitution enacted by parliament providing for the control of all relevant departments for the full control of its administration. It is ridiculous and a mockery to say a country is self-governing while another country tampers with its administration. The control of police, transport, posts and telegraphs by the Republican government makes self-government in our Transkei a mockery. It is a big ruse which should be exposed to those who are being persuaded by radio and pro-Republican government press to believe that the homelands are self-governing.

A self-governing state should have the boundaries of its territory defined. How can the Transkei be said to be self-governing when the Republican government owns portions of land within the confines of its territory? I refer to all the towns of the Transkei, Port St Johns and Matatiele included, which are controlled by the Republican government. This foreign control of our towns is detrimental to the best interests of our people. Instead of providing sites for Transkeian citizens whose accommodation is so inadequate that the situation has assumed alarming dimensions, the Republican government is building houses for whites who are entering the Transkei in large numbers - a situation which is contrary to the promises made when the policy of separate development was first mooted.

At this juncture may I say categorically that without

the land formerly under the jurisdiction of the chief magistrate of the Transkei known as Kaffraria Proper including the districts of Elliot, Maclear, Matatiele Farms and Mount Currie, there can be no independent Transkei. As you may have read in the press and Hansard the following resolution moved by me was passed by the Legislative Assembly in May 1972:

'That the government should consider the advisability of requesting the Republican government to grant independence to the Transkei comprising the following districts and towns: Elliot, Maclear, Mount Currie, Elliotdale, Engcobo, Flagstaff, Bizana, Butterworth, Lusikisiki, Kentane, Mount Ayliff, Mount Fletcher, Matatiele, Nqamakwe, Mqanduli, Ngqeleni, Qumbu, Tsolo, Tsomo, St Marks, Xalanga, Port St Johns, Tabankulu, Umtata, Willowvale, Idutywa, Libode, Mount Frere, and Umzimkulu and should forthwith initiate consultation between the two governments.'

The Transkeian cabinet has sent the resolution with strong recommendations to the Republican government but has not been furnished with a written reply. The Honourable the Prime Minister has declared in interviews with delegations of the Transkeian government that he will not comply with the demands of the Transkei insofar as land claims are concerned, but will grant independence on the land now occupied plus any other land to be allocated in terms of the Native Trust and Land Act of 1936. Hence the controversy over land has now widened the gap in the strained relations between the two governments brought about by the Republican government's negative attitude. We are determined, with the backing of this congress and the general voters of the Transkei, to pursue the claim for land until the Republican government becomes aware of the un-Christian attitude it has shown in arrogating to the white community all South African land and leaving the bulk of the black population with fragmented patches of stony and dry land.

We shall remain the subjects of the Republican government bearing in mind that South Africa belongs to both black and white. My government, if returned to power at the October elections, will continue to expose the hollowness of the Republican government's policy and their determination to maintain white domination at all costs. We shall continue to administer the affairs of the Transkei in all departments under our charge to the best of our ability and in the best interests of the poor people of the poor land. The argument that we chose the land we occupy is an extravagant distortion of the true facts. All the land we occupy, together with that now occupied by white farmers and which we now claim, formerly belonged to the British government and later to the South African Bantu Trust in terms of the 1936 legislation.

With regard to my proposed federation plan with other homelands and the Republic in Southern Africa, I wish to point out that this is not a new thought. It was voiced by the late Dr Verwoerd in the form of a commonwealth of South African nations. But my own idea is that of a federal parliament similar to that of the United States of America with representatives from the independent states of Southern Africa. The Republican government does not appear to be happy about this proposal and its reactionary attitude seems to have captured the imaginations of other homelands leaders. However, the unison of the thinking of the two leaders of the biggest homelands, KwaZulu and the Transkei, is consoling as it has brought support from the Zulus and Xhosa-speaking tribes of the Transkei in the midst of strenuous attempts from certain quarters to disrupt our unity. The separation of the black people on ethnic grounds is a retrograde step as it has revived tribal rivalries.

When the Native Representative Council was established in 1936, it represented the voice of the black people in South Africa. The same will happen when we establish a federal government of equal and independent states. We are opposed to the United Party federal policy which places the white parliament in a superior position over the black states. We are also opposed to the Progressive Party policy which stands for a qualified franchise. We stand for the principle of one man one vote in all stages of our government.

The question now remains to be asked: where does the Transkeian Democratic Party stand in the aforesaid political situation? This is the question asked by all reasonable men who have a clear concept of the South African situation. Will they continue to stab us in the back in our struggle for the liberation of the black man?

Manifesto of Paramount Chief K.D. Matanzima, Transkei General Election, 1973

Politics in the Transkei have reached the stage where the voters have to decide conclusively whether the policy hitherto followed by the Transkeian National Independence Party under the leadership of Paramount Chief K.D. Matanzima is to be the pattern for South Africa's solution of the intricate problem of race relations facing this country in the eyes of the world.

I submit that the policy of separate development, now the basis for future development of all homelands, has demonstrated in no uncertain terms that if carried out to its logical conclusion, will demonstrate to the world that black and white in South Africa can live together side by side peacefully and respectably.

To achieve this goal, the following principles should be given full cognisance by all races in this country:

1 / That South Africa belongs to black and white equally and all its wealth should be shared by all inhabitants without discrimination.

2 / That the homelands should be developed to full independence and that the division of land in terms of population numbers is basic for the fulfilment of such independence.

3 / That as whites established the Union of South Africa in terms of the 1910 South Africa Act, so should the blacks establish their own union of black South African states by way of federation of the homeland governments and those governments already independent in Southern Africa.

4 / The freedom of the individual irrespective of colour or creed should be the motto of the Transkeian citizens and this should be attained irrespective of whether the Transkei is independent or merely self-governing, i.e. freedom to seek work anywhere in the Republic of South Africa and freedom from pass laws.

5 / The opening of the door to industrialists by means of attractive incentives for the purposes of establishing major industries in the homeland in order to employ Transkeian citizens is basic to economic

viability.

6 / The creation of an infrastructure for agricultural development, e.g. the establishment of co-operative farmers' associations, irrigation schemes and soil reclamation.

7 / The concern of the black leaders for the amelioration of the political, social and economic position of the urban blacks should be stepped up. This will always be a major concern of my government.

8 / The general improvement of living conditions by increasing wages is of paramount importance. This has been my concern since the establishment of the Transkeian government. The ultimate aim is equal pay for all races in Southern Africa irrespective of colour for work undertaken.

9 / Friendly relations amongst the population groups is of the utmost importance in the interests of South Africa as a whole.

10 / The involvement of the Transkeian citizens in commerce and industry by formation of companies in order to pull together capital to meet the demands of modern trade technicalities.

11 / The urbanisation of the landless class to afford them employment in the Transkeian towns which are being taken over for their occupation. For the first time in the history of South Africa, our people are able to purchase freehold title properties in twenty five of the Transkeian towns. These towns will in due course be owned and controlled by the Transkeian government.

12 / Building of schools, both primary and secondary, and universities. Free education for the black child will result in a high percentage of literacy.

13 / The tarring of Transkeian roads to stimulate tourism on the Transkeian Wild Coast.

14 / The eradication of the causes of criminal behaviour, e.g. drunkenness caused by drugs and excessive drinking.

15 / The building of a civilised society based on African traditions and customs.

'Unity is Strength.'

Transkei National Independence Party: Manifesto of Candidates, Transkei General Election, 1973

1 / I/We pledge myself/ourselves to give full support to the cabinet in its efforts to develop the economy of the Transkei.

We shall activate the Transkeian citizens in farming, building of roads and bridges, building of clinics, building of schools with government subsidy, provision of water supplies for domestic and agricultural use, compulsory education, commercial undertakings, irrigation schemes.

2 / I/We pledge assistance to the Transkeian government in its claim for additional land comprising the districts of Elliot, Maclear, Matatiele Farms, Mount Currie and Port St Johns.

3 / I/We shall struggle, in support of the government, to remove from the statute book all discriminatory laws which are a source of inhumanity, e.g. pass laws, influx control regulations, discrimination in wages and salaries, restrictions on movement of stock.

4 / I/We shall assist the government to activate the establishment of industries in the Transkei so as to provide work for Transkeian citizens and augment the revenue of the country.

5 / I/We shall fight for the establishment of farmers' co-operatives, land bank, trading companies, to step up the economy of the country.

6 / I/We stand for complete independence and the federation of the black states. Complete equality amongst all races is our objective.

Imbumba Yamanyama. 'Unity is Strength.'

Transkei Democratic Party: Statement of Objectives in the Constitution

(a) To ensure harmonious and cordial relationships among the various races which constitute the inhabitants of the Transkei by forming a government on the principles of democracy of government of the people, for the people and by the people.

(b) Creating a sound economy - a solvent state; means of livelihood for everyone.

(c) To ensure the protection of minorities by constitutional entrenchments.

(d) To seek the agricultural and industrial development of the Transkei as part of the Republic of South Africa.

(e) To ensure a developing educational system fitting the individual into human society which is universal.

(f) Improved employment opportunities, equal pay for equal work, and promotion based on merit.

(g) The development of a judiciary free from political bias and committed to international standards of justice.

(h) Increased and state-subsidised health services.

(i) The continued retention of the Transkei as part of the Republic of South Africa.

(j) The establishment of friendly and diplomatic relations with countries committed to the western way of life and civilisation.

(k) The development of a non-racial loyalty to the government of the Transkei and the republican government of the Republic of South Africa.

(l) The establishment of cultural bodies with a view to adjusting Bantu customs and traditions into western culture and patterns.

(m) The maintenance and perpetuation of the institution of traditional chieftainship.

(n) Freedom of speech and religion, freedom of movement and assembly.

Transkei Democratic Party: Statement, General Election, 1968

The Democratic Party, as it goes to the Transkei Electorate in the forthcoming General Election on 23 October 1968, again re-affirms its policy of multi-racialism. The party feels that its policy, based on goodwill and fellowship with all races that must live together in South Africa to eternity, is a policy of understanding and acceptance of the reality that South Africa is multi-racial.

We stand for the upliftment of the African in South Africa by co-operation and interplay of influences for good among South Africans of all races.

We believe that the economic involvement of the African in a single South African economic state is a reality which cannot be disentangled, and that the African's upliftment is assured by his greater participation in the economic upsurge of South Africa. A closed Transkei economy is neither feasible nor realistic.

For this reason we believe that the African should be allowed free access into South Africa's labour centres to serve as unskilled workers, to train and serve as skilled and semi-skilled workers in the complex South African community.

We believe that the African is as loyal as every other South African citizen is loyal, and shall neither encourage nor connive at any activity calculated to undermine the security of our country.

We believe in the need for an intensive and extensive programme of education for the African in the Transkei and elsewhere so that he may become a worthy South African citizen, contributing to progressive evolution positively and constructively.

We believe in the security, unity and sanctity of family life which will be assured when families, in spite of the stresses of economic evolution, will be kept together as a unit.

We believe that, given the opportunity in South Africa, including the Transkei, the African will provide the man-power for phenomenal industrial development in our country.

We firmly believe that governing bodies must be wholly elective so that in them the African may be heard to pledge his patriotism, to express his wishes, desires and aspirations through men and women placed in these bodies by the vote of the people of the electorate.

We strongly urge an agricultural programme, linked up with demonstration and propaganda by field workers, that will increase the yield of the land.

The poor and the needy, the sick and the infirm, the weak and the starving, the old and the aged, are all the responsibility of the state, and of those who are more favourably placed in life. More than anything else, had they had equal opportunity, they would have overcome the adversities of life.

We believe that the Transkei's future is full of promise so long as it continues to remain an integral part of the Republic of South Africa.

These beliefs which are our convictions and are the basis of our programme for the future will be realised, as we have sought to realise them in the last five years as an Opposition in the Transkei parliament, by constitutional means and round-table consultations with the South African government.

On Being a South African

K.M.N. GUZANA

(Address delivered to the students of the University of Port Elizabeth on 15 August 1973)

My reactions to the words 'South African' may be just as docile as yours, for the words connote, broadly speaking, what we all claim to be. Just as an American, an Englishman or a Frenchman has a sense of elation and well-being when identified with his country of origin, so do we react similarly when we are identified as South Africans. The two-word phrase conjures up the idea of unity, of oneness, a belongingness to a part of the world around which we expend some pride and sentiment. Yet I have known what the reaction is when we identify ourselves as South Africans beyond the borders of the Republic of South Africa. There is a considerable raising of eyebrow, a curiosity over your geographical identity, disbelief and even cultured hostility towards us - this in contrast to the reaction that an Englishman, for instance, arouses in America. Thank heaven that when we travel beyond our borders, we carry a passport which benevolently describes one as a South African citizen.

Because our identity outside South Africa stimulates speculation, sometimes hostile, we might do well to look at ourselves closely, honestly asking ourselves the questions: why this reaction to a South African? do we deserve this description of being South African as fully and justifiably as the insular Englishman is so called and as the man from France is known as a Frenchman? Let us join together in underscoring some of the common denominators of all South Africans.

Firstly, we are all born in South Africa. Whether we be Capetonians, Durbanites, Transvalers or lusty Free Staters, there is a common neutralising denominator of being the children of the land called South Africa.

Secondly, broadly speaking we are subjects of one government and if this should raise in your mind the question of Bantustan governments in South Africa, let me hasten to remind you that the central government is still supreme.

Thirdly, we have - again in a broad sense - a Christian teaching recognising one Christ although we show this allegiance in various and devious ways.

Fourthly, we all subscribe to a greater or a lesser degree to the tenets of western civilisation and all that it stands for.

The list is not exhaustive by any means, but it serves to emphasise and strengthen our claim to being South African. Those who have had to leave South Africa under peremptory instructions to do so, or out of righteous choice and have marshalled themselves into forces anti-South African, betray a strong desire to be with us whether it be by fair or foul means. They wish to return to a changed South Africa and introduce to us a new concept of what a South African should be - quite different from the present South African whose rights and privileges, duties and obligations, limitations and dispensations, justice and dignity, security and affluence are trimmed by race and colour consciousness. For let us face the truth, no matter how unpalatable it may be, that we have first class South Africans, second class South Africans and third class South Africans. When faced with this classification, the typical first class South African shrugs his shoulders, blames the government and all in authority for these inequalities, thus assuming an attitude of non-involvement. He lifts his eyes above the rugged terrain of prejudice, hardship, and corrosive indignities suffered by lesser South Africans, explains all this by reminding the critical observer of our traditional way of life.

Tonight let us try to look closely at the present attitudes and see if you and I cannot diagnose the malady that afflicts South Africans. Is there not in us an arrogance of attitude towards one another, born of a righteous sense of achievement and a feeling of superiority that refuses to countenance change? Have we not brought Christianity to dark and superstitious South Africa; is western civilisation not our heritage benevolently offered to less favoured South Africans as bounty and largesse for which the latter have to be forever grateful in humility? Do we not owe it to our forebears to maintain and preserve these bequests and keep them untarnished for the next generation? After all, the other South Africans will taint and possibly ravish this heritage and posterity might well be the universal heirs of a civilisation and a way of life second-graded by misguided humanitarianism. We owe it to posterity to maintain the status quo even if our consciences revolt against the traditional way of life which wounds and hurts. And because of this unholy reverence for a cruel and inhuman tradition, black South Africans - I use the adjective black for lack of an accurate word - develop a counter-arrogance born of frustration and despair, manifesting itself in rejection and exclusivity, in emphasis on black identity to measure up to and counter balance the arrogance of the white South African. To me this is a dangerous polarisation of attitudes that makes our claim to being South Africans a mockery and a sham. Our attitudes and prejudices which we think preserve our heritage for posterity are the very corrosive agents which may leave an empty and hollow inheritance to our children.

Then our attitudes and actions are conditioned by race and colour. We have the white South African, the off-white South African, the brown South African and the black South African with corresponding attitudes and actions scaling down from being exemplary to downright hideousness as we move into the shadow of blackness. I have always wondered what would happen if all the laws based on race and colour were to be expunged from the statute books tomorrow, next month or next year! Would the South African live in a Utopia? I say no, for in our hearts and minds would be left the sediment of race and colour prejudice and it would take a long time to clean the mess of our inner selves.

In this context I am reminded of the recent case of agony and despair, the frustration and the fear which were the lot of white parents whose child began to fade in complexion into horrifying and progressively degrading blackness. Classmates began to tease and torment her, playmates began to shun her, there were whispers behind her back and challenges about her identity. Race classification hovered menacingly over the whole family; friends, relatives and acquaintances had perforce to give assurances and moral support and pledge unaltered social relationships. I ask the question: Why all this? Does colour have something to do with the inner man, the real being in us to the extent that life grows progressively into a sinister hell for those not so white, those who are brown and even black? Ladies and Gentlemen how would you feel if after this evening you were to shade away into the colour of the other South African? Would you commit suicide? Would you emigrate to the Argentine? What would you do, I ask you? I shudder when I contemplate the consequences in the South African situation.

Here let us in passing count some of the many indignities that stem from our depressing obsession with race and colour. Because the other South African is not white:

(a) he must deliver my message via the back door even if I have to descend from the inner sanctuary of my residence to the kitchen door level to receive it;

(b) at the butchery I buy my cutlets, but do not forget to purchase a part of the carcass which goes under the name 'servants' meat';

(c) though he has entered the public building before me through his door and is being attended to, I must get precedence on my arrival;

(d) he is tolerated while he is of service to me, but must fade away and his existence be forgotten when night falls and for all time when he ceases to be useful;

(e) I feel self-conscious and awkward if he recognises and approaches me in public - why did he ever know me and I know him?;

(f) even though she nursed and cared for me into the night in babyhood, cuddled me to sleep and sang me a soothing lullaby in some language not intelligible when mother went to the cinema, she has no claim to equality with me as a South African.

And so on and so on - the list is endless.

All these manifestations of colour and race prejudice are not underpinned by legislation. You cannot honestly pass on the responsibility to some inhuman legislator. We are in the dock; we stand accused - what is our plea? Guilty.

I am afraid that my handling of the subject thus far has tended to be depressing and I feel we must now put together our South African, sort the pieces out, and rearrange them in such a way that we produce a South African who is worthy of the name. I must confess that in South Africa more than at any time before, and in spite of the law and law enforcement, there is now a breeze of change which manifests itself in self-examination and a refusal to conform, a growing awakening to the inhumanity of our sectional South Africanism. Let me pause here to state how much the black South African has warmed to the students of the University of Cape Town and other like-minded students in other universities who have unwittingly bared themselves to physical pain, have suffered weals and bruises, have been tugged by the hair and by the leg for the sake of educational equality for all South Africans. What they have in education they value: but when they have it exclusively they know that they do not have it fully. Theirs was indeed a noble and acceptable sacrifice.

The term dialogue has become threadbare and some of us turn away from it because to them dialogue is an intellectual and social exercise (with political nuances) that salves the consciences of the participants.
I reject this attitude, for dialogue involves for me reciprocal acceptance. It substitutes hope for despair, induces warm relaxation in place of cold rigidity and opens wide the flood-gates of goodwill and understanding. For us it connotes a willingness to negotiate, a readiness to run the gauntlet of suspicion and antagonism for the greater reward of Christian neighbourliness; we are on the threshold of negotiation which presages concessions. There is a meeting of minds, a meeting of sentiments, a meeting of feelings. But because our journey in this direction is bound to be harassed by historical and emotional conservatism, let us accept the fact that rewarding results are not so quick and as precise as bombing an enemy stronghold. If we disagree, there lies the justification for dialogue, not a reason for abandonment of the effort, for those who disagree with us do not necessarily hate us, nor are they our enemies.

A very common error which bedevils good and Christian acts on the part of one South African for the benefit of another South African is the predilection for condescending patronage. Many South Africans who have been 'do gooders' to the benefit of distressed fellow South Africans have withdrawn into themselves because of chilling ingratitude and suspicion on the part of those who have been benefitted. I believe the reaction of the recipient is justified because he feels bound to accept in humiliation and self-condemnation. If this is the case, can we not do our good deeds, can we not undertake humanising and developing projects with a justified expectation of genuine appreciation if the other party is convinced that he is in it for his own good; that he will get out of it as much as, if not more than, what he puts into it; that you are both in it for what you will both get out of it, and not that he gets all whilst your reward is an easy conscience. Any project motivated differently is bound to collapse in ruins as hand-outs are no longer acceptable and purposeful participation is fundamental.

One of the tragedies of the South African way of life is a refusal to concede that we must all share the responsibility for the maintenance and preservation of the western way of life. None of us will gainsay the fact that all racial groups in South Africa have been touched and influenced to a greater or lesser degree by western ways. The past 300 odd years have exposed the black South African to persistent and continuous orientation western-wise and this has meant a progressive abandonment of traditions and customs typically African. Today the black South African's fulfilment is in the classroom and the university, in the workshop and in the factory, in his religion and the redeeming Christ and when the suggestion is made that he should develop along his traditional way of life he is resentfully bewildered. He has made his choice and the white South African must accept credit for this. He now wants recognition in that new and thrilling society, with all its complexities and bewilderment. He is as eager to perpetuate this newfound way of life as any other South African. There is therefore a need to share the rights and privileges, the duties and obligations which devolve upon those who share the same objectives, the same aspirations and treasure the same values.

I may be wrong, but I have come to the conclusion that what we hold as supreme ideals for ourselves proliferates with sharing. We hold dearly the sanctity and unity of family life, freedom of movement and access, respect for the individual, human dignity, security of residence and earnings, and freedom from fear. These are the hallmarks of cultured and civilised society and we treasure them as a golden thread that is woven into our lives. Any denial of one or more of these ideals is to say the least dehumanising. Yet I have wondered to what extent the white South African enjoys these endowments of citizenship: and I have asked myself the question as to whether, by seeking to keep them to himself, he is not in fact diminishing his enjoyment of them: and whether his enjoyment of them is not relative to the lack of enjoyment of them by the black South African. Is it not possible that in making these fundamental ideals of society divisible on ethnic grounds we diminish and devalue them? When this happens, as it is happening to us South Africans we are not wholly South African. Let me draw an analogy for clarity. Society has a well-tried method of ridding itself, albeit temporarily, of undesirables via the law courts into prison. The state employs officials who are not guilty of any breach of the law, to restrain and keep the prisoner in relative confinement. Consequent upon this guard and prisoner relationship, the guard's freedom of movement and association are at once circumscribed by the degree to which limitations of movement and association are imposed on his prisoner. In effect, his freedom is no greater than that of his prisoner; and also his liberty, his conversation, his circle of associates - all limited by restrictions not imposed on him but on his prisoner. Thus those who for their comfort and restful ease at night would have black South Africans confined to the townships must have some of their number patrol the periphery of the townships and walk the city streets, those who will not allow one section of South Africans to watch an international match in progress must have some of their number manning the entrances and the fences, thus missing the exhilaration of watching South Africans win. South Africans who enjoy race and colour-circumscribed rights and privileges enjoy them in part and for brief moments, and never wholly.

One of the many factors which constantly circumscribe our well being as South Africans is the constant reminder that the enemy is hidden along our borders ready to launch an assault on us if we should but wink an eye. Consequently South Africans, and lately, of all races have stood guard along our frontiers in continuous vigilance and many have paid the supreme price for our safety.(1) To them we owe a reverent gratitude. Threatening forces on our borders, do not however confine the area of battle to that part of South Africa alone and we must count ourselves lucky by comparison that hundreds have not been killed by bombs, bullets or boobytraps, nor have many died daily from hunger and exposure within the Republic. Let this not induce complacency for there is a battle field in South Africa, in our homes, our streets and alleyways, in our townships and rural settlements, in the cities and in towns where the call for a change of heart is as loud and clear as the call to arms. In this battlefield we cannot count the dead and the wounded, for here the casualties are invisible; they are the wounded heart, the inner hurt, the frustrated effort, distress, misery and despair of the future.

In conclusion may I present a South Africa in which there will live South Africans freed from the prison of their privileges. It will be:

(a) a South Africa in which dialogue and negotiation have replaced confrontation and conflict;

(b) a South Africa in which people can move freely and easily across racial borders, and

(c) a South Africa in which force is relied on less and less as an instrument of national policy.

NOTE

(1) In 1972 the South African Police included specially trained black detachments for service in the Caprivi Strip and other border areas.

THE NON-INDEPENDENT HOMELANDS: CISKEI

Change for Development

LENNOX L. SEBE

(Excerpts from an address on the occasion of the visit by the Gazankulu Cabinet, 29 August 1973)

This is an historic occasion. This is the first time a Chief Minister and Cabinet Ministers from another homeland have visited the Ciskei. Meetings and dialogue between homeland leaders can do nothing but good for the progress of the African people.

The winds of change, of which one has heard so much, are now blowing strongly in the homelands - stronger in some than in others perhaps, but nevertheless blowing encouragingly. The next decade is going to produce spectacular changes in Southern Africa - changes which even a few short years ago were undreamed of, and appeared impossible. In recent months I have been privileged to have had the opportunity of discussing many problems with the Prime Minister of South Africa and the Minister for Bantu Administration and Development. I am satisfied that the government of the Republic of South Africa is genuine in its declared policy of homeland development and independence. I am satisfied that insofar as the homelands are concerned the sky is the limit for the African people. The ball is at our feet.

Having given you these encouraging words let me immediately sound a word of caution. We have heard so much in recent years of constitutional development, but what does this mean to the man in the street, the man in the rural areas, struggling to keep his family and himself clothed and fed? He has been caught up in the excitement of elections, he has heard much talk of independence and constitutional development, but in a few years time he is going to pause and wonder just what all this has in fact meant to him. Then, unless he can see better job opportunities, unless he is better able to get the things he needs - more pay, better food and clothing, better schooling for his children, in fact a better standard of living for himself and his family - dissatisfaction and unrest will follow.

Now let us take a brief look at Africa as a whole. After World War II when the European empires fell to pieces and colony after colony gained independence, the demand for industrialisation and modernisation grew to a shout. This demand was further intensified by the population explosion in the underdeveloped countries, and the realisation that people need not wait for someone to invent the improvements so desperately needed. The machines and methods needed in an undeveloped country are nearly all in use somewhere already, if only someone would get them and teach the people how to use them. Then there is the communist pressure trying to draw the developing countries into the new style empire of the communist blocs. That pressure cannot be held back by clinging to the old traditional way of life. It can be avoided only by development and modernising under conditions of freedom while there is yet time.

Development is not simply a matter of learning how to use radios and automobiles, and in time how to manufacture them. Development touches every side of national life - political, social and even religious. Development leads to changes. Whether these inevitable changes will be peaceful or violent depend on industrial and agricultural progress and job opportunities, and on how quickly the old families, especially the younger members, can learn to accept their new places in the changing world around them. Whatever the political changes and pressure, a sound development programme requires progress in industry as well as agriculture balanced as well as may be possible. The expanding population cannot all be employed in agriculture and, as a rule, new employment has to be sought in industry and in the service occupations.

In order to achieve the development I envisage a properly thought out and well correlated development plan, embracing all departments of government, is essential for all homelands. Other countries have done it, why can't we? By 1959 India had launched her third five-year development plan and this has been followed by a series of five-year development plans - with the necessary evaluation and reappraisal in between. This is what is required in the homelands and this is what I intend instructing the various departments of government in the Ciskei to get on with as soon as possible.

I suggest we must, as soon as possible, adopt the system of programme budgeting - a five-year development plan must be drawn up in the broadest sense and this plan must then dictate the budget. In other words instead of available funds dictating development programmes, development programmes must dictate the funds that must be found. If funds are not available from our own resources, then funds must be found in the form of foreign aid. I understand there is nothing to prevent the homelands seeking foreign aid, and I have accordingly been in touch with various overseas donor agencies. I hope to make further contact with donor agencies during my forthcoming visit overseas, and I will be raising this subject at the summit conference to be held in Umtata later this year.

I must now touch on a subject which, from time to time, enjoys headlines in the daily newspapers - I mean the land question. The Republican government has set aside large sums of money for the purchase of land to add to the homelands. This will take several years to accomplish. Then, if there are still problems in this field, I believe they will be resolved by dialogue with the government of the Republic of South Africa around the conference table. There is nothing that cannot be achieved by dialogue in a spirit of Christian sincerity. Violence and terrorism are in fact foreign to us. We Africans are by nature a friendly, amiable and hospitable people, stoical and long-suffering in the face of hardship and adversity. The terrorism and violence one hears about further north are something foreign, something that is being imposed on Africa from without. Something evil that is being imposed not in the interests of Africa, but in the base interests of those wishing to involve the developing countries in their new style communist empire. So once again let me warn you of the jackal in our midst who cries peace, peace, while all the time he means something different.

Some of you may have read in the newspapers a few weeks ago that the State President of South Africa had called on the white people of South Africa for a change of attitude toward the black people. He called on all people to work tirelessly to foster happy and friendly race relations. More recently my good friend Chief Matanzima made a similar call to the black people of the Transkei for a change of attitude toward the white people. Let me re-echo these calls. In this troubled and sorely distressed world let us unite in our endeavour to make the southern tip of Africa the happiest, most peaceful and most prosperous place in it.

Manifesto of Lennox

1 / Introduction

(a) I stand for the aspirations and wishes of the Ciskeians. These should be achieved within the framework of the policy of separate development.

(b) For this goal I have sacrificed a career in the Department of Education so that you should not be found leaderless during this stage of constitutional development. I, therefore, stand as a symbol of sacrifice for your interests.

2 / Political rights and privileges

(a) Promise of equal rights, privileges and treatment for all Ciskeians in the Ciskei and in the urban areas.

(b) To struggle for the recognition of all hereditary chiefs irrespective of ethnic group.

(c) To negotiate areas/land for resettling of the recognised chiefs and their people.

(d) To protect the existing rights and privileges of all chiefs.

(e) To raise salaries of chiefs and headmen.

(f) To grant full authority to township councils to run civic matters without any interference.

(g) To maintain law and order in the Ciskei.

(h) To struggle for more land for the Ciskei.

(i) To see to it that the consolidation of the Ciskei is not prejudicial to the interests and welfare of the Ciskeians.

3 / Fair deal for public servants

(a) Ciskeian public servants to enjoy similar privileges to those enjoyed by their counterparts in the Republic by:

(i) Seeing that they get the same subsistence and travel allowances.

(ii) Providing more transport vehicles so that there should be more progress and more efficiency in the various departments.

(b) To see to it that all promotions are based

strictly on ability and merit.

(c) That no civil servant will have his chances or promotion prejudiced on account of his ethnic extraction.

(d) To see to it that public servants are granted more scholarships to further their studies with full pay.

(e) To champion higher salaries and leave bonuses for public servants, viz. clerks, magistrates and prosecutors, etc.

(f) To allow public servants to buy a house anywhere in the Ciskei.

4 / Education

(a) Promotions to the inspectorate will depend on experience, qualification and merit, and creation of more posts.

(b) To narrow the gap in salaries between Ciskeian teachers and those of other racial groups.

(c) To employ married female teachers permanently.

(d) To encourage the building of schools on the rand for rand basis or any other workable formula likely to assist poor and struggling communities.

(e) To offer scholarships to teachers who wish to further their studies.

(f) To grant study leave with full pay to all employees of the department.

(g) To encourage in-service training courses for teachers.

(h) To encourage inspectors to hold conferences where members of the inspectorate will read papers on various subjects.

(i) To grant autonomy to professional organisations and consult their views on all educational matters, viz. conditions of service, syllabuses and examinations.

(j) To introduce compulsory free education for Ciskeian children of school-going age.

(k) To supply free books in all Ciskeian schools.

(l) To establish special schools for the deaf and blind in the Ciskei, with improved conditions of employment.

5 / Health services

(a) To build modern clinics.

(b) To provide more transport for medical officers and nurses.

(c) To grant study leave with full pay to nurses so that they should further their studies in (i) intensive nursing care, (ii) hospital administration, (iii) radiography, (iv) ward administration, (v) public health.

(d) To encourage employment of more health officers and nurses in the clinics in the remote areas, and creation of more higher and responsible posts especially in hospitals.

(e) Build more hospitals.

6 / Social services

(a) To erect playgrounds and build recreationsl halls.

(b) To build cinemas and parks.

(c) To build swimming pools.

(d) To improve township roads and to construct better roads to rural locations.

(e) To see to it that street lighting is provided in all townships.

(f) To prevent gangsterism and tsotsi-ism. Social workers will be employed to work among the young to encourage sport like boxing, dancing etc., and working conditions of social workers will be improved to stop high rate of resignations. More scholarships will also be provided for them.

7 / Agriculture and forestry

(a) To promote co-operative farming.

(b) To train Ciskeian youth in veterinary surgery.

(c) To encourage meat industry in the Ciskei.

(d) To build big breeding stations for cattle, sheep, fowls, pigs, and to sell the stock to the Ciskeians at reduced prices.

(e) To train Ciskeians as foresters by establishing a forestry school with better facilities.

(f) To subsidise hardworking farmers with loans/ grants on the same basis as the land bank.

(g) To give seeds and fertilisers to successful farmers at half price.

(h) To create a scheme for Ciskeian farmers to buy insecticides at low prices.

8 / Stimulation of the economy of the Ciskei

(a) To encourage industries on an agency basis to

create avenues of employment for the Ciskeians.

(b) To encourage industrialists to pay high wages to workers.

(c) To encourage healthy working conditions in factories.

(d) To encourage trade boards to settle wage disputes.

(e) To encourage industrialists to recognise workers' associations as mouthpieces of fellow workers.

(f) To encourage labour inspectors to visit factories to investigate working conditions.

(g) To encourage Ciskeians to own businesses in the Ciskei by granting trading rights to aspiring businessmen.

(h) To encourage friendly countries to the Republic to establish industries in the Ciskei.

(i) To accelerate the industrial development of the Ciskei, foreign aid will be solicited from countries like the U.S.A. through the required channels.

9 / Relations with other governments

(a) To maintain healthy diplomatic relations with the Republican government and other homeland governments.

(b) To see to the protection of the Ciskeians in the cities.

(c) To see to it that Ciskeians who have been working in the cities for a long time are allowed to remain there with their families.

(d) That widows and the aged are not ejected from the cities after they have spent their lives in the cities.

(e) To petition the Republican government to regard doctors, lawyers and businessmen as people doing essential services in the urban areas and that there should be no restrictions on their remaining there.

(f) To petition the Republican government to grant higher pension benefits to the old, aged and sick.

10 / Internal relations

(a) To create mutual trust among all people in the Ciskei.

(b) To establish healthy relations amongst all people by organising occasions which will bring all Ciskeians together.

(c) To promote institutions which will bring together and unite the people of the Ciskei.

(d) To honour and respect those institutions which have played an important role in the lives of the people in the Ciskei.

11 / Conclusion

I wish to remind the voters of the Ciskei about my achievements as head of education and as head of agriculture and forestry.

Ciskei National Independence Party: Principles

The party stands for:

1 / The maintenance of Christianity, democracy and the rule of law.

2 / The promotion of unity of the Ciskeian citizens both within and beyond the borders of the Ciskei, regardless of ethnic extraction.

3 / The establishment of diplomatic and consular relations with foreign countries in consultation with the government of the Republic of South Africa.

4 / The preservation of friendly relations between the Ciskei homeland and the Republic of South Africa as well as other homeland governments and friendly foreign states.

5 / The preservation of the institution of enlightened Christian chieftainship which serves as a symbol of traditional leadership and a rallying point for tribal unity; and the operation of such chieftainship along modern democratic lines.

6 / The protection of the rights and privileges of chiefs and the maintenance of their automatic membership of the Ciskeian Legislative Assembly.

7 / A policy of economic, social and educational development of the Ciskei and the establishment of councils of experts to advise in connection with the implementation of such a policy.

8 / The provision of additional land commensurate with the increasing population of the Ciskei such that the physical boundaries of the territory for the time being, include the Kei River in the east, the Indian Ocean in the south, the Great Fish River in the west, and the Bamboos Storm Mountain in the north.

9 / The drawing up of a well worked-out plan of granting independence to the Ciskei homeland with the full pilotage of the government of the Republic of South Africa.

10 / The principle of federation of all African homelands within the Republic of South Africa after they have gained full independence status after due

consultation with them.

11 / Full scale implementation of the policy of separate development by the republican government with a view to improving the lot of Ciskeian people, economically, socially and educationally and further to gaining additional land in which to develop towards effective self-determination.

Ciskei National Independence Party: Objectives in Draft Constitution

(a) To unite the citizens of the Ciskei into one solid body for the purpose of fostering closer relationship by studying together, exchange of views on political, economic, social and educational problems at national level.

(b) To study local issues, viz. water supplies, roads, schools, clinics, chieftaincy disputes or any issues which may affect the residents of a locality.

(c) To educate the party members about their party policy at rallies, study circles, party socials and research groups.

(d) To see to it that party members are registered as voters for elections.

(e) To ensure that on the election day the voters know how to reach the polling stations.

(f) To see to it that the party members can be identified by the returning officer.

(g) To see to it that the party members are aquainted to/with the party symbol; in the case of the party the tiger shall be the symbol.

(h) To raise funds for the party by concerts, bazaars, levies or any other method which the party might decide upon.

(i) To form party branches throughout the Republic.

Policy Statement of Chief Justice T. Mabandla, Ciskei General Election, 1973

I have submitted the following policy statement to my cabinet. It has been adopted unanimously by members of the cabinet. I therefore proceed to offer it to the electorate of the Ciskei and wish to call on all candidates who offer themselves for election and who endorse the policy which I hereby announce to contact me without delay. This policy will be the principle on which the future government of the Ciskei will be based and for which the electorate will be requested to vote:...

It has been no mean achievement to develop from a rather obscure system of government, administered mainly from Pretoria, to a self-governing status, with a fully fledged government and administration, manned to a very large extent by our own people. All over the Ciskei we perceive development, and the feeling of national unity among our people has already manifested itself. Never again shall we be satisfied to take the backseat in the affairs of our people. We are very proud to have been responsible for the piloting of this development, and for the fact that we consulted the leaders of our people at every phase thereof. We are striving to become more sophisticated in the art of state-craft, and we aim at achieving the final goal - independence - in as short a time as possible, not only in the constitutional sense, but also in the economic and cultural fields.

All these beneficial developments have taken place under the guiding principle of separate development, which was adopted by the leaders of our people, and which we adopted as the mandate of our day to day responsibilities, and which has been the foundation stone on which constitutional development was based. We still subscribe to this policy of separate development, and we wish, in broad terms, to outline future policy as follows:

1 / We pledge ourselves to observe the Ciskeian constitution as the charter of our future development on constitutional matters. It is in terms of this constitution that we shall always dedicate ourselves to preserve the office of chieftainship, and to promote the

traditional system of authority, whilst observing democratic norms as the most equitable form of modern government. We shall always regard this constitution not as a finality, but as a prelude to complete independence for the Ciskei. For a meaningful independence we shall strive for a clear definition of the boundaries of the Ciskeian territory and for a fair and just programme of consolidation.

2 / We recognise the fact that the citizens of the Ciskei belong to the Xhosa National Unit, and that there is a close affinity between ourselves in the Ciskei and our 'brothers' in the Transkei. History has so fated it that we were and still are divided, but there is every indication that this division will, and must, be terminated at some time in the future. We unequivocally declare that amalgamation will not be effected except by an expressed desire and mandate of the leaders and citizens of the Ciskei through the Legislative Assembly

3 / We do not subscribe to any policy aimed at integrating the Ciskei into:

(a) A multi-racially integrated state and society;

(b) A federal or confederate system of government, embracing a number of Bantu national units.

But for sound economy, for security and for diplomacy we shall endeavour to sustain friendly ties with the Republic of South Africa, and any other neighbouring independent state, provided that such friendly ties will be reciprocated on the basis of equality. Further, we shall promote treaties, when necessary, between the Ciskei and the Republic of South Africa and/or any other friendly independent state for mutual benefit on such matters as defence, state security, trade and infrastructure for industry, major health projects or schemes, etc. We shall maintain cordial relations with any non-Ciskeians residing within the borders of the Ciskei.

4 / By way of consultation and dialogue, we shall observe a close liaison with the republican government, which has thus far been our guardian, and will move towards more and greater responsibilities in close cooperation with the republican government.

5 / At home we shall strive to improve agriculture by the introduction of more scientific agricultural methods for maximum land yield and remuneration from stock. We acknowledge the fact that agriculture is the backbone of economy in the Ciskei, and that no nation can afford to

ignore the vast importance of agriculture in the national household...

6 / We shall endeavour to get the best possible labour conditions for our migratory labourers, who annually go to work in the Republic. We shall exert ourselves to the utmost to remove legal, technical and administrational discrepancies and impediments, affecting our labourers in the Republic.

7 / It is our firm belief that the trend of education in the Ciskei will determine every facet of our national development. We also believe that until the bulk of our citizens are educated, and until the quality of their education is indisputable, self-government or independence for the Ciskei will be meaningless. We shall endeavour to improve on the tremendous advances we have made so far. Specifically our future education policy is aimed at:

(a) The reduction of teacher-pupil ratio.
(b) A diversification of avenues of study to meet all the demands of a self-sufficient nation.
(c) Elimination of double session and the 'platoon system'.
(d) Compulsory primary and secondary education up to the age of 16.
(e) Extension of facilities for adult education.
(f) Providing more and better classrooms at both primary and post-primary levels.
(g) Better conditions of service and salaries for teachers.
(h) Provision of free books for all, and bursaries for post-primary education.
(i) Negotiations to extend university and medical school facilities for many.

We aim at producing an educated Ciskeian who can be serviceable anywhere in the world, when his academic qualifications are needed.

8 / We appreciate that industrial development for the Ciskei merits a very high priority. We have taken note of the Republican government's policy of decentralisation of secondary industry, towards border areas. We have already reaped great benefits from this policy of decentralisation. Bearing this in mind, we shall continuously prevail on the Republican government to apply this policy meticulously, thus channelising considerable industries to the Ciskei, which is

admirably situated for border industry in many respects. We shall unceasingly petition the Xhosa Development Corporation to:
(a) establish commercial and industrial concerns within the boundaries of the Ciskei under the agency sytem, to enhance economic stability in our country;
(b) accelerate the process of training Bantu personnel in such industries, so that eventually such industries will be manned by Bantu;
(c) accelerate taking over of business concerns from non-Bantu within the Ciskei for an eventual take-over by Bantu businessmen.

In order to improve our economy in the Ciskei it is our firm belief that the earning power of all our employees must be improved. We firmly believe in the principle of equal pay for equal work. We shall continue to negotiate with the Republican government, and to exert pressure on employers of our citizens for the fulfilment of this principle. We shall continue our efforts to improve the earnings of our chiefs and headmen to a standard commensurate with their status and responsibilities.

9 /
(a) We are committed to improve the present conditions in the already existing townships and settlements,
(b) we shall strive to abolish the means test when one applies for Old Age Pension,
(c) we shall continue to see to it that our people are not resettled until essential facilities and services are provided such as lighting, water, post office facilities, schools, clinics, etc., and that they are resettled within reach of possible employment. We shall endeavour to improve the quality of dwelling houses provided for our people in townships. In view of the fact that Bantu sport is beginning to attract world attention, we shall strive to provide enough and suitable sport facilities. We shall also see to the provision of suitable centres of entertainment.

10 / We believe that South Africa is a permanent home for many nations, and that the people within must live in freedom from internal strife and tension, and from external invasion.
(a) We shall also associate ourselves with all the efforts of the Republican government to maintain law and order, and to defend South Africa against subversive

intrusions.
(b) We shall do all in our power to promote good relations within the different tribes making up the national unit of the Ciskei. For unity and strength tribalism must not come into the national affairs of the Ciskei. We shall play our part to make the Ciskei, and South Africa, a happy home for all its inhabitants...

Ciskei National Party: Policy

Broad Principles

1 / The party recognises and upholds the Christian faith and its practical application to the national and political life of the country.

2 / The party upholds the principle of full freedom for the individual to develop to the best of his ability and the principle of equality of all people before the law.

3 / The party strives to maintain friendly relations with the Republic of South Africa and any other neighbouring state on the basis of full equality.

4 / The party strives for a society in which there is just and equal treatment of all men and undertakes to fight against all forms of discrimination by reason of race, tribe, colour or creed.

5 / The party undertakes to preserve the system of chieftainship, and to promote the traditional system of authority, while practising the modern democratic form of government.

6 / The party upholds the principle of self-determination for the black people and for all other people in this country.

7 / For a meaningful independence the party strives for a clear definition of the boundaries of the Ciskei and for a fair and just programme of consolidation or release of land by the Republic of South Africa for black occupation.

8 / The party stands for and seeks co-operation between the Ciskei and other black states in South Africa and for the ultimate amalgamation of these black states.

9 / While the party stands by the policy of separate development, it will always remain flexible to changing political circumstances, and will thus adjust its policy to suit any current trends.

Education

The party strives for a progressive educational system and for the following objectives:

1 / Reduction of the teacher-pupil ratio.

2 / Diversification of avenues of study to meet all the demands of a modern, developing state.

3 / Compulsory primary and secondary education from six to sixteen years of age.

4 / Elimination of double sessions and the platoon system.

5 / Extension of facilities for adult education.

6 / More and better classrooms at primary and secondary levels, and provision of adequate and fully equipped technical and agricultural schools.

7 / Better conditions of service and better salaries for teachers and the removal of all forms of discrimination against female teachers.

8 / Home language as medium of instruction from Sub A to Std. 2, then English as medium from Std. 3 to the highest level of education.

Agriculture

The party strives to make full use of the agricultural potential of the Ciskei by the introduction of more scientific methods of agriculture and pastoral farming, particularly in the following respects:

1 / Irrigation schemes on an extensive scale.

2 / Subsidies for farmers by means of a land bank or other scheme.

3 / Employment of more demonstrators and other trained agricultural personnel.

4 / Co-operative societies for co-operative buying and selling.

Industry and Commerce

1 / The party strives for the establishment of commercial and industrial concerns within the boundaries of the Ciskei to promote economic stability.

2 / The party seeks to accelerate the process of training black personnel in such commercial and industrial concerns so that these concerns may be taken over by blacks as soon as possible.

3 / The party strives for the improvement of wages and salaries of all workers on the basis of equal pay for equal work.

4 / The party strives for the recognition of trade unions as negotiating instruments on behalf of workers.

Social Welfare

The party strives for

1 / The improvement of old age pensions and the abolition of the means test for old age people.

2 / Provision of adequate social amenities, including sports facilities, in urban and rural areas.

3 / Adequate and state-subsidised health services for all Ciskei citizens.

4 / Employment of trained social workers in towns and rural villages to help improve the social life of the people.

The Problems of Homeland Transition

JUSTICE T. MABANDLA

(Paper was written especially for this book)

What the black man of the 1970s thinks is very difficult to extract from the complex political situation in this country. The following factors contribute, to varying extents, towards the difficulty: the banning of organisations like the A.N.C. and the P.A.C. and silencing of their voice; the advent of the new political concept of viewing South Africa as a multi-national state; the policy of separate development as the only officially acceptable platform of expression for the black man; the not-so-high standard of education and political awareness of the leader who is the offshoot of separate development. Before they were banned the P.A.C. and the A.N.C. represented the opinion of the blacks in South Africa.

This opinion is based on the fact that South Africa was one country to which belonged many racial groups. These organisations were products of a freely expressed African mind. What the leaders of these organisations wanted and said could easily be accepted as honest and genuine since the movements originated from them. These organisations were then banned, and in many ways their leaders and followers were silenced. When this happened the sound of their voices did not die down. It was simply abruptly muted.

This move by the government has had the effect of splitting the blacks into those who were silenced; those quiet ones who shared the views of the banned but afraid to suffer a similar fate; those who had never had any opinion or voice at all, and to this group belonged the majority of the black population. One certain thing was that all of them had come to know what offended the government, and what one had to do or say to qualify for a banning order.

As this stage came the idea of a multi-national South Africa, and it came down from the ruler, the government. The blacks who were in a position to accept or reject the new concepts belonged to the last two groups above. The already banned or silenced could have no say. In terms of this new dispensation the tribal chief and his tribesmen were to occupy top positions, although the great majority are uneducated. With the passage of time a small black elite has come into the picture, and its voice is beginning to come out loud and clear. But the activities and the conduct of these leaders must strike a balance between their personal wishes, the wishes of the Republican government and the needs of the black masses. The middle course in this regard has been very difficult to follow. I was a member of the Ciskeian Authority long before it developed into the present constitutional form - the Legislative Assembly. The said Authority was reconstituted in 1968, and by that time only the Transkei had already advanced to the status of a Legislative Assembly. The Ciskeian Territorial Authority was composed of 84 members: 42 chiefs and 42 tribesmen. Six were elected into the Executive Council, each leading one of six departments.

I must repeat that when the political idea of multinationalism came into being those blacks who were in a position to make the policy a working philosophy or proposition, were the illiterate and the politically ignorant; the elite, who were in the minority, were very much aware of the conduct or utterances which might result in the banning of opposition to the government. The black personnel responsible for the running of the policy of separate development can be classified as:

(a) those who accept the policy, while indifferent to its aim and finality; they enjoy the minor benefits within their immediate surroundings, such as an M.P.'s salary at the end of the month or state grants for some projects;

(b) those who accept the policy only as a medium for free expression, in order to voice what would be difficult outside the enclosure of expressed government policy, and, finally;

(c) those who accept the policy as a 'while we wait' device.

For a number of reasons I do not think that separate development was ever meant to reach complete independence. If it was, I feel that at this stage the Republican government will not be happy to fulfil such finality. It has always been expressed that the chief motive of the policy of multi-nationalism is to ensure the security of the white man and his civilisation in the midst of a very frightening majority of blacks. But the difficulties presented by the process of consolidation of land and the definition of homeland boundaries may well bring about the collapse of the policy. The status quo has existed for too long to be dismantled overnight. If the apportionment of land is pushed at any cost, the whites who may be affected will be offended. This attitude is going to be a problem in any attempt at consolidating the land. I do not see how separate development will materialise without a satisfactory consolidating of land and definition of boundaries.

There are other problems. For a very long time the blacks will not have the manpower to run their own affairs. Fulfilment of independence for the homelands will need full-scale preparation over a long time. The black man is lacking in those matters which count most in a state of independence. Any independence will be difficult to operate while each such government must depend to a large extent on foreign manpower. It is difficult to see the independent black homelands becoming economically viable. Their citizens have not got the know-how and the capital. Any foreign aid would have to be long term. On the other hand foreign investment becomes unlikely when the would-be investors cannot be certain about the future stability of the homelands.

For centuries the whole life of South Africa has been interwoven in every sense. Inter-relationship between one service and another has been entrenched in the whole set-up of this country. This refers to such matters as defence, foreign affairs, transport and agriculture. How these and many others will be maintained by treaties, or segmented into separate nationhoods, or allowed to rely on unpredictable neighbourliness between the homelands and the Republic of South Africa is difficult to imagine. Such considerations will make homeland independence a difficult project to work out.

The problems posed to South Africa by international bodies such as the United Nations, the Commonwealth of Nations and the Organisation for African Unity and by some of the independent African states, must make South Africa reluctant to let the black homelands go entirely free. What guarantee would South Africa have that the independent homelands would not serve as launching-grounds to attack South Africa, when South Africa will no longer have any say in the affairs of the various black homelands? All in all I do not think that the black homelands will ever be completely independent.

On the other hand there have been advantages. Zoning the blacks into their respective homeland governments has had the useful effect of decentralising their development. This trend seems to be yielding a much faster tempo of physical development than would be the case while the attitude was still 'so much has been done for the Bantu'. So many schools for the Transkei; so many universities for KwaZulu and other homelands; so much money for the budget of Lebowa, etc. All this amounts to better and faster physical development.

Avenues opened up for the needs of separate development have afforded a welcome all-round training for the black man in South Africa. Such diversification of training will make the blacks suitable for any other eventual political arrangement. The black man has found himself training for industry and commerce, for parliamentary procedure, for legal occupations (as magistrates and prosecutors), and for special subjects in the field of education and many other opportunities. All those were outside the reach of the black man before separate development. The policy has made it possible for an outward expression of the black man's thoughts. This has been from public platforms, press interviews, radio service, visits to countries abroad and dialogue with the Republican government. This has been a great step indeed.

I am convinced that the guerilla movements are not serving the best interests of the black man in this country. One will admit that they have been incited by laudable motives - to free their people and themselves from oppression. But the sympathy and the support they receive from countries with a communistic bias is a dangerous indication. For a time these sympathisers and supporters will seem to be for the same cause as the 'freedom fighters'. The truth is that they have ulterior motives. They are for world supremacy. Communists have no interest in the liberation of the black; they will do anything to push their influence into this country, and any other country, for that matter. Because they get support, food, blankets and arms from communists, the guerilla movements seem to be blind to any other eventuality.

But in my view, we might best solve our common problems by working positively so that homeland governments may end up as additional provincial councils when there will be a common central government in South Africa.

Bantu Affairs Administration Boards

A. DUNJWA

(Address to the Department of African Law and Government at the University of Stellenbosch, May 1974.)

My address does not purport to give a full and coherent exposition of the application of the policy to the urban blacks. Rather it should be regarded as an analysis of some of the thorny problems experienced by urban blacks in the field of Bantu Administration. I shall endeavour to give constructive criticism during the course of this paper. Allow me in passing to thank those local authorities who in the past have handled Bantu Administration to the best of their ability.

The Advent of Bantu Affairs Administration Boards

These boards are new organisations and, naturally, like all new organisations, they will have their teething problems. With the advent of these boards recently, there is much talk of free movement of blacks in cities. The black people have become motivated and are looking forward to good things, at long last. They are looking forward to more and better job opportunities, a better standard of living, better amenities, fewer police raids, more schools and, above all, better race relationships.

A keen student of Bantu Administration today is bound to ask himself this question: what can be done to ensure the implementation of the various enactments affecting the black population in the urban areas in such a way as to guarantee the necessary control by enlisting the positive co-operation of all parties concerned and thereby eliminating the friction and ill-will which tend to vitiate urban life at the present time? Most of the measures referred to are embodied in the Native Urban Areas Act of 1945, which is administered in conjunction with other legislation, e.g. the Bantu Labour Regulation Act.

The work that is done by the Bantu Affairs Administration Boards is probably the most important work that can be done by officials in South Africa today. The officials of these boards are the people who are dealing directly between the white people and the blacks of the cities, and on the work they do and the spirit in which they do it will be decided, possibly for all times, the pattern in which our relationships will develop. What they do as officials is not perhaps within their control. It is laid down for them. It is the law of the country. But how they do it, is for each individual to decide. This is a thorny problem which is interwoven inseparably with our country's policy and politics. Consequently it is obvious that an official of the Bantu Affairs Administration Boards is morally and legally bound to implement to the best of his ability the policy of the government of the day.

In my opinion, mercy, sympathy and understanding can enter into human relationships that are established by these boards. The Bantu Affairs Administration Board is a special type of organisation exclusively concerned with black interests - unlike other departments which are concerned with activities affecting the whole population including blacks.

Let us have as a background to this problem the indisputable fact that the economic interests of whites and blacks are interwoven and cannot be separated in an urban society. Further, the development of the blacks is essential for the welfare of the cities.

I appreciate some of the difficulties encountered by officials of these boards. I know also that all the legislation that they have to apply is unpopular. This is a fact and we must just face it. I am not here commenting on the need or justification for any particular legislation. I am merely referring to problems that the official who applies these laws has to cope with. The official responsible for black administration forms the target for attacks by two antagonistic communities. On the one hand you have members of the European community who are, with certain exceptions, unsympathetically disposed towards black citizens. As a result, attempts to make the living conditions for blacks more agreeable by the provision of amenities such as sports grounds, swimming pools, libraries, schools, transport facilities, recreation, provision of health services, and combating of evils which arise from the abuse of liquor, e.g. tsotsism, are often criticised in unrestrained language as a waste of money or as too much money spent on blacks. On the other hand, there is the fact of the developing black community constantly agitating for those very amenities. The officials of these boards must appease both sides for the sake of preserving good race relationships. This requires a united-progressive front.

The urban black today is not what he was ten or twenty years ago. He reads books and papers, he is educated. He knows the laws and regulations that govern him. In other words he knows which side his bread is buttered on. As a result, he questions every piece of legislation affecting him, especially when he is not a party to the making of that legislation.

There are two attitudes possible in administrative matters. The first is where the letter of the law is strictly enforced and nothing more. This is by far the easier attitude to adopt. The official here is always right. The black man's problems are no concern of his. He is merely there to carry out the law and get his fat cheque at the end of the month.

The other attitude is to consider the laws and regulations at one's disposal as weapons with which to combat evils and the development of undesirable conditions, but otherwise to apply them with due consideration of surrounding circumstances and the problems which beset human beings. Here, the black man's problems, his objects and circumstances must be considered, and the likely effects of any decision carefully weighed. Hence I say, there is a dire need for change of heart.

This attitude requires patience and the use of discretion. I want to concede here that this adds to the official's worries and loads him with additional responsibilities, yet, for the sake of building up better relationships between black citizens and these boards, I think the latter attitude, though more onerous, is justified. I also share the frustration of those genuine administrators who seek to encourage change, improvement of conditions and opportunities for blacks but cannot do so because of the policy of these boards.

The greatest urge that motivates man's action on earth is, as Professor John Dewey puts it, 'a desire to be important'. That being the case, we should realise that nothing will provoke antagonism and resentment more easily than the slighting of a black man's desire to be considered 'somebody'.

At the moment, black confidence in the Bantu Affairs Administration Boards' system of justice and civil administration is badly shaken. It grieves me for instance to see a white official of these boards or a white policeman in full pursuit of a black man in the township just because the latter cannot produce his reference book. My plea therefore to these officials is: treat even the humblest black man with due respect for his personal dignity. Be tolerant even towards those who vex you. I say this in terms of the great contribution of Christian morality - the necessity to do unto others as you would have them do unto you.

It is most unfortunate that the Bantu Affairs Administration Boards appointed, or that the central government should appoint, only white personnel in the key positions of these boards. In our opinion there are today black administrators who qualify for some of these key positions in the field of Bantu Administration. Whether this be government policy or merely a question of job reservation it is to be regretted, because as long as the blacks are not directly represented on these boards, they will continue to view them with suspicion. Urban blacks are not a party to the policy-making of Bantu Affairs Administration Boards and they are not happy about it.

The boards are a specialised type of organisation exclusively concerned with black interests. Specialised knowledge is most essential in Bantu Administration today. The days when officials were appointed because of their knowledge of the 'Bantu mind' are gone, never to come back again. What is the position with regard to the knowledge or understanding of the Bantu languages by these officials? How many have taken a diploma in Bantu studies? It is most essential that these officials should know the blacks, should be accustomed to their affairs, norms, traditions and customs. Training is therefore a useful short cut to this objective.

Nowadays things have changed from the old order when whites even went to school with blacks and played with blacks. Today, the Bantu Affairs Administrator is living away from the people he governs. He is residentially separated from them by law. Mr Mears, one-time Secretary of Bantu Affairs, once pointed out that many officials of the Department were there by sheer accident. They had no special interest in the work they did. Some of us feel the same today. The solution to this problem would be to train the blacks, who, since they belong to the culture, can better manage the affairs of their own people. The employment of blacks in administrative capacities has been envisaged as a fundamental policy for a long time, e.g. during the General Hertzog and General Smuts regimes. A fundamental point which I would like to repeat is that I have not lost hope in a 'change of heart'.

The Problem of the Pass Laws

What is the black man's conception of the word 'pass'? In other words how does a black man define the word 'pass'?

To him it is a legal document to which he objects because it is a document carried only by a particular section of the people and which is connected with the restrictions of the liberties of his movements. He further resents having at all times to carry it on his person since mere failure to do so is, in itself, a punishable or criminal offence.

The black man in the urban areas traces all his problems with the white man to the pass laws and their application to the black community. Let me from the very outset concede that pass laws have in the past been considered necessary to secure control over the black population and to provide a safeguard against crimes. Later these laws, amplified and extended, have been used to maintain order, to detect desertion, to identify on behalf of their relatives blacks who have become lost, and to trace the heirs of those who have died leaving assets which should properly be distributed at their homes.

It has been argued by officials of the boards that the main function of the pass laws is to stop the influx into the urban areas. I do not want to dwell on the pass laws but wish to say that we need a complete re-orientation in the approach to this problem.

I now want to submit that if the purpose of the pass laws is to stop the influx of blacks into the urban areas, they should not be applied to those blacks who already qualify under Section 10 of the Act, and who, in my opinion, do not require these restrictions.

Undoubtedly the pass laws are causing tremendous frustration, humiliation and bitterness amongst our black people.

Let us admit that there are numerous reasons why the blacks want to come into the cities, e.g. lack of employment opportunities in the homelands. It is my humble opinion that this problem cannot be solved by the application of the pass laws but by, inter alia, creating more employment for blacks.

Perhaps it might be difficult for the Bantu Affairs Administration Boards for both ideological or practical reasons to scrap the whole system of the pass laws (which many blacks feel ought to be done). But to alleviate the situation it might be suggested to the government by the officials of the boards that, at least, police raids for passes in the black townships be minimised.

The mere non-production of the reference book should, in my opinion, not constitute a criminal offence. The emphasis must be shifted from compulsory measures and from restrictive laws to machinery for advice, guidance and voluntary registration. Steps must be taken to ensure that everybody has some fit and proper place to which he is entitled to go.

While, on the one hand, the object should be to reduce restrictive measures to a minimum in respect of law-abiding people there should, on the other hand, be strong and energetic action aganist idlers, disorderly persons and other lawless elements. A really efficient system of identification should be instituted both to assist and protect the honest man and to facilitate action against disorderly elements. Where these measures can be put into operation on a general basis without racial discrimination, so much the better.

The principle of establishing an aid centre in any city is quite a commendable one provided, of course, it does the work for which it is intended. Black people suspected of having contravened the regulations constituting technical offences should first be referred to these aid centres before being arrested and charged at police stations. I feel very strongly that an aid centre can help tremendously towards the solving of this problem, particularly if the person in charge of an aid centre is a legally qualified official of the Bantu Affairs Administration Board.

We are all responsible and reasonable persons and we know that the severity of each offence must be determine on its own merits and the surrounding circumstances. In certain circumstances it could at the most be a technical offence and the administrative or controlling machine would not be thrown out of gear if the offender were given an opportunity to obtain and produce the required document (compare with the production of driver's licence in cases of car accidents), in which case there would be no need for resorting to such drastic action as arrests. On the other hand, circumstances may be such as to justify such action. It is now left to the official concerned to use his sense of justice and 'fairplay' to react as circumstances may dictate.

Permanently Settled Urban Black Population

It is my candid opinion that a policy based on the proposition that all black people in towns are temporary migrants, is a false policy because the proposition itself has in the course of time proved to be false. The main cause resulting in permanent black urbanisation is the development of industry in cities. Unfortunately this conception of towns as being exclusively for European settlement has dominated some of the major provisions of the Native Urban Areas Act. Urban black policy has been largely shaped as formulated by the Stallard Commission of 1922 - which in my opinion is very much out of step. Problems should be dealt with as they arise. Life is an evolutionary process and not a revolutionary one.

One of the major practices the world over in contributions made to the discussion of South African policy is the recommendation that the existence of permanent black urbanisation should be accepted as a fact and that the policy should be adjusted accordingly. The Bantu Administration Boards should view the migrant system of labour as a temporary measure which will disappear in the course of time.

Let us not hesitate to acknoweldge the fact of permanency in the urban black's population because Section 10 of the Act provides the incubator for a growing future town-born black population. The Act itself has therefore created the permanency in our urban population. I think it is only realistic to acknowledge and recognise this permanency. It does not matter whether for policy purposes we adopt the principle that blacks should be permitted to urban areas purely for employment purposes. The mere fact that blacks are required in urban areas for employment purposes, establishes blacks as a permanent section of the cities.

I am, of course, aware of the fear raised by some officials of the boards, namely, that if blacks are allowed to settle permanently in towns then they would have to be given municipal franchise and be entitled to share in the management of national interests and, if so admitted, who knows if they will not use their positions to secure the removal of all features that perpetuate their subordinate positions? Let us be more practical in our urban administration. Put more responsibility into the hands of the black urban population.

I believe that the official policy of these boards is directed towards discouraging the growth of a permanent black population by perpetuating the system of migrant labour; restricting accommodation in urban areas for families, and by placing obstacles in the way of the migration of females into towns.

But one has to face realities. If you employ a black man, then you have to look well after him. You have to see that he is healthy and that he has good accommodation. If you don't do that, he is a burden to you.

The housing problem is here stressed as the most important and urgent need of the city blacks. A most serious position is developing in almost every urban area. There are big families living in very small houses. The position is getting worse daily. The position is deteriorating so rapidly that if it is allowed to continue we are going to have one of the worst and greatest slums that this country has ever known. You will never be able in the foreseeable future to accommodate the natural increase in the black population unless something specific is done. The central government should undertake a vigorous housing programme. Blacks should be allowed to build their own houses where they qualify and should be financially assisted to do so. The government should embark on a massive plan to build family houses. Some firms and employers of black labour are prepared and are ready to grant building loans to their employees.

It grieves me to see widows ejected from houses when their husbands die. The endorsing out of widows not exempted in terms of Section 10 should in my opinion be reviewed. Let us accept these widows as householders in whose names the houses must be registered at the death of their husbands.

Educational Facilities

We are all aware that education is the key to the success of every nation, hence education is given priority by blacks in their townships. We appreciate what private organisations like TEACH, ASSECA and others are doing for black education but we feel strongly that the central government should play a major role in this field. We need more schools in our urban townships. We need technical and training colleges. Many children from cities do not gain entrance in homeland institutions because of the vast population of the homeland children.

Labour Problems

To overcome some of the difficulties inherent in administration, there should be better mobility of labour and this could be done by enlarging the labour areas. The boundaries of the Bantu Affairs Administration Boards in each district should be extended. In fact, the less we hear of 'prescribed areas' and 'proclaimed areas' even for blacks who qualify in urban areas, the better. We want our black labour to move freely. The blacks can see no reason why a man who qualifies under Section 10 should not be permitted to work in any other city in the Republic. I fail to see, for instance, why a man who lives in Stellenbosch cannot take up employment in Cape Town. The Bantu Affairs Administration Boards must accept the fact that blacks in towns remain part and parcel of the urban economy. Is there not a moral obligation on these boards to give blacks the certainty of continuous permanent employment in cities?

Consultation between Whites and Blacks

There is lack of effective consultation between white officials and black citizens in most urban areas. I want to suggest that most blacks have much more common sense and intelligence than whites are traditionally prepared to concede to them. The officials of the department must keep this in mind when they endeavour to establish and maintain consultation.

The importance of effective communication cannot be over-estimated. Without effective communication there can be no agreement between human beings. What happens when a strike is called? It simply means that communication between employers and employees is cut off. The basic truth is that whilst communication is maintained between officials of these boards and black citizens, understanding and agreement can be reached; without communication, it cannot.

Advisory Boards and Urban Bantu Councils

In most urban areas these bodies are regarded by most blacks as 'dummy bodies' acting only in an advisory capacity. They are in fact 'creatures of statute' and as such their powers are circumscribed or limited to those which are expressly conferred upon them by the statute which creates them. Members of these boards are often referred to as 'stooges' of the local authority. How best can these boards be reorganised so that they can continue to perform a useful function as a link between the Bantu Affairs Administration Boards and the black population? If these boards are still considered necessary, then certain administrative and legislative duties and functions should be conferred on them. After all the whole purpose of these boards originally was to provide blacks with an opportunity of taking part in the process of local government. If you deny them these rights, then you will find the black population at loggerheads with the Bantu Affairs Administration Boards.

We must now look for possible alternatives to these boards which black people admit do not function properly. The important thing to do is to get the genuine leaders of the black people and not the 'Fanagalo' members appointed or nominated from above.

The government should in my opinion replace these boards with more meaningful boards that command the respect of the black citizens in the townships. These new boards could be used as a useful barometer for black public opinion in regard to proposals which it has in mind for its black population. In this respect, a judicious and conscientious use of this power would result in the building up of bonds of confidence between the Bantu Administration Boards and their black citizens.

I now venture to say that we must consider whether with the passing of the years and the changed circumstances which exist today, the time has arrived when some change should be made and a system evolved whereby elected leaders of the black people in the townships are given powers which are not purely of an advisory nature. The blacks over the years have developed sufficiently and now manifest a desire and capacity to play a greater part in the administration of their own affairs in their urban townships, and it would be wise if a system could be devised whereby the government could hand over a large measure of executive responsibility to the blacks themselves for the administration of their own affairs.

The administration of the vast black townships is still regarded as a sub-section or an appendage of the Bantu Affairs Commissioner concerned. This is indeed a disturbing feature to most blacks. Although these officials may be capable, dedicated and understanding persons, they do not in my opinion possess appropriate training in urban administration. The operation of the system of Bantu Affairs Administration Boards within the framework of a government department or as agents of the central government is going to be extremely difficult in practice.

The Need for a Judicial Commission

Assuming that the 'change of heart' referred to earlier will be effected, it would be proper to appoint a judicial commission to enquire into the legitimate needs and grievances of blacks in the urban areas. This would ease the tension in the relationship not only between the Bantu Affairs Administration Boards and blacks but also between the races and groups in general. This would be particularly so if the recommendations of such a commission are carried out or a reasonable explanation given where they cannot be carried out.

A judicial commission headed by a judge or consisting of judges is an important body free from control of the political parties, with wide experience in the selecting and weighing of the evidence before it. Such a body, therefore, is able to present the true state of affairs.

Finally, I would be failing in my duty if I were not to refer to the tragedy in South Africa of dealing along party lines with the so-called black problem in urban areas. It is hoped that the Bantu Affairs Administration Boards will be removed from the field of party politics and that black affairs will be dealt with on a national basis.

THE NON-INDEPENDENT HOMELANDS: KWAZULU

My Role within Separate Development Politics

M. GATSHA BUTHELEZI

(Excerpts from an address to the Scandinavian Institute for African Studies, Uppsala, Sweden, December 1972)

I assume that most people are curious to know what separate development looks like through the eyes of one like myself, who is participating in the implementation of this policy. It is probably one of the most controversial policies pursued by a country in our time. Because of the mass media many people know of South Africa and her policy of apartheid, although that word now tends to be substituted by separate development, particularly within South Africa. I have great reservations about the philosophy of apartheid which is behind the policies in whose implementation I am participating. I am not saying this because I am in Sweden, it is something I made quite clear from the moment I was elected by my people to lead them and this was embodied in my inaugural address at Nongoma, KwaZulu. I have since then repeated this, not only before the Prime Minister of South Africa, Mr B.J. Vorster, but on every possible occasion.

This policy is not one of options and to pretend that the question of accepting or not accepting it ever arises at all, is grossly misleading. What is worse, such pretence gives the South African white minority who rule us undue credit by giving the impression that we have any latitude in this matter at all. In my opinion, to say that we have 'accepted' apartheid, by serving our people within the framework of the South African government's policy, would be as nonsensical as to say that when great African leaders like the late Chief Albert Lutuli, Dr Z.K. Matthews and others, served their people within the framework of the United Party government's policy of segregation as members of the Native Representative Council, they did so because they 'accepted' the segregationist policies of that government. Nothing could be farther from the truth.

It is also a well-known fact that when African political organisations like the banned African National

Congress and the Pan-African Congress were militant in the early sixties they were clamped down on for the very reason that the authorities in South Africa could not tolerate the militant way in which they articulated the wishes and aspirations of their people, despite the fact they were leading an unarmed people. There was a void which lasted for almost ten years in the African political scene as no politics were allowed except within the framework of separate development.

Operating as I do with my reservations clearly spelled out, I therefore do not believe that I have in any way sold my soul like Dr Faust, to the devil, if I may use the expression. On the occasion of the inauguration of the Zulu Assembly I also defined what I considered to be the implications of this policy, if its propounders intend to carry it out with any degree of honesty. Foremost among these was the question of land. As the 'homelands' stand at present, it is a crude joke that anyone can seriously consider them to be countries in the making. They all need to be consolidated if this is a serious experiment and this is the only point on which all homeland leaders agree. I further made it clear at my inauguration that I expected us to have full human dignity and freedom. This leaves the ball in the Republican government's court, which is where it is as far as I am concerned. I also wish to place on record that these so-called 'homelands' are areas into which we were pushed after conflicts and wars with the ancestors of the present whites. It is nonsense to call them our traditional homes. They have not been set up by the Nationalist Party government alone. All that they have done is to romanticise the old reserves by giving them a new Christmas wrapping as 'homelands'.

When my people asked me to lead them despite my well-known views, I felt that I just could not dare to refuse. It was one of those moments in history where I felt caught between the devil and the deep blue sea. It is therefore one of those events where I think history will be the best judge of my actions in agreeing when I was called in to serve. I did so because no other chance of serving my people in politics was allowed. I did so also because I felt that when there is as much suffering as exists in that situation, it is a moral obligation to alleviate the suffering of human beings in however small a degree. For the moment I have scope for articulating the wishes and aspirations of my people for the first time since Sharpeville. I think this is important even at the risk of these instruments ending up as 'talking shops' in the same way in which the Native Representative Council was ultimately looked on by its members.

At present we find that the challenge is to do the utmost one can do towards the development of our people. The 'homelands' are the only machinery through which one can legally make this attempt in South Africa. It might rightly be said that the most we can achieve in this direction would be to nibble at the edges. This I consider much better than folding arms and crying about it. We are drawing the attention of white South Africa to the cruelty of denying us our share of the wealth which we help to produce.

More than seventy per cent of our people receive wages below the poverty datum line. We are at present engaged in warning South Africa about the dangers of the kind of polarisation of wealth and poverty which exists at present. At the moment the ratio of black to white wages is 1:4. The dangers in the perpetuation of this situation are obvious if one takes the history of the human race as a guide. We feel that it is our duty at this time for our people to look at themselves as black workers instead of on an ethnic basis. Once this solidarity becomes a reality we have enough faith to know that our voice will be heard. We do not underestimate the reaction of the powerful should this moment be reached.

We are also concerned about disparities in white and black educational opportunities. Whites have free and compulsory education with all the wealth they command. No such facilities are anywhere in sight for blacks. In 1968 about R14,48 per head was spent on black children. In the same year expenditure per head for white children in the four provinces of the Republic of South Africa was as follows: R191 in the Transvaal, R244 in the Orange Free State, R266 in the Cape and R288 in Natal. According to Hansard, (February 1970) this represents R228 per white child, if we take the number of white pupils in each province into account. Or in simple terms it means that fifteen times more is spent on a white child than on an African child.

When we look at the health of the people we also see a grim picture. There is a doctor for every 44 400 Africans, one coloured doctor for every 6 200 coloureds, one Indian doctor for every 900 Indians and one white doctor for every 400 whites. Fewer than 12 African doctors a year are trained for a population of 15 million. I have been approached by a number of black doctors with the request that we should launch a fund to establish a private school with a science bias, in order to get as many candidates for the medical school as possible. According to an editorial of the latest edition of the 'Bantu Education Journal', the sum of R500 million is estimated as being required to eliminate the numerous inequalities and evils we suffer under Bantu Education. We are trying to impose taxes on ourselves to do as much as we can. But this will certainly not go very far.

There is a group of white South Africans who are getting concerned about the situation and have launched funds known as the Teach Fund in Cape Town, the Learn Fund in Durban and the Rand Bursary Fund in Johannesburg. This will not solve the problem. But we feel that there is scope for friends within South Africa and all the countries that have diplomatic relations with South Africa to help us to relieve the situation. It is of no use to be over-righteous about apartheid, if we get no concrete assistance while apartheid lasts. In other words we feel it is not enough to condemn apartheid, as it will not crumble like the walls of Jericho merely by people shouting, without doing something concrete to alleviate our plight. While the problems of South Africa remain unresolved we feel we should be helped as blacks to help ourselves. The ritual of resolution after resolution at the United Nations condemning apartheid has not the same euphoric effect as it had on blacks say twenty years ago. We realise that like the Afrikaners we must also attempt to lift ourselves by our own bootstraps. The difference with us is that we do not even have the bootstraps, which they had after the Anglo-Boer war.

Those of us who have qualms of conscience about apartheid and yet are working within the framework of the policy do so only because it gives us the only opportunity of awakening our people to help themselves. We can only judge who are our friends, not by any torrents of crocodile tears, but by concrete contributions towards our campaign as blacks to try and stand on our own feet despite the situation in which we find ourselves. There is a lame excuse which has become threadbare in our eyes and that is the excuse that if we are helped, those who do so are strengthening apartheid. We are living within apartheid not out of choice and anyone interested in us will help us where we are. We will sink deeper into the apartheid seas if we are to look at the situation from that angle, unless we are helped right where we are to keep our heads above water. Many people say South Africa is rich and can do these things for us. What a specious argument! After all there is both white and black South Africa, and people should know who are wallowing in wealth and who are wallowing in poverty.

There is also the argument that the situation should be allowed to deteriorate and thus bring about a revolution soon. Some of us are not committed to a violent confrontation. I belong to this group. We do not pretend that this might not overtake us if we do not make a serious effort to solve our problems in South Africa. We find it rather strange for anyone outside South Africa to prescribe this for us. It seems to us that in the final analysis the South African problems will be solved, whether peacefully or violently (may God forbid this), within South Africa by those within the country. The question of whether it will be a peaceful denouement or a violent confrontation can be dictated by the extent to which we are or are not assisted right now to stand on our own feet as blacks.

We have not given up the concept of blacks as an entity. That is why, although we are the so-called homeland leaders, Chief Minister Matanzima and I have pledged ourselves to work towards a federation of the Transkei amd KwaZulu and with whoever wishes to join us. It must be mere definition of such a goal, however remote it might be in the opinions of others, particularly our critics, that keeps the concept of black unity alive as something we must strive for. I mention this to show that we have not abandoned anything which was precious to patriots who have passed on the African political scene before us.

It must always be remembered that there is no situation in any country where politics cannot be defined as the art of the possible. Also in a situation like ours, even more so it remains the art of the possible. We are doing what is possible, no more and no less. This I venture to say is what politics is about anywhere and in any situation.

Explaining Our Case to Africa

M. GATSHA BUTHELEZI

(Article in The Cape Times, 16 January 1974)

I have always said it is extremely beneficial to talk to the people at the kind of international conferences I have had the privilege to attend.

Addis Ababa was no different, but it was more important to me as a black man from South Africa that I participated in a conference like this on the continent of Africa. From the moment we arrived in Nairobi, en route to Addis, we were made to feel at home. In Nairobi, one of the people I met was Mr Oliver Tambo, the Head of the African National Congress-in-exile in London, who was on his way to Lusaka.

While we all work for change in South Africa we are committed to radically different ways of bringing about such change. While we were all for change, we agreed to differ on the methods of effecting such a change.

Mr Tambo was expected to attend the conference at Addis, but did not. Neither did the other members of what are called liberation movements outside South Africa. These included Mr Herbert Chitepo of the Zimbabwe African National Union, whom I later met in Dar-es-Salaam, and members of Frelimo.

The significant thing for me at the African-American dialogue conference was the opening address by His Imperial Majesty Haile Selassie I. Also of significance was an address by the Deputy-Secretary of the Organisation for African Unity, Mr Kamanda Wa Kamanda.

Another important speech was made by Congressman Charles Diggs. Both he and Mr Kamanda condemned the policies pursued in Southern Africa which includes Southern Rhodesia, Mozambique, South Africa and South West Africa.

It may interest readers to know that some of these gentlemen referred to Southern Rhodesia as Zimbabwe and to South Africa as Azania. In their speeches they expressed support for what they called 'the armed struggle' in Southern Africa.

The Americans were concerned about the effect of the policies of their country on African issues and problems. Both white and black Americans are sensitive about anything in American policies that might appear to have the effect of perpetuating black oppression in Southern Africa.

I appreciated the anger of black men everywhere caused by racial discrimination anywhere. I can also appreciate that any racialist policies pursued anywhere against blacks is an affront to their dignity.

However, I thought it might also be of interest to them to know the effect on blacks of some of the actions they recommend or prescribe ostensibly in the interests of blacks here.

I tried to show why we are not committed to a violent change. I conceded that the policies pursued here are kept going through force, and tried to show how impossible it is for us as blacks to pursue the course of violence.

I had not gone to the conference to convert anyone, but I had gone there to be exposed to the thinking of other people and in return I expected them to bear with mine. This, I think, they did beyond my expectations and in this respect I felt that my participation in the dialogue was a success.

If one puts this against the usual walkouts that South Africans experience at conferences of this sort then it should be clear that it is not hyperbolic on my part to say that this was a successful encounter. While others with views dissimilar to mine did not change their views, they listened to what I had to say. They applauded what I said at the conference and in conversations during breaks.

The fact that Lij Endalkachew Makonnen, the Ethiopian Minister of Communications, expressed his appreciation openly was in itself a milestone. It must be remembered that Minister Makonnen is the former Ethiopian United Nations representative who was also a runner-up for the position of Secretary-General when U Thant retired.

My invitation to the African-American dialogue also gave me an opportunity I have been hoping to get for a long time of meeting leaders of independent Africa. I was also delighted to meet the youth of Ethiopia at the Haile Selassie I University in Addis Ababa.

I encountered a deep concern about the situation here,

and in some cases amazing ignorance of what the whole game in South Africa is about. I was also deeply impressed by the depth of concern in general about Africa's problems. More than one student queried the oppression of blacks by blacks in certain parts of Africa.

I can only thank my friend, Dr Megussey, the Head of the Department of Political Science, who invited me to the University. I was touched when he said, in passing a vote of thanks, that Gatsha in Amharic means 'shield' by way of encouraging me at the end of my encounter with the students.

We had several meetings with officials of the Organization for African Unity, and we also paid an official visit to O.A.U. headquarters.

We discussed the homelands policy and our attitude to it. We explained the effects of the oil embargo and our attitude to violence as a means of bringing about change.

They emphasized that they expected us to suffer as a price of our liberation. They said that they understood our position but that some of our utterances on issues like the oil embargo gave them the impression that we were apologists for South Africa.

I stressed that we were not spokesmen for South Africa as we had no credentials to be so. But we could speak with authority on what would happen to our people as a result of actions such as the oil embargo.

It was while we were visiting the O.A.U. headquarters that Mr Peter Onu an O.A.U. assistant secretary, gave me a telex message announcing the banning of my cousin Dr Manas Buthelezi. This could not have been more ill-timed. It shook and soured me and made me silent when this was shown as an example that no dialogue can solve problems in South Africa.

KwaZulu Executive Council: Comments on Land Consolidation

(To the Honourable the Commissioner-General, Mr P.H. Torlage, Commissioner-General for the Zulu and Swazi National Units)

1 / When we met the Honourable the Prime Minister on 28 June 1971, in the Hon. Commissioner-General's presence, the Chief Executive Councillor speaking on behalf of the Executive Council, made it clear to the Hon. the Prime Minister, Mr B.J. Vorster, that consolidation of land in KwaZulu on the basis of the 1936 Native Land and Trust Act would, if pursued, place us as leaders of our people in an invidious position. He explained that the quota promised by the Hertzog government in 1936, was promised as additional land to existing Native Reserves long before present policies which envisage the setting up of separate states were ever contemplated. The Chief Executive Councillor expressed the feelings of the Executive Council and of the majority of the Zulu people when he said that the 1936 land quota cannot be accepted as adequate to set up a separate country with any possibility of viability. In other words we cannot be convinced that the Republican government seriously wants us to set up as a country, if it can only do so on the basis of the 1936 quota promised by the Hertzog government.

2 / The plan for consolidation as presented to us by Mr Pepler on behalf of the Hon. the Minister, on 2 June 1972, we find difficult to accept, in view of the above views clearly expressed to the Hon. the Prime Minister in the presence of both the Hon. the Minister of Bantu Administration and Development and Education, Mr M.C. Botha, and the Hon. the Commissioner-General for the Zulu and Swazi National Units, Mr P.H. Torlage. That is if we have any say in the matter. It is unacceptable on moral grounds as we can hardly accept that what was promised by Dr Hertzog before separate development was ever expounded as a policy, is good enough to cover up for any failure to face up to the implications

of seriously setting up KwaZulu as a country.

3 / The Zulu people just like other black people in the Republic still expect to get the quota promised under the 1936 Land and Trust Act. They can, however, hardly be expected to correlate the fulfilment of those promises by the Hertzog government in 1936 to the consolidation of KwaZulu in terms of the present government's policy under a completely new commitment of the country under present policies.

4 / The use of state lands for consolidation seems to be an attempt to placate white voters by touching as little of their land as possible. We have never doubted in our minds that state lands would automatically fall into KwaZulu. It hardly seems fair that hectares from state lands should be counted by the government for the purposes of fulfilling promises under the 1936 Land Act or for consolidation under the policy of separate development. This we state in view of the amount of land that is already owned by the white minority in this country and the little percentage that falls under our areas.

5 / The idea of splitting up land under irrigation near Jozini Dam between whites and us left us completely flabbergasted at what appears to us to be white avarice gone mad. Whites are already so wealthy in South Africa that we would have thought that it would hardly dent white wealth to give all the lands under irrigation at Jozini to the Zulu people. We did not expect Ubombo and neighbouring areas to be made white merely for the purposes of sharing the Jozini Dam Scheme with us, who are starting almost from scratch.

6 / The game reserves are an integral part of KwaZulu and just like state lands we thought they would automatically fall into KwaZulu where they belong. We were shocked to find them split up between whites (Hluhluwe) and blacks (Mfolozi), as they are one complex. Since we have no industries we thought reserves could contribute towards the alleviation of our poverty as a tourist attraction. We see examples of the great possibilities in this respect in the free African countries like Kenya, Tanzania and Zambia. It seems more reasonable to keep game reserves as one complex and to give them to us as such, instead of destroying them by splitting up the complex.

7 / If the Republican government seriously wanted

KwaZulu to be a viable state, then Richards Bay should be our port so that we can get an outlet to the sea and also give us a possibility of getting anywhere near economic viability. We are shocked at the idea of giving all the coast to whites and leaving us with hardly any beaches. This is more serious as it underlies white mistrust of blacks to the extent of deliberately making them landlocked. If we are mistrusted in this way, what reason do we have to trust those who display such a mistrust of us?

8 / The scheme involves the removal of too many of our people and very few whites comparatively speaking. This even involves the removal of people who have fairly recently been removed to places like Paulpietersburg.

9 / The idea of taking away places like Groutville, Ifafa and others, which have developed sugar-cane farming, seemed grossly inconsiderate in terms of our general underdevelopment as a people. How can our most developed farming land be taken away and given to whites who already have so much?

10 / Stanger is to Zulus a national shrine as it is the resting place of King Shaka, the founder of the Zulu nation. The Afrikaners have their own sacred places and this is our most sacred ground and one would have expected more sympathy from them in this regard.

11 / The whole idea of having corridors of white territories cutting us apart does not convince us that the government wants to consolidate seriously. This position we find completely unacceptable.

12 / We find it almost ludicrous, if it was not so tragic, that all rich places that fall logically within a consolidation plan for KwaZulu from our point of view should not have fallen within KwaZulu to enable those whites who wish to keep their land and fall under KwaZul to do so. This is not such a horrible idea. We know many dedicated nationalists who own land in Swaziland and Botswana, and who have not turned black or changed their citizenship, accept that they must abide by the laws of those countries.

13 / Even at draft-level, we wish we had been involve as a people most affected, to help in making proposals, and a joint commission of both whites and Zulus should have been appointed.

14 / To have an all-white commission nominated by an all-white government to decide on our future means that

it is only the interests of the whites which are well safeguarded. Anyone who contradicts this would only imply that whites are angels and not humans like us, if they would not be influenced mainly by the interests of their own people.

15 / As far as we are concerned separate development is a political operation. It is a political solution for South Africa's problems prescribed by the present government. Therefore, with all due respect for considerations as to suitability of land for agriculture and other industries, all we are concerned with, for the purposes of this policy for the moment, is a political map of KwaZulu, and once we have this, it will be for us to know what to do once we have a country with clear-cut boundaries.

16 / In view of the foregoing we wish to repeat that the scheme for the consolidation of KwaZulu as presented to us at present, is unacceptable to us. We recommend a Natal and KwaZulu referendum of people of all races on this question.

In Defence of the 'No Opposition' Policy

M. GATSHA BUTHELEZI

(Excerpts from letter by Chief M. Gatsha Buthelezi in the Natal Mercury, 31 August 1971)

In an interview I had with one newspaper, I said that at this stage we will not have an opposition because with problems of development we are facing, and faced as we are with white minority rule in South Africa, we cannot afford deliberately to create apparatus for petty bickering among ourselves.

At present we debate every issue thoroughly and everyone expresses his opinion honestly and votes according to the best dictates of his conscience.

This is Zulu democracy at work based on a consensus of opinion. At present members are free to tear to shreds any proposal placed before the Assembly without being tethered by any party affiliation.

I am sorry to have to talk like an egoist, but it is a fact that I read and passed Constitutional Law for non-degree purposes. The Westminster model of Great Britain, which Nsika Khumalo thinks is so perfect, developed by trial and error; it was not artifically and deliberately created. In other words it developed spontaneously as the constitutional development of the British people evolved.

In my interview, I said that as time goes on and as policies change we will encourage the emergence of an opposition. I added that I was educated in the western tradition and think an opposition does keep the government on its toes; but that at present it was a luxury a black man in this country can't afford.

I dispute the innuendo that all white things are perfect and that all black things are imperfect. I am not impressed, for example, with what Mr Wilson in Great Britain has done in connection with the entry into the European Common Market. He is now opposing what was his own policy when he was in power merely because he is now the leader of the opposition!

I never said anything about having a one-party state.

In fact I said we are for the moment going to operate on a non-party basis. I therefore leave it to readers, to judge whether I deserve Nsika Khumalo's puerile animadversions.

Mr Khumalo should know that some of us operate within this system for the sake of our people and because we have no choice. The cards are so stacked against the black man in South Africa that I feel we are going nowhere as black people, if Mr Khumalo can misdirect his energies on me on a thing he has in any case misunderstood, instead of attacking the real 'niggers in the woodpile' of our South African situation.

KwaZulu Executive Council: The Role of the Zulu King

(Statement by the Executive Council of the KwaZulu Legislative Assembly on the petition allegedly sent by the Zulu Paramount Chief to the Honourable the Minister of Bantu Administration requesting the suspension of the Chief Executive Councillor, Chief M. Gatsha Buthelezi, in 1973)

Yesterday the Honourable the Commissioner-General informed the Chief Executive Councillor that the Minister has not received the petition. He further informed him that when they read in the press that the petition had allegedly been typed in the offices of the Department of Information in Durban, they had investigated the allegation. They received information that a 'junior' member of the staff had typed the letter on the instructions and request of one Mr David Zulu from Umlazi. Mr David Zulu is the Secretary of the Paramount Chief's Royal Council. At one time the Paramount Chief requested this Executive Council to make finances available in order to employ him as his personal secretary. The Executive Council could not accept his name because of certain alleged subversive activities of the Royal Council against the KwaZulu Government; particularly during preparations for Shaka's Day in September last year and Mr David Zulu's involvement in particular.

The Chief Executive Councillor was informed by the Hon. W.S.P. Kanye, Liaison Officer between us and the King, that the Paramount Chief denies any knowledge of the petition alleged to have been sent or written by him

Yesterday certain Usuthu Tribal Councillors, Messrs. N. Shamase and A.M. Nhleko, came to see the Chief Executive Councillor in his office, because of the deep concern that has been caused by the alleged petition throughout KwaZulu. They informed the Chief Executive Councillor that they had just been with the King and had asked him if he knew anything about the letter or petition, but that he denied any knowledge of it.

The Chief Executive Councillor wrote the King a forma

letter asking him to state whether he knew anything about the petition to the Minister requesting his removal and he denied it.

We wish to declare our unswerving loyalty to the monarchy. At the same time we wish to stress that loyalty to a king and loyalty of the king to his subjects is a reciprocal game. It can never be a one-sided affair. Any king is a custodian of the monarchy as an institution and should see himself as such. He must realise that he should not either personally or through others do something that thwarts the will of his people, for this is certainly a collision course. The institution of the monarchy is too great to be allowed to go to the rocks by even a king in office. We see ourselves as having a duty to the nation in this respect even if it may mean taking very drastic steps.

The Royal Council was only a few months ago exposed by Prince Layton Zulu, and all their plots to have us unseated were revealed in the press. It was alleged that some of these plots were hatched at the King's Palace, at Mbelebeleni, KwaMashu, and these allegations have not been denied by the King or the Royal Council.

We are not in terms of our constitution in a position to make any deductions on the King's role on the above facts out of respect and loyalty to his office. We however feel that we have to condemn in the strongest terms the role the Royal Council has played since the time of the coronation. It is quite plain that they consider themselves to be of more importance than the Zulu people. Hence all the attempts they have been engaged in in attempting to thwart our efforts as the true voice of our people and all their plots to undermine us as the government of KwaZulu. Their actions are subversive in the true sense since they pretend that they are not a political party, which they are in fact. Their political role is not even veiled. What perturbs us is that they are not on their own. In other words they are a front for certain manipulations.

We condemn the idea of the republican government's employees involving themselves in subversive actions against us. This has been going on for some time, including political campaigning by a Zulu member of the Department of Information in Durban against the Chief Executive Councillor.

For the Zulu people to be convinced of the innocence

which their King declares, we have passed a resolution requesting the King to sever all connections with the Royal Council and, if possible, to dissociate himself publicly from them and/or their actions. We hope the King will be gracious enough to do this not in our interests but in his own personal interests. We feel that our next steps in this matter will depend on his actions now.

No Confidence in KwaZulu Executive Council

CHARLES HLENGWA

(Excerpts from text of intended motion by the leader of the Umkhonto KaShaka Party, presented in Soweto, 1974)

My motion is based on the following facts which I regard as detrimental to good government and to the interest of KwaZulu:

At a welcome function of the Chief Executive Councillor held at the Jabulani amphitheatre, Soweto, the Honourable the Chief Executive Councillor delivered a speech which he concluded with the following words:

'I would like to leave a message to the people of Soweto: we have agreed that the white people of South Africa are our vanguard in every respect, so we always follow their example. For God's sake don't be deceived and allow yourselves to be divided on the basis of ethnic grouping. The whites of South Africa have different cultures and backgrounds and yet when it comes to matters of this country, whether it be Union, Republic or politics, they are all united on the basis of their colour. If you allow yourselves to be divided on the basis of ethnic grouping then I conceive, ladies and gentlemen, that you are the biggest bunch of fools that the Almighty ever created.'

Should we gather from these words that the Honourable the Chief Executive Councillor was speaking as a Zulu, propagating Zulu nationalism, Zulu unity, Zulu development, Zulu independence? Or should we come to the conclusion that he was speaking as their self-appointed leader of a black nation, an integrated society made up of Indians, coloureds and blacks in which Zulus who are proud of the fact that they are Zulus have no place, where Xhosas are not welcome or where Tswanas are unwanted ... where only blacks who have lost their national pride, their traditions, their language are welcome?

What did the Chief Councillor have in mind when he called on the Indians to join us? Here I am referring to a speech by the Honourable Chief Executive Councillor to an Indian gathering in Lenasia, Johannesburg, on the

23 November 1972, as was reported in the Rand Daily Mail of 24 November 1972. At this meeting, and I quote from the Rand Daily Mail:

'1 / He offered unity with Indians, even at "grass roots level" and called for common strategies - not against anyone, but for upliftment;

'2 / He warned Indians against believing that they were better off without the other black groups, and promised them stability Indians had not enjoyed in Uganda;

'3 / He appealed to them to share their commercial, industrial and managerial skills with Africans, and offered them industrial partnership in KwaZulu when it achieved sufficient autonomy.'

At the same meeting in Lenasia he said, and I quote his exact words:

'We must act in the realm of the possible. The fact is that I am able to articulate the wishes and aspirations of our black patriots who are languishing on Robben Island and the patriots who have died for our country. While I do this, I am immune because I am leader of a budding homeland.'

The Honourable Chief Executive Councillor said that he is articulating the wishes and aspirations of his black patriots who are held on Robben Island and those who died for 'our country'. Who are these 'black patriots' who are serving sentences on Robben Island? Are they Zulus? What are their wishes and aspirations which our Chief Executive Councillor says he is articulating? Is it the development of KwaZulu? Is it the unity of KwaZulu? Is it the adoration of our King and the preservation of our customs? Has it anything to do with KwaZulu? If so, why are the patriots of our Chief Executive Councillor serving prison sentences on Robben Island and why is our Chief Executive Councillor immune, as he put it, because he is the leader of a budding homeland? For which country did the patriots of our Chief Executive Councillor die? Was it for KwaZulu, and if so, were they Zulus and how and why did they die?

On his recent visit to Swaziland the Honourable the Chief Executive Councillor delivered words of thanks to the Prime Minister, Prince Makhosini, at a cocktail party given in his honour. I quote from his address:

'I think it would be a terrible omission, your Excellency, if I do not take advantage of this occasion to thank His Majesty and his government for giving political asylum to many of our brothers who ran away from political persecution to seek your protection. Those of us who are still struggling within South Africa are daily conscious of the importance of Swaziland's role in giving sanctuary to your brothers from South Africa. Africa will never forget it and when the day comes when the history of our times is written, Swaziland will be given a place of honour for doing this for the sons and daughters of mother Africa.'

Allow me to ask the question once more: on whose behalf did our Chief Executive Councillor thank the Swaziland government for giving sanctuary to political refugees? Are they Zulus and if so, why did they flee this country? Did they flee because they were loyal to our King, because they were working for the upliftment of our Zulu people, the development of KwaZulu and for the independence of our nation?

We are aware of the fact that the Chief Executive Councillor has on a number of occasions had discussions with Mr Sonny Leon of the Coloured Labour Party. I wish to ask the Chief Executive Councillor this question: Have you, Sir, also invited the coloureds to join us and offered them industrial partnership in KwaZulu as you did to the Indians?

Having referred to our Chief Executive Councillor's condemning of 'ethnic groupings' and therefore also condemning of a united Zulu nation because we are an ethnic group, his call on the Indians to join us, his associating himself with prisoners on Robben Island and with political refugees in Swaziland, may I ask where does the Umtata summit and his declaration of faith which he co-signed with Mr Harry Schwartz of the United Party fit in?

Has he signed the Umtata Manifesto (calling for a federation) as the Chief Executive Councillor of KwaZulu? If so, who gave him the mandate to peddle away our land, our nationality or future independence?

In Cape Town, addressing the South African Institute of Race Relations, he again advocated a federation of states in Southern Africa. In his speech he visualised three types of states. Giving an example of a state wherein the interests of blacks would be paramount, he referred to Natal, where the Zulus, Europeans, Indians and coloureds would form the Zulu state and in which the minority groups, namely the Europeans, Indians and coloureds, would have a joint say in the government of the Zulu state.

He therefore does not visualise a pure autonomous Zulu nation or Zulu state, but an integrated society of Zulus, Europeans, Indians and coloureds. If this should ever happen, what would become of our proud Zulu nation? Will we become a nation of half-castes, losing our culture, language and identity? Where does our father, the King, fit in? Will he still be regarded as the King of such a state and therefore also become the King of Europeans, Indians and coloureds? What will become of our chiefs - will they also be regarded as chiefs serving over Europeans, coloureds and Indians? Has the signing of the declaration of faith with Mr Schwartz been sanctioned by the Zulu nation? The Chief Executive Councillor did not enter into a similar agreement with the National Party. Why? Is it because the Chief Executive Councillor rejects the policy of self-determination, of Zulu independence, as advocated by the Nationalists, and that he subscribes to the policy of the United Party which boils down to continued 'Baasskap', serfdom, under a white parliament?

Various newspapers have reported that our Chief Executive Councillor is working towards the establishment of a newspaper to be called 'The Black Voice - Iswi Lomnyana'. It is said that the Edendale Lay Ecumenical Centre is playing an important role in the establishment of this newspaper. I would like to ask the Chief Executive Councillor whether this will be a Zulu newspaper or whether it will be directed to the black masses of Southern Africa? Where will the funds come from? Is is true that certain foreigners are playing a leading role in the technical planning of this newspaper?

I have no doubt that I speak on behalf of every person who is proud of the fact that he is a Zulu in condemning the KwaZulu Executive Council for its delaying tactics in our constitutional development.

The Transkei will receive its independence as an autonomous state within the next few years. Bophutha-Tswana, Lebowa, Gazankulu, Venda and the Ciskei are well on the road to independence. Where do we stand? We, the biggest national unit in the Republic of South Africa, are the least developed, constitutionally and otherwise. Whose fault is it? Are we, the Zulus, so primitive and so stupid that we are far behind? Or are our leaders so busy with their own little fights with the republican government and with their own ideologies that KwaZulu and the interests of our nation are of no consequence? If all the time which our Chief Executive Councillor has spent in attending church and other meetings abroad, if all the time and energy he has spent in writing articles in newspapers on non-Zulu subjects, if all his time spent in addressing Progressive Party meetings, Indian, European and other gatherings and even acting in films, if all this time were spent and all this energy directed to the upliftment of our people and the development of our country, we, the Zulus, would have been the most advanced of all the homelands and we would already have been a prosperous nation.

I have now received information that the KwaZulu Executive Council has requested the central government not to hold elections when the term of office of this Legislative Assembly expires during 1975. The Executive Council wants to progress from an executive council to a cabinet in terms of chapter two of the Promotion of Self-Government Act without letting our people exercise their rights to elect a government of their own choice by means of a general election. The argument has been advanced that a general election could not be held until such time as all our people have been issued with citizenship certificates.

Where it has become clear from this motion that our Chief Executive Councillor has come forward not as a leader of the Zulu people but as the spokesman of the blacks in South Africa, I find it strange that he has not objected to the other homelands making use of reference books as a means of identification in the various and successful general elections that they have conducted. It is only in the case of KwaZulu that such interim means of identification has been rejected - and we are still lagging behind, we are still not developing and we are still not given our democratic right to exercise our vote. Are these the signs of the birth of a one-party state or are we being kept on ice for an integrated society in which the Zulu identity will be lost for ever?

Having noted with sadness and regret the failure of this Executive Council to recognise the traditional supremacy of the Zulu King, its failure to effect a democratic government and to honour and protect Zulu traditional political institutions and the rights and privileges of chiefs, and its dismal failure to work for the unity, development and independence of the Zulu nation, I hereby propose a motion of no confidence in the Executive Council of KwaZulu.

Issues in KwaZulu

M. GATSHA BUTHELEZI

(Excerpts from address delivered at the general conference of the National Cultural Liberation Movement (Inkatha) at Bhekuzulu College, Nongoma, 18 July 1975)

We have tremendous problems which face us as blacks. This machinery gives us a chance of coming face to face with these problems right from the grass roots. In the past we have tended to hope that we can be helped by others to solve our problems. It is, of course, true to say that no people stand on their own in the present world. At the same time there are those problems in the history of a people, which only the people concerned can solve. We have tended to hanker far too much for foreign cultural patterns in the past, which in any case were kept by those who brought them for their own exclusive use. It is clear that hopes for only a change of heart, on their part, will not carry us far.

This means therefore that this is the time for us to wrestle with our problems of development in our own way through our own indigenous cultural patterns. Western civilisation is impressive in its emphasis on the rights of the individual. On the other hand our culture stresses the rights of the individual as a member of the group. Clearly group survival is of paramount importance in our society, and individual rights are important in order to promote the continued existence of the group, rather than just that of individuals. That is why our extended-family system, which is a source of so much banter and sarcasm in western societies, is geared towards the survival of the entire group.

In a society such as that of South Africa, where we are excluded from most of the fruits of our labours and from other privileges, as a racial group, it is clear to me that our cultural pattern of reacting to this as a group is the only answer we have. This is not a situation where our efforts should be geared towards what each individual rakes off for himself. The system which puts us as a racial group beyond the pale of life's bounty is a vicious one. It cannot be tackled successfully by individuals or cliques but we have to mobilise each and every individual in our society, be it male or female, be it young or old, if we can hope for any success in the foreseeable future.

Let me emphasise that our efforts are geared towards self-upliftment on all fronts and at every level of our society. They are geared towards correlating our efforts with those of our brothers in the whole of Southern Africa. It is not good enough to condemn what others do unto us, if we have not learnt not to do the same things to our people in all matters where we have any latitude.

Lest people should think I am talking through my hat, let me illustrate what I mean here by our cultural pattern geared towards group survival. I will mention simple things such as weeding parties, amalimo, in which neighbours come together to assist each other in the planting of crops, in the weeding of crops and in harvesting. I can also refer to simple things such as the sisa custom, where a man with more cattle than his neighbour loans some of his cows to a neighbour so that he can also have milk. I can go on talking about these cultural patterns for a long time. The stockfell parties, although very crude manifestations of these indigenous cultural patterns, are a modern example, and also ukuholisana, where individuals share salaries by giving their salaries, or part thereof, to others on certain month-ends.

It is clear that unless we join hands in our community development we can never hope to survive. It should not be difficult to develop modern co-operative societies in our communities as these fall in line with our own cultural patterns.

It seems to me that one day we will be faced with the problem of deciding to what extent the people must have a stake in the control of the means of production, and in sharing the fruits of that production. In my budget speech in the Assembly last year it will be recalled that I stated that I believed in free enterprise. At the same time I do believe that in our areas of influence the people must, without stifling private enterprise, have a stake. I believe in these things because I am convinced that we have suffered so much injustice and deprivation that it would be tragic if we strive for freedom only in order to replace white exploitation with black exploitation. There are instances where black exploitation exists; where this is the case we must seek to eliminate it. If our efforts are not geared towards them we might as well forget about waging any battle towards the elimination of poverty, disease and ignorance which are hall-marks of our present state of oppression.

I think I need to say these things at the very outset, because I believe it would be a terrible mistake if we emphasised our political problems to the exclusion of those other problems which keep us in a state of deprivation, about which we can do something even now, to liberate ourselves.

I consider it a pity that some supposed liberals in the mass media have tried to confuse issues by emphasising the political thrust in our struggle to the exclusion of the educational, social and economic fronts of the struggle. Whilst it is the KwaZulu Legislature that has set us up, we would be fools to concern outselves only with KwaZulu politics, as much as it would be foolish to ignore KwaZulu politics. A fine balance is needed here and this machinery, Inkatha, does provide us with solutions if we use its machinery in a constructive way.

Inkatha provides the machinery within which the people as a whole have a right to participate in national decision-making at all levels. It provides a forum for African democracy based on consensus. We Zulus have a lovely expression, which sums up this thought very well, when we say, 'injobo enhle ngethungelwa ebandla'. One Zulu-English dictionary translates this saying as 'the umutsha is sown in the company of others from whom you may receive tips and advice'. In other words, only those things thrashed out with others can produce meaningful solutions. This is what we are here to do.

On the political scene I have stated at various meetings of the National Movement, that the system of self-rule worked out for us has run into problems which many of us anticipated. In the first place those who have set us up, as a KwaZulu government, have done so without being prepared to give us a country where such governing can take place. After the so-called final consolidation plans, we still end up as pieces of separate uncontiguous territory scattered all over our province, which in its entirety was our Zulu land. This raises a number of issues. This being the case it has been considered necessary for us to revive the National Cultural Movement in order to enable our entire people to participate with us in thinking through these imponderables.

A view has been expressed in this connection that we should seek independence. To me, and my government, it seems a farce to ask for independence of separate pieces of inadequate territory for the largest ethnic group in South Africa. This puts to great doubt the sincerity of the government. Although we as the Legislative Assembly have rejected the idea of independence under these circumstances, it is important to know exactly how the people as a whole feel about this issue. The National Cultural Liberation Movement gives us this opportunity of knowing where people as a whole stand on this issue.

We have further suggested a federal formula, as a compromise solution for South Africa, and this has also been rejected out of hand by the government. There are some voices which want to present me and my Assembly as not representing the true wishes of the Zulu people on this issue. A spurious comparison is made with the Transkei, when such a comparison does not apply at all. The Transkei is today one geographic bloc of territory, not as a result of any act of benevolence on the part of the present government. It is such a bloc by a sheer accident of history. In spite of this, it is still a 64 000-dollar question whether it can be a viable country, able to stand on its own amongst other nations. It is true that there are many nations that are not economically viable that have flags, national anthems, and are represented at the United Nations.

For us in South Africa the problem is made complex by the fact that we blacks have contributed towards the growth of the South African economy. Our decision in KwaZulu, and elsewhere, must be whether to decide to sign away our claim to this economy we have helped to develop in exchange for a flag, a national anthem, and representation at the United Nations, and even a unit of the army which in terms of modern warfare may be nothing more than a posse of a police force. I admit that even we in KwaZulu need such a defence force. The hub of the problem is whether these things are worth the signing away of what many of us see as our birthright? We do not want to appear to be forcing our qualms of conscience on these issues down anybody's throat. This National Movement provides the forum for the expression of our national consensus on these crucial issues.

If we can not reach any meaningful fulfilment through the instruments of separate development, what is the next step? A view is expressed by some people that one must have nothing to do with the system. This implies choice. I am not convinced that such choices are open to black people of this land. To pretend that we have open choices amounts to giving the powers-that-be more credit than they deserve. The pressures brought to bear on us to make us conform need no cataloguing here as they are by now too well-known to the whole world. Many questions come to mind: for example, after the Republican government has created machinery whereby various taxes paid by blacks are channelled to the coffers of these reserves' governments, what does one do? Do we refuse to take the responsibility to work out, as we do now, some kind of budget for the departments assigned to us? This is not an ideal situation even with the additional cash given to us as budgetary subsidies. Do we then miss the opportunity of doing the best with what we get out of this whole mess in order to be able to say that we are ideologically clean? Does this eliminate the danger of certain elements assuming authority in our name and presenting apartheid to the world as acceptable to us?

These are but a few questions that need to be faced in wrestling with these questions. For example, for those of us who are hereditary chiefs, if one wants to 'get out of the system' as some people are urging, what does this mean? Does one abandon one's people to the wiles of anyone who may be imposed on them? Or does one suffer and struggle with them in the misery in which fate has placed them at this age and hour?

We need a body like this National Movement where we can come face to face with these questions and think them through as a national group. If this means action, then we can only take collective action if we are properly organised. The time for short-lived dramas or traumas is over. Careful thought should precede collective action. If the decision is non-action, we also need to think this one through and through, together.

It is now accepted that our people will have to help themselves. Where do we find them? Right where they are, I suppose, in these reserves, and in the ghettos called townships and locations. We have not created the reserves or these ghettos, and the fact that the system is abhorrent to us, does not sound a plausible excuse to me for keeping out of the people's struggles, just to be able to say we have not contaminated ourselves with the system. Ideological cleanliness may be a virtue, but to strive for it whatever the cost is to one's people may cheapen it to nothing more nor less than a cheap and arrogant vice.

Many divisions have been created between us by many things which are enumerated in our preamble. The National Movement gives us the opportunity to tackle these questions jointly. The black struggle is not something that can simplistically be reduced to a struggle between patricians and plebeians, or between urbanites and peasants or between intellectuals and the hoi polloi. We have no such segmentations in our society except in theory. Our colour levels us all, in a country where racism has been institutionalised almost to perfection. We have one struggle whether we like it or not, whether we are rural or urban, whether we are chiefs or commoners. We have a tryst with destiny to resolve these problems together as people suffering under the same oppression.

As far as our education is concerned, we have set up a committee to go into the problems of our education. We feel that too much stress was put on formal education in the past. Blue-collar jobs are vital if any country is going to develop. There is great dignity in labour, and blacks need technical training in order to participate in the industrial growth of the country. Job reservation is not the only barrier stopping us from doing certain jobs. We have no artisans worthy of that name. A new re-think on our whole system of education is called for by these circumstances.

Although only 30 per cent of KwaZulu is arable we need to step up the training of our youth in agriculture. It is not sufficient to assist farmers through our extension officers; we need a more thorough training in agriculture from Form I right up to university. At the same time the churches have through the Health and Welfare Association gone into rural community development. This is overdue and highly appreciated. We need a complete re-orientation to face up to this kind of thorough training in rural community development. Some people use the excuse that we need not be given more land, because we cannot even use what we have. While this is too over-simplistic a view, it is still true that we can do much better than we are doing at present to produce enough to feed ourselves. These are basic issues, which are the very first things, if one talks about development. The pilot project in rural development should not be something seen as a thing only of local interest. We should all set our eyes on it, as it should set a pattern for our development.

We think our Women's Brigade and our Youth Brigade should be seen as segments of the National Movement that should spearhead our development at grass roots, if our community development projects are to get off the ground.

As far as the question of education is concerned, I think it is the only issue, apart from land, on which the whole question of government sincerity revolves. The Minister has announced that he is going ahead with the Pretoria-imposed medium of instruction of our children in the urban areas. They did not even have the decency to inform the black leaders that the issue had been decided unilaterally once and for all by them. Just like most of you we read about it in Hansard and in the newspapers. So much for dialogue and détente within South Africa.

Article 26 of the Universal Declaration of Human Rights states:

'1 / Everyone has the right to education. Education shall be free, at least in the elementary and fundamental stages. Elementary education shall be compulsory. Technical and professional education shall be made generally available and higher education shall be equally accessible to all on the basis of merit.

'2 / Education shall be directed to the full development of the human personality and to the strengthening of respect for human rights and fundamental freedoms. It shall promote understanding, tolerance and friendship among all nations, racial or religious groups, and shall further the activities of the United Nations for the maintenance of peace.

'3 / Parents have a prior right to choose the kind of education that shall be given to their children.'

The attitude of the government, as displayed through the Minister of Bantu Education, is a direct contravention of Article 26 of the Universal Declaration of Human Rights, in that he arrogates to himself a right which, according to this Declaration, is a prerogative of the African parents to choose the kind of education that shall be given to their children. No white child is educated through the medium of two languages on a 50 - 50 basis. If this is not evidence of white oppression of black people, then I do not know what the word oppression means.

There are issues such as machinery for negotiation and labour relations for our people. We feel that our people should have trade unions, if the trade unions for whites and other racial groups are regarded as effective machinery for negotiations, as we understand them to be. Trade unions are not machinery for staging strikes, but for negotiation in order to avoid strikes. A lot is being said about works committees. These are not effective in most cases, and the appeal made recently by the Federated Chambers of Industry for black trade unions echoed what is in our hearts on this issue.

In South Africa there is one doctor for every 44 400 Africans. This reveals the extent to which our health needs are not met. We realise that missionary hospitals attempted to meet these needs in the past. There is now an impressive health scheme with emphasis on preventive medicine which the Health Department is implementing. We are impressed with it, but the take-over of mission hospitals in KwaZulu seems to be a fly in the ointment at the moment. We have no health department at present and have been told when we recently asked for one that we are not ready for it. Our wish was that the take-over of mission hospitals be postponed until we have a health department. We are afraid that we may lose some doctors, if the take-over is implemented immediately, which would aggravate a delicate situation in terms of our medical needs. The Health and Welfare Association community development project includes a clinic. We in KwaZulu intend seconding some of our nurses and extension officers as part and parcel of this project. We are now in the process of getting a Red Cross organisation going in KwaZulu. An investigation of how this may be interwoven with the brigades, is going to be carried out.

In all these things we need your advice and guidance. We feel that the forum is provided by the National Movement to express these openly so that our thinking can be one on all these vital issues.

There is a big fallacy that we in KwaZulu are

delaying elections deliberately. Of course nothing could be further from the truth than this wild rumour, which unfortunately is being deliberately and falsely propagated by people in very high places. The KwaZulu Legislative Assembly decided to use citizenship certificates for elections. This was decided because the reference books or 'dom-passes' are hated by all Africans. Even this is a compromise as electoral divisions will still be determined on the basis of the reference books. These citizenship certificates are being issued for us by the Department of Bantu Administration and Development, and at present only 451 001 have been issued. Now we have done all we can to step up the issuing of these certificates, but as we have no computers, and have to rely on Pretoria's computers, we still cannot determine the rate at which these certificates are issued. I have been aware since the launching of the now defunct Shaka's Spear Party that attempts by Pretoria are being made to blame me for the slow rate at which these citizenship certificates are issued. In 1974 and 1975 at the Ordinary Sessions of our Assembly, I suggested that we should abandon our decision to use these certificates and instead use 'dom-passes'. At each session my suggestion was rejected by the KwaZulu Legislative Assembly. On these issues, I want to be acquainted with your own thinking on these decisions by our Assembly.

A lot of propaganda is being sold to the South African public and overseas visitors that I am delaying KwaZulu independence. When we asked to move into the second phase of constitutional development the Minister of Bantu Administration and Development rejected the Assembly's decision. His excuse was that we had to move to that phase only after elections, and yet most other Legislatures moved into the second phase before the elections. The Minister stated that unless we can tell him the date of the elections, he cannot allow us to move into the second phase, and yet it is his computers which issue these citizenship certificates, and he is in a better position than we are to give us an idea of when the elections are likely to be. All these sins are heaped on my head by sections of the Afrikaans press, and even a Sunday English newspaper has joined them.

As far as international relations are concerned, you are all aware that my very first visit overseas, in 1963, had nothing to do with the government homelands policy. I went overseas to attend the Anglican congress in Canada and later I was in London and Scandinavia with my wife as guests of the churches.

You will recall that my passport was taken away shortly after my return, and that all pleas for the return of the passport failed. I had been invited to the United States on a Leadership grant in 1964. I had not been invited as a leader under the homelands policy of the government, but as a hereditary leader of my tribe and of the Zulu people, who tried to concern himself with problems affecting all Africans.

It was not until 1971 that my passport was returned to me. I visited Italy, Germany and Britain. There have been subsequent visits to the United States and Europe which all of you are aware of. I have also been to a number of African countries since my passport was returned.

Whenever I went abroad the main issue was of course this whole question of apartheid, and what my own position is in all this. One big issue has been the question of investments: whether multi-national corporations in the United States, Britain and other European countries with subsidiaries in South Africa should withdraw their investments. The rationale is that by having investments in South Africa these countries strengthen apartheid through their industries. So a lot of pressure is brought to bear particularly by the churches and organisations opposed to apartheid, which include our banned organisations, the African National Congress and the Pan-African Congress.

My view was that pressures were plausible in so far as they made people conscious of the evils of apartheid. I supported pressures on the corporations if geared towards helping my people to advance towards economic justice. I told my audiences and the mass media that the pass system and influx control made every job for an African vital, since we have no choice, and since we are recruited on a contractual basis. This meant, I explained, that we could not sell our labour in an open labour-market and, what is more, we were exploited since we have no trade unions, which means that we have no effective machinery for negotiation for the maintenance of labour relations. I have never supported investments on any terms. So I supported pressures to push industries to improve wages, to give my people fringe benefits, to enable them to have pension schemes, and trade unions. I have been severely criticised for this stance by some people. I would like to have your thoughts on this issue as well.

The National Cultural Liberation Movement (Inkatha)

SIBUSISO BENGU

(Reprinted from Reality, September 1975)

The National Cultural Liberation Movement, known in Zulu as Inkatha Yenkululeko Yesizwe (abbreviated as Inkatha) traces its origin from King Solomon, Dinuzulu's son, who founded it in 1928. In its original form Inkatha was conceived as a movement that would organise the Africans of Zulu origin into a cultural unit, regaining whatever had been lost of the traditional values.

It was through the foresight of the Hon. Prince M.G. Buthelezi, Chief Executive Councillor for KwaZulu and President of the Movement, that Inkatha was revived early this year. At a meeting attended by representatives of various sections and interests in African society at KwaNzimela, Melmoth, in March 1975, the movement was officially launched and Chief Buthelezi was unanimously elected its first president to lead an interim central committee of 25 members.

Article 1 of the movements preamble declares Inkatha a cultural movement. It is, therefore, necessary for us to take a closer look at the concept of culture. Generally speaking the term 'culture', especially in this country, conveys an idea of artistic and intellectual creations in a given society. In this sense it is possible to speak of some people as being 'cultured' and others 'uncultured'. Anthropologists, however, have long given the term 'culture' a wider meaning to include religion, family, customs, general knowledge and aptitudes, utensils, habitats, dress, etc. Culture is therefore understood by Inkatha as a generic term for the values people uphold at the present time since it is now an accepted fact that there is evolution in culture as in biological development. Inkatha does not attempt to re-live the past or find a way of switching the clock back, it merely declares that since culture embraces the totality of values, institutions and forms of behaviour transmitted within a society, as well as material goods produced by man, national unity and model for development should be based on values extrapolated from the people's culture and adapted to present-day needs and situations.

It is, therefore, easy to understand why blacks in Southern Africa seek to liberate themselves through their culture. Not only do Africans wish to liberate themselves from poverty, ignorance, hunger, disease, neo-colonialism and cultural domination by their white masters but they are also desirous of liberating themselves from what I choose to call 'mental whiteness' or a 'colonial mentality', that is, a sense of rejection of things African. Inkatha can be seen as part of the cultural identity movement that is sweeping Africa today. The Africans' basic concern is not what others expect them to do but what they are called upon by reason and by nature to do. Instead of Africans endeavouring to be carbon copies of others, they want to be distinctively themselves.

Since Inkatha deprecates all attempts to imitate closely the whites it should not be looked upon as an anti-white movement. Through Inkatha we do not want to cut ourselves off from other groups and the rest of the world in pursuit of an African identity. Certainly we live in a world in which there is increasing interdependence and exchange of ideas.

Inkatha accepts the fact that we as Africans have many things to copy from the western economic, political and educational patterns of development. Certain western patterns have, however, to be put to the test to see if they work in an African situation. The experience independent African states have had with the western partisan political system makes us in our liberation struggle accept the challenge we face, to find, in a democratic way, a system that will suit our temperament. At this stage we cannot help but reject the cultural domination and arrogance responsible for the belief that only the western partisan political system is perfect. There is evidence that many African leaders reject foreign ideologies and are beginning to think out their own ideology and political systems. Their disillusionment with party politics and other experiments with the western democratic institutions has given rise to the current search for African values even in politics.

In the South African situation meaningful democracy will be the kind that will allow Africans to work out their own system based on their cultural values. In South Africa and probably elsewhere, Africans have lost confidence in the western, so-called democratic, systems which in their application have become the preserve of the whites and have left the Africans out in the cold. Inkatha is, therefore, not a political party for we do not believe in partisanship at all. As politics is merely one of the many fronts we are using in our liberation efforts Inkatha is a national movement which is open to all. Our doubts about the suitability of the partisan system mean that we reject multi-partyism as well as single-partyism. We believe in the representation of different sectors of society in the national movement. No cut-and-dried system of government is ready for presentation to the world at this stage. All we maintain is that we are capable of devising our own arrangement and pattern which will meet our political requirements.

Working on various fronts such as the educational, economic, political and spiritual ones, our movement purports to abolish all forms of colonialism, racism, intimidation, discrimination and segregation based on tribe, clan, sex, colour or creed and to ensure the acceptance of the principles of equal opportunity and treatment of all people in all walks of life.

With us in this part of the continent political liberation will only be meaningful if it comes with the total liberation of our people. Please note that this is not a tribal movement. To us culture means more than mere tribal ties. There is no reason why African cultural assertiveness should not manifest itself on a macro-cultural level - that is, the continental level or the sub-continental or regional levels.

One of the main objectives of Inkatha is to fight for the liberation and unification of Southern Africa. KwaZulu, as our President has taken pains to point out, is merely a launching-pad. The movement aims at fostering the spirit of unity among the people of KwaZulu throughout Southern Africa, and between them and all their brothers in Southern Africa, and to co-operate locally and internationally with all progressive African and other nationalist movements that strive for the attainment of African unity.

After a thorough study of the complex South African situation, we, through our National Cultural Liberation

Movement, propose to adopt and follow new non-violent strategies for the ultimate and complete liberation of the Africans. We hope we shall be understood as saying that we want to explore all non-military fronts in our struggle. In this sense non-violence does not mean non-action but rather various self-help activities which stem from the people. After mobilising the people the Inkatha leaders will work out a clear and well-graduated programme of positive action.

Inkatha (The National Cultural Liberation Movement): Resolutions, 1975

(Bhekuzulu College, Nongoma, 18 and 19 July 1975)

INKATHA RESOLVES

1 / That this conference fully supports the decision of the KwaZulu Legislative Assembly not to ask for independence for the separate pieces of inadequate portless land for the Zulus.

2.1 / That this conference appreciates and supports the stand taken by the Legislative Assembly in insisting that Article No. 26 of the Universal Declaration of Human Rights be adopted as a fundamental principle in our system of education.

2.2 / That the medium of instruction for the Zulu children living in 'white' areas be changed to conform to the requirements of the KwaZulu Legislative Assembly.

2.3 / That special schools be established to teach mathematics and science so as to increase the number of African medical and technical students.

2.4 / That more emphasis be placed on differentiated education in our post-primary schools.

2.5 / That farm schools be so controlled that children attending these schools are not required to leave school to perform compulsory labour on the farms.

2.6 / That the importance of agriculture and the dignity of labour be given a prominent place in our system of education.

2.7 / That enough pre-schools be established.

2.8 / That the Department of Bantu Education be requested to cater adequately for the Zulu children living in the Orange Free State.

2.9 / That post-primary school pupils be encouraged to attend vacation schools where they will receive instruction on nation building.

2.10 / That members of Inkatha give their fullest support to communities everywhere to erect more classrooms and undertake to urge our government to find more resources for revenue.

3.1 / That the South African Government be requested

to hand over the Department of Health to the KwaZulu Government.

3.2 / That an appeal be made to the South African Government to refrain from taking over mission hospitals in KwaZulu, until the KwaZulu Government takes over the Department of Health, because this taking over may lead to a loss of many doctors at present engaged in the Health Service.

3.3 / That the KwaZulu Government should extend and establish community health schemes structured to involve the Women's Brigade and Youth Brigade.

3.4. / That the paucity of African students being admitted for medicine at the University of Natal be discussed with the university authorities and that other universities be used for training our medical students.

4 / That this conference endorses the policy of the KwaZulu Government on the industrial development of KwaZulu. This conference in its awareness of the dangers entailed in the polarisation of wealth and poverty in any society, accepts that the people must have a stake in the wealth of their land. With this realisation in mind, this conference accepts the KwaZulu Development Corporation, as the economic arm of the government of KwaZulu for the economic development of KwaZulu.

4.1 / That this conference urges the KwaZulu Government to be vigilant to ensure that the KwaZulu Development Corporation, should be in the control of KwaZulu Government along certain lines of the National Development Corporation of Tanzania, which allows partnerships with private firms that permit up to and not more than 50 per cent of the equity by the firms concerned.

4.2 /That this conference accepts the idea of tripartite companies in which the people of KwaZulu can also participate.

5 / That this conference appreciates the fact that the United Nations has probably been the most important body in the world that has kept the issue of racial discrimination in South Africa before the eyes of the international community since the founding of the United Nations; whilst appreciative of this, this conference wishes to bring before the eyes of the world the fact that South Africa is an area of social, cultural and political change; whilst admitting that black people in South Africa are not a free people, this conference consisting of elected representatives of the Zulu people

wishes to state that only they and they alone can judge who their legitimate leaders and spokesmen are, within the situation in which they find themselves.

5.1 / That this conference rejects the allegations so often flung around that no one, in the situation here, speaks for blacks. They accept unreservedly the leadership given in the situation by their leader Chief M.G. Buthelezi in advancing their interests, and in interpreting their aspirations and those of other blacks in this difficult situation. While appreciative of admissions made by the South African Ambassador at the United Nations, Mr R.F. (Pik) Botha, that racial discrimination is indefensible, they deplore the failure of the South African Government to give blacks in South Africa meaningful decision-making machinery and a just share in the wealth of their country. This conference would like to warn the South African Government that it is making it increasingly difficult for the Zulu people not to instruct their leader to join those who urge the expulsion of South Africa from the United Nations, something he has not done so far. This conference urges the government to give blacks of South Africa a right to determine their destiny, and freedom which at present remains the prerogative of whites, in order to avoid forcing the decision on them, of joining those who are urging such expulsion of South Africa from the world body.

6 / That on the policy of investment or disinvestments in South Africa, this conference expresses its appreciation for the pressures that are brought to bear on the multi-national corporations to force them to help blacks to reach economic justice. This conference wishes to express its support for constructive engagement rather than disengagement. In taking this view, the conference is influenced by the restrictions imposed on blacks only and implemented through the pass laws and influx control regulations. These regulations make every job for an African vital, since they cannot bargain freely unlike members of other races in a free labour market, and are denied the right to have trade unions. The pressures on the industries should therefore be geared towards equal pay for equal work, fringe benefits and pension schemes for black workers, bursary schemes for the workers and their children and support for efforts to persuade the government to recognise existing and the establishment of new African trade unions. This

conference, whilst highly appreciative of the efforts of all organisations and agencies that keep the apartheid scourge before the eyes of the international community, wants to emphasise that in the final analysis the actual liberation of blacks will have to be performed by blacks themselves within the borders of South Africa, whatever methods the people decide to use to effect their liberation.

7 / That this National Conference of Inkatha Yenkululeko Yesizwe

(i) urges the Central Committe to establish a regular informative brochure aimed at:

(a) giving a clear perspective of our past history as the black people of South Africa;

(b) giving a perspective of African democracy in action in the past and as envisaged by Inkatha;

(c) giving periodical corrections to misguided views which appear in news media from time to time; and further

(ii) urges KwaZulu Legislative Assembly to set up a KwaZulu radio broadcasting station to keep the citizens of KwaZulu well informed in educational, cultural and financial spheres of KwaZulu life;

(iii) waives the application of constitutional Clause 17 (1) in Chapter III which reads: 'All members of the Central Committee shall be full-time National Headquarters officials of the movement'.

8 / That this National Conference of Inkatha views with concern the concerted efforts of certain exiled South Africans who denigrate Chief Buthelezi as a puppet or stooge of Mr Vorster's regime. This conference therefore rejects with contempt such allegations and wishes to place on record their deep and sincere appreciation of Chief Buthelezi's stand, his forthright fight for his black people and his wise and strong political leadership of the Zulu nation. This conference further accept him as the unchallenged leader of the 4½ million Zulus in their struggle for their cultural, economic, educational and political liberation. This conference further empowers him, or his representatives, to speak and act freely on behalf of the 4½ million Zulus within and outside the borders of South Africa and this conference accepts also his commitment to the liberation of all black people of South Africa.

9 / That Inkatha requests the KwaZulu Government to

approach the Republican Government and discuss the question of the R3 levy which is KwaZulu Government levy on all Zulu males. This conference is concerned that there is no provision for the collecting of the R3 levy in white areas while there is provision for the R2,50 tax by the Republican Government.

10 / That the National Cultural Liberation Movement does all in its power to bring an end to the mental and legal slavery of our womenfolk, especially that slavery based on the Natal Code.(1)

11 / That this conference fully supports the KwaZulu Government in its decision to invite Checkers to establish businesses in certain areas in KwaZulu on terms proposed by the government.

12 / That although this conference rejects the policy of separate development, it fully supports the KwaZulu Government in its fight for the liberation of the black people.

12.1 / That this conference recommends the planning of a new non-violent strategy for the ultimate and complete liberation of the Africans.

NOTE

(1) The Natal Code refers to code of law collected during the nineteenth century in Natal in order to clarify traditional law and custom for administration by the courts. This code encapsulates the low status of the woman in tribal society.

THE NON-INDEPENDENT HOMELANDS: BOPHUTHA-TSWANA

BophuthaTswana Today

LUCAS M. MANGOPE

(Excerpts from address delivered to commerce students of the Universities of Cape Town and Stellenbosch on the occasion of the Peter Kruger Memorial Lecture, 9 August 1972)

The 600 000 or so Tswana people in the Republic of Botswana are blood brothers of ours, who speak the same language and enjoy the same customs. On account of an artificial boundary, we have, however, no official connection whatsoever. Our villages, unlike those of the Nguni, are as a rule compact, but for administration purposes are divided into wards or 'kgotlas', each of which is headed by a headman, who is responsible to the chief and tribal council for law and order in his ward. Tribal organisation based on the leadership of chiefs and headmen is of the utmost importance. The chief of the tribe is the 'father' and personification of the tribe. The chief is supposed to be the repository of tribal tradition and custom. He is the symbol of authority, who exercises his power in council and is responsible for the welfare of the tribe. We say the chief is the tribe and the tribe is the chief. Altogether my homeland has 63 chiefs. For very good reasons my government decided to continue the republican government's practice of respecting the autonomy of tribes within tribal areas, and provision for this autonomy is enshrined in our constitution.

In the main we are rather small and wiry in stature (I believe I am an exception), because of the hard natural conditions we have to overcome in order to survive. We are a quiet, peace-loving and law-abiding people, especially in respect of laws we accept and understand. It is obvious that we particularly love our tribal laws, for to us they make sense. As leader of my people, I would like to emphasise the need for consultation with us on all laws that affect us before they are passed by the republican parliament. I am disturbed by the number of my people who fill up the republic's prisons for contraventions of laws about which we were never consulted, and some of whose need we do not feel. It is gratifying to note that white conscience is beginning to be disturbed over this matter.

Our new constitution, especially prepared by us with a view to the attainment of self-government, provides for a Legislative Assembly of 72 members, 48 of whom are designated by Regional Authorities, while the remaining 24 are elected by Tswana people inside and outside BophuthaTswana. We have been severely criticised in certain quarters for the large number of designated members, but we believe we must lead our people from what they know to what they do not know, for the concept of a general election is unknown in our traditional administration. Anything that grows changes, and as we grow in knowledge and experience we may feel the need for change in this respect.

Our education is not compulsory and free; it is, on the contrary, voluntary and very expensive when considered in terms of our earning power, and yet we find that there is a great eagerness and enthusiasm to acquire knowledge. You will see our children along the roads on a cold and frosty morning, miles away from school, hurrying on foot to be in time, so that they do not miss any opportunities. It does not seem to me that the white children always appreciate this gift of knowledge, which they can have for the asking. White children have had a natural basic training, around the meal tables in the family, by looking at books, going on holiday, seeing films before even reaching school. These sources of basic knowledge have yet to be experienced by many of my people.

Since the inception of Bantu education some eighteen years ago, our children have been taught in the medium of Setswana for the first eight years of their schooling and in English and Afrikaans, on an equal basis, in their secondary and high school years. That this arrangement has not been altogether acceptable to my people, is evidenced by repeated motions from various regions over the years for a revision of this system (regions are constituents of the Legislative Assembly). At the last sitting of the Legislative Assembly this year, a resolution was unanimously passed to have the system investigated, with a view to reverting to English and Afrikaans as media of instruction in our primary schools

This will no doubt cause much difficulty and perhaps even disruption of our education system, for most of our present day teachers are products of the present system. Much care will have to be exercised. While we are concerned about the deteriorating standard of English and Afrikaans, which languages are a source of knowledge in the form of books, especially text books, our own language is highly treasured as God's heritage, which we would like to preserve and develop, all the more because by Act of the republican parliament, we reserve the right to declare it a third official language in BophuthaTswana, a right my Legislative Assembly eagerly exercised.

Most of our post-matriculation students attend the University of the North at Turfloop, but by reason of our school population and because we believe that the physical presence of a university or university branch is an important part of the cultural and economic development of a people, the Tswana have started a university fund, and already R85 000 has been contributed voluntarily to it.

On 29 July 1972 the Potchefstroom Students Representative Council came over to Mafeking and to our pleasant surprise donated R1 000 towards this fund. Anything that grows changes, and as the number of our educated grows, we hope to afford our children the natural basic training that you enjoy, which is so conducive to study and which so readily facilitates educational progress.

Political growth has led to a change of my homeland's name from Tswanaland to BophuthaTswana, which means 'the place where the Tswana people abide', and which was given to the homeland by our Legislative Assembly. BophuthaTswana is composed of nineteen separate areas of land which are situated in the Western Transvaal and North-Eastern Cape. There is an isolated area at Thaba Nchu in the Orange Free State - our Caprivi Strip - in terms of distance from our headquarters. All in all, it is at present a land area covering 3 754 018 hectares or 36 197 square km made up, as I have indicated, of bits and pieces, which makes administration extremely difficult. We have been informed by the republican government that consolidation proposals will be made known soon. We sincerely hope that real and proper consultation and negotiations will take place and that we shall be involved in determining the boundaries of BophuthaTswana. I consider the question of adequate land for my people absolutely basic to the success of the policy of separate development, for without an equitable distribution of land amongst the different nations of our country we should not expect those peaceful and harmonious relations between whites and blacks which all of us so very much desire.

The land allocation to the Tswana people in terms of the Land Acts of 1913 and 1936 is altogether insufficient and much too small to constitute an independent sovereign state, which in terms of policy, we aspire to. These two Land Acts in my opinion were intended to be the Native Reserve of those days. I maintain that our population has since greatly increased and that an amendment of these Acts is necessary, especially because in terms of policy, the Tswana in urban areas are ultimately to settle in BophuthaTswana.

Anything worthwhile that one has done and paid for, one is proud of, and one feels it is truly one's own. Though unable to say exactly what our repayment ability is, the Legislative Assembly at its last session authorised my cabinet to negotiate with the South African government for a loan of R5 million payable over a period of five years, for we feel we should ourselves contribute towards the building of our own capital. We would like our capital to be built as soon as possible since Mafeking is totally inadequate, even for our present needs. We are aware of the economic climate throughout the world and realise that eventually the costs of building a capital will be far in excess of our contribution of R4 million. The intention is to build this new capital at Heystekrand, and with a character of its own, which to us is an immensely important consideration. The other R1 million we propose to expend on building extra schools for, as it happens, the building of schools is the financial responsibility of the individual communities or tribes which is a crippling burden on their meagre resources. We still have, as I have pointed out, to negotiate over this loan with the South African government. We should rather experience the effects of such a loan from our South African government than from a foreign government, at this stage.

I wish to state humbly that my people and I are aware of the fact that we stand on the threshold of an exciting but challenging future, a future that will no doubt extend to the utmost the manhood in us. Man's supreme and most crucial task in our age, in my opinion, is to build a common ground of understanding, that is essential for the promotion of the world. The existing and ever-increasing gap between the have and have-not nations of the world confronts humanity with a serious problem that threatens the attainment of peace and stability throughout the world.

Even here in South Africa our greatest national responsibility is to foster understanding and harmonious co-existence among our various racial and ethnic groups. We can only achieve success in this momentous task by ensuring a more equitable distribution of our national wealth, and a more balanced economic development programme over the rest of our country. Unbalanced and unfair distribution of wealth can only bring friction and lasting instability to a country. South Africa is a rich country, but only the white areas fall within this category. Our Bantu homelands can only be rightly construed as underdeveloped and backwards, within a properous and dynamic economy.

Until recently it has been the exclusive responsibility of successive white governments to hatch plans and propose solutions for the development problems of Bantu areas. Their traditional approach has not always been rational and completely objective. One has suspected that it has, to a great extent, been motivated and governed by considerations of self-interest and self-preservation, rather than by the actual needs and circumstances of the black people. For too long we were regarded as 'the Native Problem'. To my mind this was a very serious misconception and an absolutely erroneous way of regarding the situation of the black people in South Africa. This misleading assertion implied that the black people were a problem, which only the white people were competent to solve.

May it be clearly accepted, once and for all, that our interests and ideals are not different from those of whites. We utterly resent being relegated to differential treatment in all spheres of life. What is hurting to a white man is equally hurting to us. The best that white South Africa desires for herself, we desire for ourselves. Rather we should be regarded as an asset and not a problem. We shall always be willing and only too glad to do the very best we are capable of towards the creation of stability and peace in our beloved country, for I believe it is only in that climate that our hopes and efforts for progress in the development of our homelands will attain fulfilment. In any plan or scheme intended for the development of our homelands, our voice and our fullest participation should be the principal sine qua non.

The mistake in the past and to a lesser extent today, has always been that we have not shared in decision-making on matters that vitally affect us. We can only be reasonably expected to give unswerving support to those projects and ventures in the planning and execution of which we are directly involved. That is what we believe the policy of separate development has for us.

African Liberation

LUCAS M. MANGOPE

(Press statement, 8 September 1972)

Up till now I have been silent regarding the African nations' expressed desires and intentions to assist and to 'liberate' their black brethren in Southern Africa.

It has been my view that as the positive aspects of the policy of separate development became more apparent, our brethren in the north would realise that the door to self-determination and eventual independence was also open to the black nations in Southern Africa and that they would then change their attitude and rather give moral support to our own efforts for the speedy implementation of a policy which promises so much. I have been sadly disillusioned.

They who know nothing about our conditions and problems in this country have individually and collectively in the world councils arrogated to themselves the right to judge, to condemn and to appear, unasked, as the champions of the oppressed peoples in Southern Africa. Now I pose the questions: How did they attain independence? With outside help or by their own efforts? Who interfered from outside to assist them? Do they regard us, their black brethren as they like to call us, too immature, too stupid, too cowardly to fight our own battles? In other words, do they think they are superior to us and that they should decide for us what is best for us? Do they think that such an ineffective lot (as they seem to think we are here in the south) should be allowed to govern ourselves when the white man's shackles have been forcibly removed? Or have they the intention of taking over the white man's guardianship?

I realise that the leaders of the African nations base their views and actions on information received from unreliable sources. I also realise that some of them are probably motivated by a desire to help, but as leader of the Tswana people in the Republic of South Africa I say bluntly that we desire no interference in our domestic affairs. To organise so-called 'liberation' movements to fight the governments in Southern Africa would not help at all.

Much violence has been done in the name of the Lord God and in the name of Allah. Man's own self-created organisation for preservation of peace, the United Nations, has failed signally because of dissension among and self-interest of its members. God's own creation, the church, has also failed because of its failure to preach God's own word. Moral support and sustenance for 'freedom fighters' are nothing more than complicity in murder of the innocent.

I and others who are leading our people in a responsible manner are daily reaping rewards for that effort, but we are not consulted by United Nations committees or African countries purporting to speak on our behalf. I and other African leaders in South Africa have spoken our minds freely. We have criticised the negative aspects of the policy of separate development, but have supported the positive aspects with hardly any publicity or acclaim in a world which arrogates to itself the right to decide what is best for us, without regard to what we ourselves wish. I prefer to be a stooge for my own people rather than of popular world opinion. I am totally against the concept of black solidarity where it implies the grouping together of blacks purely because their skins are black, as against whites purely because their skins are white. To me that is an intolerable racist attitude. But in South Africa I am absolutely in favour of rejection of outside interference in our affairs.

I challenge anyone, the United Nations included, to say that any responsible black leader in South Africa supports the activities of terrorists or, as they are conveniently called, 'freedom fighters' or the barring of our sportsmen from international competition, or the withdrawal of investments.

BophuthaTswana National Party: Manifesto, BophuthaTswana General Election, 1972

1 / CHARACTER OF PARTY

The party:

(a) acknowledges that loyalty to BophuthaTswana and the existence of mutual understanding, the infusion of a sense of common purpose and unity, amongst all citizens of BophuthaTswana are not only essential pre-conditions for development, but also some of the major objectives of the party;

(b) aims to build a strong and secure BophuthaTswana Nationalism based on a fair and equal treatment of, and unbiased recognition of the rights and privileges of, each and every BophuthaTswana citizen;

(c) aims to be and shall always be the political home of all BophuthaTswana citizens within or without the borders of BophuthaTswana.

2 / ECONOMIC CONSIDERATIONS

A. The party will strive to exploit all possible channels that can, directly or indirectly, contribute towards the realisation of an economically sound BophuthaTswana.

B. Agriculture

(a) The party believes that 'with the provision of timely and adequate credit facilities, technical assistance, training and facilities for the marketing and distribution of products, the land will become for the man who develops it the basis of his economic stability, the foundation of his increasing welfare, and the guarantee of his freedom and dignity'.

(b) The party will

(i) promote the exploitation of all the land available to BophuthaTswana to its maximum potential with a view to achieve maximum productivity;

(ii) promote the establishment of voluntary economic organisations like co-operatives since they are essential in providing access to sources of credit, ensuring reasonable prices for farm products and making consumer goods available at lower cost. Credit facilities to farmers; e.g. for implements, fertilisers, etc. will enable them to improve their farming techniques thereby enhancing increased productivity;

(iii) strive for the establishment and/or improvement of irrigation schemes and negotiate with the Republican government for usage of water emanating from sources outside the borders of BophuthaTswana; e.g. the take over of the Klipvoordam in Hammanskraal, the Houwater dam in Pilanesberg; the improvement of the Taung irrigation scheme and the take over of the Lindleyspoort dam for the purpose of generating our own electricity in BophuthaTswana etc.;

(iv) investigate the marketing of consumer goods so as to ensure the highest possible benefit to the farmer;

(v) strive to improve the quality of livestock by granting farmers financial assistance for the purchase of studstock;

(vi) strive to improve services at cattle sales since they are hitherto not always satisfactory and to encourage citizens to become auctioneers themselves;

(vii) encourage the production of more milk in BophuthaTswana by, for example, the establishment of milk-schemes where possible so that BophuthaTswana citizens should themselves provide dairy products to all institutions within BophuthaTswana;

(viii) clamour for as much land as shall meet the needs of BophuthaTswana;

(ix) institute a land board which will

(a) investigate all land requirements of BophuthaTswana and represent the BophuthaTswana government in negotiations with Republican government for more land;

(b) represent the BophuthaTswana government in all deliberations appertaining to the consolidation of BophuthaTswana - with the background knowledge that some citizens are presently expected to make a living out of 2-3 morgen of land.

C. Commerce and Industry

The party will strive for

(a) and encourage the establishment of border industries since they ease the unemployment problem facing BophuthaTswana;

(b) and encourage the establishment of industries within the borders of BophuthaTswana where citizens shall have the right to buy shares with a view to ultimate take over of those industries and employees the right to be appropriately trained without the hindrance of job reservation laws;

(c) political stability within BophuthaTswana so as to enable industrialists to establish industries within the borders of BophuthaTswana without any fears;

(d) and clamour for a reasonable living wage to be paid out to employees by both border industries and those within BophuthaTswana and, also, to represent the urban BophuthaTswana citizen in the struggle for the betterment of his earnings and conditions of employment;

(e) and see to it that entrepreneurs who are citizens of BophuthaTswana be given first preference in the establishment of industries;

(f) the establishment of a National Industrial Corporation Fund with a view to financing capable BophuthaTswana entrepreneurs;

(g) the representation of BophuthaTswana opinions and views in the decision-making processes of institutions like the Bantu Investment Corporation of S.A. and the right for citizens to become directors and/or buy shares in B.I.C. undertakings like the Ga-Rankuwa Brewery;

(h) the reduction of the 7½ per cent interest presently charged on all B.I.C. loans;

(i) and see to it that capable BophuthaTswana citizens are free to establish their own businesses without prior consultations with the B.I.C.;

(j) and see to it that the B.I.C. monopoly of having the sole right to purchase business sites in BophuthaTswana be done away with and all business sites be surveyed and sold directly to capable and interested citizens;

(k) the appointment of our own licencing boards consisting of citizens;

(l) and see to it that only BophuthaTswana citizens qualify for trading rights in BophuthaTswana;

(m) and see to it that the Bantu Mining Corporation and private mining houses do more prospecting and mining in BophuthaTswana so as to exploit, to the full, its rich mineral endowment;

(n) and see to it that all mining taxes paid out to the Republican government for mining in BophuthaTswana be paid out to the BophuthaTswana government - this holds for any other industrial undertaking in BophuthaTswana for which the Republican government benefits by taxation;

(o) and see to it that preference is always given to BophuthaTswana citizens in the allocation of all mining sub-contracts, e.g. cartage, etc., available in BophuthaTswana.

3 / EDUCATION

(a) The party believes it would be to the best interests of BophuthaTswana, at all times to give priority over the evolvement and implementation of a sound, suitable and acceptable educational system.

(b) The party will strive for the implementation of compulsory education as soon as possible since it believes it is the best method to eradicate illiteracy.

(c) The party will do its utmost to ease the teacher-shortage problem and grant bursaries to and encourage as many students as possible to join the teaching profession.

(d) In order to ease the school-shortage problem the party aims to negotiate with the central government for a loan of about one million rand so as to supplement the present efforts of communities and tribal authorities.

(e) The party aims to agitate for the diversion of the B.I.C. Bantu beer profits to our school building programme.

(f) The party believes that not only does our high school population warrant the establishment of our own university but that its physical presence is also essential for our economic and cultural development.

(g) The party will strive for the erection of a technical high school and see to it that students produced by this school get apprenticed accordingly.

(h) Since the party admits that educational progress is largely dependent on the quality and contentment of the teaching personnel, it aims to build a contented and happy teaching profession by, inter alia, improving salaries and creating better conditions of service.

(i) The party will not venture to debar teachers from founding an organisation that would cater for the interests of all BophuthaTswana teachers.

4 / SOCIAL WELFARE

(a) The party aims to strive for

(1) increased old-age pensions;

(2) the establishment of old-age homes where possible;

(3) the accommodation of, training of, and the provision of recreational facilities for the disabled;

(4) the establishment of as many clinics with maternity

depots as are necessary;
(5) the creation of more training facilities for nurses;
(6) the appointment of our own doctors as district surgeons and senior medical officers at the same salaries paid out to their colleagues of the same status;
(7) the employment of as many social workers as possible and the creation of good working conditions of service;
(8) the construction of a stadium of world standard which would enable us, amongst other things, to produce sportsmen of world rank.

(b) The party aims to negotiate with the central government for a loan of about four million rand for the erection of a capital which would have a character of its own and be of our own liking.

(c) The Party will see to it that the housing programme in BophuthaTswana makes provision for a variety of tastes in size, comfort, etc..

(d) The party realises the immense significance of the absence of community halls in some areas and aims to attend to this matter actively.

(e) The party is satisfied that there are some areas in BophuthaTswana which are well-suited for the establishment of holiday resorts and aims to get these areas accordingly developed by either private enterprise or the BophuthaTswana government.

(f) The party will see to it that police stations and other institutions meant for the safety and well-being of citizens be put up where necessary.

5 / CITIZENSHIP

The party will see to it that the Tswana and all those non-Tswanas legally domiciled in BophuthaTswana qualify for citizenship.

6 / CIVIL SERVICE

(i) All posts in the civil service of BophuthaTswana are meant for BophuthaTswana citizens and the party will strive to see to it that all non-citizens of BophuthaTswana are replaced by suitable citizens;

(ii) the party will see to it that previous experience and salary are taken into consideration when new appointments are made and strive for the general improvement of salaries;

(iii) the party will strive for the permanent appointment of married women, lady teachers included;

(iv) the party will see to it that civil servants are, as far as possible, housed with due regard to their rank and status.

7 / RELATIONS WITH REPUBLICAN GOVERNMENT

(1) The BophuthaTswana National Party firmly re-affirms its acceptance and support of the positive aspects of the policy of separate development, e.g. separate but equal development in all spheres of life, and the government of the party will function within the framework of this policy.

(2) The party will, as far as is humanly possible, strive for cordial relations with the government of the Republic of South Africa and differences shall be settled around a conference table.

Seoposengwe Party: Manifesto, BophuthaTswana General Election, 1972

(a) We accept the policy of separate development only for the implied promise of handing back to us our homeland (forefathers' land) and particularly for the promise of granting BophuthaTswana its ultimate sovereign independence.

(b) We consider the greatest asset of BophuthaTswana to be its human material and propose to give that a top priority in our sense of values as well as first consideration in our programme of development of a free, dignified, and contented human being second to none in every respect. Our touchstone is the motto 'Nihil nisi optimum' (Nothing will do unless it be the best).

(c) We believe that a government must come from the people, i.e. it must be elected by the people, for the people, and must act on behalf of the people. In other words a government must identify itself with the needs and aspirations of the people.

Further, it is our pledge, among other things, to work for the fulfilment of the points stated below.

1 / EDUCATION

In order to accelerate the tempo of Development to Independence it is essential to embark upon a crash programme for the raising of general educational standards throughout BophuthaTswana.

It is a praiseworthy effort to campaign for a university but in our sense of priorities, it is the student body rather than buildings that constitutes a university. In order to achieve this desired end, we feel, we must first insist upon the immediate introduction of a system of free and compulsory education, at least, at the primary schools level, as well as adult literacy.

This will in turn ensure a sound secondary education system with a higher percentage of students undergoing higher academic, vocational, and technical training from which a university can draw its supply of students.

2 / LAND

(a) The old idea of native reserves has now given place to the modern concept of the Bantu homelands.

Unlike a reserve a homeland is a completely new concept that has gained in dimension. It is a consolidated large mass of land rather than the scattered fragments of land dotted all over the country as we know them today.

(b) Batswana still know very well their early 19th century historical and geographical homeland and they would welcome the handing back of their land to its rightful owners as early as possible, so as to make independence feasible and meaningful.

(c) Any demarcation of the boundary of their land and its consolidation should be with the express consultation and participation of the parties concerned to ensure that their views are taken into consideration.

3 / ECONOMY

We believe that the success of an independent state cannot be achieved without a sound and dynamic economy. Therefore we propose that:

(a) In major plans and schemes for the exploitation of the mineral wealth and the establishment of industries, the BophuthaTswana government should have the final say as to whom to approach for the exploitation of such minerals, and the siting of such industries or growth points.

(b) Entrepreneurship by aliens should be allowed but kept short of BophuthaTswana government getting so used to it as to become unable to accept Tswana entrepreneurship at a later stage.

(c) The Bantu Investment Corporation should operate initially in BophuthaTswana until such time as a Batswana Development Corporation shall have been established not only in name but in fact.

4 / ADMINISTRATION

(a) In view of the vast expanse of BophuthaTswana territory we feel that general administration should be more decentralised. Local bodies such as regional authorities, tribal authorities, urban councils, school boards, school committees, licensing boards, agricultural boards, health boards etc. should take over some of the duties which take much of the Cabinet Ministers' time.

Decentralisation will give more people participation in the running of their own country.

(b) Our central, regional and local governments should act as employment agents to help find employment for the many potential tax-payers who are at present unemployed.

(c) There should be a gradual phasing out of aliens

by replacing them with Tswana nationals. This process should start from the bottom and be applied gradually, until the higher positions are reached in every department of state.

Tswana National Party: Manifesto, BophuthaTswana General Election, 1972

VOTE FOR MMASE ROSE MODISE (Taung Constituency)

If you vote for me, I promise to fight for you in Mafeking for the following:

1 / Factories for Taung, especially Pampierstad, so that people can be employed.

2 / Machines for reaping. Hands are too wasteful.

3 / Taung must have a Tswana Superintendent for the distribution of irrigation waters.

4 / An enquiry into the plight of the people of Majeng and the conditions of their removal.

5 / Disability and old-age pensions for all Tswanas to be increased.

6 / Better education and building of a Tswana university.

7 / At Mafeking in the BophuthaTswana Legislative Assembly.

8 / In all urban areas.

9 / For a Tswana Industrial Development Corporation, controlled by Tswanas, to replace Bantu Investment Corporation.

THE NON-INDEPENDENT HOMELANDS: LEBOWA

Challenges in Homeland Development

CEDRIC N. PHATUDI

(Excerpts from an address on the occasion of the Golden Jubilee Celebrations of the African Teachers' Association of South Africa, held at Inanda Seminary, Durban, 18 December 1971)

In Africa, the main political trends in the sixties are familiar and only a brief and not an elaborate treatment of these should suffice. Radical changes took place. European colonial powers withdrew from the scene, giving way to governments by black independent states. The tremendous changes affected black states in west, central and east Africa and reached out also to the black states of Botswana, Lesotho and Swaziland. In some instances the withdrawals were followed by bloody upheavals and civil commotions. The events in the Congo, Ghana and Nigeria may be recalled. Other instances however, did not have dire consequences. On the contrary, the spirit of 'uhuru' was channelled constructively. It could now be said that the former colonial peoples are determining their own fate. This is a stage of development which is not only desirable but necessary as it works towards the fulfilment of the political aspirations of the people of the black states concerned.

The impact of these political changes was felt even in the Republic of South Africa. Hitherto the latter firmly believed in and rigidly carried out a 'segregation policy'. The revolutionary changes all round this continent compelled the Republic of South Africa to modify in some measure its policy of segregation. A policy known under more than one name was adopted. In some quarters the policy is called 'apartheid'. In others it is known as 'self-determination in own areas'. And yet another name is 'separate freedoms'. In pursuance of this policy, the republican government has passed legislation for seven budding Bantu Legislative Assemblies. The most senior of these Legislative Assemblies is that of the Transkei. The intention or purpose of this legislation is that the various Bantu groups, each with its own language and background, should have self-rule in its area but within the confines of the Republic of South Africa.

Whether or not this political structure will work out successfully and harmoniously is the problem of the seventies and possibly of the early eighties. The crux of the matter is that the South African Bantu desires and demands full-fledged independence like that of Lesotho, Botswana and Swaziland. In this connection, not even the Transkei has reached the mark! There are admittedly intractable though not insurmountable problems. I wish to invite attention to some of these briefly. Many a politician, black or white, tends to stress differences and to ignore similarities. The differences thus stressed are, strictly speaking, not vital though they have some emotional, not rational, content. Things like tribal, ethnic, denominational, language and colour differences may be cited. But, all these become unimportant when the nature or similarity of man as man, the child of God, is taken into account. Man's basic needs are the same all around the world. In seriously providing for his needs man has built not only a moral world but also a scientific and technological world which unites and does not divide men all around the globe. Alongside this man builds an economic and commercial world which unites men as well. He seeks to communicate. He seeks dialogue everywhere. If he does not do so, he will invite his own doom. And South Africa is no exception. It is, therefore, reasonable and wise for the politicians of the various national groups within this country to reverse the trend and stress the similarities or unities and not to stress differences. In other words, the common goals, the common destiny, of man be put before the nations. That is the challenge of the seventies and possibly of the early eighties. The totality of the human personality, the totality of the universe and the totality of God Himself should teach us to think more in wholes than in scattered bits and pieces.

There is yet another problem, namely, that there are some black politicians who blame the white politicians for all the difficulties and shortcomings in this country. This approach now misfires since the battle has moved on. The white politician has conceded that the policy of underdog and topdog, the essence of the segregation policy, has failed and that the black politician must take up the cudgels himself and work out his destiny in spite of heavy and numerous problems in his way under a policy of 'separate freedoms'. Thus there is not much point in blaming a generation past or present but there is point in positively facing the realities of the existing political situation. Indeed, there is yet another group of black politicians, who accept and praise the policy of separate development or separate freedoms, husks and all, forgetting that in all history there is no policy that man down the ages has ever evolved that is free from imperfections. Consequently not unlike previous policies that were tried, the present policy has merits and demerits and it is our duty to use that which is good in it and to improve upon the imperfections. That will be the meaning of progress in political life and that is the challenge of the future.

Policy Statement

CEDRIC N. PHATUDI

(Address delivered in the Lebowa Legislative Assembly, 28 May 1972)

Everybody in Lebowa, in South Africa, and, I dare say, in the world, is aware of the sweeping and rapid changes that are occurring in political arrangements and economics and also in social relationships. In the circumstances people are called upon to make quick adjustments to meet the demands of the times but people unfortunately are painfully slow in their reaction. In fact many people in this country in particular prefer to cling to a dying past than to respond quickly and intelligently to a challenging present and unknown future. The position is an interesting one indeed.

The proposals regarding the consolidation of Lebowa territory have been placed by His Excellency the Commissioner General before the various Regional Authorities in Lebowa but these proposals have not been placed before this legislature for attention. It is understood that those proposals have been rejected by all the Regional Authorities concerned but I maintain that this honourable house must be afforded an opportunity to examine and debate the issue so that Lebowa's standpoint may be known. Maybe a special committee may be chosen to go into this matter carefully and to report to parliament. As things are, there are now fourteen pieces of land constituting the territory of Lebowa. I gather that according to the proposals of the republican government the fourteen pieces are to be consolidated into five. Eventually, therefore, the territory of Lebowa will consist of five pieces should these proposals be accepted. I must point out that assuming Lebowa will consist of five pieces when consolidated, it will be impossible to govern effectively a country consisting of five scattered pieces. I maintain that consolidation should be complete and not a half measure. Five pieces are definitely a half-measure. Strictly speaking it is not consolidation, but it is a partial consolidation which is unsatisfactory. Complete and satisfactory consolidation must mean putting the five pieces together into one coherent mass of area. This could be achieved without mass removal of people if black and white people in Lebowa and Northern Transvaal generally will accept one another. That is, if the citizens of South Africa will not allow themselves to be the victims of superiority and/or inferiority complexes and if our people and our white neighbours will think for themselves and not have others think for them. Mutual trust and confidence in one another must be engendered now as never before.

I believe the blacks and the whites must and can live together in peace and harmony and happiness in this part of South Africa not on the basis of competition but of co-operation and mutual trust. The people of Lebowa must accept this challenge and responsibility and so should and can our white neighbours. Nobody should lose in this arrangement provided we hold proper dialogue in this regard. Indeed I believe that a satisfactory way can be found which will be in the interests of all the population groups concerned. I must emphasise that it is the policy of this government to live in peace and happiness as well as in co-operation with all our neighbours be they white or black. We will make this point quite clear to the Republican government at the earliest possible opportunity.

Flowing from the whole problem of consolidation is the question whether Lebowa should receive additional land or not. My own view is that with the growing population of Lebowa, more land is essential. Whatever arrangements were made under the 1936 Land Act, circumstances have changed so much under the policy of separate freedoms that the decisions arrived at without consultation with the black people at the time are not answering our purposes now. I am certain that the late General Hertzog was a reasonable man. He realised that land had to be given to the black man. Using the statistics and circumstances obtaining during that time he came to that conclusion. If he were given statistics and circumstances of our day, I feel certain he would be willing to change his formula. He would be realistic. I do not think at all that the late General Hertzog did all the thinking absolutely for the present generation and for all future generations of the Republican government in this regard. On the contrary, he did the thinking only of his contemporaries. We must, therefore, do our own thinking over these questions in the light of the realities before us.

Spokesmen of the Republican government are understood to say that additional land cannot be considered for Lebowa or any of the homelands unless and until the homeland concerned proves that it can use profitably and properly whatever area of land is provided for it. I am afraid that this condition or view is irrelevant. It is for the government of the homeland concerned to see to that and not the Republican government. A fair and just redistribution of land should have no strings attached by the Republican government. Once we have our territory, in fair and just measure, it will be our duty to put it to proper and advantageous use. No other government must interfere with us except by invitation or request.

There is poverty in Lebowa. This state of affairs is frustrating. The Lebowa government must tackle this problem vigorously. The Republican government has plans for the establishment of border industries and industries within our homeland. We are most grateful for these plans. But progress in bringing these plans to actuality is painfully slow. What is the reason for this slow progress? The industrialists are hesitant and have some doubts apparently. The Lebowa government is anxious to have industries both within and outside the borders. My government has tentative plans already to have dialogue with the industrialists. We want to come to some understanding with them. It will be unfortunate if we will be compelled to seek assistance beyond our borders when we could comfortably find help at home.

It must be emphasised that it is urgent that the Lebowa government must do away with the burden of poverty in this territory. When people are suffering, it is unreasonable to counsel them to exercise more and more patience ad infinitum. It is also the determination of the Cabinet to look into the question of mining operations in Lebowa at the earliest opportunity. Tentative plans for contacts with the authorities are already under way.

Agriculture is a vital industry for Lebowa. Though many inhabitants are involved in this industry not enough is being produced. The Department of Agriculture and Forestry will step up efforts in this regard. During this session a bill will be placed before this honourable house for attention. Allied with the question of agricultural industry is the problem of migratory labour. Young Lebowa citizens, including girls, are moved in open lorries or vans to various areas of employment under unsatisfactory conditions of life and renumeration. This and allied questions are receiving attention. The crux of this situation may however be summed up this way: a man leaves farming because he finds it does not pay. He goes to seek work in the urban areas. There too, while living in a hostel where his family is not permitted to join him, he finds work that does not pay. That is the dilemma. We must find ways urgently and not just gradually. Our people in the urban areas have many difficulties and it is the policy of this government to attend to those difficulties. We will co-operate fully with our urban boards.

As far as education is concerned, a bill is being prepared and will be placed before this honourable house in due course. In the meantime, however, the Department of Education is giving attention to the burning question regarding the shortage of trained manpower, including artisans, technicians and teachers.

Lebowa is a self-governing territory. Her citizens everywhere must show respect to others, be they white or black, but other people are expected to do likewise to Lebowa. This government expects Lebowa citizens to be accorded common decencies and human dignity everywhere, including the urban areas. We will not tolerate indignities or humiliations. With respect, however, I place on record, Your Excellency, the Commissioner General, our appreciation of the happy relations between us and the officials seconded to us by the Republican government.

Manifesto of C.N. Phatudi, N.S. Mashiane, S.S. Mothapo, and C.L. Mothiba, Lebowa General Election, 1973

As candidates seeking election for the constituency (district) of Thabamoopo we are glad to present this our manifesto to all voters.

1 / We firmly believe that parliament demands dedicated work from each member of parliament. It is not a place where a member sits and relaxes or even dozes. If elected we will render devoted services to the Thabomoopo electorate at all times.

2 / Chieftainship: This is our traditional binding force. We firmly believe in upholding this institution. Its revered place and dignity must be accorded. Thus it is our determination to serve faithfully all chiefs and members of the royal family.

3 / Special Customs: We undertake to respect interests or customs of our people, for instance the initiation schools and religious ceremonies.

4 / Education, Health, Trade and Commerce, Social Services, and Agricultural and Technical Services: If elected, we undertake to give top priority to these vital matters.

5 / Labour and Employment Opportunities are the spine of any society. We undertake, therefore, to work for the improvement of the lot of the electorate specially in these matters.

6 / Transport and Communications: We firmly believe that for any people to do well in modern times, healthy and ready contacts must be opened and maintained. Consequently, if elected, we undertake to take good care of transport facilities and communication media.

7 / Efficient Parliament: We firmly believe that Lebowa parliament must be efficient to build a great country. If elected, we undertake to build a great Lebowa.

Manifesto of Collins Ramusi and Hebron Leshabane, Lebowa General Election, 1973

Sekgosese, at last the time has come to state what we stand for:

1 / All the people of Lebowa, irrespective of tribe, nationality, colour or creed want an ordinary decent life for themselves and others. This is our belief.

2 / The people of Lebowa and their chiefs want to be respected by all. We believe in the same concept.

3 / The people of Lebowa and their chiefs want education, land, wealth, water, hospitals, clinics, transport, roads, pensions, trade and commerce, social services, technical and agricultural services, plus a self-respecting strong government. We will help in the attainment of all these projects.

4 / The people of Lebowa and their chiefs reject apartheid because it is an unethnical, dangerous, inhuman system. We reject it outright.

5 / The people of Lebowa and their chiefs firmly believe that all men and women were created equal and that the people of Lebowa are members of a single human race. Hence the people of Lebowa and their chiefs fully accept that South Africa will always remain as an integrated society. Long live integration.

6 / The people of Lebowa and their chiefs have never rejected their own fellow Africans in other parts of South Africa and they will continue to live and work harmoniously with all fellow Africans and other races in South Africa and elsewhere. We love our neighbours as ourselves.

7 / The people of Lebowa and their chiefs reject the pass laws, job reservation, discrimination based on the colour of the skin, and all humiliating practices that are being carried out against our people.

8 / We will do everything in our power to enable our people to work in any place in South Africa for civilised wages, without influx control.

9 / We will refuse to be used as puppets or stooges of the government of the Republic of South Africa in any form or shape. We shall make sure that our members

of parliament are not turned into civil servants by the government of the Republic of South Africa.

10 / We undertake to inform our people of all important happenings within or outside parliament.

11 / We believe that the human race is one family which is dependent for its survival on the unity of all men and women in a civil society. We cannot and must not live half slave and half free.

Lebowa People's Party: Manifesto

1 / The party acknowledges the sovereignty and guidance of Almighty God in the destiny of peoples and desires the development of the people of Lebowa along Christian-national lines as well as African culture without prejudice to the right of the individual citizen to freedom of thought, conscience and religion.

To this end, it seeks to unite in political co-operation all who, whether hitherto members of the Lebowa People's Party or standing outside, are prepared to endorse the party's aims and principles, and to accept in good faith the obligations arising therefrom.

2 / AIM OF THE PARTY

It shall be the aim of the party to ensure, in the government of Lebowa:

(a) The realisation of aspirations and convictions of the people of Lebowa, with the motto, 'The people first';

(b) that no discrimination based on race, religion, language, colour or tradition shall be tolerated;

(c) the promotion and safeguarding of the welfare of Lebowa and her people in so far as this can be done by political means. This is to be founded on a common and undivided loyalty and devotion to Lebowa and her interests, on mutual trust and on the recognition of equal rights for all;

(d) that the people be united in our faith that the best way of ruling our people is not through any arbitrary, offensive and oppressive rules of man;

(e) the people of Lebowa shall strive to promote friendly relations with other nations, especially fellow South Africans irrespective of their colour, race or religion, and those who share with them the heritage of African and Western civilisation under the guidance of God the Almighty;

(f) that with our united aim (to remain a united people) it is our fervent desire and aim to promote political unity and co-operation for the promotion of harmonious relations with our neighbours for the common good of all,

and that tranquillity, love and peace should be maintained amongst our people in Lebowa and in South Africa;
(g) the essential equality and dignity of every human being in the face of law irrespective of race, colour or creed, and the maintenance of his fundamental rights;
(h) the promotion of social progress and the improvement of living standards through the energetic development of a modern economy based on free enterprise whereby resources can be fully utilised.

3 / ECONOMIC AND LABOUR POLICY

(a) Lebowa shall be economically developed in respect of all needs by the provision of credit facilities, technical assistance, training, marketing and proper distribution of products for the welfare of all people;
(b) we stand for the energetic development of a modern economy based on free enterprise. Economic and labour policy should be directed to the conquest of poverty by increasing the national income, maintaining a high and stable level of employment and hence improving the living standards of all sections of the population;
(c) we stand for the organisation and utilisation of economic organisations, irrigation schemes, provision of water and electricity supply, modern farming and high quality livestock farming, dairy schemes, etc.;
(d) there shall be no job reservations in Lebowa and the people of Lebowa shall reject, where possible, any job reservation outside Lebowa. The people of Lebowa shall initiate, support and encourage training schemes for employment within or outside Lebowa.

4 / COMMERCE AND INDUSTRY

(a) We shall strive for the establishment and encouragement of various industries in Lebowa for the employment, development and betterment of Lebowa and its peoples;
(b) no one shall be debarred from establishing an industry inside (or outside) Lebowa on the grounds of race, colour or creed;
(c) the Bantu Investment Corporation shall not have the monopoly of purchasing business sites in Lebowa. Lebowa peoples who are both willing and capable shall be allowed to purchase such sites. We shall strive for Lebowa Development Corporation under Lebowa government;
(d) adequate means of communication in the form of telephones, roads, rail, etc. will be the aim of this party.

5 / MINING

The Lebowa People's Party desires to encourage the exploitation of our mineral resources in every possible way, with due consideration for the welfare of the worker and for the government's claim to its rightful share in the country's mineral wealth.

6 / LANGUAGES

The official languages in Lebowa shall be:
(a) Northern-Sotho
(b) English
(c) Afrikaans

7 / NATIONAL HEALTH

The Lebowa People's Party envisages the introduction and encouragement of a comprehensive and efficient system for the protection and advancement of the people's health in Lebowa.

8 / EDUCATION

The Lebowa People's Party, believing as it does in the maintenance and extension of Western civilisation, has as the objects of its education policy the following:
(a) the fostering amongst all citizens of Lebowa an appreciation of the basic tenets of that civilisation;
(b) the development of the individual to the full extent of his capacity in order that he make the maximum contribution to his own welfare and to the people to which he belongs;
(c) the promotion in the children of each group of an understanding and appreciation of the cultures, traditions, backgrounds and aspirations of the other groups, thereby fostering better relationships amongst the people of South Africa.

The aim of the Lebowa People's Party in this respect will be:
(i) to do away with the unacceptable and unsound system of Bantu Education and in its place to evolve and implement a sound, suitable and acceptable system of education;
(ii) to provide adequate facilities for free primary and secondary schooling; and to extend the provisions for compulsory school attendance as the facilities become available;
(iii) to ensure that technical and university education is available; provision being made for bursaries or loans

for deserving students to assist them to attend such institutions; and special attention being paid to the catering for brilliant students;

(iv) to dedicate ourselves to the vigorous school building programmes in every part of Lebowa so that illiteracy may be eliminated.

(v) to ensure adequate salary scales and equitable conditions of employment for all teachers.

9 / WELFARE SERVICES

It will be the aim of Lebowa People's Party to:

(a) provide adequate old-age pensions;

(b) cater for the aged and disabled;

(c) establish clinics, hospitals, grants-in-aid, relief funds, gratuity benefits and other benefits which may be considered necessary from time to time;

(d) provide nurses' training facilities, doctors, pharmacists, engineers, technicians, mechanics, electricians and other craftsmen;

(e) train social workers, sports administrators, community workers and other public workers required for the smooth running of our welfare needs;

(f) establish communal halls and other public buildings for public use. The building of holiday resorts and other places of recreation in Lebowa for the enjoyment of all;

(g) creches, nursery schools, etc. will also receive urgent attention.

10 / CITIZENSHIP

Every person who was born in, resides in or chooses Lebowa as his home, shall be a Lebowa citizen irrespective of his race, colour or creed. The people of Lebowa acknowledge that everyone who lives with them is their fellow citizen.

Statement by the Hon. Chief M.M. Matlala, Lebowa General Election, 1973

Nobody contemplated the possibility of a government for Lebowa twelve years ago. The government of Lebowa came into being in 1962 with the application of a law which stipulated that, because the Republic of South Africa contained various national groups with different laws, customs and cultures, there was only one way of handling matters – namely separate development – which meant that each of these different national groups would govern itself and that none would be governed by another. The situation in which we find ourselves, i.e. our possession of a parliament and cabinet, is the result of separate development. I believe, and I emphasise the fact that there could be only one way: separate development.

The traditional leaders and leadership of the Lebowa government are in the hands of the chiefs, because they form the basis for the government, provide guidance, and carry out the laws in the tribal areas of Lebowa. For this reason it is my intention to protect the chieftainship, and to strengthen and extend it.

Those who despise and belittle the chieftainship, who despise the traditional culture and customs of the chiefs and their subjects, are enemies of Lebowa, and, what is more, there is no place for them in Lebowa. However, we do not close the doors against adjustment of the chieftainship to the demands for modern forms of government.

According to the laws of the Republic of South Africa, each of its nations is entitled to independence like other nations of the world. I would like to point out to the people of Lebowa that the time is past when Lebowa had been governed by another nation. The sun of being governed has set and today the sun of self-government is shining. In view of the fact that the status of Lebowa has been increased rapidly since 1969, it is my objective that Lebowa should obtain full independence as soon as possible.

The absence of employment opportunities near Lebowa is a painful problem. It is the breeding ground of disease, hunger and death, and is also an obstacle in the way of development.

It is my intention to negotiate on behalf of the

government of Lebowa with the government of the Republic of South Africa in order to remove the obstacles in the way of proper employment opportunities and employment alternatives so that we would be in the same position as all the inhabitants of South Africa. The country will not be able to develop with poor and unattractive employment opportunities and conditions.

On behalf of Lebowa it is already the intention to negotiate with the government of the Republic on the carrying of identity cards instead of the present reference book which has served its purpose.

All people are entitled to education; not only some of them. Education is the root and basis of modern life. All children of Lebowa should receive education. Children should therefore be compelled to attend school, and bursaries should be increased for the benefit of promising and hard-working pupils. I shall also strive for the establishment of teacher-training institutions because there is a country-wide shortage of teachers. I am also of the opinion that, unless we increase the salaries of teachers, they will increasingly leave the profession, as they are doing now.

Any country could put itself on its feet if its people had employment opportunities and attractive salaries. It is my intention to bring to the attention of the employers and inhabitants of South Africa that people should be paid what they are worth, and that laws which prevent this should be repealed. I shall also negotiate with the government on the abolition of job reservation.

The majority of the people of Lebowa subsist on agriculture and cattle farming. It is therefore necessary to negotiate with the government on the expansion of our territory in order to obtain a revival of agriculture stock farming.

It is my intention to attend to health services and the care of the old and to ensure that officials employed by the Lebowa government are receiving proper guidance and training to occupy in future the positions of the whites who are now assisting the Lebowa government.

It is a known fact that we have no suitably qualified people for appointment as magistrates. Training of a sufficient number of people is striven for.

It is my intention on behalf of the Lebowa government to make available bursaries for the training of engineers so that roads, bridges and dams can be built.

THE NON-INDEPENDENT HOMELANDS: GAZANKULU

The Hour of Decision

H.W.E. NTSANWISI

(Address to the Progressive Party Annual Congress, Durban, 3 September 1973)

As this is a unique occasion in South African party politics, I would like to congratulate your leaders on the bold and courageous step that they have taken in inviting me and my colleagues to observe for ourselves the Progressive Party at work in what I consider its earnest endeavour to tackle the problems of co-existence, co-operation and interdependence in South Africa. Indeed there may be different ways of attempting to solve the problems which confront us here in South Africa. However, it is becoming evident that the hour of decision has arrived and that for the good of the country black and white should take that decision together.

We have now more than abundant evidence to the effect that the unilateral action which has always been exercised by whites is no longer acceptable to the black people of today. Black consciousness is gaining momentum day by day and any constructive effort to bring about change must take this black awareness into consideration. This means that the black man must be consulted in all things that affect his life. Meaningful dialogue is the operative expression.

There are many facets of life which need radical change in this country in the economic, political, educational and social spheres. It is imperative that all people in South Africa receive equal opportunities for development and self-expression in these fields. It is also imperative that in order to end discontent, frustration and resentment, all people irrespective of race, colour and creed must take part in decision-making and legislation.

Many of you may think that it is already too late and that the discontent and the resentment are already too deep. Judging from the mood of some of our people - especially our young people - it may be thought that it is futile to try to work together. We have radicals amongst the blacks just as you have radicals amongst the whites. But I think it is for the pragmatic individuals on either side to come together and it is on you, the whites, that rests the responsibility for reducing tensions and creating an atmosphere of meaningful co-operation. The fact that for some 300 to 500 years we blacks have been forbearing is surely some indication to you that black people are far more pragmatic and patient than whites may think.

But time is running out; Africa is impatient; the outside world is becoming impatient and pressures from the outside are increasingly isolating the white community to such an extent that you cannot expect any understanding or friendship in the event of armed intervention against you. Admittedly white South Africa has an army that can cope with intervention but this military preparedness is no long-term guarantee of your security here. Your security depends on us, your black fellow citizens. Our security depends on you, our white fellow citizens. But we can stand together against outside intervention if you convince us of your sincerity to share fully the benefits of this richly endowed country. And when I say fully I do not mean just the creation of a few fragmented ethnic homelands - some of which are not economically viable units. I mean sharing in every sense, in its Christian sense. The homelands are here to stay and if the homelands must succeed they must be made economically viable; they must be the natural habitat of their inhabitants.

You will see in the near future an ever greater awareness amongst recognised black leaders, a growing unanimity of purpose and action. The proposed summit meeting of the black leaders of the homelands is to my mind only a beginning of an attempt to make the whites of all political parties, and the world at large, realise that these leaders are not simply the puppets of the liberal forces or the stooges of the Republican government but are thinkers in their own right.

We leaders have to walk a tightrope every day of our lives between the dictates of pragmatism and the dictates of our own consciences which demand that we talk to you before it is too late. If you consider our demands on land, better educational facilities, job opportunities, the rate for the job, and abolition of discrimination based on colour as unrealistic, remember that the extremists amongst us would have them far more radical. Indeed an uncompromising stand by us black leaders is tending to command far more respect today than any attempt to build bridges. What the whites in South Africa do not understand is that we are considered stooges of the South African government by the outside world and leaders of the Organisation of African Unity because we are prepared to play a part in the apartheid conspiracy by accepting the leadership of the homelands. Yet when I speak here in defence of human dignity - I am told by those who wield the real power that I am speaking nonsense - I should know that the sky is not the limit for the black man. It is this relationship of paternalism between black and white leadership which creates in us frustration and helplessness.

I appeal to white South Africa to accept our human dignity, our dignity as feeling human beings, our dignity as men and women who are striving for the same spiritual and material goals as yourselves. I repeat, all that we black people want is to be treated like men and women. We believe in our hearts that we are men - men who can stand on our own feet and control our own destinies. We are not interested in the paternalistic attitude of the white men; we shall not and cannot be satisfied with the crumbs that fall from the overlord's table; we wish to share the loaf of bread. The African eagle will not for ever live on chicken feed. What we want is not favours or privileges but rights. We want to be afforded the opportunity to pay our passage through life.

I believe that white and black in South Africa, although divided into different ethnic homelands, have one common homeland - South Africa - to which they should and must share one common allegiance and loyalty if we are to survive. I have pointed out all these things not in anger or bitterness but because I firmly believe that there can be no real progress and happiness in the crucial race relations in this country unless the hurt to human dignity which abounds in many of the restrictive measures which apply to blacks in this country is pointed out in forthright terms for all, irrespective of party affiliation, to see and understand and take some concrete action to counteract this explosive race problem before our borrowed time runs out.

The black man may be lacking in the technical skills that keep computers going but we have something to offer the white man in teaching him how to behave towards his fellow man. The black and white keys of the piano can and will play a harmonious tune if only you will join in contributing to the tune and if you allow the black notes to embellish that tune.

We blacks do not ask you to abdicate your cultural heritage or your traditions but we ask you to abdicate your paternalism, your feelings that it is for the white man to decide when and where the black man is sufficiently mature to join him on an equal footing.

Dikwankwetla Party: Extracts from the Manifesto

1 / POLITICS, ADMINISTRATION & LAND

The Party will:

(a) adhere to the principles of Christianity and democracy and therefore believes in the orderly development of the Basotho;

(b) strive for the extension of Qwaqwa jurisdiction to all Basotho areas within the Republic of South Africa, and for the consolidation of those areas in order to form one government with them;

(c) preserve the institution of enlightened chieftainship and promote effective tribal administration as well as co-operation between tribal authorities and the national government of QwaQwa;

(d) give the right to representation and expression to all citizens of QwaQwa.

2 / ECONOMICS

The Party will:

(a) vigorously strive to promote the economic development of QwaQwa by means of:

(i) the establishment of industries within QwaQwa;

(ii) the establishment of a QwaQwa Development Corporation;

(iii) the provision of technical assistance and credit facilities, training facilities for marketing in order to convert the traditional subsistence economy to a market-oriented economy with a view to the enlargement of agricultural output;

(iv) the establishment of co-operatives;

(v) the development of the necessary infrastructure;

(vi) the promotion of tourism;

(b) negotiate the necessary financial and technical means from the Republic and other western countries in order to achieve the objectives as stated above;

(c) promote the implementation of the principle of equal pay for equal work;

(d) negotiate better opportunities and benefits for the citizens of QwaQwa who are employed in the Republic of South Africa.

3 / EDUCATION & CULTURE

The Party will:

(a) promote the language and culture of the Basotho;

(b) strive for free and compulsory education on the level of primary education;

(c) since it believes that vocational and technical education is indispensable for the physical development of QwaQwa, also provide the necessary training facilities in that respect and create facilities for adult education.

4 / SOCIAL WELFARE

The Party:

(a) realises that the system of influx control causes discomfort and will therefore negotiate with the Republican government with a view to the promotion of a proper family life for QwaQwa citizens in the white urban areas;

(b) will strive for increased old-age pensions;

(c) will promote the establishment of clinics in QwaQwa as well as recreational facilities at places where such facilities are considered necessary.

THE NON-INDEPENDENT HOMELANDS: VENDA

Venda Consciousness

PATRICK R. MPHEPHU

(Speech, translated from Afrikaans, to welcome the State President)

Mr State President and Mrs Fouché, it is a happy day for the Venda people to welcome you here today. We are proud to greet you and to say that the Venda celebrate your visit. I give you the greetings of my people and ask God's blessing for your happy stay in Sibasa, and a safe return when you leave us.

What you will see and hear today is only a small token of the appreciation in which you and your government are held for your willingness to acknowledge my people as a separate group of people who wish to stand on their own feet. Perhaps you are not aware of it, but I can assure you that the Venda people were a few years ago, not aware of their own identity as a people. They stood in danger of being swamped by other groups. This degeneration had already gone so far that the individual Venda no longer respected his language and traditions. As a people we were in the process of disappearing.

Thus we thank you and the government of the Republic who have allowed the Venda people to revive, so that we might as a people welcome you to this beautiful land with the knowledge that we will progress even further on the road to development. We have, through your action, regained our pride, and we thank you that you have come to visit us today. This day will be remembered by the Venda people as a great day in the history of the Venda: when the State President visited us for the first time.

We realise that there are people in South Africa as well as in other countries who distrust the political set-up in our land, and hope to see it fail. Your visit here is an indication that it can succeed, and that white and non-white can live together contentedly in this land, but only if we are willing to clasp each other's hands, and together build a future for our different national groups. Therefore we offer you a hand of friendship on this auspicious day. Be also assured that you will be welcome in the future whenever it may please you to visit us.

We are all aware that there are still many problems that must be solved, but if we tackle them together, then nothing stands in the way of their successful solution. The Venda people are anxious to take our new steps, but we also realise that our feet have not yet found firm ground. We thus ask you not to let go our hands and let us walk alone. From our side we are willing to work hard, since we realise that a people cannot develop, if they themselves are not strong. Only if a nation has self-respect can it expect that others will respect it. We will show you then that indeeed we have self-respect, and that we can stand on our own feet.

On Terrorism

PATRICK R. MPHEPHU

(Address delivered during an exhibition of weapons used by terrorists, Sibasa Stadium, 16 March 1972)

The ceremony master, officers of the government, parents and children, I greet you all. We have gathered here to listen to what an ex-terrorist has to say about his active participation with the terrorists. We all know that South Africa, Rhodesia and Portugal are hated most by the terrorists and the countries which support them. A question might arise: what are terrorists? In short, we can say they are the people who do not abide by the laws of the country. Usually we find that alien countries influence the citizens of a country to fight against their own government. They attract them by promising to give them bursaries to further their education overseas. But when they are overseas they do not go to schools but undergo military training so that when they return they can fight against their own people.

This man who is amongst us was flattered by being promised educational advancement; instead he was being sent to a military camp. The result is that he had to run away. Where is the education he was promised? He passed his Junior Certificate but was later enticed by the African National Congress which did not help him except to make him its slave. Therefore we parents and school children should be aware of this, because there are people who will cheat us by promising many things.

Let us guard our country against any invasion by the terrorists. You remember, we were once issued with photographs depicting the attire and shoes used by the terrorists as camouflage. We Vendas are just at their borders. We must help the government to fight these people because by failing to do so we are going to cry in the end when we are attacked. Therefore in order that Venda should not be taken, it is the task of every Venda citizen, young and old, to help the government in its fight against the terrorists.

Mphephu Faction: Policy Declaration, Venda General Election, 1973

(Issued under the aegis of the Chief Minister, Chief Patrick R. Mphephu)

We, the acknowledged leaders of the Venda people, hereby declare that the following principles form the foundation upon which we will build the future of the Venda nation.

(A) NATIONAL UNITY

1 / Our motto is, Venda first! Venda forever!

2 / We believe that national unity is the only foundation upon which a great and prosperous future for the whole Venda nation can be built.

3 / All Venda, both within and without the boundaries of Venda, will be bound together into a solid political unit.

(B) POLITICAL DEVELOPMENT

1 / We believe that the basic principles of the political system of the Venda are the best basis for the development of a true democratic government.

2 / We do not believe in the formation of political parties, because these will create division and dissatisfaction amongst the Venda.

3 / Political parties will undermine and destroy the existing political system of the Venda.

4 / The system of the tribal head-in-council and of headmen-in-council should be extended to lead the whole Venda nation to complete freedom and independence.

5 / The Venda government will continue to train its people to obtain the necessary knowledge and experience in order that the Venda in Venda will be taken care of by their own government.

6 / No effort shall be spared to fulfil the ideals of freedom, self-reliance and independence, in all facets of the lives of the people.

(C) VENDA CULTURE

1 / We will preserve and elevate the fine culture of the Venda so that the Venda nation will never lose its heritage.

2 / Attention will be given to the history of the Venda. Important historical sites and places of national beauty will be preserved for posterity.

3 / Dzata day will be declared a national holiday in Venda.

(D) ECONOMIC DEVELOPMENT

1 / Venda has already been placed on the road to comprehensive and stable economic development. This road will be followed with ever-increasing intensity and vitality.

2 / With the intention of accelerating economic independence, special attention will be given to all aspects of the following matters.

(a) The establishment of a Venda Development Corporation with Venda citizens as members of the Board of Directors.
(b) The making available of training facilities in selected centres in Venda where Venda citizens, by means of short courses, can be equipped with the knowledge necessary for the development of the people and the nation.
(c) The establishment of a well-organised chamber of commerce in Venda for the promotion of trade by the appointment of personnel trained in commerce who will provide training courses and after-training guidance to Venda.
(d) The provision of credit facilities for capable businessmen.
(e) The provision of technical help and guidance in all aspects of business administration.
(f) The development of industries.
(g) The development of the mining industry.
(h) The development of agriculture and animal husbandry.
(i) The development of an efficient distribution and marketing system.

(E) EDUCATION

1 / The education of the Venda is the most important task of the government, the nation and the private citizen.

2 / Education encompasses more than mere booklearning.

It includes experience, background, a healthy insight, good manners and a sound character. A man or woman of letters is not necessarily an educated person.

3/ The purpose of educating a child is:
(a) to develop the child spiritually and intellectually so that he will develop into a responsible and useful citizen;
(b) to develop the child in such a manner that he will remain a loyal Venda and will be able to earn a good livelihood.

4 / To reach this goal the cabinet has already decided to introduce compulsory free education in both primary and secondary schools. The co-operation of all concerned is requested to implement this.

5 / In order to realise the ideal of education for each Venda citizen in the shortest possible time, special attention is being given to the following:
(a) The establishment of a network of primary schools and high schools throughout Venda.
(b) The establishment of a system of adult education.
(c) The establishment of training colleges for the training of a greater number of teachers.
(d) The erection of technical colleges and trade schools and eventually a university for the Venda people.
(e) The making available of more bursaries for students at training colleges and universities.

6 / Regular attention will be given to the revision of the educational system to bring it in line with the requirements of the time.

7 / The right of a parent to have a say in the education of his children has already been recognised by us. We expect parents to carry out their obligation in this matter in a responsible way.

8 / Special attention is already being given to the training of many more fully qualified teachers in Venda.

This policy will be accelerated in particular by the following measures:
(a) More training facilities for teachers.
(b) Study loans.
(c) A systematic improvement in salaries, conditions of service and general living conditions for teachers.

9 / Where possible white teachers will be replaced by Venda personnel.

10 / The government has already commenced with a five-year plan which includes (amongst other projects)

the following:
(a) The construction of a new teachers training college with hostel facilities - R1 500 000.
(b) The building of the Dimani Agricultural High School with all the necessary equipment - R1 200 000.
(c) The construction of permanent buildings for the Tshavhakololo College for the sons of chiefs - R1 200 000
(d) Extensions to high schools and government schools - R300 000.
(e) The construction of a new secondary school at Sibasa - R40 000.
(f) The construction of a new higher primary school at Sibasa - R30 000.
(g) The erection of a technical high school for vocational training - cost not yet known.

(F) AGRICULTURE AND CATTLE BREEDING

1 / Agriculture is the basis of the Venda national economy. Venda possesses a great agricultural potential. As in the past the government will continue to assist the Venda to make efficient use of this potential wealth.

2 / It is our policy to assist Venda farmers to farm more efficiently and scientifically to ensure that production can be appreciably increased.

3 / The three centres at which sixty farmers receive free training in respect of their farming methods are to be extended.

4 / Although a number of fine dams have already been built, it is our policy to appreciably accelerate the building of dams for irrigation purposes.

5 / We shall continue to promote at an accelerated pace the improvement of livestock - especially cattle, sheep and goats.

6 / For this purpose attention is to be given to:
(a) The establishment of credit facilities for the farmers.
(b) The expansion of technical aid and extension work.
(c) The establishment of co-operative and other agricultural organisations.
(d) The development of meat, vegetable, fruit and other canning factories.
(e) The establishment of an efficient system of marketing to ensure the disposal of surplus products.
(f) The purchase of good bulls and rams for the improvement of livestock.

(g) The purchase of high-quality seed.

7 / We are pleased to mention that control over forestry (and especially control over the Tate Vondo Plantation) has now been placed in the hands of the Venda government. We shall continue to carry out the good work already in progress.

8 / It gives us pleasure to mention that Venda now has its own veterinary services and we shall extend these services to the advantage of all Venda farmers.

9 / Attention will be given to the development of a good market for the distribution of the Venda farmers' products.

10 / Special attention is drawn to the fact that fish breeding has been established in Venda. This activity will provide an additional source of food and revenue for the Venda nation.

11 / We will continue with the expansion of our sisal project which has already proved to be a good source of revenue for the Venda.

(G) SOCIAL WELFARE

It is our aim:

1 / to increase old-age pensions and care for the aged and infirm;

2 / to accommodate and train people with physical defects;

3 / to establish more clinics;

4 / to establish more training facilities for nurses and to improve existing facilities;

5 / to train our own doctors;

6 / to train and employ more social workers;

7 / to establish sports grounds and social centres.

(H) CIVIL SERVICE

1 / All posts in the civil service are meant for Venda citizens, and we will endeavour to replace as quickly as possible all non-Venda citizens in the civil service by suitably qualified VhaVenda.

2 / We will ensure that previous experience and salaries are taken into account in making appointments, and will endeavour to improve salaries and conditions of service generally.

3 / We will ensure that civil servants are properly housed, with due regard for rank and status.

(I) EMPLOYMENT AND CONDITIONS OF SERVICE

We shall endeavour to get the best possible labour conditions for our workers who are employed in the Republic.

(J) RELATIONS WITH PEOPLES OUTSIDE VENDA

Although 'Venda First' is our motto, we shall endeavour:

1 / to follow a policy of friendship with all other peoples, collaboration in, and deliberation on matters of common concern;

2 / with regard to the Republic of South Africa, the help that is offered will be accepted, and the good relations which already exist will be extended.

(K) TOWNSHIP DEVELOPMENT

We shall endeavour to establish properly planned townships throughout Venda. Provisions will be made inter alia:

1 / for the necessary services such as electricity, water, streets and sewage;

2 / for school and church premises, recreation facilities, business and industrial centres;

3 / for stands where individuals can build their own houses.

(L) PHYSICAL DEVELOPMENT

We aim to improve and extend roads, water services, communication media and transport facilities.

(M) LAW AND ORDER

We shall ensure:

1 / that action be taken against any individual or organisation which threatens security in Venda or which disturbs the peace;

2 / that Venda police be trained and given such experience as will enable them to take over gradually the functions of the South African Police.

(N) LIAISON WITH VENDA CITIZENS OUTSIDE VENDA

We shall maintain existing links and extend them to the benefit of all Venda citizens.

Mphephu Faction: Manifesto of Candidates Supporting Chief Mphephu, Venda General Election, 1973

A / FOR A NATION TO BE SELF-GOVERNING AND AUTONOMOUS IT MUST HAVE THESE PREREQUISITES:

1 / Land

That nation must have its own land with well-defined and fixed boundaries.

2 / Language

Such a nation must have a language of its own.

3 / Culture

Such a nation must have its own culture and customs.

4 / A Political System

Again such a nation must have evolved a political system which is the basis of its government.

As Venda has all these prerequisites, it is a country and a nation which has its own parliament, and is self-governing.

B / WHAT WE INTEND TO DO FOR VENDA

(a) Our aim shall be to see to it that the basis or foundation on which Venda and its government rest is not tampered with. We shall continue to build and improve Venda, its government, language and culture on the above proven and true foundations.

(b) The Unity of Venda: We will see to it that Venda society is not divided into sections or classes; instead there should be co-operation and unity between a chief and his subjects at all times.

(c) A Venda that can accommodate us all: We will strive for a Venda that is big enough for us and which can accommodate us comfortably. We will negotiate with the central government for satisfactory boundaries or ask that Venda revert to its original boundaries.

(d) A Free Venda: To achieve the above aim, we will negotiate with friendly foreign powers to invest money in Venda in order to make Venda economically viable.

(e) A Peaceful Venda: In order to achieve internal security and peace, Venda will co-operate with other governments for the protection of Venda. There shall also be economic co-operation with other friendly governments.

(f) A Productive Venda: To make Venda productive and self-sufficient, large dams and irrigation schemes shall be undertaken at suitable sites. Where there are no rivers, boreholes will be sunk to provide enough water for crops. Venda has the potential to provide enough fruit, milk, meat and grain for its people and even for export.

(g) A Prosperous Venda: Our aim shall be to exploit the mineral wealth in Venda, cultivate tea and sisal. We will explore the possibility of growing other crops which can be of economic value to Venda.

(h) An Industrialised Venda: We will endeavour to our utmost to establish industries and factories at suitable points in which large numbers of men and women will be employed.

(i) Literacy: Our aim shall be to increase the number of schools of all types until illiteracy is wiped out. Compulsory education will be speeded up. A University of Venda will be established as soon as possible.

(j) A Beautiful Venda: Our aim shall be to build holiday resorts and rest camps in order to foster a tourist trade. Artificial lakes will be created and natural ones beautified as tourist attractions.

(k) A Contented and Healthy Venda: In order that every Venda should be happy, contented and healthy, we shall end all slave wages! We will see to it that every Muvenda is paid a living wage.

(l) A Co-operative Venda: Every Muvenda has a right to life, happiness and freedom of worship. Every Muvenda should be free from fear; fear of his chief and vice versa; fear of the uneducated and vice versa. All Venda citizens should learn to respect one another. There shall be no distinction before the law. All Venda citizens should know the value of co-operation.

C / CONCLUSION

(a) These aims when achieved will end poverty and fear, which are caused by ignorance and lack of education

(b) These aims when achieved will bring about tangible progress in Venda.

(c) These aims will bring about complete happiness, complete freedom and prosperity to every Venda citizen.

These are what we will achieve!

Venda Independence People's Party: Manifesto, Venda General Election, 1973

PREAMBLE

1 / The party candidates firmly stand for the undivided loyalty and respect for the chiefs of Venda, the symbols of tribal unity; and will work for the co-operation and consultation with them and the central government of the Republic of South Africa.

2 / The party candidates stand for promoting and advancing the dignity, rights, socio-economic and cultural well-being of Venda through responsible negotiation with the chiefs, the Venda government and the central government of the Republic of South Africa.

3 / The party candidates will challenge all barriers frustrating the peaceful development of Venda.

EDUCATION

'Education is the key for tomorrow.'

1 / Free and compulsory: The party stands for free and compulsory education for Venda children.

2 / Medium of instruction: The party will challenge all outside interferences on the rights of parents to decide the medium of instruction for their children.

3 / Accommodation and bursaries: The party stands for improved accommodation for pupils and adequate bursaries for the varied and various fields of learning.

4 / Higher and technical education: The party will work tirelessly for a more intensive system of higher and technical education for Venda.

5 / The teacher: The party, recognising the high value to the nation of the work performed by the teachers of all grades, stands for the elevation of their status, emoluments and conditions of service, in conformity with the importance and dignity of their profession.

6 / Educationists and planners: The party will strive for closer unity and effective participation of all educationists in the planning of a dynamic educational programme which should be a quarter of a century ahead in adjusting to the needs of the rising industrial giant of our country instead of the unfortunate reality of

being a quarter of a century behind.

The quality of leadership depends on education.
Vote V.I.P. candidates for enlightened leadership.

ECONOMY

'Seek ye the Economic Kingdom and all things shall be added.'

1 / The party will encourage free enterprise and will attract more wealthy investment and development capital to Venda ... in consultation with the central government of the Republic of South Africa.

2 / The party will relentlessly work for the protection of the interests of the Venda citizens against unfair competition and exploitation by the unscrupulous aliens.

3 / The party will work for the elevation of the living standards of the Venda citizens, so that the material and moral power should not decline.

4 / The party will strive for some form of ownership rights of the mineral wealth of Venda.

5 / The party will challenge all the existing irregularities frustrating the granting of business licences to the potential Venda entrepreneurs.

6 / The party will promote the exploration of facilities for encouraging the establishment of new industrial undertakings in Venda.

Good business - good job opportunities - good government
good candidates - go together.

LABOUR AND EMPLOYMENT

'Every Venda must sweat and swear with his "blood, tears and sweat".'

Dignity of Labour

1 / The party holds that it is the duty of the government to provide suitable work for all. Conversely in recognition of the principle that work is honourable, it shall be the duty of every member of the state to work to the best of his strength and ability.

2 / The party will challenge all the influx control regulations ... and fight for employment opportunities for all Venda citizens.

3 / The party firmly opposes the cheap migratory labour system.

AGRICULTURE

'Land is the fulcrum of Venda life.'

1 / The party stands for the development of a scientific agricultural programme that will assure the farming community of its existence; through improved land, stock management, marketing, co-operatives, anti-soil-erosion measures, quality and other aspects of ranching to raise incomes.

2 / The party stands for the restoration of the authority of Venda chiefs as spiritual and economic leaders of their tribes, responsible for the equitable distribution of arable land and opposes the present unfortunate usurping of their powers by the agricultural officers.

3 / The party will work for the improvement of our traditional wealth ... by fostering interest in cattle farming amongst the citizens of Venda.

4 / The party will challenge the exploitation of Venda cattle farmers by the unscrupulous cattle buyers.

HEALTH AND WELFARE

'Health is better than wealth.'

1 / The party shall strive for the promotion of the principle of 'Common Interest Before Self'.

2 / The party will fight for increase of the old-age pension and will establish old-age homes according to modern standards.

3 / The party stands for improved health services and the promotion of child welfare services.

4 / The party stands for improved co-ordination of services between hospitals and the patient's home, through a well-organised social welfare programme of activities.

5 / The party will challenge the influx control regulations which shake root and branch the smallest social unit ... the family, by separating husband and wife. The party will fight for a house for every married Venda man working in the urban centres.

REMOVALS

1 / The party will oppose the removal and resettlement of the Venda chiefs and their subjects without consultation from their traditional residential areas they have for so long cherished.

2 / The party will challenge the unsatisfactory manner of paying out compensations for people's property

after removing from their homes they occupied for many years.

3 / The party will resist the removal of Venda tribes from their long-established homes to undeveloped areas without proper consultation, proper alternative accommodation, health facilities and other conveniences.

NATIONAL UNITY

'One Venda nation - One Venda country.'

1 / The party stands for a united one Venda nation with one country; and shall promote a spirit of brotherhood and social co-operation for the good of all.

2 / The party pledges unbending and undivided loyalty in supporting the sacred position and authority of all Venda chiefs and acknowledges them as the symbols of tribal unity and the natural traditional leaders in Venda society.

3 / The party stands for the elimination of all meaningless tribal barriers and class distinctions.

4 / The party will cherish and defend the best of the past - patriotism, respect for authority, personal responsibility; embrace and foster the best of the future - science and technology, the new freedoms of mind and spirit.

5 / The party recognises freedom of thought and religion, but firmly condemns the ideologies that threaten or undermine the Venda democratic traditions. But it is irreconcilably against all secret political organisations; because it is its firm conviction that the activities of these organisations work against the spirit of 'One Venda nation - One Venda country'. 'Those who are not with us are against us.'

FOREIGN POLICY

'Love thy neighbour...'

1 / The party will work for closest co-operation with the central government of the Republic of South Africa and other nations, without in any way endangering Venda's own honour, self-respect and national principles. 'The enemies of negotiation are the enemies of peace.'

2 / The party realises fully that the white potential in Venda must be fully explored and used more intensively to improve the creative power and to broaden productivity amongst the citizens of Venda. 'Use what you have - until you get what you want.'

3 / The party will challenge all who appease the enemies of Venda.

Mphephu Faction: Whither the Venda Party?, Venda General Election, 1973

A. Vhavenda beware! A strange thing is going about in Venda. It has sugar on its tongue and a deadly sting in its tail.

1 / The name is foreign and ridiculous. Who now speaks of a Venda Party - V.I.P.!

2 / The basis of the constitution is foreign and dangerous to the Venda. It is the barb which threatens to destroy the Venda.

3 / The symbol of the party is foreign to the Venda. We have beautiful symbols; why should we borrow the symbol of another nation?

B. With this constitution nothing will ultimately be left of the proud past of the Venda, and their future will be doomed to failure. This barb will destroy the soul of the Venda people.

C. The political system of the Venda is based on the Chieftainship-in-Council and the Headman-in-Council. This proud system is ignored in the constitution. In the highest policy-making body - the Supreme Council - provision is made only in the last paragraph 7 A(8) that Venda chiefs, who are members of the party, will be honorary members. The chiefs can also be honorary members of the Regional Councils. This is a great insult to the Venda chiefs.

According to common practice and the Oxford English Dictionary an honorary member is not a full-fledged member. Normally he may speak, but he has no vote. Nothing is said in the constitution about the headmen.

A Venda must be very stupid if he or she does not realise that with the constitution of the Venda party - V.I.P. - a process of undermining the traditional institutions of the Venda is being started.

D. The unity of the Venda nation is threatened. The whole

constitution of the Venda Party - V.I.P. - carries this message and evidence that it will sow great dissension and bitterness among the Venda. Unity has always been the strength of the Venda. Do not allow this party with a foreign spirit to destroy the unity of the Venda.

E. Venda, be alert. Do not be misled by sugared words and empty promises.

Work for Chief Mphephu and vote for his faithful team who have proved that they do not serve their own interests, but have worked hard and faithfully towards the building up of Venda and towards the development of a great Venda nation.

F. Vote for our well-known, capable, honest and faithful Venda candidates.

Venda Politics Today

J.P. MUTSILA

(Abridged Statement, Venda General Election, 1973)

To date, the Government in Venda is run by white government officials through a helpless cabinet. Chief Patrick Ramaano Mphephu said so during the visit here by the Republic's Prime Minister, Mr B.J. Vorster. Inter alia, he said that the Venda people were not yet mature enough to run their own government. He emphasised that the Europeans should stay here for as long as possible.

According to him, the position is still as bad as at the time of Mr Vorster's visit. Hence, the oncoming elections are being fought between the enlightened Vendas and the officials of the Venda Government through helpless selected candidates, who, according to themselves, have been advanced with money and ministerial conveyance to fight elections.

What is more, some of the European staff in the Venda Government are secretly and at times openly canvassing for the candidates of the Venda Government.

The Venda Independence People's Party (V.I.P.), which has bounded its policy of action, has found sympathy with the majority of the Venda electorate, both at home and in the urban areas. In addition to the V.I.P., there is a group of progressive people who have combined to make a concerted effort with limited ability for the sake of success.

Up to now, candidates of the V.I.P. and others have been so successful in their campaign that it is strongly rumoured that the Venda Government intends, if the present tempo is maintained, to declare a state of emergency two days before the date of elections.

Thus the Ministers go about calling opposition candidates traitors, sewer-flies, wolves, jackals, etc.

The followers of the V.I.P. and other groups should be warned not to heed the tantalisations of the Venda Government, for that is just a casus belli. The destiny of Venda is in the hands of the Venda themselves and not in the hands of the government officials.

I am proud to declare that the Venda nation is itself ready to handle its own affairs without the aid of the government officials. If the present cabinet is not yet mature, the people are long mature.

Through this medium, I wish to advise the voters to vote early and also to examine their reference books to ascertain that their books have been endorsed on the right places. That is on letters E for the males and on D for the females.

THE NON-INDEPENDENT HOMELANDS: SWAZI TERRITORY

Political Development amongst the Republican Swazis

D. LUKHELE

During 1932 the King of Swaziland, King Sobhuza II, who was by then a Paramount Chief of the Swazis during the colonial days, invited the Republican chiefs to Entonjeni, and Dr I. Seme, an African attorney, drafted a petition which was sent to the South African parliament. The purpose of the petition was to ask the South African government to grant certain Swazi chiefs land in the Transvaal. Some of the chiefs were granted land with their subjects and others remained as labour tenants on white-owned farms.

Developments at Nkomazi, an area populated by Swazis, led to acceptance of the Bantu Authorities Act and formation of tribal authorities; the same applied at Nsikazi. They again formed themselves into regional authorities, bodies that concern themselves with administrative matters.

During 1968 a movement came into being amongst the Swazis of the white areas, with their chiefs, called the Swazi National Council of the Republic of South Africa, and Mr D. Lukhele was chosen as a national organiser. Arrangements were made to meet the Honourable Minister of Bantu Administration and Development, Mr M.C. Botha, at Pretoria. Two interviews resulted and discussions were held with the Honourable Minister on the following issues: land, self-government, and the prosecution of squatters on certain lands owned by black land-owners. Mr D. Lukhele was the chief spokesman on both occasions. The Honourable Minister suggested to the Swazi delegates a plan to resettle all Swazis inside Swaziland; that there are lands that are owned by whites in Swaziland and that the Republican government was prepared to purchase those lands for the Swazis. This offer was twice rejected by the Swazis. The Republican Swazis requested land inside the Republic as other national groups had done. They regarded themselves as citizens of the Republic and felt that the government was now dumping them onto a foreign state.

The Swazis of the Republic met on certain occasions

in order to unite. This was accomplished during 1971 and a single body was formed of the Swazi National Council, the Nkomazi Regional Authority, and the Nsikazi Regional Authority.

After unity was effected a committee, known as the Swazi Interim Committee, was formed to achieve self-government for the Swazis. This committee has on several occasions met the officials of the Department of Bantu Administration and Development and the Honourable Commissioner General of the Zulu/Swazi Unit. But at these meetings it has been proved that the government is not in a position to accept proposals from the Swazis.

The government discussed the consolidation of land, and proposed an area bordering Swaziland stretching from Amsterdam to the Portuguese border. Although the proposed land was not acceptable to the Swazis because of the system of give and take applied by the government, the Swazis decided at last that 'Thy will be done'.

The Commissioner General, the Honourable Mr P.H. Torlage, suggested that Swazis living in white areas must reside in Swazi homelands in order to meet the requirements of the law. And this is the only way in which Swazis could be given a Swazi Territorial Authority. But up to date nothing has materialised.

Since 1932 the Swaziland people have had no interest in the problems of the Republican Swazis. Because of land difficulties, many Swazis cross the border and settle in a land they believe is theirs and a land that belongs to the King. But, alas, they are arrested by the police in Swaziland and are charged for entering Swaziland illegally and are evicted.

During 1972 at the Incwala ceremony a medical doctor of Springs, Dr L.A.M. Gama, was appointed by His Majesty to be his personal representative. Dr Gama was born and brought up at Daggaskraal in Amersfoort district and obtained his medical degree at the University of the Witwatersrand in Johannesburg. He has been a member of the Swazi National Royal Club, an organisation said to have been founded by His Majesty Sobhuza II during 1972 for cultural purposes, with headquarters at Sophiatown, Johannesburg.

This organisation, the Swazi National Royal Club, has been at loggerheads with the Swazi National Council. Thus the appointment of Dr Gama was received with suspicion by the Republican Swazis, and the Department of

Bantu Administration and Development asked its officials to assist Dr Gama. The matter was first referred to the Swazi Interim Committee, a body representing all the Swazis of the Republic. There was a misunderstanding about the acceptance of Dr Gama because the people introducing him were politicians from Swaziland, namely the Assistant Minister of Local Administration, Mr S.M. Tshabalala, and Senator M. Nhlabatsi, and because he was a leader of all the Swazis of the Republic of South Africa appointed because the King had received frequent requests from Republican Swazis.

With regard to the first reason, Dr Gama's introduction by Swaziland politicians was not acceptable because Swaziland is an independent state and Republican Swazis do not take part in Swaziland politics. With regard to the second reason, no request from the Republican Swazis or chiefs was ever forwarded to His Majesty asking for a leader or representative. A memorandum was presented to the Bantu Affairs Commissioner of Barberton informing him and the Department of Bantu Administration and Development about the decision of the Swazis.

Swazilanders were not prepared to lose face but continued their efforts and asked again for the assistance of the local Bantu Affairs Commissioner, who called a meeting at Nkomazi Regional Authority and another at Nsikasi to introduce Dr Gama. The Swazi National Council was invited to take part in the discussion. It was said by the Bantu Affairs Commissioners that only royalty is in effect entitled to say 'yes' or 'no' about the question of Dr Gama.

Before the Dlamini clan emigrated to Swaziland the land was occupied by certain Sotho clans, and the ruling house was the Masekos, i.e. Amangcamane under their leader Khubonye. Sobhuza I fled to Swaziland with his Ngwane clan; the Ngcamane Chief Khabangobe Maseko afforded Sobhuza I protection and residential facilities. The son of Sobhuza I, Mswati, however conspired against the Ngcamane (about 1840) and murdered their Chief (Amangcamane) Mgazi, son of Khabangobe. The Ngcamane were subdued with very little resistence. A small group together with the Chief's son Sidinga fled to the Transvaal and some fled to Malawi. That is why you will find the Masekos there.

The Dlamini clan became powerful under the leadership of Mswati and subdued many tribes. As a result the people were named after him 'the people of Mswati', the land of the Swatis. The ruling clan in Swaziland is the house of Dlamini. The Dlaminis are monopolising political power in Swaziland. Almost the whole cabinet is dominated by the Dlaminis, and the Nxumalos, who are closely related to the King. It is a pity that political power is centred in the royal house and that the King, instead of being a constitutional monarch, is used as a political instrument.

In Swaziland the only political party existing now is the Imbokodwa National Movement; the Ngwane Liberation Movement led by Dr Zwane has been banned. It was banned because one of the King's sons, Prince Mfanasibile, was defeated at the polls by Mr Thomas Ngwenya, who has been denied his citizenship in Swaziland and sent back to the Republic.

These are the fears that the Swazi National Council and other Swazis have regarding the appointment of Dr Gama as the King's representative. In January 1974 the Swazi Interim Committee sent a letter to the Hon. Commissioner General asking him to convey their decision to the Hon. Minister of Bantu Administration and Development, i.e. that the Swaziland government be officially informed about the rejection of Dr Gama by the Republican Swazis. This is not to be taken as disloyalty to His Majesty but as an indication that the Republican Swazis who are Christianised prefer to choose their own leaders. Some traditionalists, however, support the King's appointee.

The King advised Dr Gama to form an organisation under the title of Swazi Nation of the Republic with headquarters at Springs. There are at least ten branches in the Transvaal that broke away with Chief Mkohshi Dlamini, who was expelled by the Swazi National Council. He has joined Dr Gama. Three chiefs followed suit: Chief Jokoma Tshabalala of Wakkerstroom and Chief Jan Mnisi of Amersfoort and Chief Funwako Dlamini of Emgindini, Barberton. Although these chiefs have joined Dr Gama, their followers are still with the Swazi National Council.

After the Swazis' rejection of Dr Gama, it was pointed out to us that he is only a cultural adviser - he does not take part in Swazi politics. But there are strong indications that he will now operate subtly until such time as the Swaziland royal house will influence the Dlamini chiefs, who out-number the other chiefs, to accept the King's choice as their leader in order that the Dlaminis retain leadership and political power. This has happened because Swazi society is docile and adheres to tradition.

The Swazi National Council's efforts to a certain extent have been successful; Swazis were divided into many groups. This is the result of tribalism. The following tribes were united under the Swazi National Council:

1 / Chief Tobias Nkosi - Ndlela tribe - Piet Retief area.

2 / Chief Robert Dlamini - Dlangamandla tribe - Sheepmoor.

3 / Chief Aaron Gama - Gama tribe - Amsterdam.

4 / Chief Wesman Nhlapo - Mlambo tribe - Ermelo.

5 / Chief Madzanga Dlamini - Kunukakuyengwa tribe - Oshoek Ermelo.

6 / Chief Jim Nkosi - Butsini tribe - Steynsdorp.

7 / Chief Enock Maseko - Amangcamane tribe - Pretoria - Witbank, Free State.

8 / Chief Elias Nkosi of Nomovovo, living in Johannesburg, plus the other three who joined Dr Gama under the Swazi Nation of the Republic.

Discussions were held by the national executive of the S.N.C. and the S.N.R., during which, in order to bring peace, the S.N.C. proposed that Dr Gama should not associate himself with any organisation or be known to be a leader of an organisation! This was unacceptable to his executive. They maintain that Dr Gama is here to create a political forum for the Swazis so that any political aspirations must come from this body, the Swazi Nation of the Republic.

Swazi Economy

A large number of Swazis live on white-owned land as labour tenants, and are dependent on the white farmers for a living. According to law they are unable to produce any goods and are forbidden to own any businesses on white farms.

Living on farms does not improve the living standards of the Swazis. Those working on forests or plantations educate their children up to Standard 2, as do those who reside on farms. Some white farmers are sympathetic to the Swazis by providing them with school books and engaging teachers out of their own money. There are certain large citrus farmers who go to the extent of sending

Swazi children to university and high school.

The Swazi National Council, in order to improve the economic standard, has its own wing of the Swazi National Chamber of Commerce and Swazi National Investment Corporation with the object of encouraging Swazis to be entrepreneurs. Educated women have been organised into a Swazi National Women's League. They contribute monthly or weekly to this fund for the assistance of poor students who are unable to continue with their education. Despite the difficulties these women are experiencing in finding money, they are succeeding slowly.

These organisations were not brought into being because we wish to be exclusive, but because the sophisticated blacks seem to be interested in running organisations of this kind in the metropolitan centres of Johannesburg, Pretoria, Durban and Cape Town. There is the Chamber of Commerce, which confines its activities to the big cities. The National Women's League is also confined to the large cities, although these people will always give the impression overseas that they are representing all blacks of the Republic.

This organisation was born due to hardships experienced by the Swazis who are not accepted in the other homelands, because even though we accuse the white man of practising discrimination it is worse amongst blacks - they overdo it in relation to other national groups. Sometimes our children are forced to be educated in a foreign language, despite the fact that we are prepared to offer our own teachers.

Swazis were compelled to request the Republic government to grant them their own homeland where they can, like other nations, have opportunities for development. Because of these circumstances Swazis are forced to accept separate development. There is a saying in Swazi, 'When a baby cries can any woman come and breastfeed her?'. The answer is No! Only the natural mother will do it; everybody will ask where the mother of this crying baby is! They may pity her but will not feed her.

Federation

On the above question the S.N.C. sent a delegate to the Bulugha conference on Federation. After receiving a report the Swazis were interested in federations in order to share the national income and power.

Amalgamation with Swaziland

Because of language ties, tradition, and wealth of the nation, there is the possibility that Republican Swazis may one day join their brothers of Swaziland, but on the undermentioned conditions:

1 / That the Republican Swazis first attain self-government in order to bargain from a position of constitutional authority, and not negotiate through the white government;

2 / that the King of Swaziland becomes a head of state without executive powers or a change of the constitution;

3 / that only one body, i.e. the constituted government, upholds the law in Swaziland and that there be an end to the double standards practised at present, i.e. Swazi national administration and its traditional laws and the Law Courts practising Western democracy.

Self-government

Perhaps very early next year the Swazis will be granted constitutional authority. At the moment (1974) negotiations are going ahead with the officials of Bantu Administration and Development.

Land Question

The Swazis demand more land in order to be productive like other national groups. At the moment there are no border industries planned for our people. We are going to have a lot of difficulty with our people who will need employment in order to support their families.

In conclusion Swazis are hopeful that the Republican government will assist them to develop their land as has been done by other national groups.

CONCLUSION

How to Promote Peace in South Africa

MANAS BUTHELEZI

(Extracts from an address to a Financial Mail investment conference, Johannesburg, November 1976)

War and peace are mutually exclusive of each other. Peace cannot prevail while war is still being waged. The fact of the matter is that there is no peace on our streets, and our homes are ceasing to be places of refuge for our children.

Parents and children alike are in a state of panic. The other day I heard one father saying that he was afraid to leave his home because he had just heard that the police were going to come that evening to collect children from house to house. He wanted to be present when the police came, even though he saw no reason why his son should be arrested. The fear was there nevertheless.

This is a symptom of the pathological condition our country is in. When the whole black community has to live in terror it is high time the whites examined the questionable security that is being created for them out of the substance of the insecurity of the black man. There is general confusion in Soweto because of what appears to the parents to be an indiscriminate arrest of their children. Whatever the political logic of the arrests of our youth, it must become clear to the authorities that no administration, however strong, can in the final analysis last without the moral support and approval of the majority of the people.

What we need now is the end to this war between the students and the police. Anyway future generations will look at it as having been a shameful and distasteful exercise. During the last days publicity has been given to Brigadier Jan Visser's appeal that steps be taken to create a harmonious relationship between the police and the community of Soweto. Before I react to it may I say that I hope he has the full backing of not only his department but also of the rank and file of his staff.

I am fully behind the brigadier if his appeal has to

be understood in the context of the sense of the ordinary meaning of words. In other words I hope that his appeal is not calculated to encourage the black community to turn the other cheek and connive at what is happening and what has happened. In further qualifying my support let me also state that I hope the appeal is not for a cosmetic dressing of the scars on our body-politic, but also includes creating fundamental good relations between the police and the students.

If that be the case we would be heading for some of the fundamental solutions of the problems of our country. Everybody knows that the relations between the police and the black community are bad not because the police are dedicated to the combat of crime - the black community is also dedicated to that - but because the police, being among the few whites who can move freely in the black community, spearhead the enforcement of a myriad of unacceptable laws, some of which are designed to silence the critics of separate development and force the black man to accept the status prescribed to him by the South African Way of Life.

May I also suggest some of the interim steps that should be taken if the spirit of the brigadier's appeal is to materialize:

(a) The police must dramatically stretch a hand of friendship to the students so as to correct the belief that the police are the enemies of students and are out to get them. This can be done first through the ministerial order that no student will be arrested at school, home or cemeteries and that there will be no street collecting of students. It is only too obvious that no black leader can attend any talks with the police while there is no assurance that he will find his children still all at home having not been picked up.

(b) There should be a withdrawal of all the charges against our children, and a pardon of all those who have been convicted. It is a futile exercise for the older generation anyway to create a situation where the majority of the younger generation will have political-criminal records. This will only serve to create an embittered younger generation with hardened attitudes. Putting political opponents in prison may of course in the short term give politicians a breather, but it does community relations no good, especially if there is anything that may tempt people to believe that it is basically a case of one racial group acting against another.

The history of this country from the Anglo-Boer War to the Second World War shows that political crimes do not stick even if one is not convicted. When the political climate has changed, prison graduates usually become national heroes. That is why a couple of men in positions of leadership in South Africa today were once political prisoners. What amazes me is that people can forget so easily the lessons of the past.

Be this as it may, it would be a height of sadism and irresponsibility on my part to condone the incarceration of our young black children in political prisons with the belief that prison experience will groom them into better future leaders. There are better ways of achieving that. I merely make this historical observation in order to demonstrate that the withdrawal of all the political-criminal charges levelled against all black children and the pardoning of all those who have been convicted is in the long term in the best interest of the country. The only thing that can be achieved if this course is not followed is future embarrassment, since no political system is eternal.

(c) Recognition and consultations with the whole spectrum of black leadership. The resources of a community are no greater than the quality of leadership it can produce. When you take away all the leaders of a people you take away its important resource. Community leaders are not installed from outside but they grow out of the community.

It is worth remembering that each one of the detained and imprisoned persons since the beginning of the present unrest has a constituency of followers and admirers. It is true that that constituency may only be black, but white people must realise that black constituencies deserve as much respect as white ones. Any attempt to improve relations between the police and the community must include a restraint in tampering with community leaders.

It is a well-known fact that there has been a trend to arrest office-bearers of black organisations operating outside government framework. This cannot happen without hurting the feelings of the people. One way of improving the relations between the police and the black community may be for a ministerial announcement that there will be no harassment of lawful black organisations by way of arresting their office-bearers unless charges can be prefered at the time of arrest and tested in a court of law.

It must have been clear by now that detentions do not serve the interests of a harmonious relationship between the community and the police, because they create suspicions that one is not charged but detained instead because one has not committed any crime. This has led to many allegations which even though not proved in court become material for rumours of all types.

Whites must realise that there is something known as black public opinion. Although it may not influence what happens in the white community, it certainly shapes the attitudes and the conduct of the black community. If for instance white institutions label a man an agitator and even invoke statutory provisions to censure him, as long as the black public opinion is such that he is regarded as a leader, this does not affect his esteem in the black community. All that can be achieved is to hurt the black community. There can never be harmonious relations between the police and the black community as long as the sensibilities and judgments of the black community are not recognised.

I am pointing these things out because I believe that they can be done now. One way of getting out of the present deadlock is for South Africa to follow the example of its own protegé, Rhodesia. South Africa must also use the prescription it has helped prepare for Rhodesian ailments. This includes dialogue with former political opponents as well as with former political prisoners after they have been released for the purpose of finding a joint solution for problems in the country.

Report Back

M. GATSHA BUTHELEZI

(A report back to the Reef Africans on the conference of black leaders with the Hon. B.J. Vorster, Prime Minister of South Africa, on 22 January 1975)

To put matters in perspective before I go into the purpose of this meeting I would like to remind my brothers and sisters gathered here that the meeting of black leaders with the Prime Minister was the second conference of its kind. The first one took place on 6 March 1974.

We are all aware that the over-emphasis on our ethnic groupings by the powers-that-be was largely a matter of the old divide-and-rule technique which is as old as the Roman Empire. That is why we as black leaders decided to meet at Umtata on 8 November 1973. We knew that black people were one people; that their problems were the same and had very little to do with ethnic grouping. We realised that we can only tackle these problems with any hope of success if we have a common front and if we adopt a common strategy. With this end in view, we approached the Prime Minister of South Africa, the Hon. B.J. Vorster, to allow us to meet him together, so that we could present black grievances on a common platform. This the Prime Minister acceded to by granting us the above-mentioned interview on 6 March last year.

We presented the black man's case formally, and through memoranda we discussed with him. It might be a good thing for me to remind you that at the March 1974 meeting we presented the following matters:

1 / (a) The meaning of independence: the discussion was led by me and in making the initial presentation I was supported by the Hon. Chief L.M. Mangope, the Chief Minister of BophuthaTswana.

1 / (b) The basic principles of consolidation: the discussion was led by the Hon. Mr L.L. Sebe, Chief Minister of the Ciskei.

2 / Racial discrimination and the discussion on this subject was led by me, and in the initial representation I was supported by the Hon. L.M. Mangope, Chief Minister

of BophuthaTswana.

3 / The wage gap and disparity in revenue and expenditure in the 'homelands': the matter was presented by the Hon. Chief L.M. Mangope, Chief Minister of BophuthaTswana.

4 / The position of the urban blacks and the problems of black businessmen in the urban areas: the discussion was led by the Hon. Dr C.N. Phatudi, Chief Minister of Lebowa, and he was supported by me in the presentation of this item, particularly as it referred to problems of the black businessman in the urban areas.

5 / The medium of instruction in African schools was presented by the Hon. Dr. C.N. Phatudi, Chief Minister of Lebowa.

6 / The phasing out of passes and influx control regulations: the discussion was presented by the Hon. Professor H.W. Ntsanwisi, Chief Minister of Gazankulu, and in this presentation he was supported by the Hon. Paramount Chief K.D. Matanzima of the Transkei.

7 / The question of departments excluded from 'homeland' governments: the discussion was led by the Hon. Paramount Chief K.D. Matanzima, Chief Minister of the Transkei.

All black leaders participated in the discussions. There was a strong divergence of opinion on most of the subjects discussed. The Prime Minister said that we were free to ask for independence, but no one amongst us came forward to ask for what the Prime Minister calls 'independence', the main reason being that most of the leaders could not accept such independence when it is based on the provisions of the 1936 Natives Land and Trust Act. Moreover, most of us felt that it would not be right to do so without a clear mandate from you. The Prime Minister stuck to his guns that he would not contemplate going beyond the provisions of the 1936 Act, which means that blacks end up with nothing more than 13 per cent of the whole area of South Africa, when they constitute 80 per cent of the population.

While we acknowledged the fact that the present Nationalist government had bought more land for black occupation than any of the previous governments, we could not accept that the mere purchase of all this land settles the question of land between black and white in South Africa. There was no clarity on whether by 'independence' the

Prime Minister on the one hand, and the black leaders on the other hand have one and the same thing in mind. The leaders spelled out point by point what they regarded as true independence. This area was never fully canvassed point by point in reply, except that the Prime Minister emphasised that he means independence in the dictionary sense of the word. Although there was a promise that during the current financial year more money would be used (three times more than previously spent), the purchases under the 1936 Act can only be completed in five or ten years' time. The main point here is that even if the full quota of land promised under the 1936 Act is purchased, we still remain not fully consolidated into compact and contiguous 'countries'.

On racial discrimination there was a very emotional and in-depth discussion on the basis that racial discrimination is an assault on the human dignity of blacks. The Prime Minister's view was that he would educate his own people, and that we should also educate our own people on attitudes. The Prime Minister said that racial friction could not be avoided through legislation, but by education. He admitted that there were some amongst his own people who addressed blacks in a crude manner. He said that the other side of the coin showed that there were certain blacks who were arrogant when they met whites.

On the point that there was a wage gap and disparity in the revenue and expenditure of these so-called 'homelands' and the revenue and expenditure for whites, it was decided to set up a committee of experts, one nominated by blacks and one by the Prime Minister. They were to go into the whole contention by black leaders that Africans in general, and the 'homelands government' in particular, are not getting a fair share of services from taxes paid directly and indirectly by Africans.

Black leaders requested the government to devise ways and means of closing the gap in salaries paid to different racial groups.

On the medium of instruction, i.e. that the language used in schools in the so-called 'white areas' should be the same as that used in the 'homelands', the Prime Minister suggested that the Minister of Bantu Administration should go into the legal constitutional and educational aspects and then report at the next meeting.

On urban blacks, and black businessmen in urban areas,

the Prime Minister suggested a full day to be set aside to discuss the problems of urban blacks, as the Prime Minister admitted that the subject was important and big enough to warrant it. That is how the conference we had with the Prime Minister on 22 January 1975 came about.

When we approached the Prime Minister initially, we did so in order to discuss black problems, regardless of whether these were rural or urban. Black oppression occurs throughout South Africa. It is something based on colour and it is a system which forces all blacks, wherever they are, to live under the most untenable conditions, under which no other racial group, even those who share discrimination with Africans, has to live.

In this context we were most surprised to find that after we had succeeded in getting the Prime Minister to discuss urban blacks with us, some blacks, baited mainly by the white press, took it upon themselves to question our credentials in speaking for our people here. The struggle of the black man is one, and even during the heyday of the banned African organisations, such as the African National Congress and the Pan-Africanist Congress, no distinction was ever made between urban and rural leadership. There were even several leaders who served as Presidents General of the African National Congress who came from rural areas. I question whether there is any black man who is not acquainted with the whole impact of black oppression in South Africa. I am dealing with this at such length because I think that it is the time for each one of us, whether he is urban or rural, to join forces, co-ordinate efforts and adopt a common strategy. This is no time for chewing the cud of mutual recrimination, purely on the basis of who should speak for whom amongst blacks. It we do not guard against this great 'divide', we will find when it is too late that we have fallen into yet another trap which seeks to weaken our full impact, and which creates an artificial barrier between oppressed people on the basis of whether they are urban or rural. This is ridiculous and farcical. Its price is too great. We cannot afford to allow it.

Urban black problems were dealt with as follows:

(a) Security of tenure and home ownership: This discussion was led by the Hon. Paramount Chief K.D. Matanzima, Chief Minister of the Transkei. The Chief

Minister supported by the Hon. Professor H.W. Ntsanwisi, Chief Minister of Gazankulu, submitted that unless black people in the urban areas, particularly second and third generation inhabitants, associated and identified themselves with a homeland, their permanency in the 'white' urban areas should be recognised. The black leaders proposed a freehold form of land tenure for blacks in urban areas. The Prime Minister did not accept the granting of freehold rights to urban blacks, his argument being that whites cannot have freehold rights in most 'homelands', and that he cannot therefore allow blacks to have freehold rights in 'white' areas. He argued that whites were not allowed to purchase land in freehold in the so-called black areas in order to protect the black population groups who were economically weak groups. He promised to look into a form of leasehold which would give blacks a right to make improvements to their houses and to get compensation for them. Most black leaders participated in the discussion, as did the Minister of Bantu Administration, his two Deputies and Secretaries.

(b) Trading rights of the blacks in the urban areas: The discussion on this item was led by me, and I was supported by the Hon. Professor H.W. Ntsanwisi, the Chief Minister of Gazankulu. I put before conference the memorandum I presented at the March conference on the subject. We went through that memorandum point by point. I requested that the one-man one-business rule be relaxed; that black businessmen should be able to own business establishments other than those providing only for the daily essentials of black residents; that the ban on the establishment of black partnerships, financial institutions and wholesale operations should be lifted, and that the licensing procedures for businessmen be the same as those for white businessmen. I further submitted for consideration and discussion a memorandum on the same subject submitted to the Minister of Bantu Administration and Development, on 31 October 1974, by Mr S.M. Motsuenyane and the National African Federated Chamber of Commerce.

The Prime Minister said that the points raised were all valid. He promised that these matters would be evaluated and laws and regulations affecting this situation would be reconsidered.

(c) Influx control regulations: The discussion was led by the Hon. Professor H.W. Ntsanwisi, Chief Minister of Gazankulu, supported by the Hon. Chief L.M. Mangope, Chief Minister of BophuthaTswana. The Hon. Paramount Chief K.D. Matanzima, Chief Minister of the Transkei, took up the question of the Bantu Administration Boards.

Professor Ntsanwisi appealed for the complete abolition of influx control and described influx control regulations as a denial of fundamental human rights. Chief Mangope pointed out that these regulations caused hardships which needed at least to be eased. Paramount Chief Matanzima pointed out that the institution of the Administration Boards had not alleviated the position of work-seekers in the urban areas. He emphasised that there were hardly enough employment opportunities in the 'homelands'. Other leaders also participated in the discussion, as did members of the Prime Minister's team.

The Prime Minister said there was no alternative to influx control and that it could not be done away with. It was the government's view that the influx control regulations protected the existing black labour force in the urban areas. He stated that an official, a Mr Meyer, was at present investigating possible amendments to the regulations. The Prime Minister invited the leaders to submit suggestions and, if it could be found, a solution for the entire system. At the Prime Minister's suggestion the leaders, excepting me, agreed to appoint three representatives from among themselves, who would sit down with the official concerned, and possibly others as well, to work out a better system. I suggested that it might be better if we, as leaders, and other blacks gave evidence and submitted memoranda on the influx control regulations, instead of joining the official in working out 'a better system of influx control'. This was rejected by the Prime Minister, and my colleagues said that the Prime Minister's suggestion was reasonable. In the light of the Prime Minister's categoric statement that the pass-laws cannot be repealed as we had suggested, I felt that I could not be a co-author of an 'improved influx control system'. I believe that one can give evidence to an official committee entrusted with the job, but not risk being the co-author of something that would still not satisfy one's people. I quite appreciate the difficulties entailed in the influx of people without jobs into cities throughout the world, but I cannot accept it in South Africa, so long as it is discriminatory, in applying only to Africans and to no other racial group. I felt that this was a question of principle.

(d) The position of professional blacks in the townships: The discussion on this was led by the Hon. Professor H.W. Ntsanwisi. He dealt with the position of professional blacks and, in particular, that of doctors. It was felt that they should be free to practise their profession in the urban areas without any difficulties. The question of disparity in pay in the case of doctors was also dealt with. The Hon. M.C. Botha, the Minister of Bantu Administration and Development, told the meeting that it was government policy to encourage professionally trained blacks to settle in the 'homelands'. The leaders felt that African professional people, such as doctors, should not be forced to go into the 'homelands' but must make their own decisions. The Prime Minister said that this policy was aimed at helping the 'homelands', but if the 'homelands' did not require this protection, the policy would be revised.

As far as salaries were concerned, the Hon. M.C. Botha pointed out that in a homeland with self-government such as the Transkei, which has its own department of health, doctors received the same salaries as white doctors. It was further stated that it was government policy to narrow the wage gap in the urban areas. Other leaders also participated in the discussion.

(e) Civic rights for blacks in the urban areas: The discussion was led by the Hon. Dr C.N. Phatudi, Chief Minister of Lebowa. He pointed out that urban blacks were sophisticated and politically conscious, and needed to have their own local government. The position as it exists at present was far from satisfactory. He was supported by the Chief Minister of the Transkei and me. I pointed out that urban councils needed to have budgets like all other civic councils. The Prime Minister asked whether this meant clothing urban councils with more responsibility and we concurred.

A suggestion was made by the Hon. M.C. Botha, on the merging of urban councils with representatives' urban boards. This matter would be looked into.

At this point I read an excerpt from the memorandum presented to us by the Mayor of Soweto, Mr Makhaya. I put to the Prime Minister his suggestion that Soweto be proclaimed a black homeland. I recalled that at a meeting I attended here in Soweto, the then Mayor, Mr

Lengene, once requested me to make representations to that effect. The Prime Minister's response was terse, and to the effect that the proclamation of Soweto as a homeland was out of the question. The Minister of Bantu Administration remarked that this would be too easy a solution. That disposed of that item.

(f) Public transport facilities: Discussions were led by the Hon. Paramount Chief K.D. Matanzima, Chief Minister of the Transkei. The Chief Minister pointed out the inadequacies of the maximum transport facilities afforded blacks from and to their places of employment. He pointed out that these had reached saturation point. He said that the contrast between these facilities and those provided for whites can only cause more and more bitter anti-white feelings. He pointed out how people had to stand in queues for long stretches of time, and how as a result they had to go to the expense of hiring taxis. The Chief Minister of the Transkei proposed an interdepartmental committee representing Transport and the Department of Bantu Administration and Development to go into the matter.

The Prime Minister pointed out that conditions were much worse in other countries. He said that the problem of moving huge masses of people at peak hours was an international problem. An interdepartmental committee does review the problem yearly, and millions were spent on improving transport facilities. It was decided that the matter would be discussed at the next meeting.

(g) Mass removals of blacks from urban areas to homeland areas: The discussion was led by the Hon. Dr C.N. Phatudi, Chief Minister of Lebowa. He complained about lack of facilities in the areas to which people were being removed. He said that people suffered when they were 'dumped', penniless, in such areas. Then certain specific removals in Lebowa were discussed at great length. The Hon. M.C. Botha, Minister of Bantu Administration and Development and of Bantu Education, told the meeting that the government objected to the use of the word 'dumping'. He said that it was a principle of the resettlement programme that no one was sent to a place where essential facilities such as water, schools and housing were non-existent. He told the meeting that people were compensated for whatever they might have to leave behind. He said the policy was to resettle only 'the workless'.

(h) Ethnic grouping in urban townships: The discussion was led by the Hon. Dr C.N. Phatudi, Chief Minister of Lebowa. He pointed out that ethnic groupings amongst blacks were taken too far by the administration in spite of the fact that our people in the urban townships were living together in one milieu. He pleaded for people to be able to live in free association in the urban townships, and not to be restricted by regulations. He said that this applied to residential areas and schools.

The Prime Minister said that in the urban areas blacks were free to associate, and that the black leaders themselves requested that in urban areas schools should be organised along lines corresponding with those of the various 'homelands'. It was stated that the matter would nevertheless be investigated.

(i) Education problems: The discussion was led by the Hon. Professor Ntsanwisi, Chief Minister of Gazankulu, and was supported by the Hon. Mr L.L. Sebe, Chief Minister of the Ciskei. The subject was sub-divided into:
(1) Medium of instruction to tally with that used in the area of the particular 'homeland' legislature to which citizens of a particular 'homeland' belong.
(2) The new rule concerning the equal use of English and Afrikaans as media of instruction.
(3) Africanisation of black universities.

Professor H.W. Ntsanwisi proposed that the medium of instruction used in schools in the urban areas should be the same as that used in the schools in the black 'homelands'. The Hon. Professor Ntsanwisi, supported by the Hon. L.L. Sebe, submitted for discussion and consideration a memorandum on the same subject, submitted to the Secretary for Bantu Education on 7 January 1974 by the Joint School Boards and Committee Boards of the Southern and Northern Transvaal Regions of Bantu Education. I pointed out that this question of not allowing our people in the urban areas to use the same medium as that used in those areas, called 'homelands', to which their taxes are channelled, and in which they are supposed to be voters, cut right across the principle of self-government offered blacks and, in fact, made a mockery of it. I was supported in this view by the Hon. Chief L.M. Mangope, Chief Minister of BophuthaTswana, who said that this was not in keeping with self-government, since the urban black population, who were denied the right to use the language which the 'homeland' legislature had decided should be used as a medium of instruction, were supposed to be citizens of those 'homelands'.

It was contended by the leaders that English was more generally used in the 'homelands' high schools and at all the black universities. A request was also made for a change in the rule concerning equal use of English and Afrikaans as media of instruction in the urban schools. A case for the administration and control of black universities to be placed into black hands, so as to bring about 'Africanisation' of black universities, was very ably presented on behalf of the leaders by the Hon. Professor Ntsanwisi. It was argued that key decision-making posts and bodies should be placed in the hands of black people. It was pointed out that black academic staff should also get equal pay with their white colleagues, especially now that this has been put right at the University of the Western Cape.

On the medium of instruction, the Hon. M.C. Botha said that the matter was extremely complicated, posing enormous practical problems involving more than 5 000 schools, and required further investigation. The matter was presently being taken up with various school boards by the Secretary for Bantu Education. I asked what the time schedule would be for putting right this question of medium of instruction, and the Minister of Bantu Administration and Development and of Bantu Education, the Hon. M.C. Botha, said that 'the matter could not be rushed'. I pointed out that the feelings of the people on this issue had been expressed for quite some time now. The Minister denied that the issue had been going on for a long time, arguing that we had mentioned it at our conference in March 1974, and that it had also been mentioned by the KwaZulu cabinet about two years ago.

The question of mother-tongue instruction for pupils of one 'homeland' residing in another was discussed at great length. A few minunderstandings, especially regarding the position in Garankuwa and Mabopane East, were cleared up. On this aspect of the matter, a meeting of the respective Chief Ministers to discuss these problems would be convened by the Deputy-Minister of Bantu Education, the Hon. T.N.H. Jansen. Most black leaders participated in this discussion.

(j) Trade unions for blacks: This discussion was led by the Hon. Chief Minister of BophuthaTswana. Before the Chief Minister could speak, the Prime Minister pointed out that this matter of trade unions had been fully canvassed in Parliament in 1974, and legislation passed. He thought it could not be taken any further.

The Chief Minister asked whether the Prime Minister meant that the matter could not even be discussed, pointing out that our people were not satisfied with works committees. Chief Mangope then placed before the conference a letter and memorandum sent by Mrs Lucy Mvubelo to the Minister pf Labour on behalf of the National Union of Clothing Workers (South Africa) on the subject of trade unions. The Minister of Bantu Administration pointed out that the Minister of Labour had dealt with the matter. The Prime Minister, however, finally offered to arrange a meeting between the leaders and the Minister of Labour, although it was not indicated when such a meeting was likely to be held, as the Prime Minister still had to approach the Minister of Labour.

(k) The détente in Southern Africa: This discussion was led by me, and was probably the most controversial part of our whole conference with the Prime Minister. I was supported by the Chief Minister of BophuthaTswana. Other leaders who participated in this particular discussion were the following Chief Ministers: the Hon. Paramount Chief K.D. Matanzima of the Transkei, the Hon. Dr C.N. Phatudi of Lebowa, the Hon. Professor H.W. Ntsanwisi of Gazankulu, the Hon. L.L. Sebe of the Ciskei.

In my presentation, I congratulated and applauded the Prime Minister of South Africa, the Hon. B.J. Vorster, and the President of Zambia, H.E. Dr Kenneth Kaunda, on their efforts to promote détente in Southern Africa. I also read excerpts from a letter from a P.A.C. refugee abroad, in which he praised the Prime Minister and expressed hopes that the Prime Minister would rise to the occasion, and that his new deal would not just be 'a repetition of the same policies that are already unacceptable to the International Community at large'.

I reminded the Prime Minister that in March 1974 he had said to us that he does not believe in racial discrimination but in differentiation and I told him that we could hardly tell the difference between the two.

I reminded him that by co-operating with his government in implementing this policy, we had been slated as 'collaborators with the oppressors' by certain elements within South Africa, and others outside South Africa. I reminded him that there were those amongst us who do not believe in apartheid as a philosophy, but who have co-operated merely because there were no other alternatives to finding a peaceful settlement. I pointed out that in view of his 'give-us-six-months' speech the hopes of blacks for meaningful change had been raised.

I told the Prime Minister that this was to us a natural corollary to his initiatives in the present détente in Southern Africa. We hoped to share power and decision-making, in a new and meaningful way. I told the Prime Minister of the assurances I was given by H.E. President Kaunda, when I visited him in December 1973, that he also believes in a peaceful change on the basis of the Lusaka Manifesto.

I reminded the Prime Minister that we had presented the Lusaka Manifesto to him, in March 1974, as a reasonable basis for a peaceful change in South Africa. I told the Prime Minister that President Kaunda had then told me that he believed in a meaningful dialogue with South Africa, but that a meaningful dialogue should take place between us within South Africa, first, before he would be interested in it. I told the Prime Minister of a similar statement by the President of Liberia, H.E. Dr William R. Tolbert Jr, to me this year, when he said that if the Prime Minister wanted to meet him as an equal he would be interested only if the Prime Minister first regarded his black brothers in South Africa as equals.

I told the Prime Minister that I had told the President of Liberia that, although the Prime Minister does meet us as equals around the table, as today, it was too early for me to judge whether we are moving towards real and meaningful equality in South Africa. I told the Prime Minister that President Tolbert had expressed the view that they would be guided by us, their black brothers, as to what stance they should adopt towards South Africa.

I told the Prime Minister that we do not regard the present government policy on consolidating these areas, on the basis of the 1936 Natives Land Act, as leading us to such real and meaningful equality. But that after his Senate speech, his Nigel speech, and Mr R.F. Botha's speech at the United Nations, in which the latter condemned racial discrimination, we were full of expectations, and that our hopes had been raised even for a more meaningful consolidation of the 'homeland' areas, and that I hoped that he would seriously consider a federal formula on the basis of properly consolidated 'homeland' areas.

I then stated that, although the item on the détente had been placed on the agenda with the concurrence of my fellow black leaders, I wanted to point out that I did not want to embarrass them by assuming that they also agree with me with regard to the part of my memorandum I was then about to read. I told the Prime Minister that I took full responsibility for this part of my memorandum. I warned: 'We have been prepared to endure abuse, in the hope that the government's policy may be a road to real fulfilment for blacks. If this road, as appears under the circumstances described above, is leading only to a cul-de-sac, then our only alternative is to seek fulfilment not in unreal "separate freedoms", but in one South Africa and in the only seat of power which is Parliament.' I went on:

'I would like to make it crystal clear that I am not saying these things in any spirit of ill-will or threats, but I feel that it is my moral duty at this point in time to point out the only logical alternatives we have, if we do not want our people to resort to civil disobedience and disruption of services in this land. Not that I intend leading my people in this direction at the moment, but I do feel, judging by the mood of my people, that it is timely that I should point out that if no meaningful change is forthcoming for them through the government's policies, this will come as a logical alternative. I believe in avoiding situations when we as South Africans can only hurt each other, with no real victors on either side. At the same time, I want to say that I cannot be expected to successfully ward off the venting of pent-up frustrations of my people, if the government continually fails to offer them anything meaningful through their policy.'

I also quoted extensively from the now famous speech by Mr R.F. Botha, South Africa's representative at the United Nations. I quoted some of these extracts to show the Prime Minister what had heightened black expectations as a result of his utterances, and the utterances of South Africa's permanent representative at the United Nations.

The Hon. Chief L.M. Mangope referred to the March 1974 conference and the Prime Minister's statement that he did not believe in racial discrimination. He asked whether we are going to be separate and equal, and wanted to know what the import of the Prime Minister's speeches was, and that of Mr. R.F. Botha, at the United Nations.

The Chief Minister wanted to know what had been done to educate the people of South Africa to avoid harmful racial incidents. The Hon. Professor H.W. Ntsanwisi praised the Prime Minister for his role in promoting détente, and hoped that this would lead to am improvement of conditions for black people in South Africa. The Hon. Paramount Chief K.D. Matanzima supported him, and also pleaded with the Prime Minister to take the black leaders into his confidence on the question of where South Africa was going. The Hon. Dr C.N. Phatudi also stressed the expectancy created by the recent speeches. The Hon. Mr L.L. Sebe expressed hopes of meaningful change and the expectancy he had encountered in his travels abroad.

The Prime Minister repeated the main theme of his speech in the Senate, dealing with peace and co-operation in Southern Africa. He outlined the reactions in Zambia and elsewhere and then dealt in detail with his speech in Nigel. Quoting from the typewritten text of the speech the Prime Minister said that he had not asked for six months for himself, or for his party, or for his policy, but for South Africa, and that even those who refused to give him that time would see where South Africa stood in six to twelve months. He was referring here not to domestic affairs of South Africa, but to the question of South Africa's position in Africa and the world. He repeated that, if peace could be achieved in Southern Africa, the black leaders would appreciate where South Africa would then stand.

The Prime Minister said that these people who now fêted the 'homeland' leaders at conferences had had their opportunity in the past and asked what they had done for the black people, the leaders, of that period. The black leaders were now recognised as such, and could discuss matters with him as equals. He said that government policy was indeed to get away from purely racial discrimination. However, he pointed out that there are many differences which existed in South Africa's multinational composition. He said that very day's meeting with black leaders, on matters of vital importance to them, was proof of how the government was trying to eliminate friction and how the black leaders shared in the considerations and decisions on matters affecting black people.

On the question of sharing power in one Parliament, the Prime Minister said that this was not the policy of his party and his government. However, black leaders would eventually have sole power in independent states. Meanwhile more and more opportunities would be created for black people to exercise power and responsibilities in the 'homelands' and to obtain experience in, for example, international affairs. The Prime Minister mentioned in this connection the recent what-he-called 'multi-national' delegation to the United Nations, and the training of black diplomats and information officers abroad.

Referring to my memorandum in which, as you have heard, I referred to civil disobedience and disruption of services if black aspirations are not met, the Prime Minister said that I should consider my position and statements. He said no one would be allowed to take the law into his hands, and South Africa would be administered on the basis of law and order.

He said he envisaged independence for all 'homelands' and promised that South Africa would, after their independence, provide financial and technical expertise to the new countries. He said that we must wait and see what happens when the Transkei gets its independence.

(1) The question of amnesty for South African political exiles and prisoners: This discussion was led by me, and most leaders participated in it. When the Prime Minister asked me what I meant by political prisoners, I said I had in mind people like Mr Nelson Mandela. I told the Prime Minister that, even on the basis of common law offenders, a remission of sentence is given after a certain period of time, and I appealed that this matter be dealt with in the same way. I pointed out that the Rhodesian political detainees had been released as a result of the Prime Minister's initiatives. I felt this was the psychological moment to release our own political detainess. The Chief Minister of the Transkei, the Hon. K.D. Matanzima, in supporting my presentation, said that special consideration ought to be given to those who left the coutry without a passport, and who now wished to return to 'homelands' such as the Transkei.

The Prime Minister said that if people left South

Africa, without having committed a crime, and were not communists, but their only crime was leaving the country without a passport, he would consider their return sympathetically, if the leaders were prepared to vouch for them. The same applied to those who left with an exit permit. The Prime Minister said that he had warned these people at the time that if they had been sentenced by a court for breaking the law and later fled the country, they would receive no mercy. Referring to one of the prisoners whose name had been mentioned, and others who are in prison with him, the Prime Minister said the prisoner in question had boasted in court of being a communist and he had not changed his mind. He said the same applied to some of his fellow-prisoners. He went on to say that all people in South Africa, blacks and whites, needed protection against the aspirations of communists such as the individual who did not, in his opinion, speak for black people but on behalf of the Communist Party.

On the question put to the Prime Minister by Dr Phatudi and others and by me, on Mr Robert Sobukwe, the Prime Minister said that Mr Sobukwe did not fall into the above-mentioned category. In other words, he was not a communist. He said that his case was reviewed from time to time. On being asked by me whether he could not initiate a special review of Mr Sobukwe's case, the Prime Minister said he would do so, although he cannot bind the Minister of Justice and vice versa.

Other issues discussed were foreign investments in 'the homelands', the powers and functions of commissioners-general and the proposed new autonomous Homeland Development Corporations. I will not go into them.

I have come here because I believe that I have a moral obligation to report to you as our constituents. I do not consider that it is good enough for me to trust that you will get titbits of what was discussed through mass media.

As you have seen, there were a few concessions on peripheral issues. I believe that it is time we hear from you whether we can adopt a new strategy in the light of the reactions by the Prime Minister to our presentation of your grievances.

At the same time, since I went so far as to issue the warning of what might happen, I felt that I needed to come and explain exactly what I said and exactly what I meant. I have not deviated from my path of non-violence: our people can never meet violence with violence, even if one assumed some wanted this. I do believe that they have other non-violent methods, which will come to hand automatically if nothing meaningful emerges for them in terms of sharing in decision-making, political power and the wealth of South Africa, which they have also worked to produce over many decades. These are not threats but responsible warnings of what is logical if the détente excludes us in terms of the sharing of wealth and decision-making referred to above.

All these things cannot be oversimplified. These things mean an uphill struggle such as the Afrikaner himself had. In many ways our struggle is, and will be, much more arduous than that of the Afrikaner. The Afrikaner at least had the advantage of a white skin, the veritable measuring-rod of security and privilege in South Africa for the last three hundred years.

What I have come to say is that we need to think seriously of the only alternatives that might be forced on us by circumstances, white intransigence, and white greed. I fear that if we are caught napping, I would never forgive myself for not issuing these warnings. These are not things I say lightly, nor are these things we can be jubilant about. These spell for us the painful path which all oppressed people have at one time or another to traverse as there are hardly any short-cuts to freedom.

Our Afrikaner countrymen who are today wielding power over us should know these things better than anyone else, since their own memories of their own subjugation less than a century ago are still so fresh. I realise only too well that, as in the case of the Afrikaner, our path to freedom is full of dangers. The Afrikaner will bear me out that this is a path fraught with suffering and, I am afraid, even with death, for some of us. The consolation I have, which I hope is well founded, is that the Afrikaner himself did not ascend to power only through bloodshed. My daily prayer for him is that God should give him the grace He gave the English, to bow to the inevitable while there is time.

Most of you might expect miracles from us. Some of you even use us to ventilate your frustrations as if we are retarding the pace of your march to freedom. That is one of the reasons why I have decided to come and tell it to you, as it is! This I am doing in the hope that you will realise that we have a great moral duty to make sacrifices for our posterity. The Afrikaner who is ruling us today is reaping the fruits of many sacrifices his forebears made for him. The way to freedom was for him sprinkled with sweat, with blood, and with tears. If we expected any less than this, it can only mean one thing, which is that we are living in a fool's paradise.

We, as your leaders, cannot demand sacrifices from you. We must liaise with you, and reach some consensus as to where we are going, and how we are getting there. We have to learn from past experiences and avoid some of the mistakes of some of our predecessors. It is no longer good enough to promote sporadic dramatic actions which will be topical in the world press for a few weeks, or even months, and then peter out. We must aim for something which will make our rulers come to terms with us not just on the basis of a makeshift arrangement, but on the basis of finding a formula for peaceful co-existence of people of South Africa, of every race, and of every colour. It is no longer good enough to blast us for not 'talking sense into the Prime Minister', as some of you would say. We want alternative suggestions given direct to us and not through mass media. This we must do, if we are all convinced that black solidarity is the answer to black oppression. We do not pretend to be demi-gods; we are human like each one of you. We are no more devils or angels than any one of you can be either of these things. We have power, and we can use it effectively, only if we do not stop at talking black solidarity, but by acting as if we really believe in it.

Biographies of Contributors

ERNEST BAARTMAN

The Rev. Ernest Baartman was born at Touws River in the Cape Province in May 1933. He was educated at Langa High School and at Healdtown, where he received a teacher's certificate. He subsequently obtained a Diploma in Theology at the Federal Theological Seminary, Alice. Currently he is general secretary of the Methodist Christian Education and Youth Department, Durban.

WILBY L. BAQWA

As industrial relations officer for a large construction company, Wilby Baqwa liaises between management and a work force of 12 000 blacks, for whose welfare he is responsible. Mr Baqwa was born in Johannesburg in 1924, and has spent most of his life there. A keen musician, he is president of the Johannesburg Bantu Music Festival, and also conducts his own music group. He has also been secretary of the S.A. Bantu Football Association.

SIBUSISO MANDLENKOSI EMMANUEL BENGU

Born at Kranskop, Natal, in 1934, Dr Bengu spent his childhood at various mission stations in Zululand. He trained as a teacher at the Umpumulo Training College and then proceeded to the University of Zululand, where he earned a B.A. degree, followed by a B.A. Hons (History) from the University of South Africa. At the end of 1974 he was awarded a Ph.D degree by the Graduate Institute of International Studies, University of Geneva. A member of the teaching profession since 1952, Dr Bengu has since 1969 been the headmaster of Dlangezwa High School. Dr Bengu served as publicity secretary of the Natal Teacher's Association for 1971/72, was president of the Students' Christian Movement in Natal for five years, and is now secretary-general of the National Cultural Liberation Movement (Inkatha).

PETER JOHN BUTELEZI

The Rt Rev. Peter John Butelezi is the Catholic

Bishop of Umtata. Born in 1930 in Newcastle, Natal, Bishop Butelezi studied in Rome at the Gregorian University and the Pontifical Biblical Institute. He has Licentiates in Philosophy, Theology and Scripture. Bishop Butelezi is chairman of the R.C. bishops' commission on Ecumenism, a member of the Executive of the S.A. Council of Churches, and a member of the Joint Committee of Wilgespruit Fellowship Centre.

MANAS BUTHELEZI

Dr Manas Buthelezi is bishop of the Evangelical Lutheran Church of Southern Africa, and chairman of the Black Parents' Association formed in 1976 after the Soweto disturbances.

MANGOSUTHU GATSHA BUTHELEZI

An hereditary chief of the Buthelezi tribe that has traditionally supplied the chief councillor to the king, and a prince of the Zulu nation, Mangosuthu Gatsha Buthelezi was born on 27 August 1928. He was raised in the Zulu Royal Palace in Mahashini, and after matriculating he attended Fort Hare University College, from where he was expelled for his forthright views and actions. He later graduated with a B.A. degree in history and administration from Natal University in 1950. Chief Buthelezi then worked as a clerk with the Bantu Administration Department in Durban until 1952, and in 1953 he was installed as an hereditary chief of his tribe. With a strict Anglican Christian upbringing, Chief Buthelezi has shown a strong interest in church work, and has held positions on the Natal Provincial Synod. In 1970 he was unanimously elected Chief Executive Officer of the KwaZulu Legislative Assembly, and in 1972 he became Chief Executive Councillor.

BARNEY IRVINE DLADLA

Barney Irvine Dladla was Executive Councillor for Community Affairs in the KwaZulu Government. He was born in Estcourt, Natal, in 1925, and spent his childhood tending his father's livestock, in between schooling. After passing a teachers' course, he taught for three years, and then joined industry. He was the first organiser of the African Chamber of Commerce in Johannesburg from 1956 to 1960. Mr Dladla was a member of the now-banned African National Congress, and in 1959 left to join the Pan Africanist Congress, also subsequently banned. On his return from Johannesburg in 1963 he was elected to the Hlanganiso Regional Authority, and then the Zulu Territorial Authority. He became a member of the first KwaZulu Executive Council in 1972. He died in 1975.

ASHTON DUNJWA

Mr Dunjwa was the Urban Representative for Ciskei and was based at Langa, a black township, in the Cape Peninsula. He is a graduate of the University of Natal.

THEOCRITUS SIMON NDZIWENI GQUBULE

The Rev. Theocritus Simon Ndziweni Gqubule is lecturer at the Federal Theological Seminary, near Pietermaritzburg, and principal of John Wesley College at the seminary. Born in Uitenhage in 1928, he matriculated and trained as a teacher in a mission school near Fort Beaufort. Mr Gqubule holds the degrees of Bachelor of Arts from Rhodes University and Bachelor of Divinity and Master of Theology from London and Edinburgh universities respectively. He has served as a pastor in the Transkei, in addition to various teaching and lecturing posts, and has long been involved with various aspects of education.

PATRICK GOODWYN GUMEDE

Patrick Goodwyn Gumede was born at Dannhauser, Natal, in 1937 and received his schooling at Mariannhill and at Roma, Lesotho, from where he matriculated. Now a businessman in Newcastle, Mr Gumede is president of the Inyanda Regional African Chamber of Commerce, which operates in Natal and KwaZulu, and vice-president of the National African Federated Chambers of Commerce. He is also Chairman of the KwaZulu Government Tender Board and served on the first Township Council of Madadeni from 1972 to 1975. A member of the Roman Catholic Church, Mr Gumede is Chairman of Christ the King Parish Council, Madadeni.

KNOWLEDGE GUZANA

Knowledge Guzana is the leader of the Opposition in the Transkei. The son of a shoemaker, he was born in 1916 in Keiskammahoek, where he received his early education. He matriculated at Lovedale Training School, and then obtained his B.A. Degree from Fort Hare University in 1939 while teaching at Lovedale. After teaching in Cape Town and Umtata, he was admitted as an attorney in 1955, and then practised in Mqanduli near Umtata. In 1963 he was elected to the first Transkeian Legislative Assembly, and helped to form the opposition Democratic Party, which elected him as its leader in 1965. Mr Guzana is also active in the Methodist Church, and was the South African delegate to the World Methodist Conference in Denver, Colorado in 1971, when he was elected to the Executive of the World Methodist Council.

CHARLES BOYIZA HLENGWA

Charles Boyiza Hlengwa is a tribal chief and a member of the KwaZulu Legislative Assembly. He was born at Camperdown in Natal on 10 March 1912, and spent his childhood on a mission reserve. He gained a teacher's certificate from the Amanzimtoti Institute and taught for the period 1934-45. His interests in community affairs are mostly concerned with agricultural matters such as Farmers' Associations and Co-operatives.

WILLIAM MOSHOBANE KGWARE

Born in 1916 on a farm in the Orange Free State, Professor Kgware went in 1937 to the University of Fort Hare, where two years later he obtained both a B.A. degree and a Diploma in Education. He also holds an M.A. degree from the Department of African Studies (1944), a University Education Diploma (1948), Bachelor of Education (1951) and the Master of Education (1954) and Doctor of Education (1969) degrees from the University of South Africa.

In 1961 he was appointed Professor of Didactics and Educational Administration and in 1969 became the first head of a Department of Comparative Education at a South African university - the University of the North, and in 1976 was appointed the first black Rector of that university.

Under the auspices of the U.S.-S.A. Leader Exchange Program, Professor Kgware visited the U.S.A. on a study and lecture tour. He has also lectured in London, Amsterdam and Kampala.

In 1964 Professor Kgware was appointed chairman of the first all-black Advisory Board for Bantu Education in the Republic of South Africa. In addition he is a member/trustee/consultant of a number of prestigious public bodies.

ERNEST PELAELO LEKHELA

The entire career of Professor Lekhela has been in the field of education. Starting as a teacher in Kimberley, where he was born in 1913, he became a school principal, an inspector of schools, a university lecturer, and is now head of the Department of History of Education at the University of the North. Professor Lekhela has a D.Ed. degree from the University of South Africa.

A one-time member of the Methodist Synod, Conference and Missionary Committee, Professor Lekhela is chairman of the Universities' Section of the Students' Christian Movement. He is vice-chairman of the South African Pedagogical Society, member of the History of Education Society and of the Historical Association (both London-based) and an active participant in many local cultural movements.

SOLOMON JOEL JACK LESOLANG

Solomon J.J. Lesolang is a member of the Bophutha-Tswana Legislative Assembly, and a businessman in Ga-Rankuwa. Born in the Pretoria district in 1906, he spent his childhood in Johannesburg. After matriculation and a teacher's course, he was a teacher from 1928 to 1945. From 1942 to 1945 he was president of the Transvaal African Teachers' Association. In 1946 he turned to commerce, and has been the treasurer of the National African Federated Chamber of Commerce since 1964. He is deputy leader of the opposition Seoposengwe Party.

DAVID MABALEKA LUKHELE

The son of a coalminer, David Lukhele was born at Newcastle, Natal, in 1926. In 1934 his parents emigrated to the Transvaal, where he received his higher primary education. He passed his senior certificate examination through correspondence courses. At present he is studying economics while employed as a salesman. A founder member of the Swazi National Council, Mr Lukhele was local secretary of the Pretoria Branch and was elected leader of the Swazi National Organisation in 1968.

JUSTICE THANDATHU MABANDLA

Justice Thandathu Mabandla was born in Rwarwa, near Alice, in 1926 and raised in the Keiskammahoek area. An hereditary Fingo chief, he has a diploma in Bantu Law and Custom, in addition to his training as a teacher.

Chief Mabandla was chief minister of the first-stage Legislative Assembly created in 1971. After the first elections in March 1973, he formed the Ciskei National Party, whose policy was to work for a just settlement of the land question, and the co-operation between black states in South Africa. When the new assembly met in May 1973, he lost the position of chief minister to Mr Sebe. Chief Mabandla's article was written especially for this book.

LUCAS MANYANE MANGOPE

The son of the chief of the relatively small Bahurutshe tribe, Lucas Mangope was born in 1923 in Motswedi in the Transvaal. He was educated at Motswedi, in Johannesburg, and in Pietersburg, where he qualified as a teacher in 1940. He is fluent in Afrikaans and English as well as Tswana. He entered politics when he succeeded his father as chief of the Bahurutshe in 1958. He became vice-chairman of the Tswana Territorial Authority when it was inaugurated in 1961, and when it was 're-constituted' in 1968 he became Chief Councillor. In the elections of October 1972, his party, the BophuthaTswana National Party, gained 72 per cent of the votes and 12 of the 16 seats against the Seoposengwe Party led by Chief Tidimane R. Pilane, the first chairman of the previously existing Territorial Authority.

KAISER D. MATANZIMA

Paramount Chief Kaiser D. Matanzima has been Chief Minister of the Transkei since 1963. He was born in 1915 in Emigrant Tembuland where he received his school education. He studied law at the South African Native College of Fort Hare. In 1944 he became articled to a firm of attorneys and passed the Attorneys Admission Examination four years later, obtaining first position in the Cape. He was installed as Chief of the Hala Tribe in 1940, was recognised as the Chief of Emigrant Tembuland in 1958, and elected Chairman of the Transkeian Territorial Authority in 1961. He played a leading role in the constitutional and political development of the Transkei and as Chief Minister requested the Republican government to declare the Transkeian Territories a self-governing territory.

ABRAM L. MAWASHA

A senior lecturer in, and at present acting director of, the Language Bureau at the University of the North, Abram Mawasha received his schooling at Lady Selborne, a location near Pretoria, where he was born in 1938. He holds the degrees of B.A., B.Ed. and M.Ed.(and the U.E.D.) from the University of South Africa, and an M.A. from the Southern Illinois University, U.S.A.

As is to be expected, his main interests in community affairs are in those connected with his profession. He is the founder of the Association of Teachers of English in African Schools, member of the English Academy of Southern Africa, of the English Language Teaching Information Centre at the University of the Witwatersrand, and of TESOL (Teachers of English to Speakers of Other Languages) in the U.S.A. Mr Mawasha is chairman of the Ford Foundation Black Fellowship Programme, a newly founded organisation based in the U.S.A. but administered from the offices of the South African Institute of Race Relations.

MANASSEH TEBATSO MOERANE

Until recently the editor of The World newspaper, Manasseh T. Moerane came into journalism after a twenty-year career as teacher and then school principal in Natal. Born at Mount Fletcher in the Cape, he was raised in East Griqualand. He holds a B.A. and a B.Econ. degree from the University of South Africa, and a B.A. Hons. from the University of Natal. He is a trustee of the South Africa Foundation, president of the Association for Educational and Cultural Advancement of the African Peoples, and a former member of the African National Congress.

ERNEST SEDUMEDI MOLOTO

Dr Moloto grew up in a rural area in the Transvaal and qualified as a primary school teacher at Stofberg-Gedenkskool in the Orange Free State. In 1942 he obtained a B.A. degree at Fort Hare University, and through private studies a B.A. Hons. (1962), M.A. (1964) and D.Litt et Phil. (S.A., 1970). He did pioneering work in secondary education, taught at the University College of the North, and eventually became one of the first Education Planners in the Tswana Territorial Authority in 1969. In 1972 he visited West German schools and universities at the invitation of the West German government. His extra-mural activities include the compilation of the BophuthaTswana Legislative Assembly's Hansard, and active participation in various educational committees and organisations.

SAMUEL M. MOTSUENYANE

The president of the National African Federated Chamber of Commerce (NAFCOC), Samuel M. Motsuenyane, was born in Potchefstroom, spending his childhood there and in Pretoria. He has a diploma in social science from the Jan H. Hofmeyr School of Social Work in Johannesburg, and a B.Sc. degree in agriculture from the University of North Carolina. He has served for nine years as national organising secretary of the African Soil Conservation Association. He started a nursery and poultry business in 1967 in the Pretoria district, and also organised the Winterveld Farmers' Association, of which he is chairman. He has been president of NAFCOC for six years, and for three years edited the journal, The African Trader. A Methodist, he has played a leading role in Sunday-school work for many years.

PATRICK RAMAANO MPHEPHU

An hereditary chief of the Mphephu house, Patrick Ramaano Mphephu was born in 1925 and spent his childhood in his tribe's traditional area. He was educated to junior certificate level. He was chairman of the Mphephu Tribal Authority and the Ramabulan Regional Authority before being elected Cheif Councillor of the Venda Territorial Authority in 1969, and later Chief Minister of Venda.

JOSIAH PHINNY MUTSILA

Josiah Phinny Mutsila was born at Maungani, in the district of Sibasa, Northern Transvaal, on 1 June 1914. He first taught and then entered the business world. He was a director of a number of companies and managing director of the Vendaland Trading Co. (Pty) Ltd. In 1973 he was elected to the Venda Legislative Assembly and became deputy leader of the Opposition Venda People's Party. He died in 1976.

LUCY MVUBELO

Lucy Mvubelo is general secretary of the National Union of Clothing Workers, which, with a membership of

24 000, is the largest South African black union. Early in her marriage, her husband was severely injured as a result of an attack by thugs, and she took on a job as a sewing hand to help feed and clothe her two children. Her interest in union work took her to her present position. Mrs Mvubelo has travelled widely, studying labour problems in other countries, and has been an indefatigable worker for the cause of non-registered labour in South Africa.

CURNICK MVELASE CURWENS NDAMSE

Curnick Ndamse, who died at the beginning of 1974, was a member of the Transkei Legislative Assembly and formerly Minister of Education in the Transkei government. Born in 1919 in Mount Ayliff, he spent much of his life in the Transkei. He had a B.A. from Fort Hare University, and also studied in the United States, where he gained an M.A. degree in education. In the sphere of education he was a high school teacher, a university lecturer, and an inspector of schools before he became Minister of Education.

TEMBA NOLUTSHUNGU

Temba Nolutshungu is youth organiser of the South African Institute of Race Relations in the Western Cape.

HUDSON WILLIAM EDISON NTSANWISI

Hudson William Edison Ntsanwisi, Chief Minister of Gazankulu, was born at Letaba, in the Transvaal, in 1920. After taking his B.A. at Fort Hare University College, in 1946, he became successively a teacher, school principal, and then inspector of Bantu Education. In 1961 he was appointed senior lecturer in Bantu languages at the University of the North. After taking his M.A. at the University of South Africa in 1966, he read linguistics at Georgetown University in the United States, and in 1967 he was appointed Professor of Bantu languages at the University of the North. In 1968 he became chairman of the Machangana Territorial Authority, and then Chief Minister of the Gazankulu Legislative Assembly.

CEDRIC NAMEDI PHATUDI

The Chief Minister of Lebowa, Cedric Namedi Phatudi, is the son of a chief of the Bakgaga. He was born at

Mphahlele in the Pietersburg district in 1912. After completing a teacher-training course in 1932, he entered teaching and in 1935 became headmaster of the Marishane Tribal School in Sekhukhuneland (now Lebowa), later advancing through various posts to become an inspector of Bantu Schools in 1965. Matriculating through private study he earned a B.A. from Fort Hare University in 1947, and in 1960 the degree of Bachelor of Education from the University of Witwatersrand. In addition to his activities in various education bodies, he has translated Defoe's Robinson Crusoe and two Shakespeare plays into Northern Sotho. He has also written a play and a novel. He has travelled in Britain, the United States and Nigeria to study educational systems. Mr Phatudi entered politics in 1969, and was responsible for education in the first Lebowa Executive Council. In 1972, when the status of Legislative Assembly was given, he became Minister of Education, and in May 1973 he was elected Chief Minister. In recognition of his services in education, the University of the North conferred on him the degree of Doctor of Education (h.c.) in May 1974.

LENNOX LESLIE SEBE

The Chief Minister of the Ciskei, Lennox L. Sebe, is a member of the Rarabe tribal group. He was born in 1926 in the King William's Town district, where he was educated. He qualified as a teacher as well as taking an agricultural diploma, but most of his working life has been in the teaching profession. Prior to entering politics in 1968 he was an inspector of schools. In 1968 he became the executive Councillor for Education, moving at the end of 1971 to the post of Minister of Agriculture in the first Ciskeian Legislative Assembly. In May 1973 he succeeded Chief Mabandla as Chief Minister.

SOL SELEPE

The Rev. Sol Selepe is a minister in the Nederduitse Gereformeerde Kerk in Afrika (Dutch Reformed Church). He was born in Johannesburg but grew up in Cape Town, where his father was a minister in the Dutch Reformed Church. After school he went to theological school in the Orange Free State, and then served as a minister to N.G. Kerk congregations in Beaufort West, Lady Grey and Allanridge. Mr Selepe later worked as a programmer of the theological correspondence course of the African Independent

Churches Association. He describes himself as being 'engaged in the struggle for liberation of the black man in South Africa.'

ENOS ZWELABANTU SIKAKANE

The Rev. Enos Z. Sikakane is a Methodist minister, and the founder and director of the Edendale Lay Ecumenical Centre in Natal. He was born in 1915 in Ladysmith, where he grew up. He holds a B.A. degree from the University of South Africa, as well as diplomas in agriculture and teaching. The Edendale Centre offers programmes in leadership training, agriculture, and workshops for IDAMASA, the Interdenominational African Ministers Association of Southern Africa.

DESMOND TUTU

The Rt Rev. Desmond Tutu was born in Klerksdorp and educated in the Western Native Township, Johannesburg. He obtained a Teachers' Diploma in Pretoria, a B.A. through UNISA in 1951, and a B.D. and M.Th. at King's College, London University in 1966. He received his theological training at St. Peter's Theological College, Johannesburg and in 1961 was ordained as a priest. He lectured at Federal Theological Seminary in Alice and at U.B.L.S., Maseru, and was appointed Dean of Johannesburg in 1975 and Bishop of Lesotho in 1976.

ALPHAEUS HAMILTON ZULU

The Rt Rev. Alphaeus Hamilton Zulu is the Anglican Bishop of KwaZulu. Born in 1905 in Nqutu, KwaZulu, he has spent most of his life in Natal. After gaining a B.A. degree and a teacher's certificate, Bishop Zulu taught for twelve years before being ordained. Active in a wide range of community affairs, Bishop Zulu is an Executive Committee member of the S.A. Institute of Race Relations, and the South African Council of Churches, and is a president of the World Council of Churches.

References and Sources

GENERAL INTRODUCTION, pp. 1-27

Dia, Mamadou, 1962: The African Nations And World Solidarity (translated from the French by M. Cook). London: Thames and Hudson.

Rhoodie, N., (ed), 1972: South African Dialogue. Johannesburg: McGraw-Hill.

Horrell, M., 1973: The African Homelands Of South Africa. Johannesburg: South African Institute of Race Relations.

Van der Merwe, Hendrik W., and D. Welsh (eds), 1972: Student Perspectives On South Africa. Cape Town: David Philip. London: Rex Collings.

WHITE AND BLACK NATIONALISM, pp. 51-61

(1) Niddrie, David L., 1968: South Africa: Nation Or Nations (Van Nostrand Searchlight book), p. 120. Princeton, New Jersey, Toronto, Melbourne, London.

(2) Adam, Heribert, op. cit., pp. 68-9

(3) Carter, Gwendolen M., Thomas Karis and Newell M. Stultz, 1967: South Africa's Transkei: The Politics Of Domestic Colonialism, pp. 180-1. Evanston: Northwestern University Press.

BLACK SOLIDARITY, pp. 77-81

(1) Brotz, Howard, (ed), 1969: Negro Social And Political Thought, pp. 203-4. New York: Basic Books.

(2) Walshe, P., 1970: The Rise Of African Nationalism In South Africa, p. 196. London: C. Hurst.

(3) Ibid, quoted from Kuper: Passive Resistance, pp. 154-6.

(4) God Bless Africa.

TRADITIONAL ATTITUDES, pp. 123-9

(1) Schapera, I., (ed), 1937: The Bantu-speaking Tribes Of Southern Africa. London: Routledge & Kegan Paul Ltd.

(2) Krige, E., 1936: The Social System Of The Zulus. Pietermaritzburg: Shuter & Shooter.

(3) Gillham, F.E.M., 1966: 'Agriculture, education and the population explosion' in S.A. Journal of Science, vol. 62 (10), p. 317.

(4) Mapham. 'Agricultural extension', a memorandum, 10 April 1972, p. 6.

(5) Kelsey, L.D. and C.C. Hearne, 1964: Cooperative Extension Work, p. 12. New York: Comstock Publishing Associates.

(6) Op. cit., p. 10.

(7) Newsletter of Department of Bantu Administration and Development: Extension News, no. 14, pp. 23-4.

(8) Lilley, H.W.L., 1967: 'Characteristics and motivational orientations of the amaNzimkwe land-occupiers of location 4 B', M.Sc. thesis, Pretoria University, p. 104.

(9) Ibid.

(10) Op. cit., p. 189.

(11) Frean, N. (economist for Cane-Growers' Association), personal communication.

(12) Lilley, H.W.L., 1973: 'Some farmer characteristics and other problems limiting efficient agricultural development in the Umbumbulu district of Natal', report for Department of Bantu Administration and Development.

(13) Op. cit., 1967, p. 54.

KWAZULU DEVELOPMENT, pp. 130-7

(1) Welsh, David, 1971: The Roots Of Segregation. Cape Town: Oxford University Press.

(2) Ibid.

(3) Brookes, Edgar H., and N. Hurwitz, 1957: The Native Reserves Of Natal. Natal Regional Survey, vol.7, p. 57. Cape Town: Oxford University Press

(4) Statement summarising major points emerging during the proceedings of the Conference: 'Towards a comprehensive development in Zululand', prepared by the Organising Secretary, L. Schlemmer, Francis Wilson and S. Kahn, p. 1.

(5) Olivier, M.J.: interview with Tim Muil in Natal Mercury, 8 June 1972, p. 8.

(6) Financial Mail, 2 June 1972.

EDUCATION FOR DEVELOPMENT, pp. 214-27

Horrell, M. et al., 1973: A Survey Of Race Relations In South Africa, 1972. Johannesburg: South African

Institute of Race Relations.

Jolly, R., (ed), 1969: Education In Africa: Research And Action. Nairobi: East African Publishing House.

Parker, F., 1972: 'Educational strategies for accelerating development in Southern Africa', keynote address to the Education Workshop held at the University of the Witwatersrand, Johannesburg, 21 March 1972.

UNESCO, Final Report of Conference of African States on the Development of Education in Africa, Addis Ababa, 15-25 May 1961.

Union of South Africa, Report of the Native Economic Commission 1930-32, U.G. 22/1932.

Van Zyl, H.J., 1972: 'Bantu Education' in N. Rhoodie (ed), South African Dialogue. Johannesburg: McGraw-Hill.

Van Zyl, H.J., 1973: 'Developments in the education of the Bantu with special reference to technical education', paper read at the symposium of 'The Optimum Involvement of Manpower in Business and Industry' held at Umhlanga Rocks, Natal, 5-9 August 1973.

Ward, W.E.F., 1959: Educating Young Nations. London: Allen & Unwin.

MEDIUM OF INSTRUCTION, pp. 234-42

(1) Brookes, Edgar H., 1930: Native Education In South Africa. Pretoria: Van Schaik.

(2) Loram, C.T., 1917: The Education Of The South African Native. London: Longmans, Green and Co.

(3) Shepherd, R.H.W., 1941: The Story Of A Century, 1841-1941. Lovedale, South Africa: The Lovedale Press.

(4) Van Lill, G.J., 1965: 'Die beheer en administrasie van Bantoe-onderwys met spesiale verwysing na die tydperk sedert Unie, 1910', p. 146. Unpublished M.Ed. dissertation, University of Stellenbosch.

(5) Inter-departmental Committee on Native Education 1935/36, Para. 33.

(6) Ibid.

(7) Cape of Good Hope, Department of Public Education, Report of the Superintendent-General of Education, 1931, C.P. 3-32, p. 46.

(8) Cape of Good Hope, Department of Public Education, Report of the Superintendent-General of Education, 1929, C.P. 1929, 3-30, p. 38.

(9) Transvaal Education Department, Annual Report, 1915, p. 43.

(10) Transvaal Education Department, Annual Report,

1931, T.P. No. 3-32, p. 15.

(11) Report of the Commission of Native Education 1949-1951 (Eiselen Commission), U.G. 37/1951, para. 921.

(12) Ibid., p. 1.

(13) Ibid., p. 19.

(14) Duminy, P.A., 1967: Trends And Challenges In The Education Of The South African Bantu, p. 135. Pretoria: Van Schaik.

(15) 1962 Annual Report, p. 8.

(16) 1964 Annual Report, p. 9.

(17) 1965 Annual Report, p. 10.

(18) 1967 Annual Report, p. 11.

(19) Kgware, W.M., 1971: 'Medium of instruction in Bantu secondary schools in South Africa'; discussion paper prepared for the meeting of the Advisory Board for Bantu Education held in Pretoria on 3 March 1971.

(20) Hartshorn, K.B., 1972: 'The position of the official languages in the education of the Bantu'. Paper presented at the National Language Teaching Conference, July 1972.

(21) Op. cit.

(22) Sunday Times, Johannesburg, 22 April 1973.

(23) Quoted by Kgware, W.M.: op. cit.

HISTORY IN BLACK SCHOOLS, pp. 245-52

(1) Steel, D.J. and L. Taylor, 1972: Family History In Schools. Sussex: Phillimore & Company.

(2) Syllabus for the Higher Primary School Course (revised 1967). Pretoria: Government Printers, 1967, p. 59.

(3) Ibid.

(4) Cicero, quoted by Lucey: History: Methods And Interpretation.

(5) Op. cit.

(6) Op. cit.

(7) Jahn, J., 1962: A History Of Neo-African Literature, p. 277. New York: Faber and Faber and Grove Press.

(8) Op. cit.

HIGHER EDUCATION, pp. 255-9

(1) Macmillan, W.M., 1927: The Cape Colour Question, p. viii. London: Faber & Gwyer.

(2) The Federal Theological Seminary trains black, 'coloured' and Asian students for the ministry in the

Anglican, Methodist, Congregational and Presbyterian Churches, and is racially integrated.

THE CHURCH CONFRONTS S.A., pp. 300-5
(1) Bonhoeffer, D., 1967: The Cost Of Discipleship, p. 36. New York: Macmillan

PROFILE OF THE HOMELANDS, pp. 364-8
(1) Laurence, Patrick, 1976: The Transkei: South Africa's Politics Of Partition, p. 101. Johannesburg: Ravan Press.
(2) Ibid., p. 102

SIGNIFICANCE OF TRIBAL SYSTEM, pp. 372-84
Breutz, P.L., 1956: The Tribes of Mafeking District.
1953: The Tribes of the Rustenburg and Pilanesberg Districts.
Bruwer, J.P., 1957: Die Bantoe Van Suid-Afrika. Johannesburg: Afrikaanse Pers.
Population Census, 1970: Press statement by the Hon. J.J. Loots, Minister of Statistics.
Proceedings of the Tswana Territorial Authority, 1961: Speech by Mr Bruce Young, Secretary, Department of Bantu Administration and Development.
Proclamation 110 of 1957: Regulations prescribing the duties, powers, privileges and conditions of service of chiefs and headmen.
Schapera, I., 1959: A Handbook Of Tswana Law and Custom. London: Oxford University Press.
South African Panorama, July 1973.

Index of Contributors

Baartman, E., 273, 293
Baqwa, W.L., 177, 180
Beard, T.V.R., 1
Bengu, S.M.E., 94, 490
Butelezi, P.J., 311
Buthelezi, M., 565
Buthelezi, M.G., 42, 51, 77, 82, 110, 130, 260, 456, 461, 468, 479, 569
Charton, N.C.J., 364
Dladla, B.I., 204, 210
Dunjwa, A., 445
Gqubule, T.S.N., 255, 320
Gumede, P.G., 158
Guzana, K.M.N., 69, 413
Hlengwa, C.B., 473
Kgware, W.M., 214
Kotze, D.A., 355
Lekhela, E.P. 245
Leshabane, H., 524
Lesolang, S.J.J., 138, 144
Lukhele, D.M., 557
Mabandla, J.T., 432, 440
Mangope, L.M., 62, 499, 505
Matanzima, K.D., 385, 398, 403, 407
Matlala, M.M., 530
Mawasha, A.L., 234
Moerane, M.T., 34, 88
Moloto, E.S., 372
Motsuenyane, S.M., 148, 161, 163, 165, 171
Mphephu, P.R., 536, 540
Mutsila, J.P., 555
Mvubelo, L., 188, 191
Ndamse, C.M.C., 266
Nolutshungu, T., 121
Ntsanwisi, H.W.E., 84, 532
Phatudi, C.N., 253, 516, 519, 523
Ramusi, C., 524
Sebe, L.L., 29, 123, 421, 425
Selepe, S., 315
Sikakane, E.Z., 306
Tutu, D., 324
Zulu, A.H., 300

Index of Organisations and Documents

Association for the Education and Cultural Development for Africans (ASSECA): Objectives and Programmes, 347
Black Academic Staff Association: University Autonomy, 287
Black Allied Workers' Union: Policy Statement, 200
Black Caucus of the S.A. Council of Churches: The Soweto Disturbances, 328
Black Community Programmes: Aims and Objectives, 330; Excerpts from Annual Report (1973), 334
Black Ministers of the Dutch Reformed Church: Statement on Apartheid, 318
Black People's Convention: Extract from Constitution, 91; Rejection of Foreign Investment, 93
Black Renaissance Convention: Declaration and Resolutions (1974), 118
BophuthaTswana National Party: Manifesto, BophuthaTswana General Election (1972), 507
Ciskei National Independence Party: Principles, 430; Objectives in Draft Constitution, 431
Ciskei National Party: Policy, 437
Dikwankwetla Party: Extracts from the Manifesto, 536
Edendale Lay Ecumenical Centre: Location and Nature, 352
Inkatha (The National Cultural Liberation Movement): Resolutions (1975), 494
KwaZulu Executive Council: Black Trade Union Rights, 202; Comments on Land Consolidation, 464; The Role of the Zulu King, 470
KwaZulu Government: Consultative Education Committee of the KwaZulu Government: Education Manifesto of KwaZulu, 228
Lebowa People's Party: Manifesto, 526
Mphephu Faction: Policy Declaration, Venda General Election (1973), 541; Manifesto of Candidates Supporting Chief Mphephu, Venda General Election (1973), 547; Whither the Venda Party?, Venda General Election, (1973), 553
National African Chamber of Commerce: Regionalisation and Bantu Investment Corporation Policy, 150
Seoposengwe Party: Manifesto, BophuthaTswana General Election (1972), 513
South African Students Organisation (SASO): Black Students' Manifesto, 97; Statement of Objectives, 98; Policy Manifesto, 99; Understanding SASO, 101; Alice Declaration: Boy-

cott of Black Universities, 106; The University - What does it mean to you?, 279; Historical Background, 281; Resolution on Black Theology, 309; Community Projects (1972), 341
The League of the African Youth: Objectives, 107; Principles, 108
Transkei Democratic Party: Statement of Objectives in the Constitution, 410; Statement, General Election (1968), 411
Transkei National Independence Party: Programme of Principles, 388; Declaration of Loyalty by Members, 391; Manifesto, Transkei General Election (1968), 392; Manifesto of Candidates, Transkei General Election (1973), 409
Transkei Teachers' Association: Statement of Objectives, 286
Transvaal United African Teachers' Association: Language and Communication: Freedom to Choose Medium of Instruction for Children, 243; State- of Objectives, 285
Tswana National Party: Manifesto, BophuthaTswana General Election (1972), 515
Venda Independence People's Party: Manifesto, Venda General Election (1973), 549
Women's Association of the African Independent Churches: Report Covering 1969-71, 349

General Index

advisory boards, 454
African Bank Project, 165-70
African literature, 29-33
African National Congress, 21, 36-9, 44-5, 110-11, 113, 355, 359, 440, 456-7, 461, 488, 540, 572
African Nationalism: see also African National Congress, Pan Africanist Congress; 4-5, 12, 35-41, 55
African People's Democratic Union of Southern Africa, 355
African Resistance Movement, 355
African Students' Association (ASA), 281-2
African Students' Union of South Africa (ASUSA), 281-2
Afrikaans: see also medium of instruction; 2, 16
Afrikaners, 34-5, 42-9, 116, 245, 256, 270, 307-8, 459, 466, 585, 586
agriculture: see also land; 123-9, 386, 389, 396-7, 408, 427, 433-4, 438, 484-5, 494, 507-8, 521-2, 531, 544-5, 551
Alexandra Township, 183, 185
All African Convention, 38, 266
apartheid: see also separate development; 3, 8-9, 13, 456-60, 516, 524; 'petty' apartheid, 11, 84-7
Association for the Educational and Cultural Advancement of the African People of South Africa (ASSECA), 347-8, 360, 453
Baartman, E., 273-8, 293-9
Bam, W., 323
Bantu Administration Act (1927), 374
Bantu Affairs Administration Boards, 445-9, 450, 454-5, 574
Bantu authorities, 356, 375-6, 378-9, 387, 441
Bantu Education Act, 216, 237
Bantu Homeland Citizenship Act, 356
Bantu Homeland Development Act, 139
Bantu Investment Corporation, 132, 139, 140, 144-5, 149, 150, 151-3, 158-60, 509, 510, 527
Bantu Mining Corporation, 140
Bantu Trust and Land Act (1936), 19, 65-6, 131, 356, 358, 367, 405, 464-5, 502, 520, 570-1, 580
Baqwa, W.L., 177-89
Bengu, S.M., 94-6
Biko, S., 111, 340
black: consciousness, 4, 14-17, 26, 27, 91-2, 97-100, 101-5, 111-12, 114, 115-16, 284, 344, 360-1, 532; heritage, 40, 71-2, 102-3, 306-8, 372-84, 408, 479-80, 490-1, 499, 523, 541, 542; theology, 15, 92, 309-10, 311-14, 337, 361
Black Allied Workers' Union, 200-1
Black Community Programmes, 330-3, 334-40, 341-6, 360

Black People's Convention, 7, 40, 90, 91-3, 328, 359-60, 363
Black Renaissance Convention, 118-20
Bonhoeffer, D., 304-5
BophuthaTswana, 7, 138-43, 357, 366, 367, 379, 499-515
BophuthaTswana National Party, 507-12
border industries, 6, 22, 144-7, 155, 434-5, 521
Botha, M.C., 139, 140, 464, 487, 557, 575, 576, 578, 579
Botha, R.F., 496, 580-1, 582
Botswana, 382
Breutz, P.L., 377
Bruwer, J.P., 373
Butelezi, P.J., 311-14
Buthelezi, Manas, 463, 565-8
Buthelezi, M. Gatsha, 1, 11, 17, 23, 25, 42-9, 51-61, 77-81, 82-3, 110-17, 130-7, 240-1, 260-5, 362, 366, 403, 456-60, 461-3, 468-9, 473-7, 479-89, 490, 496, 497, 569-86
Cape Peninsula Students' Union, 281
capitalism: see free enterprise
chiefs, 361, 364, 372-84, 385, 388, 410, 425, 430, 432-3, 437, 441, 483, 499, 523, 530, 541, 553
Chitepo, H., 461
Christian Institute of South Africa, 330
churches: see also black theology; 293-9, 300-5, 309, 313-14, 315-17, 318-19, 337-8, 377-8
Ciskei, 358, 365, 366, 367, 421-55
Ciskei National Independence Party, 430-1
Ciskei National Party, 437-9
coloured people, 2, 80-1, 475, 476
Coloured Persons Representative Council, 10
communalism, 15, 92
communism, 295-6, 394, 423, 443-4
compounds, 181-2, 183, 322
consolidation of homelands: see land
Constitution of the Bantu Homelands Act, 5
de Wet Nel, M., 139-40
Diggs, C., 461
Dikwankwetla Party, 357, 536-7
Dingane's Day, 307-8
Dladla, B.I., 23, 204-9, 210-13
Dlamini clan, 559-61
Dunjwa, A., 445-55
Durban Students Union, 281
Dutch Reformed Church, black ministers of, 318-19
Edendale Lay Ecumenical Centre, 88, 352-3, 476
education: see also medium of instruction, universities; 15, 92, 97-8, 99, 107, 108-9, 115, 121, 134, 214-27, 228-33, 253-4, 266-71, 273-8, 285, 338, 347-8, 395, 426, 434, 437-8, 458, 500, 510, 513, 528-9, 531, 542-4, 549-50, 577-8
Eiselen, W.W.M., 140
entrepreneurs, problems of, 140, 145-7, 150-6, 158-60, 163-4, 169-70, 171-6, 365, 377, 386, 390, 396, 570, 573

exploitation, 88, 93, 103, 119
Federal Theological Seminary, 118, 258-9
federation: possibility of, 3, 17, 51-61, 67-8, 112, 406, 407, 409, 430-1, 433, 475-6, 482, 562; of KwaZulu and Transkei, 460
foreign investment, 93, 189, 199, 488, 496
free enterprise, 480, 527, 550
Freire, P., 273-4, 274-5
Frelimo, 2
Fynn, H.F., xx, 26
Gama, L.A.M., 558-61
Gazankulu, 361, 366, 532-5
Gqubule, T.S.N., 255-9, 320-3
Gumede, P.G., 158-60
Guzana, K.M.N., 69-76, 399, 413-20
Haile Selassie I, 461
Handbook On Black Organisations, 335
health education, 339, 341
Herstigte Nasionale Party, 1
history, teaching of, 245-52
Hlengwa, C., 473-8
homelands: see also individual homelands, political leaders and parties; 4, 5-26, 62-8, 74, 112, 130-5, 361-3, 364-586; citizenship of, 12, 356, 487, 511; public services, 364-5, 394-5, 425-6, 511-12, 545, 555; relations with Republic, 365-6, 386, 388-9, 392, 393, 398-402, 403-6, 428, 430, 433, 512, 531, 546, 569-86
Imbokodwa National Movement, 560
Indians, 474, 476
influx control: see urban areas
Inkatha, 15, 25, 96, 362, 481-2, 482-3, 484, 485, 490-8
Institute of Industrial Education, 210, 212
Inter-denominational African Ministers' Association of South Africa (IDAMASA), 360
International Labour Organisation (I.L.O.), 188, 211
Inyanda regional African Chamber of Commerce, 158-60
Jolobe, J.J.R., 33
Jordan, A.C., 33
Kamanda, K.W., 461
Kaunda, K., 579, 580
Kgware, W.M., 214-27, 239
KwaZulu, 20, 25, 112, 130-5, 158, 160, 358-9, 361-2, 366, 367, 379, 456-98
labour: see also exploitation, migratory labour, trade unions, wages; 177-9, 180-7, 188-90, 191-9, 200-1, 204-9, 366, 367, 376, 390, 396, 397
land, 5, 13, 18-21, 35, 37-8, 40-1, 47, 65-6, 74, 112, 131-2, 358, 359, 366-7, 382, 399-400, 401-2, 404-6, 409, 423, 425, 430, 437, 442, 457, 464-7, 481, 494, 501-2, 508, 513-14, 519-21, 557, 558, 570-1
League of the African Youth, 15, 107, 108-9
Lebowa, 516-31
Lebowa People's Party, 526-9
Lekhela, E.P., 234-42, 245-52

Lembede, A., 39
Leon, S., 10-11, 475
Leshabane, H., 524
Lesolang, S.J.J., 138-43, 144-7
Lesotho, 18, 20, 22, 368, 381-2
Lukhele, D., 557-62
Lusaka Manifesto, 580
Luthuli, A., 45, 456
Mabandla, J.T., 432-6, 440-4
Makonner, L.E., 462
Mandela, N., 583
Mangope, L.M., 15, 62-8, 357, 367, 403, 499-504, 505-6, 569-70, 573-4, 577, 579, 581-2
Mashiane, N.S., 523-5
Matanzima, K.D., 13-14, 16, 17, 52, 258, 357, 385-7, 398-402, 403-6, 407-8, 423-4, 460, 570, 572-3, 574, 576, 579, 582, 583
Matlala, M.M., 403, 530-1
Mawasha, A.L., 234-42
Mbiti, J., 306, 307
medium of instruction: see also education; 2, 233, 234-42, 243-4, 328, 359, 485-6, 494, 500-1, 562, 570, 571, 577-8
migratory labour, 10, 51, 72, 134-6, 185-7, 320-3, 365-6, 397, 434, 522, 550
Moçambique, 2, 461
Moerane, M.T., 34-41, 88-90
Moloto, E.S., 372-84
Mopeli, K.T., 357
Mota, W., 357, 359
Mothapo, S.S., 523-5
Mothiba, C.L., 523-5
Motsuenyane, S.M., 148-57, 161-2, 163-4, 164-70, 573
Mphephu, P.R., 538-9, 540, 546, 555
Mphephu Faction, 541-6, 547-8, 553-4
Mqhayi, S.E.K., 33
Mulder, C.P., 6, 9, 403
Mutsila, J P., 555-6
Mvubelo, L., 188-90, 191-9, 212
Namibia, 18, 27
Natal Code, 498
National African Chamber of Commerce, 15, 147, 149, 155-7, 161-2, 163-4, 166, 168-9, 174, 360, 573
National Council of African Women, 15
National Cultural Liberation Movement: see Inkatha
National Union of South African Students (NUSAS), 111, 281-3
Native Education Commission (1949-51), 216, 266-7
Natives Land Act (1913), 18-19, 37-8, 266, 356, 400, 502
Natives Representative Council, 356, 379-80, 381, 406, 456, 458
Ndamse, C.M.C., 266-72, 399-400
Ngwane Liberation Movement, 560
Nolutshungu, T., 121-2
Non-European Unity Movement, 21, 281, 355
Ntsanwisi, H.W.E., 84-7, 361, 403, 532-5, 570, 573-4, 575, 577, 578, 579, 582
Nxumalo, J.A.W., 210-11
Organisation of African Unity, 8, 59, 368, 442, 461-3, 534
Pan Africanist Congress, 39, 355, 359, 440, 456-7, 488,

572
pass laws: see urban areas
Phatudi, C.N., 253-4, 516-18, 519-22, 523-5, 570, 575, 576, 577, 579, 582, 584
Pityana, B., 17, 111
Plaatje, S., 19, 37-8
police, relations with black community, 565-8
Poqo, 355
Promotion of Economic Development of the Homelands Act, 7, 140
Qwaqwa, 166, 357-8, 359, 365-6, 536-7
Ramusi, C., 524
Rhodes, C.J., 35, 43
Rhodesia: see Zimbabwe
Schapera, I., 374, 375
Schwartz, H., 475, 476
Sebe, L.L., 29-33, 123-9, 357, 367, 421-4, 425-9, 569, 577, 579, 582
Selepe, S., 315-17
self-help, 77-81, 89-90, 104, 163-4, 165, 167, 168, 345, 359, 360
Seme, Pixley Ka I., 44, 557
Seoposengwe Party, 513-15
separate development, 5-26, 52, 60-1, 74, 119, 148, 171-2, 355-60, 362, 385, 389, 392, 398, 399, 403-6, 407, 432, 440-3, 456-60, 464-5, 498, 505, 506, 513, 516-17, 530, 562, 566, 579-80
Shaka, xx, 14, 26, 35, 42, 466
sharing: see also communalism; 21, 92, 103, 118, 407, 480, 533
Sharpeville, 111
Shezi, N.M., 111
Sigcau, B., 387
Sikakane, E., 306-8
Small, A., 257
Smith, I., 2
Sobhuza II, King, 557, 559-61
Sobukwe, R.M., 45, 111, 584
South African Bantu Trust, 138-9, 153, 406
South African Council of Churches (S.A.C.C.), 326, 328, 330
South African Federation of Trade Unions, 190
South African Pedagogical Society, 223
South African Students' Organisation (SASO), 7, 15, 97-8, 99-100, 101-5, 111, 114, 115, 280, 281-4, 309-10, 328, 341-6, 355, 359-60, 363
South West Africa: see Namibia
Soweto, 2, 16, 183-4, 328-9, 349-50, 565-6, 575-6
Stallard Commission, 185, 451
Status of the Transkei Act, 20
Swazi Territory, 557-62
Swaziland: 22-3; relations with (Republican) Swazi territory, 557-61
Tambo, O., 461
Tiro, A., 111
Tolbert, W.R., 580
Tomlinson Commission, Report of, 146-7, 173
Torlage, P.H., 558, 560
trade unions, 7, 12, 15, 23, 119, 188-90, 191-9, 200-1, 202-3, 205-9, 210-13, 486, 496, 578-9
traders: see entrepreneurs

traditional leaders: see chiefs
Transkei, 5, 7-8, 16, 20, 21, 22-3, 357, 358, 359, 361, 364, 365, 366, 367, 368, 385-420, 460, 482
Transkei Constitution Act, 5, 356
Transkei Democratic Party, 406, 410, 411-12
Transkei National Independence Party, 388-90, 391, 392-7, 401, 409
Transkei People's Freedom Party, 361
Transkei Teachers' Association, 286
Transvaal United African Teachers' Association, 243-4, 285, 360
tribalism and tribal culture: see black heritage, chiefs
Tswana National Party, 515
TUCSA, 212-13
Tutu, D., 324-7
Umkhonto KaShaka Party, 473-8, 487
Umkonto we Sizwe, 355
Umtata Declaration, 16, 17, 358, 423, 475
universities, black: see also names of individual institutions; 106, 115, 221-3, 231-2, 233, 255-9, 260-4, 270-1, 279-80, 287-92, 495, 578
University Christian Movement (UCM), 232-3, 360
University of Botswana, Lesotho and Swaziland, 292
University of Durban-Westville, 255, 257
University of Fort Hare, 105, 110, 222, 236, 256, 258-9, 260, 263, 270-1, 292
University of the North (Turfloop): 106, 222, 257, 501; Black Academic Staff Association, 287-92
University of the Western Cape, 255, 257, 260-1
University of Zululand (Ngoye), 105, 222, 257, 292
Unlawful Organisations Act (1960), 355
urban areas, Africans in, 10, 12, 47, 130, 135-6, 150-6, 169-70, 172, 174-5, 182-7, 363, 377, 400, 445-55, 502, 509, 522, 570, 571-7
urban bantu councils, 454
Venda, 361, 379, 538-56
Venda Independence People's Party, 549-52, 553-4, 555-6
Venda Party, 361
Verwoerd, H.F., 5, 9, 48-9, 267, 406
violence, 460, 461, 540, 565
Vorster, B.J.: 1, 6, 9, 41, 55, 82, 112, 131-2, 403, 456; conferences with homeland leaders, 363, 399, 405, 464, 569-86
wages, 23, 40, 46-7, 78, 119, 132-3, 141-2, 143, 189, 191-4, 213, 408, 435, 458, 571
white attitudes, 5, 27, 69-76, 85, 94-6, 300-2, 316, 324-5, 326-7, 414-19, 423, 448-9, 503, 571
white politics, 1, 3, 5-6, 69-76
Women's Association of the African Independent Churches, 349-51
works committees: see also trade unions; 196-7, 205-6,

207
World Council of Churches, 298
Xhosa Development Corporation, 139
Young, B., 374-5
Yu Chi Chan Club, 355
Zimbabwe, 2, 18, 27, 461, 568
Zulu: see also KwaZulu, Buthelezi, M.G.; 44-5, 307-8, 468, 473-8; role of king, 470-2, 477-8
Zulu, A.H., 300-5